PROJECT MANAGEMENT HANDBOOK

Edited by

David I. Cleland
Professor
Engineering Management
School of Engineering
University of Pittsburgh

William R. King
Professor of Business Administration
Graduate School of Business
University of Pittsburgh

VNR VAN NOSTRAND REINHOLD COMPANY
NEW YORK CINCINNATI TORONTO LONDON MELBOURNE

Library of Congress Catalog Card Number: 82-7030
ISBN: 0-442-23878-9

Manufactured in the United States of America

Published by Van Nostrand Reinhold Company Inc.
135 West 50th Street, New York, N.Y. 10020

Van Nostrand Reinhold Publishing
1410 Birchmount Road
Scarborough, Ontario M1P 2E7, Canada

Van Nostrand Reinhold
480 Latrobe Street
Melbourne, Victoria 3000, Australia

Van Nostrand Reinhold Company Limited
Molly Millars Lane
Wokingham, Berkshire, England

15 14 13 12 11 10 9 8 7 6 5 4 3 2 1

Library of Congress Cataloging in Publication Data

Main entry under title:
Project management handbook.

   Includes index.
   1. Industrial project management—Addresses, essays,
lectures.   I. Cleland, David I.   II. King, William
Richard, 1938–
HD69.P75P75   1982   658.4′04   82-7030
ISBN 0-442-23878-9   AACR2

Preface

The purpose of this handbook is to provide project managers and those individuals concerned with project management in both public and private organizations a reference guide for the fundamental concepts and techniques of managing projects.

Like all good handbooks, this is a reference source for practical how-to-do-it information. A manager or professional who has a problem with project management can turn to this handbook and find the help needed to solve the problem.

However, there are other important uses to which this handbook can be put. The field of project management has been growing so rapidly in recent years that anyone who wishes to learn more about the discipline is faced with an abundance of published information. The handbook contains the writings of an uniquely qualified group of people who have made significant contributions to the theory and practice of project management.

Thus, in such a rapidly developing field, even experienced project managers are faced with the challenge of keeping up with current developments and selecting those concepts and techniques that are most appropriate for their needs.

Those who are not experienced project managers, but who must play a role in the process of project management—functional managers, general managers, project team members and support staff—have an even more difficult task, for they must "keep up" in a rapidly expanding field that is not their special area of expertise. So, the *Project Management Handbook* is also addressed to their needs.

Students of project management may use the *Handbook* as a self-study aid, for it has been organized to facilitate an overall program of learning about the field as well as to provide a quick reference source on specific topics.

The *Project Management Handbook* seeks to provide guidance for all varieties of projects—from the largest and most complex systems development efforts, to the personal "research project." Its emphasis, however, is organizational in the sense that much of the material deals with the integration of projects into an overall managerial framework.

In addition to serving the needs of those who are directly concerned with project management, this book will be useful to top managers who wish to motivate and establish a philosophy of project management within their organizations. There are different types of project management, ranging from the simplistic use of expediters to sophisticated multiproject organizational approaches; the high-level manager who believes that one of these forms will be useful will find the *Handbook* to be a sound guide for planning for the evoluation of project management in the organization.

The handbook provides information on both the theory and practice of project management. While primary emphasis is on the pragmatic aspects of managing projects, this pragmatism is casted in a sound, theoretical framework of managerial thought.

In the editors' opinion, the proportion of project participants who require access to a handbook in this field is greater than for any other managerial group. This is because of the relative newness of the field, the lack of adequate training programs, and the general awareness that, unlike some other disciplines, there is a practical body of knowledge which can serve to support all aspects of the project management process.

As one leafs through the pages of the *Project Management Handbook*, the number and variety of the factors and forces with which the project manager must deal become clear. Their very number appears at first to make it impossible for one individual to master the art and science of managing projects. However, in reading further one becomes aware of the creativity and ingenuity which the authors have brought to bear on project management. For most of the problem situations that a project participant will face, this handbook has information that can be of help. Certainly, no one would claim that the state-of-the-art of this field has stabilized. Further evolution will continue. Nevertheless, the reader will find that there are workable solutions to the situations that arise in project management.

This handbook is the result of the cooperative efforts of a large number of people. The qualifications of the individual contributors are clear from the biographical sketch given on the title page of each article. The topic content of the handbook is broadly designed to be relevant to the general organizational contexts in which project management is found. Accordingly, some of the parochial subjects of project management in specific industries are not included. For example, configuration management and value engineering—two key concerns of project managers in the aerospace industry—are not treated. The editors believe that the parochial interests of a particular industry's project manager's needs can be best served by studying the literature of that industry.

Whatever its value to the reader, the *Project Management Handbook* reflects the experiences and considered judgments of many qualified individuals about the pivotal factors and forces surrounding project management. Eight interdependent areas of project management are developed:

1. *An Overview of Project Management.* The framework of practice and theory in which contemporary project management is found.

2. *Project Organization.* The alignment of resources to support project objectives, particularly in terms of the matrix organization.
3. *Organizational Strategy of Project Management.* The deployment of resources to support broader organization missions, objectives, and goals.
4. *Life Cycle Management.* The management of projects as they fit into broader and longer-range organizational purposes.
5. *Project Planning.* Planning to include the development of goals, strategies, and actions to allocate project resources.
6. *Project Control.* The means to determine the harmony of actual and planned cost, schedule, and performance goals.
7. *Behavioral Dimensions of Project Management.* The development of a climate whereby the project people work together with economic, social, and psychological satisfaction.
8. *The Successful Application of Project Management.* An examination of what counts for success in project management.

We thank the contributing authors who have given so importantly and unselfishly through their practical how-to-do-it presentations of the forces and factors involved in project management.

The editors are deeply indebted to Claire Zubritzky, who managed the administration involved in the development and production of this handbook. We are also indebted to Olivia Harris, whose contributions, both to the *Handbook* and to the milieu in which we work, were substantial.

We thank Dr. Albert G. Holzman, Chairman of the Industrial Engineering Department, Dr. M. L. Williams, Dean of the School of Engineering, and Dr. H. J. Zoffer, Dean of the Graduate School of Business, all of the University of Pittsburgh, who provided us with the environment to pursue this effort.

Contents

Section I

Overview of Project and Matrix Management

This introductory section of the handbook presents an overview of project and matrix management. Project management is viewed as a powerful tool that is particularly useful in terms of the management of the many interfaces that exist within an organization, and between an organization and its environment.

However, despite the power of the concept and its history of successful application, project management is not presented as a panacea. Rather, it is a tool which, when properly used under appropriate circumstances, can aid the organization in the achievement of its major goals.

In Chapter 1, Peter W. G. Morris explains the need for project and matrix management in an insightful chapter on "interface management." He discusses project and matrix management in conceptual terms and provides, as well, numerous real-world illustrations and prescriptions for the successful management of interfaces.

In the second chapter, Linn C. Stuckenbruck discusses project integration in the matrix organization by emphasizing the proactive nature of integration; that it does not just happen, but must be made to happen. He discusses how a project management system can be implemented in the organization and what the project manager must do to properly begin the project.

In Chapter 3, Arthur G. Butler, Jr. discusses the pros and cons of project management by reviewing the evolution of the project management concept, the uses to which it has been put, and its alternatives. He emphasizes both the functional and dysfunctional potentials of project management in a variety of dimensions such as conflict, patterns of interaction, power, status, influence and control.

1. Managing Project Interfaces—Key Points for Project Success

Peter W. G. Morris

One of the most important qualities of a project manager is a mature understanding of the way projects develop. This allows the nature of project activities to be better understood, problems to be seen in perspective, and needs to be assessed ahead of time.

To some extent this understanding of project development is intuitive, though it clearly also depends upon specialist knowledge of the project's technology and industry. It can, however, also be acquired in large part from formal study of the development process of projects, since all projects, regardless of size or type, follow a broadly similar pattern of development.

The organizational framework underlying a project's development is the subject of this chapter. The intent of the chapter is to illustrate the types of issues that are normally encountered as a project develops and to suggest ways in which these issues should be handled.

THE SYSTEMS PERSPECTIVE AND PROJECT MANAGEMENT

The chapter employs a systems framework: project structure is divided into major systems components, and the management of these components is looked at from a systems perspective. What is the systems approach?

A system is an assemblage of people, things, information, etc., grouped together according to a particular system "objective." Thus, one has the elec-

Peter Morris undertook research into project management at Manchester University, England in the late 60's, gaining his Ph.D. in 1972. He has worked both as a manager and as a consultant on a variety of projects around the world ranging from telecommunications and petrochemical projects in the Mid East, North Africa and Europe, steel projects in Latin America, and construction, MIS and aerospace projects in North America and Europe. Dr. Morris specializes in project planning, organization and control at the Arthur D. Little Program Systems Management Company, Cambridge, Massachusetts.

trical system, the digestive system, a high pressure weather system, an air conditioning system, a weapons system, a system for winning at cards.

A system may be logically broken down into a number of subsystems, i.e., assemblages of people, things, information, or organizations required to achieve a defined system *sub*-objective, like the switching, outside plant, building, transmission, and subscriber subsystems in a telephone system. The subsets of each subsystem may then be identified—cables, poles, microwave, and transmission and distribution equipment for the transmission subsystem—thereby creating sub-subsystems. Subsets of these subsets may then be identified, and so on.

Properly organized and managed, the overall system acts in a way that is greater than the sum of its parts. The systems approach emphasizes treating the system as a whole.

The systems approach has its origin in the late 1920s and 1930s. Biologists noticed similarities in the way that living organisms interacted with and controlled their environments. Similar patterns were simultaneously observed, by Gestalt psychologists, in the way the human mind organized sensory data. Both the mind and living organisms have to adapt to changes in their environment. Systems of this type are known as "open" systems. Before long it was seen that all social systems operate as open systems.[1]

During the 1950s, work in economics, psychology, sociology, anthropology and other disciplines developed these open system ideas by elaborating such concepts as self-organization, purposive systems, the importance of goals and objectives, the hierarchical classification of systems and subsystems, and the importance of systems' boundaries and interfaces (2)*. At the same time, this "systemic" view of the world was enriched by a parallel (but initially separate) set of disciplines which had their origin in the industrial and military applications of the scientific method during and immediately after World War II. This was the essentially numeric set of disciplines, such as cybernetics, control theory, operations research, systems analysis and systems engineering, concerned with modelling real life situations so that complex behavior could be more accurately described and forecast. Slowly both streams merged, encouraged

---

[1]Open systems are "open" to the effects of their environment. On the other hand, closed systems, which are the other major system type (including for example, much of physical chemistry and many types of machines), operate independently of their environment. In open systems, events rather than things are structured; there is a constant energy and information exchange between the system and its environment; the system organizes to minimize entropic decay; equilibrium with the environment is achieved through a process known as homeostasis; and there is a tendency towards differentiation. Closed systems operate in almost exactly the opposite manner (1).*

*Numbered references are given at the end of this chapter.

greatly by the enormous growth in the ability of the computer to apply these systems ideas with powerful effectiveness, so that the systems approach is now an established and vigorous influence on management and research.

The systems perspective has contributed substantially to the development of project management. Most importantly, the emphasis on viewing a system as a whole has frequently been behind the recognition of the need for an across-the-board integrating role—i.e., for project management itself (3).[2]

Secondly, systems thinking has shown how projects should work as successfully regulated organizations—the need for clearly defined objectives, the recognition that projects are organizations in constant change and the need to define and manage the major subsystems and their interfaces. A third important contribution is that the dynamic control needs of projects are now better understood—the importance of feedback, the progressive development of information and multilevel project control. And a fourth contribution is the widespread use of systems techniques—systems analysis, systems engineering, work breakdown structures, and simulation models.

Interface Management, as it is used in project management today,[3] is an outgrowth of the first two of these influences of systems thinking on project management. Interface Management identifies:

- The subsystems to be managed on a project.
- The principal subsystem interfaces requiring management attention.
- The ways in which these interactions should be managed successfully.

The emphasis on identifying key interfaces and on focusing on interface performance has grown as it has been increasingly realized that all projects share a common pattern of interfaces derived from a common pattern of subsystem

---

[2]The development of project management by the U.S. military is an illustration: the systems ideas developed initially for technical purposes were adapted to generate the organizational flexibility and control missing in the existing military bureaucracy. This can be seen in each of the steps in the U.S. military's development of project management—the Atlas Program, begun in 1954; Peck and Scherer's study of the US and Soviet weapons procurement processes in the late 1950's (4); the development of PERT by the US Navy in 1958; the introduction of project organizations in the Navy, Air Force and Army in the late 1950s/early 1960s; McNamara's extensive study and implementation of program management and project control techniques in the early 1960s; and Laird's and Packard's process-oriented focus on the needs of the total project life-cycle in the late 1960s/early 1970s.

[3]Interface Management is generally used now in a broader sense than it was ten or twenty years ago. In the 1960s and early 1970s Interface Management generally referred simply to ensuring that system interfaces matched (i.e. had the same specifications, were not missing any equipment, data etc.) Today it is used in the sense of defining systems—organizational, managerial and technical—and of actively managing their interrelationships.

interaction.[4] This is true no matter what the type of project, be it a theater production or an aid program, an election or a major capital investment program.

There are three sets of subsystems on any project: those deriving from the project's life cycle, its management levels, and its operational characteristics.

PROJECT LIFE CYCLE

Project management teaches that to achieve the desired project objective one must go through a specific process. There is no exception to this rule. The process is known as the project "life-cycle."

Projects (like people) have a life-cycle that involves a gradual buildup as definitions are established and working characteristics developed, a full-bodied implementation as the work is accomplished, and a phasing out as the work is completed and the project winds down. This cycle (Figure 1-1) is invariant, although (as with people) sometimes not fully recognized or respected.

A project starts as an incipient idea which is explored for financial and technical feasibility in the *Feasibility Stage*. Capacity is decided, locations chosen, financing arranged, overall schedule and budget agreed, and preliminary organizations set-up. At the end of the first phase there is usually a formal "go/no-go" decision. In the second, *Design* phase, the work is organizationally and managerially similar to the first phase, only it is more comprehensive and detailed. The technical definition of the project is expanded (albeit generally still at a fairly strategic level); schedule, budget and financing is reappraised; contracting strategy is defined; permits are sought; and infrastructure and logistics systems are defined.

In phase three, *Manufacture, Construction and Installation* (often called *Production*), equipment is procured, civil work is undertaken, and equipment and facilities are installed. This phase differs dramatically from the previous two. First, whereas the *Design* and *Feasibility* phases were organic and evolutionary in character, the *Production* phase is highly mechanistic (5). The aim is not to develop new technical options but to build as efficiently as possible the thing which has been defined in the *Design* phase. Second, there is a large—often vast—expansion in organization (whereas there may have been only dozens or hundreds of persons active in the first two phases, there may be thousands or even tens of thousands involved in this third phase.) And third, the

---

[4]Note that an interface is technically defined as the space between interacting subsystems. Even though there might be a common set of subsystems on all projects, this does not necessarily mean there will be a common set of interfaces. The extent that there is depends on the commonality of subsystem interaction. This chapter will show that subsystem interaction does in fact follow a common pattern on most projects.

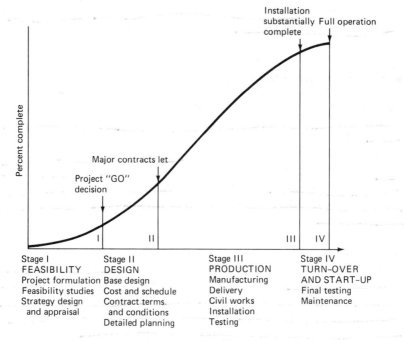

Figure 1-1. Project life cycle.

characteristic mode of control changes from one of "estimating" costs and durations to one of tight "monitoring" of quality, schedule and cost to keep actual performance within the target estimates.

The fourth and final phase, *Turn-Over and Start-Up*, overlaps the third phase and involves planning all the activities necessary for acceptance and operation of the project. Successfully synchronizing phases three and four can prove a major management exercise. The cost of capital locked up in the yet uncommissioned plant, and the opportunity costs of both, underutilized operating systems such as sales, operating plant, personnel etc., and a possible diminishing strategic advantage while competitors develop rival products can prove enormous.

Between each of these four life-cycle phases there are three distinct "change points" (what shall later be called "dynamic project interfaces"):

- From *Feasibility* to *Design*: the "go" decision.
- From *Design* to *Production*.
- From *Production* to *Turn-Over & Start-Up*.

The project on either side of these change points is dramatically different—in mission, size, technology, scale and rate of change—and these differences create their own particular different characteristics of work, personal behavior, and direction and control needs. Thus, importantly, the management style of each of the four main life-cycle phases is significantly different.

PROJECT MANAGEMENT LEVELS

The four phases have a set and important managerial relation to each other. The work of the *Feasibility* stage is highly "institutional" (top management) in kind—decisions taken in this phase will later have an overriding impact on the health of the investing enterprises. In *Design* the work is of a "strategic" nature, laying the axes upon which the detailed, "tactical" work, of the third, *Production* phase will rest. Interestingly, the fourth phase, *Turn-Over & Start-Up*, exhibits a mixture of all three managerial levels of work: institutional, strategic and tactical.

These three levels of management activity have been recognized as distinct levels of management since at least the time of Talcott Parsons, the eminent American sociologist. Parsons made the point that each of the three levels has an essential role to play in any successfully regulated enterprise: the technical/tactical level (III) manufactures the product, middle management (II) coordinates the manufacturing effort, whilst at the institutional level (I) top management connects the enterprise to the wider social system (6). Each of the three has a fundamental role to play in the management of every project (although it is true that the levels tend to become more blurred on the smaller projects). Yet surprisingly most project management literature deals only with Levels II and III. There is little in the literature that treats such Level I issues as: the role of the owner and his financer; relations with the media, local and federal government, regulatory agencies, lobbyists and community groups; the sizing and timing of the project in relation to product demand and the cost of finance—all issues that became crucially important during the 1970s.

The distinction between Levels II and I is quite critical since it is essentially the distinction between the project and its outside world (Figure 1-2). Levels II and III deal almost exclusively with such familiar project activities as engineering, procurement, installation, testing and start-up—Level III providing the technical input, Level II providing both a buffer from the outside world and guidance in how to avoid external pitfalls. But no project exists in isolation from outside events. Level I provides the coordination of the project with outside events and institutions. Level I actors typically include the project owner and his finance team, government agencies, community groups, very senior project management and one or two special project executives specifically charged with external affairs, such as Public Relations and Legal Counsel.

The involvement of each of these Levels is different during each of the major phases of the project life-cycle. During the *Feasibility* stage, the owner and his

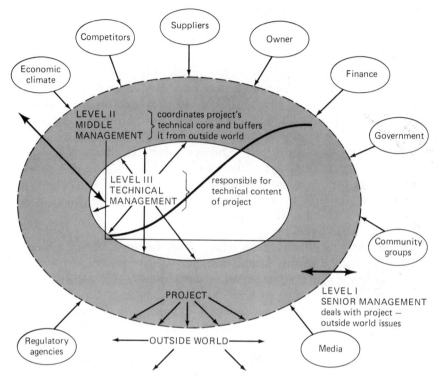

Figure 1-2. The three levels of project management.

team (Levels I and II) have to make crucial decisions about the technical performance and business advantages they are to get for their investment—and indeed, whether the project should "go" at all. Once the decision to go ahead is taken the weight of the work moves to the design team (Levels II and III). During *Production* engineering reaches a detailed level. Both project management (Level II) and technical staff (Level III) are now at full stretch, while the owner (Level I) takes a more reduced "monitoring" role. Finally, during *Turn-Over and Start-Up*, all three Levels are typically highly active as engineering work gets completed (Level III), often under intense management pressure (Level II), while high level coordination is required at the owner level in coordinating the initiation of Start-Up activities.

The responsibilities of these Levels thus focus on two main areas of activity: Levels II and III on the technical and middle management work within the project, and Level I on the senior management work at the project/outside world interface.

PROJECT OPERATIONAL SUBSYSTEMS

The work of these two essentially distinct levels of project management activity tends to follow a pattern which is similar on many projects.

At the project/outside world level, the concern is to ensure that the project is commercially viable and, as far as possible, is provided with the conditions and resources necessary to succeed. The principal areas of work at this level are:

- Ensuring satisfactory *Project Definition* (which includes both technical content, cost and schedule requirements).
- Preparing for *Operations & Maintenance*.
- Preparing for *Sales & Marketing*.
- Ensuring appropriate *Organization* structures and systems, both for the project and for operations.
- Facilitating relations with important *Outside Groups* such as government and community groups, financial institutions, and the media.
- Ensuring appropriately skilled *Manpower* for both the project and future operations.
- Ensuring that the total enterprise is *Commercially Sound* and "adequately" "financed."

Work within the project, on the other hand, focuses more on accomplishing the tasks within the strategic parameters developed and managed by senior management. At the intra-project level, the principal subsystems are:

- Realizing the desired *Project Definition*—i.e., assuring that the project is produced to technical specification, on time, and in budget.
- Creating the *Organization* needed to execute the project—this includes both the formal organization structures, contractual relationships, systems of information flow and control procedures, and also informal patterns of working relationships and communication.
- Minimizing external disruptions from the *Environment*—by, for example, acquiring adequate materials inventory to provide buffer stocks against delivery disruptions, handling union negotiations, obtaining necessary regulatory approvals, or warning top management of future financing needs.[5]

---

[5]The effects of environment on a project can be profound, and continue to provoke keen theoretical analysis and discussion. Of particular interest is the problem of how organizations behave in a constantly and rapidly changing environment. Theorists describe such environments as turbulent and call the type of systems that operate in such environments "Multistable" (7). Large or complex projects in particular suffer many of the consequences predicted for multistable systems,

•/Providing an adequate *Infrastructure* to accomplish the project (facilities, transportation, communication, utilities).

STATIC AND DYNAMIC INTERFACES

The likely existence of these subsystems in a project, no matter how it unfolds, enables us to categorize certain interfaces as on-going or "static"—they are not a function of the way the project develops but represent relationships between on-going subsystems (like engineering and procurement, on Level I and Level II). There is another group of interfaces, however, which arise only as a function of the pattern of activity interdependencies generated by the way the project develops. These we may identify as life-cycle or "dynamic" interfaces.

Dynamic interfaces between life-cycle (or activity) subsystems are of the utmost importance in project management, first because of the continuous importance of the clock in all projects, and second because early subsystems (like *Design*) have a managerially dominant role on subsequent ones (like *Manufacturing*). Dynamic interrelationships require careful handling if minor mistakes in early systems are not to pass unnoticed and snowball into larger ones later in the project.

Boundaries should be positioned where there are major discontinuities in technology, territory, time, or organization (8). Major breakpoints in the project life-cycle—as, for instance, between each of the four major phases, and also between activity subsystems within each phase (for example between manufacture, inspection, delivery, warehousing, installation and testing)—provide important dynamic interfaces. These serve as "natural" check points at which management can monitor performance.

Most major dynamic interfaces are in fact used in this way: for example, the Project Feasibility Report, the initial Project Technical Design, the formulation and negotiation of the "Production" contracts, and Testing and Hand-Over. Review points such as design-freeze points, estimates-to-complete, and monthly progress reports, may also be introduced for purely control purposes without there being any "natural" discontinuity. Each in its own way represents a response by project management to control the project's momentum across its dynamic interfaces.

Whereas the important dynamic interfaces are relatively sharply defined for

---

such as large subsystem interaction, continuous objectives redefinition, rich internal feedback processes, high impact of external factors (often causing the subsystems to have to act in an apparently less-than-rational way), and great organizational change, often of a step-function size. All these characteristics can be found on today's superprojects such as TAPS, the SST program, and the North Sea Oil program.

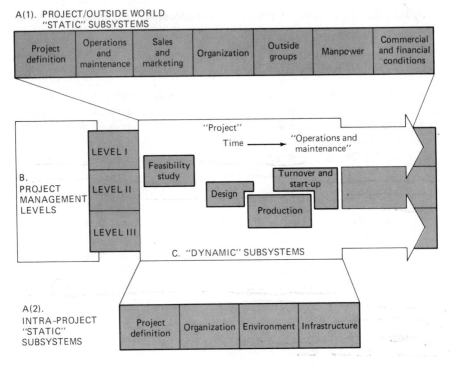

Figure 1-3. The three sets of project subsystems.

Level II and III management, at Level I they are less distinct. Level I management is certainly partly driven by the anatomy of the project's internal development, but it also has its own dynamic interfaces for each of its own principle subsystems. Operation, Sales, many of the Outside Groups, Manpower, Finance and Commercial issues each have their own often distinct life-cycles. (For example: the process of recruiting and training manpower; preparing annual financial plans.) Thus at Level I, dynamic interfaces do not become less important; rather they become more varied and less clearly defined. They are still crucial to the project's success.

Static interfaces too are less clearly defined at Level I than at Levels II and III, partly due to the wider scope of concern of Level I (which gives rise to much multifaceted subsystem interaction, as, for example, between Operations, Sales, Manpower and Finance) and partly due to the disruptive effect of the outside environment.

Figure 1-3 sketches the three principle sets of project subsystems which have now been identified: the three levels of management, static subsystems, and dynamic subsystems.

PROJECT INTEGRATION

Some interfaces are clearly larger and more important than others. Organization theorists describe the size of an interface not in terms of, for instance, a small change point or a major one, but in terms of the degree of *differentiation* between subsystems. Typical measures of differentiation include differences in:

- Organization structure.
- Interpersonal orientations.
- Time horizons.
- Goals and objectives (9).

Thus, a panzer division can be differentiated very clearly from a sunday school picnic on all dimensions. The R & D wing of a company can be similarly differentiated from the marketing wing. The architect can be differentiated from the building contractor.

Now it is very rare (and perhaps tragic) for a panzer division to have to integrate with a sunday school picnic, but it is annoyingly often (or so it may seem) that R & D has to integrate with marketing, and inevitable that architects must integrate with contractors. Why? Because the activities of the groups create certain technical, organizational and environmental *interdependencies*. These interdependencies may be almost accidental or may be deliberately organized. *Integration* becomes important when the degree of organizational interdependence becomes significant. Research has shown that tighter organizational integration is necessary when:

- The goals and objectives of an enterprise bring a need for different groups to work closely together.
- The environment is complex or changing rapidly.
- The technology is uncertain or complex.
- The enterprise is changing quickly.
- The enterprise is organizationally complex.

The amount of integration actually required at an interface depends both on the size of differentiation across the interface and on how much "pulling together" the interfacing subsystems need.

Certain project subsystems can be differentiated from one another quite markedly. For example, the project/outside groups interface is marked by very strong differences in time horizons, goals and objectives, interpersonal orientations, and structure—this is why the conflict over many environmental and regulatory issues is so drastic on many large projects: the aims and mores of the environmentalists are far, far removed from those who are trying to build the project. The design group often functions quite differently from the construction group—the former's interest might be elegant engineering, time might not be money, and quality may be paramount; the construction crew may be of less elitist thinking, have strong incentives not to waste time, and may often work in a tougher organizational milieu. Similarly, there are major differences in perspective between operations and project personnel, between the project finance team and project engineering, between a construction manager and project management, and so on. It is, in short, possible to establish the degree of differentiation between each one of the projects interacting subsystems, and in so doing thereby establish which are the principle project interfaces (10).

Despite the insights of management theorists, choosing the degree of integration—the amount of "pulling together"—required across an interface still calls for considerable judgement. This is inevitable. There is no easy answer to the question, how much management is enough? There are some pointers, however. James D. Thompson, in a classic book (11), observed that there are three kinds of interdependency, each requiring its own type of integration. The simplest, "pooled," only requires that people obey certain rules or standards. The second form, "sequential," requires that interdependencies be scheduled. "Reciprocal" interdependence, the most complex kind, requires mutual adjustment between parties (Figure 1-4). In project terms, subsystems which are in continuous interaction require liaison in order to achieve the necessary integration, whereas those that just follow on from one another can follow plans and schedules.

There is a range of devices which can be used to achieve liaison (12):

- Liaison positions.
- Task forces.
- Special teams.
- Coordinators (or permanent integrators).
- Full project management.
- Matrix organizations.

Each of these options provides stronger integration than the last.

The primary function of *liaison positions* is to facilitate communication between groups. Other than this, the liaison position carries no real authority and little responsibility. *Task forces* are much stronger. Task forces provide mission-oriented integration: a group is formed specifically for a particular task and upon completion of the task the group disbands. *Special teams* are like task forces but attend to regularly recurring types of problems rather than specific issues. A *coordinator*, or permanent integrator, provides a similar service as a liaison position but has some formal authority. He exercises this authority

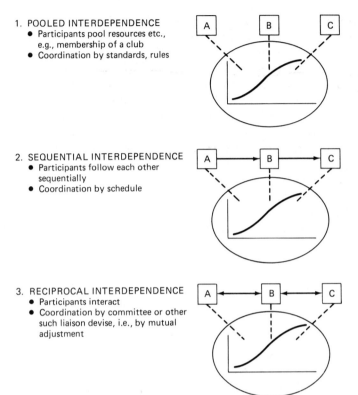

1. POOLED INTERDEPENDENCE
   - Participants pool resources etc., e.g., membership of a club
   - Coordination by standards, rules

2. SEQUENTIAL INTERDEPENDENCE
   - Participants follow each other sequentially
   - Coordination by schedule

3. RECIPROCAL INTERDEPENDENCE
   - Participants interact
   - Coordination by committee or other such liaison devise, i.e., by mutual adjustment

Figure 1-4. The three types of interdependence.

over the decision making processes, however, not over the actual decision-makers themselves. This is a subtle point, but an important one, and it often causes difficulties in projects. The coordinator cannot command the persons he is coordinating to take specific actions. That authority rests with their functional manager. He can however influence their behavior and decisions, either through formal means such as managing the project's budget and schedule, approving scope changes etc., or through informal means such as his persuasive and negotiating skills. The full project manager role upgrades the authority and responsibility of the integration function to allow cross-functional coordination. The integrator—the project manager—now has authority to directly order groups to take certain actions or decisions. Matrix organizations are, by general consent, considered about the most complex form of organization structure. Matrix structures provide for maximum information exchange, management coordination, and resource sharing. Matrixes achieve this by having staff account simultaneously to both the integrating (project) managers and the functional managers whose work is being integrated. Both project managers and functional managers have authority and responsibility over the work, albeit there is a division of responsibility: the functional manager is responsible for the 'what' and 'by whom', the project manager decides the 'when' and 'for how much'. Unfortunately the person who often comes off the worst in the matrix is the poor soul (at Level III) who is actually doing the work. He reports to two bosses—his project manager and his functional manager—which is not in itself necessarily a problem except when, as often happens, the project manager and functional manager are themselves in conflict. (Like, for instance, over how much should be spent on the project). Matrix structures generate considerable conflict and suffer from constantly changing boundaries and interfaces (13).

The relative merits of the matrix organization vis-a-vis the fully-fledged project organization is one of those hardy perennials of project management. Various writers at various times have offered all kinds of reasons why one or other form is better. Three points seem to stand out however. First, the full project management role—with a project manager in overall command of the project—does offer stronger leadership and better unity of command. It is better for achieving the big challenge. Second, the matrix organization is more economical on resources. For this reason alone it is often almost unavoidable on large or complex projects. Third, it is quite common to find a fully-fledged project manager sitting on top of a matrix structure (Figure 1-5)—the two forms are not incompatible but in fact, fit rather well together: the top project manager (Level I) providing the leadership and ultimate decision making authority, the matrix providing maximum middle management (Levels II and III) integration.

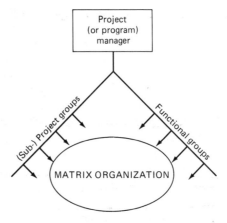

Figure 1-5. Typical use of the project management and matrix organizations simultaneously.

The challenge in moving through this range of liaison devices is very clear. Achieving greater integration requires increased attention to interfacing parties. Interfaces tend to become increasingly difficult to manage as one moves through the continuum. Let's look now at some experience of managing project interfaces.

MANAGING PROJECT INTERFACES

Interface Management is not, it must be admitted, a well developed theory of management well supported by a tight body of research and experience. It is in many ways more a way of looking at project management which is useful and is supported by general experience and research. The insights which are offered below are therefore illustrative rather than comprehensive in their exposition of Interface Management.

Keep Static Interfaces Clearly Defined

On projects, problems require solutions within short time frames, organizational conflicts abound, and compromises are inevitable. In such an environment, boundaries can blur. It is therefore a fundamental principle of Interface Management to maintain the static interfaces clearly defined.

In the Apollo program there was a constant need to reinforce organizational boundaries. When General Phillips was appointed director of the Apollo Program in 1963, he found that the program was organized entirely along project grounds: one group for the Lunar Excursion Module, one for the rocket and so on. This created a number of problems, particularly with the wide geographic dispersion of the program. The program was therefore reorganized to stress its functional and geographic needs as well as its project requirements. Five functional divisions were created—systems engineering, checkout and test, flight operations, reliability and quality assurance, and program control—with project offices in Houston, Huntsville and Cape Canaveral. A matrix organization was thus created which reported to a strong but small program office in Washington DC (Figure 1-6). This office, of only about 120 persons, managed a program which consisted at times of upwards of 300,000 persons. It did so by very clearly defining lines of responsibility and authority and program interface relationships, and by insisting that work be delegated and accounted for strictly in accordance with these lines and procedures (14).

Organizational checks-and-balances also help keep organization interfaces clearly demarcated. There are four groups which must always be organizationally distinct on projects: project management, project control, the functional groups, and subprojects. Project management should be separate since its role as an integrator requires it to maintain an independent viewpoint and power

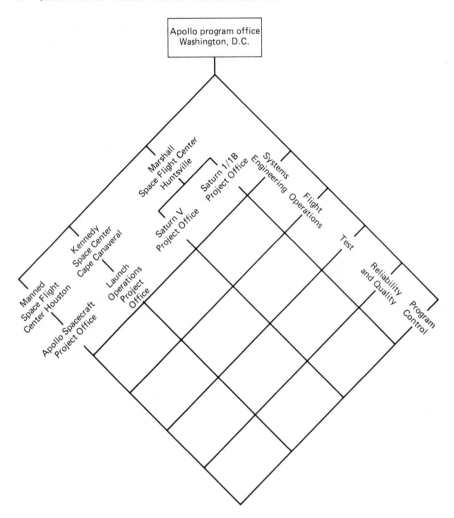

Figure 1-6. Apollo program organization.

base. The Project Control Office should be independent since its job is to report accurate and objective data on project progress. If positioned as part of another group, say project management or construction, there will be a tendency to downplay poor performance because management will inevitably hope that things will improve. Functional groups—engineering, contracting, production, testing, reliability, contracts, etc.—represent the "engine room" of the project: the place where technical progress is accomplished. On a large project or program which is divided into subprojects there is usually a number of important

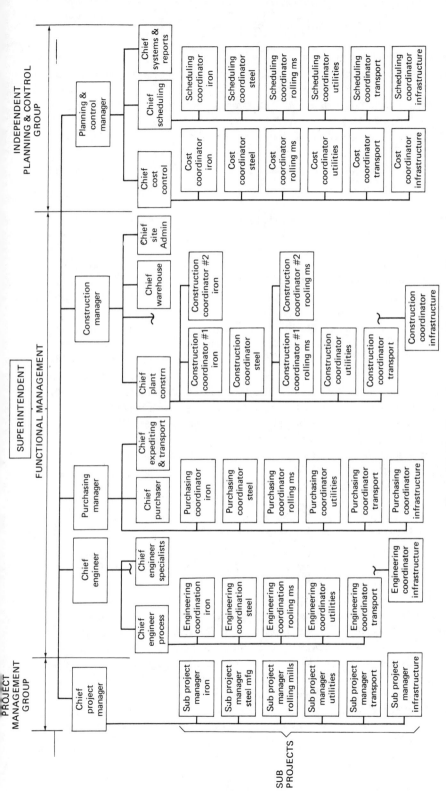

Figure 1-7. The four principal project groups on the Acominas project.

schedule interlinkages and competition for scarce resources between the sub-projects. Often budget and personnel are swapped between the subprojects. Subproject boundaries should be clearly defined and their interfaces closely monitored by senior management if subproject performance is to be properly controlled.

The organization structure used for the $3.5 billion Acominas steel mill project shows these four principle groups very clearly, (Figure 1-7), as does the Apollo organization shown in Figure 1-6. (The Acominas case is described in more detail below.)

Early Firm Control of Technical Definition Is ESSENTIAL to Project Success.

Ultimately, the investor wants what he asked for, when he asked for it, at the price he agreed to pay. This is what he pays project management to achieve for him. Time and again projects fail because the technical content of the program is not controlled strictly enough or early enough.

Software development projects (particularly large, complex ones) are extremely difficult to manage at the best of times since their work content (residing for most of the project in the project team's heads) is not as tangible as in other projects. Unless the system design is very carefully defined and communicated, the system often ends up technically inadequate, late and very costly. The software development life cycle consists of five basic phases: concept definition, design, development, evaluation, and operation. The first phase involves problem definition and feasibility study; the second, specification of user functions and technical system design; the third, coding, integration testing, user documentation, etc. Many software projects rush the first two phases and move too quickly into coding. Subsystem interfaces are then wrongly designed and code is inappropriately written. Project management techniques are now being increasingly applied to software projects. Configuration management is being used to help specify the technical content of the system as it develops and to control all changes as they arise. Software development techniques are also now emphasizing the careful, top-down evolution of the system's design and programming.

Figure 1-8 shows a model of the official British building process life-cycle ("official" in the sense that this is the life-cycle published by the Royal Institute of British Architects—The RIBA Plan of Work (15)). Interestingly, there is in practice no obvious checkpoint at the interface between Sketch Design and Detailed Design. There are no clearly recognized discontinuities in either technology, territory or time at this interface, nor are there any major organizational changes. Yet the outline design developed in the Sketch Design phase determines the character of the building, and thus lays the foundations for many of the technical problems which may subsequently arise during the pro-

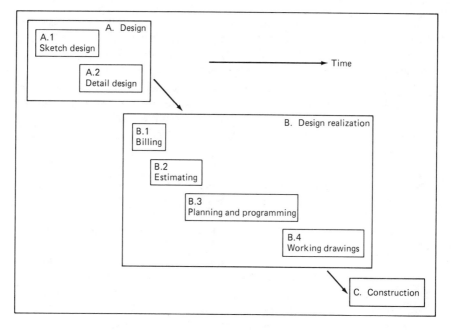

Figure 1-8. Model of the "official" British building process.

ject. If this dynamic interface is not properly controlled—and sadly often it is not—the danger of design errors cropping up unexpectedly later in the project is high (16).

Churchill Falls is often lauded as an example of a successful project. The praise invariably centers on its tight control of design. An ambitious project in northern Canada, the project consisted of retaining the flow of the Churchill River through a series of vast reservoirs and dams over a 2,500 square mile basin in Upper Labrador. The project was begun in earnest in 1966 for a budget of $550m and was completed eight and a half years later on budget and ahead of schedule. The project was marked by an early and very intense coordination between project management, engineering, construction management and finance (including insurance)—each of which was conducted by quite separate companies. At the time of arranging project financing the state of project documentation was such that there were "virtually no questions unanswered" (17). Following this exhaustive initial design there was continuous close review by construction management of the engineering design as it developed, and intensive engineering to achieve cost savings wherever possible.

Firm control of design is achieved through configuration management—most specifically, the use of Work Breakdown Structures and Change Control. Configuration management documents the technical design of the project, ensures regular design reviews, and rigorously checks the technical cost and schedule impact of all changes before approving them. Configuration management has been used primarily in the U.S. aerospace and defense industries; it is only slowly being applied to other types of projects. It is not used in the building and civil engineering industries for example (although the British Quantity Surveying profession does do a part of the WBS work in preparing Bills of Quantities). Applying configuration management to non-aerospace industries is currently one of the major interest areas of project management practice.

The Skills Required in Managing Dynamic Interfaces Vary Depending on the Management Level and Stage of the Project

The Trans Alaskan Pipeline (TAPS) remains one of the largest and most ambitious of recent super-projects. Although constructed in the three years between 1974 and 1976 (at a cost of approximately $8 bn) the project had in fact been on and off since 1968. Senior management was required to concentrate on a series of strategic issues of startling variation: firstly, on engineering (how to prevent hot oil damaging the Alaskan permafrost and how to design for seismic damage), and then moved through political support (the project manager actually moved to Washington DC to advise the political effort that eventually resulted in the 1973 TAPS Act), infrastructure development (transportation, camps, equipment supply, and union negotiations), organization issues (the development of a highly decentralized matrix organization once construction began), environmental regulations, and finally, engineering and construction again. The sequence of issues is interesting: firstly, achieve agreement on the technical concept and political support for the project; secondly, assure adequate infrastructure and organization; thirdly, resolve environmental, construction and engineering issues as the project is built. This is essentially the institutional, strategic and tactical sequence already noted as typical for all projects. At the middle management level however (where managers were responsible for anything up to $4 bn of work!), work centered either on resolving engineering and construction problems or on issues of organization and leadership. Nowhere was the organizational concern more clearly evident than in the change at about 15% of the way through construction from a 9-tiered, centralized, functional organization to a 4-tiered, decentralized, matrix organization (Figure 1-9). The result was a highly flexible construction organization relying, like Apollo, on a small cadre of senior managers (18). Emphasis was on leadership, horizontal and informal communication, simple structures and tight reporting relationships—and getting the job done.

The TAPS pipeline matrix organization tells of an experience very similar to that of Apollo and Acominas. Acominas is a steel plant nearing completion

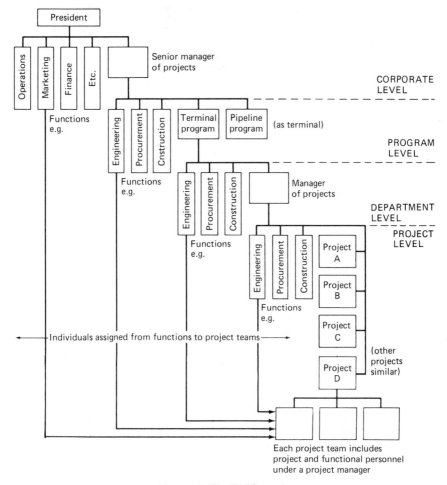

Figure 1-9. The TAPS matrix.

(as of 1982), at a cost of over $4.5 bn, in central Brazil. The project schedule was, like TAPS and Apollo, tight. The project staff, numbering about 400, were organized on a matrix basis, operating simultaneously at three distinct levels (Figure 1-10). Like TAPS, Acominas was initially organized along primarily functional lines. Functional managers took the lead in developing the engineering design, planning the project, and negotiating the contracts. As contracts were signed and the project moved in to the production phase, however, responsibility was delegated to the project management teams (19).

The TAPS/Acominas organization development leads to three important observations about the development of projects.

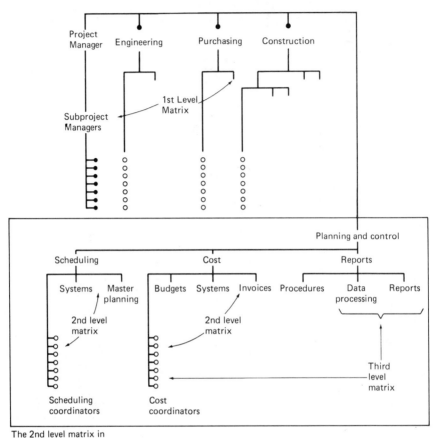

Figure 1-10. The multi-level Acominas matrix.

1. **Typically, Large Projects Require A Decentralized Organization During Production With Centralization Before And After.**   Both projects exhibited the same pattern of centralization—decentralization—centralization. (The final centralized phase during *Turn-Over and Start-Up* has not been discussed here.) The initial, design phase requires unified strategic decision-making. During production the volume of work becomes so great that responsibility must be delegated: the organization becomes decentralized under the project and functional matrix control. Finally, at *Turn-Over*, the volume of work decreases while the need for unified integration with Operations' *Start-Up* creates the need for centralization once again.

2. **The Project Organization Must Change According To The Needs Of The Project's Size, Speed And Complexity.**   The Acominas matrix was planned to change at the onset of production—about one-and-a-half years after it was set up, which fits with the time it usually takes to "grow" a matrix (20). Research suggest that while the timing of the organization change is a function of the project's schedule, the severity of the change depends on the project's size, speed and complexity (21).

3. **Once Decentralized, Projects Require A Substantial Management Superstructure To Effect The Necessary Coordination.**   Projects decentralize, essentially, to ease the pressure on decision making. Once decentralized, informal controls and communication tend to proliferate and there is a rapid growth in the number of meetings and committees. With this growth in informal decision-making there is more need than ever for careful configuration management and budgetary and schedule control. Formal reporting will clearly lag actual events considerably, but in an informal organization there is a danger of assuming that things are happening when in fact they may not be. (Also, informal reporting will tend to concentrate on strategically important items only; formal reports should provide a regular update on all aspects of project progress.) It is, therefore, vital to ensure full, regular reporting during this decentralized phase.

The character of a project thus varies both at different stages of its development and at different levels of management. The skills which are required in managing the project's evolution vary depending on the level of management and stage of the project.

Each Major Project Change Point Requires its Own Distinctive Total Management

Changing from one major life-cycle phase to another—from *Feasibility* to *Design, Design* to *Production*, and *Production* to *Turn-Over and Start-Up*—is a major event. The *Feasibility–Design* transfer is economically the most important step in the project's life. Major federal acquisitions have long placed great importance on the need for very thorough feasibility studies. Thorough agency needs-analysis and exploration of alternative systems is now mandatory federal practice. Yet while the importance of a thorough feasibility study is now generally recognized, it is suprising how many projects do become committed to and move into *Design* on the basis of a totally inadequate feasibility study. Two of the most notorious of recent projects exhibit this clearly. Concorde was conceived almost entirely by the British aircraft establishment, largely on the wings of technological fascination using financial data of seemingly the most spurious kind. The proposal was championed ardently by one or two senior British ministers who effectively resisted Treasury pressure to review the financial assumptions. Once the French government joined the project (invited by a British minister partly because of lack of Treasury support for the project (22)), the political momentum became virtually unstoppable. Final commitment to the project was made on the basis of a twenty page report which was "little more than a sketch" (23). At this stage the research and development was estimated to cost £150m to £170m; the final cost is some £2,000m. Likewise, the Sydney Opera House was committed to on the basis of a totally sketchy design backed by strong political support. New South Wales' prime minister, John Cahill, saw the Opera House as an imaginative political act. A design competition was held and Utzon's design was selected as winner. The design was, however, little more than diagrammatic. There was little evidence of structural feasibility and no cost estimate. A quantity surveyor was therefore asked to prepare one, which he did "under duress in a few hours" (24) arriving at a figure of $A 7 million. The final cost, after drastic redesign (resulting in so reducing the scenery space that opera cannot be fully staged in the building) was $A 102 million.

The transition from *Design* to *Production* is less clear-cut than that from *Feasibility* to *Design*. It is also much broader in scope and involves much fuller management attention. At this interface management must be fully active in all the major project subsystems: project definition, organization, environment, and infrastructure. The overriding preoccupation should be that the strategic parameters are properly set as the interface is crossed, since once *Production* begins the scale and pace of events increase dramatically. So important is this interface to project implementation success that it requires "total" management attention: planning, organizing, directing and controlling. Contracting— the key interface activity in fact—offers a good example. The contracting process must be supported by project management through integrated planning, thorough negotiating, and close monitoring. Often contracting is not managed but just happens, thus swamping the project with work and delaying it considerably. (Acominas had to sign 400 contracts during an 18–24 month period. Accomplishing this was a major management achievement in its own right.)

Turn-Over and Start-Up probably receives considerable non-profit planning and control. The meshing of the two important phases of project construction and operations is complex and has large cost implications. All Level I subsystems must be complete and activated as soon as *Turn-Over* occurs. Yet despite the obvious importance of smoothly transitioning from *Production* to *Turn-Over* it would appear rare that a project planning group prepares and monitors integrated plans for crossing this interface. This might be partly because of the substantial differences in *Start-Up* between aerospace programs and large new capital expansion facilities (factories, telecommunication systems, ports, etc.) which may have depressed the evolution of program management ideas on this important area of work.

Ensure Full Working-Out of the Static Subsystems at Each Stage of the Project Life

"Static" project subsystems (technical definition, organization, environment and infrastructure) must be fully worked out at each phase of the project's life-cycle. Unfortunately this does not always happen, often because the habits of an industry or organization have institutionalized a culture of neglecting certain "essential" subsystem considerations.

Movie productions are notorious, for example, for overrunning budget. The most common reason for their doing so is that there is a culture of allowing the director to work-out how the film will develop as he shoots it—there is neither "design" nor "schedule." (No-one on the set, including the director, knew how Casablanca was going to end until the end of shooting; Francis Ford Coppola did not have the ending of *Apocalypse Now* worked out even as he entered the editing room.)

The tendency for architectural design to dominate the British building process has already been commented upon. Figure 1-11 compares two basically well-managed, large, complex building projects (25). The first (A) was managed by architects working under the RIBA's Plan of Work. Since the Plan of Work assumes competitive bidding by the main contractor, it does not mention the use of any form of construction management advice prior to construction bidding. Thus the architects did not schedule the project nor seek any form of production advice during the early design phases. Project B, however, used a large U.S. A/E firm which was familiar with project management practice and employed both systems design techniques and a management contractor. As a result there was early project scheduling and production advice so that the technical definition subsystem was fully worked out early in the project.

Planning Must be Phased to the Stage of the Project Life-Cycle

The differing nature and requirements of the various project life-cycle phases require that different issues be addressed as the project unfolds. Project planning cannot be done comprehensively, once-and-for-all, at the beginning of the project. The uncertainty during the early stages of a project is too great. Instead, planning must be incremental (26). Initial planning must concentrate on building viable planning bases for each principal subsystem; detail being added later in phase with the project schedule (Figure 1-12).

The Apollo Mission's "Phased Project Planning" explicitly recognizes this

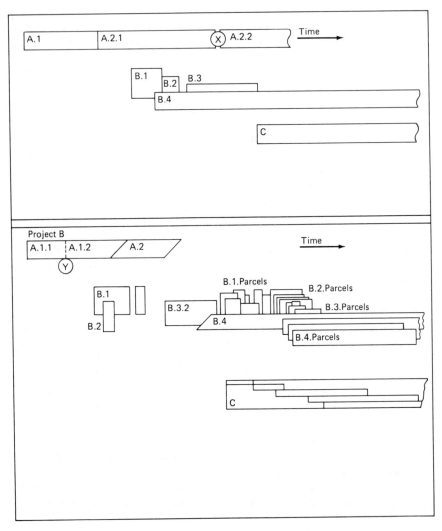

Figure 1-11. Comparison of two British building projects. (For Subsystem Coding refer to Fig. 1-8)

(27)—major life-cycle phases were identified and planning review checkpoints positioned along the life-cycle (Figure 1-13)—as have subsequent U.S. aerospace manuals (e.g. DOD 3200.9, DOD 5000.1, AFSC 800-3, to mention just three).

Apollo was fortunate in that it had nearly a decade for NASA to develop its systems and program planning. Many projects are less fortunate. The North Sea Oil program, for example, was implemented on a crash basis, and made

worse by the short summer weather window for towing and positioning platforms in the North Sea. Oil companies found themselves having to develop a
new generation of rigs, which involved the use of new technology, working in
a harsh and poorly documented environment, without adequate codes of practice or regulations—all within a very tight schedule. A slippage of just a few
weeks could result in the delay of the whole program for nearly a year. To
speed up the program, projects were often sanctioned on the basis of preliminary design data and manufacturing was overlapped with design as much as
possible. While the program could probably have been managed more efficiently if there had been a longer start-up time to acquire environmental design
data, develop codes and put project management systems and procedures in
place (as has been suggested (28)), the economic pressure on distributing
North Sea Oil as soon as possible effectively precluded this option. In this program, the project life-cycle not only determined the sequence and degree of
planning appropriate at a given stage, it set an absolute limit on the time available for planning.

**Control Needs Vary Depending on the Level of Control and Stage of the
Project**

As the tasks of the different levels of project management vary, so do their
control needs. Level III management uses frequent, often daily, control of key
performance factors such as earth moved, concrete poured, pipe laid, vessels
installed, tests completed, together with basic cost data. At Level II further
data is required in addition to the Level III "key drivers": for example, inven-
tories, drawing approvals, transportation, camp capacity, security, accidents,
contract management, changes pending and approved, contingency reserves.
These are data not needed on such a frequent basis as the "key drivers" data.
Level I interests are broader still: exception reporting on progress (i.e. report
problems and poor trends only), interface relationships with other subsystems
(e.g. between subprojects, between operations planning and project progress),
training, cash flows, etc. (29).

"Control" has a meaning which is greater than merely monitoring. It is used
in the broader context of setting standards, monitoring, and correcting for
deviations between actual and planned performance. This more complete interpretation of control is the one used in cybernetics. (The word "cybernetics"
itself derives from the Greek "to steer"). The nature of control during *Feasibility* and *Design* is different from that during *Production* and *Turn-Over*. As
has been already noted, the need during the early stages of a project to plan,
design and estimate correctly is very large. The costs during these early phases
are small compared with the total project cost, and so the need to monitor them
(at least from a project as opposed to design point of view) is correspondingly

PLANNING SYSTEM \ PLANNING STAGE	FEASIBILITY	PROJECT STRATEGY	DESIGN	PRODUCTION	TURN-OVER & START-UP
ECONOMIC EVALUATION	• Benefits • Risk	• Continue Appraisal with View to Changing Project Specifications if Necessary	• Impact on other Business Functions Assessed • Adjustments Made as Necessary		• Assess Project Cost for Product Pricing Purposes
PROJECT DEFINITION	• System Specs • Base Technology • $ Estimate • Project Schedule	• Outline Design • Configuration Definition • Budget by Major Areas • Milestone Schedule • Detailed "Planning" Schedule	• Futher development of Outline Design, Schedule and Budget	• Detailed Contract Specs and Drawings • Overall Schedule Requirements • Detailed Budget/Contract Bids	• Operating Manuals • Training • Primary Materials Preparation • Hand-over Schedules • Test Schedules • Move
FINANCE	• Potential Sources	• Principal Sources • Major Payments Schedule	• Detailed Sources • More Detailed Cash Requirements	• Detailed Payments Schedule by Creditors & Currency	• Annual Financial Operating Plan
ENVIRONMENT	• Initial Impact Assessment	• Definition of Environmental Impact Statement • National & Local Government Support Assessed • Local Population Attitude Assessed • Supplier Situation Assessed	• Schedule of Approvals Required • Government or Community Support Groups Identified	• Permit Expediting System • Expediting Schedules • Pubic Relations	• Marketing • Personnel • Inventory Planning • Safety Procedures • Outstanding Legal Issues

ORGANIZATION & SYSTEMS	• Initial Project Outline	• Overall Concepts for: —Contractor Strategies —Design Fabrication, Construction —Labor & Materials Sources • Principal Responsibilities Determined • Major Information Systems Identified • Key Personnel Identified	• Contract Negotiating Plan • Some Major Contracts Signed • Union Discussions • Possibly Some Long Lead Materials Ordered • Responsibilities Matrix • Manpower Plan • Systems Design Schedule	• Contract Terms and Conditions • Owner Organization Detailed • Detailed Staffing Plans	• Operations Organization Development and Start-up • Project Organization Phase-out • Wind-down of project personnel
INFRASTRUCTURE & SUPPORT	• Assess Extent of Support Required	• Preliminary Plans for: —Labor Relations —Camps —Logistics	• Further Definition of: —Labor Relations —Camps —Administration —Transport, Logistics & Warehousing • Support Organization Outlined • Permits Requested	• Detailed Definition of: —Labor Relations —Camps —Transport, Logistics, etc. • Construction Schedules/ Contracts for Camps, Power, Transport, etc. • Service Contracts Identified • Support Organization Defined	• Wind-down and sell-off of project camps, etc. • Plan for housing, transport, physical & social welfare of operating personnel

Figure 1-12. Project planning development.

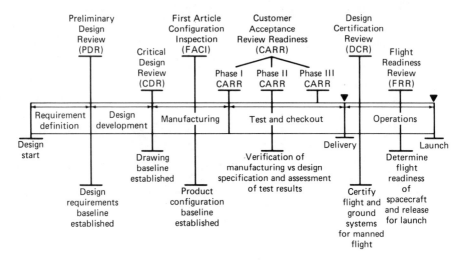

Figure 1-13. Apollo's phased program planning.

small. Later, during *Production*, however, the crucial control need is the monitoring of performance to ensure that quality is being achieved and resources are being deployed on schedule and in budget. Hence the nature of control changes during the project life-cycle from predicting to monitoring.

Personnel Issues Will Vary, Again Depending on the Level of Control and the Stage of the Project

Conflict is inherent in every project since the primary project objectives—quality, cost and schedule—are themselves in conflict. Quality costs money and requires time; crashing a schedule costs money. Also, projects engender contractual and community conflict. And there rarely seem to be sufficient resources to accomplish the project.

Studies in the mid 1970s (30) have shown how the pattern of conflict varies during the project life-cycle (Figure 1-14): schedule and priorities dominate the early phases, with technical issues coming to the fore later (and with cost as a consistently low-conflict item). One should not assume that this pattern applies for all projects, however—one would normally expect greater conflict over technical issues earlier in the project, the conflict pattern might vary by type of project (and contract type), cost pressures may be generally more dominant than they were on the projects studied, and personal issues are probably stronger on matrix and overseas projects. Despite such necessary caveats, the findings are extremely valuable: they provide solid evidence that the type of conflict varies according to the stage of the project life-cycle.

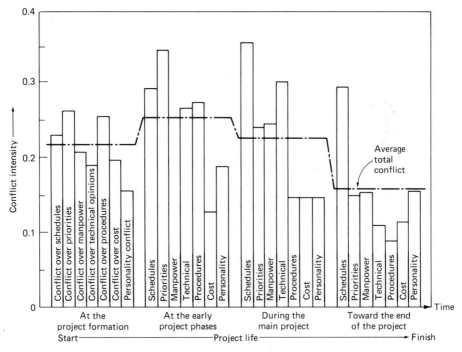

Figure 1-14. Relative intensity of conflict over the project life-cycle.

Similar research (31) has also studied how the factors which are (a) most important and (b) most inhibiting to project success vary with the life-cycle stage (Figure 1-15). It too has shown that personal issues vary with the stage of project life-cycle.

The nature of conflict also differs according to the level of management. All the research on project conflict undertaken to date either concentrates on Level II/III management or has been in the aerospace industries, which are more sheltered from external pressures. Conflict at Level I is usually totally different, requiring other modes of resolution. Most of the behaviorial work in projects to date assumes a normative, mechanistic view of the world: a world where people make rational decisions based on trade-offs of costs and benefits, and where open dialogue between men of goodwill leads to amicable solutions. While this approach is largely valid for most intra-project conflict and behavioral issues, it is often inappropriate for dealing with outside world issues. The Level I manager will as often as not find himself having to deal with people having completely different value systems to those of the project's. Hence while the more mechanistic approach to personal issues is appropriate to Levels II and III, Level I often requires a more political approach.

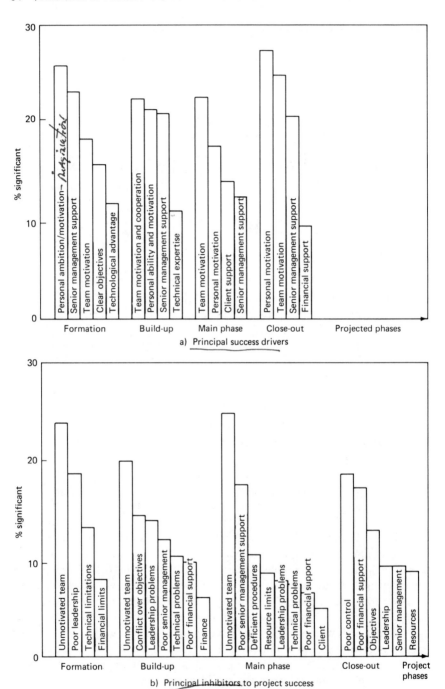

a) Principal success drivers

b) Principal inhibitors to project success

Figure 1-15. Behavioral drivers during the project life-cycle.

POSTSCRIPT: BEYOND THE SYSTEMS FRAMEWORK

In describing the major points in a project where management attention is required, this chapter has used a systems framework of project development. Yet in doing so, it has been seen that at times the systems model itself begins to break down.

The mechanistic systems model of organizational behavior is appropriate for the highly managed, intra-project activities of Levels II and III. Behavior at the Level I, project/outside world interface, however, requires a subtler, more political model: a model based on the recognition that group interests and power systems can shape organizational behavior as radically as owner goals, technical issues, finance or any of the other "systems" factors (32).

As environmental issues and regulatory requirements continue to affect projects so powerfully, and as long as inflation forces project sponsors to more directly share the risk of project cost control, political externalities will continue to have a decisive role in the successful management of projects. In consequence, project management writing and research during the 80's might be expected to draw increasingly on political models of organization behavior to better understand the key points for project success.

REFERENCES

1. Katz, D. and Kahn, R. L. *The Social Psychology Of Organizations* (Wiley. New York, 1966), pp. 14–29.
2. Kast, F. E. and Rosenzweig, J. E. *Organization and Management. A Systems Approach* (McGraw Hill. New York, 1970).
3. Lorsch, J. W. and Lawrence, P. R. *Studies In Organization Design* (Irwin Dorsey. Homewood, Ill., 1970).
4. Peck, M. J. and Scherer, F. M. *The Weapons Acquisition Process; An Economic Analysis* (Harvard University Press. Cambridge, Mass., 1962).
5. The organistic/mechanistic classification of organization types was developed by Burns, T. and Stalker, G. M. in *The Management Of Innovation* (Tavistock. London, 1961).
6. Parsons, T. *Structure And Process In Modern Societies* (Free Press. Glencoe, Ill., 1960).
7. See for example:
   Metcalf, J. L. "Systems Models, Economic Models and the Causal Texture of Organizational Environments: An Approach to Macro-Organizational Theory." *Human Relations,* Vol. 27 (1974), pp. 639–663. Also, Emery, F. E. and Trist, E. L. "Sociotechnical Systems." *Systems Thinking,* ed. Emery, F. E. (Penguin. Harmondsworth, 1969), pp. 241–257.
8. Miller, E. J. "Technology, Territory and Time: The Internal Differentiation of Complex Production Systems." *Human Relations,* Vol. 12(3) (1959), pp. 270–304. Also, Miller, E. J. and Rice, A. K. *Systems of Organization, The Control of Task and Sentient Boundaries* (Tavistock, London, 1967).
9. Lawrence, P. R. and Lorsch, J. W. *Organization and Environment; Managing Differentiation and Integration* (Harvard University Press, Cambridge, Mass., 1967).
10. Morris, P. W. G. "Organizational Analysis of Project Management in the Building Industry." *Build International,* Vol. 6(6) (1973), pp. 595–616.
11. Thompson, J. D. *Organizations in Action* (McGraw-Hill. New York, 1967).

12. This list is based on Galbraith, J. R. *Organization Design* (Addison-Wesley. Reading, Mass., 1973).
13. Davis, P. and Lawrence, P. R. *Matrix* (Addison-Wesley. Reading, Mass., 1977).
14. See for instance Baumgartner, J. S. "A Discussion With The Apollo Program Director, General Sam Phillips." *Systems Management,* ed. Baumgartner, J. S. (The Bureau of National Affairs. Washington D.C. 1979).
15. Royal Institute of British Architects, *Plan of Work, Handbook of Architectural Practice and Management* (RIBA. London, 1963).
16. Morris, P. W. G. "Systems Study of Project Management." *Building,* Vol. CCXXVI (6816 and 6817) (1974), pp. 75–80 and 83–88.
17. Warnock, J. G. "A Giant Project Accomplished - Design Risk and Engineering Management." *Successfully Accomplishing Giant Projects,* ed. Sykes, A. (Willis Faber. London, 1979), pp. 31–61.
18. Moolin, F. P. and McCoy, F. "The Organization and Management of the Trans Alaskan Pipeline: The Significance of Organizational Structure and Organization Changes." *Proceedings of the Project Management Institute Conference, Atlanta, 1980* (Project Management Institute. Drexel Hill, PA, 1980).
19. Reis de Carvalho, E. and Morris, P. W. G. "Project Matrix Organizations, Or How To Do The Matrix Swing." *Proceedings of the Project Management Institute Conference, Los Angeles, 1979* (Project Management Institute, Drexel Hill, PA, 1979).
20. See, for instance Davis, P. and Lawrence, P. R. *Matrix,* op. cit. Also, Whitmore, K. R. *Matrix Organizations in Conventional Manufacturing - Marketing Companies,* M.S. Thesis. (Sloan School of Management. MIT. Cambridge, Mass., 1975).
21. See Reis de Carvalho, E. and Morris, P. W. G., op. cit.
22. Hall, P. *Great Planning Disasters* (Weidenfeld and Nicolson. London, 1980), pp. 87–108.
23. See Hall, P., op. cit. and Edwards, C. E. *Concorde: Ten Years and a Billion Pounds Later* (Pluto Press. London, 1972).
24. Hall, P., op. cit. p. 141.
25. Morris, P. W. G., op. cit.
26. Horwitch, M. "Designing and Managing Large-Scale, Public-Private Technological Enterprises: A State of the Art Review." *Technology in Society,* Vol. 1 (1979), pp. 179–192.
27. Seamans, R. and Ordway, F. I. "The Apollo Tradition: An Object Lesson for the Management of Large Scale Technological Endeavors." *Interdisciplinary Science Review,* Vol. 2 (1977), pp. 270–304.
28. Department of Energy, *North Sea Costs Escalation Study* (Her Majesty's Stationery Office. London, 1976).
29. Morris, P. W. G. "The Use and Management of Project Control Systems in the 80's." *Project Management Quarterly,* Vol. XI (4) (December, 1980), pp. 25–28.
30. Thamhain, H. J. and Wilemon, D. L. "Conflict Management in Project Life-Cycles." *Sloan Management Review* (Summer, 1975).
31. Dugan, H. S., Thamhain, H. J. and Wilemon, D. L. "Managing Change Through Project Management." *Proceedings of the Project Management Institute Conference, Atlanta, 1980* (Project Management Institute. Drexel Hill, PA, 1980).
32. Mintzberg, H., "Organizational Power and Goals: A Skeletal Theory," *Strategic Management,* eds. Schendel, D. E. and Hofer, C. W. (Little, Brown and Company. Boston, Mass., 1979).

2. Project Integration in the Matrix Organization*

Linn C. Stuckenbruck†

INTRODUCTION

Projects range from very small to extremely large, and can vary greatly in complexity. The larger and more complex the project, the more likely that it will be multidisciplinary, that is, the project will involve many different areas of expertise. Complex multidisciplinary projects are likely to be organized in the matrix mode. The matrix is used to achieve optimum efficiency in the utilization of project resources, though it also enlarges the potential for organizational conflict. All of these factors tend to further increase project complexity and to multiply the problems of the project manager.

It is a management axiom that the principal job of every manager is to create within the organization an environment which will facilitate the accomplishment of the organization's objectives (1).‡ Certainly the job of the project manager fits this role very well. In addition, managers are responsible for the generally-accepted functions of planning, organizing, staffing, directing and controlling. Since every manager has these functions, how does the job of the project manager differ from that of the line or discipline manager?

The project management concept is based on vesting in a single individual the sole authority for the planning, resource allocation, direction and control

---

*This chapter includes material from Chapters 6 & 9 from *"The Implementation of Project Management: The Professional's Handbook"* (Addison-Wesley Inc., 1981).

†Dr. Linn C. Stuckenbruck is with the Institute of Safety and Systems Management at the University of Southern California where he teaches project management and other management courses. Prior to this he spent seventeen years with the Rocketdyne Division of Rockwell International where he held various management and project management positions. He holds a PhD. from the State University of Iowa, and has recently published a book entitled: *"The Implementation of Project Management—The Professional's Handbook,"* published by Addison-Wesley Publishing Company.

‡Numbered references are given at the end of this chapter.

of a single, time-and budget-limited enterprise. But this statement does not indicate any major difference between the job of the project manager and that of the line or discipline manager. What does make a difference is the complexity of most projects, and the project manager's necessary preoccupation with the integration of a given project. This chapter will discuss the problems of obtaining a fully integrated project and point out the various actions that the project manager must initiate to ensure that the process of project integration is carried out.

THE INTEGRATION FUNCTION

As has been indicated, projects vary greatly in complexity, though all but the simplest projects have a common element—they must be integrated. The process of systems integration is difficult to separate from general good management practice. However, integration can be defined as the project manager's most important responsibility: to ensure that a particular system or activity is assembled so all of the subsystems, components, parts and organizational units fit together as a correctly functioning, integrated whole, according to plan. All levels of management have this goal, but the project manager must be preoccupied with it because he has the direct responsibility to ensure that it occurs. This job of integration is most important and most difficult when the project is organized in the matrix mode. Then, the project manager's problem becomes one of interface management. What he does to solve his problem can be described by the more general term—systems integration.

LIVING WITH THE MATRIX

The matrix is a complex organizational form that can become extremely intricate in very large projects. The conventional hierarchical–functional management structure usually finds itself in difficulty when dealing with large projects. Pure project organization is a solution when the project is very large, but it is not always applicable to smaller projects. Therefore, management in an effort to obtain the advantages of both project and functional organizational forms has evolved the matrix, which is actually a superimposition of a project organization upon a functional organization. The matrix is not for everyone. It should only be utilized if its advantages outweigh the disadvantages of the resulting organizational complexity.

Why is systems integration difficult in the matrix organization? What's different about the matrix? Since the matrix is such a complex organizational form, all decisions and actions of the project manager become very difficult, primarily because he must constantly communicate and interact with many functional managers. The project manager discovers that the matrix organization is inherently a conflict situation. The matrix reveals the presence of conflicting project and functional goals and objectives. In addition, the project manager finds that many established functional managers who contribute to the project feel threatened, and continual stresses and conflicts result.

Matrix organizations will not work automatically, and an endless number of things can go wrong. Since most matrix problems occur at the interfaces between the project manager and his functional managers, the project manager has to effectively work across these interfaces if he is going to accomplish his integrative function.

Integration doesn't just happen, it must be made to happen by careful planning, and by designing it into the system. It requires more than just a fitting together of components; the system has to function as a whole. Integration cannot be an afterthought, and it does not consist only of actions that can be accomplished after the subsystems are completed. The critical actions leading to integration must take place very early in the project's life cycle, particularly during the implementation phase. In a "pure" project organization, there is no question as to who initiates these actions; the project manager runs his own empire. In a matrix organization, however, the project manager encounters particular difficulties and problems in effecting integration.

The matrix organization has evolved to cope with the conflict inherent in any large organization—the needs of specialization versus the needs of coordination (2). These divergent needs cause inevitable conflict between functional and top management, and often lead to nonoptimizing decisions. All major decisions must be made by top management, which may have insufficient information. The matrix organization grew out of the necessity for someone to work with the experts and specialists. The project manager assumes the role of "decision broker" (2) whose job it is to solve problems through the experts (functional managers and their specialists), all of whom know more about their particular field than he.

Recognizing that the matrix is a complex organizational form is just the first step. The next step is getting the organization to function. Its successful operation, like that of any management function, depends almost entirely on the actions and activities of the various people involved. In a matrix, however, the important actions and activities are concentrated at the interfaces between the various organizational units. The most important of these interfaces are between the project manager and top management, and between the project manager and the functional managers.

INTERFACE MANAGEMENT

The project manager carries out his task of systems integration primarily by carefully managing the many diverse interfaces within his project. Archibald indicates that "the basic concept of interface management is that the project manager plans and controls (manages) the points of interaction between various elements of the project, the product, and the organizations involved." He defines interface management as consisting of identifying, documenting, scheduling, communicating, and monitoring interfaces related to both the product and the project (3).

The complexity that results from the use of a matrix organization gives the project manager many more organizational and project interfaces to manage. These interfaces are a problem for the project manager, since the obstacles he encounters are usually the result of two organizational units going in different directions. An old management cliche says that all the really difficult problems occur at organizational interfaces. Here the problem is complicated by the fact that the organizational units are usually not under the project manager's direct authority, and some of the important interfaces may be outside of his company or enterprise.

TYPES OF INTERFACES

There are many kinds of project interfaces. Archibald divides them into two types—product and project—and then further divides them into subgroups, of which management interfaces are a major division. The problem of the overall project/functional interface is thoroughly discussed by Cleland and King who point out the complementary nature of the project and the functional or discipline-oriented organization. "They are inseparable and one cannot survive without the other" (4).

There are three general categories of interfaces that the project manager must continually monitor for potential problems: 1. personal or people interfaces, 2. organizational interfaces, and 3. system or product interfaces (5).

1. *Personal Interfaces*. These are the "people" interfaces within the organization. Whenever two people work on the same project there is a potential for personal problems and conflict. If the persons are both within the same line or discipline organization, the project manager has limited authority, but he can demand that the line supervision resolve the problems that arise. If the persons are not in the same line or discipline organization, the project manager finds himself in the role of mediator, with the ultimate alternative of insisting that line management resolve the problem or remove one or both of the individuals from the project team. Personal interface problems become even more troublesome and difficult to solve when they involve two or more managers.

2. *Organizational Interfaces*. Organizational interfaces are the most troublesome types of interfaces since they involve not only people but also

varied organizational goals and conflicting managerial styles and aspirations. Each organizational unit has its own objectives, its own disciplines or specialties, and its own functions. As a result of these differences, each organizational unit has its own jargon that is often difficult for other groups to understand or appreciate. Misunderstanding and conflict can easily occur at the unit interfaces. These interfaces are more than purely management interfaces since much day-to-day contact takes place at the working level. Purely management interfaces exist when important management decisions, approvals or other actions will affect the project. Organizational interfaces also involve units outside the immediate company or project organizations such as the customer, subcontractors, or other contractors on the same or related systems.

3. *System Interfaces*. These are the product, hardware, facility, construction, or other types of non-people interfaces inherent in the system being developed or constructed by the project. They are interfaces between the various subsystems in the project. Here the problem is intensified because the various subsystems are usually developed by different organizational units. As pointed out by Archibald (3) these system interfaces can be actual physical interfaces existing between interconnecting parts of the system, or performance interfaces existing between various subsystems or components of the system. System interfaces may actually be scheduled milestones involving the transmission of information developed in one task to another task by a specific time, or the completion of a subsystem on schedule.

MANAGEMENT INTERFACES

Each of the three types of interfaces that have been described pose important problems. Problems become particularly troublesome when personal and organizational interfaces are combined into what may best be called management interfaces. Management interfaces have personal aspects because normally two individuals are involved, such as a project manager and a particular functional manager. And management interfaces also have organizational aspects because the respective managers lead organizations which probably have conflicting goals and aspirations.

There is a great difference between the conventional organization chart (whether it be hierarchical or matrix) and the actual operation of a real-world organization. The conventional hierarchical organization chart, or matrix organization chart, clearly shows many of the management interfaces, such as superior/subordinate, and project management/worker relationships. But, conventional management charts only suggest some of the other important interfaces. These interfaces, shown by the double-ended arrows in Figure 2-1, consist of

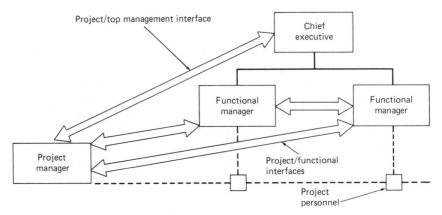

Figure 2-1. The multiple management interfaces in the matrix.

project manager/functional manager interfaces, project manager/top management interfaces, functional manager/functional manager interfaces, and sometimes even project manager/project manager interfaces.

Most important are the interfaces between the project managers and the various functional managers assisting the project. These relationships are almost inevitably adversary since they involve a constantly shifting balance of power between two managers on essentially the same reporting level.

The interface with top management is important because it represents the project manager's source of authority and responsibility. The project manager must not only have the real and unqualified support of top management, but must also have a clear and readily accessible communication link with them. The project manager must be able to get the "ear" of top management whenever necessary.

The interfaces between the various functional managers are important because they are the least visible to the project manager, and he might not be immediately aware of a trouble spot.

THE INTEGRATION PROCESS

Systems integration is related to what Koontz and O'Donnell call "the essence of management-coordination, where the purpose of management is the achievement of harmony of individual effort toward the accomplishment of group goals" (6). However, doesn't every manager have this function? Yes, but the project manager must be preoccupied with it. The project manager's major responsibility is to assure that a particular system or activity is assembled so that all of the components, parts, subsystems and organizational units fit together as a functioning, integrated whole, according to plan. Carrying out this responsibility comprises the function of systems integration. Integration is an action that is important to the success of any project whether hardware is involved or not. Any project involving many people, many organizational units, and many subsystems must be carefully and thoroughly integrated if the system is going to fit together as projected.

The management function of integration was identified and described by Lawrence and Lorch. They pointed out that with the rapid advances in technology and the greater complexity of systems to be managed, there is an increased necessity both for greater specialization (differentiation) and for tighter coordination (integration) (7)(8). An effective manager has a need for both; however, since they are essentially antagonistic, one can usually be achieved only at the expense of the other. This can be described as a trade-off between these two functions, as shown in Figure 2-2.

It has been suggested that the ideal high performance manager appears on the arrow midway between differentiation and integration, and is probably typical of high performance top management. It is also true that line or discipline management usually appears closer to the differentiation arrow, and that the project manager will be closer to the integration arrow. This model illustrates the need for the project manager as integrator.

The role of the project manager in the matrix organization has been analyzed by Galbraith (9)(10), Lawrence and Lorsch (7)(8)(11)(12) and Davis and Lawrence (3). They point out that the horizontal communication in a matrix organization requires an open, problem-solving climate. However, as pointed out by Galbraith (9)(10), when the sub-tasks in an organization are greatly differentiated a matrix structure may be required to achieve integra-

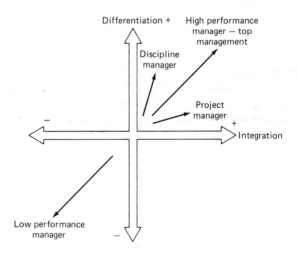

Figure 2-2. Measuring managerial performance.

tion. The integrator coordinates the decision processes across the interfaces of differentiation. The project manager as the integrator is necessary to make the matrix organization work.

Problem solving and decision making are critical to the integration process since most project problems occur at subsystem or organizational interfaces. The project manager is the only person in the key position to solve such problems, and provides "1. a single point of integrative responsibility, and 2. integrative planning and control." (5) The project manager is faced with three general types of problems and the subsequent necessity for solving them:

1. Administrative problems usually involving the removal of road blocks or the setting of priorities. A major effort is necessary to resolve organizational conflicts involving people, resources or facilities.
2. Technical problems which necessitate making key decisions, deciding on scope changes, and making key trade-offs among cost, schedule or performance. Decisions are necessary to select between technical alternatives which impact project performance.
3. Customer or client problems which involve interpretation of and conformance to specifications and regulatory agency documents.

The integration process becomes more critical and more difficult in the matrix where problem solving cannot be accomplished without considerable interaction on the part of the concerned managers. A great deal of negotiation is necessary if all project interfaces are to be managed and all real and potential conflicts resolved. It is imperative that the project manager function as an effective integrator if the matrix is to work.

THE BALANCE OF POWER

Having implemented a matrix organization, top management must recognize that it has placed a new player in the management game—the project manager. Conflict will naturally arise from the adversary roles between the project manager and the functional managers who participate in the project. This relationship can best be described as a balance of power between the two managers involved (Figure 2-3). This relationship has also been described as a balance of interest and a sharing of power (14). But this does not imply that the shared power is ever truly balanced, because in reality the balance of power is a dynamic, constantly changing condition that cannot be static even if so desired.

There is no way to assure a balance of power at every managerial interface. Theoretically, it should be possible to divide authority and responsibility more or less equally between the project and functional managers, which would imply a very clear balance of power. This is not only very difficult; it doesn't

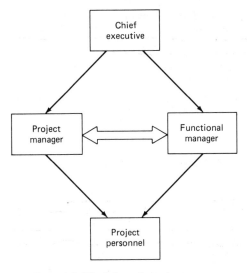

Figure 2-3. The balanced matrix.

happen very often. Various authors have attempted to delineate the authority and responsibilities of both project and functional management in order to assure a balance of power (4). Certainly such a delineation can indicate where major responsibilities lie, but it cannot guarantee a balance of power. In fact, there are many reasons why it is almost impossible to have a true balance of power between functional and project management. Not the least of these reasons is the fact that a matrix consists of people, and all people, including managers, are different. Managers have differing personalities and differing management styles. Some management styles depend on the persuasive abilities of the manager while others depend on or tend to fall back on strong support from top management.

Since the project, program or creation of product is usually the most important of all of a company's activities, the project manager is very important. He or she is the one who puts the company in a position where it can lose money or make a profit. Therefore, in terms of the balance of power, it would seem that the scales would always be tipped in the project manager's direction, particularly when he or she has the firm support of top management. Not necessarily so! In fact, not usually so, at least in a matrix organization. In a pure project organization, there is no question as to who holds the power. But in a matrix organization the functional manager has the aid of powerful forces; it is the functional manager who is normally perceived by project personnel to be the real boss. This is inevitable since functional management is part of the management hierarchy which goes directly up to the president of the company, and is therefore perceived to be "permanent" by the employees. After all, the functional organization represents the "home-base" to which personnel expect to return after the completion of the project.

Strong top management support of the project manager is necessary to get the matrix to work, and even this support will not guarantee project success. However, the matrix will not work without it. The project manager must get the job done by any means at his disposal even though he may not be perceived as the actual boss.

THE PROJECT/FUNCTIONAL INTERFACE

The secret of the successfully functioning matrix can thus be seen to be not just a pure balance of power, but more a product of the interface or interface relationships between the project and individual functional managers. Every project decision and action must be negotiated across this interface. This interface is a natural conflict situation since many of the goals and objectives of project and functional management are so different. Depending on the personality and dedication of the respective managers, this interface relationship can be one of cooperation or conflict. Neither a domineering personality nor a power play approach is the solution. The overpowering manager may win the local skirmish, but usually manages, sooner or later, to alienate everyone on the project. Across the project/functional interface, cooperation and negotiation are the keys to successful decision making. Arbitrary and one-sided decisions by either the project or functional manager can only lead to or intensify the potential for conflict. Unfortunately for the project manager, he can accomplish little by himself; he must depend on the cooperation and support of the functional managers. The old definition of a successful manager as "one who gets things done by working through others," is essential for successful project management in the matrix organization.

In a matrix organization, the project manager's most important interface is with the functional managers. The conventional matrix two–boss model does not adequately emphasize this relationship. Obviously, the project manager and the functional manager cannot give conflicting orders. The two managers must communicate with each other on a daily basis, and usually more often. The organizational model shown in Figure 2-3 shows the managerial relationship as a double-ended arrow indicating that the relationship is a two-way street. Consultation, cooperation and constant support are necessary on the part of both the project and functional managers. This is a very important relationship, a key to the success of any matrix organization, and one which must be carefully nurtured and actively promoted by both project and functional management.

STRONG VS. WEAK MATRICES

Achieving an equal balance of power between project and functional management may in most cases be a desirable goal. Certainly it should be a way of minimizing potential power struggles and possible conflicts. There is no way to be certain that there is an equal balance of power, and it is probably rarely achieved. However, it can be approached by assuming that the project manager has the full support of top management and that he reports at a high enough level in the management hierarchy.

When it may not be desirable to have an equal balance of power the scales can be tilted either way. For instance, a project may be so important to the company, or the budget and schedule so tight, that top management feels the project manager will need to be in a very strong position. Or perhaps the project manager sees that he must tilt the organizational balance of power in his favor to obtain better project performance. On the other hand, top management may decide that functional management could use more backing. In either case, the balance of power can be tilted in either direction by changing any one or any combination of the following three factors:

1. *The Administrative Relationship.* The levels at which the project and functional managers report, and the backing which they receive from top management.

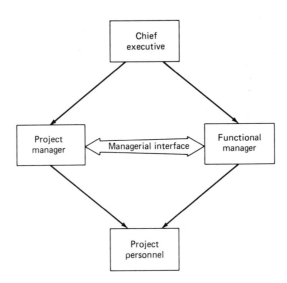

Figure 2-4. The balance of power in a strong matrix.

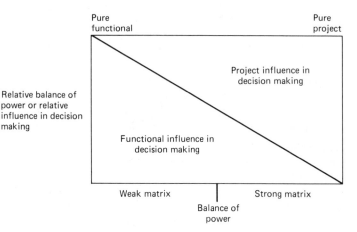

Figure 2-5. The balance of power in weak and strong matrices.

2. _The Physical Relationship_. The physical distances between the various people involved in the project.
3. _The Time Spent on the Project_. The amount of time spent on the project by the respective managers.

These three factors can be used to describe whether the matrix is strong or weak. The strong matrix is one in which the balance of power is definitely on the side of project management. This is shown by the model in Figure 2-4. A weak matrix is one in which the balance of power tilts decisively in the direction of line or functional management.

The managerial alternatives can be shown as a continuum ranging from pure project to functional (Figure 2-5) (15). The matrix falls in the middle of the continuum, and may range from very weak to very strong depending on the relative balance of power.

THE CRITICAL ACTIONS OF INTEGRATION

The integration process is difficult to separate from general good management practice. However, the integration process consists of a number of critical actions which the project manager must initiate and continually monitor. In most cases the project manager is the single point of integrative responsibility, and is the only person who can initiate these actions. These critical actions are of two types: 1. those which are essentially just good project management practice and which must extend over the entire life of the project, and, 2. specific one-time actions which must be taken by management (usually the project manager or a member of top management) to get the project started on the right foot. Those actions that extend over the life of the project will be discussed first. Among the most important of these actions are: (18)

- Planning for integration.
- Developing an integrated work-breakdown structure, schedule and budget.
- Developing integrated project control.
- Managing conflict.
- Removing roadblocks.
- Setting priorities.
- Facilitating project transfer.
- Establishing communication links.

Planning for Project Integration

Integration doesn't just happen—it must be planned. The project manager must develop a detailed planning document that can be used to initiate the project, and to assure that all project participants understand their roles and responsibilities in the project organization.

The project manager is the only person in the key position of having an overview of the entire system, and who can foresee potential interface or other integration problems. After identifying the interfaces the project manager will keep them under close surveillance in order to catch and correct any integration problems that occur. Particularly important in the project plan is the clear delineation of the project requirements for reporting, hardware delivery, completion of tests, facility construction and other significant milestones.

An important part of the project plan should be the integration plan. This may even be a separate document if a single department or even a separate contractor is responsible for project integration. In any case, the integration plan should define and identify all interface problems, interface events, and interrelationships between tasks and hardware subsystems. The plan should then analyze the interrelationships between the project's tasks and its scheduled sequence of events.

The project manager must continually review and update the administrative and technical portions of the project plan to provide for changes in scope and direction of the project. He must see that budget and resource requirements are continually reviewed and revised so that project resources will be utilized in the most effective manner.

The most complete and well integrated project plan is worthless if not implemented. Only the project manager can be sure that all task managers are aware of their roles and responsibilities in project success. Continuous follow-up by the project manager is necessary to ensure adherence to the project plan and awareness of any necessary revisions.

Developing an Integrated Work Breakdown Structure, Schedule and Budget

Solving the project manager's problems starts with the subdivision of every project into tasks which are capable of being accomplished. Creating this Work Breakdown Structure (WBS) is the most difficult part of preparing a project plan because the project manager must ensure that all of the tasks fit together in a manner that will result in the development of an integrated workable system. Too often a WBS is prepared by breaking up the project along easily differentiated organizational lines with very little thought as to the fitting together of the final system. However, the WBS is the "organization chart" which schematically portrays the products (hardware, software, services, and other work tasks) that completely define the system (16). Therefore, it is best to break up the project along subsystem lines for the top level breakdown, while putting lower level "work packages" within single organizational units.

This process of breaking up a project into tasks and work packages, that is, creating a WBS, is just the first step. The WBS must then be carefully integrated with the schedule and budget if the project is to succeed. Each work package must have an integrated cost, scheduled start and scheduled completion point. The WBS serves as the project framework for preparing detailed project plans, network schedules, detailed costing, and job responsibilities. A realistic WBS assures that project integration will take place.

Developing Integrated Project Control

The most prolific planning is useless if project control is ineffective. Whatever type of planning and control technique is used, all the important interfaces and interface events must be identified. Interface events such as hardware or facility completions will be important project milestones. The project network plan must be based on the interface events in order to facilitate analysis of the entire project on an integrated basis. Resource allocation and reporting periods can then be coordinated with interface events, and schedules and budgets can be designed.

Managing Conflict

The project manager has been described as a conflict manager (17). This does not mean that he should constantly be a fire fighter, though he cannot avoid his role in resolving conflicts, particularly when they involve project resources or project personnel. Conflicts are very likely to occur in the temporary project environment where the project manager is often the new player who has not had time to develop good working relationships with the functional managers. The conflict potential is also increased by the great differences in project functional goals and objectives, and by the unavoidable competition between projects for resources.

It is inevitable that problems occur at organizational and subsystem interfaces. These problems may or may not result in actual open conflict between individuals or organizations. A common occurrence is personal conflict between the two managers involved at the interface. Conflict situations occur primarily when the concerned groups or managers lose sight of the overall project goals or have different interpretations of how to get the job accomplished. The project manager must continually be on the lookout for potential and real conflict situations and resolve them immediately if he is going to have an integrated project.

Removing Roadblocks

Roadblocks are inevitable in a complex organization, and are the result of conflict situations. Resolving the conflict situation will eliminate many roadblocks, but others are always set up intentionally or unintentionally by managers and other personnel not directly involved with the project. These roadblocks may be the result of conflicting needs for resources and personnel, or conflicting priorities for the use of facilities and equipment. Administrative roadblocks often occur because managers outside the project do not understand or sympathize with the project manager's urgency. Such roadblocks are difficult to deal with, and the project manager may be forced to go to top management to get a satisfactory resolution.

Setting Priorities

In order to resolve or prevent conflict situations the project manager is constantly faced with the problem of setting priorities. There are two types of priorities that concern the project manager:

1. The overall company or organizational priorities which rate his project needs in relation to other projects within the organization.
2. The priorities within his project for the utilization of personnel, equipment and facilities.

The first type of priority may be beyond the control of the project manager, but it is a problem with which he must be continually concerned. Pity the poor project manager who is so busy getting the job done that he forgets to coment his relationships with top management. The result may be a low project priority that dooms his project to failure. The second type of priority is within the project organization and therefore within the project manager's control. These priority problems must be handled on a day-to-day basis, but in a manner that will promote the integration of the system.

Facilitating Project Transfer

Project transfer is the movement of a project through the organization from the conceptual phase to final delivery to the customer. Project transfer doesn't just happen, it must be carefully planned and provided for in the scheduling and budgeting of the project. The project manager has the responsibility of assuring that transfer takes place without wasteful effort and on schedule. The steps in a typical project are shown in Figure 2-6.

The movement of the project from block to block entails crossing organizational interfaces, an action which must be forced it it is to happen on schedule. The basic problem is that of making certain that the project is transferred quickly, without organizational conflict, without unnecessary redesign or rework, and without loss of relevant technology or other information. Experience has shown that the utilization of people who can move with the project across organizational interfaces is the best method of assuring effective project transfer. The project manager has two alternatives to facilitate project transfer: 1. The designation of suitable qualified personnel who can move forward with the project, i.e. change their role as indicated by the left to right dashed arrows. 2. The utilization of personnel who can move backward in the organization and serve as consultants or active working members of the project team. When the project moves ahead they serve as transfer agents who guide the project forward through the organization. Various possible personnel transfers are shown by the right to left solid arrows in Figure 2-6. Great importance must be placed on having customer, manufacturing and/or construction representatives take part in the design phase.

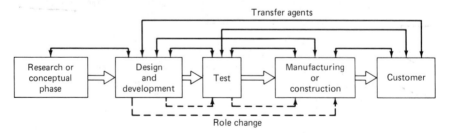

Figure 2-6. Project transfer.

Establishing Communication Links

The last of the integration actions, that of constantly maintaining communication links, is perhaps the most difficult and troublesome—because it involves the necessity for considerable "people" skill on the part of the project managers. Most project managers find that they spend at least half of their time talking to people—getting information, clarifying directives, and resolving conflict and misunderstanding. Much of this time involves the project manager's critical responsibility for maintaining all communication links both within and outside his project in order to assure project integration. Internal communication links must be maintained between each subdivision of the project, and the project manager must make sure that all of his team members talk with each other. In addition, the project manager is personally responsible for maintaining communication linkages outside his project. Many of the external communication links can be personally expedited by the project manager, and in most cases the communication consists of written documents.

Communication linkages internal to the project, however, must function continuously, with or without documentation, whether the project manager is personally involved or not. These internal communication linkages are most important to the health of the project since they involve the technical integration of the subsystems of the product or project. However, there are usually very real communication barriers across any two such subsystem interfaces. In order to ensure that problems don't accumulate and build up at these interfaces, the project manager must act as a transfer agent or a communications expediter. The model shown in Figure 2-7 illustrates the interface problem.

The project manager must serve as the bridge to make sure that communication barriers do not occur. These barriers can be caused by a variety of circumstances and occurrences which the project manager must watch for. A

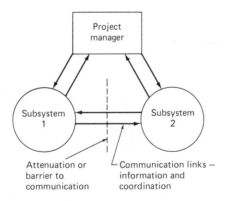

Figure 2-7. The project manager as communications expediter.

communication barrier may or may not result in actual conflict; this depends upon the individuals involved.

The project manager is the one person always in a position to expedite communication linkages. He can be seen as a transfer agent when he completes a communication link by transferring information and project requirements across an interface. Considering the number of interfaces in a complex, multidisciplinary, matrix-organized project, this process becomes a major effort for the project manager. The only saving grace is that many of these interfaces will be trouble free, with good communications, and the problems will not all occur at the same time.

Communication barriers may be caused by a variety of circumstances and occurrences. Some of the causes of communication barriers are:

1. Differing perceptions as to the goals and objectives of the overall system. Lack of understanding of project objectives is one of the most frequent and troublesome causes of misunderstanding. It can be directly attributed to insufficient action on the part of the project manager, since he has the major responsibility for defining project objectives. Even when these objectives are clearly stated by the project manager, they may be perceived differently by various project team members.

2. Differing perceptions of the scope and goals of the individual subsystem organizations. Again it is the responsibility of the project manager to clarify these problems, at least as to how they impact his project.

3. Competition for facilities, equipment, materials, manpower and other resources. This can not only clog communication routes but can eventually lead to conflict.

4. Personal antagonisms or actual personality conflicts between managers and/or other personnel. There may also be antagonism toward the project manager by line managers who perceive a threat to their authority or their empire.

5. Resistance to change or the NIH (not invented here) attitude may also detrimentally affect communication links between organizational units.

As indicated in Figure 2-8, the project manager has four important communication links: 1. upward to top management, 2. downward to the people working on the project, 3. outward to line managers and other projects at the same level in management, and 4. outward to the customer or client. The project manager has a major responsibility for maintaining communications with the chief executives in his organization. They must be provided with timely, up-to-date progress reports on the technical and financial status of the project. Similar reports must be provided to the client or customer, particularly if the customer is outside the company (i.e., the government).

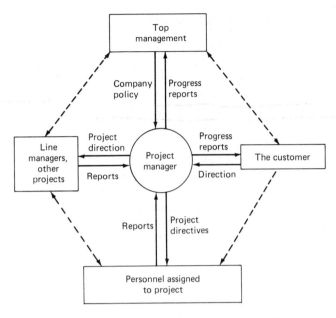

Figure 2-8. The project manager's communication links.

The other important communication link is with the people working on the project. The project manager must keep them informed by means of project directives and personal communications. In addition, there is a continual stream of reports from the discipline/line-organization manager and specialists working on the project. Many of these reports concern details, and the reports can be evaluated by administrators and assistant project managers. However, the ultimate decisions as to the worth of the report, and whether it should be included in progress reports to the customer and/or top management, is in the hands of the project manager. His communicative skills therefore must include the ability to accurately and rapidly evaluate, condense, and act on information from many sources.

Attenuation in these communication links at the organizational interfaces must be minimized. This means that the project manager must have an open line to top management. Conversely, he cannot have too many line managers interpreting his instructions and project goals to the people working on the project. Without open communication links, the project manager will surely fail. There are also a number of important communication links outside the scope of the project. The four most important such links are shown by the dashed arrows in Figure 2-8. The project manager has to recognize the existence of, and the necessity for these communication links. Rather than fight them, he should endeavor to make use of these relationships.

IMPLEMENTING PROJECT MANAGEMENT

To achieve successful project integration, it is also very important that the project get started on the right foot. Here again there are a number of important actions that must be taken, both by top management and by the project manager (19). The secret of project success is dependent on taking these critical actions as early as possible in the project life cycle. For the most part these actions are inseparable from the normal actions that must be taken to implement any successful project. However, most of the important decisions and actions are made during the project implementation phase. If the right decisions are made at this time, the project can be expected to run smoothly and integration will take place as planned.

The most important decisions, and resulting actions, are those made by top management. Many of these decisions must be made well before the project is actually started. Not all of them are entirely concerned with the integration function, but they are all necessary for the successful implementation of matrix project management. The most critical ones which must be undertaken by top management are:

1. Completely selling the project management concept to the entire organization.
2. Choice of the type or form of project organization to be utilized.
3. Issuance of a project charter to completely delineate project vs. functional authority and responsibilities.
4. Choice of project manager.
5. Choice of the right functional managers to participate in the project and/ or matrix organization.
6. Supply adequate resources to the project organization such as finances, equipment, personnel, computer support, etc.
7. Continuing support to the project manager.

The above list is more or less in the order that the decisions or actions must be undertaken, and most of them must be completed prior to the actual implementation of the project.

Now that top management has successfully established project management and has given it full support, the action passes to the newly appointed project manager. There are a number of specific actions that he must initiate to start the project on the road to success, and to ensure project integration. The project manager is the single point of integrative responsibility, and is the only person who can initiate and monitor these actions. The most critical of these actions are:

1. Issuance of the Project Implementation Plan.
2. Creation of the project Work Breakdown Structure (WBS).
3. Development of the project organization.
4. Issuance of the Project Procedures Guide.
5. Issuance of a Project Material Procurement Forecast.
6. Issuance of Work Authorizations.

These actions are more or less sequential, although they are strongly inter-related, and must be worked on at the same time. The most important consideration is that documentation implementing the above actions be issued as early in the project life cycle as possible. Hopefully, much of this effort would have been accomplished prior to the initiation of the project, such as during proposal preparation. Even so, a great deal of effort is required during the "front end" of a project to accomplish these actions, and ensure that project integration takes place.

CONCLUSIONS

The project manager must do his job of project integration in spite of complexity, and this job is the most difficult in a matrix organization. Project integration consists of ensuring that the pieces of a project come together at the right time, and that it then functions as an integrated unit. To accomplish this integration process, the project manager must make a number of positive actions to see that integration takes place. The most important of these actions is that of maintaining communication links across the organizational interfaces—proving once again, that the principal function of the project manager is to serve as a catalyst to motivate his project team.

Project integration is just another way of saying interface management, since it involves the continual monitoring and controlling of a large number of project interfaces. The number of interfaces can increase exponentially as the number of organizational units increase, and the life of the project manager in a matrix can become very complex indeed. Interfaces usually involve a balance of power between the two managers involved. This balance of power can be tilted in favor of either manager, depending on the desires of top management. The project manager must continually keep his eyes on the various managerial interfaces affecting his project. He must take prompt action to ensure that power struggles don't degenerate into actual conflict. It takes very little foot dragging to sabotage the best project. Integration doesn't just happen, it must be made to happen.

REFERENCES

1. Koontz, Harold and Cyril O'Donnell *Principles of Management: An Analysis of Managerial Functions* (McGraw-Hill. New York 1972), p. 46.
2. Sayles, Leonard R. "Matrix Management: The Structure with a Future." *Organizational Dynamics* (Autumn, 1976), pp. 2–17.
3. Archibald, Russell D. *Managing High-Technology Programs and Projects* (John Wiley and Sons. New York 1977), p. 66.
4. Cleland, David I. and William R. King, *Systems Analysis and Project Management* 2nd Edition, (McGraw-Hill. New York 1975), p. 237.
5. Archibald, p. 5.
6. Koontz and O'Donnell, p. 50.
7. Lawrence, Paul R. and Jay W. Lorsch *Organization and Environment: Managing Differentiation and Integration* (Harvard University, Division of Research, Graduate School of Business Administration. Boston, 1967).
8. Lawrence, Paul R. and Jay W. Lorsch "New Management Job: The Integrator." *Harvard Business Review*, (November-December, 1967), pp. 142–151.
9. Galbraith, Jay *Designing Complex Organizations* (Addison-Wesley. Reading, Mass., 1973).
10. Galbraith, Jay *Organization Design* (Addison-Wesley. Reading, Mass., 1977).
11. Lawrence, Paul R. and Jay W. Lorsch *Developing Organizations: Diagnosis and Action* (Addison-Wesley. Reading, Mass., 1969).
12. Lorsch, Jay W. and John J. Morse *Organizations and their Members: A Contingency Approach.* (Harper and Row. New York, 1974). pp. 79–80.
13. Davis, Stanley M. and Paul R. Lawrence *Matrix.* (Addison-Wesley. Reading, Mass., 1977).
14. Davis, Stanley M. "Two Models of Organization: Unity of Command versus Balance of Power." *Sloan Management Review,* (Fall, 1974), pp. 29–40.
15. Galbraith, Jay R. "Matrix Organization Design." *Business Horizons,* (February, 1971), pp. 29–40.
16. Cleland and King, p. 343 .
17. Kerzner, Harold *Project Management: A Systems Approach to Planning, Scheduling and Controlling* (Van Nostrand Reinhold Co. New York, 1979), p. 247.
18. Stuckenbruck, Linn C. "Project Manager—The Systems Integrator." *Project Management Quarterly,* (September, 1978), pp. 31–38.
19. Stuckenbruck, Linn C. *The Implementation of Project Management: The Professionals Handbook* (Addison-Wesley. Reading, Mass., 1981). Chapter 6.

3. Project Management—Its Functions and Dysfunctions

Arthur G. Butler, Jr.*

PROJECT MANAGEMENT—THE CONCEPT

Introductory

Project management (PM) has evolved as a device to overcome, through "purposeful conflict," a "cultural lag" in the art of managing the development, acquisition, and introduction into effective use of technically complex systems (1). Although used in a broad range of undertakings, such as development of new commercial products and construction projects, full recognition of its value as a distinctive tool for management of technologically sophisticated activities awaited application to the defense weapon-systems acquisition process during and after World War II.

It was once possible for a defense development agency to provide aircraft specifications to selected contractors, have each develop a prototype, award a production contract to the successful contractor, and purchase all the competitors' models. As costs sky-rocketed and system technology became more sophisticated, the agencies shifted source selection competitions into earlier, lower-cost stages of the weapon system development cycle, moving first away from prototype competition, and then from design competition toward what has been called "management competition" (2).

Only rarely has the government maintained an in-house system development

*Arthur G. Butler, Jr., is Dean for Business Affairs of Santa Fe Community College in Gainesville, Florida. He received his PhD in economics and business administration from the University of Florida, MBA from Stanford Graduate School of Business, and baccalaureate degree from the U.S. Naval Academy. He served on the management faculty at the University of Florida and as head of the management faculty at Georgia Southern College. His work has appeared in the *Academy of Management Journal* and other periodicals, and as contributions to several books.

and acquisition capability. With some noteworthy exceptions, defense and space-systems agencies have contracted with industry for their needs, determined requirements and specifications, and managed contractual efforts through special coordination and control techniques. The management discipline has benefited from requirements in these contracts that sophisticated tools be employed to manage contracted time, cost, and performance parameters.

The managerial role of planning, organizing, and controlling activity tends not to be overwhelming when each member of the organization can focus on a relatively explicit task. For more complex work efforts, however, where a high degree of sub-task specialization is involved, not only must each specialized area be managed, but the activities of those separate areas must be integrated into an effective whole. With extraordinary advances in the state-of-the-art came more complexity, and the scope of managerial activity has come to involve a multiplicity of intraorganizational, intercompany, and even interindustry interactions.

Certain characteristics appear to be common in development of major systems that illustrate the massive coordination requirements which form the predominant management challenge in such endeavors: 1) growing size and complexity of systems; 2) increasing need for specialization of skills—scientist-engineer, technician, manager; 3) diversity of organizational and personal goals which promotes conflicts among managers and scientists-engineers in many areas (e.g., budget, cost, design change, delivery schedules); and 4) the difficult process of adapting the organization to rapid environmental change (3).

The need to develop efficient and effective practices for management of large research and development (R&D) projects has long been recognized, but certain environmental factors have made it difficult to achieve this objective: 1) uniqueness of creative endeavors; 2) lack of experience-based standards for conduct of purpose-oriented R&D under severe time-cost-performance constraints; 3) lack of assurance that efficiency/effectiveness in individual sub-projects will produce like results in the system as a whole; thus, 4) unsatisfactory bases for generalization of procedures to guide future efforts (4).

Thus, uncertainty plays a dominant role in management of R&D projects and the situation is exacerbated by long lead times required for development of military systems. Additionally, uncertainty exists concerning the nature of the military threat the system is designed to meet and the national defense policy which must be supported in that future period.

The traditional line-functional structure typical of most large organizations has not demonstrated a capability for assuring consistent success in developing and acquiring sophisticated systems. It is difficult in such an organization, however flexible its managerial style, to maintain a substantial team of creative specialists who do not fit neatly into a structure where work tends to be highly structured and role behavior tends to be carefully prescribed. This structure performed reasonably well as long as available managerial skills and resources could be focused on one or a few special projects whose technical requirements were not drastically different from the regular line of endeavor. With further technological advance, however, both government and industry had to adapt to multiple programs and projects of more and more complexity. Managers perceived the need for a structure that was tailored to the project task (e.g., systems management without undue functional constraints) which would integrate centrally the technical expertise of many interrelated functional groups.

Thus, PM evolved largely from the need to develop and produce large, costly, complex systems on a compressed time schedule. Lacking an elaborate conceptual foundation, PM tends to operate through organizational arrangements which vary depending on the balance desired between the new project structure and established functional components. In the Manhattan Project, the ballistic missile programs, and the Polaris submarine-missile program, the technique emerged as an essential ingredient of their high-priority efforts, and large PM organizations were superimposed upon functional structures in both government and industry.

Uses and Objectives

Modern executives must be cognizant of the myriad nonstructured activities necessary to complete a major project within time, cost, and performance parameters. The status of these projects, which typically are born in the R&D component, may vary from concepts to near completion. As the executive learns that he cannot keep current on all work efforts for which he is responsible, a project leader may be assigned to each major project to coordinate its progress in the several disciplines of the organization. The project leader becomes a focal point for information concerning his particular project and interacts with the diverse intraorganizational and extraorganizational activities involved. Influence tends to follow information as the latter accumulates with the project leader.

As projects are added, the executive depends increasingly on his project leaders to keep him informed and to coordinate relevant activities in the several functional groups. It could be said that "purposeful conflict" develops between a project leader and functional submanagers to highlight problems and identify needs for remedial trade-offs among the time, cost, and performance parameters of a particular project. The executive will usually expect project and functional managers to resolve operating problems among themselves, but bring major unresolved issues to him to enable him to manage by exception.

Government and industry have long employed quasi-project managers in the guise of "special coordinators," "monitors," and "expediters." Since authority assigned to these positions was typically not directive in nature, and since their usual concern was with bottlenecks, they had to resort to indirect measures (e.g., persuasion) to convince responsible personnel to take whatever action the "coordinator" felt was appropriate. Evolution of PM was probably delayed by failure of managers to fully understand its purpose. Early titles used for the managerial integrator were misleading, and the scope of his responsibility was rarely clear. Some confusion was also generated by differing interpretations of what constitutes a "pure project" or a "pure functional" type of organization, which may be viewed as extreme positions on a continuum of task-management approaches.

PM has been variously defined, but the technique does not appear to have been sufficiently conceptualized to permit formulation of a definition that would command a consensus. Attempts have ranged from the fairly simple assertion that project is a general management activity encompassing planning, control, supervision, and the engineering or manufacturing involved in producing the end item, to the comprehensive definitions adopted by the Department of Defense (DOD) for management of the weapon-systems development and acquisition process (5).

The usual goal of PM is to provide sustained, intensified, integrated managerial attention to complex organizational ventures that require focus of a substantial portion of total organizational resources on a specific objective which typically: 1) involves a high degree of interdependence among specialized work tasks; 2) requires integration of these specialized efforts as a major if not the predominant managerial consideration; 3) must be completed in accordance with relatively severe cost, schedule, and cost constraints; 4) promises severe performance penalty or loss to the organization if unsuccessful.

With introduction of PM into large functional organizations came significant changes in prevailing authority and responsibility patterns. In the extreme case of "maximum intensification" of managerial attention, the project manager was charged with complete responsibility for development and acquisition of the weapon system, and was granted authority to direct all project-related effort throughout the organization, subject only to the overall project plan approved by top management. At the other extreme, the so-called project manager was assigned coordinative (or simply monitoring) responsibility for integration of project-related efforts, but existing patterns of functional responsibility and directive authority remained intact. In most instances, the project manager was required to "sub-contract" with the functional organization, at least in part, for specialized efforts required for successful completion of the project. It has been the unusual case where the project manager enjoyed the design, development, production, test, and support capabilities fully equal to the requirements of his project (i.e., to enable him to operate as an independent product division). Normally, he must obtain these specialized services on a task-and-fund basis whether it be by intraorganizational assignment of work packages or by contract with an outside concern.

Typical Ingredients

Broad acceptance of the PM concept in the DOD was tempered somewhat by the enjoinder that discretion be used in establishing projects. The pertinent DOD directive made it clear that such discretion is vital because the net result of converting all or most major work packages into systems/projects would be decimation of the functional organizations and loss of capability to handle on-going, non-projectized work. A significant reason underlying the adoption of PM was to achieve some degree of relative priority among major work efforts throughout the DOD with full recognition that, as projects multiply, relative priorities tend to become more difficult to determine and ultimately perhaps less meaningful.

Since many years may elapse between the time need for a product is perceived and the time such product is finally in use, a basic element of project success is recognition of the point in time when the project method is required for a given work effort; that is, when to form a project as opposed to assignment of the task to the regular functional organization. There appear to be no simple rules to follow, but several general criteria have been suggested for consideration (6).

Magnitude. PM is appropriate for undertakings concerned with a specific end product, such as a complex weapon system, a move to a new plant site, a corporate acquisition, or development of a new product for the market. The question of size is a relative matter; however, when an undertaking requires substantially more resources than are normally available for conduct of routine business, project techniques appear to be appropriate. Although the functional elements required to produce the end product may exist, a given function may be overwhelmed by the diversity and complexity of such a new task. PM provides a logical approach to definition of organizational relationships and problems which will be encountered in integration of the work to be done, particularly since the organization must continue normal operations during the project's life.

Unfamiliarity. The project method may not be necessary for a given work effort unless it constitutes an unusual undertaking for the organization. For example, a minor engineering change for an existing system might be effectively accomplished by the regular structure, but complete re-design of a major system would probably be suitable for PM. In the first instance, each functional manager concerned could draw on past experience and available resources to accomplish his portion of the work. In the latter case, the significance of cost, schedule, and technology constraints may warrant designation of a project manager to integrate the functional activities required to accomplish the objective.

Interrelatedness. A decisive criterion for establishment of a project is the extent to which the constituent tasks of the work effort are interdependent. If the effort requires integration of many functionally separated activities which are critically interrelated, PM techniques appear worthy of consideration. For example, early planning for development of a new product might require completed sales forecasts before plans could be developed for manufacturing processes, industrial facilities, special tooling, and marketing strategy. In the absence of an agency responsible for coordinating all these activities, if credible estimates are not forthcoming, or if conflicting plans are submitted by different departments, then the singleness-of-purpose of PM would seem appropriate.

Organizational Reputation. The stake of the organization in the venture is an important consideration in deciding whether the use of PM would be cost-effective. For example, if failure to complete the contract on time and within cost and performance constraints would seriously damage the company's stature in the industry, the case for using PM would appear to be strong. Furthermore, in the case of defense contracting, the contractor is dealing with a single customer whose adverse reaction to unsatisfactory performance could be catastrophic in terms of future awards.

Summary. PM is a device for managing significant, unique work efforts, but it is no panacea. Before decisions are made to employ project techniques, specific aspects of the organizational environment should be carefully weighted and evaluated, including: objective of the planned effort; potential for methods improvements; size and complexity of the project; and status of active and prospective projects.

In short, the traditional vertical relationships of an organization often prove to be inadequate to manage the complexity of a single but significant venture, and the horizontal relationships appropriate to the technology involved must be established. PM provides horizontal and diagonal relationships which may not have been previously prescribed, but balance between functional and project components must be preserved.

Organizational Alternatives

Organization is essential for effective management of R&D efforts, but contemporary theories and practices are often unable to cope with the operational objectives and requirements of modern technology. The so-called principles of organization may be valid, but they should often be rearranged, modified, and supplemented to develop improved organizational methods, sensitivity to legitimate operational needs, and an optimum level of desired innovation.

Some writers have advocated a "hands-off" philosophy toward management of R&D, insisting that the most effective performance results from minimal managerial intervention. The general argument contends that while management of some functional areas must necessarily be productivity-centered, the central managerial thrust in R&D cannot be toward accomplishment of prescribed jobs according to predetermined standards; thus, the primary managerial emphasis should be placed on motivation, encouragement, and participation with individual professionals.

While there may be some merit in this philosophy, there is considerable evidence that managerial principles which are applicable to other enterprise activities also apply to R&D. In other words, although motivational problems may be less obvious or less critical in the production-oriented approach, they do exist. Sound organizational structure is basic to effective managerial control, since it provides a foundation for planning and coordination, assignment of duties and responsibilities, and measurement of the effectiveness of each unit in implementing plans established for it. Since R&D has discrete objectives, and since its work is difficult to plan and its effectiveness difficult to measure, a sound organizational structure would appear to be all the more essential.

There is no consensus on the desirability of PM as a means for achievement of a given level of managerial attention and emphasis. One survey of companies which have used the concept revealed the following alleged advantages of "projectizing" a significant organizational undertaking (7): 1) better visibility of efforts and more intensive focus on results; 2) improved coordination and control of the diverse work efforts; 3) higher morale and better mission orientation of project employees; 4) accelerated development of managers under conditions of broad project responsibilities; 5) better customer relations; 6) shorter product development time; 7) lower total program costs; 8) improved quality and reliability of end product; 9) higher profit margins; and 10) better control over project security.

The same survey, however, reported alleged disadvantages which tend to contradict the claimed advantages: 1) a tendency for functional groups to neglect their jobs and permit the project organizations to do their jobs for them; 2) excessive shifting of personnel between projects because of changes in relative priorities; 3) duplication of functional skills between projects and functional components; 4) more complex internal operations; 5) inconsistency in the application of company policy; 6) lower utilization of personnel; 7) higher program costs; 8) more difficulty in management; and 9) lower profit margins.

A major attraction of the "pure" project organization is that it provides complete line authority over the project; that is, project participants work directly for the project manager. A major disadvantage is that costs in a multi-project company would tend to be prohibitive as resources would be widely duplicated. Since no reservoir of specialists would be provided in a functional component, project managers would tend to retain personnel on the project long after their services were necessary. Furthermore, there would be no functional group to plan for the future and form a basis for company capability to win new and profitable programs.

The project is usually established when the need for the system is conceived, and the project manager is assigned responsibility for its development, test, production, and delivery to the customer. When all units of the system have been delivered and accepted, the project (in theory) is discontinued and project personnel are released to other activities. The actual organization for PM and the level to which the project manager reports will depend on the commitment of top managers to the project approach, considerations with respect to the significance of the work effort, and the like.

It is not uncommon for the PM organization to change during the life of the project and adapt to the predominant need of the various stages of development; that is, a small development-oriented organization may be used during the early life of the project, to be replaced by a production-oriented staff during the manufacturing phase, and changed finally to a support-oriented staff when the system becomes operational. The project may also become a long-term or even a permanent effort.

As previously suggested, the organization for PM may take any of a number of forms on a continuum, the extremes of which are rarely found in practice. Between the extreme cases on the continuum ("pure" project or "pure" functional) lies an infinite variety of project-functional combinations. Each of these forms has certain advantages and disadvantages, and no one form is best for all applications, or even necessarily best for a given project throughout its lifetime. The essence of project organization is versatility; that is, the project organizes around the task and, as the task changes, so must the scope of the project organization.

The matrix organization is a mixed project-functional structure, some variant of which is used widely in companies engaged in developing complex systems. The mixture can lie anywhere between the two extremes on the continuum, the precise structure being determined by the specific task requirements of the project. The project manager may report to the chief executive in a line capacity and his staff tends to vary in number from only a few to several hundred people, depending upon the degree to which project activities are to be centralized.

In the matrix organization, the project manager has authority over the functional managers regarding the "what" and "when" of project-related activities; the functional managers determine "how" support will be provided. The functional managers are responsible to both their line supervisors and the project manager which appears to represent a significant departure from the traditional scalar principle and the line-staff dichotomy until the project-specific nature of the authority/responsibility relationship with the project manager is clearly recognized. It is significant that the functional manager may be supporting several different project efforts simultaneously, and is confronted with the whole host of problems associated with development of a workable system of priorities.

Organizational authority thus flows vertically, horizontally, and diagonally through the company and there are similar relationships between the project manager and project contributors who are organizationally positioned outside the parent company. In this dual-management process, deliberate conflict is recognized as a mechanism for achieving effective trade-off decisions.

The matrix organization has many advantages: 1) the project is emphasized as the focal point for all project-related matters; 2) flexible utilization of manpower is provided by a reservoir of specialists in functional organizations; 3) specialized expertise is available to all programs as dictated by relative importance of need; 4) project personnel have a functional home when no longer needed on a given project; 5) responsiveness to project needs is generally better as lines of communication are established and decision points are centralized; 6) management consistency among projects can be maintained through deliberate conflict operating in the project-functional environment; and 7) better balance between time, cost, and performance can be obtained through the built-in checks and balances (deliberate conflict) and continuous negotiations between the project team and the functional organizations.

There are also disadvantages to matrix organization: 1) balance between the functional and project organizations requires continual surveillance to ensure that neither seriously dilutes the other; and 2) balance between time, cost, and performance parameters must be monitored to ensure that neither group favors cost or time over technical performance (8).

Matrix organization may be viewed specifically as a form of organizational pluralism overlaid temporarily on the traditional hierarchical model to facilitate its adaptation to professional work (9). Rather than separating people into professional groups, matrix organization separates certain work activities into projects, and these projects then compete for organizational resources to accomplish their specific assignments. A significant feature of matrix organization is that while professional groups tend to constitute a permanent commitment for the employee, project groups are temporary systems which may have a life expectancy of only a few years. Generally, an employee is assigned to a project for its limited life, but he may be assigned only as long as his specialty is needed in the project effort. His temporary rank in the matrix hierarchy may differ from his relative rank in his permanent department, and, in some cases, his position or role in the matrix structure may require him to call upon his permanent supervisor to provide certain project-related services. As one project assignment is completed, the employee may return to his "permanent" assignment in a functional department, or he may be assigned to another project. In some cases, an employee may be assigned part time to two or more projects simultaneously.

In the matrix structure, people have multiple roles, and there is a potential for confusion about these roles. It has been noted that this approach dilutes functional authority and increases requirements for coordination and control. In order to overcome the confusion which arises from complexity and multiple roles, all persons involved with matrix organization must clearly understand the roles of project employees and the project manager, and this can be accomplished largely through training and experience.

Matrix organization focuses on adaptive, short-run systems which are operated by a carefully selected set of professionals who contribute diverse skills to the project effort. The project group is organized around a problem to be solved, and its manager is more a coordinator and linking-pin between occupational groups than a command authority. The project manager must be familiar with the language of the different groups involved and be able to communicate and mediate between these groups (10).

The project manager accomplishes his objectives by working primarily with professional employees and managers, and his use of authority tends to differ from what is observed in the simple subordinate-superior relationship. PM tends to confirm the observation that " . . . simply being in an executive hierarchy does not mean that one can freely direct those below him," and higher-level managers depend more on their subordinates and peers than traditional theory explains. The decisions made in large projects are too complex for an individual, acting unilaterally, to make a thorough analysis of all factors governing important choices. The project manager must depend on many others to provide decision premises, analyses, alternatives, and proposed courses of action (11).

Framework for Analysis

The foregoing discussion has dealt with certain alleged limitations of functional organizations largely in terms of organizational behavior. Comparative organizational effectiveness has not been examined, as such, primarily because of the limited extent to which satisfactory criteria have been developed for such assessment and the fact that research has not yet confirmed any consistent and reliable association between the several measures of employee satisfaction and the various tentative measures of organizational performance. Accordingly, no attempt is made here to assign any cause-and-effect relationships between employee behavior and organizational performance, whether or not PM has been used.

The major difficulties which functional organizations have experienced in their attempts to provide appropriate managerial attention to multiple projects

the capability of his department to perform in the first place; 7) these employees are returned to the functional department after the "hot project" is completed, precisely when the functional executive no longer needs them so desperately; 8) "they have learned less structured work habits and will no longer be satisfied in my more structured organization"; 9) "their pay grades and salary levels have escalated and therefore my costs will increase, even if I could get an increase in the budget to cover them"; 10) "their aspiration levels have been upgraded and I have no means of satisfying them because the PM concept has supplanted my department at the top of the pay and status schedules"; and 11) "while my man was in the project office, he got into trouble with my submanagers by pushing work for the project, and I would just as soon not have him back anyway!"

On the other side, the project manager is not likely to have much sympathy for the problems of the functional executive. He is fully aware of his dependence upon the functional organization for fulfillment of project objectives on time, within cost and profit goals, and in accordance with performance specifications. The pressure is typically on him to perform, and to ensure that no "surprises" reach higher levels of management with regard to his highly significant work effort. He maintains sustained pressure on the functional executives, probably using their own personnel for the purpose because they have the necessary expertise for application of just the right kind of pressure. His objective is fairly well circumscribed, and he knows that the simple measure of his success is completion of the project according to plan. He will tend to use every available device and control technique to accomplish that objective. This is why he was given the job in the first place; the situation is highly competitive; and conflict was not unexpected.

PM seems to present an ideal environment for conflict. Classical organization theory emphasizes formal structure, procedures, departmentation, authority structure, job descriptions, interdependence of roles, and incentives for members of the organization. Conflict occurs, for example, when an individual has two superiors, or when two departments have legitimate but competing claims on common but scarce resources, or when the demands and activities of two or more organizational roles are otherwise not compatible. Conflict also occurs when insoluble problems arise in the decision-making, information processing, communication, search, and other organizational subsystems, or when two or more groups or individuals disagree on choices, or their choices are incompatible.

Applying this rationale, it is clear that the functional manager will perceive disagreement with the project manager whether they overtly disagree over issues of mutual concern, or their high degree of interdependence makes them aware of a lack of agreement. Actual disagreements are likely to increase when goals differ. Thus, other things equal, perceived disagreement between the two managers will increase with differences in goals and with increasing interdependence of their formal roles.

Role interdependence is an essential attribute of formal organization. It is a measure of the extent to which one party depends on another for work inputs or decision premises and tends to be high when both parties compete for scarce resources, when frequent consultation is required by job descriptions, or when the formal system sets up a widely-shared norm of consensus. Goals are a criterion for decision making; that is, for recognizing and structuring problems, for generating alternative choices, for evaluating acceptability of alternatives, or for making final choices.

If, for instance, the project manager uses his own goals to select problems for solution, for generating alternative choices, for evaluating acceptability of alternatives, or for making final choices, and the functional manager uses different (or differently weighted) goals for this purpose, the two managers are likely to see the entire process differently. Further, a major source of conflict in organizational subsystems is the departmental drive for autonomy. The high degree of interest shown by the project manager in affairs of the functional manager tends to induce in the latter a perception of potential "invasion" or "expansion" motives on the part of the former. On the other hand, the functional manager may adopt an "insulation" attitude under pressure; that is, he may deny responsibility for work efforts attributed to him by the project manager (14).

These conditions which give rise to conflict are quite completely satisfied in the project manager—functional manager relationship. Goals differ and there is a high degree of role interdependence. The propensity to conflict tends to be high.

Structure and Built-in Conflict

Many areas of intraorganizational, interorganizational, and interpersonal conflict exist in functional organizations, with or without PM. While these are significant, this discussion is intended to focus on those aspects of PM in functional organizations which engender new or intensify existing conflict. Nevertheless, the two areas of conflict are not clearly separable for a rather simple reason: the PM organization is one more structure within the larger organization, and all the sources of conflict are potentially present even if the arrangement were called something else. Oversimplifying somewhat, the chief differences between the former and latter areas of conflict may be summarized as: conflicts associated with change; conflicts associated with power and status relationships; and conflicts associated with concentration of professional employees, perhaps of differing disciplines, in a more or less autonomous group effort which has a limited life.

By emphasizing work flow and systems considerations which have significant cross-functional relationships, PM tends to violate established managerial practices with respect to hierarchical authority and responsibility, procedural arrangements and accommodations, departmentation definitions, incentive systems, unity of command and direction, span of control, resource allocation patterns, and assignment of performance goals. Established work groups are disrupted, staffing patterns tend to be duplicated, and functional departments are forced into interaction in an environment which stresses interdepartmental consensus (e.g., without conflict). Functional executives and their key subordinates are required to participate in the forward planning of activities which previously had been accomplished more or less unilaterally, and this increased participation of others in this area tends to engender fear of invasion or absorption.

Changed Patterns of Interaction

Attitudes toward Change. An important distinguishing characteristic of the PM environment is the prevalence of change. People tend to resist change, but, in activities associated with R&D, as contrasted with many other functions, change is a normal part of the operation while routine is minimal. The professional tends to thrive in this environment and probably would be bored if he were involved in less dynamic work; however, this continual transformation of work is not an unmixed blessing. For example, while a new project with unexplored facets and extensive resources may be stimulating, an expiring project or a situation with limited prospects for challenging assignments represents unwanted change. Similarly, peripheral (i.e., not work-related) changes in physical facilities, administrative procedures, and "trivial" circumstances like parking arrangements tend to be more disconcerting to the professional employee than to people who are engaged in more routine activity, and consequently are more strongly resisted by the former.

It has been observed that " . . . the words 'direct' and 'manage' strike terror in the technological breast, for they signify something less than reverent regard for the favored sacred cow of science, freedom of inquiry." Since no enterprise can afford random approaches to R&D, managers must take a common sense approach to the creative process, not one which is dictated by preconceived notions of what constitutes management and science, but one which is sensitive to the " . . . human dynamics—including conflict—which are the very fabric of individual or group creativity."

According to this argument, a skilled leader understands change and the dynamics of human growth, including conflict. Growth is uncomfortable, and, since change is required for growth and since there are alternative paths to any goal, conflicts are certain to develop; nevertheless, the argument holds, most management authorities either avoid the subject of conflict altogether or consider it in a distorted light. In fact, the whole purpose of management is frequently to disrupt " . . . an unsatisfactory set of conditions—conditions that by definition are harmful to the firm, even though its employees are most content with the status quo."

Researchers, for example, should not be surprised to learn that conflict often produces good, since conflict is a certain indicator of difference, and something different is precisely what the researcher is searching for. To avoid conflict, which is a distinct and detectable behavior pattern, is to ignore potentially profitable points of view (15).

Pressureful Environment. Establishment of the project manager adds a source of pressure for the functional executive, and the source may or may not be perceived by the functional executive as legitimate. In effect, he is forced into continuing interaction with a powerful role which he had no part in creating, and this new role exerts pressure for change while the functional executive tends to have a vested interest in the status quo. In short, this new environment disrupts the whole range of established ways of work, including accommodations of interpersonal relationships in which functional executives are involved. In this connection, the establishment of multiple projects severely complicates the functional executive's problem of assigning relative priorities for work efforts in the functional department, since he tends to have no control over the process whereby the relative importance of the several projects is assessed. The difficulty tends to be further complicated where relative priorities have not been established for all projects, because project managers will then tend to exert situational pressures in accordance with their individual perceptions of urgency.

Intra-team Considerations. The project manager tends to be the focal point for authoritative pressure to perform where, in the past, such pressure was spread over the several functional executives. It is likely that attempts by the project manager to divert such pressure to supporting agencies will be only marginally successful; a significant factor which is associated with project visibility. The project manager must organize a cohesive work team of professionals from diverse disciplines who work for him in perhaps a limited sense, and who have their own difficulties in adjusting to new working relationships within the project team, with their parent departments, and with other organizations who are associated with project-related work efforts. He tends to inherit problems of goal integration which accompany these professional employees to their new assignment; moreover, their professional reference groups tend to remain either in the functional department or with some other professional group outside the project team. In fact, these individuals may have been reluctant to leave their previous assignments for this and many other reasons.

Occupational conflicts tend to increase when professionals of diverse disciplines are required to work together as a team, especially when there are strong pressures for consensus and team results. A similar tendency exists when professionals and nonprofessional technicians of the same or related discipline are required to function as a team under such conditions. This latter tendency is frequently demonstrated as nonprofessional technicians in the logistic support functions seek to participate with professional engineers in pre-production planning of major weapon systems.

The project manager, and in some cases the functional executive, tends to experience continuing problems of conflict throughout the life of the project: conflict between professional standards of performance and the multiple managerial criteria which govern project cost, delivery, and performance; conflict associated with the frustration of individuals in their attempts to serve varied objectives and goals in a conflictual environment; the need to maintain effective communications which is difficult in the face of conflict; the need to encourage creativeness among professional employees in an environment which emphasizes pressure toward achievement of specified results within visible and effective constraints; the need to preserve the professional employee's commitment to his expertise when he becomes a member of the project team, which is essentially a managerial device rather than an arena for exercise of individual professional skills; the difficulty of maintaining affective neutrality in an environment where there is competition for loyalty to the project (or to the functional department, or to the profession); the need to provide adequate incentives for professional members of the project team when the work effort has a limited life, where advancement opportunities within the organization are either non-existent or obscure, and where violation of other commitments may be required to enhance the individual's opportunity to advance in other hierarchies (e.g., functional or professional); the lack of security or a clear picture of future employment prospects beyond termination date of the project; and a continuing struggle over areas of responsibility and authority, as, for example, whether a function should be performed in the functional dedepartment or by the project team.

Power, Status and Influence

At the root of much of the fundamental conflict associated with the project manager/functional executive relationship is the struggle for power and status among managers. There seems to be no question that the functional manager has lost both power and status, along with some degree of autonomy; however, there is more. The functional executive has actually experienced a sort of role reversal and has been placed in the position of receiving task assignments from the project manager; that is, the status of work-initiator accrues to the project manager and his group. The potential for conflict increases when external forces (i.e., top managers) require decisions which must be reached by internal compromise of preferred courses of action. Additionally, the propensity for conflict increases with the interdependence of members and the areas which they represent or control, and with the variety of professions involved. The project manager tends to be the problem definer and takes the lead in resolving such conflicts.

Since his authority does flow horizontally across existing vertical superior-subordinate relationships, the project manager is likely to find conflict and struggle regarding allocation of resources to his project. He generally has no explicit authority to resolve interfunctional disputes; but, as the focal point for the flow of project-related information, he may exercise influence beyond that which has been specifically delegated to him in the form of formal authority.

The project manager must make major and minor trade-off decisions involving cost-schedule-performance criteria. This requirements-balancing process tends to create internal and even extraorganizational conflict because there tends to be a significant lack of clear-cut lines of demarcation in the areas under consideration, and functional interests are not likely to be optimized in trade-off decisions in an environment where a given functional interest constitutes only one of many inputs to the decision-making process. The functional manager understandably tends to be parochial since he must support all projects either impartially or in accordance with established relative priority, and such "project-intensive" decisions will usually fall short of his desires.

Success in PM is usually measured by achievement of successful events in the planned network of accomplishments. The project manager needs to know what is to happen, when it should happen, and who is responsible to see that it happens. If he is to maintain control over his project, he must assure himself that events occur as they should, he must know in advance whether schedule is or is not likely to be met, and he must be able to act positively to keep the events flowing on schedule. Individuals commonly keep their work-related problems to themselves until it is too late to correct the situation, even through intensive application of effort and resources. To assure authenticity of communication, the project manager must instill confidence that managerial assistance based on a "confession of difficulty" will not be accompanied by punishment.

Communication in the project environment is difficult under the best of circumstances, primarily because of the complexity and interrelatedness of task responsibilities. The principal tool for communications is the project plan which is typically worked out in substantial detail early in the life of the project. Development of the plan is itself a source of conflict, for it is here that all interested parties are convened to make their contributions to the overall project blueprint. It is from this planning effort that the approved execution program, and therefore project authority, is likely to emerge; therefore, the struggle for power, status, and incorporation into the plan of participants' goals is likely to be at its highest level of intensity.

New Patterns of Control

PM drastically revises the work-initiation-and-control patterns in the organization as the functional executive becomes the recipient of tasks from the project manager, and is no longer able to determine on his own what needs to be done as well as how it is to be done. In fact, the basic information necessary to make functional decisions tends to be available to the project manager in the form of system requirements, and is not necessarily available to the functional managers in the desired context. Such information is usually available in a more specific perspective only in the form of functional task assignments received from the project team. In any event, the functional executive tends to assume a subordinated role to the extent that his role is prescribed and his performance is evaluated by the project manager as integrator of project work efforts; however, simultaneously, he is responsible to his formal superior for overall performance of the organizational function.

Developing estimates for the planning and control of project efforts is complicated by many factors, including the lack of precedent in R&D work, unpredictable technical problems, program changes resulting from new technology or shifting requirements, uncertainty of the time cycle, the inherent optimism of professionals, the human productivity variable, and bias of estimators. To promote project approval, professionals have a tendency to underestimate time and resources needed, as well as the extent of the technical problem to be solved, and to minimize difficulties as well as to overstate potential project benefits. Thus, in addition to deciding on the desirability and feasibility of the proposed project, the manager must often evaluate the capability of individual professionals to perform as planned (estimated).

In the absence of reliable quantifiable measures of their intangible contributions, performance of professionals in R&D projects is often evaluated by subjective standards constructed by managers. The most accurate source of information tends to be people who are technically and operationally closest to the situation; however, professionals tend to be reluctant to disclose existence of technical difficulties; to be overly optimistic about achievement; to report misleading information as a simple expedient; and to delegate reporting tasks to less-qualified personnel. It also appears that individuals can be instrumental in developing techniques for control of other functions, but can provide no means of evaluating the quality of their own performance.

R&D professionals want recognition, but, while professional and organizational acceptance may or may not be compatible, both must be based on an intelligent appraisal of performance. The professional can normally expect organizational recognition only from some type of review and evaluation; some responsible official must determine his contribution and have authority to reward his effort. This is not as obvious as it may seem in light of 1) the professional's reluctance to expose his performance to audit, and 2) the lack of adequate criteria for evaluating his contribution (16).

Competition for Professional Personnel

The task of staffing the project team is often very difficult. Other projects may be competing for the limited talent available, and the functional executive who "owns" such talent is under increasing pressure as the number and size of projects increase. Optimally, he would try to satisfy all requirements, but he is necessarily constrained by the requirement to maintain his own work force in the specialized area. For good and sufficient reason, the functional manager may be unwilling to release the personnel that the individual project manager feels he needs.

On the other hand, the employees themselves may be reluctant to leave their present positions. It is not uncommon for employees to be hesitant in this regard: they may fear termination of employment or less desirable jobs at the end of the project; they may be particularly reluctant to transfer if they have a good record in their present job; they may fear that their present supervisor will not be receptive to their return home; and they learn that the project manager does not always control their pay increases and other personnel matters of vital interest to individual workers.

PM tends to dilute the personnel resources of the functional departments as premium professional employees are selected for assignment to project teams. This has a double consequence: 1) the project manager tends to use the functional executive's own best people to determine tasks for and evaluate performance of the functional organization; and 2) the functional executive's capability to respond to such work assignments has been curtailed. These problems tend to be complicated by important situational variables discussed earlier in this section.

Functional Dependency

The project manager will also experience conflict along many of these same lines, but perhaps more importantly, he tends to be almost totally dependent on functional departments for fulfillment of his project needs. Even if he does have clear-cut project authority, he usually must exercise it across functional boundaries through his management team; that is, the type of influence that he wields tends to be significantly different from, say, the influence that is associated with hierarchical authority. In fact, all members of the project team occupy boundary positions—that is, they deal continuously across departmental and even company lines—and these positions have been demonstrated to be inherently stressful. Additionally, to the extent that project authority is not clearly defined, all project participants are vulnerable to role ambiguity, and this too is a common source of stress.

Specialization leads people to develop expectations associated with their respective work environments, and the work orientation of a department tends to determine the kinds of managers it will attract, the way those managers assess human problems, and the kind of work they consider to be most important. It has been observed that an individual's standards for judgment are influenced by his location in organizational space; "community centrism" develops as the norms of cultural subgroups influence if not determine the values and frames of reference of group members; and the "system centrism" of any social organization will affect its members' knowledge, experiences, attitudes, and judgments. This pervasive phenomenon has also been described as a process of selective perception that produces a bias with which project managers must contend in conducting their boundary activities (17).

Professional Expectations

Since the project manager, members of the project team, managers of professionalized functional departments, and many others who must interact in the project environment are likely to be professionals, it would be interesting to investigate the attitudes toward PM held by each of these groups of individuals. In the absence of systematic research, however, much of what can be said in this area can only be deduced from other generalizations about the expectations of employed professionals.

Professionals tend to seek autonomy while avoiding (or resisting) the hierarchical authority relationship typical of functional organizations—i.e., the superior-subordinate relationship—thus, to the extent that team members were subject to hierarchical authority in their former assignments, and to the extent that authority in the project environment is collegial, it could be expected that the goal of autonomy would be served by assignment to project teams.

It may be, however, that professional employees in the functional departments are permitted substantial freedom to pursue their individual tasks, and it may also be that the collegial atmosphere does not prevail in the project team. It has been observed that the tendency in many professionally oriented organizations is to organize professionals into groups which are homogeneous with respect to specialty, and that this type of structure tends to permit collegial authority relationships in the professional group, at least with respect to the decisions that are most significant to them; that is, decisions related to pursuit of individual technical activities. The point is that the professional who leaves his parent functional organization to become a member of the project team may not be serving his autonomy goal.

There is evidence that PM may be the type of activity that promotes a more authoritative approach to team performance than is generally expected. Furthermore, the individual professional may be the sole representative of his discipline on the project team while his reference group remains in the functional department. There is intense pressure for careful, well-structured planning, and tight, responsibility-fixing controls designed to maintain the integrity of cost-performance-delivery parameters of the project. The project has high visibility because of its significance to the organization, and failure of performance to conform to plan tends to result in increased pressure to improve performance of individual professionals. Although rigid rules and regulations may not be invoked to control daily performance, it may be that equally constraining behavior results from tightly defined accomplishment goals and milestone-type control systems.

Of course, many individuals thrive in this type of pressureful environment. To the extent that the project manager and members of his team are this type of individual, then they are likely to derive substantial satisfaction from their endeavors. At least this would tend to be true if they are accorded proper recognition and status by their superiors in terms of their accomplishments. Progress reporting can be psychologically demanding, however, and project personnel may resent the constant "over-the-shoulder" type of integrative effort typical of many projects.

In any event, it is difficult to see that the functional executive and his remaining professional employees would enjoy any of these more favorable possibilities. The significant work effort defined as the project has been removed from their area of control; that is, their scope has been substantially narrowed. They may feel that their intrinsic worth has been ignored by managers, and that the residual workload is either "hack" work or piece-work which has been assigned as tasks by the project team. Pressure for performance is intensified, and it comes from individuals who may have previously been subordinates in the same departmental organization. Autonomy has been degraded in any event, at least autonomy in any field of endeavor which is worthwhile from the professional viewpoint. One cautionary remark, however: to the extent that basic research activities are excluded from the project scope, which appears to be more common than not for large-scale endeavors, establishment of significant developmental efforts as projects may have removed enough pressure for results from the functional department that more, not less, autonomy may result in the research effort.

A further point might be made with respect to the project manager, at least to the one who is highly committed to professional standards. The integration task would appear to require a relatively strong commitment to organizational goals. Furthermore, the typical criteria for project efforts—cost-performance-delivery—tend to be organizationally oriented, with the possible exception of the performance parameter (before trade-offs). Associated with these elements is the reported reluctance of the scientific professional to seek out responsibility for implementation activities. The selection problem is clear: the project manager of developmental efforts, particularly those which extend to delivery of the finished product, cannot avoid implementation responsibility.

Recognition, influence, challenging work, and the like are alleged to be missing when the professional occupies a circumscribed role in the functional organization; thus, it might be expected that assignment to the project team with its obvious challenge, closeness to decision-making authority, and opportunity to be recognized through project visibility might operate to enhance the professionals' motivation. Again, however, it may not be true that the particular functional organization in which the professional is employed is deficient in this regard. The incentive system may be more or less satisfactory.

A high degree of expertise is desired by the project manager and it is reported that he typically gets the better talent in the organization. It may not be true that this superior talent is used in the best way, from the professionals' point of view. The project team is a management team, and the individual professional may have deserted his opportunity to perform technical work when he becomes a member of that team, even though he retains his professional orientation. He simply may not have the opportunity to exercise his technical talents directly as he deals in the managerial activities of task assignment, progress control, evaluation, and so on.

It appears that the opportunity for recognition is much greater in the visible project environment, and to the extent that the project manager shares credit for performance, his professional team members will be recognized at the highest organizational levels. This may or may not satisfy these individuals, however, since they may prefer acclaim from their professional colleagues rather than management. Whether they will have an opportunity to participate in the activities of their professional associations is another question which would have to be answered empirically.

It may be true that assignment to the project team brings an increase in pay and status for project team members, and this eventuality would produce further differential rewards between the project team and the functional departments. When these professionals return to their parent organization, whether or not the elevated pay and status continues, someone will tend to be dissatisfied.

Institutional Allegiance

Much has been written about the dual-loyalty problem, generally subsumed under the heading of "cosmopolitans and locals," although there is not much evidence concerning the extent to which this phenomenon has any connection with the value of contributions made by professionals to their employing organizations. It could be argued that commitment to one's skills might be sufficient for organizational purposes, at least to the extent that managers are capable of defining the skills required to perform the tasks necessary to achieve organizational purposes.

The findings of research into labor-management relations with respect to dual allegiance raise an interesting question: Is there something peculiar about professionals that would prohibit a simultaneous enthusiasm toward professional standards, where they are appropriate, and organizational standards, in their place? Or is it only the rank-and-file employee that can be simultaneously enthusiastic (or antagonistic) toward both the worker association (union) and the employing organization? If professional employees are antagonistic toward organizational purposes and standards, is there not also a possibility that they have a like attitude toward professional standards as well as any other restraint on individuality?

The concept of partial inclusion is too rarely brought into this discussion, perhaps because it conflicts with the notion that employees ought to be loyal to their organization. Nevertheless, since allegiance is apportioned in the mind rather than allocated among claimants from some fixed amount, it appears to be quite possible for an individual to be loyal to more than one organization at the same time just as it is probably impossible for a person to be totally loyal to one organization to the exclusion of all others with which he is associated (18).

Some writers seem to suggest that the integrative decision, which is made by managers, is somehow less crucial than the technical decision, which is made by professionals. Perhaps the search for knowledge, the avowed goal of the scientist, may be of such social significance that it transcends organizational purposes and should be of more fundamental importance than the constraining integrative decision. On the other hand, it would not be difficult to argue convincingly that in the organizational setting, where the purpose is not the search for knowledge, as such, the managerial decision which overturns the researcher's proposal in favor of action which is compatible with organizational goals should prevail.

In this connection, it is interesting to note that classical organization theorists reasoned that decisions would be made by experts. Difficulties arose, however, in defining individual roles with sufficient specificity that qualifications could be established for role incumbents, and then came the problem of selecting role occupants who possess those precise qualifications. There is little assurance that the selection problem will solve itself even if role requirements are relaxed and an attempt is made to hire individuals who are capable of fitting into the organic structure and who will naturally fill the necessary roles as the task evolves.

TOWARD A BALANCED CHOICE

The six tentative propositions that have guided this analysis are presented as a basis for evaluating the costs and benefits associated with PM (19). It appears that the following are warranted propositions:

1. PM tends to achieve intensified management of complex, nonroutine organizational efforts which, because of their crucial significance to the organization, require positive assurance of sustained, integrated administration of rather severe cost, schedule, and performance constraints.
2. PM in traditional functional structures tends to produce interorganizational and interpersonal conflict, and, in some instances, to exacerbate conflicts that already exist in the organization.
3. Valuable insights into the interpersonal relationships between managers and professional employees may be obtained by empirical analyses of these conflict situations.

Unfortunately, unresolved problems of quantification and measurement abound, and while there is considerable evidence to support these observations and the fact that these phenomena do occur as predicted, the extent to which their validity has been demonstrated ranges from near zero to limited. For example, there are virtually no objective assessments of how much the introduction of PM has improved the integration of such work efforts, nor of the net cost or net benefit that accrued from the structural change.

For these same reasons, the following propositions must be more cautiously labeled as probably warranted, but with reservations:

4. The high degree of single-purpose managerial attention desired cannot reasonably be expected to emerge from the traditional functional organization.
5. The degree of "purposeful conflict" associated with PM tends to be constructive in mitigating the so-called "cultural lag" in the art of management—that is, in serving a relatively short-term purpose that is highly significant to the organization without destroying the long-term viability of the supporting base for ongoing organizational effort (i.e., the traditional functional structure).
6. Professional employees of the organization have been party to, as well as victims and beneficiaries of, the induced conflict.

Clearly, many managers have decided to use PM for the reasons suggested in these propositions, but it is not altogether clear that the desired results cannot be obtained with the basic framework of the functional structure. The question appears to require comparative operational studies which examine projectized undertakings together with the "excluded alternative" arrangements, and these are very difficult to arrange. Similarly, whether PM is the answer to the "cultural lag" is problematical as is the question whether a viable functional structure can be maintained at reasonable cost over the long-term with establishment of multiple projects. In any event, the crucial question of relative priorities among work efforts remains, and it appears that this question persists under either approach.

Finally, if the motives generally attributed to professional employees can be accepted as reasonably accurate, some professionals do appear to have been victims and some have been beneficiaries of the PM approach. The extent to which these effects have been contrived, of course, is not known.

REFERENCES

1. Cleland, D. I. and W. R. King *Systems Analysis and Project Management* (McGraw-Hill. New York, 1968).
2. Peck, M. J. and F. M. Scherer *The Weapons Acquisition Process: An Economic Analysis* (Harvard University. Boston, 1962), pp. 350–351.
3. Kast, F. E. and J. E. Rosenzweig (eds). *Science, Technology and Management* (McGraw-Hill. New York. 1963), p. 308.
4. Glennan, T. K., Jr. "Research and Development," in Stephen Enke (ed)., *Defense Management* (Prentice-Hall. Englewood Cliffs. 1967), pp. 269–289.
5. "Systems/Project Management," Washington, D.C., Department of Defense Directive 5010.14 dated May 4, 1965.
6. Cleland and King, *Op. Cit.*, pp. 154–157.
7. Middleton, C. J. "How to Set up a Project Organization," *Harvard Business Review,* 45. pp. 73–82.
8. Cleland and King, *Op. Cit.*, p. 172. See also Rensis Likert and J. G. Likert, *New Ways of Managing Conflict,* (McGraw-Hill. New York. 1976), pp. 203–216.
9. Davis, Keith. *Human Relations at Work: The Dynamics of Organizational Behavior* (McGraw-Hill. New York. 1967), pp. 295–298.
10. *Ibid.*
11. Simon, H. A., D. W. Smithburg, and V. A. Thompson. *Public Administration* (Alfred A. Knopf. New York. 1950), p. 404.
12. Goodman, R. A. "Ambiguous Authority Definition in Project Management," *Academy of Management Journal,* 10:395–407, 1967.
13. Kahn, R. L., D. M. Wolfe, R. P. Quinn, J. D. Snoek, and R. A. Rosenthal. *Organizational Stress: Studies in Role Conflict and Ambiguity* (Wiley. New York. 1964).
14. Pondy, L. R. "Theory of Organizational Conflict," *Academy of Management Journal,* 9:246–256, 1966.
15. Sprague, P. A. "Man as a Research Tool," in C. D. Orth, III, J. C. Bailey, and F. W. Wolek (eds), *Administering Research and Development* (Homewood: Richard D. Irwin, Inc., and The Dorsey Press, 1964), pp. 351–355.
16. Roman, D. D. *Research and Development Management* (Appleton-Century-Croft. New York. 1968), pp. 360–408.

17. Katz, Daniel and R. L. Kahn. *The Social Psychology of Organizations.* New York: Wiley, 1966; Sherif, Muzafer (ed). *The Psychology of Social Norms.* (Harper and Row. New York. 1936); March, James and H. A. Simon. *Organizations.* (Wiley. New York. 1958).
18. Stagner, Ross. "Dual Allegiance as a Problem in Modern Society," *Personnel Psychology,* 7:41–47, 70–71, 1954; Katz and Kahn, *Op. Cit.,* p. 284; Allport, F. H. *Institutional Behavior* (Chapel Hill: University of North Carolina Press. 1933).
19. Butler, A. G., Jr. "Project Management: A Study in Organizational Conflict," *Academy of Management Journal,* 16:84–101, 1973, from which a number of other thoughts expressed herein are derived.

Section II

The Project Organization

This section emphasizes the organizational dimensions of project and matrix management.

In Chapter 4, Harvey F. Kolodny traces the evolution that often occurs from "pure" functional organizational forms, through the introduction of projects, to a matrix organization. He also describes the behaviors that are required of the key actors in this evolutionary process.

Then, Chapter 5 presents F. A. Hollenbach's description of the project organization of Bechtel Power Corporation. He provides details of team makeup, individual responsibilities and organization. The project manager's responsibilities in various phases of the project are delineated as are the qualifications and characteristics of the project manager. Client involvement, in the project and external influences on the project and the organization are also treated.

Chapter 6 presents Russell D. Archibald's depiction of the project office and project team—integral elements of the organization for projects that warrant a full-time project manager. He presents detailed specifications of the duties of the various project participants.

In Chapter 7 Richard L. Patterson expands on the role of the assistant project manager in terms of sets of needs—those of the project, the client, the contractor and the individual. While these are presented in terms of structuring a role for the assistant project manager, they are more generally relevant to other dimensions of the project as well. Various projects in which this role was made operational are described.

4. Evolution of Project and Matrix Organizations*

Harvey F. Kolodny†

Matrix organizations have become common in a wide variety of organizational sectors. From a restricted beginning in the aerospace industry, matrix applications have proliferated and now flourish in multinational corporations, financial institutions, hospitals and health-care agencies, and governmental and educational institutions. Effective management of a matrix organization calls for the use of behavioral skills and structural mechanisms in ways that constrast sharply with those of traditional forms of organizations. Nevertheless, most matrix organizations arise out of these traditional forms. This article develops a model of the evolutionary process, and of the behaviors required of the key actors in each stage of that process.

Not all organizations follow an evolutionary path to its logical conclusion. Some stop along the way because they have found the appropriate form for their situation. Others skip stages or go directly to the last stage. This is a feasible action and there are successful matrix organizations that have utilized it(4).* However, there is not significant empirical evidence as yet to suggest that shortcuts along the evolutionary path necessarily get the organization and its total behavioral and structural support systems to the appropriate form any faster than does a step-by-step approach.

Learning new behaviors takes time. For those who take giant steps, the price in human dislocation can be high, not only for the obvious victims of the accel-

---

*Portions of this article were previously published in "Evolution to a Matrix Organization" *Academy of Management Review,* V4, N4, 1979, 543–553 and "Managing in a Matrix" *Business Horizons,* March, 1980.
†Harvey F. Kolodny, D.B.A. is Associate Professor of Organizational Behaviour in the Faculty of Management Studies at the University of Toronto. He is a graduate electrical engineer from McGill University with extensive industrial experience in engineering industries. Harvey completed his M.B.A. at the University of Sherbrooke and his Doctorate in organizational behaviour at the Harvard Business School. His research, teaching, and consulting have been in the areas of organization design, improving the quality of working life through new organizational designs and, particularly, in the design, implementation, and management of matrix organizations.
*Numbered references are given at the end of this chapter.

erated change rate, but for the managers and changers themselves. They may be forced to adapt themselves at a pace too rapid for their cognitive and emotional capacities to keep up with. They may also pay a heavy psychological penalty for too quick a rate of change; and it will show when the difficulties in managing the matrix structure arise years after the design has been put in place (10).

Stages of Evolution

Most matrix designs combine two of the three dominant organization forms in our society: function, product, and geographic. I examine the evolution from a functional, or specialist organization basis to a combined function-and-product matrix form. The evolutionary mode presented here has four distinct states: function, project, product/matrix, and matrix.

PROJECT ORGANIZATION

Galbraith (8) provided an early descriptive example of how an organization evolves from a functional to a matrix form. The process begins with the organization's inability to respond in timely fashion to problems in its environment: variations required in the product lines, uncertainty in the competitive marketplace, complexity in the product-market relationships, and technological changes that threaten critical products with obsolescence. More often than not these environment-stimulated problems cut across departments in the organization. They demand complex and frequently interdependent responses from these different segments. The vertically structured hierarchy cannot cope with the horizontal coordinating requirements quickly enough. The organizational answer is to decentralize decision making around a specific task and to assign that task to a specific coordinator, often called a project manager.

This action usually takes some of the pressure off the top of the organization and the philosophy is soon extended to other tasks, activities, and projects. In essence, the organization acknowledges that a second orientation, one that is concerned with task coordination, cost, delivery, and performance is too important to be treated as a secondary concern by those functional managers whose primary orientation is to their specialist activities. The organization learns that explicit structural actions must be taken to ensure that the management of its projects (and sensitivity to the clients who are concerned about them) is not reduced to too low a level of priority because of the traditional specialist orientations of the functional managers.

Project organization decentralizes decision making to the level of the project team-leader or project manager. This is the level where knowledge relevant to the decision issues can be brought together and where a close monitoring of activities is possible. Project managers acquire and assemble the relevant resources; they plan, organize, and control the tasks and activities; and they take responsibility for the results of their projects or tasks (5). Through project organization it becomes possible to handle the large amounts of information that otherwise overload the vertical hierarchy.

Centralization—sometimes through control systems, sometimes through physical location rearrangements, and often just through the superordinate role of the project manager—serves as a way to integrate and resolve the conflicting opinions that inevitably come about when different persons or groups are assembled to serve on a task group or project team. PERT, CPM, and a variety of network and control methods serve as procedural frameworks for some of these centralizing tendencies in project organization systems (20).

Project or program managers (PM) tend to be selected from the functional area that is dominant in that particular organization. Hence, in technical organizations engineers become the PMs. In consumer marketing companies it is the marketers who get the job. In insurance companies it is actuaries. In hospitals it is doctors. There are many reasons for this: 1—Project managers must be from the dominant specialty if they are to maintain credibility in the organization (where most of the power lies with the dominant function(s)); 2—They must be able to order the problems (but not solve them); 3—They are the people best able to determine a good fit between the requirements of the sub-environment they face (e.g., the market sector) and the resources or technical strengths that the organization possesses; 4—The clients and sub-environments expect that it is just those type of people with whom they will interact.

Just because the PMs are so often drawn from the ranks of the dominant specialist function, there are problems created for their roles. The PMs can only be effective if they *do not* become their own specialists, e.g., their own project engineers. There's a great tendency for them to want to do just that. If they do, however, they will not pay adequate attention to their sub-environment, to the particular external world they were given explicit responsibility to manage. In effect, they must become general management oriented. They must be wise enough in their knowledge of how the dominant specialty works to put priorities on problems; but they must be broad enough to see themselves in charge of a total program or product line, not merely its specialist aspects.

Despite decentralized decision making and tight local aspects, the project or task seldom achieves complete autonomy (12). Many projects are not large enough to contain all their own resources. Furthermore, each project is unique and moves through different stages. At each of these stages a project requires a different set of resources. The need to share resources becomes a clear requirement of the situation. Resource sharing is accomplished through decentralized support of the projects, support that can come from a variety of sources: functional units within the organization, outside consultants, subcontractors, suppliers, customers, and the like. The project organization design places a premium on the ability to support projects flexibly and adaptively.

Project organization is a stage of unfreezing bureaucratic behavior, a stage anticipating movement to a new kind of behavior. It is a period when learning new behavior begins for the organization's members. Adjustments in processes and behaviors, rather than structural alterations, best characterize this stage.

The next stage is a "changing" stage, one in which the behaviors unfrozen in the project organization phase are shaped to a different pattern. Figure 4-1 illustrates the process. There is also a decision point at this next stage. One path is followed if the tasks of the organization will continue to be a stream of temporary projects. In this case, the design is refrozen into a permanent project organization form. If many of the tasks undertaken will be ongoing ones, however, the organization will continue on a different path in its evolutionary development.

The belief expressed by the design emphasis in Figure 4-1 is that structural mechanisms can induce and reinforce desired behavior. The sequence proposed begins with behaviors that are initially frozen and maintained by a bureaucratic structure. They are then unfrozen by relaxing these bureaucratic constraints through the introduction of project organization. The new and desired behaviors are subsequently induced or reinforced through the use of structural mechanisms (which are described next). Finally, in the matrix stage, the design emphasizes both structural and behavioral mechanisms.

Ultimately, matrix organization is a way of behaving. When the members of the organization learn the required behaviors, the organization's structural mechanisms become relatively redundant. They exist to reinforce existing behavior patterns and to induce desired behavior in new members; but they take a background role to the stronger effects of the learned new behaviors.

PRODUCT/MATRIX ORGANIZATION

The second step on the evolutionary road to matrix structure differs from the previous stage on several counts: the task activities are permanent, and the

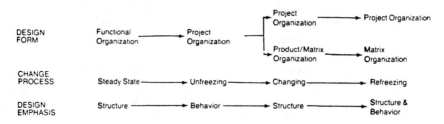

Figure 4-1. The stages of evolution to a matrix.

primary organizational emphasis is on building the structural devices that will shape and maintain the new and desired behavior patterns. It is a stage where the support systems that accompany the organization design are put in place and learned. It is also a time when the individuals in the organization acquire enough understanding of how the system works to begin making their own decisions, based on the data of experienced or observed behaviors.

Project organization aims to complete a temporary task in a fixed amount of time, for a predetermined cost, and according to a tightly specified set of performance standards. In the end, project managers aim to put themselves out of business. Product/matrix organization, in contrast, takes an idea or a product or a particular kind of technology and aims to develop it so it can grow "as large and as long and as profitable as possible" (9). A product manager becomes a "mini-general manager," a person responsible for the complete business, for its profit and loss, its current operations, and its future potential.

In the stage called product/matrix organization, some or all of the following support systems are put in place:

- Dual evaluation/reward systems.
- Dual accounting/control systems.
- Comprehensive team-building.
- Interpersonal skill development programs.
- Extensive meeting networks to disseminate information.
- New planning systems with both strategic and operating orientations.
- Physical territory re-structuring.

After the unfreezing stage, many matrix managers must begin a new stage of learning new behaviors. One of the most affected groups are the two-boss persons. For some of them, the ambiguity of the job is a re-awakening, an opportunity to flower and bloom, to carve out a role that fits better than anything hierarchical organization ever offered them. For others, it is a disaster. It is not just that they have acquired a complex role that they cannot learn. It is more that the clear career trajectory they once viewed has been suddenly truncated—just above the level where they are currently positioned. The dyadic superior-subordinate behaviors of bureaucracies die hard. Unfortunately, organizations often have insufficient tolerance for the time that it takes for supervisors to learn to become "coordinators" in their new two-boss roles. As a consequence, for some would be two-boss persons, the coming of matrix spells the end of a career.

Can people not learn the needed new behaviors? Some can, and do so very well by themselves. Others cannot. And sadly, the re-training skills of many organizations are just not adequate to help the latter group. Many of this group would be better off continuing their careers in a more traditional form of organization.

The personnel implications of the preceding paragraph are frequently not as frightening as they at first appear. Not everyone need be involved in the new matrix structure. In a conventional manufacturing organization, those actively involved in the dual orientations of two-boss roles may be as few as five percent of the organization's members. They will comprise the product and functional managers and their next level of subordinates and not very many others. In the eyes of the rest of the employees, the organization will continue to function quite traditionally. For example, a two-boss person may be both a manufacturing manager for a program and a member of the functional manufacturing group. He or she may have several or several hundred subordinates reporting through a traditional hierarchical structure. The vast majority of those people might go on about their work quite oblivious to the existence of a matrix structure at the top.

Alternatively, if the matrix is in a professional organization, e.g., a consulting firm where planners, architects and engineers are shared across different projects, everyone, including the office secretaries, may feel the effects of the matrix design.

MATRIX ORGANIZATION

For organizations evolving from functional to product forms or from centralized to divisionalized forms the stages are clear. However, when organizations have some systems centralized and others decentralized (14) the distinction between stages requires a closer examination of the support mechanisms—the control systems, the reward systems, profit and loss responsibility, and so on. Furthermore, when an organization moves from a product/matrix organization to a matrix organization, where the differences are more behavioral than structural, the distinctions between stages become increasingly difficult to identify.

Most processes and behavior that reach maturity under matrix structure existed to some extent in the project and product/matrix states. The balance of power that is so dominant a phenomenon in a mature matrix is first evident as a dilution of functional power under project organization. For example, in the product/matrix structure it surfaces as a trend in the direction of increasing authority, responsibility, and power for the product manager. Or, in another example, the team functioning that begins with the advent of project organization becomes elaborated into a spectrum of teams, task forces, committees and meetings when the organization reaches the matrix stage. For many, multi-team membership becomes a normal matrix way of life. As such, distinguishing explicit stages in an evolutionary process where the discriminating characteristics are primarily behavioral is a problematic undertaking. Nevertheless, under matrix organization one can expect to see some or all of the following.

HIGH FLEXIBILITY AND ADAPTABILITY. Not only do projects and products phase in and out, but new functional groups develop either out of new demands (e.g., if computers are built into the products, the computer programming might surface as a new function) or as existing functional groupings become more differentiated (11). The organization becomes increasingly morphogenic. It grows and acquires and divests itself of different organizational units. And it recombines resources in a wide and unanticipated variety of ways.

INTENSIVE BOUNDARY TRANSACTIONS. Not only do the product managers acquire the right to sub-contract outside the organization for services that could be supplied in-house (but in some way do not meet the requirements of the product groups), but also functional groups acquire equivalent rights to sell their services outside (11). In effect, the matrix organization transacts far more extensively across its many boundaries with the environment than it did as a functional, project, or product/matrix organization. Not only are there a larger number of product/project and functional managers in intensive interaction with their local environments, but because much of the decision making has been decentralized to the level of these managers, top management has more time to interact with the external forces it faces for the organization as a whole. The result is that more managers are carrying out the boundary transactions that are normally considered the primary functions of management (15). The mature matrix organization approaches more and more the ideal of an open system (2). Scott (16) illustrates a similar phenomenon, observing that the number of transactions across an organization's boundary increases as it grows from entrepreneurial to functional to product forms.

RESOURCES SHARING, MULTIPLE TEAM MEMBERSHIP, AND INTERPERSONAL SKILL DEVELOPMENT. As a kaleidoscope recombines its elements into different forms that stay within its own confines so does the matrix provide a framework in which its members combine and recombine into a complex variety of teams, task forces, projects, programs, product groupings, functional homes, and a variety of ad hoc arrangements that overwhelm the ability of any organization chart to capture (6), (7), (8). Matrix members complain of the continuous process of meetings but through them learn the collaborative skills needed to function in an ever-interacting environment. They also learn to resolve conflicts because each team is multidisciplinary and differences in orientation must be managed. They learn interpersonal and communication skills because the multiple team memberships allow time enough only for clear and unambiguous communication and no time to resolve problems that are a consequence of emotional or personality differences (18), (4). They learn problem-solving and group-process skills as consensus decision making replaces individual and authority-based decisions. As members come to value the different inputs to a task, they also come to realize that these inputs cannot be used effectively unless the team members acquire participative skills.

PRO-ACTIVE BEHAVIOR. Functional managers in the matrix "unlearn" reactive behavior and learn, instead, to go to product and project managers in anticipation of their needs (9), (11). No longer the exclusive repository of a functional skill, because product managers can buy services outside, the functional managers learn to sell their services. The increased responsiveness makes the matrix more of a marketplace: negotiations are constantly being conducted with respect to the assignment and priorities of people, equipment, facilities, and other resources. At the same time, product managers become increasingly pro-active about their subenvironments. Already engaged in the task of fitting their product/project technology or specialist skills to their particular market or customer segments, they take the additional step of attempting to reduce uncertainty (17) or equivocality (19) in their subenvironment. Hence we see aerospace program managers who take offices in the client's plant or bring the client into their facility (1). We see human service coordinators who engage a client's "social network" to support the client with at least some minimal level of structure and stability (3). And we see program managers in schools of education who co-opt both of their key environments by bringing into their faculty school teachers as adjunct professors, and professors from other faculties and departments within their university (13).

Functional managers, long the repository of their particular skill within their organizations, must stop functioning like librarians, i.e., waiting for people to come to them because they control the source of a particular skill, knowledge, or discipline for the organization. If PMs are to truly manage their sub-environments, they need functional managers as support, i.e., to manage the people and other internal aspects of the product team. Functional managers are equipped to do this because they normally have a long-run view of the organization. They should be able to anticipate a product manager's functional needs.

However, this requires a *proactive* stance from functional managers. They have to learn to say to PMs: "How can I help you?" Such requests, directed to PMs who are often younger than the functional managers and hold less seniority in the organization, are difficult for a functional manager to learn to make. If they don't learn, the matrix often degenerates into acrimonious "we-they" squabbles as the product managers, overloaded with both internal and external issues to manage, fault the functions for not being sufficiently supportive. To forestall this, functional managers must learn to go to the product managers. For some functional managers, this entails radically new behavior. The CEO must often intervene to keep the peace while the new roles are being learned and understood. The personal stress can get quite high.

The person at the apex of the matrix is the CEO. The matrix organization succeeds or fails according to how well the CEO understands its workings. A key element of that understanding is the maintenance of the appropriate balance of power.

Power must shift with the environment. When economic times are tough, the power must swing to the product side. It is the product managers who have the short term profit and loss orientation necessary for survival. When the environment is benevolent then it is the functions that must have the resources to advance the states-of-the-art in their specialties. During good economic times, an organization's competitors will also be investing in their own functional areas. The organization cannot afford to lag too far behind if it is to maintain its competitive position. The functional competencies are, in the end, what the organization "is about", in other words, what it brings to bear against the environment in order to give itself a justification for existing, for carving out a niche or domain in the larger society. Functional competence can occasionally be diminished when short-run survival is the issue; but in the long run it must be carefully guarded. Power balancing in the matrix is a matter of the *appropriate* balance for the particular situation.

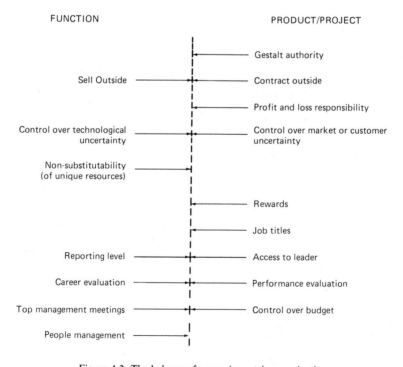

Figure 4-2. The balance of power in matrix organizations.

To maintain the appropriate balance the CEO need tools—organization mechanisms, support systems or processes—that can help to shift the emphasis, when it needs to be shifted. However, it is not a single organizational issue that establishes an appropriate balance. It isn't even several. It is many. Understanding the issues and knowing how to manipulate them is what gives the CEO the ability to adjust the power balance. Figure 4-2 illustrates a typical set of organizational issues (processes, systems, even concepts) that balance power in a product-function matrix structure. For the CEO who understands how to manipulate them, they are the levers for change. (Table 4-1 describes the issues in Figure 4-2).

It is worthwhile to examine the process whereby the organizational devices

Table 4-1. Some Variables Used to Balance Power in a Matrix Organization.

FUNCTION		PRODUCT/PROJECT	
		Gestalt Authority	Product managers are responsible for something *whole* which, no matter how small, is a type of perceived authority no funetional manager obtains.
Sell Outside	The right to sell resources outside the organization, making the functional manager who does so also a product manager.	Contracting Outside	The right to buy/access resourses outside the organization, even when same are available inside.
Control over Technological Uncertainty	Control over important environmental uncertainties for the specialist areas gives off significant perceptions of power.	Control over Product-Market Uncertainty	Control over important environmental uncertainties for the market segments of the different product lines gives off significant perceptions of power.
		Profit and Loss Responsibility	A measure of performance congruent with the way the organization itself is measured, suggesting high importance.
Non-substitutability (of unique resources)	Control over the availability and development of resources not available elsewhere gives off significant real and perceived power.		

Table 4-1. (*Continued*)

FUNCTION		PRODUCT/PROJECT
	Rewards	Rewarding product managers more than functional managers and signalling same to the organization shifts power to the product side.
	Job Titles	A fictitious perception of power accruing to the seemingly large group of similarly titled program managers, whose different goals rarely cause them to cooperate.
Reporting Level	Functional managers report directly to the CEO; a relationship obvious to the organization.	Access to Leader	Product managers usually report into managers of product managers who serve as their functional bosses (of how to manage products and programs) while the CEO is their product boss and, as such, always provides them with direct access to himself or herself.
Career Evaluation	The functional managers exercise a powerful influence over the career trajectories of most people in the organization.	Performance Evaluation	The product managers provide crucial inputs to the short-run appraisal of product/program people, particularly when such people are physically located with the product group.
Top Management Meetings	Frequent (often weekly) operations meeting to manage the organization comprise the CEO and the first level functional managers, but usually not the product managers.	Control over Budget	Product managers often have control over the budgeted dollars and negotiate with functional managers for needed resources.
People Management	Hiring, firing, training, promoting, career trajectory decisions belong to the functional managers.		

Figure 4-3. The self-supporting matrix.

in a mature matrix organization become consistent with each other and congruent with the design. As functional managers become pro-active and go to the product-project managers, the latter have less need to look inward on the organization. They have more time to focus on the boundary management problems, the interface between their product groups and the relevant customer/market segment. As product managers pay more attention to their individual businesses, the CEO finds less need to be concerned about how those individual businesses are being managed. The CEO finds more time to do the primary CEO job: managing the long-range concerns of the organization, and scanning and being sensitive to aggregate environmental changes. This necessarily means more interaction with the functional managers who hold the organizational responsibility for appropriate development of longer-term resources.

With this re-assessment of functional manager relevance on the part of the CEO, and with increased confidence from the product managers that the functional managers will be doing the job well, the mature matrix organization becomes increasingly self-supporting (Figure 4-3). The words of one CEO emphasize this outcome: "The necessity for product managers to go bashing functional managers has largely disappeared. The system has become supportive. I know that we'll all live longer for it. It's now a real beauty to observe. You can see people anticipating talking to others about a need that they can see others are going to have, and asking how they can help" (9).

REFERENCES

1. Barlow, Edward. "The Optimum Balance Between Program Organizations and Functional Organizations to Promote Technology Transfer." *IEEE Transactions on Engineering Management*, (16(3) 1969), pp. 116–121.

2. Bertalanffy, Ludwig von. *General systems theory: Foundations, Development, Applications* (Braziller. New York, 1968).
3. Curtis, Robert W. "Team problem solving in a social network." *Psychiatric Annals* (1974).
4. Davis, Stanley M. and Lawrence, Paul R. *Matrix*. (Addison-Wesley. Reading, Mass., 1977.)
5. Flaks, Marvin, and Archibald, Russel D. "The electronic Engineer's Guide to Project Management." *Electronic Engineer* (April-August, 1968), parts 1-5.
6. Gabarro, John J., and Lorsch, Jay W. Northern Electric Company, Limited, (A), (B), (C), and (D) (ICCH 9-413-062, 063, 064, 065). (Intercollegiate Case Clearing House. Boston, 1968).
7. Galbraith, Jay R. "Environmental and Technological Determinants of Organization Design." In Jay W. Lorsch and Paul R. Lawrence (Eds.). *Studies in Organization Design.* (Irwin. Homewood, Ill. 1970), pp. 113-139.
8. Galbraith, Jay R. "Matrix orgainzation design." *Business Horizons* (14(1), 1971) pp. 29-40.
9. Kolodny, Harvey F., and Lawrence, Paul R. Canadian Marconi Company-Avionics Division (ICCH 9-474-158). (Intercollegiate Case Clearing-House. Boston, 1974).
10. Kolodny, Harvey F., and Lawrence, Paul R. Diamond Instrument Company (ICCH 9-474-071). (Intercollegiate Case Clearing-House. Boston, 1975).
11. Kolodny, Harvey F. "Evolution to a Matrix Organization." *Academy of Management Review* (V9(4), 1979) pp. 543-553.
12. Middleton, C. J. "How to Set Up a Project Organization." *Harvard Business Review,* (45(2), 1967), pp. 73-82.
13 Overing, Robert. "Toward a Redefinition of Teacher Education." *Interchange,* (4(2/3), 1973), pp. 19-27.
14 Perrow, Charles. "The Bureaucratic Paradox: The Efficient Organization Centralizes in Order to Decentralize. *Organizational Dynamics* (5(4), 1977), pp. 3-14.
15. Rice, A. K. *The Enterprise and its Environment* (Tavistock. London. 1963).
16. Scott, Bruce R. "Stages of Corporate Development—Part 1." (ICCH 4-37-294). (Intercollegiate Case Clearing House. Boston, 1971).
17. Thompson, James D. *Organizations in Action.* (McGraw-Hill. New York, 1967).
18. Thompson, Paul H., and Lorsch, Jay W. "The TRW Systems Group." (A), (B), and (C) (ICCH 9-414-013, 014, 015). Intercollegiate Case Clearing House. Boston, 1967).
19. Weick, Karl E. *The Social Psychology of Organizing.* (Addison-Wesley. Reading, Mass. 1969.)
20. Weist, Jerome D. "Project Network Models: Past, Present, and Future," *Project Management Quarterly,* (7(4), 1977), pp. 27-36.

5. The Project Management Organization in Bechtel Power Corporation

F. A. Hollenbach*

This chapter is based on project management methods used within the Bechtel Power Corporation during the engineering and construction of nuclear and fossil-fueled power plant projects. Although the discussion here relates specifically to these projects, it is believed that the matrix organization approach to project management can be applied equally well by any company which has numerous projects in progress. The matrix approach requires strong functional organizations to provide a common pool of people to support the projects and to provide standard controls and approaches.

EVOLUTION OF PROJECT MANAGEMENT

For years, power projects, which were much smaller and less complex than they are today, were performed within the Bechtel Power Corporation without a project manager. These small organizations were made up of people who had worked together for many years. The project engineer led the project during the design phase. After major construction was underway, this role shifted to the project superintendent. The division manager fulfilled the role of the project manager by providing the coordination necessary to attain overall project objectives.

Today's projects are so complex, of such long duration, and draw upon so many specialized skills that it is no longer possible to manage them as informally as in the past. The working environment has also changed, with employ-

*Fred Hollenbach is vice president and deputy division general manager in Bechtel Power Corporation's San Francisco Power Division. He holds a bachelor of science degree in chemistry and physics from Muhlenberg College. He is a member of the American Nuclear Society, the Commonwealth Club of California, is a past president of the Northern California Chapter of the Project Managemen Institute, and is on the Board of Directors of the Engineers Club of San Francisco. He is a registered professional engineer in the state of California.

ees being more educated and specialized than previously. The "boss" cannot possibly know every phase of the operation; he must now rely on a team of people of various disciplines to fulfill the needs of the project.

IMPLEMENTATION OF THE MATRIX APPROACH

Under the project management concept, specialized services are "borrowed" from the functional organizations (departments) on an as-required basis to pursue and complete project requirements. Experience has shown it is best to bring the project team together in one location.

The functional organizations (engineering, construction, services, procurement, etc.) provide the varied and specialized resources required by the project. The departments have available specialized groups, standards, techniques, computer programs, etc., that can maximize the capabilities of the available human resources, permit more consistency among the projects, and minimize the repeating of mistakes.

Thus, the functional organizations provide the basic foundation from which project-oriented activities are carried out; the project manager integrates the team's efforts to meet project objectives. The project manager's authority cuts across functional and organizational lines.

The project manager, serving as a focal point for project activities, determines the "when" and the "what" of the work; the functional managers, in supporting all the projects, determine "how" the work will be done.

PROJECT TEAM

Under the project management concept, representatives from each of the division's functional departments are assigned to the project team, as shown in Figure 5-1. This results in a dual working relationship; that is, each member of the team derives expert functional guidance and administrative control from the department manager while receiving project direction from the project manager, who represents division management. The team includes the following key personnel:

- Project manager.
- Project engineer.
- Project field construction manager.
- Project construction coordinator.
- Project startup engineer.
- Project quality assurance engineer.
- Project cost and schedule supervisor.
- Project administrator.

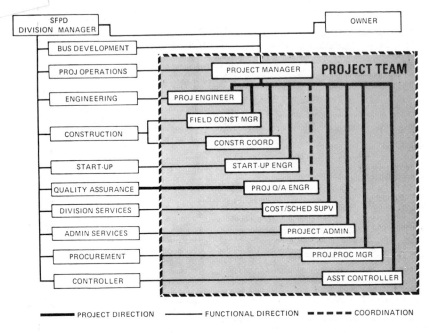

PROJECT DIRECTION ———— FUNCTIONAL DIRECTION ▪ ▪ ▪ ▪ ▪ COORDINATION

Figure 5-1. Typical project team organization.

- Project procurement manager.
- Project assistant controller.

These project personnel work closely with their counterparts in the client's project organization.

The project team is a service oriented group requiring expert organization, strong leadership, and the continuous support of senior management. To be successful, it must include a sound communications network. Frequent staff meetings are required to plan and implement project activities and monitor progress. Communications between the project team and senior management ensure active management support. Communications with the client are equally essential. Project costs and schedules, the quality of the work, and the many problems that inevitably arise demand continual communication.

The major responsibilities of the team members are defined in the following paragraphs.

Project Manager

The project manager is responsible for the overall execution of the project based on the contract, client requirements, regulatory agency criteria, and specific corporate commitments. A detailed description of his specific duties is given later.

Project Engineer

The project engineer is responsible for Bechtel's engineering effort on the project. This effort includes preparing the technical scope documents describing the project, developing the engineering plan and budget, and developing the project design including drawings and specifications. It includes preparing technical reports and providing technical support of licensing applications. Finally, the effort includes preparing material requisitions for permanent plant equipment, materials, and engineered subcontracts along with bid evaluations and recommendations for award; ensuring the quality of design; providing technical support to other departments and to the client; monitoring and controlling the engineering program; and providing support during construction. A typical project engineering organization is shown on Figure 5-2.

Project Field Construction Manager

The project field construction manager is responsible for all of the company's activities at the jobsite. This includes supervision of direct-hire labor, admin-

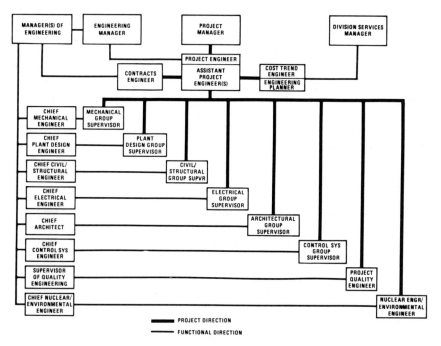

Figure 5-2. Typical project engineering organization.

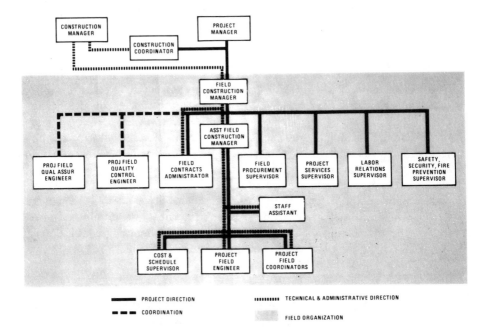

Figure 5-3. Typical project construction organization.

istration of construction contracts, field engineering, field procurement, job safety, construction quality control, jobsite accounting, and receipt and temporary custody of separately purchased plant equipment and materials. He maintains liaison with client personnel resident at or visiting the site. He is responsible for the construction plan, cost control, and forecasting for all jobsite costs. Figure 5-3 depicts a typical construction organization for a project requiring only construction management services.

Project Construction Coordinator

The construction coordinator, located in the home office, assists the construction manager in evaluating job costs and schedules. He coordinates the activities of jobsite personnel with home office design engineering, procurement, cost and scheduling, and construction personnel.

Project Startup Engineer

The project startup engineer is responsible for planning the preoperational testing services for the project. He coordinates the work of the company's startup engineers at the jobsite and provides technical instruction and guidance to client personnel for preoperational testing services following completion of construction.

Project Quality Assurance Engineer

The project quality assurance engineer is responsible for developing and implementing the quality assurance program for the job and monitoring and auditing the quality control activities of the engineering, procurement, construction, materials, and fabrication groups on the project. He can initiate stop-work action when warranted.

Project Cost and Scheduling Supervisor

The project cost and scheduling supervisor is responsible for the preparation of project estimates, budgets, and schedules and for forecasting and monitoring job costs and progress. He implements a material quantity program and directs the preparation of economic studies. He is responsible for evaluating trends, predicting their effect on ultimate job completion, advising the project manager of possible remedial measures, and preparing periodic reports for company and client management concerning the status of the project.

Project Administrator

The project administrator is responsible for providing, staffing, and administering all the administrative/clerical services required by project team members including document control and records management; ensuring the effectiveness of administrative interfaces between the various entities supporting the project; and ensuring that all applicable corporate, client, and project procedures are followed as well as producing the project procedures manual and other internal procedures.

Project Procurement Manager

The project procurement manager is responsible for all procurement functions required by the project including home office and field procurement, subcontracting, expediting, traffic, and inspection.

Project Assistant Controller

The project assistant controller is responsible for all finance and accounting matters on the project such as general accounting, payroll, accounts payable, billings, employee accounts, timekeeping, accounts receivable, and cost and commitment records. He provides functional guidance and advice to the project field accounting managers and conducts periodic examinations of field accounting activities.

PROJECT MANAGER

A project manager responsible for the direction of a major project (such as the construction of a power plant) has responsibilities equivalent to that of the chief operating officer of a corporation handling a cash flow in excess of $100,000,000 per year. He must administer the activities of large numbers of people while planning, directing, and monitoring a complex, highly technical enterprise to the satisfaction of a quality minded, profit motivated Board of Directors and a knowledgeable, demanding client.

He is the direct communications link between the client's organization and his own company's engineering and construction personnel. His major goal is to keep the project within budget, on schedule, and completed to quality standards acceptable to the client and the company.

Precontract Award Period

The project manager's responsibilities and functions usually begin during the precontract phase of negotiations. He assists in preparing the proposal by identifying the technical elements of the project, performance commitments, client functions, and key project personnel. He coordinates the activities of the business development and legal representatives from the date the proposal is submitted. He obtains applicable data from engineering, procurement, administration, construction, startup, the services, and other concerned groups to develop the scope of the contract. He supports business development efforts during contract negotiations by conferring with the client regarding the level of the company's involvement with subcontracts, purchasing of major items, other purchasing, scheduling, construction, startup, plant manuals, client training, and construction equipment and tools.

Contract Execution Period

During the contract execution phase of the project, the project manager must develop the overall project plan and obtain the concurrence of the various functional groups participating in the project. He is responsible for development of the project procedures manual, the summary and detailed project schedules, and the project budget based on detailed budgets supplied by the functional participants. He reviews and approves accounting releases and client billings, ensuring conformance to the contract and company policies, and ensures that change orders are promptly prepared in conformance with the contract before obtaining the client's approval. He must monitor the work progress to ensure that it conforms with the budget and schedule, initiating corrective action as needed. He must monitor equipment procurement plans and schedules and the performance of all major subcontractors. He reviews, approves, and issues all project forecasts; issues required reports to the client and his company management; and monitors job performance to ensure attainment of quality workmanship.

Contract Closeout Period

During the contract closeout phase, the project manager is responsible for ensuring that the company has fulfilled all contract requirements; he coordinates turnover of the completed plant and obtains formal acceptance by the client before obtaining the contract release from the client and closing out the project.

Project Manager's Qualifications and Characteristics

The success of a project manager is measured by client satisfaction as a result of getting the job done on time and within budget. Successful project managers all have certain personality traits that ensure success whether the project is large and complex or small and uncomplicated. Although these traits are often an inherent part of one's personality, many of them can be learned and improved through experience. Successful project managers also use specific management practices that have been developed within the company over the years.

The project manager should be a person who can create and lead a stimulated, aggressive project team. He can only gain the respect of the team and the functional managers because of his overall performance, personality, and contribution to the team effort.

He must, of course, understand the technology involved in the project. He should be able to focus on the key issues of a problem without getting involved in the minor details. It is important that he possess initiative, imagination, and ingenuity. He must be willing to make difficult decisions and accept risk. He must be willing to compromise, be openminded, and reasonably unemotional. He cannot allow himself to become flustered when he has to deal with a large number of issues at one time. He must be able to communicate concisely in writing and orally.

He must be people-oriented; that is, he must be concerned with the behavior of his team members and their reactions. He must provide recognition to individuals when tasks are well done. It is important that he encourage initiative and decision-making by subordinates. He should be compassionate in dealing with errors or the problems of individual team members.

Any number of good management practices are available to the project manager. He should assess, review, and communicate the objectives and goals of the project on a regular basis. Interfaces should remain simple and clearly understood. A current project plan should be available that is understood and accepted by the people responsible for the performance of the work. Budgets and schedules should be realistic and the product of the organization doing the work. The project manager will actively and conscientiously support an adequate quality assurance/quality control program.

A good project manager will be forthright in his dealings with the client, other agencies, and the project team. He will make no excuses. He will not make decisions that should be made within a functional entity. He will document all important instructions to the project team and summarize in writing all significant understandings or decisions reached in discussions with the client.

A project manager should be a leader rather than a dictator. He should delegate responsibility but, at the same time, require that methods to measure the plan, budget, and schedule be established and monitored. Differences should be resolved face to face. Problems should be identified early. Most importantly, a good project manager will not assume things will happen; he will make them happen.

As a prerequisite, a good project manager should have substantial experience in the industry. He should have been exposed not only to engineering and construction, but to costing and contract methods. He should have a general knowledge of the company along with an area of expertise in a specific field of its business. He should be efficient when conducting business. He must be willing to accept increasing responsibilities, to work hard, and to go "where the action is."

Weakness in any of these areas must be overcome as quickly as possible in order to gain the confidence of the project team and the client.

CLIENT INVOLVEMENT IN THE PROJECT

The primary consideration on a project is the client; therefore, the project manager and his team must constantly be aware of the pressures the client faces, the client's organization, and most important, the degree of client involvement in the project.

In response to a more demanding environment and to try to ensure cost effective project performance, the electric utility industry has established a trend toward active participation in its construction projects. This more active role has taken one of several forms.

The first alternative involves establishing a project management team to actively monitor the performance of the architect/engineer and constructor and directly manage the resources employed to design and construct the plant. This approach normally requires a project management team of between 25 and 100 persons having both management and technical skills.

The next approach has been to integrate utlity project management with the architect/engineer and constructor management groups. Under this arrangement, utility managers play an active role in the day-to-day supervision of engineering and/or construction work. An even higher level of technical and managerial skills is needed by the utility's project management team which, although varying widely in size, is often one and one-half to three times larger than required in the first alternative.

Finally, a few utilities have established in-house groups to perform the work. This approach is found most often in large utilities. They typically have major ongoing construction projects, requiring a total work force of several hundred or even thousands and a full range of both managerial and technical skills.

Each of these alternatives provides a greater role for the utility than in the past and requires a larger and more highly skilled staff in both the technical and managerial aspects of power plant construction.

This trend is equally true for industry in general. Most companies are taking a more active role in the management of their projects.

Clients are especially concerned about progress monitoring because of their need to report to regulatory agencies and closely monitor their cash flow. As a result, a project management information system has been developed to continually monitor progress of the design, procurement, construction, and startup of a large project. A primary objective of the system is to accumulate, in an auditable form on an ongoing basis, actual project costs. Another function of the system is to report at least once a month project cost and schedule variances, probable project cost when completed, changes in the planned date of resource availability, and experience and trends in labor productivity. The system produces detailed information necessary for preparing cost estimates of future projects and resolving contract adjustments for scope changes on the project in progress.

EXTERNAL INFLUENCES IMPACTING PROJECT MANAGEMENT

National and international affairs significantly influence the management of projects. For example, compliance with governmental regulations can be very costly to a project. Because projects must be designed and built to conform to current regulatory requirements, the clients are obligated to install and pay for the systems required by those requirements. Some of these systems are extremely costly not only in actual dollar value but in the time it takes to install them. If a regulation change causes a change in the scope of work, the work schedule will undoubtedly slip. Every time a schedule slips, the cost of a project increases.

It is important to minimize the influence of this type of change on a project. Changes come from every direction: from the government, the client, the suppliers, etc. The project manager must anticipate and control these changes so the project can proceed without constant interruption and according to a carefully planned schedule and budget.

ADVANTAGES OF THE MATRIX APPROACH

A company may decide to employ the matrix approach to project management for any number of reasons.

Basically, this management technique helps a company remain competitive because it reinforces the company's ability to get a better return for its human investment. The matrix form can ensure effective project direction through the use of dedicated project team management as well as efficient project execution through the control of human resources and technical standards by functional groups.

The project team is solely responsible for the work of the project, yet it is able to obtain technical support and direction from the functional organizations which provide standardized tools and specifications.

The matrix organization provides a "home" for project personnel between assignments and allows for the most efficient allocation of personnel between projects. A strong functional organization allows specialization for an individual and provides broader opportunities than are available on a single project. It also provides well-trained people to support project requirements.

MATRIX ORGANIZATION IMPLEMENTATION PROBLEMS

Several problems were observed in implementing the project management concept.

Because responsibilities cut across functional and project lines and project team members serve two masters, conflicts arise. To eliminate difficulties concerning responsibilities and interfaces, matrices were developed to define the responsibility interfaces between the key project team members and functional managers. These matrices cover activities in all phases of management of the project. Many problems have been eliminated by a clearer understanding provided through the use of the responsibility interface matrices.

Another problem when implementing the project management concept was the lack of understanding and agreement with the project management philosophy and policy. To resolve this problem, a project manager's manual was issued. The principal objectives of the manual are to provide a statement of project management policy and make available to project managers a document that describes their responsibilities. In addition to providing learning and working tools, the manual promotes a uniform project management approach on all jobs; makes multidivisional projects easier to manage; facilitates interdivisional utilization of project managers; and promotes a more uniform approach to similar types of projects.

FACTORS UNIQUE TO THE MATRIX APPROACH

Several factors are unique to project management within a matrix organization.

The matrix organization concept is relatively new and deviates from traditional theories; consequently, its usefulness is often qestioned.

Because responsibilities cut across functional and organizational lines, conflicts occur.

The specific interest of a specific project sometimes conflicts with the best interests of the company as a whole.

Although assigned the overall responsibility for project performance, the project manager requires extensive participation by organizations outside his control.

CONCLUSION

The large number, high value, and complex nature of projects require increasing diversity of personnel skills; therefore, the use of a functional organization overlaid by a project management organization appears to be the most effective method for handling today's business.

BIBLIOGRAPHY

Hollenbach, F. A., and D. P. Schultz *The Organization and Controls of Project Management,* presented at the "Realities in Project Management" Proceedings of the 1977 Project Management Institute International Seminar/Symposium, 1977.

Allen, R. D., *Bechtel Project Management Techniques for Nuclear Projects,* (San Francisco, California: Bechtel Power Corporation. June 1977).

Bechtel, *Conflict Management in a Matrix Organization,* seminar presented at the Bechtel Power Corporation, San Francisco, California, 1979.

Hollenbach, F. A., *Project Management and Client Relations,* seminar presented at the Bechtel Power Corporation, San Francisco, California, 1974.

Allen, R. D., *Project Management Challenges in the 1980s* (Project Management Quarterly, December 1980).

6. Organizing the Project Office and Project Team: Duties of Project Participants*

Russell D. Archibald†

The approach described in this chapter is based on typical major project situations involving the design, manufacture, assembly, and testing of complex hardware and software systems. This presumes the following conditions:

- The project (or program) warrants a full-time project manager.
- The project office is held to minimum size, with maximum use of functional contributors in existing departments.

This chapter summarizes the functions of the project office and the project team under these conditions, describes the duties of key persons involved in the project, and discusses their relationships.

The situation frequently occurs wherein one project manager is responsible for several projects, or, when multiple small projects exist, the general manager will retain the project manager responsibility himself. In still other situations, a manager of projects is appointed. In such cases, a centralized Operations Planning and Control function is recommended.

FUNCTIONS OF THE PROJECT OFFICE AND PROJECT TEAM

The project office supports the project manager in carrying out his responsibilities. Thus his basic charter, organizational relationship, and the nature of

---

*Adapted from Chapter 6, "Organizing the Project Office and Project Team," *Managing High Technology Programs and Projects,* by Russell D. Archibald (John Wiley & Sons, Inc., New York, 1976).
†Mr. Russell D. Archibald has directed major domestic and international programs with the Bendix Corporation and ITT; has consulted on program management to numerous large and small companies in eleven countries, as well as the U.S. Air Force; and has written and lectured extensively on this subject over the past 22 years. He is presently a Private Consultant in project management, international business development and strategic growth management.

the project itself will influence the makeup of the project office. The presence or absence of other projects, and of a central planning office, will also affect the organization of the project office.

The *project team* includes all functional contributors to the project, as well as the members of the project office. The general functions to be carried out during completion of the overall project by members of the project team are:

- Management.
- Product design and development.
- Product manufacture.
- Purchasing and subcontracting.
- Product installation and test.

The relationships of these functions to the project manager are shown in the generalized project organization chart in Figure 6-1. Each of these functions is discussed in the following paragraphs.

Management

The management functions are simply those necessary to enable the project manager to fulfill his basic responsibility: Overall direction and coordination of the project through all its phases to achieve the desired results within established budget and schedule.

Product Design and Development

The basic purpose of this general function is to produce adequate documentation (and often a prototype product or system) so that the product may be manufactured in the quantity required within the desired cost and schedule. These functions may be defined as

- Systems analysis, engineering, and integration.
- Product design.
- Product control (quality, cost, configuration).

Systems analysis, engineering, and integration functions include: system studies; functional analysis and functional design of the system or product; and coordination and integration of detailed designs, including functional and mechanical interfaces between major subsystems or components of the product.

Product design functions include the detailed engineering design and development functions needed to translate the functional systems design into specifications, drawings, and other documents which can be used to manufacture,

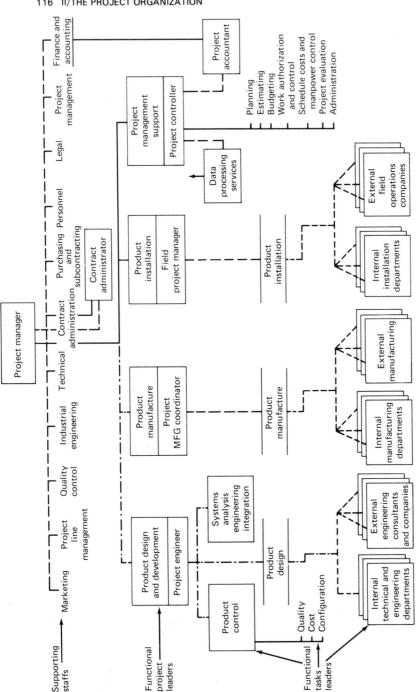

——— Project office members recommended in most cases.
······ May or may not be members of project office.
- - - - Not usually members of project office.

Figure 6-1. Generalized organization of the project team.

assemble, install, and test the product. This may also include the manufacture and test of a prototype or first article system or product, using either model shop or factory facilities on a subcontract basis.

Product control functions include: product quality control, using established staff specialists and procedures; product cost control, including value engineering practices; product configuration control including design freeze practices (to establish the "base line" design), engineering change control practices, and documentation control practices.

It should be noted that the term "product" refers to *all* results of the project: hardware, software, documentation, training or other services, facilities, and so on.

The project office in a specific situation may perform none, a few, or all of these product design and development functions, depending on many factors. Generally a larger share of these functions will be assigned to the project office (together with adequate staff) when the product is new or unusual to the responsible unit, or when there is little confidence that the work will be carried out efficiently and on schedule within established engineering departments. When several engineering departments, for example, from different product lines or different companies, are contributing to the product design and development, the functions of systems analysis, engineering and integration, and of product control, should be assigned to the project office.

Except in the situation described above, these functions should be performed by project team members within existing engineering departments, under the active coordination of the project manager.

Product Manufacture

This general function is to purchase materials and components, fabricate, assemble, test, and deliver the equipment required to complete the project. These functions are carried out by the established manufacturing departments within the project's parent company or by outside companies on a subcontract or purchase order basis.

The project manager, however, must coordinate and integrate the manufacturing functions with product design and development on one hand and field operations (if any) on the other. *The lack of proper integration between these areas is the most common cause of project failure.*

In order to achieve this integration, it is necessary to appoint a project manufacturing coordinator or equivalent who will, in effect, act as a project manager for product manufacture. He is a key project team member. He may be assigned full time to one major project or he may be able to handle two or more projects at one time, if the projects are small.

It is recommended that the project manufacturing coordinator remain within the appropriate manufacturing department. When two or more divisions or companies perform a large part of the product manufacture, each must designate a project manufacturing coordinator, with one designated as the lead division for manufacture. If it is not possible to designate a lead division, then the coordination effort must be accomplished by the project office.

Purchasing and Subcontracting

This function is sometimes included with the product manufacture area, but it is normally important enough to warrant full functional responsibility.

A separate project purchasing and subcontracting coordinator with status equivalent to that of the manufacturing coordinator should be appointed to handle all purchasing and subcontracting matters for the project manager. This person should be a part of the purchasing department where he can maintain day-to-day contact with all persons carrying out the procurement functions.

Product Installation, Test, and Field Support

Many projects require field installation and test of the system or equipment, and some include continuing field support for a period of time. In these cases, a field project manager (or equivalent) is required.

When field operations are a part of the project, this phase is usually clearly recognized as being of a project nature and requiring one person to be in charge. This field project manager is almost always a member of an established installation department (or equivalent) if such a department exists within the responsible company. Since engineering and manufacturing operations frequently overlap the installation phase, the overall project manager's role continues to be of critical importance to success while field operations are in progress. However, in the relationship between the project manager and the field project manager, the project manager retains the overall responsibility for the coordination of the entire project. For projects involving major construction, a Field Project Manager will be required whose duties and responsibilities are equivalent to the project manager as outlined earlier.

Assignment of Persons to the Project Office

As a general rule, it is recommended that the number of persons assigned to a project office under the supervision of the project manager be kept as small as possible. This will emphasize the responsibility of each functional (line) department or staff for their contribution to the project and retain to the maximum degree the benefits of specialized functional departments. It will also increase flexibility of functional staffing of the project, avoid unnecessary payroll costs to the project, and minimize reassignment problems when particular tasks are completed. This will enable the project manager to devote maximum effort to the project itself, rather than supervisory duties related to a large staff.

With adequate project planning and control procedures, a highly qualified project staff can maintain the desired control of the project. In the absence of adequate planning and control procedures to integrate the functional contributions, it is usually necessary to build up a larger staff with as many functionl contributors as possible directly under the project manager in order to achieve control. Experience indicates that this is an expensive and frequently awkward approach, and it aggravates the relationships between the project manager and contributing functional managers.

The persons who should be assigned (transferred) permanently to the project office are those who:

- Deal with the management aspects of the project.
- Are needed on a full-time basis for a period of at least 6 months.
- Must be in frequent close contact with the project manager or other members of the project office in the performance of their duties.
- Cannot otherwise be controlled effectively, because of organizational or geographic consideration.

The recommended assignment location of each of the key people on the project team follows.

Project Manager.   The project manager is always considered the manager of the project office (which could be a one-man office).

Project Engineer.   The project engineer may be assigned to the project office in charge of product design and development where the product is new to the company or where several divisions are involved, as discussed earlier. Otherwise, he should always remain within the lead engineering department.

Contract Administrator.   The contract administrator should remain a member of the contract administration staff, except on very large programs extending over a considerable period of time. He may be located physically in the project office while remaining with his parent organizaion.

Project Controller.   The project controller should always be assigned to the project office, except where he is not needed full time or where a centralized planning and control function adequately serves the project manager.

Project Accountant.   The project accountant should remain a member of the accounting department, except on very large programs extending over a considerable period of time. Like the contract administrator, he may physically be located in the project office while remaining with his parent organization.

Manufacturing Coordinator. The manufacturing coordinator should remain a member of the manufacturing organization, preferably on the staff of the manufacturing manager or within production control. When more than one division is to contribute substantially to product manufacture, it may be necessary to assign him to the project office to enable effective coordination of all contributors.

Purchasing and Subcontracting Coordinator. This coordinator should remain a member of the purchasing department in most cases.

Field Project Manager. The field project manager should remain a member of the installation or field operations department, if one exists, except under unusual circumstances that would require him to be assigned to the project office.

Project Team Concept

Whether a person is assigned to the project office or remains in a functional department or staff, all persons holding identifiable responsibilities for direct contributions to the project are considered to be members of the project team. Creating awareness of membership in the project team is a primary task of the project manager, and development of a good project team spirit has proven to be a powerful means for accomplishing difficult objectives under tight time schedules.

The Project Organization Chart

Figure 6-2 shows a typical representation of a project team in the format of a classic organization chart. This type of representation can be confusing if not properly understood, but it can also be useful to identify the key project team members and show their relationships to each other and to the project manager *for project purposes*. This recognizes that such a chart does not imply permanent superior-subordinate relationships portrayed in the company organization charts.

PROJECT MANAGER DUTIES

The following description of project manager duties is presented as a guide for development of specific duties on a particular project. Some of the duties listed

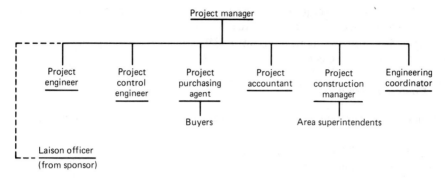

Figure 6-2. Typical construction project task force.

may not be practical, feasible, or pertinent in certain cases, but wherever possible it is recommended that all items mentioned be included in the project manager's duties and responsibilities, with appropriate internal documentation and dissemination to all concerned managers

General

- Rapidly and efficiently start up the project.
- Assure that all equipment, documents, and services are properly delivered to the customer for acceptance and use within the contractual schedule and costs.
- Convey to all concerned departments a full understanding of the customer requirements of the project.
- Participate with responsible managers in developing overall project objectives, strategies, budgets, and schedules.
- Plan all necessary project tasks to satisfy customer and management requirements.
- Assure that all project activities are properly and realistically scheduled, budgeted, provided for, monitored, and reported.
- Identify promptly all deficiencies and deviations from plan.
- Assure that actions are initiated to correct deficiencies and deviations, and monitor execution of such actions.
- Assure that payment is received in accordance with contractual terms.
- Maintain cognizance over all contacts with the customer and assure that proper staff members participate in such contacts.
- Arbitrate and resolve conflicts and differences between functional departments on specific project tasks or activities.
- Maintain day-to-day liaison with all functional contributors to provide communication required to assure realization of their commitments.

- Make or force required decisions at successively higher organizational levels to achieve project objectives.
- Maintain communications with higher management regarding problem areas and project status.

Customer Relations

In close cooperation with the customer relations or marketing department:

- Receive from the customer all necessary technical, cost, and scheduling information required for accomplishment of the project.
- Establish good working relationships with the customer on all levels: management, contracts, legal, accounts payable, system engineering, design engineering, field sites, and operations.
- Arrange and attend all meetings with customer (contractual, engineering, operations).
- Receive and answer all technical and operational questions from the customer, with appropriate assistance from functional departments.

Contract Administration

- Identify any potential areas of exposure in existing or potential contracts and initiate appropriate action to alert higher management and eliminate such exposure.
- Prepare and send, or approve prior to sending by others, all correspondence on contractual matters.
- Coordinate the activities of the project contract administrator in regard to project matters.
- Prepare and participate in contract negotiations.
- Identify all open contractual commitments.
- Advise engineering, manufacturing, and field operations of contractual commitments and variations allowed.
- Prepare historical or position papers on any contractual or technical aspect of the program, for use in contract negotiations or litigation.

Project Planning, Control, Reporting, Evaluation, and Direction

- Perform, or supervise the performance of, all project planning, controlling, reporting, evaluation and direction functions.
- Conduct frequent, regular project evaluation and review meetings to identify current and future problems and initiate actions for their resolution.

- Prepare and submit weekly or monthly progress reports to higher management, and to the customer if required.
- Supervise the project controller and his staff.

Marketing

Maintain close liaison with Marketing and utilize customer contacts to acquire all possible marketing intelligence for future business.

Engineering

- Insure that Engineering fulfills its responsibilities for delivering, on schedule and within product cost estimates, drawings and specifications usable by manufacturing and field operations, meeting the customer specifications.
- In cooperation with the Engineering, Drafting, and Publications Departments define and establish schedules and budgets for all engineering and related tasks. After agreement release funding allowables and monitor progress on each task in relation to the overall project.
- Act as the interface with the customer for these departments (with their assistance as required).
- Assure the control of product quality, configuration, and cost.
- Approve technical publications prior to release to the customer.
- Coordinate engineering support related to the project for Manufacturing, Installation, Legal, and other departments.
- Participate (or delegate participation) as a voting member in the Engineering Change Control Board on matters affecting the project.

Manufacturing

- Insure that Manufacturing fulfills its responsibilities for on-schedule delivery of all required equipment, meeting the engineering specifications within estimated manufacturing costs.
- Define contractual commitments to Production Control.
- Develop schedules to meet contractual commitments in the most economical fashion.
- Establish and release manufacturing and other resource and funding allowables.
- Approve and monitor production control schedules.
- Establish project priorities.
- Approve, prior to implementation, any product changes initiated by Manufacturing.

- Approve packing and shipping instructions based on type of transportation to be used and schedule for delivery.

Purchasing and Subcontracting

- Insure that Purchasing and Subcontracting fulfills their responsibilities to obtain delivery of materials, equipment, documents, and services on schedule and within estimated cost for the project.
- Approve make-or-buy decisions for the project.
- Define contractual commitments to Purchasing and Subcontracting.
- Establish and release procurement funding allowables.
- Approve and monitor major purchase orders and subcontracts.
- Specify planning, scheduling, and reporting requirements for major purchase orders and subcontracts.

Installation, Test, and Other Field Operations

- Insure that Installation and Field Operations fulfill their responsibilities for on-schedule delivery to the customer of materials, equipment, and documents within the cost estimates for the project.
- Define contractual commitments to Installation and Field Operations.
- In cooperation with Installation and Field Operations, define and establish schedules and budgets for all field work. After agreement, release funding allowables and monitor progress on each task in relation to the overall project.
- Coordinate all problems of performance and schedule with Engineering, Manufacturing, and Purchasing and Subcontracting.
- Except for customer contacts related to daily operating matters, act as the customer interface for Installation and Field Operations departments.

Financial

In addition to the financial project planning and control functions described:

- Assist in the collection of accounts receivable.
- Approve prices of all change orders and proposals to the customer.

Project Closeout

- Insure that all required steps are taken to present adequately all project deliverable items to the customer for acceptance and that project activities are closed out in an efficient and economical manner.

- Assure that the acceptance plan and schedule comply with the customer contractual requirements.
- Assist the Legal, Contract Administration, and Marketing or Commercial Departments in preparation of a closeout plan and required closeout data.
- Obtain and approve closeout plans from each involved functional department.
- Monitor closeout activities, including disposition of surplus materials.
- Notify Finance and functional departments of the completion of activities and of the project.
- Monitor payment from the customer until all collections have been made.

PROJECT ENGINEER DUTIES

General

The project engineer is responsible for the technical integrity of his project and for cost and schedule performance of all engineering phases of the project. Specifically, the responsibilities of the project engineer are:

- Insure that the customer performance requirements are fully understood and that the company is technically capable of meeting these requirements.
- Define these requirements to the smallest subsystem to the functional areas so that they can properly schedule, cost, and perform the work to be accomplished.
- Insure that the engineering tasks so defined are accomplished within the engineering schedules and allowables (manpower, materials, funds) of the contract.
- Provide technical direction as necessary to accomplish the project objectives.
- Conduct design review meetings at regular intervals to assure that all technical objectives will be achieved.
- Act as technical advisor to the project manager and other functional departments, as requested by the project manager.

In exercising the foregoing responsibilities, the project engineer is supported by the various engineering departments.

Proposal Preparation and Negotiation

During the proposal phase, the project engineer will do the following:

- Coordinate and plan the preparation of the technical proposal.
- Review and evaluate the statement of work and other technical data.
- Establish an engineering proposal team or teams.
- Within the bounds of the overall proposal schedule, establish the engineering proposal schedule.
- Reduce customer engineering requirements to tasks and subtasks.
- Define in writing the requirements necessary from Engineering to other functional areas, including preliminary specifications for make or buy, or subcontract items.
- Coordinate and/or prepare a schedule for all engineering functions, including handoff to and receipt from Manufacturing.
- Review and approve all Engineering subtask and task costs, schedules, and narrative inputs.
- Coordinate and/or prepare overall engineering cost.
- Participate in preliminary make-or-buy decisions.
- Participate in overall cost and schedule review.
- Participate, as required, in negotiation of contract.
- Bring problems between the project engineer and engineering functional managers to appropriate engineering directors for resolution.

Project Planning and Initiation

The project engineer is responsible for the preparation of plans and schedules for all engineering tasks within the overall project plan established by the project manager. In planning the engineering tasks, he will compare the engineering proposal against the received contract. Where the received contract requirements dictate a change in cost, schedule, or technical complexity for solution, he will obtain approval from the director of engineering and the project manager to make the necessary modifications in engineering estimates of the proposal. During this phase, the project engineer will:

- Update the proposal task and subtask descriptions to conform with the contract, and within the engineering allowables prepare additional tasks and subtasks as required to provide a complete engineering implementation plan for the project.
- Prepare a master engineering schedule in accordance with the contractual requirements.
- Prepare, or have prepared, detailed task and subtask definitions and specifications. Agree on allowables, major milestones, and evaluation points in tasks with the task leaders and their functial managers.
- Through the functional engineering managers, assign responsibility for task and subtask performance, and authorize the initiation of work against

identified commitments based on cost and milestone schedules, with approval of the project manager.

- Using contract specifications as the base line, prepare, or have prepared, specifications for subcontract items.
- Participate and provide support from appropriate engineering functions in final make-or-buy decisions and source selection.
- Prepare, or have prepared, hardware and system integration and acceptance test plan. Review the test plan with Quality Assurance and advise them as to the required participation of other departmens.

Project Performance and Control

The project engineer is responsible for the engineering progress of the project and compliance with contract requirements, cost allowables, and schedule commitments. Within these limits, the project engineer, if necessary, may make design changes and task requirement changes in accordance with his concept and assume the responsibility for the change in concert with the functional engineering managers and with the knowledge of the project manager. No changes may be made that affect other functional departments without the knowledge of that department, documentation to the project manager, and the inclusion of the appropriate charge-back of any variance caused by change. He maintains day-to-day liaison with the project manager for two-way information exchange. Specific responsibilities of the project engineer are to:

- Prepare and maintain a file of all project specifications related to the technical integrity and performance.
- Prepare and maintain updated records of the engineering expenditures and milestones and conduct regular reviews to insure engineering performance as required.
- Initiate and prepare new engineering costs-to-complete reports as required.
- Establish work priorities within the engineering function where conflict exists: arbitrate differences and interface problems within the engineering function, and request through functional managers changes in personnel assignments if deemed necessary.
- Plan and conduct design review meetings and design audits as required, and participate in technical reviews with customer.
- Prepare project status reports as required.
- With the project manager and other functional departments, participate in evaluation and formulation of alternate plans as required by schedule delays or customer change requests.
- Assure support to Purchasing and Subcontracting, Manufacturing, Field

Operations, and support activities by providing liaison and technical assistance within allowables authorized by the project manager.

- Modify and reallocate tasks and subtasks, open and close cost accounts, and change allowable allocations within the limits of the approved engineering allowables, with the concurrence of the functional managers involved. Provide details to the project manager of all such actions prior to change.
- As requested by the project manager, support Legal and Contracts Administration by providing technical information.
- Review and approve technical aspects of reports for dissemination to the customer.
- Authorize within the approved allowables the procurement of material and/or services as required for the implementation of the engineering functional responsibility.
- Adjudicate technical problems and make technical decisions within scope of contractual requirements. Cost and schedule decisions affecting contractual requirements or interface with other functions are to be approved by the appropriate engineering function manager with the cognizance of the director of engineering (or his delegate) and the project manager.
- Approve all engineering designs released for procurement and/or fabrication for customer deliverable items.
- Bring problems arising between the project engineer and engineering functional managers to the engineering director for resolution.
- Bring problems arising between the project engineer and functions outside engineering to the project manager for resolution, with the cognizance of the director of engineering and the director of the other functions.

CONTRACT ADMINISTRATOR DUTIES

General

Contract administration is a specialized management function indispensable to effective management of those projects carried out under contract with customers. This function has many legal implications and serves to protect the company from unforseen risks prior to contract approval and during execution of the project. Experience dictates that well-qualified, properly organized contract administration support to a project manager is vital to the contiunuing success of companies responsible for major sales contracts.

Contract administration is represented both on the project manager's team and on the general manager's staff. A director of contract administration has the authority to audit project contract files and to impose status reporting requirements that will disclose operational and contractual problems relating to specific projects. The director of contract administration is also available to provide expertise in the resolution of contract problems beyond the capability of the contract administrator assigned to a given project.

The project contract administrator is responsible for day-to-day administration of *(a)* the contract(s) that authorize performance of the project and *(b)* all subcontracts with outside firms for equipment, material, and services to fulfill project requirements.

Proposal Preparation

- When participation of an outside subcontractor is required, assure that firm quotations are obtained based on terms and conditions compatible with those imposed by the customer.
- Review with the Legal and Financial Department all of the legal and commercial terms and conditions imposed by the customer.
- Review the proposal prior to submittal to assure that all risks and potential exposures are fully recognized.

Contract Negotiation

- Lead all contract negotiations for the project manager.
- Record detailed minutes of the proceedings.
- Assure that all discussions or agreements reached during negotiations are confirmed in writing with the understanding that they will be incorporated into the contract during the contract definition phase.
- Assure that the negotiating limits established by the Proposal Review Board (or equivalent) are not exceeded.

Contract Definition

- Expedite the preparation, management review, and execution of the contract, as follows:
  Clarify the contract format with the customer.
  Establish the order of precedence of contract documents incorporated in reference.
  Set the date by which the contract will be available in final form for management review prior to execution.
  Participate with the project manager in final briefing of management on the contract terms and conditions prior to signature.

Project Planning Phase

- Establish channels of communication with the customer and define commitment authority of project manager, contract administrator, and others.

- Integrate contract requirements and milestones into the project plan and schedule, including both company and customer obligations.
- Establish procedures for submission of contract deliverables to customer.
- Establish mechanics for monthly contract status reports for the customer and management.

Project Execution Phase

- Monitor and follow up all contract and project activities to assure fulfillment of contractual obligations by both the company and the customer.
- Assure that all contract deliverables are transmitted to the customer and that all contractually required notifications are made.
- Record any instance where the customer has failed to fulfill his obligations and define the cost and schedule impact on the project of such failure.
- Identify and define changes in scope and customer-caused delays and force majeure, including:
  —Early identification and notification to customer.
  —Obtaining customer's agreement that change of scope or customer-caused delay or force majeure case has actually occurred.
  —In coordination with the project manager and the project team, preparing a proposal that defines the scope of the change(s) and resulting price and/or schedule impact for submittal to the customer for eventual contract modification.
- Assist in negotiation and definition of contract change orders.
- Participate in project and contract status reviews and prepare required reports.
- Arrange with the customer to review the minutes of joint project review meetings to assure that they accurately reflect the proceedings.
- Assure that the customer is notified in writing of the completion of each contractual milestone and submission of each contract deliverable item, with a positive assertion that the obligation has been fulfilled.
- Where the customer insists on additional data or work before accepting completion of an item, monitor compliance with his requirement to clear such items as quickly as possible.

Project Closeout Phase

- At the point where all contractual obligations have been fulfilled, or where all but longer term warranties or spare parts deliveries are complete, assure that this fact is clearly and quickly communicated in writing to the customer.
- Assure that all formal documentation related to customer acceptance as required by the contract is properly executed.

- Expedite completion of all actions by the company and the customer needed to complete the contract and claim final payment.
- Initiate formal request for final payment.
- Where possible, obtain certification from the customer acknowledging completion of all contractual obligations and releasing the company from further obligations, except those under the terms of guaranty or warranty, if any.

Project/Contract Record Retention

Prior to disbanding the project team, the project contract administrator is responsible for collecting and placing in suitable storage the following records, to satisfy legal and internal management requirements:

- The contract file, which consists of:
  Original request for proposal (RFP) and all modifications.
  All correspondence clarifying points in the RFP.
  Copy of company's proposal and all amendments thereto.
  Records of negotiations.
  Original signed copy of contract and all documents and specifications incorporated in the contract by reference.
  All contract and modifications (supplemental agreements).
  A chronological file of all correspondence exchanged between the parties during the life of the program. This includes letters, telexes, records of telephone calls, and minutes of meetings.
  Acceptance documentation.
  Billings and payment vouchers.
  Final releases.
- Financial records required to support postcontract audits, if required by contract or governing statutes.
- History of the project (chronology of all events—contractual and noncontractual).
- Historical cost and time records that can serve as standards for estimating future requirements.

PROJECT CONTROLLER DUTIES

The primary responsibility of the project manager is to plan and control his project. On some smaller or less complex projects, he may be able to perform all the planning and controlling functions himself. However, on most major projects, it will be necessary to provide at least one person on his staff who is well qualified in project planning and control and who can devote his full attention to these specialized project management needs. This person is the project controller. (A number of other equivalent job titles are in use for this position.) On very large or complex programs or projects the project controller may require one or more persons to assist him in carrying out his duties and responsibilities.

If a centralized operations planning and control function exists in the company, that office may provide the needed planning and control services to the project manager. In that case the project controller would be a member of the Operations Planning and Control Office and would have available to him the specialists in that office. In other situations the project controller may be transferred from Operations Planning and Control to the project office for the duration of the project.

The duties of the project controller are described in the following sections.

General

- Perform for the project manager the project planning, controlling, reporting, and evaluation functions as delegated to him, so that the project objectives are achieved within the schedule and cost limits.
- Assist the project manager to achieve clear visibility of all contract tasks so that they can be progressively measured and evaluated in sufficient time for corrective action to be taken.

Project Planning and Scheduling

- In cooperation with responsible managers define the project systematically so that all tasks to be performed are identified and heirarchically related to each other, including work funded under contract or by the company, using the project breakdown structure or similar technique.
- Identify all elements of work (tasks or work packages) to be controlled for time, manpower, or cost, and identify the responsible and performing organizations and project leaders for each.
- Define an adequate number of key milestones for master planning and management reporting purposes.
- Prepare and maintain a graphic project master plan and schedule, based on the project breakdown structure, identifying all tasks or work packages to be controlled in the time dimension, and incorporating all defined milestones.
- Prepare more detailed graphic plans and schedules for each major element of the project.

Budgeting and Work Authorization

- Obtain from the responsible manager for each task or work package a task description, to include:

Statement of work.

Estimate of resources required (man days, computer hours, etc.).

Estimate of labor, computer, and other costs (with assistance of the project accountant).

Estimate of start date, and estimated total duration and duration between milestones.

- Prepare and maintain a task description file for the entire project.
- Summarize all task manpower and cost estimates, and coordinate needed revisions with responsible managers and the project manager to match the estimates with available and allocated funds for the project in total, for each major element, and for each task.
- Prepare and release, on approval of the project manager and the responsible functional manager, work authorization documents containing the statement of work, budgeted labor, and cost amounts; scheduled dates for start, completion, and intermediate milestones; and the assigned cost accounting number.
- Prepare and release, with approval of the project manager, revised work authorization documents when major changes are required or have occurred, within the authorized funding limits and the approval authority of the project manager.

Work Schedules

- Assist each responsible manager or project leader in developing detailed plans and schedules for assigned tasks, reflecting the established milestone dates in the project master plan.
- Issue current schedules to all concerned showing start and completion dates of all tasks and occurrence dates of milestones.

Progress Monitoring and Evaluation

- Obtain weekly reports from all responsible managers and project leaders of:
  Activities started and completed.
  Milestones completed.
  Estimates of time required to complete activities or tasks under way.
  Changes in future plans.
  Actual or anticipated delays, additional costs, or other problems that may affect other tasks, the schedule, or project cost.
- Record reported progress on the project master plan and analyze the effect of progress in all tasks on the overall project schedule.
- Identify major deviations from schedule and determine, with the respon-

sible managers and the project manager, appropriate action to recover delays or take advantage of early completion of tasks.

- Obtain monthly cost reports and compare to the estimates for each current task, with summaries for each level of the project breakdown structure and the total project.
- Through combined evaluation of schedule and cost progress compared to plan and budget, identify deviations that require management action and report these to the project manager.
- Participate in project review meetings, to present the overall project status and evaluate reports from managers and project leaders.
- Record the minutes of project review meetings and follow up for the project manager all resulting action assignments to assure completion of each.
- Advise the project manager of known or potential problems requiring his attention.
- Each month or quarter obtain from each responsible manager an estimate of time, manpower, and cost to complete for each incomplete task or work package; and prepare, in cooperation with the project accountant, a revised projection of cost to complete the entire project.

Schedule and Cost Control

- When schedule or budget revisions are necessary, due to delay or changes in the scope of work, prepare, negotiate, and issue new project master plan and schedules and revised work authorization documents, with approval of the project manager, within the authorized funding limits and the approval authority of the project manager.
- In coordination with the project accountant, notify the Finance Department to close each cost account and reject further charges when work is reported complete on the related task.

Reporting

- Prepare for the project manager monthly progress reports to management and the customer.
- Provide cost-to-complete estimates and other pertinent information to the project accountant for use in preparing contract status reports.
- Prepare special reports as required by the project manager.

PROJECT ACCOUNTANT DUTIES

The basic function of the project accountant is to provide to the project manager the specialized financial and accounting assistance and information needed to forecast and control manpower and costs for the project. The project accountant duties are as follows:

- Establish the basic proedure for utilizing the company financial reporting and accounting system for project control purposes to assure that all costs are properly recorded and reported.
- Assist the project controller in developing the project breakdown structure to identify the tasks or project elements that will be controlled for manpower and cost.
- Establish account numbers for the project and assign a separate number to each task or work element to be controlled.
- Prepare estimates of cost, based on manpower and other estimates provided by the controller, for all tasks in the project when required to prepare revised estimates to complete the project.
- Obtain, analyze, and interpret labor and cost accounting reports, and provide the project manager, project controller, and other managers in the project with appropriate reports to enable each to exercise needed control.
- Assure that the information being recoded and reported by the various functional and project departments is valid, properly charged, and accurate and that established policies and procedures are being followed for the project.
- Identify current and future deviation from budget of manpower or funds, or other financial problems, and in coordination with the project controller notify the project manager of such problems.
- Prepare, in coordination with the project manager and the project controller, sales contract performance reports as required by division or company procedures on a monthly basis for internal management purposes, and for submission to any higher headquarters.

MANUFACTURING COORDINATOR DUTIES

General

The general duties and responsibilities of the manufacturing coordinator (sometimes called the project leader—manufacturing) are to plan, implement, monitor, and coordinate the manufacturing aspects of his assigned project (or projects, where it is feasible for him to coordinate more than one contract).

Specific Duties

- Review all engineering releases before acceptance by manufacturing to insure they are complete and manufacturable (clean releases), and that all changes are documented by a formal written engineering change request.

- Participate in the development of project master schedules during proposal, negotiation, and execution phases, with particular emphasis on determination of requirements for engineering releases, critical parts lists, equipment requirements, and so on, to insure meeting delivery requirements.
- Monitor all costs related to assigned projects to assure adherence to manufacturing costs and cost schedules. Analyze variances and recommend corrective action. Collect needed information and prepare manufacturing cost to complete.
- Develop or direct the development of detailed schedules for assigned projects, coordinating the participation of manufacturing and product support engineering, material planning, fabrication, purchasing, material stores, assembly, test, quality control, packing and shipping, in order to insure completion of master project schedule within budget limits; provide information and schedules to different functional groups in order for action to be initiated.
- Approve all shipping authorizations for assigned projects.
- Provide liaison between the project manager and Manufacturing; diligently monitor manufacturing portions of assigned projects and answer directly for manufacturing performance against schedules; prepare status reports and provide information needed to prepare costs to complete as required.
- Take action within area of responsibility and make recommendations for corrective action in manufacturing areas to overcome schedule slippages; obtain approval from the project manager for incurring additional manufacturing costs.
- Coordinate requests for clarifications of the impact of contract change proposals on manufacturing effort.
- Participate in the preparation and approval of special operating procedures.
- Review and approve for manufacturing all engineering releases and engineering change notices affecting assigned projects, and participate in Change Control Board activity.
- Represent project manager on all Make/Buy Committee actions.

FIELD PROJECT MANAGER DUTIES

General

The field project manager (or equivalent) has overall responsibility for constructing required facilities and installing, testing, and maintaining for the specified time period, and handing over to the customer, all installed equipment and related documentation as specified by the contract. This includes direct supervision of all company and subcontractor field personnel, through their respective managers or supervisors.

Specific Duties

- Participate in the development of project master schedules during proposal, negotiation, and execution phases, with particular emphasis on determination of equipment delivery schedules and manpower and special test equipment needs.
- Monitor all field operations costs for the project to assure adherence to contract allowables. Analyze variances and recommend corrective actions. Collect needed information and prepare field operations cost to complete.
- Develop or direct the development of detailed schedules for all field operations: coordnating the equipment delivery schedules from Manufacturing and subcontractors with field receiving, inspection, installation, testing, and customer acceptance procedures, wtih due regard for transportation and import/export requirements, to insure completion of the master project schedule within budget limits; provide information and schedules to different functional groups or departments in order for action to be initiated.
- Provide liaison between the project manager and Installation and Field Operations; diligently monitor field operations portion of the project and answer for performance against schedules; prepare status reports.
- Take action and make recommendations for corrective action in field operations and other areas to overcome schedule slippages; obtain approval of the project manager for incurring additional intallation costs.
- Coordinate requests for clarifications of the impact of contract change proposals on field operations.

7. Developing the Role of the Assistant Project Manager by Assessing the Needs of Project Clients

Richard L. Patterson*

INTRODUCTION

In the many discussions and papers on the subject of project management and related management concepts, techniques and procedures there appears to be a dearth of information on the role of the Assistant Project Manager.

The reasons for this condition are not necessarily clear nor are they really germane to our discussion—but isn't it about time we took a closer look at this fellow? Shouldn't we delve into questions like who needs him and why? What function does the Assistant Project Manager perform? Where does he fit into the organization? And finally, what is his personal stake in his role?

Three basic principles evolve almost immediately during any analysis of the role of the Assistant Project Manager, namely:

- The role must provide for the accomplishment of substantial and productive functions within the scope of the total project.
- The role must fulfill certain basic needs of both the Client and the Contractor.
- The role should provide a meaningful challenge to the holder and at the same time encourage his personal growth and development.

---

*Mr. Patterson spent nine years as a project manager for Bechtel Power Corporation. During this time he managed the design, procurement and construction of two multi-unit, coal-fired power generating stations, each costing over $500 million. These assignments gave him first-hand experience at effectively utilizing assistant project managers. Mr. Patterson is now Division Manager of Quality Assurance of the Los Angeles Power Division of Bechtel Power Corporation. He is a registered Civil Engineer and a member of the ASCE and the Project Management Institute.

138

SPECIFIC NEEDS OF THE PROJECT

A Project Manager is primarily concerned with the successful completion of his project. It is from the real life world of the project itself that the specific needs for an Assistant Project Manager arise and from which his basic role is ultimately defined.

Essentially most of our larger engineering and construction projects today, and especially those in the power generation field, challenge the Project Manager's span of control at their very outset. Some of the more significant factors which strain this span include:

- The extreme physical size of many of today's projects
- The large capital costs and lengthy schedules of the projects.
- The significant financial exposure of the Client during the project cycle.
- The range and complexities of the technologies involved.
- Special services required of the Contractor in addition to his normal offerings and demonstrated capabilities.
- Geographic spread of the basic project and the major subcontractors' efforts.
- Special procurement considerations such as:
  —Client/Contractor legal relationships and divisions in procurement responsibilities or activities.
  —Extensive supplier/subcontractor qualification, inspection, expediting or test requirements.
  —Extensive commercial evaluations and negotiations to obtain satisfactory escalation provisions.
  —International as well as national procurement activities with attendant financial, legal or administrative considerations.
- The tremendous impact of regulatory agencies and their proliferation at national, state and local levels.
- The increasing public interest and the scrutiny of intervenors into more and more elements of a project.
- Construction and construction-related activities including such factors as:
  —Labor relations and union matters.
  —Site logistics and support.
  —Housing and associated socioeconomic considerations.
  —Insurance.

These typical and basic strains on project management generally prevail throughout the average power project life cycle and obviously require the continuing attention of the Contractor's and the Client's management. But it is also important to note that most large and long term projects go through several major changes in emphasis and many shifts in the tenor of their operations during their life cycles.

For example, in the early stages of a power project we may be concerned with such factors as site selection, housing requirements, fuel transport, major long lead hardware procurement, environmental reports, criteria development and basic estimates and schedules associated with the conceptual design. As the final design is developed the project emphasis shifts to detailed engineering demands with particular attention devoted to engineering calculations, drawings and the preparation of detailed specifications. Subsequently, project concern will center upon the qualification of vendors and subcontractors, the preparation of bid packages, bid evaluations and material availability, while the design, costs and schedules undergo continuing and strengthening refinements. In the meantime, field mobilization must be planned and the site prepared. Then, with the pouring of the first major concrete the activity in the field increases very rapidly. Now special attention must be focused on the timely delivery of hardware and materials, and getting the necessary engineering drawings to the field to ensure orderly and effective progression in a total construction effort that may involve several thousand workers. As construction advances, the project emphasis again shifts; this time to the installation and checkout of equipment, the resolution of equipment problems, and the progressive startup of the plant.

These typical project patterns are not exempt from the unexpected or unusual problems which also serve to change management plans and expectations. Further, it should be emphasized that with each changing project pattern there is usually both a qualitative and quantitative impact upon project management. The special skills, technology, or professional requirements change with each new pattern. Similarly, the intensity of project management attention and devotion to certain project areas must shift with each change in the project pattern.

Naturally, both the Contractor and the Client desire that the Project Manager bring to the project the widest (and deepest) possible personal exposure and professional experience in all facets of the job. However, it is a rare individual who can fulfill all the demands of today's major projects.

In such cases the capabilities and experience of an Assistant Project Manager can be used to complement and supplement those of the Project Manager in one or more areas of concern and during one or more major time frames of the project. Proper matching of skills and background coupled with timely assignment can greatly strengthen the Contractor's project management and the true span of control.

GENERAL NEEDS OF THE CLIENT

The Client desires that the needs of the project be satisfied as discussed in the previous section. He also has some very specific needs of his own.

The Client has a concern in the day-to-day availability of the Project Manager. In the Project Manager's absence the Client invariably requires assurance that adequate management attention is being given to the project operations and that a designated and capable individual—within management—is available to respond to his needs.

Similarly, the Client has an overriding interest in the continuity of his project and generally looks with favor on the presence of a designated assistant in the Contractor's organization who can eventually (and smoothly) move into the Project Manager's shoes, if and when required. Some Clients may actively participate in the actual selection of this assistant by establishing certain qualifications or criteria for the role, or by other means.

The very fact that the Client has brought a Contractor on board is presumptive of his needs. Normally the statement of work and related contract documents will identify these needs adequately. However, it is not always possible to fully define certain key concerns or overriding needs, especially in regard to personnel qualifications, staffing and organization.

While the Client may have no direct interest in the personal growth or development of each individual within the Contractor's organization, he does have a general and continuing concern for the overall strength and depth of the Contractor's project team.

In this respect, it is not uncommon for the Client to view the Contractor's organization as an extension of his very own. In this context then, the Client frequently demonstrates a strong advocacy for furthering the growth and development of certain of the Contractor's people in parallel with his own in-house plans. Specifically, the establishment and development of the role of Contractor's Assistant Project Manager usually fits very nicely into the Client's personnel plans and policies.

GENERAL NEEDS OF THE CONTRACTOR

The Contractor's senior management, as well as many others within and without the Contractor's organization, will normally view the Project Manager as the primary contact (and expert) on his assigned job. And rightly so!

It naturally follows that the Project Manager is frequently sought out or solicited for reports, reviews, audits, special information or documents and similar efforts by his own management. In addition, he is frequently called upon to head up meetings or conferences or to participate to a greater or lesser degree in related activities sponsored by others, both within and without his own organization. Obviously, he must be particularly concerned with those key management plans and operations which interface directly with his assignment.

Progressive companies will provide opportunities for deserving Project Managers to participate in executive management training courses and seminars to prepare them for positions of greater responsibility.

These demands upon the Project Manager's time make him less available to his own project organization which must deal with a multitude of questions on a day-to-day basis. Under such circumstances the assignment of an Assistant Project Manager to fill in for the Project Manager in his absence can ensure timely monitoring of operations, lend mature judgment and guidance to project personnel, provide for appropriate approvals (signature) where required, and do much to alleviate any work delays or encumbrances which might otherwise be brought about by the Project Manager's absence.

On many key projects the Contractor may have a further and naturally selfish need for the presence of an Assistant Project Manager. On long term projects it is especially prudent for management to plan for the ultimate replacement of the Project Manager as the latter may move on to further challenges. The assignment of an Assistant Project Manager on a timely basis then becomes the Contractor's primary tool for achieving project continuity. Subsequently, an efficient transition or change in project management with no unsettling Client or project team disturbances can be made when required.

The successful Contractor is also alert to foster the personnel growth and professional development of his own people. It is usually the more talented and motivated employees who actively seek out the promotional routes to management, and who must be reassured, at timely intervals, by appropriate assignments of increasing responsibility and growth potential.

The role of an Assistant Project Manager, if properly structured, on a selected project can provide excellent training for the development of future Project Managers and at the same time maintain the dedication and motivation of the individual employee by providing him with meaningful challenges and opportunities. It should be noted that we stress the fact that the role must be properly structured, and for the benefit of all—the Contractor, the Client, the Project and the Individual.

THE NEEDS OF THE INDIVIDUAL

Senior engineering and construction personnel on their way toward a management career will be attracted to the role of Assistant Project Manager if the position will:

- Provide challenging work assignments.
- Utilize their professional skills, talents and experience.
- Call for (tangible) productive work to achieve recognizable goals.
- Permit their professional development and growth.

A stimulating work environment must be afforded the Assistant Project Manager. His care and feeding, particularly if the role represents his first assignment with "manager" in the title, is of particular concern and may markedly affect project operations.

From the individual's standpoint—and ideally—all the foregoing factors should be equally represented in the assigned role. Regrettably, all projects do not necessarily present such a balanced offering. However, it is extremely fortunate that most of today's large projects do offer a wide variety of experience to the young managerial candidate. By ensuring that the Assistant Project Manager is given adequate exposure to diverse elements of the project to enhance his growth and development, the Contractor's Management can frequently compensate for occasional shortcomings in other specific areas of concern to the individual.

STRUCTURING THE ROLE

Structuring the role of an Assistant Project Manager on a specific project may turn out to be a challenging task. The interplay among the management, personal and project variables and tradeoffs must be carefully evaluated.

The individual candidates for the role will normally have clear cut concepts of their personal requirements. However, as we pointed out earlier it is a rare situation or project which will completely satisfy the personal needs of every candidate for the role or neatly supplement or complement the personal capabilities of the Project Manager.

While the general needs of the Contractor and the Client loom large and important, the specific needs of the project become the more compelling and should invariably establish the basic structure of the Assistant Project Manager's role.

However, it should be noted that within the total project needs there will usually be several marked variations in the relative priorities assigned to the various requirements. Moreover, there may be a wide disparity between disciplinary or functional needs on the project which cannot be easily reconciled or encompassed by the placement of any one individual. Finally, not all requirements can be neatly compartmentalized nor effectively segmented from many other portions of the project to provide a nicely fenced-in area for the role of the Assistant Project Manager.

The timing of the assignment of the Assistant Project Manager is influenced primarily by the requirements of the project, which vary with time.

For the most part, the project scope and schedule can serve to identify the need dates for special assistance or added attention to certain project activities or events. In the case of very large and complex projects it may be desirable to staff the position coincident with the assignment of the Project Manager. On smaller or less complex projects, and especially those on a low burner in their early phases it will usually be more prudent and cost effective to delay the assignment. In either case a project learning curve for the Assistant Project Manager should be considered so that when he is required to perform as Project Manager, he will have had time to assimilate the necessary project background and experience to enable him to perform satisfactorily.

While we have so far discussed the role of the Assistant Project Manager as that of a singular individual, it should now be apparent that on certain demanding and complex projects two or more Assistant Project Managers may very well be required.

Throughout our discussion we have also consistently used the title "Assistant Project Manager." However, there is no mandatory requirement for this usage. Other titles appropriately matched to the Contractor's and Client's job classification and organizational concepts would also be suitable. Examples might include:

- Deputy Project Manager.
- Associate Project Manager.

INTERPRETING THE ROLE

When the basic structure and background needs of the role of the Assistant Project Manager have been reconciled, his position can be implemented and integrated into the project organization.

Essentially there are three elementary organizational arrangements which should be considered, as shown in Figure 7-1. In the first case, the Assistant Project Manager is placed in a staff position relative to the Project Manager. This position is indicative of a more confined or segmented role and connotes a less than full time backup for the Project Manager. This arrangement is most beneficial when an experienced staff person is assigned to the project to concentrate his expertise on specific problems. It provides only a minimum opportunity for training the Assistant Project Manager to take over the role of a Project Manager.

In the second case, the Assistant Project Manager is placed in a separate box directly below the Project Manager and with all line functions passing through his office. This organization is more indicative of a strong and rigid role for the Assistant Project Manager; it encompasses all project functions and full time backup for the Project Manager. However, because of its rigidity this organizational approach may not necessarily increase the Project Manager's span of control and could tend to make the position of Assistant Project Manager a bottleneck.

In the third case, the Assistant Project Manager is placed in the same box with the Project Manager and directly beneath him. This arrangement reflects full time backup for the Project Manager and a stronger measure of togeth-

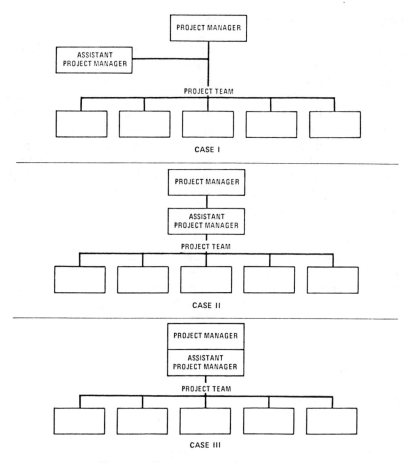

Figure 7-1. Elementary organizational arrangements.

erness. The opportunity for increasing the Project Manager's span of control is greater through a sharing of the many duties. At the same time the Assistant Project Manager may give special attention to certain functional, disciplinary or other aspects of the project.

There are obvious merits in each approach and there can be several variations of these organizational concepts. In any case, the overriding concern of management should be to design or select the organizational arrangement which will respond best to the project needs and contribute most to project and Contractor/Client Team performance.

Some variations in the role of the Assistant Project Manager can be illustrated by a brief description and discussion of their actual employment in the engineering and construction of three current power generating projects.

ARIZONA NUCLEAR POWER PROJECT (ANPP)

This project for Arizona Public Service (and other participating utilities) consists of three 1300 MW nuclear units (Palo Verde 1, 2 and 3) sited in south-central Arizona about 60 miles from Phoenix.

A unique feature of the project will be the use of reclaimed sewerage water from the City of Phoenix, which will be transported to the site by a large pipeline, to meet the extensive project cooling water makeup requirements.

A simplified version of the basic organization chart is shown in Figure 7-2. The water reclamation and pipeline effort is being handled by another division of the company under the supervision of a separate Project Manager. This Project Manager reports to the ANPP Project Manager for coordination with the Prime Contract and its supporting documents and for coordination of his efforts on other contractual matters, budgets, procedures, procurement and field support.

The scope, complexity, cost and schedule of the total project merit the full time attention of two Assistant Project Managers.

In this arrangement, Assistant Project Manager A , with a strong background in engineering and project field engineering, directs his primary attention to:

- Engineering.
- Procurement.
- Legal and Insurance.
- Quality Assurance.

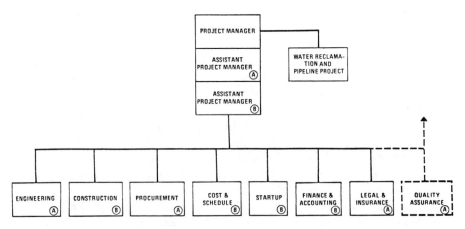

Figure 7-2. Simplified basic organization chart, Arizona Nuclear Power Project.

Assistant Project Manager B, with extensive experience in cost engineering, subcontract management and planning and scheduling, including home office and field efforts, concentrates his attention on construction, startup, finance, accounting and cost, and schedule matters.

Both Assistant Project Managers are exposed to the entire range of project operations.

SAN ONOFRE UNITS 2 AND 3

This project for Southern California Edison and San Diego Gas and Electric consists of two 1100 MW nuclear units sited on the coast of California about 60 miles south of Los Angeles. The project has been exposed to numerous major criteria changes due to the many new regulatory guides issued by the NRC since its inception, and was exposed to extensive public scrutiny by various intervenors and the California Coastal Commission in its early design and licensing stages.

While the project site and Client and Contractor headquarters are within reasonable commuting distances of each other there are a few significant geographical spreads in the project—for example, the turbine generators are furnished by English Electric.

A simplified version of the basic organization chart is shown in Figure 7-3. There is one very experienced Assistant Project Manager on this project who functions throughout the complete spectrum of the project, but is used extensively on procurement, startup and legal and insurance matters. The Assistant Project Manager has also recently been engaged in extensive restructuring/

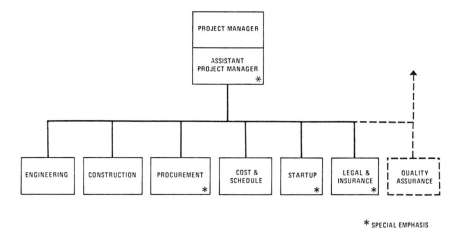

* SPECIAL EMPHASIS

Figure 7-3. Simplified basic organization chart, San Onofre units 2 and 3.

renegotiating of certain major subcontracts with companies experiencing serious financial and production difficulties which posed major problems to the project.

The Assistant Project Manager has a strong background in estimating, cost and schedule control, finance and accounting matters and engineering administration. Nonetheless, he participates fully in all phases of the project and is a full backup for the Project Manager.

In the later stages of the project a senior project manager was brought in to provide added management support during critical construction completion and startup activities. The senior project manager is in a direct line position over the project manager and assistant project manager. With the original management team intact to direct the day-to-day operation of the project, the senior project manager has the freedom to concentrate his efforts on specific problem areas and make key company, client and supplier contacts as necessary.

This type of an arrangement shows how the project management concept and organization can be kept flexible to respond to the specific needs of the project.

CORONADO UNITS 1 AND 2

This undertaking for Salt River Project consists of two 350 MW coal-fired units sited in eastern Arizona. Four coal sources located along an existing main line railroad are currently being investigated. There is a separate design and construction management contract for a 43 mile railroad to handle unit trains of coal from the main line to the site. The railroad effort was designed and the construction managed by another division of the company.

A simplified version of the basic organization chart is shown in Figure 7-4.

In this situation the primary project manager functions as a manager of projects. At one time he had responsibility for three projects.

The primary long-term project is the design, procurement and construction of the Coronado Generating Station. During the early stages of Coronado, construction and startup work were being completed on the three 700 MW coal-fired units of the Navajo Project for the same client. A separate assistant project manager for the completion of Navajo worked under the general guidance of the Coronado Project Manager to provide central contact and consistancy of approach with the client.

The other division of the company assigned a project manager to direct the design, procurement and construction management of the railroad spur. This project manager also worked under the general guidance of the Coronado Project Manager in order to maintain consistency in client relations, project procedures and also to obtain close coordination between the field activities.

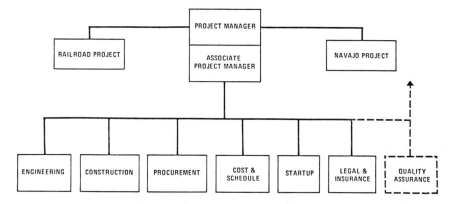

Figure 7-4. Simplified basic organization chart, Coronado units 1 and 2.

The Project Manager on the Coronado Project is assisted by an Associate Project Manager who is thoroughly integrated into the basic project. The Associate Project Manager has previous management experience and a strong background in project engineering. In day-to-day operations he concentrates upon the technical engineering interface with the Client and engineering-construction interfaces. The latter effort helps to achieve proper understanding and effective operations between these two major components of the project. Typical routine duties assigned the Associate Project Manager are listed in Figure 7-5.

SUMMARY

While we may have overlooked the role of the Assistant Project Manager in our formal discussions in the past it is readily apparent that he can be a key man in the organization and can do much to improve the total management and performance of the project team.

The role of the Assistant Project Manager may vary considerably from project to project. There does not appear to be a universal approach which can satisfy all projects. Some of the major considerations in defining the role include:

- Special needs of the project.
- Client needs.
- Contractor needs.
- Capabilities and availability of the Project Manager.
- Capabilities and interests of the Assistant Project Manager.
- Geographic spread of activities.
- Various contractual arrangements and their implications.

ENGINEERING

KEEP CURRENT ON ALL STATUS AND PROGRESS

PROVIDE CONTINUOUS MONITORING TO ENSURE THAT THE DESIGN IS CONSISTENT WITH

    COST REDUCTION GOALS

REVIEW MAJOR STUDIES AND BID EVALUATIONS

REVIEW AND CONTINUOUS ENGINEERING AUDIT OF PAST JOB PROBLEMS

ATTEND DESIGN MEETINGS AND ASSIST IN CLIENT PROJECT ENGINEERING RELATIONS

CONSTRUCTION

KEEP CURRENT ON ALL STATUS AND PROGRESS INCLUDING HOUSING FOR CONSTRUCTION

    PERSONNEL

PROCUREMENT

REVIEW AND COORDINATE INSPECTION, EXPEDITING AND EQUIPMENT DELIVERIES

PARTICIPATE IN AND CONDUCT BIDDER REVIEW OR PRE-AWARD CONFERENCES AS REQUIRED

COST AND SCHEDULE

CONDUCT INITIAL REVIEW FOR PROJECT MANAGEMENT APPROVAL:

    TRENDS

    CHANGE NOTIFICATIONS

    PROJECT FINANCIAL STATUS REPORT

REVIEW, COORDINATE AND MONITOR FOR FULL IMPLEMENTATION:

    COST AND SCHEDULE PROGRAMS (EMPHASIS ON ENG & H.O. COST CONTROL AND

    ENGINEERING PROGRESS REPORTING)

    SCHEDULE PREPARATION

CONTINUOUSLY MONITOR THE TREND PROGRAM FOR IMPLEMENTATION AND IDENTIFICATION

    OF COST TRENDS AND COST REDUCTION ITEMS

COORDINATE IMPLEMENTATION OF BECHTEL-SUGGESTED COST REDUCTION AND EFFICIENCY

    MEASURES FOR OUR OPERATIONS

INSURE THAT NON-REIMBURSABLE COSTS ARE BUDGETED AND CONTROLLED

COST AND SCHEDULE (Continued)

PREPARE CURRENT COMMENTS FOR PROJECT FINANCIAL STATUS REPORT

COORDINATE PREPARATION OF PFSR AND FORECASTS

CLIENT COMMENTS ON BECHTEL BILLINGS

STARTUP

KEEP CURRENT ON ALL STATUS

QUALITY ASSURANCE

REVIEW AND COORDINATE

LABOR RELATIONS AND SAFETY

REVIEW AND COORDINATE PREPARATION OF AFFIRMATIVE ACTION PROGRAM

INSURANCE

REVIEW AND COORDINATE

ADMINISTRATION AND CORRESPONDENCE

COMMUNICATION WITH CLIENT AS REQUIRED

REVIEW AND COORDINATE PREPARATION AND FULL IMPLEMENTATION:

    EXTERNAL PROCEDURES

    INTERNAL PROCEDURES

PREPARE MINUTES OF PROJECT REVIEW MEETINGS

PREPARE MINUTES OF EXECUTIVE STAFF MEETINGS

PREPARE MONTHLY REPORT

PREPARE WEEKLY REPORT TO MANAGEMENT

COORDINATE AND IMPLEMENT CONTRACT CHANGES INCLUDING NECESSARY COST ESTIMATES

PROJECT TEAM SPACE ARRANGEMENTS

USE OF COMPUTER IN FIELD OFFICE

PUBLISH ACTION ITEMS REPORT

Figure 7-5. Associate Project Manager routine duties.

Notwithstanding the many differences in the three examples we have cited, two very consistent factors stand out:

- All the Project Managers encourage the Assistant Project Manager to actively participate in all facets of the project.
- The experience and capabilities of the Assistant (Associate) Project Managers are being effectively concentrated on those areas of their expertise, while being exposed to the total project.

In the final analysis, the key requirement for the role of the Assistant Project Manager is to provide flexibility on the part of Contractor's Management and the Client in best meeting the needs of all.

Section III

Organizational Strategy and Project Management

Project management is a tool for executing overall organizational strategy. Therefore it is inadequate to view project management only within the confines of the project. It must be considered within the context of the overall organization and its strategy.

In Chapter 8, William R. King describes the inter-relationships of the various elements of business strategy. He demonstrates a method that can be used to ensure that the projects embarked on by an organization are those that are most compatible with its overall mission, strategy and goals.

In Chapter 9, Dale R. Beck continues this theme by discussing the formation and implementation of a particular project from the viewpoint of both top management and project management.

William E. Souder's Chapter 10 deals with techniques for evaluating and selecting projects. Project selection is the mechanism by which the organization ensures that it selects the "right," or the "best," projects for funding. A wide range of techniques are reviewed, each of which addresses a different objective and set of measures that may be applied. (The strategic "program evaluation" approach of Chapter 8 is another technique that may be used.)

8. The Role of Projects in the Implementation of Business Strategy

William R. King*

There is a good deal of anecdotal evidence concerning business strategies that have failed because they were not implemented or because they were inappropriately implemented. Since projects and programs are the vehicles through which strategy is implemented, such failures strike at the heart of the value of project management to the organization.

In an audit of the existing and planned programs in the central research laboratory of a major diversified firm, the author found:

- Programs and projects that could not be associated with any business or corporate objective or strategy.
- Programs and projects which apparently fell outside the stated mission of the corporation or the charter of the laboratory.
- Projects whose funding levels could not reasonably be justified in terms of the expected benefits to be produced.

Such observations have so frequently emanated from less formal analyses in other companies as to suggest the existence of a faulty linkage between corporate plans and strategy and the programs and projects through which they should be implemented.

---

*Dr. William R. King is Professor of Business Administration in the Graduate School of Business at the University of Pittsburgh. He is the author of more than a dozen books and 100 articles in the fields of strategic planning, information systems and project management. Additional biographical material may be found in the current editions of *Who's Who in the World, Who's Who in America,* and other standard references.

THE CHOICE ELEMENTS OF CORPORATE STRATEGY

Because of the semantics jungle which exists in the area of business policy and strategy, it is necessary to rather precisely define the terms to be used. The *choice elements of corporate strategy*—those choices that must be explicitly or implicitly made in the corporate strategic planning process—are the *Organization's:*

Mission—the "business" that the organization is in.

Objectives—desired future positions on roles for the organization.

Strategy—the *general direction* in which the objectives are to be pursued.

Goals—specific targets to be sought at specified points in time.

Programs/Projects—resource-consuming sets of activities through which strategies are implemented and goals are pursued.

Resource Allocations—allocations of funds, manpower, etc. to various units, objectives, strategies, programs and projects.

These informal definitions are meant to provide a common framework for communication rather than to define the "correct" terminology. Various firms may use different terminology, but none can escape the need to make choices of each variety. (These strategic choice elements are treated in more detail elsewhere.*)

Most organizations conduct planning processes which are aimed at explicitly choosing all or some of these strategic choice elements. However, many firms fail to deal with all of the choice elements in the detail and specificity which each deserves.

Often, for instance, missions are dealt with implicitly, as in the case of the firm that responds to the mission concept by stating their mission to be: "We make widgets." Such a product-oriented view of the organization's business ignores new market opportunities and perhaps, the firm's generic strengths. It is these opportunities and strengths which form the most likely areas for future success. Thus, it is these opportunities and strengths, rather than the current product line, which should define the mission.

Strategies are almost always explicitly chosen by firms, but often strategies are thought of in output, rather than input, terms. In such instances, strategies may be described in terms of expected sales and profits rather than in terms of strategic directions such as product redesign, new products or new markets.

Thus, the elements of strategic choice are inescapable in the sense that the

---

*See William R. King and David I. Cleland, *Strategic Planning and Policy,* Van Nostrand Reinhold, 1978, Chapters 3 and 6–9 from which portions of this material are adapted with the permission of the publisher.

avoidance of an explicit choice about any of the elements means that it is chosen implicitly. However, many firms make poor or inappropriate choices, both explicitly and implicitly, because they do not have a clear awareness of the relationships among the strategic choice elements and their innate interdependence.

RELATIONSHIPS AMONG THE STRATEGIC CHOICE ELEMENTS

One of the most important conditions for the effective implementation of plans has to do with the relationships among the strategic choice elements. If these relationships are well defined, carefully analyzed and conceived, the plan is likely to be implemented. If they are not, the plan is likely to be a voluminous document that requires substantial time and energy to prepare, but which is filed on the shelf until the next planning cycle commences. Indeed, many plans are so treated precisely because they do not carefully spell out the relationships among various strategic choice elements and therefore do not provide the appropriate information that is necessary to guide the many decisions which must be made to implement the plan and to develop and manage the projects and programs which are the operational essence of the plan.

Figure 8-1 shows the elements of strategic choice in the form of a triangle which illustrates that the mission and objectives are the highest level elements. They are supported by the other elements—the strategies, goals, programs and projects. The strategic resource allocations underlie each of these elements.

Figure 8-2 shows an illustration of these concepts in terms of a business firm. The mission chosen is that of "supplying system components to a world-wide non-residential air conditioning market." Note that while this mission statement superficially appears to be product-oriented, it identifies the nature of the product (system components), and the market (world-wide non-residential air

Figure 8-1. Relationship of strategic choice elements.

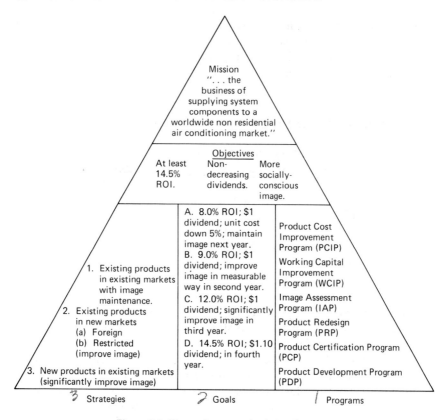

Figure 8-2. Illustrative strategic choice elements.

conditioning) quite specifically. By exclusion, it guides managers in avoiding proposals for overall systems and strategies that would be directed toward residential markets. However, it does identify the world as the company's territory and (in an elaboration not shown here) defines air conditioning to include "air heating, cooling, cleaning, humidity control and movement."

Supporting the base of the triangle are strategies, goals, and programs. The firm's strategies are stated in terms of a three-phase approach. First, the company will concentrate on achieving its objectives through existing products and markets while maintaining its existing image. Then, it will give attention to new markets for existing products, foreign and restricted, while improving the company's image. "Restricted" markets may be thought of as those that require product-safety certification before the product can be sold in that market. Finally, it will focus on new products in existing markets while *significantly* improving its image.

Clearly, this is a staged strategy; one that focuses attention first on one thing and then on another. This staging does not imply that the first strategy element is carried through completely before the second is begun; it merely means that the first element is given primary and earliest attention, then the second and third in turn. In effect, the first element of the strategy has its implementation *begun* first. This will be made more clear in terms of goals and programs.

At the right base of the triangle, a number of the firm's programs are identified. Each of these programs is made up of a variety of projects or activities. Each program serves as a focus for various activities having a common goal. For instance, in the case of the Product Cost Improvement Program, the associated projects and activities might be as follows:

- Quality Control Project.
- Production Planning Improvement Project.
- Production Control System Development Project.
- Plant Layout Redesign Project.
- Employee Relations Project.

All of these projects and activities are focused toward the *single* goal of product cost improvement.

In the case of the Working Capital Improvement Program, the various projects and activities might include a "terms and conditions" study aimed at revising the terms and conditions under which goods are sold, an inventory reduction project, etc. Each of the other programs would have a similar collection of projects and activities focused on some single well-defined goal.

The goals are listed in the middle-lower portion of the triangle in Figure 8-2. Each goal is stated in specific and timely terms related to the staged strategy and the various programs. These goals reflect the desire to attain 8.0% ROI (a step along the way to the 14.5% objective) next year, along with a $1 dividend (the current level), a unit cost improvement of 5%, while maintaining image. For subsequent years, the goals reflect a climb to 14.5% ROI, a steady and then increasing dividend, and an increasing and measurable image consistent with the staged strategy that places image improvements later in the staged sequence. This is also consistent with the program structure, which includes an "Image Assessment Program," a program designed to develop methods and measures for quantitatively assessing the company's image.

Figure 8-3 shows the same elements as does Figure 8-2, with each being indicated by number, letter, or acronym. For instance, the block labeled 1 in Figure 8-3 represents the first stage of the strategy in Figure 8-2, the letter A represents next year's goal, etc.

The arrows in Figure 8-3 represent *some* illustrative relationships among the

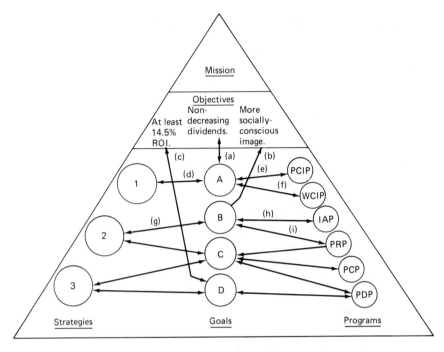

Figure 8-3. Relationships among illustrative choice elements.

various objectives, programs, strategy elements, and goals. For instance, the arrows a,b, and c reflect direct relationships between specific timely goals and broad timeless objectives:

a. A, next year's goals primarily relate to the objective of nondecreasing dividends.
b. B, the second year's goals relate to the "more socially conscious image" objective.
c. D, the quantitative ROI figure is incorporated as a goal in the fourth year.

Of course, each year's goals relate implicitly or explicitly to all objectives. However, these relationships are some of the most direct and obvious.

Similarly, arrow d in Figure 8-3 relates the first year's goals to the first element of the overall strategy in that these goals for next year are to be attained primarily through the strategy element involving "existing products in existing markets." However, arrows e and f also show that the Product Cost Improvement Program (PCIP) and the Working Capital Improvement Program (WCIP) are also expected to contribute to the achievement of next year's goals.

The second year's goals will begin to reflect the impact of the second strategy element (existing products in new markets) as indicated by arrow g in Figure 8-3. The effect of the Product Redesign Program (PRP) is also expected to contribute to the achievement of these goals (arrow i) as is the Image Assessment Program (IAP) expected to provide an ability to measure image by that time. The other arrows in Figure 8-3 depict other rather direct relationships whose interpretation is left to the reader.

From this figure, relationships among the various strategic decision elements can be seen:

1. Goals are specific steps along the way to the accomplishment of broad objectives.
2. Goals are established to reflect the expected outputs from strategies.
3. Goals are directly achieved through programs.
4. Strategies are implemented by programs.

Thus, the picture shown in Figure 8-3 is that of an interrelated set of strategic factors that demonstrate both *what* the company wishes to accomplish in the long run, *how* it will do this in a sequenced and sensible way, and *what performance levels* it wishes to achieve at various points along the way.

STRATEGIC PROGRAM EVALUATION

Figures 8-1 to 8-3 make it clear that the various elements of strategic choice are mutually supportive. However, there remains the question of how this high degree of interdependence can be effectively attained.

Certainly, an understanding of the logical relationships that are depicted in these figures should itself lead to better subjective choices in the planning process. However, while subjective judgement can be appropriately applied at the higher levels of strategic choice because these elements are tractable, it is an inadequate basis for choice at the lower levels of program/project selection and funding.

In other words, no formal techniques are needed in choosing among alternative missions and objectives because these choices must inherently be made on a primitive basis of the personal values and goals of management and other stakeholders. At this level, there are only a few viable options from which choices must be made.

At the level of programs, projects and resource allocations, quite the opposite is the case. There are many contenders and combinations of contenders to be considered. Thus, some formal approach may be useful. Indeed, such an approach is not only practically useful, but it forms the integrating factor in the array of strategic choice elements.

The intergrating factor is a strategic program evaluation approach *which directly utilizes the results of the higher level strategic choices to evaluate alternative programs, projects and funding levels.* "Project selection" approaches are well-known and widely used in industry for the selection of engineering projects, R&D projects, and new product development projects. However, if program/project evaluation is to be the key link in unifying the array of organizational strategic choice elements, the evaluation framework must itself be an integral element of the strategic plan.

Thus, potential projects and programs must be "filtered" through the application of strategic crietria that are based on the higher-level choices that have previously been made—the organization's mission, objectives, and strategies. The output of this filtering process is a set of rank-ordered project and program opportunities that can serve as a basis for the allocation of resources.

Other important criteria must come into play in implementing this evaluation process. These criteria are those that are *implicit* in a good specification of the organization's mission, objectives and strategy. However, they must be *specifically addressed* if program and projects are to truly reflect corporate strategy. These criteria are:

1. Does the opportunity take advantage of a *strength* that the company possesses?
2. Correspondingly, does it avoid a dependence on something that is a *weakness* of the firm?
3. Does it offer the opportunity to attain a *comparative advantage* over competitors?
4. Does it contribute to the *internal consistency* of the existing projects and programs?
5. Does it address a *mission-related opportunity* that is presented by the evolving market environment?
6. Is the level of *risk* acceptable?
7. Is is consistent with the established *policy guidelines?*

A Strategic Program Evaluation Illustration

A strategic program/project evaluation framework based on these criteria is shown as Table 8-1. In the left-most column of the table is a set of evaluation criteria that relates to the example in Figures 8-2 and 8-3. The body of the table shows how a proposed new program to begin manufacturing of system components in Europe might be evaluated.

The "criteria weights" in the second column of the table reflect their relative importance and serve to permit the evaluation of complex project characteristics within a simple framework. A base weight of 20 is used here for the major

Table 8-1. An Example of Strategic Program Evaluation.

PROGRAM PROJECT EVALUATION CRITERIA		CRITERIA WEIGHTS	VERY GOOD (8)	GOOD (6)	FAIR (4)	POOR (2)	VERY POOR (0)	EXPECTED LEVEL SCORE	WEIGHTED SCORE
Fit with mission	Product	10	1.0					8.0	80
	Market	10	1.0					8.0	80
Consistency with objectives	ROI	10	0.2	0.6	0.2			6.0	60
	Dividends	5		0.2	0.6	0.2		4.0	20
	Image	5			0.8	0.2		3.6	18
Consistency with strategy	Stage 1	10					1.0	0	0
	Stage 2	7	1.0					8.0	56
	Stage 3	3					1.0	0	0
Contribution to goals	Goal A	8					1.0	0	0
	Goal B	6	0.8	0.2				7.6	45.6
	Goal C	4		0.8	0.2			5.6	22.4
	Goal D	2					1.0	0	0
Corporate *strength* base		10				0.8	0.2	1.6	16
Corporate *weakness* avoidance		10				0.2	0.8	0.4	4
Comparative advantage level		10	0.7	0.3				7.4	74
Internal consistency level		10	1.0					8.0	80
Mission-related opportunity		10	1.0					8.0	80
Risk level acceptability		10				0.7	0.3	1.4	14
Policy guideline consistency		10			1.0			4.0	40
Total score									690

criteria related to mission, objectives, strategy and goals. Weights of 10 are applied to the other criteria.

Within each major category, the 20 "points" are judgementally distributed to reflect the relative importance of subelements or some other characteristic of the criterion. For instance, the three stages of strategy and the four subgoals are weighted to ensure that earlier stages and goals are treated to be more important than later ones. This implicitly reflects the *time value of money* without requiring a complex discounting calculation.

The first criterion in Table 8-1 is the "fit with the mission." The proposal is evaluated to be consistent with both the "product" and "market" elements of the mission and is thereby rated to be "very good," as shown by the 1.0 entries in the upper left.

In terms of "consistency with objectives," the proposal is rated to have a 20% chance of being "very good" in contributing to the ROI element of the objectives (see Figure 8-2), a 60% chance of being "good" and a 20% chance of being only "fair," as indicated by the likelihoods entered into the third row of the table. The proposed project is rated more poorly with respect to the "Dividends" and "Image" elements.

The proposal is also evaluated in terms of its expected contribution to each of the three stages of the strategy as outlined in Figure 8-2. In this case, the proposed project is believed to be one which would principally contribute to stage 2 of the strategy. (Note that only certain assessments may be made in this case since the stages are mutually exclusive and exhaustive.)

The proposal is similarly evaluated with respect to the other criteria.

The overall evaluation is obtained as a weighted score that represents the sum of products of the likelihoods (probabilities) as the 8, 6, 4, 2, 0 arbitrary level weights that are displayed at the top of the table. For instance, the "consistency with objectives-ROI" expected level weight is calculated as

$$0.2(8) + 0.6(6) + 0.2(4) = 6.0$$

This is then multiplied by the criterion weight of 10 to obtain a weighted score of 60. The weighted scores are then summed to obtain an overall evaluation of 690.

Of course, this number in isolation is meaningless. However, when various programs and projects are evaluated in terms of the same criteria, their overall scores provide a reasonable basis for developing a ranking of projects that reflects their consistency with strategy. Such a ranking can be the basis for resource allocation since the top-ranked program is presumed to be the most worthy, the second-ranked is the next most worthy, etc.

SUMMARY

The strategic program evaluation framework that is developed and demonstrated here provides the integrating factor that is necessary if strategic plans are to be effectively implemented. The critical element of the evaluation approach is its use of criteria which ensure that programs will be integrated with the mission, objectives, strategy and goals of the organization as well as criteria that reflect critical elements of strategy such as business strengths, weaknesses, comparative advantages, internal consistency, opportunities and policies.

9. Implementing Top Management Plans Through Project Management

Dale R. Beck*

INTRODUCTION

The concept of Project Management is one of the most significant new management techniques developed in the post World War II era. Project Management is a comparatively new approach having been developed and refined as a result of the complexity of modern day government, military and business issues. Solving complex problems is a challenge of integrating interdisciplinary efforts toward a common goal.

Problems facing organizations today cannot be neatly placed within subunits of the organization for resolution. Solving problems and exploiting opportunities, requires input and contributions from many areas of the organization. Project Management is geared toward solving problems and exploiting opportunities *through interdisciplinary efforts*.

But Project Management is not top management. Project Management depends on top management for authority, direction and support. Top management, in turn, depends on Project Management for timely, and cost effective achievement of results. plus quality

Some of the forces acting on businesses and other organizations today are regulatory thrusts, competitive pressures, technological changes, economic factors, resource scarcity, consumerism, equal employment issues, and demographic changes. All of these forces have existed for a number of years, but managing organizations has become extremely difficult because of the number

---

*Dale R. Beck is Director of Pricing for Ross Laboratories, Division of Abbott Laboratories, Inc. His former position was Manager of Project Management with Ross Laboratories where he had responsibility for managing over 100 projects. Mr. Beck has been a member of the Project Management Institute and served as Vice President of the Project Management Institute, Ohio Chapter. He has presented and published many papers on project management. Mr. Beck is a graduate of the University of Michigan and has an M.B.A. from the University of Cincinnati.

and strength of these forces. Project Management has evolved in order to manage efforts required to deal with these outside environment forces, in addition to freeing top management to deal with these forces. Project Management frees top management time by performing some of the functions top management used to perform such as implementing policy changes, introducing new products, constructing new facilities, and developing new marketing and sales programs.

Another factor which has accelerated the trend of using Project Management is the need for organizations to respond quickly to changes in environmental and internal forces. To be successful, an organization must quickly implement decisions made by top management. Competitive forces provide an example of how business must respond quickly. If a company introduces an innovative and successful new product, a competitor frequently introduces its own new product to block the competitive success, to protect itself from loss of business, and to capitalize on the opportunity.

Another aspect of complexity affecting organizations today are increasingly specialized work functions. Organizational efforts require inputs from numerous units and departments of the organization. Accomplishing these efforts thus impacts on many other areas of the organization. Departments are no longer independent. Almost any significant effort embarked on by an organization's sub-unit impacts on many other areas. For example, an effort to improve productivity in one department will likely affect the productivity level of many other departments within that same organization. Project Management represents a method of integrating the inputs from many departments and of optimizing the effect upon the entire organization of a change. In other words, through the project team approach Project Management can reach a consensus as to how an organized effort can be implemented so that the result maximizes the project objective.

Because of the number of departments involved in a project, the need for communications increases extensively. With only two or three departments the communications are relatively simple. When sixteen specialized departments are involved in a project, a much greater level of communications must be utilized to keep everyone informed. This is necessary in order to reach decisions based on inputs from people who need to take part in those decisions. Project Managers have learned to handle communications by on the job experience.

Because of the complexity of the world in which organizations operate today, top management, in order to bring about change in an organization, has been open to delegation of some of its authority. Project Management has been successful in filling a need of top management: to bring about change by solving problems and exploiting opportunities. Top management must concentrate on planning, on directing the organization to respond to environmental forces in a timely way. Project Management is a tool of top management that brings about results through interdisciplinary efforts.

TOP MANAGEMENT PERSPECTIVE

Top management oversees the course of the organization by setting objectives, choosing from among alternative strategies, developing plans for achievement of objectives and ensuring that control systems are in place to track progress compared to plan. The control systems must be designed so that red flags appear if significant deviations from planned performance occur. Accounting and financial reports are the basis for most business control systems. These financial controls are an aspect of department managers' performance in all areas of business. Another type of control system vital to many organizations is a decentralized management by objectives (MBO) program. A mark of a good MBO program is shown by its highlighting of exceptional as well as sub-standard performance.

Project Management is a type of management control system. Top management can use Project Management to ensure that its key plans and projects are accomplished productively. Top management expects these results from Project Management:

1. Attainment of project objectives in a timely manner and within budget.
2. Progress reports with deviations from plan highlighted.
3. Significant decisions brought to top management for approval.
4. Alternative choices researched by Project Management and laid out for decisions.

Project Management can fit in very well with management by objectives (MBO). MBO emphasizes clear identification and achievement of objectives throughout an organization. At the same time each project has one or more project objectives. The project objective can be included with other objectives and worked toward in the same way as nonproject objectives.

Project Management provides an effective method of achieving objectives. When a project is identified, top management usually has a number of choices as to how to manage it. Top management may assign a project to any of a number of functional areas within a business. For example, let's consider a manufacturing company as our organization. Research and Development, Quality Assurance, Marketing, or Manufacturing may be assigned responsibility to manage the project. In this case the project objective is to introduce a new product. Each functional discipline would expand its role and manage the project from its own perspective. If top management assigns the responsibility to manage the project to Research and Development, this functional area might take a long time to design and develop the new product. Research and Development may try to perfect the design of the new product, but will never be able to do so. The product will be thoroughly researched and documented. It will be tested and retested. The new product introduction date will probably be delayed due to Research and Development efforts to overdesign the product. The cost of the project will probably be over budget as the testing goes on. However the project objective will be achieved and the new product will be well designed.

If top management assigns this same project to Quality Assurance the effect upon the business would be a little different from the effect of R&D managing the project. Quality Assurance will design the new product so that there is little chance of any defects ever showing up. It will be well designed but not perfected from Research and Development's theoretical standpoint. Instead, Quality Assurance will be a little more practical by testing production on the manufacturing line to determine what kinds of problems develop. Because of Quality Assurance's goal to minimize the risk of defects, the product will probably be expensive to produce. The project schedule and budget may be overrun because of Quality Assurance's desire to design many controls and check points into its manufacture.

If top management assigns this same project to Marketing, it will be designed with all the bells, whistles, options, colors and sizes one can imagine. Marketing's objective is to make it as easy as possible to sell the new product in response to what they see as the needs of the customer. However, Marketing is also interested in introducing the new product as soon as possible, in order to nullify any advantage a competitor might hold, or to gain a competitive advantage if no such product is yet available. Marketing is not as concerned about the thoroughness of Research and Development's design effort, or about the risk of a product quality deviation occurring. Since Marketing wants the product introduced as soon as possible, the new product is likely to be introduced on schedule and within budget. The major problem is that product integrity, quality and specifications may be suspect because of Marketing's hurry to introduce the new product.

If top management chooses to assign the project to Manufacturing, their main concern is to make the product as simple and as inexpensive to produce as possible. Manufacturing's interest is to design the new product to be manufactured using existing production methods and facilities. In contrast to Marketing's desire to provide a variety of product options, colors, etc., Manufacturing will opt for "one size fits all". They want to avoid production changeovers to different products and will seek to simplify inventory control by allowing only one basic product. The risk here is that the new product although produced efficiently will not sell because it will not meet the needs of the customer. It is in the interest of top management to assign this project to an area of the organization that is not biased toward their regular responsibilities. Project Management can take responsibility for this project because it is unbiased, and because there should be less confusion as to the priority of its effort as compared to other responsibilities. In other words, any functional area which would take on responsibility for a new product project would have to decide what the priority of this project is compared to its regular responsibilities. Project Management on the other hand needs to prioritize this project in with its other regular projects. Where there is any confusion by the Project Manager as to the priority of any one project, clarification should be achieved by communication with top management.

There are other reasons why Project Management should have a role in an organization. The solution of problems is enhanced as the Project Manager becomes expert in handling interdisciplinary efforts. As the Project Manager builds experience his or her knowledge of all areas of the organization increases and it is that knowledge base that may be called upon to solve problems as projects unfold.

In effect, the project manager takes on the role of a general manager. Whereas the general manager of an organization has overall responsibility for the success of the organization, the Project Manager has overall responsibility for the success of the project. The general manager has responsibility for all functions of the organization, financial, marketing, sales, research and development, manufacturing, quality assurance and personnel. In the same way, the project manager has responsibility through project team members for all areas of the organization which have any impact on the overall project. It makes sense that experience as a project manager enhances the practice of general management later in one's career.

Given that each organization has overall goals and objectives which top management is seeking to achieve, what is the role of Project Management as seen from the top management perspective? Top management expects Project Management to bring together the resources of the organization, decide the direction to take on the project, and achieve the objective of the project in a timely and productive manner. By assigning a project to Project Management, top management thereby increases the profile and priority of the project. Normally, any project that is assigned to Project Management is important, and there are a finite and often limited number of projects that can be assigned to Project Management at one time. Functional area representatives on the project team recognize that the project is important, for it would not have otherwise been assigned to Project Management.

Project Management can serve another role if called upon by top management. If the situation in an organization is such that functional areas are somewhat complacent toward a particular issue, top management can assign resolution of the issue to Project Management. In this role Project Management will serve as a catalyst to raise the level of awareness, to stir some controversy, and to encourage the organization to start moving toward the particular issue that top management wants to focus on. On the other hand, if an issue is already at a peak level of awareness and attention in the functional areas, even to the point where visible and heated arguments and conflicts have taken place in regard to the particular issue, Project Management can fill another role: that of peacemaker. In this capacity, Project Management, with the support and knowledge of top management, can convene a gathering of the interested parties to approach the issue and to resolve the conflict. Sometimes this can be achieved by clearing the air, providing opportunity for better understanding of objectives, and by emphasizing clear communications. Note that in either of these two situations, top management could always step in. By having Project Management available, top management can, in effect, delegate responsibility to handle particular projects. This frees up time for top management to focus attention on issues that are of paramount importance, such as long range planning.

But realistically there are some risks in assigning project to Project Management. Depending upon the personalities involved it is possible that Project Management can become mired down in the technical details of the project, overwhelmed by powerful functional groups, or fall victim to power plays. These situations can develop for whoever is managing the project, whether it is project management or another area. No one is expert in all technical areas and organizational politics can always play a role in the success or failure of a project. The skillful project manager will be alert to these situations and learn how to deal with them.

Project Management does not have line authority as traditionally defined in terms of the manufacture and sale of products. However it has something just as important; implied authority from top management. As long as project management is responsive to top management, and as long as top management provides the support where necessary, project management can perform its job without having direct traditional line authority.

Other types of skills that successful project managers exhibt include—leadership skills, people handling skills, general administrative skills and computer systems skills. All these skills enhance Project Management's role in the eyes of top management. Depending on where Project Management reports in the organization and its importance relative to the functional area, the project manager can serve the role of expeditor, coordinator, project supervisor, project manager, project general manager, or project director. These titles reflect generally increasing levels of responsibility for the project manager and are likely to be coupled with an increasingly higher level of reporting within the organization.

In order for Project Management to function successfully within an organization it must have the overall support of top management. The relationship is somewhat cyclical. In order for top management to support project management, project management must be successful, and in order for project management to be successful it must have the support of top management. It is up to project management to take the inititative to build a successful track record and to communicate with top management when support is needed. It is also necessary for Project Management to provide feedback to top management on performance in relation to achieving project objectives. Just as in any other position of responsibility Project Management needs to communicate the key status of its efforts so that top management is informed.

The relationship between top management and project management must be based on a clear and mutual understanding of the objectives of Project Management and of the objectives of projects. This can best be achieved by Project Management's written description of its authority and its written statement of project objectives improves the chance of success of Project Management in the organization. A description of the role of the project manager should be included within the written statement of project authority. In this way Project Management and other areas can have a better understanding of its responsibility, its accountability to top management and its authority in making decisions relative to the projects. Some decision areas should reserved for top management. In this circumstance Project Management would recommend a course of action for approval by top management. Other decisions should be made by the project manager with input from the project team members. Still other decisions need to be made by the functional area managers. In order for Project Management to be successful in an organization, these decision areas must be understood by top management, project management, and functional managers.

Just as in other areas of an organization, project managers must understand how they are individually to be measured, even though the success of the project depends not only on the project manager but on the project team members. The project manager must be able to influence and motivate project team members to high levels of achievement. Like all managers, the project manager gets things done through people. The difference is that in some cases the project team members do not report directly to the project manager, and the wide variety of technical backgrounds of the project team members requires the project manager to be a generalist.

In summary, top management's role is to oversee the course of the organization by setting objectives, by making decisions on alternative strategies and by developing and approving plans for achievement of objectives. Top management also must ensure that control systems are instituted to track progress as compared to planned efforts. Project Management is, in effect, a control system of top management. Project Management's role is to attain project objectives in a timely manner and within budget. To be successful, Project

Management must seek the support of top management when necessary and maintain its own credibility through successful performance. The next step is to turn the situation around and look at the organization from project management's perspective.

PROJECT MANAGEMENT PERSPECTIVE

Just as top management has its set of values and perspectives in relation to its role in the organization, so does Project Management. Ideally, top management's and Project Management's views of the role of project management are identical. However, this is not always the case. If the role or character of project management differs from top management's expectation, problems will arise and top management will likely step in and correct the situation. *To avoid this, a clear understanding of the authority and responsibility of the role of Project Management should be adopted as a written policy of the organization.* Project Management needs the authority to develop an overall plan for a project, to obtain a commitment for resources, to direct the project team and to integrate its efforts to solve problems. In addition, Project Management needs the authority to make decisions on balancing risks and resolving problems, and the authority to interact with any area to ensure successful achievement of project goals.

After a clear statement of authority is written and agreed to by top management, there should be little confusion or conflict as the project management area goes about fulfilling its function. This statement of authority should be communicated throughout the organization. Without such a statement, Project Management could be continually struggling with other areas of the business over resource allocation, manpower utilization, and scheduling. The priority of projects should be communicated since Project Management's efforts are among the most important of the organization. Project Management's responsibility is to clearly define the project objective and develop a plan to achieve that objective; to utilize manpower and other resources effectively; to direct and control project team efforts to achieve results; to provide effective leadership, motivation, and management; and to establish and maintain two-way communication between Project Management and project team members.

To create the ideal situation of authority and responsibility, Project Management and top management should agree on the role of Project Management. Perfect agreement is not realistic. For this reason Project Management should communicate key decisions for top management's approval. In this way, top management in effect has an opportunity to redefine the authority of Project Management by approval or disapproval, by delineating where Project Management authority ends, or by redirecting its efforts to other areas of the organization which top management wants to emphasize.

Project Management has a role in the overall planning of an organization.

Project Management's perspective is future oriented since, in terms of project objectives, it focuses most of its energies forward—although these efforts are expended in the present. It rarely looks at the past since each project is unique. It is unnecessary to review the results of earlier projects except to determine performance as to project objective, schedule and budget. Since Project Management has a role in the planning of the organization, it can be viewed as an extension of top management which holds primary and ultimate responsibility for planning, including long range planning.

If Project Management undertakings were not unique they would be handled routinely by other areas of the organization. As Project Management makes decisions, the key decisions are reviewed by top management. Some of the areas that Project Management is involved in are very sensitive, and Project Management with its close contacts to top management can investigate options such as new approaches, new management techniques, new methods of conserving resources and improving productivity. Any of these approaches may be necessary to be reviewed and approved by top management.

Project Management has a definite role in the planning of an organization. It is future oriented, involved with improving management techniques and in carrying out the plans of top management. But in carrying out these plans conflict is inevitable. Conflict is a part of everyone's job. It can be especially apparent in the position of the Project Manager because of the variety of sources of conflict inherent in the project management area. Project conflict can be caused by the lack of understanding of objectives, or due to the diversity of project team members. It can be due to a traditional conflict between the functional department and project organizations. Conflict can also be caused by a lack of authority, or confusion as to the authority of project management as described earlier. Conflict can also be caused by a wide variety of communications problems. But conflict can be healthy; problems can be resolved through open discussion of conflict. Conflict can lead to creativity, which can lead to an increased level of confidence on the part of people involved in the conflict and to development of those individuals. The project manager should approach conflict directly by involving the participants, working on a base of understanding as to what is to be accomplished, and searching for some level of agreement to begin the discussion. When conflicts are not resolved, they surface and resurface in later stages of a project. They can continually throw the project team on to tangents of dealing with the conflicting issues and parties instead of the business of accomplishing the project directly.

Occasionally if Project Management is not able to manage the conflict itself, top management needs to step in and work it out. This should be avoided by Project Management at all costs because it reflects poorly on Project Management's ability to work things out. Another key point is that Project Management as discussed earlier prides itself on being unbiased. It is constantly working out issues for the good of the overall organization, not for any one functional department represented by a project team member. Occasionally however, project management needs to take a stand and may side with a particular functional department. In this case Project Management is aiding in the resolution of conflict by making a decision and taking a stand. Project Management must be sure that it is making this decision in behalf of the project itself and not because of the personalities involved. The project manager must go through the project while maintaining objectivity and unbiasedness.

Project Management also has a definite role in the area of control. One way of looking at Project Management is to consider it a control technique. In its role, top management is planning, directing and setting objectives for the organization. Project Management is interpreting those plans, directives and objectives and serving as a control function by seeing that the plans are met. A middle step between a plan and a control function is a schedule, and the project manager with extensive input from the project team members is responsible for putting together the project schedule. The control loop starts when project management feeds back information on the progress of the project from the project team members to top management. Top management either accepts those results or decides that changes must be made. These changes in performance and plans are redirected to project management who in turn interprets them and reschedules the project and communicates them to the project team members. This process can be recycled a number of times if necessary until top management approves the entire project and the objective is ultimately achieved. Project Management itself is a control device because it controls the project team and that part of the organization that is impacting and involved in the particular project.

We should now shift gears from the overall perspective of Project Management in terms of its authority, responsibility, planning, conflict resolution and controlling efforts, to the key step in any project, that is the overall formation of the project and the direction the project should take.

PROJECT FORMATION AND DIRECTION

The key step in any project is the first step, and that is understanding the objective of the project, communicating that objective to project team members, and thoroughly considering alternative approaches to the project before jumping in and working the project itself. It is very important to sit down and thoroughly think through the project before jumping in. The project manager needs to move along the learning curve on the project very quickly. In order to do so the project manager should gain as much information as possible about the project from the client.

The client is the person or group of persons that are requesting and have approved Project Management's undertaking the project. The client can be top management or it can be other functional areas of the organization. In some cases the project client is Project Management itself where it has identified a project and gained approval for the project from top management. In construction companies the client is an organization outside the construction company. Project Management needs to discuss in detail the specific project objective and have it written down and approved by the project client. The Project Manager also needs to ask as many questions as possible of the client to learn everything there is to know about the project particularly the criteria for success, the expected budget and schedule. Later on, as key decisions arise or problems or opportunities develop the project manager needs to consider carefully who the client is and check with the client on key decisions.

At the outset, after approval for undertaking the project has been granted, the project manager may want to go through a checklist and gather information on the project. The project manager will early on be required to make several decisions with the valuable input of the project team members. Some of these decisions are, what is the target date for completion of the project; what is the project budget; where will the resources come from; who will the project team members be; who will develop the plan for the project or provide the systems support, etc. The input of information gained by the project manager during this formation stage will be valuable in making these early decisions.

The project manager should determine the complexity, size and uniqueness of the project. All of these aspects will impact, for example, on the number of project team members, who they will be, the budget, and the schedule.

In the process of gathering the information at the outset of the project, the project manager should interview the key functional managers who are expected to lend project team members to this particular project. The project manager should communicate the fact that top management has approved the project, and obtain the approval of the functional managers who will be supplying the resources to undertake the project, especially those who will provide the manpower resources.

Uncertainty is an element present at the outset of every project. Sometimes it is present in greater degrees than others. It is especially prevalent when the project is unique because nothing similar has ever been accomplished by Project Management before. Uncertainty is also present to a high degree if this is the first project undertaken by the project manager or, even more so, if it's the first project ever undertaken by the organization's Project Management's department. The checklist referred to earlier, and extra effort by the project manager to gain as much information as possible early on, will serve to cut through this level of uncertainty and ambiguity. If the project manager does not sort through ambiguity, its effect will be felt later on, especially by the project team itself, due to a lack of clarity about the mission of the project as communicated by the project manager.

If the project manager is unsure of how to approach the project after gathering as much information as possible, it is a good idea to go back to management and cut through the uncertainty with the aid of top management. One way of going about this is by developing written strategies or options to be undertaken in approaching the project. Top management can then approve one of the options for implementation. For example, if the project manager feels a need to clarify one of the basic assumptions in regard to the introduction of a new product, he or she may ask top management whether they want the product to be manufactured inside or outside of the organization's facilities. Or top management may delegate that decision to the project team for later approval after gathering information.

But uncertainty and ambiguity cannot be eliminated from any project. The project manager must sense when he or she has a much information as possible, and what strategy should be taken to approach the project. The project manager should then decisively strike forth in terms of selecting project team members and developing them into a cohesive unit in order to accomplish the project.

In some organizations project team members are assigned by Project Management. In other organizations they are assigned by the functional management groups. Still in other areas, there is a joint decision. Any of the three approaches are acceptable as long as the project team members are from the right areas of the organization, as long as they understand their responsibility, as long as there is a liaison between project management and the functional areas, and as long as they have the authority to speak for the functional areas in dealing with Project Management.

The next step after selecting the project team members and after communicating to them the information that the project manager obtained during project formation, the next step is to develop a detailed plan or schedule. Development of the detailed plan may take several iterations. It may be necessary for the project manager to develop a rough draft of the project plan with the aid of the project team members. This can sometimes be done by working backwards from the project's last step to the point of the present status of the project.

Decision making on an every day level is another important aspect of successful Project Management. On a project, decisions are made at various levels of detail and various levels of importance. Decisions should be made at the appropriate organizational level depending upon the importance of the decision. Project Management must be able to determine the impact and importance of a problem and see that the decision is made by the right person. Some decisions for example, are made at the level of a project team member and are moved up to the project manager and/or the functional manager for approval. Other decisions are made by the project manager and may be moved up the line for top management's approval. Still other decisions are reserved for top management itself.

Sometimes a state of flux develops around a particular problem which is waiting for a solution or a decision. If the project manager is not effective in resolving the problem and seeing that a decision is made, a delay in terms of time and an increase in cost is likely to impact the project.

Team or consensus decision making is a part of every successful project. In the act of pulling together a project team and meeting on a regular basis, trust develops between the project team members and a climate is set for consensus decision making. This in most cases has a positive effect on the project. However, in some cases, due to friendliness shown between certain project team members, there may be a bulldozing effect when another project team member suggests an unpopular idea. Team members may roll over the idea and not allow it to surface for discussion, and in the end after the idea is lost, the project may be sub-optimized or indeed end in failure. For example, if a team member suggests there may be substantial regulatory and government risk from introducing a new product in a certain form, other members of the team may bulldoze over the idea. The product is then introduced. If the regulatory risk materializes the new product, and in a sense the project, is a failure.

The project manager plays a strong role in synthesizing information in a form that makes sense and can be approved by top management. This synthesizing in can be visualized in a way by using the example of an air traffic controller. The controller gathers various forms of information, makes many decisions, and at times passes information up the line to a supervisor for approval as can happen when planes start to stack up and flights need to be rerouted to other airports.

In summary, implementing a project involves providing a climate for feedback information from project team members, synthesizing the information, interpreting it, and Project Management's making some decisions. The project also involves referring some decisions for approval to top management, bringing about course corrections on the project and communicating these corrections to team members.

The project manager should convene a meeting of all the project team members to develop an understanding of the present status of the project as well as the desired status after the project has been achieved. Then it is a matter of getting from the present state to the desired state, the path of events and activities becomes the project schedule. It is very important to have the project team members directly involved in development of the project schedule. In order for them to work hard toward achievement of the project objective they need to have "ownership" in the schedule that was developed to achieve the objective.

One way of doing this is to delegate sections of the schedule to key project team members. Another way is to have a number of brainstorming sessions using a flow chart and easel, and to allow the project team members to help draft alternative schedules.

After the project schedule has been drafted and approved by all the project team members, Project Management should seek approval from top management. The project schedule needs to be written down so there will be a clear understanding among all the key areas of what events and approaches project management will be using. The key areas that need to know the project schedule include not only Project Management and the project team members, but top management, the client, and the functional department managers who supply the resources. If the project is very complex or entails a great deal of ambiguity, Project Management should seek an opportunity to propose the schedule to top management and obtain their feedback and approval. In this process the project manager should seek to resolve any leftover conflicts identified during the stages geared toward project formation and development of the detailed schedule. The types of conflicts that may still be left over include authority issues, resource issues, and even project objective issues. Once the detailed plan has been developed and approved and any left over conflicts have been resolved, the project manager and the project team are ready to move on to the next stage of the project which is implementing the project itself.

IMPLEMENTING THE PROJECT

Implementing a project which has been well formed, designed and set up is much easier than implementing one which is poorly designed. Implementing a project is really tracking and controlling actual project performances as compared to plan, and constantly monitoring key events which are part of the project schedule. Referring to Figure 9-1, a project manager implements and controls a project by adjusting the performance of the project in response to top management expectations and other environmental factors such as competitive conditions, research and development obstacles, and other events which arise in the course of the project that cannot be predicted at the onset. At the beginning of a project, top management has a set of expectations for performance of the project. At the beginning of a project, since actual accomplishments have not taken place, project management and the project team's performance is usually at a different level from that of top management's expectations. As the project unfolds and time moves to the right on the chart, Project Management achieves target dates and portions of the project are completed on schedule, thus approaching top management's expectations.

Over the same period top management's expectations are adjusted based on the feedback and accomplishments that the project management area achieves.

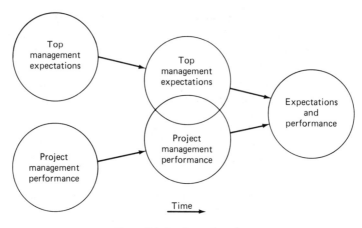

Figure 9-1. Implementing plans.

These expectations are not necessarily reduced, but are simply changed from the original set of expectations that were the first goals of top management. In the chart there is an overlap where the top management expectations and project management performance partially coincide. By the end of the project, as there is less and less uncertainty in the end as project management achieves its objective, top management's expectations are adjusted. They become more realistic with the result that top management expectations and project management performance coincide exactly.

As the project unfolds, feedback is an indispensable vehicle to accomplish project objectives. The project manager must use both informal and formal feedback systems to monitor progress. Formal control systems and communications devices can be developed by the Project Management area and used in the functional department to communicate the status of the project to Project Management. These systems may be elaborate reports or charts. Project Management may use as an alternative more informal feedback and mechanisms which could all be verbal as opposed to written. In this case the project manager would rely on his or her persuasive capabilities to obtain information on the status of the project. Without feedback the project manager would not know what is going on and would lose control of the project. The feedback information can be positive or negative as when a target date is achieved or not achieved, or neutral as purely status information. In the case of neutral information, the project manager should determine the significance of the information and, with the help of project team members, determine the potential impact on the project. As significant feedback information comes to the project manager and target dates are achieved it becomes necessary to update and change the project schedule. Like an air traffic controller, the project manager assimilates all the information that comes in and maintains an awareness of the status of the project. The project manager (like the air traffic controller) must then communicate any necessary changes back to the project team. The project manager should also communicate with the project team even when no changes are required, to provide assurance that things are moving along smoothly.

Occasionally information which is fed back to the project management area results in a determination that a significant change from the schedule will be necessary. At this point the project manager must become immediately involved in efforts to sort out the information, to determine its impact on the plan, to look at alternative schedule options, to develop recommendations and to communicate them to top management for approval.

The project manager must provide a climate for accepting all types of feedback information from the project team members. If the project manager reacts negatively to negative feedback, project team members may withhold further information from the project manager; this would have disastrous consequences.

Occasionally feedback brings significant new information which requires a major change in plans to be made for the project. For example, the feedback information could supply the results of a major R&D product test on a new product which has failed. Or a competitive product similar to a new product under development may have suffered a regulatory setback thus affording a temporary opportunity. The likely reaction to this type of feedback would be a midcourse correction or change in plans or schedule.

In Figure 9-2 there is, on the left, a point A where the project begins and

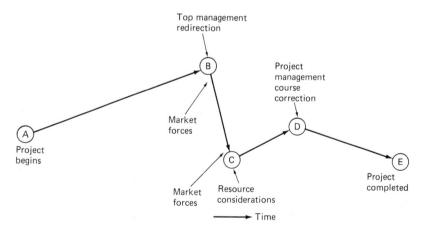

Figure 9-2. Mid-Course corrections.

then moves along to the right to a point where top management directs Project Management to alter the course of the project. Note that the direction of the line from point B to point C is not exactly the same direction as the arrow that represents the direction that top management wanted. This is because in this example top management overreacted slightly to the course the project team was moving along, and the project team recognized that it needed to change its course significantly from the prior course. At the same time the market forces were pushing the project team in almost the opposite direction. At point C the market forces increased in intensity and although resource considerations were going against the market forces, the resource considerations as shown in the line from C to D were overcome and the project was redirected somewhat similar to the original line from A to B. At point D Project Management was close enough to the end goal and was able to redirect the course toward achievement of the project at point E. The main point of this diagram is that the project team starts out on its project and then as the project unfolds deals with various forces that push in different directions. Ultimately, if the project manager correctly interprets and weighs these forces, achievement of the project goal will take place.

After these new course corrections are made at points B, C and D, the project manager must clearly and comprehensively inform the project team members, and in some cases the functional department, as to the details of the directional changes that have been approved by top management.

The whole idea of setting up a climate for feedback by the project team members, the evaluation of that feedback and the mid-course corrections, is a system of control exercised by Project Management.

PROJECT COMPLETION

This chapter has discussed the formation of a project and its implementation. This section will deal with the completion of the project. Sometimes project completion is very well controlled and presents no problems to the project manager. Other times there are problems in defining exactly when the project has been completed and when the client should take responsibility for it. For example, if the project objective is clearly specified and project specifications are identified then project completion should also be easy to define. As the project nears completion, the project manager needs to involve the client extensively. During the transition period when the project manager is winding down the project and the client is getting up to speed in taking responsibility for the project, cooperation is essential.

Occasionally during the completion stage of a project a problem develops because the project team has so much enthusiasium and momentum built up that it is rolling along like a locomotive and the project manager is unable to

stop it. This can be difficult especially if another project is not available to occupy the same people that had been project team members on the first project. The project manager must clearly communicate to the project team members that the project has been achieved and he must redirect their efforts elsewhere, preferrably to a new project.

It is very important that the project be critiqued when it is completed. The expected criteria and results of a project should have been defined upfront. The results should be measured by the project manager with the assistance of the project team members. Questions about what worked and what didn't work and how to have better accomplished the project should be asked as a part of the project team critique. If the information is available, actual results are relatively easy to compare to planned results such as the achievement of target dates. Measurement of project results usually takes place in goals and project specifications, cost and time. The information on the results serves to assist the planning of future projects which may be similar to the one just completed, and also provide an opportunity for project management to stand up and receive some recognition for a job well done. Other questions that can be incorporated in the critique of the process include how the team handled problems, whether individual members blocked the project team's progress, which team members were especially effective in providing direction and energy for the project, whether the project manager led effectively, what the project manager did that assisted the project, what if anything the project manager did to salvage the project, and overall, were the Project Management methods and techniques useful and effective? The project manager should communicate the results of the critique to top management for review and include any suggestions for change.

At completion of the project the project manager has an excellent opportunity to provide recognition for the project team members. Since project team members may report to functional managers and not to the project manager, the project manager may not have direct input into salary increase levels for project team members. However the project manager does have many opportunities to recognize project team member performance, including writing letters of appreciation to the team member. Other forms of recognition include verbal comments of appreciation to project team members or the project team member's supervisor, plaques or certificates commemorating contributions to a successful project, written articles in the organization's newspaper or newsletters, and luncheons or banquets when the project is completed. Recognition should be an everyday process so that when the project is implemented the project manager can recognize the special contributions of project team members as they occur. This recognition may either be in public at a project team meeting or in private. The purpose of the recognition is to provide feedback for an assignment or task that has been done exceptionally well. Since feedback is

sometimes negative, positive recognition brings more balance to communication. The project manager should deal in a very direct manner with the project team members by providing performance feedback to them either positively or negatively as the case warrants. But recognition helps motivate project team members toward improved levels of performance.

SUMMARY AND CONCLUSIONS

Project Management has a definite place in organizations today. Its importance will increase in the future. Competitive situations, emphasis on productivity, solving problems and exploiting opportunities will become more and more important in the future. The complexity of issues facing organizations will continue to increase. This in turn will make the jobs of top managers more and more difficult. Project Management has a vital role in implementing the plans and goals of top management. Project Management can be viewed as a type of management itself. Top management expects project management to attain its objectives in a timely manner and within budget. Top management expects timely progress reports. Top management expects significant decisions to be brought to the appropriate level for decisions and alternative choices and recommendations to be delineated by Project Management.

Project Management must deal with authority, responsibility, planning, controlling and conflict issues in carrying out the plans of top management. How well the project manager handles authority and responsibility issues, and how skilled the project manager is in planning, communicating and managing conflict, influences the likely success of a project.

The project itself may be looked at in terms of three stages. The project formation and direction stage is where the objectives must be clearly identified and understood by the project management itself and top management. The implementation stage is where feedback can result in midcourse corrections brought about by project management and where decision making is initiated by Project Management. The third stage is the completion of the project where emphasis should be placed on shutting the project down effectively, measuring its results and providing recognition to the team members.

The net result of this discussion boils down to: "Does Project Management bring about results?" "Does it deliver the goods?" "Is it efficient and is it better than the alternatives?" These questions must be answered by each organization, but many organizations in a wide variety of fields have decided that Project Management does indeed bring about results effectively. It *must* be responsive to top management because if it weren't top management would eliminate it and try another management approach.

10. Project Evaluation and Selection

William E. Souder*

INTRODUCTION

Today's projects often entail large organizational commitments. These can easily become tomorrow's failures if a wrong choice is made.

Thus, it is important to select only the very best projects. Inferior projects should be identified and screened out early in the decision process. This chapter presents several methods and techniques that can be used to help distinguish superior projects from inferior ones.

PROJECT SELECTION: A MULTI-FACETED DECISION PROCESS†

The term "project selection" has many different connotations. Figure 10-1 depicts a range of project selection activities which may occur. New project proposals may arrive from a variety of sources: employees may submit ideas for new projects, customers may suggest ideas, etc.

As Figure 10-1 shows, a new project idea may be either temporarily backlogged or put through a screening model. A screening model provides useful preliminary information for distinguishing candidate projects, on the basis of

*Dr. William E. Souder is a well-known authority in the fields of R&D management, systems analysis and organization behavior. He teaches systems management and organization behavior and directs the Technology Management Studies Group at the University of Pittsburgh, where he is Professor of Industrial Engineering. Dr. Souder is the author of over sixty papers and two books on R&D management, engineering analysis and organization behavior. He is chairman of the Institute of Management Science's College of R&D Management, a director of the Product Development Management Association, and associate editor of *Management Science,* and *Transactions on Engineering Management,* and a member of the editorial boards of several other journals.

†Portions of the subsequent material are adapted from Souder, Wm. E., *Management Decision Methods for Managers of Engineering and Research,* New York: Van Nostrand Reinhold Company, 1980, pp. 137–162 and Souder, Wm. E., "Project Selection, Planning and Control", in the *Handbook of Operations Research* (New York: Van Nostrand Reinhold Company, 1978), pp. 334–444.

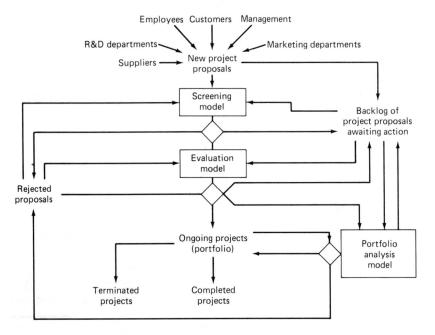

Figure 10-1. Illustration of a project selection decision process.

a few prominent criteria. An evaluation model provides a more rigorous and comprehensive analysis of candidates which survive the screening model. A portfolio model can be used to determine an optimum budget allocation among those projects which survive the evaluation model.

As shown in Figure 10-1, acceptable projects may be backlogged at several points, to await the release of critical manpower or other resources. Backlogged projects will normally be retrieved at some later point in time. But rejected projects will not. However, new information or changed circumstances may suddenly make a previously rejected project more attractive, or may cause a previously backlogged project to be rejected.

Thus, project selection consists of three kinds of decision making: screening, evaluation and portfolio analysis. As we move from screening to portfolio analysis, more factors are considered and the procedures become more complex. A variety of outcomes may occur as a result of each kind of decision, as illustrated in Figure 10-1. As time passes, these three types of decisions may be repeated many times in response to changing information states, changes in the available resources and funds, changes in project achievements, or the arrival of new project proposals.

Table 10-1. Example of a Profile Model.

CRITERIA OR REQUIREMENTS	EXTENT TO WHICH PROJECTS X AND Y MEET THE CRITERIA		
	High	Medium	Low
Reliability	X		Y
Maintainability	Y	X	
Safety		X	Y
Cost-Effectiveness	X	Y	
Durability	X		Y

X = project X's score   Y = project Y's score

SCREENING MODELS

Profile Models

An example of a profile model is shown in Table 10-1. Note that the ratings are qualitative in nature. No numerical assessments are made. Rather, the project proposals are compared on the basis of a subjective evaluation of their attributes. These evaluations could be done by one individual or by group consensus. Alternatively, the profiles developed by several informed individuals could be compared (1), (2).*

Profile models are simple and easy to use. They display the project characteristics and ratings in such a way that they are easily communicated and readily visualized. For instance, in Table 10-1 it is apparent at a glance that project X is generally a high-performer, superior to project Y on all the criteria but one.

On the other hand, a profile model does not tell us anything about the trade-offs among the criteria. For example, the profile model in Table 10-1 does not tell us if the high performances of Project X on reliability, cost-effectiveness and durability compensate for its medium performances on maintainability and safety. Thus, there is no way to get a single overall score or rating for each project.

Checklists

Table 10-2 shows an example of a checklist. This type of model assumes that the decision maker can distinguish between several finite levels of the criteria or requirements (3), (4). Each candidate proposal or project is then subjec-

---

*Numbered references are given at the end of this chapter.

Table 10-2. Example of a Checklist.

CRITERIA OR REQUIREMENTS	TOTAL SCORE	CRITERION SCORES[a]				
		−2	−1	0	+1	+2
Project X	+5					
Reliability						✓
Maintainability				✓		
Safety				✓		
Cost-Effectiveness					✓	
Durability					✓	
Project Y	−2					
Reliability			✓			
Maintainability					✓	
Safety				✓		
Cost-Effectiveness					✓	
Durability				✓		
Project Z	+5					
Reliability					✓	
Maintainability					✓	
Safety				✓		
Cost-Effectiveness					✓	
Durability					✓	

[a]*Scoring Scale:*
+2 = Best possible performance
+1 = Above average performance
 0 = Average performance
−1 = Below average performance
−2 = Worst possible performance

tively evaluated by the decision maker and assigned a criterion score on each requirement. The criterion score is ascertained from a pre-designated scoring scale that translates subjective evaluations into numerical scores. A total score is obtained for each project by summing its criterion scores. In general, for a checklist model

$$T_j = \sum_i s_{ij} \qquad [1]$$

Here, T_j is the total score for the *j*th project and s_{ij} is the score for project *j* on the *i*th requirement or criterion.

Checklist models improve on profile models by providing both a graphic profile of check-marks and an overall total score for each candidate project. An analysis of target achievements and a comparison of several candidate projects is facilitated by the total scores. For instance, a total score of +2 or greater may be specified as a cut-off point for acceptable proposals. Projects could be priority classified by specifying total score ranges, e.g., $T_j > +3$ is a high priority project, $+1 \le T_j \le +3$ is a medium priority project, etc.

Scoring Models

It is a short step from checklist models to scoring models. In a scoring model, each of $j = 1, \ldots, n$ candidate projects are scored on each of $i = 1, \ldots, m$ performance requirements or criteria. The criterion scores for each project are then combined with their respective criterion importance weights w_i to achieve a total score T_j for each project. Projects may then be ranked according to their T_j values.

For example, a simple additive scoring model would be

$$T_j = \sum_i w_i s_{ij} \qquad [2]$$

where s_{ij} is the score for project j on the ith criterion, and w_i is the criterion weight. This model is illustrated in Table 10-3.

The influence of the weights becomes apparent if one compares the results for the Weighted Scores in Table 10-3 with the results for the Total Scores in Table 10-2. The Criterion Scores in Table 10-3 contain the same information

Table 10-3. Example of an Additive Scoring Model.

CRITERION, i	CRITERION WEIGHT, w_i	$\times$	CRITERION SCORE,* s_{ij}	$=$	WEIGHTED SCORE
Project X:					
Reliability	4		5		20
Maintainability	2		3		6
Safety	3		3		9
Cost-Effectiveness	5		5		25
Durability	1		4		4
				$T_1 =$	64
Project Y:					
Reliability	4		1		4
Maintainability	2		5		10
Safety	3		2		6
Cost-Effectiveness	5		3		15
Durability	1		2		2
				$T_2 =$	37
Project Z:					
Reliability	4		5		20
Maintainability	2		5		10
Safety	3		2		6
Cost-Effectiveness	5		4		20
Durability	1		4		4
				$T_3 =$	60

*Scale: 5 = Excellent, . . . , Poor = 1

as the Criterion Scores in Table 10-2. The difference is simply a scale transformation; each Criterion Score in Table 10-3 is +3 larger than its counterpart in Table 10-2. The Weighted Scores in Table 10-3 show that projects X and Z do indeed differ. The checklist model (Table 10-2) did not show any difference between the Total Scores for these two projects. Scoring models are more accurate because they take the tradeoffs between the criteria into account, as defined by the criterion weights (2),(4),(5).

Frontier Models

Figure 10-2 illustrates the outputs from a frontier model for seven different projects. The projects are plotted in such a way as to show their relative risks and returns. "Risk" expresses the project's chances of failure. This may be measured as $1-p$, where p is the project's probability of success. Or it may be measured in terms of the likelihood that the project will *not* achieve some desired level of output, profit, etc. "Return" expresses the project's anticipated profits, sales or some other measure of value which the decision maker wishes to use.

The efficient frontier in Figure 10-2 tracks the path of the most efficient return/risk ratios. For example, project 5 (denoted as X_5 in Figure 10-2) is more return/risk efficient than project 2 (denoted as X_2). Project 5 has the same return as project 2, but it has a lower risk level. Similarly, project 3 is

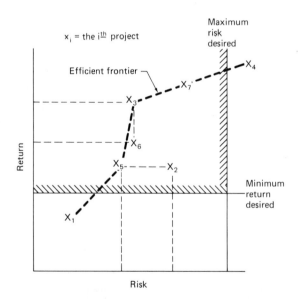

Figure 10-2. Illustration of a frontier model.

more return/risk efficient than project 6 because of its higher return at the same risk level as project 6. The maximum desired risk and the minimum desired return levels established by the organization are also depicted in Figure 10-2. Acceptable projects must fall in the region formed by these boundaries. Thus, Figure 10-2 shows that a decision maker should accept projects 3, 5 and 7 and reject the others.

Frontier models are often very useful for examining return-risk trade-offs within the organizational objectives. For instance, Figure 10-2 shows that the high risk and high return project 4 is ruled out by its high risk level. Yet its incremental return/risk ratio is the same as the acceptable projects 3 and 7. (All of these projects lie on the same line.) Thus, the decision maker may want to make an exception and retain project 4 for further study and analyses.

Frontier models may be used to indicate the need for greater diversification in idea generation and project proposals (3), (5). For example, Figure 10-2 shows that the acceptable projects are primarily of the medium to high-risk variety. Whether or not the portfolio ought to be more diversified must be resolved on the basis of the organization's goals and objectives. A frontier model can only point out trends and situations for further analysis (3), (6), (7).

Using Screening Models

Screening models are very useful for weeding out those projects which are the least desirable. Since screening models are quick and inexpensive to use, they can economize on the total evaluation efforts by reducing the number of projects to be further evaluated. Because they require a relatively small amount of input data, they can be used where the projects are not well understood or where a minimum of data are available.

However, screening models don't provide much depth of information. And they usually are not sensitive to many of the finer distinctions between projects. Rather, screening models are like a coarse seive that provides a partial separation but permits some undesirables to pass through. Thus, screening models can be very useful for some applications. But the decision maker should not expect them to provide a comprehensive or complete analysis.

EVALUATION MODELS

Economic Index Models

An index model is simply a ratio between two variables, and the index is their quotient. Changing the values of the variables changes the value of the quotient, or the index.

An example of a commonly used index model is the return on investment (ROI) index model

$$\text{ROI Index} = \frac{\sum_i R_i/(1 + r)^i}{\sum_i I_i/(1 + r)^i} \qquad [3]$$

where R_i is the net dollar returns expected from the project in the ith year, I_i is the investment expected to be made in the ith year, and r is an interest rate. The numerator of equation [3] is the present worth of all future revenues generated by the project, and the denominator is the present worth cost of all future investments.

Some other examples of index models are shown in Table 10-4. Ansoff's model uses both dollar values and index numbers as input data. The index numbers T and B are judgments. Olsen's index is a variation on Ansoff's index that uses all dollar input data. Viller's index is a kind of return on investment model, discounted by the compound likelihood of the project's success. Disman's index looks at the expected earnings over and above the cost to complete the project (2), (5).

The single-number index or score that is produced by an index model can be used to rate and rank candidate projects. An example of the use of an index model is shown in Table 10-5. The index model is:

$$V = \frac{P \times R}{C}, \qquad [4]$$

Table 10-4. Examples of Index Models.

Ansoff's Index

$$\text{Project Figure of Merit} = \frac{rdp(T + B)E}{\text{Total Investment}}$$

Olsen's Index

$$\text{Project Value Index} = \frac{rdp\ SP\ n}{\text{Project Cost}}$$

Viller's Index

$$\text{Project Index} = rdp\left(\frac{E - R}{\text{Total Investment}}\right)$$

Disman's Index

Project Return $= rp(E - R)$

Key: r = the probability of research success, d = the probability of development success, p = the probability of market success, T and B are respective indexes of technical and business merit, E = the present worth of all future earnings from the project, S = annual sales volume in units, P = unit profit, n = number of years of product life, R = present worth cost of research and development activities to complete the project

Table 10-5. Example of the Use of an Index Model.

	RETURN (R)	COST (C)	PROBABILITY OF SUCCESS (P)	$V = \dfrac{P \times R}{C}$	RANKING
Project 4	$ 80,000	$2,000	.7	28	1st ⎱ tie
Project 5	70,000	1,000	.4	28	1st ⎰
Project 1	120,000	2,000	.2	12	2nd
Project 3	10,000	1,000	.7	7	3rd
Project 2	10,000	1,000	.3	3	4th

where V is the index. Four projects are evaluated using this model, and their relative rankings on the index V are shown in the last column of Table 10-5. Two projects, project 4 and project 5, are tied for 1st place in the rankings.

These hypothetical results point up some of the weaknesses of index models. One such weakness is the implicit trade-offs that often occur. For example, in computing the V index, project 5's lower cost compensates for its lower probability of success. This is why project 5 is as good as project 4 on the V index. However, any decision maker who wishes to avoid high risks would never rank project 5 as high as project 4. Note that project 5 has a risk of failure of $1 - P_5 = 1 - .4 = .6$. In fact, instead of ranking it 1st, the risk-averse decision maker might completely eliminate project 5 from any consideration at all. Thus, the index model in Table 10-5 may be completely inappropriate for some decision makers. It could lead them to make completely wrong decisions relative to their objectives.

This example shows that all index models should be carefully examined for their internal trade-offs. Unless the trade-offs are representative of those the decision maker would actually be willing to make, the model is inappropriate.

Another weakness of many index models is the insensitivity of the index to changes in some of their parameters. As an illustration, let us examine what happens to the V index as one goes from project 4 to project 1 in Table 10-5. The return increases by 50% (from $80,000 to $120,000). The risk goes from $1 - P_4 = .3$ to $1 - P_1 = .8$, for a 167% increase. Yet the V index falls by only 57%: from $V_4 = 28$ to $V_1 = 12$. Thus, these analyses show that this index model is relatively insensitive to risks. In fact, this is a biased model; it is biased toward obscuring risks.

Still another weakness of index models lies in their inability to consider multiple objectives. Because of this, an index model may be inappropriate. For example, suppose that the decision maker also wishes to diversify the portfolio, in addition to achieving high V values. Then, the decision maker might accept project 3 (Table 10-5) because it is a relatively inexpensive way (low cost project) to get a high probability project. Having some high probability projects in the portfolio may be important. This may be especially true if the high-cost of high-risk project 1 is included in the portfolio. Yet the index model ranked project 3 next to last, because it could not incorporate this other objective for diversification into its analyses.

Of course, no index model can include everything. Index models are appealing because of their simplicity and ease of use. That is, they are attractive because they don't include everything. But the decision maker should be wary; index models can be deceptively appealing. Before placing great faith in the outputs from an index model, the decision maker should make sure that the model is unbiased and appropriate.

Risk Analysis Models

A risk analysis model provides a complete picture of the distribution of outcomes for each alternative project. An illustration of a risk analysis approach to the comparison of two candidate projects is shown in Figure 10-3. Project 1 has a most likely lifetime profit of $100,000,000, and project 2 has a most likely lifetime profit of $150,000,000. However, there is only a .4 probability that project 2 will in fact achieve the $150,000,000 level. There is a .8 probability that project 1 will achieve the $100,000,000 level. Project 2 provides an opportunity to achieve a larger profit than project 1. But it also carries some downside risk relative to project 1. In fact, there is a .3 probability that project 2 will yield lower profits than project 1, as shown in Figure 10-3. Given these data, a risk averter would be inclined to select project 1. Project 1 has a high

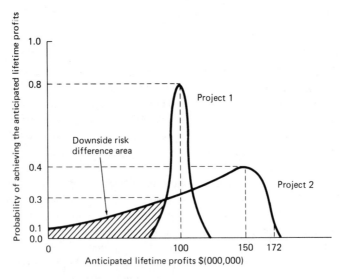

Figure 10-3. Illustration of risk analysis.

chance of achieving a moderate profit, with very little chance of anything less or greater. A gambler would be more inclined to select project 2, which has a small chance at a larger profit. Thus, the risk analysis approach makes the risk-averter and gambler strategies more visible, thereby permitting a decision maker to consciously select decisions consistent with one of these chosen strategies.

A picture like Figure 10-3 is usually not difficult to construct from a relatively small amount of data. Common methods for developing performance distributions for risk analysis include curve fitting techniques, Monte Carlo simulation methods and modeling techniques (2), (8).

Value-Contribution Models

An example of a value-contribution (V-C) model is given in Table 10-6. Value-contribution models permit the decision maker to examine the degree of contribution which a project makes to the organization's hierarchy of goals.

To develop a V-C model, first list the organizational goals as a nested hierarchy. For instance, as shown in Table 10-6, there are two supergoals: short range and long range. Within each of these two super-goals, there are several sub-goals. Within the short range super-goal, the organization desires to achieve new product dominance, a profitability target, and to reduce their present environmental impacts. Within the long range super-goal, the organization desires to maintain their technological state-of-art and market share.

The second step in developing a V-C model is value-weighting the goals. In the model illustrated in Table 10-6, the long range and short range super-goals are respectively value-weighted as $V = 60$ and $V = 40$. Note that these values must sum to 100. That is, the value-weights are determined by allocating a total of 100 points among the super-goals according to their relative importance. In Table 10-6, the value-weights indicate that the short range super-goal is one and one-half times as important as the long range super-goal. Within each super-goal, the total points are similarly spread among the sub-goals, in such a way as to indicate their relative importance. The complete set of value-weights thus indicates the level of value contribution which a project could make. For instance, a perfect project would score 30 on "Achieve New Product Dominance." Thus, a project with a perfect contribution to all the goals would have a total value contribution score of 100 points.

The actual scaling and scoring of the candidate projects within a V-C model can be done individually or by consensus. Value-weights and scoring scales can be constructed using value assessment methods or scoring model techniques (2), (3).

In the illustration in Table 10-6, project A is short-range oriented, project B is more long-range oriented and project C is about evenly oriented to both the

Table 10-6. Value-Contribution Model.*

| PROJECT COSTS $ (000) | SHORT RANGE ORGANIZATIONAL GOALS (V = 60) | | | LONG RANGE ORGANIZATIONAL GOALS (V = 40) | | TOTAL VALUE-CONTRIBUTION SCORE |
	ACHIEVE NEW PRODUCT DOMINANCE (V = 30)	ACHIEVE THE PROFITABILITY TARGET (V = 20)	REDUCE ENVIRONMENTAL IMPACTS (V = 10)	MAINTAIN THE TECHNOLOGICAL STATE-OF-ART (V = 25)	MAINTAIN MARKET SHARE (V = 15)	
			SCORES			
Project A	$100	30	20	5	15	5	75
Project B	200	15	10	10	20	10	65
Project C	150	25	10	5	15	10	65

Normalized Value-Contribution:

Project A: 75 ÷ $100,000 = $75.0 × 10^{-5}

Project B: 65 ÷ $200,000 = $32.5 × 10^{-5}

Project C: 65 ÷ $150,000 = $43.3 × 10^{-5}

Rankings:

Project A 1st

Project C 2nd

Project B 3rd

*V = the goal value-weight

long and the short range. Project A has perfect scores on the new product dominance and profitability sub-goals. It has less-than perfect scores on the other
goals. But because project A is more oriented toward the short range, it contributes more toward these higher-valued sub-goals. Thus, it has the highest
overall total value contribution (last column of Table 10-6). Since the total
costs of the projects vary, the total value contribution scores must be normalized by dividing them by their respective project costs. These resulting normalized value contribution scores may then be used to rank the candidates, as
shown in the lower half of Table 10-6.

V-C models permits the decision maker to think in terms of the goal-orient-
edness of the candidate projects, and the levels of goal achievements. V-C
models may also be useful when the decision maker is trying to assemble a
balanced portfolio of several projects. For instance, the results in Table 10-6
show that projects A and B together provide the maximum contributions to the
short range sub-goals, and they jointly make major contributions to the long
range sub-goals.

Using Evaluation Models

Evaluation Models are useful when the decision maker feels a need to have a
more detailed and in-depth analysis than screening models can provide. Evaluation models permit the decision maker to make much finer discriminations
between the candidate projects. On the other hand, evaluation models generally require a much greater volume and detail of data than screening models.
Some evaluation models require finite numbers for life cycle sales volumes,
probabilities of success and other parameters that may be very difficult to
estimate.

In spite of the difficulties in applying them, evaluation models clearly have
a place. There are times when it is difficult to make a decision without the kind
of data and information that go into an evaluation model. Thus, by using the
model as a guideline, the decision maker will be urged to more carefully search
out and analyze the proper information. In many cases, using an evaluation
model with only approximate data and rough estimates can be revealing and
helpful to the decision maker.

PORTFOLIO MODELS

The Portfolio Problem

Table 10-7 illustrates the use of a portfolio model. The objective is to determine
the best allocation of the available funds among the three alternative candidate
projects. Projects A, B and C each have four alternative funding levels: $0,

Table 10-7. Illustration of a Portfolio Model.

AVAILABLE FUNDS = $300,000			
ALTERNATIVE FUNDING LEVELS FOR EACH PROJECT	EXPECTED PROFITS ($M)		
	PROJECT A	PROJECT B	PROJECT C
$ 0	$ 0	$ 0	$ 0
100,000	100	120	10
200,000	250	285	215
300,000	310	335	350
Optimum Portfolio	*Expected Profits*		
Project A $100,000	$100M		
Project B 200,000	285M		
$300,000	$385M		

$100,000, $200,000 and $300,000. The expected profits from the projects vary with these funding levels, as shown in Table 10-7. The higher funding levels result in improved products, which yield higher expected profits.

Several alternative allocations of the available $300,000 are possible. For instance, the funds can all be allocated to project C, for an expected profit return of $350M. In this case, the other two projects would be zeroed-out—no money would be spent on them. The available funds could also be spread evenly across the three projects. This would yield an expected profit return of $100M + 120M + $10M = $230M. This is inferior to the above alternative of funding only project C at its upper limit. Continued searching will show that the optimum allocation is to fund project A at its $100,000 level, project B at its $200,000 level, and to zero-out project C. This portfolio yields the largest possible total expected profits, as shown in Table 10-7. There is no other allocation of the available funds that will achieve higher total expected profits.

It should be clear from this illustration that there are occasions when it may be more fruitful to purposely fund some projects at their lowest levels (project A) or to completely reject other projects (project C), in order to marshal funds for more productive uses (project B). The simple problem shown in Table 10-7 can be readily solved by enumerating and comparing all the alternative allocations. But when there are many candidate projects or alternative funding levels, operations research techniques and mathematical programming models are often used. These models have the advantage that various constraints may be included to insure that the portfolio is balanced for risk, or that exploratory research projects will not be disadvantaged in competing with other projects.

Mathematical Programming Methods for Portfolio Problems

In a portfolio model, candidate projects are implicitly prioritized by the amount of funds allocated to them. The general format of all such models is

$$\max \sum_j v_j(x_j) \qquad [5]$$

$$\text{subject to } \sum_j x_j \le B \qquad [6]$$

where x_j is a project expenditure, B is the total budget for $j = 1, \ldots, n$ candidates (projects) for funding, and the value function, $v_j(x_j)$, can be nonlinear, linear, or single-valued. In the single-valued case (one value of v_j and one cost x_j for each jth project), the portfolio model is an index model with v_j as the prioritizing index.

A variety of "values" may be used in equation [5] above. Many portfolio models use expected values, so that equation [5] becomes

$$\max \sum_j v_j p_j(x_j), \qquad [7]$$

where $p_j(x_j)$ is the probability of achieving v_j. Other portfolio models use a total score; e.g., a T_j "value" from a scoring model. In addition to equation [6], a typical constraint is

$$b_j^- \le x_j \le b_j^+, \qquad [8]$$

where b_j^- and b_j^+ are lower and upper project expenditure bounds. Also, portfolio models have been developed for multiple time periods, e.g.,

$$\max \sum_{ij} v_{ij}(x_{ij}) \qquad [9]$$

$$\text{subject to } \sum_{ij} x_{ij} \le B, \qquad [10]$$

where $i = 1, \ldots, m$ time periods.

Literally hundreds of portfolio models have been proposed in the literature. Several literature reviews are available, which summarize and evaluate these models (5), (9), (10), (11), (12).

GROUP AND ORGANIZATIONAL MODELS

Need for Structured Group Processes

Project selection decisions that are performed in organizational and group settings are often deeply influenced by many human emotions, desires, and departmental loyalties. Many different parties normally become involved in the project selection decision making process, either as suppliers of decision data and information, as champions of projects, as influencers, or as decision makers. Unless a spirit of trust and openness is felt by these parties, it is not likely that essential information will be completely and openly exchanged. Each involved party must come to appreciate the interpersonal needs of the other participants, and the larger missions of the organization vis-a-vis their own wants. In order to achieve a total organizational consensus and commitment to a final decision, those involved must fully comprehend the nature of the proposed projects. This means that they must have a depth of factual knowledge. It also means that the parties must have a complete awareness of their own feelings, since much of the decision data are highly personal. Many decision settings fail because the participant's feelings are not crystallized and they have not fully exchanged their feelings. Thus, there is a need for a technique that bridges these behavioral gaps, which are peculiar to organizational and group decision making settings. A structured decision making approach called the QS/NI process has been found to meet this need (2), (3).

The QS/NI Process

Though complex psychometric phenomena underlie it (1), (2), (3), the mechanics of the Q-sorting (QS) method are relatively simple, as outlined in Table 10-8. Using this procedure, each participant sequentially sorts the projects into five priority categories.

Each individual who "Q-sorts" a set of candidate projects does so according to his own perceptions and understandings of their relative value. The result is a kind of prioritizing of the candidate projects, according to their perceived value (1), (2).

The nominal-interacting (NI) decision process begins with a "nominal" period in which each individual in the group silently and anonymously Q-sorts the candidate projects. These results are then tabulated in a tally chart and displayed to the entire group. The tally chart focuses on the group consensus process and the agreement-disagreement statistics, without revealing who voted for what.

The group is then given an "interacting" period in which they discuss the results in the tally chart. During this period, they may share and exchange data and rationales, they may challenge each other, etc. To help guide the group in their accomodation patterns, group process measures may be taken and periodically fed back to the group. These measures generally indicate whether the group is becoming more or less cohesive, and what they can do to improve their team potency. It is left up to the group to decide whether or not to take these potency-improving actions (2), (13), (14).

This QS/NI sequence of an individual Q-sort in a nominal setting followed by a group discussion or interacting period can be repeated for several rounds.

Table 10-8. The Q-Sorting Method.

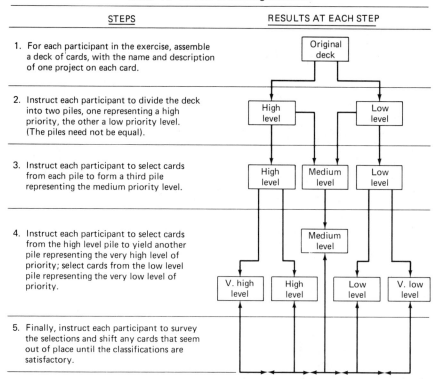

STEPS	RESULTS AT EACH STEP
1. For each participant in the exercise, assemble a deck of cards, with the name and description of one project on each card.	Original deck
2. Instruct each participant to divide the deck into two piles, one representing a high priority, the other a low priority level. (The piles need not be equal).	High level Low level
3. Instruct each participant to select cards from each pile to form a third pile representing the medium priority level.	High level Medium level Low level
4. Instruct each participant to select cards from the high level pile to yield another pile representing the very high level of priority; select cards from the low level pile representing the very low level of priority.	Medium level V. high level High level Low level V. low level
5. Finally, instruct each participant to survey the selections and shift any cards that seem out of place until the classifications are satisfactory.	

Experience shows that two or three rounds are needed to stimulate complete information exchange, but more than four rounds dissipates the participants. The first nominal Q-sort period permits individuals to document their own thoughts and value judgements. The subsequent first interacting period confronts the group with a diversity of opinions to be resolved. The second nominal Q-sort period permits each individual to privately re-structure his or her thoughts. The second interacting period provides an opportunity to refine opinions and work toward consensus. A third nominal Q-sort period provides the environment for closure and consensus. A consensus will usually emerge as the members adopt ideas and opinions from each other, acquire more information and interpersonal understandings, or become influenced by the enthusiasm of the group. The tally chart itself is consensus-inducing for those members who identify with the group effort (1), (2), (13), (14).

Table 10-9 presents an illustration of the tally charts for two rounds of the QS/NI process, for a twenty-person group, voting on seven projects. The arrows trace the changes in the individual Q-sorts from the first to the second

Table 10-9. Illustration of Results From the QS-NI Process.

	Projects	A	B	C	D	E	F	G
Categories	Very high priority							
	High priority							
	Intermediate priority							
	Low priority							
	Very low priority							
1st round	K.S. test[a] D =	.10	.15	.25	.10	.05	.15	.40
	p =	>.20	>.20	<.15	>.20	>.20	>.20	<.05
	Consensus?[b]	No	No	T	No	No	No	T
2nd round	K.S. test[a] D =	.40	.60	.40	.65	.40	.35	.25
	p =	<.05	<.01	<.05	<.01	<.05	<.05	<.15
	Consensus?[b]	Yes	Yes	Yes	Yes	Yes	Yes	No

[a]Kolmogorov-Smirnov one-sample test of significance. The null hypothesis is that the cumulative observed distribution of votes (for that project) is not different from the cumulative rectangular distribution 4, 8, 12, 16, 20. D is the largest absolute difference between the observed and rectangular distributions for any category, divided by N. See: Sidney Siegel, *Nonparametric Statistics* (McGraw-Hill: New York, 1965), pp. 47–52.

[b]Group consensus for a single category exists where it contains 50% more votes than any other category and $p \leq .10$ in the K.S. test ($p \leq .10$ can exist for bimodally distributed votes). T indicates a tendency for consensus, in that two adjacent categories contain $\geq 2/3$ of the votes.

Table 10-10. Guide to Applying Project Selection Models.

TYPE OF PROJECTS:	RELEVANT TYPE OF MODEL OR PROCESS								
	Checklists	PROFILES	SCORING	FRONTIER	INDEX	RISK ANALYSIS	VALUE-CONTRIBUTION	PORTFOLIO	QS-NI
Exploratory	X	X	X						X
Applied				X	X	X			X
Development						X	X	X	X
Type of Decision Problem:									
Screening	X	X	X	X	X				X
Prioritizing					X	X	X	X	X
Resource Allocation							X	X	

nominal period. Note that the degree of consensus actually declined during this part of the exercise for project G. In this case, the discussion revealed a heretofore hidden lack of information and a fundamental lack of comprehension of this project by some of the subjects. This proposal was returned to the submitter for additional work, followed by re-submittal. A consensus was reached on this re-submitted project at the end of a third round of the QS/NI process. As shown in Table 10-9, the other projects rapidly converged to a strong consensus. Note the high incidence of "block voting" or coalition voting among these data, in which small clusters of 3 to 5 persons are voting alike and changing their votes in a like manner. This is a common phenomenon in QS/NI exercises. The QS/NI process usually reveals a great deal about group interaction patterns and interpersonal power play strategies. Coalitions, and advocate and adversary positions are usually made very visible by the QS/NI process (13), (14).

SUMMARY

The selection of the best projects is a very important decision problem for project managers. Today's projects entail very large commitments which have the potential to become enormous regrets if an inferior project is selected. A large number of techniques and models have been developed to aid in project screening, evaluation and selection decision making. As Table 10-10 shows, the choice of one type of method over another will depend on the nature of the projects being assessed and the decision problem at hand (1), (2), (3), (5).

REFERENCES

1. Souder, W. E. "Field Studies With a Q-Sort/Nominal Group Process for Selecting R&D Projects." *Research Policy, 5,* No. 4 (1975), pp. 172–188.
2. Souder, W. E. *Management Decision Methods for Managers of Engineering and Research* (New York. Van Nostrand Reinhold Company, 1980), pp. 27–36, 64–73, 137–162.
3. Souder, W. E. "A System for Using R&D Project Evaluation Methods." *Research Management, 21,* No. 5. (1978), pp. 29–37.
4. Moore, J. R. and Baker, N. R. "An Analytical Approach to Scoring Model Design: Application to Research and Development Project Selection." *IEEE Trans. on Eng. Mgt., EM-16,* No. 3 (1969), pp. 90–98.
5. Souder, W. E. "Project Selection, Planning and Control." in *Handbook of Operations Research: Models and Applications,* J. J. Moder and S. E. Elmaghraby (eds.) (New York. Van Nostrand Reinhold. 1970), pp. 301–344.
6. Markowitz, H. *Portfolio Selection* (New York. Wiley. 1960).
7. Sharpe, W. F. "A Simplified Model for Portfolio Analysis." *Management Science, 9,* No. 1: 277–293 (1963).
8. Hertz, D. B. "Risk Analysis in Capital Investment.," *Harvard Business Review, 42,* No. 1. (1964), pp. 95–106.
9. Dean, B. V. *Project Evaluation: Methods and Procedures* (New York. American Management Association. 1970).
10. Baker, N. R. and Freeland, J. "Recent Advances in R&D Benefit Measurement and Project Selection Methods." *Management Science, 21,* No. 10. (1975), pp. 1164–1175.
11. Souder, W. E. "Analytical Effectiveness of Mathematical Programming Models for Project Selection." *Management Science, 19,* No. 8. (1973), pp. 907–923.
12. Souder, W. E. "Utility and Perceived Acceptability of R&D Project Selection Models." *Management Science, 19,* No. 12. (1973), pp. 1384–1394.
13. Souder, W. E. "Effectiveness of Nominal and Interacting Group Decision Processes for Integrating R&D and Marketing." *Management Science, 23,* No. 6. (1977), pp. 595–605.
14. Souder, W. E. "Achieving Organizational Consensus With Respect to R&D Project Selection Criteria." *Management Science, 21,* No. 6. (1975), pp. 669–691.

BIBLIOGRAPHY

Ansoff, H. I. "Evaluation of Applied Research in a Business Firm." in *Technical Planning on the Corporate Level,* J. R. Bright (ed.) (Harvard University Press. Cambridge, Massachusetts 1962).

Augood, Derek. "A Review of R&D Evaluation Methods." *IEEE Transactions on Engineering Management, EM-20,* No. 4 (1973), pp. 114–120.

Baker, N. R. and Freeland, J. "Recent Advances in R&D Benefit Measurement and Project Selection Methods." *Management Science, 21,* No. 10 (1975), pp. 1164–1175.

Cetron, M. J. and Roepcke L. H. "The Selection of R&D Program Content." *IEEE Trans. on Eng. Management, Em-14* (December 1967), pp. 4–13.

Clarke, T. C. "Decision Making in Technologically Based Organizations: A Literature Survey of Present Practice." *IEEE Transactions on Engineering Management, Em-21,* No. 1 (1974), pp. 9–23.

Dean, B. V. and S. S. Sengupta. "On A Method for Determining Corporate Research and Development Budgets," in *Management Science Models and Techniques* C. W. Churchman and M. Verhulst (eds.) (New York. Pergamon Press. 1960) pp. 210–225.

Gear, A. E.; Lockett, A. G.; and Pearson, A. W. "Analysis of Some Portfolio Selection Models for R&D." *IEEE Transactions on Engineering Management, EM-18*, No. 2 (1971), pp. 66–76.

Gee, R. E. "A Survey of Current Project Selection Practices." *Research Management, 14*, No. 5 (September 1971), pp. 38–45.

Harris, J. S. "New Product Profile Chart." *Chem. and Eng. News, 39*, No. 16 (April 17, 1961), pp. 110–118.

Hart, A. "Evaluation of Research and Development Projects." *Chem. and Ind.*, No. 13 (March 27, 1965), pp. 549–554.

Hess, S. W. "A Dynamic Programming Approach to R&D Budgeting and Project Selection." *IRE Trans. on Eng. Management, EM-9* (December 1962), pp. 170–179.

Merrifield, Bruce "Industrial Project Selection and Management." *Industrial Marketing Management, 7*, No. 5 (1978), pp. 324–331.

Murdick, R. G. and Karger, D. W. "The Shoestring Approach to Rating New Products." *Machine Design* (January 25, 1973), pp. 86–89.

Rosen, E. M. and Wm. E. Souder "A Method for Allocating R&D Expenditures." *IEEE Trans. on Eng. Management, Em-12* (September 1965), pp. 87–93.

Rubenstein, A. H. "Studies of Project Selection in Industry." in B. V. Dean (ed.) *Operations Research in Research and Development* (New York. Wiley. 1963), pp. 189–205.

Souder, Wm. E. "R&D Project Selection: A Budgetary Approach." *Trans. CCDA* (Spring 1966), pp. 25–43.

———, "Planning R&D Expenditures with the Aid of a Computer." *Budgeting, XIV* (March 1966), pp. 25–32.

———, "Solving Budgeting Problems with O.R." *Budgeting, XIV* (July/August 1967), pp. 9–11.

———, "Selecting and Staffing R & D Projects Via Op Research." *Chem. Eng. Progress, 63* (November 1967) pp. 27 (reprinted in *Readings in Operations Res.*, W. C. House, Auebach 1970).

———, "Experiences with an R&D Project Control Model." *IEEE Trans. on Eng. Management, EM-15* (March 1968), pp. 39–49.

———, "Suitability and Validity of Project Selection Models." Ph.D. Dissertation, St. Louis University, St. Louis, Missouri (August 1970).

———, "R²: Some Results from Studies of the Research Management Process." *Pro. AMIF* (March 1971), pp. 121–130.

———, "A Comparative Analysis of Risky Investment Planning Algorithms." *AIIE Trans., 4*, No. 1 (March 1972), pp. 56–62.

———, "A Scoring Methodology for Assessing the Suitability of Management Science Models." *Management Sci., 18*, No. 10 (June 1972), pp. 526–543.

———, "An R&D Planning and Control Servosystem: A Case Study." *R&D Management, 3*, No. 1 (October 1972), pp. 5–12.

———, "Effectiveness of Mathematical Programming Models for Project Selection: A Computational Evaluation." *Management Sci., 19*, No. 8 (April 1973), pp. 907–923.

———, "Acceptability and Utility of Project Selection Models in Development R&D." *Management Sci., 19*, No. 12 (August 1973), pp. 1384–1394.

———, "Autonomy, Gratification and R&D Outputs: A Small Sample Field Study." *Management Sci., 20*, No. 8 (April 1974), pp. 1147–1156.

———, "Achieving Organizational Consensus With Respect to R&D Project Selection Criteria." *Management Sci., 21*, No. 6 (February 1975), pp. 669–681.

———, "Experimental Test of a Q-Sort Procedure for Prioritizing R&D Projects." *IEEE Trans. on Eng. Mgt.*, Vol. EM-21, No. 4 (November 1974), pp. 159–164.

————, "Field Studies With a Q-Sort/Nominal Group Process for Selecting R&D Projects." *Research Policy,* Vol. 5, No. 4 (April 1975), pp. 172–188.

————, "Effectiveness of Nominal and Interacting Group Decision Processes for Integrating R&D and Marketing." *Management Science,* Vol. 23, No. 6 (February 1977), pp. 595–605.

————, "A System for Using R&D Project Evaluation Models in Organizations." *Research Management,* Vol. 21, No. 5 (Sept. 1978), pp. 29–37.

————, "An Appraisal of Eight R&D Project Evaluation Methods" to appear in *Corporate Strategy and Product Innovation,* R. Rothberg, (ed.) (Macmillan, 2nd. edition. 1981).

Sullivan, C. I. "CPI Looks at R&D Project Evaluation." *Ind. and Eng. Chem., 53,* No. 9 (September 1961), pp. 42A–46A.

Villers, Raymond *Research and Development: Planning and Control* (Financial Executives Research Institute, Inc. (1964), pp. 30–38.

Watters, L. D. "Research and Development Project Selection: Interdependence and Multiperiod Probabilistic Budget Constraints." Ph.D. Dissertation, Arizona State University, Temp. (1967).

Section IV
Life Cycle Management

One of the important reasons for the efficacy of project management is the changing mix of resources that is demanded over the life cycle of a project.

In Chapter 11, William R. King and David I. Cleland portray the project life cycle as an important rationale for project management. They present various life cycle concepts and show how the life cycle places demands on organizations that require a "new" form of management—the project management approach.

In Chapter 12, John R. Adams and Stephen E. Barndt review a set of organizational variables in terms of their impact on projects in various stages of the life cycle. They present a series of propositions that are based on their assessments of the results of studies of more than 20 R&D projects. These propositions allow one to predict the behavior of projects throughout their life cycle.

In Chapter 13, Herbert F. Spires considers an important, and often neglected, phase of the project life cycle—divestment. The phasing out of a project may be either a "natural" part of the life cycle or it may be extraordinary. In either case, phase-down creates unique problems that are associated with no other phases and with few other endeavors in life.

11. Life Cycle Management[1]

William R. King[*]
David I. Cleland[†]

"Life cycle management" is a term that describes project management in terms of one of the most salient project characteristics—the life cycle. The life cycle of a project is an important factor in determining the need for, and value of, a project management approach.

BASIC LIFE CYCLE CONCEPTS

There are a variety of life cycle concepts that are in common use. These life cycles serve to illustrate the need for life cycle management.

Sales Life Cycles

Perhaps the best known life cycle is the sales life cycle. A product moves through various phases of sales life cycle after it has been placed on the market. One of the authors[2] has referred to these life cycle phases as *establishment, growth, maturation,* and *declining sales* phases. Figure 11-1 shows these phases in terms of the sales revenue generated by the product during its period of slow establishment in the marketplace, followed by a period of rapid sales increase, a peaking, and a long, gradual decline. Virtually every product displays these

---

[*]Dr. William R. King is Professor of Business Administration in the Graduate School of Business at the University of Pittsburgh. He is the author of more than a dozen books and 100 articles in the fields of strategic planning, information systems and project management. Additional biographical material may be found in the current editions of *Who's Who in the World, Who's Who in America,* and other standard references.

[†]Dr. Cleland is a Professor of Systems Management Engineering in the Industrial Engineering Department at the University of Pittsburgh. He is author/co-author of eight books and has published numerous articles appearing in leading national and internationally distributed technological, business management and educational periodicals. Dr. Cleland has had extensive experience in management consultation, lecturing, seminars, and research.

[1]Portions of this chapter have been paraphrased from *Systems Analysis and Project Management,* 2nd Edition, (McGraw-Hill Book Company, New York, 1975) by David I. Cleland and William R. King.

[2]William R. King. *Quantitative Analysis for Marketing Management* (McGraw-Hill Book Company, New York, 1967), p. 113.

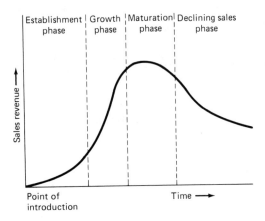

Figure 11-1. Product sales life cycle.

dynamic characteristics, although some may have a sales life cycle which is so long or short that the various phases are not readily distinguishable. For example, a faddish product such as "super balls," "hula hoops," or "flying saucers" will have a very high-peaked sales curve with a rapid decline. Many such products will have a long, slow decline after an initially rapid decline from the peak. With other products, the maturation phase is very long and the declining sales phase very gradual. But the general life cycle concept is virtually unavoidable for a successful product. Without product improvements competition will eventually lure away customers and consumers' attitudes, habits, and needs will change as time passes.

Of course, the sales portion of the life cycle of a product is really only one aspect of its entire life. Indeed, only products which are marketing successes ever get to experience the sales life cycle of Figure 11-1.

Systems Development Life Cycle

All products—sales successes or otherwise—begin as a gleam in the eye of someone and undergo many different phases of development before being marketed and subjected to the sales life-cycle considerations of Figure 11-1. For instance, the U.S. Department of Defense (DOD) and the National Aeronautics and Space Administration (NASA) have extensively defined and detailed phases which should be encountered with hardware systems development. Their system development life-cycle concept recognizes a natural order of thought and action which is pervasive in the development of many kinds of systems—be they commercial products, space exploration systems, or management systems.

New products, services, or roles for the organization have their genesis in ideas evolving within the organization. Typically, such "systems" ideas go through a distinct life cycle, i.e., a natural and pervasive order of thought and action. In each phase of this cycle, different levels and varieties of specific thought and action are required within the organization to assess the efficacy of the system. The "phases" of this cycle serve to illustrate the systems development life-cycle concept and its importance.

The Conceptual Phase. The germ of the idea for a system may evolve from other research, from current organizational problems, or from the observation of organizational interfaces. The conceptual phase is one in which the idea is conceived and given preliminary evaluation.

During the conceptual phase, the environment is examined, forecasts are prepared, objectives and alternatives are evaluated, and the first examination of the performance, cost, and time aspects of the system's development is performed. It is also during this phase that basic strategy, organization, and resource requirements are conceived. The fundamental purpose of the conceptual phase is to conduct a "white paper" study of the requirements in order to provide a basis for further detailed evaluation. Table 11-1 shows the details of these efforts.

There will typically be a high mortality rate of potential systems during the conceptual phase of the life cycle. Rightly so, since the study process conducted during this phase should identify projects that have high risk and are technically, environmentally, or economically infeasible or impractical.

The Definition Phase. The fundamental purpose of the definition phase is to determine, as soon as possible and as accurately as possible, cost, schedule,

---

Table 11-1. Conceptual Phase.

1. Determine existing needs or potential deficiencies of existing systems.
2. Establish system concepts which provide initial strategic guidance to overcome existing or potential deficiencies.
3. Determine initial technical, environmental, and economic feasibility and practicability of the system.
4. Examine alternative ways of accomplishing the system objectives.
5. Provide initial answers to the questions:
   a What will the system cost?
   b When will the system be available?
   c What will the system do?
   d How will the system be integrated into existing systems?
6. Identify the human and nonhuman resources required to support the system.
7. Select initial system designs which will satisfy the system objectives.
8. Determine initial system interfaces.
9. Establish a project organization.

Table 11-2. Definition Phase.

1. Firm identification of the human and nonhuman resources required.
2. Preparation of final system performance requirements.
3. Preparation of detailed plans required to support the system.
4. Determination of realistic cost, schedule, and performance requirements.
5. Identification of those areas of the system where high risk and uncertainty exist, and delineation of plans for further exploration of these areas.
6. Definition of intersystem and intrasystem interfaces.
7. Determination of necessary support subsystems.
8. Identification and initial preparation of the documentation required to support the system, such as policies, procedures, job descriptions, budget and funding papers, letters, memoranda, etc.

performance, and resource requirements and whether all elements, projects, and subsystems will fit together economically and technically.

The definition phase simply tells in more detail what it is we want to do, when we want to do it, how we will accomplish it, and what it will cost. The definition phase allows the organization to fully conceive and define the system before it starts to physically put the system into its environment. Simply stated, the definition phase dictates that one stop and take time to look around to see if this is what one really wants before the resources are committed to putting the system into operation and production. If the idea has survived the end of the conceptual phase, a conditional approval for further study and development is given. The definition phase provides the opportunity to review and confirm the decision to continue development, create a prototype system, and make a production or installation decision.

Decisions that are made during and at the end of the definition phase might very well be decisions to cancel further work on the system and redirect organizational resources elsewhere. The elements of this phase are described in Table 11-2.

Production or Acquisition Phase.   The purpose of the production or acquisition phase is to acquire and test the system elements and the total system itself using the standards developed during the preceding phases. The acquisition process involves such things as the actual setting up of the system, the fabrication of hardware, the allocation of authority and responsibility, the construction of facilities, and the finalization of supporting documentation. Table 11-3 details this phase.

The Operational Phase.   The fundamental role of the manager of a system during the operational phase is to provide the resource support required to accomplish system objectives. This phase indicates the system has been proven

Table 11-3. Production Phase.

1. Updating of detailed plans conceived and defined during the preceding phases.
2. Identification and management of the resources required to facilitate the production processes such as inventory, supplies, labor, funds, etc.
3. Verification of system production specifications.
4. Beginning of production, construction, and installation.
5. Final preparation and dissemination of policy and procedural documents.
6. Performance of final testing to determine adequacy of the system to do the things it is intended to do.
7. Development of technical manuals and affiliated documentation describing how the system is intended to operate.
8. Development of plans to support the system during its operational phase.

economical, feasible, and practicable and will be used to accomplish the desired ends of the system. In this phase the manager's functions change somewhat. He is less concerned with planning and organizing and more concerned with controlling the system's operation along the predetermined lines of performance. His responsibilities for planning and organization are not entirely neglected—there are always elements of these functions remaining—but he places more emphasis on motivating the human element of the system and controlling the utilization of resources of the total system. It is during this phase that the system may lose its identity per se and be assimilated into the institutional framework of the organization.

If the system in question is a product to be marketed, the operational stage begins the sales life cycle portion of the overall cycle, for it is in this phase that marketing of the product is conducted. Table 11-4 shows the important elements of this phase.

The Divestment Phase. The divestment phase is the one in which the organization "gets out of the business" which it began with the conceptual phase. Every system—be it a product system, a weapons system, a management system, or whatever—has a finite lifetime. Too often this goes unrecognized, with the result that outdated and unprofitable products are retained, inefficient

Table 11-4. Operational Phase.

1. Use of the system results by the intended user or customer.
2. Actual integration of the project's product or service into existing organizational systems.
3. Evaluation of the technical, social and economic sufficiency of the project to meet actual operating conditions.
4. Provision of feedback to organizational planners concerned with developing new projects and systems.
5. Evaluation of the adequacy of supporting systems.

Table 11-5. Divestment Phase.

1. System phasedown.
2. Development of plans transferring responsibility to supporting organizations.
3. Divestment or transfer of resources to other systems.
4. Development of "lessons learned from system" for inclusion in qualitative-quantitative data base to include:
   a Assessment of image by the customer
   b Major problems encountered and their solution
   c Technological advances
   d Advancements in knowledge relative to department strategic objectives
   e New or improved management techniques
   f Recommendations for future research and development
   g Recommendations for the management of future programs, including interfaces with associate contractors
   h Other major lessons learned during the course of the system.

management systems are used, or inadequate equipment and facilities are "put up with." Only by the specific and continuous consideration of the divestment possibilities can the organization realistically hope to avoid these contingencies. Table 11-5 relates to the divestment phase.

Taken together Tables 11-1 through 11-5 provide a detailed outline of the overall systems development life cycle. Of course, the terminology used in these tables is not applicable to every system which might be under development, since the terminology generally applied to the development of consumer product systems is often different from that applied to weapons systems. Both, in turn, are different from that used in the development of a financial system for a business firm. However, whatever the terminology used, the concepts are applicable to all such systems.

LIFE CYCLE MANAGEMENT

Life cycle management refers to the management of systems, products or projects throughout their life cycle. In the context of the sales life cycle, life cycle management is usually called "product management." In the development life cycle, it is usually called "project management." In all cases, life cycle management is needed because the *life cycle reflects very different management requirements at its various stages.*

The traditional hierarchical organization is not designed to cope with the constantly changing management requirements dictated by life cycles. It is established to effectively direct and control a much less dynamic milieu.

Variability of Input and Output Measures for Various Stages of the Life Cycle

The dynamism that is inherent in the life cycle is made apparent when one considers the variability in the measures that may be used to appropriately describe the inputs to, and outputs from, a system as it goes through its life cycle.

Such measures vary widely. For instance, in developing a new product, one might characterize the various phases of the project life cycle in terms of the proportional composition of the work force assigned to the activity. In the beginning, research personnel predominate; subsequently, their role diminishes and engineers come to the forefront; finally, marketing and sales personnel become most important.

Basic life cycle concepts hold for all projects and systems. Thus an organizational system develops and matures according to a cycle which is much like that of a product. The measures used to define various phases of an organization's life cycle might focus on its product orientation, e.g., defense versus nondefense, its personnel composition, e.g., scientists versus nonscientists, its per-share earnings, etc. For a management information system, the life cycle might be characterized by the expenditure level during the developmental phase together with the performance characteristics of the system after it becomes operational.

A hardware system displays no sales performance after it is in use, but it does display definite phases of operation. For example, Figure 11-2 shows a typical failure rate curve for the components making up a complex system. As the system is first put into operation, the failure rate is rather high because of "burn in" failures of weak components. After this period is passed, a relatively constant failure rate is experienced for a long duration; then, as wear-outs begin to occur, the component failure rate rises dramatically.

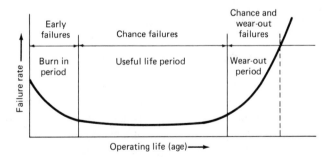

Figure 11-2. Component failure rate in a system as a function of age.

Perhaps a comparison of Figures 11-1 and 11-2 best illustrates the pervasiveness of life-cycle concepts and the importance of assessing the life cycle properly. Figure 11-1 represents a sales life cycle for a product. The most appropriate measure to be applied to this product's sales life cycle is "sales rate." Figure 11-2 shows the operating life cycle of a hardware system—for instance, a military weapons system. The concept is the same as that of Figure 11-1, but the appropriate measurement is different. In Figure 11-2 the "failure rate" is deemed to be the most important assessable aspect of the life cycle for the purpose for which the measurement will be used.

Life Cycle Management Dimensions

The variability of the various input and output measures and the fact that different measures may be more appropriate at one stage of the life cycle than at another suggest that project management must focus on certain *critical generic project dimensions*. These dimensions are *cost, time and performance.*

Cost refers to the resources being expended. One would want to assess cost sometimes in terms of an expenditure rate (e.g., dollars per month) and sometimes in terms of total cumulative expenditures (or both).

Time refers to the timeliness of progress in terms of a schedule which has been set up. Answers to such questions as: "Is the project on schedule?", "How many days must be made up?", etc., reflect this dimension of progress.

The third dimension of project progress is *performance:* i.e., how is the project meeting its objectives or specifications? For example, in a product development project, performance would be assessed by the degree to which the product meets the specifications or goal set for it. Typically, products are developed by a series of improvements which successively approach a desired goal, e.g., soap powder with the same cleaning properties but less sudsiness. In the case of an airplane, certain requirements as to speed, range, altitude capability, etc., are set and the degree to which a particular design in a series of successive refinements meets these requirements is an assessment of the performance dimension of the aircraft design project.

Managing Over the Life Cycle

Since the mix of resources (inputs) and outputs associated with a project varies through the life cycle, the implication is strong that the appropriate techniques and strategies of management also vary during the various phases. Indeed, the need for management flexibility across the life cycle is one of the primary reasons that the traditional hierarchical organization is inadequate in dealing with project-intensive management situations.

The specific implications to project management are presented elsewhere in

Table 11-6. Fox's Hypotheses About Appropriate Business Strategies over the Product Life Cycle

	FUNCTIONAL FOCUS	R&D	PRODUCTION	MARKETING	PHYSICAL DISTRIBUTION
Precommercialization	Coordination of R&D and other functions	Reliability tests Release blueprints	Production design Process planning Purchasing dept. lines up vendors & subcontractors	Test marketing Detailed marketing plan	Plan shipping schedules, mixed carloads Rent warehouse space, trucks
Introduction	Engineering: debugging in R&D production, and field	Technical corrections (Engineering changes)	Subcontracting Centralize pilot plants; test various processes; develop standards.	Induce trial; fill pipelines; sales agents or commissioned salesmen; publicity	Plan a logistics system
Growth	Production	Start successor product	Centralize production Phase out subcontractors Expedite vendors ouput; long runs	Channel commitment Brand emphasis Salaried sales force Reduce price if necessary	Expedite deliveries Shift to owned facilities
Maturity	Marketing and logistics	Develop minor variants Reduce costs thru value analysis Originate major adaptations to start new cycle	Many short runs Decentralize Import parts, low-priced models Routinization Cost reduction	Short-term promotions Salaried salesmen Cooperative advertising Forward integration	Reduce costs and raise customer service level Control finished goods inventory

217

Table 11-6. Fox's Hypotheses About Appropriate Business Strategies over the Product Life Cycle (continued)

FUNCTIONAL FOCUS	R&D	PRODUCTION	MARKETING	PHYSICAL DISTRIBUTION
			Routine marketing research; panels, audits	Reduce inventory and services
Decline	Withdraw all R&D from initial version	Revert to subcontracting; simplify production line Careful inventory control; buy foreign or competitive goods; stock spare parts	Revert to commission basis; withdraw most promotional support Raise price Selective distribution Careful phase-out, considering entire channel	
Finance				

	PERSONNEL	FINANCE	MANAGEMENT ACCOUNTING	OTHER	CUSTOMERS	COMPETITION
Precommercial-ization	Recruit for new activities Negotiate operational changes with unions	LC plan for cash flows, profits, investments, planning; full costs, revenues Determine optimum lengths of LC stages thru present-value method	Final legal clearances (regulatory hurdles, patents) Appoint LC coordinator		Panels & other test respondents	Neglects opportunity or is working on similar idea

Stage						
Introduction	Staff and train middle management Stock options for executives	Accounting deficit; high net cash outflow Authorize large production facilities	Help develop production & distribution standards Prepare sales aids like sales management portfolio		Innovators and some early adopters	(Monopoly) Disparagement of innovation Legal & extra-legal interference
Growth	Add suitable personnel for plant Many gievances Heavy overtime	Very high profits, net cash outflow still rising Sell equities	Short-term analyses based on return per scarce resource		Early adopters & early majority	(Oligopoly): A few imitate, improve, or cut prices
Maturity	Transfers, advancements; incentives for efficiency, safety, and so on Suggestion system	Declining profit rate but increasing net cash inflow	Analyze differential costs revenue Spearhead cost reduction, value analysis, and efficiency drives	Pressure for resale price maintenance Price cuts bring price wars; possible price collusion	Early adopters, early & late majority, some laggards; first discontinued by late majority	(Monopoly) competition First shakeout, yet many rivals
Decline	Find new slots Encourage early retirement	Administer system, retrenchment Sell unneeded equipment Export the machinery	Analyze escapable costs Pinpoint remaining outlays	Accurate sales forecast very important	Mainly laggards	(Oligopoly) After 2nd shakeout, only few rivals

this volume (Chapters 5, 6). Table 11-6 shows a broad set of management strategies, developed by Fox,[3] that are associated with a five-stage life cycle:

1. Precommercialization.
2. Introduction.
3. Growth.
4. Maturity.
5. Decline.

The first stage of Fox's life cycle may be roughly thought of as the development life cycle that has itself previously been treated in terms of a number of states. The remaining four stages represent the sales life cycle.

Table 11-6 clearly indicates the extreme variability in management strategy and outlook that is necessitated by the dynamics of the life cycle. The prospect of such flexibility being developed in the context of a traditional hierarchical organization, designed primarily to ensure efficiency and control, is remote. Therefore, the implications of life cycles to both the need for, and practice of, project management are straightforward.

Overall Organization Management Implications

An organization can be characterized at any instant in a given time by a "stream of projects" that place demands on its resources. The combined effect of all the "projects" facing an organization at any given time determines the overall status of the organization at that time.

The projects facing a given organization at a given time typically are diverse in nature—some products are in various stages of their sales life cycles, other products are in various stages of development, management subsystems are undergoing development, organizational subsystems are in transition, major decision problems such as merger and plant location decisions have been "projectized" for study and solution, etc.

Moreover, at any given time each of these projects will typically be in a different phase of its life cycle. For instance, one product may be in the conceptual phase undergoing feasibility study, another may be in the definition phase, some are being produced, and some are being phased out in favor of oncoming models.

The typical situation with products which are in the sales portion of their overall life cycle is shown in Figure 11-3, as projected through 1995 for the sales levels of three products, A, B, and C. Product B is expected to begin sales

---

[3]Fox, Harold W., "A Framework for Functional Coordination," *Atlanta Economic Review,* Vol. 23, No. 6 (1973), pp. 10–11. Used with permission.

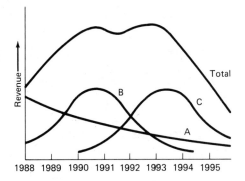

Figure 11-3. Life cycles for several products.

in 1988 and to be entering the declining sales phase of its cycle after 1991. Product A is already in the midst of a long declining sales phase. Product C is in development and will not be marketed until 1990. At any moment in time, each is in a different state. In 1991, for example, A is in a continuing decline, B is beginning a rather rapid decline, and C is just expanding rapidly.

Whatever measure is chosen to represent the activity level or state of completion of each of the projects in the stream facing an organization—be they products, product-oriented projects, management system-development projects, or decision-oriented projects—the aggregate of all of the projects facing the organization represents a stream of projects which it must pursue. Although the same measures (e.g., revenues, resources employed, percent completed, etc.) will not normally be applicable to all projects, the idea of a stream of projects—each at a different phase of its life cycle—is applicable to assessing the state of any dynamic organization.

The overall management implications of the stream of projects are clear from Figure 11-3. Top managers must plan in terms of the project stream. Since overall results are the sum of the results produced by the various projects, this planning must not only be in terms of long-run goals, but also in terms of the various steps along the way.

Most organizations do not wish to have their overall results appear to be erratic, so they must be concerned with the "sum" of the project stream at various points in time. A number of projects, each of which is pursuing a future goal quite well, might in sum, not appear to be performing well at some points before they have reached their respective goals. In each case, for instance, although the progress of each may be adequate, each may still be a phase of its life cycle where it is consuming more resources than it is producing results.

Thus, the problems associated with the overall management of an organization that is involved in a stream of projects are influenced by life cycles just as are the problems associated with managing individual projects.

12. Behavioral Implications of the Project Life Cycle*

John R. Adams†
Stephen E. Barndt‡

INTRODUCTION

During the last several decades, the technology needed to design and develop major new products has become increasingly more diverse and complex. The increasing diversity arises from the need to integrate an ever widening variety of professional and technical specialties into new product design. The increasing complexity results from the rapid rate at which knowledge has grown in each major technical specialty contributing to the product, a growth which in turn has spawned a large number of more specialized professional subareas as specialists strive to remain current in ever narrowing technical fields. The increasing technical sophistication of major new products is widely recognized. What is not well known, however, is that the increasing diversity and complexity have caused extensive innovation in management systems for developing those products, resulting in the application of project management techniques to most major, advanced technology, nonrepetitive efforts aimed at designing and developing new products or services.

---

*Portions of the material presented in this chapter were published earlier in "Organizational Life Cycle Implications for Major R & D Projects," *Project Management Quarterly,* Vol. IX, No. 4 (December 1978), p.p. 32–39.

†Dr. John R. Adams holds the Ph.D. in Business Administration from Syracuse University, and is currently an Associate Professor of Organization and Management at Western Carolina University, North Carolina. He is also the Director for Educational Services of the Project Management Institute. Dr. Adams has published a number of articles on various aspects of project management, risk and uncertainty analyses, weapon systems acquisition, and logistics management in nationally distributed journals, and is a frequent speaker at national professional and at Department of Defense symposia. His experience includes management of major weapon systems acquisition programs and supervision of a major Air Force research laboratory.

‡Stephen E. Barndt is an Associate Professor of Management at the School of Business Administration, Pacific Lutheran University, Washington. Dr. Barndt, who earned his Ph.D degree from The Ohio State University, has directed research into the behavioral aspects of project management and has published articles on that subject, among others. In addition, he has co-authored texts on project management and operations management. Dr. Barndt's project management experience includes performing as an assistant program manager and as an R & D project administrator.

The form of management known as project management was designed to "... provide sustained, intensified, and integrated management of the complex ventures" (1)** and to pull together a combination of human and nonhuman resources into " ... a temporary organization to achieve a specified purpose" (2). A project organization is established for a limited period of time to accomplish a well defined and specified set of objectives—to bring a new idea for a product through its conceptual and developmental phases and into its full implementation. When these carefully defined objectives are accomplished, the product is completed and the project organization is terminated. Thus a project has a clear, finite, and well defined life cycle, a fact which has long been used to differentiate "projects" from the more traditional, long term "functional" organization.

The field of management, as it applies to complex organizations, has been the beneficiary of a growing body of knowledge. In particular, a great deal of research has been conducted in recent years to define organizational variables and evaluate their effect on the ongoing, functional organization. Little of this general material has reached the project management literature, however, and little specific research has been conducted to identify the particular organizational factors crucial to the project management field. This is not too surprising, since the modern concept of a project cutting across corporate, industry, and governmental boundaries to develop advanced technology products is not much more than two decades old. A number of detailed topics relevant to such organizations, such as selecting an appropriate project manager (3), developing an effective, cross-functional, network-based management information system (4), and implementing an appropriate project form of organization (5), have recently been more or less intensively investigated; and research efforts on such specialized project management topics continue. Little has been done, however, to understand the broader implications of the project life cycle. In particular, no comprehensive study exists which investigates how the project life cycle may influence and change the anticipated effects of those organizational variables traditionally used to analyze functional organizations.

This chapter reviews a set of accepted organization theory variables for their potential impact on projects across the project life cycle. It then integrates the results of several independently conducted but mutually supporting cross-sectional studies involving over 20 major research and development (R & D) projects. The studies were designed specifically to analyze the differing impact of such accepted organization theory variables over the several life cycle phases of major R & D projects. The purpose is to suggest a set of propositions which will allow the practitioner and theoretician to predict the behavior of projects through their life cycles in terms of accepted organization theory variables, and

---

**Numbeied references are given at the end of this chapter.

thus better prepare to manage the unique organizational problems likely to be identified and generated by the fact of the project life cycle's existence.

RESEARCH PROGRAMS AND PROJECTS

The concept of advanced technology research and development projects has resulted from the need to develop ever larger and more complex military, space, and commercial systems products whose production and marketing strategies fail to fit within the constraints of a purely functional organization structure. The largest of these involves efforts, such as the manned moon landing program, which are simply too large for any single organization to deal with alone. These programs are typically sponsored and funded by a government organization such as the National Aeronautics and Space Agency (NASA), the Department of Transportation (DOT), or one of the Department of Defense agencies (the Army, Navy, or Air Force). The government agencies provide the funds and overall managerial coordination. Private corporations, on the other hand, act as sub-contractors and develop their own individual projects which are responsible for achieving major portions of the overall program's goals. For example, when a new aircraft is being developed, there may be one major company responsible for developing the airframe, another for developing the engine, a third for the avionics system, while still another develops the maintenance and support subsystems for the overall program. Similarly, in large privately sponsored projects such as developing new commercial aircraft, ocean-going ships, or offshore resource locating and extracting platforms, one firm might typically perform as the prime, integrating contractor. Specific hardware and other development tasks are then performed on a contract basis by other firms or other divisions of the same firm. Each contributing organization thus supports its own major project whose output must contribute to the overall program objectives, while the sponsoring agency concentrates on coordinating the activities of the contributing organizations to meet overall schedule, budget, and performance objectives. In this situation the term "program" refers to the overall effort to achieve the end objective, a new aircraft or a "man on the moon," while the term "project" refers to an individual organization's activities leading to its specialized goals in support of the program. The basic theory of the life cycle applies to both projects and programs, with the program milestones reflecting major accomplishments in one or more of the supporting projects.

THE PROJECT LIFE CYCLE

Special purpose project organizations are molded around the specific goal or task to be accomplished in support of the program. The essence of project management lies in planning and controlling one-time efforts, and thus encompas- ses the managerial aspects of both projects and programs. The project orga- nization exists only to solve some specified problem, generally one in which the "parent" or sponsoring organization has little or no prior experience. This description summarizes most current major developmental efforts, and explains the dependence of such efforts on the concepts of project management. Both projects and programs draw from the same management theory base. In this chapter, therefore, the term "project management" is used to apply to the man- agement of both "projects" and "programs."

In current major project management efforts, the sponsor usually needs to develop some new product or system within critical predetermined (a) perfor- mance specifications, (b) time constraints, and (c) budget limitations. These, then, define the project's goal. Once the goal is satisfied, the project loses its purpose for existing and is dissolved. The project organization thus exhibits a predictable life cycle: it is frequently said to be "born" when the sponsoring organization accepts responsibility for the problem and decides to accomplish the goal through project management; it "grows" and expands through the planning and initial execution phases as larger increments of money, personnel, production facilities, managerial time, and other such resources are devoted to the effort; it declines as the goal nears completion and resources that are no longer required are reassigned to other work efforts; and it "dies" when respon- sibility for the new product or system is turned over to the ongoing functional organization—the ultimate "customer" of the entire project. The project orga- nization itself exists primarily to focus the undivided attention of key manage- ment and technical specialists on the task of resolving the specified problem across the life span of that problem's existence (6).

As a project proceeds through its life cycle it passes through an identifiable sequence of phases, distinguished from each other by the type of tasks char- acteristic of each phase and frequently by formal decision points at which it is determined if the project has been sufficiently successful in the earlier phases to continue on into the next (7). Different authors identify from three to six separate phases, and there is no agreement on terminology. Nevertheless, gen- eral agreement does exist to indicate that each project phase involves different management considerations and presents different tasks to be performed (8). It should be noted that this involves two distinctly different views of the project. Table 12-1 identifies four project phases and specifies the general actions that must be taken by the sponsoring organization's management, and later by the senior project management, during each phase. Figure 12-1, on the other hand, identifies the same life cycle phases but defines them in terms of the type of tasks that must be accomplished in that phase to prepare for transition into the next. In modern, major, high technology research and development programs, the transition points between phases may be marked by formal program

Table 12-1. Managerial actions by project phase.

PHASE I CONCEPTUAL	PHASE II PLANNING	PHASE III EXECUTION	PHASE IV TERMINATION
Determine that a project is needed.	Define the project organization approach.	Perform the work of the project, (i.e., design, construction, production, site activation, testing, delivery, etc.)	Assist in transfer of project product.
Establish goals.	Define project targets.		Transfer human and nonhuman resources to other organizations.
Estimate the resources the organization is willing to commit.	Prepare schedule for execution phase.		
	Define and allocate tasks and resources.		
"Sell" the organization on the need for a project organization.	Build the project team.		Transfer or complete commitments
			Terminate project
Make key personnel appointments.			Reward personnel

reviews held by the highest level of management in the sponsoring organization. These reviews are designed to authorize the resource expenditures necessary for the project to proceed into the next phase. It thus appears reasonable to classify projects according to the phase of the life cycle they are engaged in at the time of study, and to analyze the major organizational variables affecting project management in terms of their impact in the different phases of the project life cycle.

RELATIVE ORGANIZATIONAL VARIABLES

A large number of variables have been investigated over the years for their effect on the ongoing, traditional type of organization. Those variables discussed below were analyzed for their relevance to project management because of their wide acceptance as important variables in analyzing organizations and because a research-based body of knowledge has developed concerning each. All of these variables—organizational climate, conflict, satisfaction, size, and structure (level of bureaucracy)—are free to change as a project progresses through its life cycle. In addition, the project-peculiar variable "phase of project life cycle," discussed previously, requires further elaboration as it relates to the more universally applicable variables.

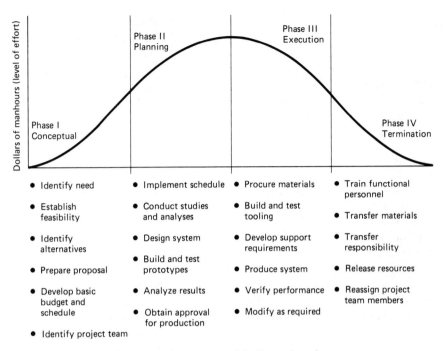

Figure 12-1. Tasks accomplished by project phase.

Organizational Climate

Organizational climate is a description of the organization as a whole (9). Litwin and Stringer defined organizational climate as " . . . a set of measurable properties of the work environment perceived directly or indirectly by the people who live and work in this environment and assumed to influence their motivation and behavior" (10). These authors went on to suggest that both satisfaction and performance are affected by climate. Hellriegel and Slocum in their review of the literature cited several studies that clearly indicated a relationship between job satisfaction and organizational climate (11). However, the nature of the relationship between climate and performance is less clear. Although Likert (12) and Marrow, Bowers, and Seashore (13) found a more positive climate to be associated with higher productivity, Hellriegel and Slocum (11) cited both support and nonsupport for this finding and concluded there was no consistent relationship. The linkage, if any exists, may be indirect. Other variables may intervene between climate and performance. In addition to job satisfaction, already mentioned, intervening variables of particular interest may include conflict sources, conflict intensity, and conflict resolution modes. Climate may "cause" individuals to perceive more or less satisfaction with their work and to consequently be motivated more or less to perform to their capability. With respect to conflict, differing sources and intensities of conflict may result from or influence the climate. The combination of climate and conflict sources may in essence dictate or at least constrain the appropriateness of conflict resolution techniques. Use of these techniques may in turn influence climate and satisfaction.

Conflict

The essence of project management is that it is interfunctional and is frequently in conflict with the normal organizational structure, leading to a natural conflict system (14). The ability of the project manager to foster useful conflict, or to convert disruptive to useful conflict, can often determine his degree of success in achieving the project's goals (15). Thus one of the project manager's key functions is to maintain, in the face of conflicting objectives, a reasonable degree of harmony among the many organizational elements contributing to the project. Research conducted by Evan is important in confirming that differences in conflict do exist between the traditional functional organization and the project organization (16). Since both size and formalization of project organizations may vary over the life cycle, it would appear logical to investigate the changes in conflict that could also develop. Thamhain and Wilemon have done so for a variety of small, industrial projects. They found that the mean intensity of conflict from all sources, the pattern of conflict arising from various specified sources, and the conflict resolution modes used by project managers all vary systematically over the project life cycle (17). The purpose of one study (18) reported later in this chapter was to extend the Wilemon and Thamhain findings to determine their relevance to the major R & D project environment.

Job Satisfaction

Payne et al. described job satisfaction as an individual's affective response to his job (9). Although long a subject of research, the relationship of job satisfaction to performance is by no means settled. The preponderance of evidence seems to indicate that the ties between job satisfaction and productivity or other measures of performance are weak or inconclusive (19). However, even the weak indicators of such a relationship should not be put aside lightly (20). In addition, there is conceptual appeal that such a link ought to exist in many situations.

Organization Size

Size has been shown to have a strong effect on perceived organizational climate in several manufacturing organizations. Payne and Mansfield, using a modified Business Organization Climate Index, reported a relatively strong positive relationship between size and most climate scales (21). Particularly noteworthy were the reported strong relationships between size and readiness to innovate, task orientation, job challenge, and scientific and technical orientation. All of these are climate dimensions that could be expected in many project organizations. Size may also be related to climate and other behavioral variables indirectly through its influence on the nature of the organization. Research has generally shown the existence of a positive relationship between size and organizational formalization (22). Increased size may dictate more links in the scalar chain, requiring greater formalization of communication and reporting systems. Increased size may also permit economies through greater functional specialization. As a consequence the larger project organization may tend to be more functionally structured or mechanistic in nature.

Level of Bureaucracy

The level of bureaucracy may be defined as a continuum ranging from a mechanistic to an organic organizational structure. A mechanistic structure refers to an organization with communication directed primarily downward, high formalization of rules and procedures, adherence to the chain of command, low intergroup cooperation, and infrequent task feedback. An organic structure is characterized by high intergroup cooperation, frequent task feedback, open communication channels, low formalization of rules and procedures, and a lack of adherence to the chain of command. The latter characteristics describe the usual conception of a project organization. However, in large projects, particularly those related to major advanced technology research and development programs, managers such as those producing program control documentation or running a project's information system may work in an environment differing little from that of the mechanistic organization where authority generally matches responsibility. A pure project manager on the other hand, operating in an organic environment, may have responsibilities that far outreach his formal authority to marshall and direct the needed resources (15). Major project organizations may thus display a mixture of organic and mechanistic characteristics which could vary over the life cycle and have a major influence on the effectiveness of managerial actions.

Phase of Life Cycle

As a project progresses from the conceptual phase through the termination phase, the relative degree of uncertainty associated with the determination and performance of tasks decreases and the extent to which routine is applied to task accomplishment increases as shown in Figure 12-2. Studies of other types of organizations have shown a general tendency for organizations with either task routineness or reduced environmental uncertainty to become more formalized and centralized, structurally (22). If the same relationship holds true in project organizations, and without the additional influence of organization size, the expectation would be that formalization (or level of bureaucracy) would increase as the project progresses. Further, since the major actions and activities change among the various phases, with differing pressures and problems arising, it should be expected that organizational climate, conflict sources, and conflict intensity would vary.

Based on the support from the literature cited above, and on several years of the authors' personal observation and research experience, Figure 12-3 was developed to demonstrate the relationships predicted to exist among the variables. As implied in the figure, size, degree of formalization (level of bureaucracy), organizational climate, and conflict source and intensity are at least partly a function of the peculiar problems and tasks that differentiate the various life cycle phases. Organizational climate is also probably influenced by the degree of formalization of structure (level of bureaucracy), the general size of the organization itself, and the sources and intensities of conflict. Conversely,

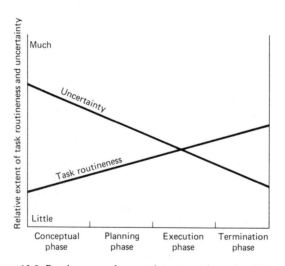

Figure 12-2. Routineness and uncertainty across the project life cycle.

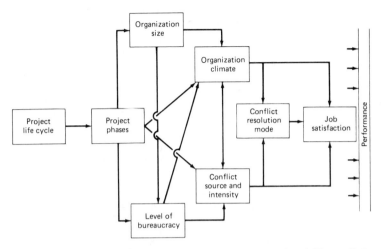

Figure 12-3. Predicted relationships among the organizational variables studied.

the intensity of conflict can be expected to increase as the organizational climate becomes less favorable. The degree of formalization of structure is expected to be a determinant of the sources of conflict as well as its intensity. The modes for resolving conflict should depend on the sources of those conflicts, their intensities, and the favorableness of the organizational climate. Job or work satisfaction is expected to be influenced by the overall organizational climate, the sources of conflict, the intensity of conflict, and the methods employed to resolve those conflicts. In general, the appropriateness of structure for task accomplishment; the extent and sources of conflict; the appropriateness, effectiveness, and acceptability of the methods employed in conflict resolution; the degree of favorableness of organizational climate; and the extent to which team members are satisfied with their work and work situation may all be expected to impact relative project performance.

PROJECT-SPECIFIC STUDIES

The authors have conducted or directed a number of studies designed to analyze the impacts of these traditionally accepted organizational variables over the several life cycle phases of major R & D projects. All of the studies examined major R & D projects in terms of three phases distinguishable from each other by the type of tasks being performed, as well as by clearly defined, formal project reviews resulting in authorization for the project to proceed into the next phase. In several cases it is possible to logically divide the third phase into a third and fourth phase, two separate phases based on the type of tasks being performed. The separate research efforts culminated in the four notable reports

Table 12-2. Research Data.

SOURCE	SAMPLE	DATA COLLECTION	PERTINENT FINDINGS
Lempke and Mann (26)	142 program managers (95% response) randomly drawn from 13 program offices representing three phases of project life cycle.	Questionnaire, personally distributed, yielded data on organizational nature of tasks, phase of life cycle, and size of organization.	Organizations are most project oriented in early phase of project life, least project oriented in middle phase of project life. Organizations are smallest in early phase, largest in middle phase.
Barndt, Larsen, and Ruppert (24) and Haddox and Long(25)	185 program managers (80% response) randomly drawn from 13 program offices representing three phases of project life cycle.	Questionnaire, mailed to subject, yielded data on organizational climate, satisfaction, organizational size, and phase of life cycle.	1. Significant differences in organizational climate exist among phases. 2. Significant differences in organizational climate exist among program offices of different sizes. Organizational climate is correlated with satisfaction.
Eschman and Lee(18)	136 program managers (68% response) randomly drawn from 20 program offices representing four phases of project life cycle.	Questionnaire, personally distributed, yielded data on sources of conflict, intensity of conflict, method of conflict resolution, and phase of life cycle.	Conflict intensity changed across program life cycle, Air Force program managers perceived less intensity of conflict than civilian project managers, and Air Force and civilian project managers agreed on conflict resolution modes across life cycle phase.

1. Findings of the Barndt, Larsen, and Ruppert study.
2. Findings of the Haddox and Long study.

summarized in Table 12-2. All data was obtained from the same organizational environment, although at different times. The sources of data were program offices of the United States Air Force charged with managing the research and development activities associated with acquiring new aircraft weapon systems. The responsibilities of these offices included conceptual studies, concept validation, hardware demonstration, prototype development, test article development and fabrication, test and evaluation, production, modification, and initial support activities. Program offices ranged in size from very small, approximately five individuals, to an office of more than two hundred.

Most data analyzed in the study was generated through use of questionnaires. Standard instruments, modified as necessary, were used to measure satisfaction, organizational climate, source of conflict, conflict intensity, and method of conflict resolution. *Measures of organizational climate* were obtained through use of the short form version of the Likert Profile of Organizational Characteristics (12). The summed score of all questionnaire items may be considered an indicator of the individual's perception of the general style or system of management prevalent in the organization. The average of the scores for all project team personnel sampled in an organization or group of organizations was considered to represent the climate relative to that of other organizations and relative to an ideal climate of openness, support, trust, and participation. *Job satisfaction* was measured by use of the satisfaction scales from the Job Diagnostic Survey short form (23). The seven scales indicated in Table 12-3 provide separate measures of the individual's affective reactions or feelings obtained from actually performing at his job. *Sources of conflict, conflict intensity,* and *method of conflict resolution* were measured using a questionnaire developed by Thamhain and Wilemon (17) modified to fit the Air Force program environment. The questionnaire includes the seven potential conflict sources and five conflict handling modes identified in Table 12-3, essentially measuring the frequency of occurrence of each. Finally, the *level of bureaucracy* was measured with a number of specifically designed questions.

The synthesis presented in this chapter involved extracting values of the major variables from the various studies and matching them with phases of the project life cycle. Analysis was necessarily restricted to identifying and demonstrating differences across life cycle phases. No attempt is made to support the existence of cause and effect relationships.

BEHAVIORAL CHARACTERISTICS OF PROJECTS BY PHASE

The combination of study results supports the existence of marked similarities in the organizational environments of major R & D projects within the identified life cycle phases, while simultaneously identifying several significant differences in the organizational environments characteristic of the separate phases. These similarities and differences are summarized in Table 12-3. Those studies which did not distinguish the execution phase from the termination phase drew most of their data for this portion of the life cycle from projects involved in tasks more descriptive of the execution phase, so it is assumed that the data presented for phases III (execution) and IV (termination) combined more nearly represents projects in phase III of the life cycle.

Table 12-3. Structural and Behavioral Characteristics of Phases.

VARIABLE	PHASE I CONCEPTUAL	PHASE II PLANNING	PHASE III EXECUTION	PHASE IV TERMINATION
SIZE (average number of managerial and technical personnel)	15 (range 11 to 18)	114 (range 49 to 169)	102 (range 42 to 207)	38 (range 30 to 46)
LEVEL OF BUREAUCRACY (average score between pure mechanistic, 1.0, and organistic, 7.0)	5.26	4.70	5.21	
ORGANIZATIONAL CLIMATE (average score, scale 0–720)	550.6-low system 4 (participative)	439.9-mid system 3 (consultative)	485.3-high system 3 (consultative)	
CONFLICT INTENSITY (on scale 0.0 to 3.0)	.704	.672	.621	.443
CONFLICT SOURCES (rank order of sources by intensity of conflict)	1. manpower resources 2. program priorities 3. technical issues 4. schedules 5. admin matters 6. cost objectives 7. personalities	1. program priorities 2. manpower resources 3. technical issues 4. schedules 5. admin matters 6. cost objectives 7. personalities NOTE: Numbers 2 and 3 tied.	1. program priorities 2. technical issues 3. admin matters 4. manpower resources 5. schedules 6. cost objectives 7. personalities	1. program priorities 2. admin matters 3. schedules 4. technical issues 5. manpower resources 6. cost objectives 7. personalities

CONFLICT RESOLUTION MODES (rank order, most to least used)	1. confrontation 2. smoothing 3. compromise 4. withdrawal 5. forcing	1. confrontation 2. compromise 3. smoothing 4. forcing 5. withdrawal	1. confrontation 2. compromise 3. forcing 4. smoothing 5. withdrawal	1. confrontation 2. compromise 3. smoothing 4. withdrawal 5. forcing
SATISFACTION (average score for general satisfaction, internal work motivation, pay satisfaction, security satisfaction, social satisfaction, supervisory satisfaction, growth satisfaction on a scale of 0–7)	Gen Sat - 5.83 IWM - 5.86 Pay Sat - 5.84 Sec Sat - 5.75 Soc Sat - 5.86 Sup Sat - 5.75 Growth Sat - 5.63	Gen Sat - 5.35 IWM - 5.98 Pay Sat - 5.50 Sec Sat - 5.30 Soc Sat - 5.41 Sup Sat - 5.70 Growth Sat - 5.10	Gen Sat - 5.29 IWM - 5.88 Pay Sat - 5.58 Sec Sat - 5.32 Soc Sat - 5.60 Sup Sat - 5.61 Growth Sat - 5.33	

Phase I

Data from projects in the conceptual phase consistently indicates that the teams are small and use a relatively organic type of structure. The overall climate is rated low in the System 4 or participative management portion of Likert's scale. Conflict intensity is highest in this phase. Manpower resources is the most noteworthy source of this conflict, with the next four sources listed grouped closely behind as generators of conflict. While confrontation (in a problem-solving mode) is the favored means of conflict resolution, smoothing and compromise are also well-used techniques. The highest levels of satisfaction are found in this phase for six of the seven measures. Thus the organizational environment of Phase I is indicative of small participative work groups, with the members working together under considerable conflict and with a relatively informal set of work rules. They resolve their differences in a generally collegial manner with apparent concern for the feelings of others, and they derive considerable satisfaction from the work.

These findings are consistent with the theory of the life cycle and with observations of projects in action. This phase is basically concerned with preplanning activities, deciding that a project is required, and establishing the overall objectives and goals. These activities take place either before or during the identification of key personnel for assignment to the project. Thus there are only a few people knowledgeable of the project, and they must work together as a small, cooperative team to identify the work that needs to be performed. This is a truly innovative portion of the project effort, and it is generally accepted that conflict and innovation are necessary partners.

Phase II

Data from projects in the planning phase indicates a substantial increase in project organization size, a multiple of five to eight relative to the sizes encountered in Phase I. The type of structure is generally organic but with significant mechanistic characteristics, while the climate is rated mid-range in a System 3, or consultative, type of organization. Conflict intensity is lower than in Phase I. Program priorities is the predominant conflict source, with the next four listed sources grouped closely together but in a clearly subordinate position. Confrontation and compromise are the preferred conflict resolution modes, while smoothing has decreased and forcing has increased in importance relative to Phase I. Internal work motivation rates high in this phase but is not supported by the other job satisfaction measures, indicating that overall satisfaction is not high in relative terms. The organizational environment of Phase II can be characterized as a relatively large work group organized along semi-organic lines with mechanistic tendencies—a consultative system. The members work together under considerable conflict which arises predominantly from project-oriented priorities, schedules, and technical issues. Differences are resolved in a generally collegial manner, but job satisfaction is not particularly high.

Here is where the project gets planned in detail, where budgets are defined and priorities are established. The work breakdown structure is developed to break the project effort into its individual tasks, while the planning and control networks are designed for imposing project priorities. The work group is expanding rapidly, so many relative strangers must work together. Simultaneously, the group is breaking into sub-units to accomplish different aspects of the task, and these subgroups must immediately compete with others for priorities and resources. There should be little surprise that conflict is high in this phase. Further, since this is only the planning and design phase, many of the participants must recognize that they will not be available several years in the future to see the results of their work. Thus commitment to the project may be difficult to obtain, and consequently job satisfaction may also be difficult to generate and sustain.

Phase III

Data from projects in the execution phase indicates that project sizes are generally comparable to but reflect a wider range than those in Phase II. The type of organization is organic with some mechanistic tendencies, while the climate is rated near the high area of System 3, a consultative but near participative type of organization. Conflict intensity is lower than in Phases I or II, but is still relatively high. Program priorities, technical issues, and administrative procedures are closely grouped as principle sources of conflict, clearly dominating the remaining sources. While confrontation and compromise remain the preferred conflict resolution modes, forcing is also an important technique in this phase. In general, job satisfaction in Phase III appears to be relatively low. It should be remembered in interpreting this data that the level of bureaucracy, the organizational climate, and the satisfaction values were generated from data sources somewhat contaminated with Phase IV-type work tasks. The organizational environment of Phase III can be characterized as a relatively large work group organized along semiorganic lines with some mechanistic overtones. The members work together under a conflict situation arising from priorities and technical issues combined with the administrative procedures necessary to resolve them. Use of power and authority to resolve differences (forcing) is increased in Phase III, while job satisfaction is reduced.

The use of power and authority to resolve differences has long been associated with a relatively low level of job satisfaction. In this phase the job must actually be accomplished. Project personnel are "under the gun" to meet the schedules, budget limits, and performance criteria that earlier planners built into the project as goals. Any mistakes made in earlier projections show up here and must be resolved, along with all technical problems that have developed. Pressures to achieve the goals are intense. Conflict would be expected to be high in this situation. Job satisfaction may be reduced as the current participants see themselves responsible for resolving situations created by the errors and optimism of earlier project personnel.

Phase IV

The data from projects in the termination phase indicates a marked, significant reduction in project size from those in Phases II and III. Conflict intensity is relatively low in this phase, with program priorities, administrative procedures, and schedules being dominant contributions. Confrontation, compromise, and smoothing are the preferred conflict resolution modes. Although not complete, this data indicates some significant differences in the organizational environment of Phase IV relative to Phases II and III. The environment can be characterized as medium-sized groups working under relatively low conflict intensities. In terminating their projects, the participants find that the principle conflicts are generated from project priorities and schedules, with the needed administrative procedures taking on increased significance. Differences are resolved in the collegial mode as was done in the earliest project phases.

This phase represents the end of the project. Those few personnel who remain are involved in turning the completed product over to someone else. Further, they are likely to be preoccupied with finding themselves new jobs, since the ones they currently hold are in the process of being eliminated. At this point, individuals are likely to experience less pressure and to perceive less need to quickly resolve conflicts through forcing. The task is essentially complete, and no amount of effort at this point is likely to change the results. In this situation, low levels of conflict are to be expected.

Reviewing the Life Cycle

Reviewing the findings for each specific project life cycle phase in comparison to each other reveals some interesting relationships. In the most general terms, the life cycle theory is supported, with marked differences occurring in the organizational environments of projects from different phases. More specific analysis indicates that project size clearly is quite different across the phases, with the planning and execution phases having by far the largest project teams, the conceptual phase the smallest, the termination phase having intermediate-sized project teams. The level of bureaucracy parallels this pattern, with the greater bureaucracy corresponding to the greater size, as would be expected.

The level of bureaucracy measure demonstrates statistically significant differences between the planning phase and the conceptual and execution phases at above the 95% level of confidence. Organizational climate also changes markedly across phases, with the early and later phases having projects more representative of System 4, while the middle phases are more System 3-oriented. Statistical tests of the organizational climate scale indicated that all scores were significantly different from each other at the 95% level of confidence (24). Conflict intensity decreases consistently across the phases. The differences between alternate phases are statistically significant above the 95% confidence level, but those between adjacent phases are not (18). Thus there would appear to be a slowly declining trend in conflict intensity across life cycle phases. Both the sources of conflict and the resolution modes change across phases in a manner consistent with the changes in size, level of bureaucracy, and organizational climate. Finally, job satisfaction in general seems to be highest for the smallest, most organic organizations and lower for those organizations most mechanistic in nature.

GENERALIZATIONS

The data referred to in this chapter were drawn from a variety of research efforts using different samples collected at different times over a two-year period. As such, the findings are not directly relatable to one another, and in some cases the observed differences are not statistically significant or cannot be tested for significance. Despite these methodological shortcomings, the synthesis, by noting important differences between projects in different phases, has served to strengthen the belief that there may be extensive variability in internal organizational environments over the life cycle of major projects. The fact that these findings are supported in the available literature as well as by the logic of careful observation lends credence to these documented results. The findings clearly indicate several differences between the projects representing various phases, and suggest others. Based on these differences several very tentative conclusions concerning the internal environments of projects over their life cycle were reached and are presented in the form of the following propositions:

- Individual project organizations tend to be relatively small in the early and late phases of their life cycle, and much larger in their middle phases. This may be a function of the different types of tasks being performed in each specific phase.
- Project organizations tend to be more mechanistic in nature and exhibit less favorable organizational climates in their mid phases than in either the early or late phases of the life cycle. The most favorable organizational

climate and the most organic type of organization is found in the initial phase of the project life cycle. This may be related to the size of the work groups found in the individual phases and to the resulting differences in organization structure.

- As the project progresses in its life cycle, the overall intensity of conflict decreases. Administrative matters and program priorities become relatively more important as sources of conflict, while manpower resources become less important sources of conflict. Cost objectives and individual personalities are relatively unimportant sources of conflict across the life cycle, although the conflicts they generate may be among the most difficult to resolve.

- As conflict resolution modes, smoothing decreases while compromise and forcing increase in relative use over most of the project life cycle. This trend reverses itself in the termination phase of the life cycle. This pattern of changes in conflict resolution modes may be associated with the changes in level of bureaucracy, size, and organizational climate which occur over the life cycle.

- Project organization size is negatively related to the extent of organic (project) orientation in the work group, perceived organizational climate, and the team member's job satisfaction.

- The perceived organizational climate in project organizations is positively related to the extent of organic (project) orientation in the work group, and to the perceived job satisfaction of the team members.

- The smaller the project, the more closely it reflects the characteristics classically recognized as representing project teams—participative, dynamic, and collegial team efforts. Larger efforts clearly display the characteristics of more bureaucratic organizations.

The above relationships suggest that major changes may occur in the organizational and behavioral environments of the single project as it progresses through the phases of its life cycle. Such changes could have numerous implications for managers of project managers and for the project managers themselves.

One major implication of the project life cycle for the manager of project managers is that the idea of choosing a single project manager to see the project completely through its life cycle may need to be discarded, at least for the major, advanced technology projects discussed here. Rather, it may be much more appropriate at the major project phase points to select a new project manager who is familiar with the types of tasks to be performed during the succeeding phase, and who may be best suited to the project environment anticipated to exist during that phase.

While his ideas are by no means universally accepted, Fiedler has shown that the relationship-motivated leader tends to achieve the best performance where tasks are unstructured, leader-member relations are either very good or very poor, and member behavior is influenced by the leader either by direct chain-of-command or through example, esteem, and expertise (27). The implication for the large research project is that a relationship-motivated project manager would achieve the best results in the conceptual or planning phases of the project, where the conditions closely match those specified by Fiedler's work. On the other hand, when tasks are better structured, the leader-member relations are relatively good, and the leader (because of a weak formal structure) can rely only to a limited extent on the direct and formal chain of command to effectively accomplish objectives, a task-motivated leader tends to obtain the best results (27). This set of conditions roughly parallels the situation in the execution and termination phases where organization climate is relatively favorable, tasks are relatively well structured, and the project manager has a less than mechanistic type of organization. Here, then, the best results might be expected from a task-oriented project manager. In addition, differences in the primary sources of conflict between the early and late phases, i.e., manpower resources and program priorities, respectively, further indicate the possibility that different managerial traits and different background experience and preparation may be called for in the project manager during different phases of the project life cycle.

During the early stages of the project, the characteristics of small size, varied tasks, a high degree of uncertainty, and the less formally structured organization appear to foster the more favorable organizational climates and higher levels of job satisfaction. The project manager is thus able to take advantage of the task commitment, the challenge, and the informality of the organic type of organization. Primary managerial functions of the project manager at this time should be to act as a communicator and facilitator, and to provide the various team members with information. The intent is to encourage participation and a team commitment to confronting and resolving conflicts. The goal should be for all team members to cooperate in accomplishing the project's goals, rather than to win an individual's point at the expense of the project.

In the later stages of the project, the project team diminishes from very large during the execution phase to very small toward the end of the termination phase. Here the project manager experiences a moderately formalized structure, perhaps as a legacy from the planning phase where rapid growth, high conflict intensities, and a great deal of environmental turbulence foster formalization in the effort to "get control of the situation." The degree of formalization in the latter phases can also be at least partly attributed to the more routine nature of the tasks during the execution phase, and to the increased importance of technical issues as a source of conflict. A lower level of satisfaction is also experienced during this period, probably due to the higher levels of routine in the work itself, the lack of glory involved in "finishing the job," and personal concerns over future employment. Organizational climate, however, remains relatively formal despite these negative influences. In these later phases, the project manager should carry out the same managerial functions necessary early in the project and, in addition, should devote attention to reducing structural formalization as the project diminishes. This must be done with great care, however, to avoid undue shuffling of personnel or the appearance of demoting professionals unnecessarily. Reducing structure, it should be noted, is not an easy task. The project manager must counteract and overcome the "natural" bureaucratic tendencies of organizations to establish formalized sets of rules and procedures for almost every activity that can remotely be considered repetitive, and by this time the project has had several years to establish such procedures.

The planning phase is characterized by a more formalized mechanistic-type structure and by large size, yet it also demonstrates high levels of uncertainty and conflict. This presents particularly challenging behavioral problems to the project manager. First, the tendency to over-structure the organization must be avoided to prevent hampering the cooperation and participative problem solving so necessary to successful projects. Second, the project manager must respond to the strong demands for establishing effective communication links. The dynamic project situation requires that project personnel generate and transmit information quickly in the face of new developments, establishing and encouraging relatively informal channels. Third, in order to facilitate a team approach to confronting and solving conflicts, the project manager needs to develop an identification with the project effort among the participants, to visibly use confrontation techniques himself, and to reward others for using these techniques. This implies a high degree of visibility and personal leadership.

In concluding this discussion of the project life cycle's behavioral implications for project managers and the managers of project managers, the authors offer these key suggestions:

- The project team size should be kept as small as possible, consistent with being able to accomplish the tasks. This requires a conscious and continuing effort, as there is a tendency to resolve problems by building a larger than necessary organization. The rationale may be to provide visibility in the parent organization, to make sure there are sufficient people to be "on top" of the situation, or simply to increase the project's power base. In any event, the increased number of personnel severely compounds the problems of effectively managing the project.
- Increased formalization of the project's structure (e.g., specialized groups, formal reports, chain of command, specified procedures) should be avoided whenever possible. The project manager should recognize and

exercise the art of trading off the advantages of specialization and efficiency of task accomplishment with the disadvantages of unfavorable organizational climate and poor job satisfaction that may result. These disadvantages may be manifested by reduced identification with the project and a lack of initiative on the part of project members, a situation which can be very costly to the project manager.

● Team members should be encouraged to work jointly to resolve conflicts in a manner that is best for the project as a whole, rather than for any one team member. This involves leadership by example, and places the greatest demands on the project manager. This means establishing open communication channels, taking time out to listen, creating challenging tasks, and praising good performance. This also means good management! The project manager should be prepared to spend a large share of the available time in leadership and communication tasks. If this leaves too little time for tracking technical, schedule, and budget issues, then the preferred solution would be to secure the services of a competent assistant manager to deal with such detail.

REFERENCES

1. Butler, A. G., Jr. "Project Management: A Study in Organizational Conflict." *Academy of Management Journal,* 16:84–101 (March 1973).
2. Cleland, David I., and King, William R. *Systems Analysis and Project Management,* third ed. (New York: McGraw-Hill Book Company, 1983).
3. Adams, J. R., and Barndt, S. E. "A Contingency Model for Project Manager Selection," in *Realities of Project Management.* Proceedings of the 9th Annual Project Management Institute Symposium, Chicago:435–442 (1977).
4. Woodworth, B. M., and Willie, C. T. "A Time Constrained Approach to Resource Leveling in Multi-project Scheduling." *Project Management Quarterly,* 7:26–33 (June 1976).
5. Youker, R. "Organizational Controls in Project Management." *Project Management Quarterly,* 8:18–24 (March 1977).
6. Stewart, John M. "Making Project Management Work," in David I. Cleland and William R. King, eds., *Systems, Organizations, Analysis, Management: A Book of Readings* (New York: McGraw-Hill Book Company, 1969).
7. Archibald, Russell D. *Managing High-Technology Programs and Projects* (New York: John Wiley and Sons, 1976).
8. Roman, Daniel D. *Research and Development Management: The Economics and Administration of Technology* (New York: Appleton-Century-Crofts, 1968).
9. Payne, R. L., Fineman, S., and Wall, T. D. "Organizational Climate and Job Satisfaction: a Conceptual Synthesis." *Organizational Behavior and Human Performance,* 16:45–62 (1976).
10. Litwin, George H., and Stringer, Robert A., Jr. *Motivation and Organizational Climate* (Boston: Harvard University, 1968).
11. Hellriegel, D., and Slocum, J. W., Jr. "Organizational Climate: Measures, Research and Contingencies." *Academy of Management Journal,* 17:255–280 (June 1974).

12. Likert, Rensis. *The Human Organization: Its Management and Value* (New York: McGraw-Hill Book Company, 1967).

13. Marrow, A., Bowers, D., and Seashore, S. *Management by Participation* (New York: Harper and Row, 1967).

14. Kast, Fremont E., and Rosenzweig, James E. *Organization and Management: A Systems Approach,* second ed. (New York: McGraw-Hill Book Company, 1974).

15. Cleland, David I., and King, William R. *Systems Analysis and Project Management* (New York: McGraw-Hill Book Company, 1968).

16. Evan, William M. "Conflict and Performance in R & D Organizations: Some Preliminary Findings." *Industrial Management Review,* 7:37–46 (Fall 1965).

17. Thamhain, Hans J., and Wilemon, David L. "Conflict Management in Project-oriented Work Environments." *Sloan Management Review.* 16:31–50 (Spring 1975).

18. Eschmann, Karl J., and Lee, Jerry S. H. "Conflict in Civilian and Air Force Program/Project Organizations: a Comparative Study." Unpublished master's thesis, School of Systems and Logistics, Air Force Institute of Technology (AU), Wright-Patterson AFB, Ohio (1977).

19. For example, see Vroom, H. Victor. *Work and Motivation* (New York: John Wiley and Sons, 1964).

20. Organ, D. W. "A Reappraisal and Reinterpretation of the Satisfaction-causes-performance Hypothesis." *The Academy of Management Review,* 2:46–53 (January 1977).

21. Payne, R. L., and Mansfield, R. "Relationships of Perceptions of Organizational Climate to Organizational Structure, Context, and Hierarchial Position." *Administrative Science Quarterly,* 18:515–516 (December 1973).

22. Ford, Jeffrey D., and Slocum, John W. Jr. "Size, Technology, Environment, and the Structure of Organizations." *Academy of Management Review,* Vol. 2:561–575 (October 1977).

23. Hackman, R. J., and Oldham, G. R. "The Job Diagnostic Survey: an Instrument for the Diagnosis of Jobs and the Evaluation of Job Redesign Projects." Technical Report No. 4, Department of Administrative Sciences, Yale University (1974).

24. Brandt, S. E., Larsen, J. C., and Ruppert, P. J. "Organizational Climate Changes in the Project Life Cycle." *Research Management,* 20:33–36 (September 1977).

25. Haddox, Donald L., and Long, Neal A. "A Study of Relationships Among Selected Organizational Variables in System Program Offices During the Weapon System Acquisition Process." Unpublished master's thesis, School of Systems and Logistics, Air Force Institute of Technology, Wright-Patterson AFB, Ohio (1976).

26. Lempke, Roger P., and Mann, Greg A. "The Effects of Tenure and Task Orientation on Air Force Program Managers' Role Stress." Unpublished master's thesis, School of Systems and Logistics, Air Force Institute of Technology, Wright-Patterson AFB, Ohio (1976).

27. Fiedler, Fred E., and Chemers, Martin M. *Leadership and Effective Management* (Glenview, Illinois: Scott, Foresman, 1974).

13. Phasing Out the Project

Herbert F. Spirer*

INTRODUCTION

It is much harder to finish than to start a project. The start of a project is a time of excitement; the team is being formed, resources allocated, the client/ customer is enthusiastic and planning efforts are supported by the natural high spirits that go with beginning a new enterprise. The finish of a project is a time of decline; both the client/customer and project personnel are looking toward other new ventures, the plans which carried the project so far are now obsolete, and where the entrepreneurial spirit once existed there is only a concern for a seemingly endless set of details. But the importance of a successful and complete closure is considerable. It is not unusual for a disproportionate share of the balance of payment due on the contract to be withheld pending termination since secondary deliverable items such as spare parts lists and procurement drawings are vital to the customer's interests. The success of future projects can be affected by the way in which project personnel are phased out of the project. A proper closure of the project provides inputs to the post-performance audit and to future project plans by providing bases for rational estimates, and can be the source of extensions of the project into new products and projects.

WHY IS THE PROJECT BEING TERMINATED?

The *natural* termination of a project is a joy to all; it occurs when the project's goals have been met. For example the microprocessor-based control system for testing of the pharmaceutical product successfully completed its acceptance

*Herbert F. Spirer is Professor of Information Management in the School of Business Administration of the University of Connecticut at Stamford. Holding degrees in engineering physics from Cornell University and in operations research from New York University, he was an engineer, project manager and engineering manager prior to joining the faculty of the University. His home study courses in project management for engineering, software development, construction and in engineering department management and quality control have been adopted by over 20 engineering and professional societies. He is a frequent lecturer and seminar leader in project management and consults to many corporations and financial institutions on project management and its integration with strategic planning. He has given papers on project management at meetings of the American Institute of Decision Sciences and the Project Management Institute.

testing in the manufacturing environment in time to support market entry, changes of scope were matched by cost and time reallocations; the new budgetary figures were met. This is a natural termination, but the project is not done yet. The operator's manual is only a copy of an edited manuscript, the parts list does not include all standard designations for parts, engineering drawings have not yet been updated, several forms required by both internal and external entities have not been completed, and so forth.

The *unnatural* termination of a project is always painful to someone; it occurs when some constraint has been violated, when performance is inadequate, or when the project's goals are no longer relevant to overall needs. If not a loss in money or failure to fill a need, it is perceived as an emotional loss with all the consequent problems. The constraints whose violation is most frequently the cause of an unnatural termination are money and time. Although the site borings indicated there should be no problem with the foundations, the partially-erected structure has shifted and the costs of correcting the situation exceed available resources; the project is abandoned. Or, the project to develop a particular experiment for a space vehicle is now projected to run for two weeks beyond the scheduled date under any circumstances. Unfortunately, this spacecraft has a narrow window of time in which to meet its planetary target; an experiment which is two minutes late is of no value.

Performance is often assessed to be inadequate as the consequence of some test of the project. The feasibility test of the prototype results in a clear demonstration of unfeasibility; a new project must be instituted with a new approach. Or, the goal is abandoned. This may be the consequence of a failed test, or the result of political or economic shifts. The decline in the price of fossil fuels can cause the cancellation of a project for synthetic fuels which is meeting all its constraints and goals.

THE TERMINATION OF A PROJECT IS A PROJECT

An understanding of the reasons for a project's termination is as important as an understanding of the goals of the project at its start. When the project manager can sight the end of a project, the task of termination itself fits the classical definition of a project as a one-time unique goal with specific resource constraints (3, p. 4; 1, p. xi).* Research (4) has shown that conflict is believed to increase on projects the less clearly project objectives are understood by project personnel.

Given a commitment to termination as a project, then the question for the project manager is to determine the "profile" of project management tools and techniques to be used to bring this subproject to successful completion. Closure

---

*Numbered references are given at the end of this chapter.

has its special problems and needs which should determine the nature of project management's plans, schedules and uses of personnel.

Just as the tools should be tailored to the special characteristics of the termination phase, so must the choice of project manager be determined by the unique characteristics of project completion. Not all managers have the necessary qualifications to match the tasks of the terminal phase. Nor do all project personnel; the staff is declining as the project comes to a close and management and direction of the decline is a key task for the project manager. The need for a profile of tools adapted to termination, an understanding of the special problems and a temperamental compatability with project closure leads to the identification of project managers uniquely suited to termination of projects. An important mission for managers of project managers is to recognize the need for transferring project authority to such persons.

EMOTIONAL PROBLEMS OF PROJECT TERMINATION

Today we know that the division of our concerns into emotional ("affective") and intellectual ("cognitive") parts is a fundamental attribute of human beings. Such a division is convenient for the management of the termination of a project. Figure 13-1 is a structure tree diagram analogous to a work breakdown structure which illustrates both the general and detailed nature of project termination issues. As can be seen from Figure 13-1, emotional issues have to do primarily with *spirit;* intellectual issues with *detail.* The difficulty of combining spirit with attention to detail accounts for many of the problems both in management and staff of ending projects.

For the project staff, both those directly reporting to the project manager and those with matrix relationships we have the following emotional issues:

- *Fear of no future work.* The fact that the project is terminating is no mystery to anyone. What is less clear is whether there is plenty of work out there for the project staff. Even when there are other projects needing support, many individuals on the project staff fear for their continued employment; there need be no rational basis for such fears. The consequence is a "philosophy of incompletion," where it seems that no one really wants to complete their task. "Foot dragging" is a common practice in termination phases. Design documents take remarkably long to retrieve, instructions are repeatedly misunderstood or not acted upon, tools disappear or are unavailable, tasks are stopped dead when the slightest impediment is met, and staff may seem to be working in slow motion.
- *Loss of interest in tasks remaining.* The start of a project involves challenging and interesting tasks: problems to be solved, new methods to be applied, resources to be allocated. The end of a project involves familiar

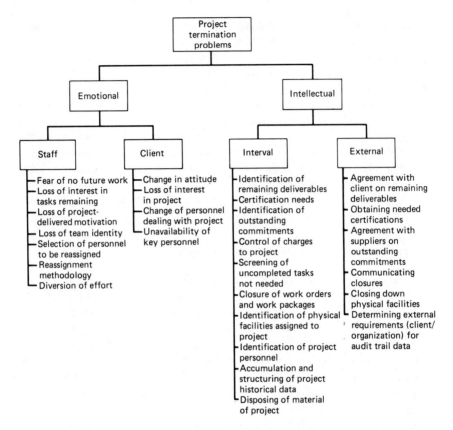

Figure 13-1. Work breakdown structure for problems of project termination.

and often tedious tasks: documents to be completed, refinement of known techniques and products, and the withdrawal of resources. The "fun" has gone out of the tasks and the result can be an inability to keep up the performance of technical people whose knowledge is needed, the continuing efforts of project personnel—often successful—to get reassigned to starting or ongoing projects with more interesting tasks, and poor performance because of the perceived dullness of the tasks.

- *Loss of project-derived motivation.* The concept of a project mission, shared among the project team members, is recognized as one of the practical advantages of a project structure (2). Organizations have supported many types of reward systems to stimulate this motivational factor, including project T-shirts, belt buckles, separate facilities, caps, project newsletters, special stationery, etc. As the project staff is reduced and activities focus on details that do not seem to relate directly to the overall goal, motivation from this source declines.

- *Loss of team identity.* As new personnel are brought into the project to carry out special tasks (e.g., the technical writing of operator's manuals) and long-term project personnel are separated, the perception of the project team as a continuing group dissipates. The closing of the project is seen to be just another job, and the drive to make deadlines is muted.
- *Selection of personnel to be reassigned.* In almost all projects, termination is accompanied by a reduction in personnel needs. A key issue for the project manager is who to reassign, who to keep. It is rare that the project manager has the luxury of making this decision solely on the basis of project needs. The needs of the organization as a whole are balanced against those of the project.
- *Reassignment methodology.* How are the personnel to be reassigned? Will there be a project reassignment office? Are personnel to be reassigned on an ad hoc basis, or will there be single or multiple mass transfers? If reassignment is not carried out consistent with the needs of termination, then many unsatisfactory situations can develop. Other managers may make "raids" on the staff, often with success because after all, "this project is running down anyway." Project team members seek new opportunities while charging time to the project and neglecting their assigned tasks. Inept reassignments can destroy morale.
- *Diversion of effort.* Other tasks have a way of seeming much more important than terminating a project, and both outsiders and insiders lower the priority of termination in their pursuit of other goals. It becomes hard to assure that project personnel are all actually devoting their time to the project; in matrix organizations the functional managers can make it quite clear to their employees how *they* perceive the priorities.

The term "client" refers to the internal or external customer (or "user") who contracts for the project and its goals. Clients are also affected by the transition of the project to a termination stage and the project manager must deal with:

- *Change in attitude.* The "steam" has gone out of the project and it carries in the customer's mind the legacy of its problems. Even where performance of the major deliverables has been satisfactory, customer's agents recall the times when compromises were made, milestones missed—memory of the petty difficulties takes over.
- *Loss of interest.* This is the counterpart of the loss of interest on the part of project staff. The excitement, the new challenges and not unimportantly, the opportunity to allocate resources generously, lie elsewhere in starting projects. There are deals to be made, authority to be delegated, technical challenges to be met, contracts to be formulated, and all the excitement of start-up to be found on new projects. To many clients and customers the closing project is a nuisance with no compensating rewards.

- *Change of personnel dealing with project.* In both technical and managerial areas, the "first team" withdraws. The lead designers move to starting projects where technical challenges exist, as opposed to the detail work of termination. The managers who are also leaders are moved out; the best inspectors, contract administrators, technicians and project officers are moved to other jobs. As the overall need for such services declines, the numbers must also fall and specialists in the project must be replaced by personnel who will do both inspection and documentation.
- *Unavailability of key personnel.* Personnel at the client/customer location whose special skills are important to tasks remaining may be unavailable due to reassignment or to geographical changes. The customer-engineer who knows the source of specifications for the exotic materials is now physically remote and does not return calls. The contract administrator who can give definitive interpretations of contractual boilerplate is no longer with the customer's organization.

RESOLUTION OF THE EMOTIONAL PROBLEMS

In large part, the emotional problems affecting termination are similar for both project staff and the client. They come from the natural shifts that must take place in response to the different needs, and how individuals see those changes affecting their self-interest and workplace activities. Despite these similarities in cause, the project manager must deal with them differently. With regard to the project staff and internal issues, the project manager has authority, influence and no small amount of power. But with regard to the client, the project manager has no authority, minimal influence and negligible power.

In carrying out termination within the performing organization, the project manager has all the managerial and leadership tools available that were there for the startup and middle phases; it is only a question of modifying them to present needs. However, with regard to the client, the project manager has primarily only two motivators: the desire of the client to "get the project off the books" with the minimum difficulty and minimum future administrative problems, and the desire not to have documentation, spare parts, and similar support functions become a problem. By recognizing the nature of the problems and the motivators available, the project manager can resolve many of the emotional problems of project termination.

No matter how spirited the project staff, how much the organization has shown its commitment to long term employment for all employees, or how large the backlog of project work, the project manager should never assume that *any* employee on the project is free from the concern for future work. Even in organizations where there has never—in decades—been a single layoff or reduction in work at the end of a project there will be such a concern, implicit or explicit. And where there has been a tradition of force reduction at the end of projects, such concern is guaranteed. Thus, even in the absence of any expressed concern for this issue, the project manager should continually communicate the truth about the prospects for future work for project staff. Of course, if there is no future work and the project manager keeps the staff going with promises of continued employment, that project manager will have serious trouble getting anything done in the future.

The project manager should make clear to the staff as a whole and then to each individual the nature of backlogged work and the pattern of reassignment. Open sessions where the project manager meets with the assembled staff and fields questions pertaining to future prospects can gain a great deal of support for project closeout work. Such a meeting should be held when the project termination phase is defined (as described below) and repeated when the project manager senses the concern rising about these issues. These concerns are often the cause behind failures to close out individual tasks, failures to follow out agreed instructions ("I don't remember you asking for that."), absences, tardiness, disappearances of workers, slow performance. The project manager should be positive, not punitive or authoritarian. Remember that whether or not the fear is rational, it is a genuine fear. It is a characteristic of leadership to be able to deal with these fears.

To offset the loss of interest in tasks, project-derived motivation and team identity, the project manager must recreate the project spirit. This can be done by the following:

- *Define the project termination as a project.* Make it clear that closeout has its own project identity. Some project managers give the closeout its own project name. Startup meetings for the beginning of the termination phase help to establish the concept that there *is* a well-defined goal to be met— closing out the job properly.
- *Provide a team identity.* Give the project a name. If the team is large and/ or widespread, have a closeout newsletter. It is not unheard of for projects to issue T-shirts, caps, etc. The modest investment in such items is well repaid. There are cases where project managers have paid for them where the organization would not, because these tools of identification increase the chances of successful completion and the personal cost is minimal compared to the project manager's long-term benefits from the success that motivation can bring.
- *Bring the team together frequently.* As discussed, the team members change as the closeout needs change and there is a tendency to allow staff to operate loosely as individuals rather than as a team with a common goal. To offset this and to improve communications, use regular get-togethers. We deliberately do not say "meetings," for this implies lengthy

sit-down sessions. Such meetings have their place in the closeout, but to maintain spirit the project manager should use stand-up sessions. These are limited in length for physiological reasons and give the project manager the opportunity to quickly introduce new members, announce reassignments, talk about new work following the termination of the project and to deal with problems and schedules within a team framework. Stand-up meetings held once a week or even daily on fast-moving projects, limited to ten minutes, can become so much a part of the project identity and process that a chance omission will result in dozens of inquiries from staff.

- *Get out to the project staff.* It is not always possible to bring all the project staff together on a regular basis. Some projects are geographically dispersed, project personnel may have assignments to other jobs or functions, and job requirements may work against full attendance. The project manager offsets these problems by getting out of the project office and providing, with his presence, the sense of identity, the connection to the project office and the communications link.

The problems pertaining to reassignment, selection of personnel to be reassigned and the method of reassignment, are essential to terminating projects. As the project terminates, you need to retain people with the greatest flexibility, the most independence, the best sense for detail and with the highest level of skill. Flexibility and skills are needed to focus on any of the different tasks that may arise. Independence is needed because of the other emotional problems pertaining to closure. And a feel for detail is needed so that no pieces are left hanging.

The methodology of reassignment should reassure personnel of their future with the organization. It should also be consistent with keeping a highly motivated work force. Together, the needs of selection and methodology for reassignment lead to the following guidelines:

- *Make each reassignment decision a conscious, deliberate choice.* Think through each reassignment decision, weighing the factors in each case. Don't make blanket decisions ("drop all electrical engineers"); they will come back to haunt you and be resented by staff.
- *Hold the best personnel.* They will be able to deal with the breadth of problems and they usually have the best feel for details.
- *Carry out reassignments openly.* Make sure that the project staff knows what you are doing to assure reassignment; don't let them find out about reassignment from someone else. Knowing what you are doing will reassure them as to their future.
- *Play an active role in reassignment.* Don't wait for the mechanics of reassignment to carry out functions in due course. Is personnel playing a lead-

ing role? Then get with them early on and offer your support.
even want to seek out opportunities for some key peopl.
organization.

To avoid diversion of effort of the project team as it reduces in size and perceived importance, the project manager must attend to the priorities of both the individual staff members and functional managers. This calls for constant communication with both, and a continuing effort to maintain their understanding of the importance—to the organization and to their own futures—of an orderly and complete closeout.

Among the staff, the project manager's task is to maintain spirit by actions within the manager's scope in dealing with the staff. However, the project manager has neither the authority nor the capacity to reward the client. The client's interest and support must be maintained by appeal to the common interest of client and project manager: a speedy and complete closeout. The project manager can get cooperation from the client personnel at all levels by stressing the following benefits from an orderly and systematic closeout:

- *Personal and organizational credit for closure.* Both the individuals and their organizations gain credit when there are no loose ends and a project coming to close is "wiped off the books" in an orderly manner.
- *Availability of future support for the project's deliverables.* A proper termination of the project means that spare parts will be available years later, manuals will be complete and drawings up-to-date.

INTELLECTUAL PROBLEMS OF PROJECT TERMINATION

The concern for *detail* is dominant among the intellectual issues. Figure 13-1 is a summary in graphic form which shows that these issues can be put into two categories: internal and external. Internal issues are those concerned with the project itself and its staff:

- *Identification of remaining deliverables.* The contract or other governing document specifies the deliverables, such as tooling, test procedures, spare parts, spare parts lists, drawings, manuals, fixtures, shipping containers, restoration of modified facilities to original form, etc. If the project manager does not match delivered items against contractual deliverables to determine what must be done, there is the danger of omissions, which will be found by contract administrators, auditors or other client representatives at a time when the costs of completion are higher.
- *Certification needs.* Certificates of conformance with environmental or regulatory standards may be a part of the contract requirements or

implicit (such as UL approval). It is not infrequent for test procedures to require multiple certifications.

- *Identification of outstanding commitments.* It can happen in any project, especially those of large scope and time duration: project closeout is almost finished and a vendor delivers a carload of components which are not needed and come as a complete surprise. The best of commitment records can miss items, cancellations are mishandled but never brought up for attention, or a genuine mistake is made. Less dramatic, but just as important is the commitment which is properly recorded, still outstanding but not needed.
- *Control of charges to the project.* Towards the end of the project, its charge accounts have become known to a large army of employees; deliberately or inadvertently they may charge to the project although not working on it.
- *Screening of uncompleted tasks not needed.* All tasks being worked on may not be needed. It is not uncommon for these "tag ends" to persist to the very end of the project.
- *Closure of work orders and work packages.* Once uncompleted but unneeded tasks have been identified, their formal authorizations must be ended. Also, tasks which have been completed may be carried on the records of the project as still open to charges; they must be tracked down and closed.
- *Identification of physical facilities assigned to the project.* During the course of the project, physical facilities—buildings, warehouses, typewriters, test equipment, machine tools, cars, trucks, etc.—may have been assigned to the project. At worst, they are incurring charges against the product although they are not needed. At best, the project management has a responsibility for their care and redirection to projects where they can provide a benefit to offset their cost.
- *Identification of project personnel.* The manager of compensation for a major company reports that the first thing he does in entering a new facility is to ask the line manager for a list of personnel, which he then compares with a physical census of employees in the operation— the two lists rarely agree. It is possible for personnel to be working on the project in a remote location or carrying out tasks which are no longer under supervision.
- *Accumulation and structuring of project historical data.* A project history can provide support in post-project disputes, is the basis for audits, puts on record technical and managerial achievements thereby making them available to others in the organization, is a guide to the management of future projects, is the basis for better estimates of costs in the future, and gives credit where it is due.

- *Disposing of project material.* The project accumulates quantities of expendables, raw materials, components, partially-finished assemblies, rejected units, files, catalogs, etc. These must be disposed of, for use if possible, or for scrap if no other use can be seen.
- *Agreement with client on remaining deliverables.* Interpretation of contractual statements is always necessary; at this stage much more is known about the exact nature of the delivered items and the specific requirements to be imposed on remaining deliverables, and there can be contractual items which are no longer needed. There may be negotiation with respect to the exact nature of the deliverables, and possible deletions and additions as tradeoffs against the deletions. Every such modification or clarification is a potential change of scope and must be treated (involvement of contracts office, sales, etc.) and documented (change order, change of scope, contract modification, letter of agreement, etc.) as such.
- *Obtaining needed certifications.* Each certification has the potential of being a project in its own right. The deliverables—in the sense of the specific documents or models required—must be determined and assembled. The appropriate path for gaining certification must be found, which is in itself a demanding task.
- *Agreement with suppliers on outstanding commitments.* As discussed in regard to internal factors, some modification or cancellation of outstanding commitments is likely as the project manager works through them. Negotiations are necessary if costs are to be kept to a minimum and satisfactory relations kept with vendors.
- *Communicating closures.* The project manager must make sure that closure of work orders and packages is fully understood and will be carried out. The shrinking of the project reduces the amount of contact among staff and a conscious effort is usually needed to assure that work has been stopped and closeout requirements met (such as accumulation of charges, test results, delivery of fixtures, etc.).
- *Closing down physical facilities.* Physical facilities external to the project can require concentrated efforts for closure. Retrieval of capital and operating equipment which has been installed or lent can be difficult. In certain space projects where equipment and facilities were maintained in other countries, closure is hampered by governments refusing to allow removal—a physical hostage for which a ransom may have to be paid.
- *Determining external requirements for audit trail data.* Different clients/ customers have different requirements for retention of records in order to make it possible to perform audits after the termination of the project. These may or may not be readily available as part of the contract. Often they must be determined through references given in the contract, or by specific agreement with the client as to what is to be kept.

RESOLUTION OF THE INTELLECTUAL PROBLEMS

To deal with these problems, the project manager brings to bear an array of analytical tools—mostly graphical—and a special set of personal skills. First we present the analytical tools for the management of termination:

- *Tree diagrams.* Tree diagrams are model hierarchies which are useful in organizing project entities when the project manager plans communication to project staff, other departments and clients. Figure 13-1 is a tree diagram and as it stands may be useful to some project managers in organizing and communicating the tasks of closeout. Figure 13-2 is another tree diagram—similar to a work breakdown structure—for organizing elements of work in a project termination. Figure 13-2 is a fragment of a particular project used here to give an example of a tree's use; the tree must fit the particular project. Tree diagrams may be used to track deliverables remaining. If there was a work breakdown structure for the start of the project, then the delivered items are crossed off; the remaining deliverables will thereby be emphasized. In the absence of such a work breakdown structure, the termination project manager can create one from the contractual documents and cross off delivered items. Similarly, tree diagrams can be used to track outstanding work orders, where the first level of the tree can be the performing departments and the same graphical approach of crossing out closed work orders can be used.
- *Matrices.* Matrix models are useful when two or three entities must be related. For example, in determination of certification needs and managing the completion of certification, the two entities may be *product* and

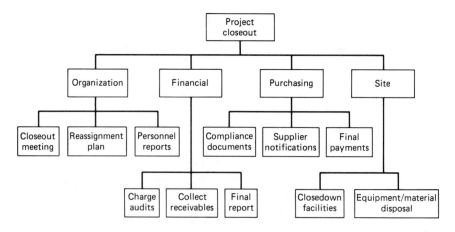

Figure 13-2. Tree diagram for a project termination.

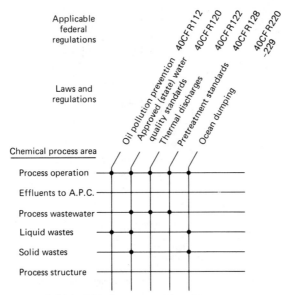

Note: Solid dot (●) indicates potential regulatory concern.

Figure 13-3. Matrix model for product versus governing specification (a portion).

governing specification. Figure 13-3 shows how a matrix model may be used to collect information concerning the relationship between product and governing specification. Once created in the process of collecting and organizing the information, this matrix becomes a reference for everyone working on the job and a means of communication. Checking the relationships for accuracy is quite easy with a model such as Figure 13-3. A typical three-entity case occurs in dealing with outside commitments, as shown in Figure 13-4. Here, the status of the commitment as well as the vendor is of interest; status is signified by the code letter in the box corresponding to the intersection of vendor and commitment. Matrix models for three entities are used to show responsibilities of differing levels. Figure 13-5 is for the assignment of level of responsibility of different individuals in meeting the records of a project. Here, the nature of responsibility and input function is shown by a code letter at the intersection points. The need for matrix models of this type is greatest when project personnel are shifting, when departmental boundaries are crossed, when it is important not to miss any details, etc., as is the case in project termination. The use of matrix models is limited only by the imagination of the project manager.

● *Lists.* Lists become the project manager's primary planning and control

	Amtel	Matarol	Pilog	State semi	Macropolis
Z80 chips	N	D			C
8080 chips	C		C		I
96K RAM	I		C		N
48K RAM	D			N	D
4K ROM	D		C		I
EPROMs	N		C		D

Note:
D, to take delivery.
N, in negotiation.
I, awaiting information.
C, closed.
Blank indicates no commitment,
past or present.

Figure 13-4. Matrix model for relationship among commitment, vendor and status.

	Vice president operations	Quality assurance manager	Director of projects	Project manager	Task engineer	Automatic equip. manager
Quality assurance manual	A	P				
QA procedure index	A	P				
QA audit schedule			P/E	R		
Drawings auto equipment	A				P	R
Drawings calibration blocks				A	P	
Spare parts specifications			A	R	P	
Calculation notebooks			A	R	P	P

Note:
P — Prepare
A — Approve
R — Review
E — Execute

Figure 13-5. Matrix model for assignment of responsibility for records in project termination.

FINANCIAL	Responsible person/dept	Due date	Remarks
Close work orders			
Close task accounts			
Audit charges			
Close payables			
Collect receivables			
Terminate commitments			
Prepare final cost summary			

DOCUMENTATION

Spare parts list			
Design drawings			
Procurement specs			
Equipment specs			
Test procedures			
Parts lists			
Maintenance manuals			

Figure 13-6. Section of checklist for project termination.

tool. This is a direct result of the nature of closeout, where every item must be accounted for finally; there can be no tasks left outstanding and undone. By screening documents and discussing with those concerned (internal and external to the project), the project manager produces listings of tasks to be done. At higher levels, these listings may be converted to trees to provide structure and quick graphic communication, to matrices where interaction is involved. To the extent that task interdependence is important, a network plan (CPM/PERT) may be prepared. But for the short term of the project termination and for weekly and daily supervision, the project manager will work from lists—checklists if they are convenient for indicating what has been done. Figure 13-6 shows part of such a checklist. It is not unusual for the project manager to have a file or notebook of such checklists, one for each major area of activity.[1] To provide a good audit trail, the dates when each task is completed should be marked

---

[1] An example of a checklist for project closeout appears in Archibald, Russell D. *Managing High-Technology Programs and Projects* (John Wiley & Sons, New York, 1976), Appendix C.

on the checklist. Micro- and mini-computers can be used to maintain such lists using "data base management" programs of modest size and cost; an adequate program package costing less than a week's pay for a clerical worker can be used on a microcomputer costing less than a month's pay for an engineer to provide continually-available listings for the project manager, free from recurring costs and the difficulties of dealing with a centralized information system.

The personal attributes needed by the project manager responsible for termination of a project include the following:

- *Knowledge of financial systems and accounting.* The concerns of the closeout project manager are primarily managerial, especially in those aspects concerned with cost and accounting. The project manager must understand cost accounting principles and systems. The manager's knowledge must go beyond the system of the project's organization, since getting agreement on outstanding commitments may often require knowledge of the vendor's accounting system. Control of charges similarly calls for understanding of cost accounting.
- *Technical knowledge of the project.* The project manager need not be capable of carrying out the design work of the project, but must be able to understand it. To specify deliverables, to screen tasks for need, to close down facilities, to safely dispose of equipment and material, the project manager must know what is going on technically; managerial skills alone are not adequate.
- *Negotiating skills.* Both internally and externally, negotiation plays a large part in closure. Without skill at negotiating, the project manager will have trouble in assisting personnel reassignment, in disposing of project material, in getting agreement on deliverables and commitments, in obtaining certifications, in closing down physical facilities and determining audit requirements. There are many successful *styles* of negotiation, and it is only necessary that the project manager be master of at least one. To have no skill at negotiation means extensive delay and cost in removing minor obstacles—and project termination is about rapidly removing obstacles at the best cost.
- *A sense of urgency concerning details.* There are many times during the initial phases of a project when details can be bypassed and when the best strategy is to focus on the "big picture." However, the termination of a project is about the trees, and not the forest. Some managers are good in dealing with the big picture, some are good with details and a rare few are good at both.

THE END IS THE BEGINNING

A complete project termination is a necessity from the standpoint of costs and goodwill. Because both project personnel and purposes are highly result-oriented, it is much too common to have the major deliverables perform well but the project end delayed for months and even years. The desire and capacity to bring the job to a close are essential parts of the success of project organizations. A timely, complete closeout of a project shows good management and sets the stage for further relationships between the client/customer and the project organization. The last task of the project manager terminating a project is to search for opportunities for either extensions of the project or new business—related to this project or not. By seeking such opportunities and documenting them, the project manager ensures that the end of one project is the beginning of others.

REFERENCES

1. Lock, Dennis. *Project Management* (Epping: Gower Press, 1979).
2. Middleton, C. J. "How to Set Up a Project Organization." *Harvard Business Review Reprint Series*, No. 67208.
3. Mulvaney, John. *Analysis Bar Charting*. Washington: Management Planning and Control Systems, 1977.
4. Thamhain, Hans J., and Wilemon, David L. "Diagnosing Conflict Determinants in Project Management." *IEEE Transactions on Management. EM-22*, Number 1 (February 1975).

Section V
Project Planning

In Chapter 14, Geoffrey H. A. Morton discusses project planning from the standpoint of human dynamics. In effect, this is an overview of project planning, since it considers the relationships among humans, their motivations, the obtaining of information and the potential for use of formal planning tools such as network planning.

Gary D. Lavold presents the work breakdown structure (WBS) in Chapter 15. The WBS is one of the basic tools of project planning. Lavold discusses its role and value in various phases of project planning.

The best-known tools of project planning—network plans—are reviewed by Joseph J. Moder in Chapter 16. Network plans, useful in both project planning and control, vary from the simple to the complex, with varying data requirements and ease of use. Moder reviews a wide range of these techniques from which the most appropriate one may be selected.

In Chapter 17, Robert S. Sullivan and Jack C. Hayya discuss stochastic network analysis—a sophisticated set of procedures that emanate from PERT—the original network planning tool that allowed for probabilities to be brought into project planning. Chapter 17 reviews and compares a number of stochastic approaches—"bounding distribution," Monte Carlo simulation and a variance reduction technique called the "antithetic variate method." (Please note that this chapter is more complex and mathematical than most of the others in the *Handbook*.)

In Chapter 18, the linear responsibility chart (LRC)—a powerful tool of organizational planning—is discussed by David I. Cleland and William R. King. The LRC is shown to have a variety of uses in the organization as well as in the project.

In Chapter 19, Harold Kerzner, discusses the pricing dimension of project planning. Pricing requires that a work breakdown structure (Chapter 15) first be developed. Then, it can be "priced out." Kerzner relates pricing to the WBS as well as to other planning tools—the linear responsibility chart (Chapter 18) and network plans (Chapter 16).

The unique issues of planning in a multi-project environment are treated by James H. Reedy in Chapter 20. He relates the problems of the multi-project environment to a system—Multiproject Management System—that may facilitate planning in this complex project situation.

14. Human Dynamics in Project Planning

Geoffrey H. A. Morton*

Our experiences with individuals, with groups and with organizations form the realm of human dynamics. These experiences reflect our history and shape our future. The purpose of this chapter is to illuminate some common, though often invisible, patterns of human dynamics in project planning. We shall look in particular at the role of the planning engineer.

The spread of project network analysis in the sixties led to the creation of a new job: the job of the planning engineer, a specialist in project planning and control. Network analysis, it was believed, would improve the management of large projects, and the planning engineer was the person to implement this novel technique. We now know that effective project planning depends more on the structure and maintenance of information systems than on the use of network analysis, and that the job of the planning engineer requires a deep understanding of the human dynamics of the project environment. The planning engineer has become an organizational psychologist.

Thus to understand the role of the planner it is also necessary to understand the behavior of the project organization. One problem with much research on organizational behavior is that, having observed that real life in organizations is complex and ambiguous, it abandons the search for general principles. But there are some basic ideas that the planner can use in his everyday work to change the course of the project.

In this chapter we will first introduce some human dimensions of project planning, and then address four problems that a planner must face, showing how he may overcome them:

1. Winning genuine commitment to project planning.
2. Planning at a manageable level of detail.
3. Collecting meaningful progress information.
4. Motivating effective remedial action.

---

*Geoffrey Morton, a consultant in the London office of McKinsey & Company, has ten years of experience in the planning of mining, manufacturing and construction projects in Africa, Europe and the Middle East.

Each of these problems exposes different facets of the human side of project management, and each problem sheds light on the skills and role of the planning engineer. Finally, we will look at the implications of effective planning for project management.

THE HUMAN SIDE OF PLANNING

It is naive to think of planning as simply an abstract, intellectual exercise divorced from the human side of the project organization. Since we manage the project by managing people, the human and technical aspects are inseparable, and the human dimensions are a legitimate concern of management. But there is a wide gap between the mechanics of network analysis and the realities of an organic world of constantly changing relationships. Emphasis on elaborate quantitative techniques without consideration for the diverse and conflicting motives of individuals and groups within the project is, therefore, a mistake.

Planning aims both to support informed decision-making and to stimulate creative problem-solving throughout the organization. When we include human factors in the analysis, we find that there is no easy way to make such a contribution. Most projects are not simple and cannot be divided up in such a way that they become simple. They are messy, and management must try to understand all their dimensions. Planning, if it is to embrace human subtleties, may turn out incomplete, disjointed and subjective.

Three human dimensions of project planning are especially worthy of consideration:

1. The subjective nature of planning.
2. The aversion to tough thinking.
3. The seductiveness of computer systems.

The Subjective Nature of Planning

Our perceptions of the future have limited reality; they are primarily illusions. Plans, therefore, are models of such illusions. So one determinant of the quality of plans—measured in terms of their value in decision-making—is the quality of the perception of the planner. Another determinant is his negotiating ability.

The process of planning is a process of resource allocation. Planning is a dynamic process by which contributing and affected groups reach agreement. This consensus is recorded in revised plans that provide a framework for decision-making for some time ahead. While planning discussions are superficially to do with programs, underneath they have much to do with the power and position of constituent groups. Indeed, some kinds of planning are entirely dependent on negotiation. The contractual duration of a project, for example, will often be solely determined by competitive and marketing considerations at the tender stage rather than by any analysis of the program.

The key resource we are allocating in this process is time. But time is a very special kind of resource. Perceptions of it are highly subjective. Moreover, it is perishable; it cannot be stored in banks or bought with money. So time, while we still have it, must be well spent. But time at the end of a project, when it has become scarce, is more valued than time at the start of a project, when it is plentiful. The planner may seek to compensate for these distortions by arguing for contingency time toward the end of the project. Hence the proportions of the ultimate program depend upon his perception and persuasiveness. The plans that result are subjective in nature.

The Aversion to Tough Thinking

Not only does planning aim to support informed decision making, but it also seeks to stimulate creative problem solving throughout the organization. This second contribution is important because there seems to be a widespread human aversion to tough thinking. Parkinson called this phenomenon his Bicycle-Shed Principle: the board of directors would much rather discuss the specifics of a new bicycle-shed for their employees that the imponderables of corporate strategy.

In the construction industry, this problem can manifest itself in an emphasis on detailed construction planning. Management wants to talk about the things that it can touch and see. But the sequence and availability of work on site is more often dictated by intangibles such as procurement decisions and design approvals. Detailed planning offers a comfortable retreat. It appears scientific, takes a long time and costs a lot of money, so it must be good—or must it? Regrettably, there is no escape from qualitative judgement, from risk, and from uncertainty. But this is a hard truth to live with.

In a project with many unknowns and many specialized functions, innovative problem-solving can occur in many places. So it is very important that the planning process should be flexible enough to accommodate creative thinking, especially at the lower levels of the organization.

The Seductiveness of Computer Systems

A further human dimension that the planning engineer in particular must address is the seductiveness of modern computer systems. To the inexperienced planner or the risk-averse manager, network planning packages look like a godsend. Vast networks and voluminous printouts offer welcome shelter from the human irrationalities of the project. But once the planner has caught his fingers in the mills of heavyweight computing, he will inexorably be drawn further and further in. There is a real danger of becoming a slave to the method.

Computers provide the ability to process bigger and bigger networks. They promise closer control through more detailed planning and through a faster response to changing conditions. Unfortunately, the bigger the network, the more rapidly it dates, the harder it becomes to collect all the necessary progress information, and the more complicated it is to change. So the more vigorously the planner defends his networks, the more certain you can be that he has lost touch with what is going on in the project, and that it is now very difficult to correct the computerized planning.

A good plan may be no more than a list of jobs scribbled on the back of a cigarette packet—if it is helpful as an action guide. One method has no more intrinsic merit than the next. But there is still the human inclination to equate more sophisticated techniques with better analysis. The planning department is often a showplace, rather like the quality control department of a manufacturing company. And just as the quality control people may be judged by the layman in terms of the expense and complexity of their electronic gauges, so the planner may be judged by his use of state-of-the-art computer tools. The more time that the planning engineer spends mastering the intricacies of the latest network analysis package, the less time he can spend on the problems of the project.

The way for the planner to avoid the thoughtless use of some of these alluring techniques is always to consider *what* is needed before he decides *how* he is going to meet that need. Then the particular method he chooses (the use of a minicomputer, perhaps) can be seen as one among a variety of alternatives. If he is clear in his own mind on the benefits he expects from a chosen technique, then the planner can assess critically whether he is realizing them in practice or not.

Computerized network analysis may now be an inescapable part of project planning. If so, then the planning engineer must continuously be wary of the seductiveness of these tools. For him, it is a human problem.

WINNING COMMITMENT TO PROJECT PLANNING

The merits of project planning have been so widely extolled that few project managers will openly express their doubts. However, public sentiments do not necessarily translate into private realities. Planning requires a significant portion of the project manager's time, and the same exercise that promises to provide a handle on the project also tracks and records management failings. Managers, who publicly avow their commitment to planning, may privately consider it expensive, time-wasting, irritating and interfering. The planner may find his efforts extremely unwelcome.

One solution for the project manager is to direct the energies of the planner along harmless paths. The insistence on very detailed networks, for example, is a useful diversion. Large networks can absorb limitless manhours and yield little of relevance to the management of the project. Sapolsky (1972) illustrates this approach to network planning. He describes how the Navy Special Projects Office developed the PERT technique on the Polaris project to sustain the myth that they had an integrated, uniquely effective management system. The project was actually managed by more direct, conventional means. But the political use of network analysis gave project management credibility and independence of action. It built "a fence to keep the rest of the Navy off."

The project manager's ambivalence towards planning can mean that planning is treated as a second-rate function. The project manager won't lose his best operations managers to planning, but looks upon it as a place to move his nonperformers: 'at least they can do little harm there.' Poor planners produce poor planning and the manager's dim view of planning is reinforced.

How is the planning engineer to deal with these problems? First, the planner must realise that project management is probably more sinned-against than sinning. Second, he must redefine his contribution. And, third, he must learn how to market project planning.

Project Management: More Sinned-Against than Sinning

Project planning took off following the development and application of network analysis on the Polaris project in 1959. Management consultants, computer companies, employment agencies and planners themselves have made the field what it is now, but they did not always make a positive contribution to project success. Project managers' suspicions about planning are not unfounded.

Consultants have made a good business out of the installation of sophisticated planning systems, designed to solve all the problems of project management. Unfortunately, methodological sleight of hand is no substitute for vision and leadership. A system is only as good as its implementation. But following a project through to completion does not offer the same profit margins, so the consultants moved on to the next unsuspecting customer.

Computer companies came close on the consultants' heels. Systems analysts and programmers found network algorithms a pleasing change from business software. Many ponderous and inflexible packages were written, with little appreciation of the requirements of project planning. The planners who used the programs found their time consumed in punching cards, debugging, and waiting for batch processing. Some of these big packages are still around today, with the apparent endorsement of the major computer companies that wrote them (and that still do not understand what project planning is about).

The demand for planning engineers to make this new technology work far outstripped the supply. Employment agencies grew up to trade in the market for planners. The shortage, and consequent high salaries, drew inexperienced and unsuitable people into the field. After all, what is a planning engineer? Network analysis—a methodology—does not constitute a new engineering discipline. So there are no degrees in planning engineering, and no professional institutions to ensure minimum standards and validate the practitioners.

Is it surprising that project managers are wary of planning? Planning has not always delivered what it promised. But what can planning contribute to project management?

Redefining the Contribution of Project Planning

We have already provided a partial answer to this question by noting planning's role in informed decision-making and creative problem-solving. Planning was traditionally defined in the context of a control system: as part of the process of setting targets, monitoring progress and taking recovery action. But recent authors, Horwitch (1979) and Stout (1980) among them, see major projects as open systems, and recognize that many of the variables that condition the success of a project may lie beyond the control of project management.

So I prefer to define the contribution of project planning in terms of its aid to decision-making: the purpose of project planning is to provide a guide to present action. This definition gives planning a strategic role, acknowledges that planning does not invariably yield control, and provides a yardstick for the assessment of our efforts. Good planning provides guidance to decision-makers, whether or not schedules slip or budgets are overspent.

McGregor (1960) makes the vital point that help is defined by the recipient. Defining planning in terms of its real purpose—service to project management—forces the planning engineer to adopt a marketing approach to his product.

Marketing Project Planning

A thumbnail definition of marketing holds that it is the business of 'identifying and satisfying a consumer need, and making a profit doing it.' Perhaps the main distinction between a marketing and a make-and-sell approach lies in this emphasis on the identification of needs. This means that the marketer must first learn to listen.

The needs of project management are so varied that the planning engineer must have the diagnostic ability to sense and assess the project manager's true requirements. Thus a simple bar chart may capture the level of reality that construction managers can relate to and understand. If so, this is what the planner should produce. Alternatively, an elaborate network may be ideal for a client, if the project manager wishes to sacrifice ease of comprehension for the extra credibility associated with sophisticated presentation.

Planning engineers tend to waste a great deal of energy debating the comparative merits of arrow versus precedence diagrams. They should get down to reality and avoid these academic debates. Different managers have different needs and different motives. The planning engineer must learn to value these differences, and value the spirit of enquiry which reveals these differences. To take advantage of such insights, the planner must have the interpersonal skills and flexibility to vary his own behavior. It is a mistake to lay too much weight on standardized planning procedures. The failures of the cook book school of project planning—which tries to prescribe a technique for all situations—can be partly attributed to insensitivity. Human nature is inherently complex and there are no foolproof recipes. So the planning engineer must find out what is required in each situation before he decides how to meet these needs. This is what is meant by marketing project planning.

The Credibility of the Planning Engineer

The credibility of the planning engineer will depend upon his colleagues' perception of him as an expert and upon their ability to identify with him. This means that he must be able to demonstrate his competence, not just with the gimmicks of computer systems, but with real problems that require sound judgment, imagination and hard work. This means that he should have a background in engineering or the operational side of similar projects, and, for many companies, it may also mean that he should be a professional engineer.

The planning engineer should offer no ready-made solutions. His credibility will be built upon thorough analysis, original thought and high personal standards of performance. Sometimes he may find that the interests of the company or of the project are not being properly served by the actions of project management. Then, like a quality controller, his sense of professional responsibility and his independent position require him to differ on important issues.

We have noted that human problems in project planning often result in plans that are far too detailed. So let us now see how the planning engineer solves the problem of planning at the right level of detail.

PLANNING AT THE RIGHT LEVEL OF DETAIL

Since too much detail is probably the commonest problem in project planning, let us develop some principles for getting the level of detail right. But, before that, we need to define what is meant by 'right.' The simple answer is that the right level of detail is the amount of detail that can feasibly be monitored.

Every time the planner adds another activity to the program, he must be sure that he will know when the activity has started, when it has finished and, while it is in progress, how long it will take to finish. Without this information the plan will be of little help to project management.

This is the golden rule: plan in the level of detail that you can monitor. Information, therefore, dictates the detail of a program. Effective planning depends on effective information systems. Structuring and maintaining information systems becomes the chief task of the planner. Because of the human issues, it is not an easy task. We shall go on to discuss the problems of securing a continuous flow of meaningful progress information but, first, here are some guidelines for this business of choosing the right level of detail.

Getting It Right: Some Don't's

Don't use prescriptions to detail the network. For example, some contracts specify that the programs should detail activities such as design, order, manufacture, delivery, installation and commissioning for each major component of the project. The thoughtless application of these formulae leads to large, uniform networks that are difficult to monitor and do not recognize special problems of the project.

Don't attempt integrated project control through network planning. Many have tried, but, unless the project is simple or small, these endeavors are doomed to failure. It is easy to see why, if you consider some of the conflicting ways in which it may be necessary to view the progress of a project:

1. By revenue (progress payments).
2. By cost (project accounting).
3. By responsibility.
4. By area (for civil engineering and construction).
5. By system (for mechanical and electrical, design, construction and commissioning).

It becomes impossible to meet the data collection requirements of networks sufficiently detailed to integrate all these elements of project control.

Don't repeat subnetworks casually. The classic example of the use of repetitive subnetworks is a housing project. This may have subnetworks of about 50 activities for each type of house. Each subnetwork is perfectly sensible and easy to monitor by itself. But combined with, perhaps, 50 or 60 houses under construction simultaneously, this approach results in a large network with too much detail for overall control.

Getting It Right: Some Do's

Do outline your program before you refine the details. The landscape artist blocks out his entire canvas first. If he started by painting one leaf in intricate detail not only would he probably never finish, but the proportions of the end result would probably be wrong.

Do detail the activities that are closest in time. If we can forecast one month ahead with a 90% probability of success, then (assuming each month's forecast is independent) we can forecast two months ahead with an 81% probability of being right, six months ahead with a 53% probability, one year ahead with a 28% probability, and three years ahead with only 2% probability. Therefore, a level of detail that is consistent across time makes no sense: detailed planning should be confined to the next few months.

Do add detail to your problem areas—those activities that are difficult, critical and within your control. There is nothing to be gained by detailing the work of a Japanese subcontractor, for example, if you cannot improve his performance and if his track record suggests that he will finish his slice of the project well ahead of the field. Rather come to grips with the vital but intangible processes that lie within your sphere of influence and that may condition your Japanese colleague's success. There is a strong temptation to plan those things that are easy or someone else's responsibility. Resist it.

Do explore every possible manual solution before resorting to the use of computers.

The Personal, Uneven Result

These recommendations lead to personal, heterogeneous plans, quite unlike the 'objective' examples quoted in textbooks. But if the planner's perception is sound and the planning useful, then this subjective, uneven result has proven its worth.

OBTAINING MEANINGFUL PROGRESS INFORMATION

We are beginning to see that planning has more to do with informed decision-making than control, and that information is the key to effective planning. The planning engineer cannot hope to command the respect of project management or produce useful plans if he does not know what is going on in the project. This requires accurate, timely and complete information, and the kind of understanding that only comes from a total immersion in every aspect of the project: human, technical, financial and contractual.

But, in trying to gather such information, the planner runs into major human problems. Why should anyone give the planner the kind of information he seeks, especially if it is sensitive and revealing? Why should any manager 'make a rod for his own back' or 'wash his dirty linen in public' by volunteering details of performance or the lack of it? The planner may be able to find unguarded information, as long as his motives are not understood. But, as soon as he starts to use this information, his right of access is likely to be challenged.

The creation and maintenance of useful information systems is the biggest test of the planner's human qualities and of his integrity. If he succeeds, he can become extraordinarily influential in guiding the path of the project. To understand the human issues, let us begin by considering the planner's sources of information.

The Use of Formal Information Systems

The planner gathers information from both formal and informal sources. The backbone of his information systems will be the organization's existing channels of information.

First, the planning engineer must persuade project management that he should promptly receive copies of every communication (memo, letter, telex, minutes of meetings, etc.) to do with the project. Ideally, the copies he receives will not be pre-screened. Often the apparently trivial items are the most significant. The extent to which he can get project managers to comply with this request will depend on their understanding of his role and their confidence in his ability to keep his own counsel. A good system for filing this information, when he gets it, is essential.

Next, the planner should attempt to place himself in the path of existing information flows: drawing transmittals, requisitions, orders, expediting reports, goods-received notices from site, etc. He has a valid reason for seeing these documents. The requisition, for example, should be routed to the procurement department via the planning function. The planner can check the recommended delivery date, indicate the priority of this material and note that an engineering activity has finished and a buying activity has begun. The planner does not keep a copy of the requisition but passes it on to the procurement function *without delay.*

These systems create an enormous amount of reading for the planning engineer. However, there is no substitute for knowledge. Reading requisitions, for example, not only provides the planner with a way of monitoring one interface between engineering and procurement, but it also gives him early indications of the materials and equipment in the project. If he does not know what he is planning, how can he plan it? Even in the process of reading requisitions, he can start to influence the project. He can challenge delivery dates that are too late for site and expedite the placement of orders for long-delivery items.

Meetings are another vital source of information for the planner. All projects have some kind of progress review meeting, which the planner attends. The planner should volunteer to write the minutes (usually an unpopular task) and make sure they record commitments to take action.

The progress meeting is a vital arena for resolution of interdepartmental conflicts, since most of these conflicts have schedular implications. The planner can offer the plans as common ground in which to work out these differences and, in the process, glean invaluable information about the true progress and motivation of each department.

With control of the minutes (especially if the minutes of one meeting become the agenda for the next), the planner has an important tool for imparting a sense of direction to the project, and for rewarding and punishing his sources of information with welcome or unwelcome recognition. The planner need not chair the meeting, and he can often be more effective if he does not (for he will then find it easier to function as a process consultant to the group). The planner's role as project historian is usually accepted as legitimate, but in the way he records and interprets progress he can change the future.

Thus by including an item week after week he can repeatedly bring it to the group's attention until satisfactory action is taken, or by dropping an item from the minutes he can shift the group's attention elsewhere. Not only does the progress meeting provide the planning engineer with information, it gives him an opportunity to shape and strengthen the group dynamics.

These three formal sources of information—distribution lists, routine documents, and project meetings—will be present in some form or other in every project organization. In addition, there are many informal sources available to the planner. He should fully exploit the potential of both the existing formal and informal information sources before he considers introducing any information systems solely to support his requirements.

The Use of Informal Sources of Information

Every informal meeting with an individual or a group is a source of information. Information is the currency in which the planner deals, and he can, and should, trade in it at every opportunity.

The very action of collecting progress information creates forces for change. In simply asking about the progress of an activity, the planner can raise the level of consciousness of his colleagues. If the activity is behind schedule, the interest of the planner may generate enough energy to put it right before the problem becomes widely known. Which information the planner seeks also sends a message to the project team. The process itself creates expectations of change and creates anxiety. The way the threat is perceived is itself informative.

In every informal contact the planner must directly or indirectly explain why he is investigating, who he is doing it for, what information he wants, how he is going to use it, how he will protect the source's confidentiality, and why the source should tell him anything at all. In the long term, the only correct answers to such questions are the truth. The planner can reward cooperation with feedback, and can do a lot to make sure that the initiative for decision-making remains at the same level of the organization as the information itself.

In his use of informal information, the planner must be unobtrusive and responsible. He needs to be persistent, patient and consistent, to take care with confrontation, to avoid surprises and to protect his sources. Progress monitoring is neither a neutral nor necessarily a benign activity. It is an intrusion in the work of the organization that can be instrumental in changing the course of the project. As his acquaintances begin to trust him, the planner—who probably knows as much about the overall project as anyone—finds himself alternating between consultant, sounding board and confessor. For example, he may learn about union corruption on site—people on the payroll but not on the job. This is something he may be able to do nothing about, but it provides insight into the psychology and performance of the organization. Or the planning engineer may learn that some goods that were apparently lost in transit were actually delivered to site, but were damaged in subsequent handling and then sold as scrap. Nobody may be willing to own up to this in public, but at least the planner can tell the project manager to stop blaming the shipper and to re-order.

To sum up, the planning engineer keeps informed by 'plugging into' formal and informal information systems. He needs many sources because he can be seriously misled if all his information comes through one channel. The quality of information he collects will depend upon his understanding and management of the human dynamics of the monitoring process.

MOTIVATING EFFECTIVE ACTION

It is often easy to win agreement to recommended action, but it can be far more difficult to effect real changes. However, with commitment, useful plans and meaningful information, the planning engineer has already begun to motivate effective action. Frequently the most important changes are the least apparent. Peters (1978) has called this 'the theory of the small win.' He argues that patterns of consistent clear-cut outcomes can be instrumental in changing the direction of an organization. So if the planner has experienced even moderate success in tackling these first three problems, he is well on his way to solving the fourth: to motivating effective action.

The planner does not derive his ability to influence the course of the project from any formal authority, but from his position at the heart of the project. To understand the nature and origin of the planner's power, it is important first of all to understand the relationship between information and decision-making in the project context.

Information and Decision-making in the Project Context

Although data, information and intelligence are words that are commonly treated as interchangeable, it will he helpful to make a distinction between them in explaining the decision-making process. Figure 14-1 suggests just such a distinction: data—an unstructured form of information—form the base of the pyramid, and intelligence—highly structured information—forms the top of the pyramid. The difference between data, information and intelligence lies in the degree of structure or of 'refinement.' Thus a number, 030681 for example, may be regarded as simply a piece of data. However if we know that the number is a date, 6 March 1981, and further that it is the actual start date of a critical activity, then the piece of data becomes more informative because it is more structured. If we also know that the date is late against some schedule, then this extra refinement transforms the data into valuable intelligence— remedial action is indicated. Hence the more structured or refined a piece of data becomes, the more relevant it is to the decision-making process.

This process of refinement is also a process of elimination. Data (numbers) that are not dates may not contain meaningful information, at least as far as the planning process is concerned. The start dates of activities that are not critical or that are within schedule may not constitute intelligence. This is why Figure 14-1 shows data as the broadbase of the pyramid and intelligence at the tip.

This distinction is important because it is planning that creates the structure. The plan defines activites, transforms data into information, and provides the vital interface between information and intelligence. The plan identifies information of least significance and filters it out. Thus planning creates intelli-

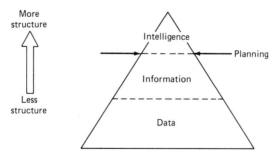

Figure 14-1. The hierarchy of information.

gence—the most refined and powerful form of information that project management receives.

But planning is highly subjective. So it is the planning engineer who is effectively conditioning the decisions, and, ultimately, the actions of project management. The planning engineer is, in a sense, a misinformation system. He decides what information to highlight for project management attention, and also what information not to pass on. He colors the attitudes and actions of management through incomplete information, by only telling half the story.

Although decision-making is the essence of management, frequently it takes place way down in the ranks. Thus the planner is very much a decision-maker. He gains power from his position as the interface between information and intelligence, and from his position at the center of the project.

Centrality and Power in Organizations

The relationship between power and centrality has been widely studied. Schein (1980) proposes a three-dimensional model of organizations (see Figure 14-2). He sees an organization as a cone. To the conventional dimensions of hierarchy and function he adds a third dimension of centrality. Centrality is a measure of an individual's inclusion in the informal structure of the organization, a measure of the degree to which he is trusted with organization secrets and allowed to influence decision-making.

The project organization is characterized by continuous changes in personnel and structure through each phase: design, procurement, construction, start-up, operation, etc. Recognizing the dynamic aspect of the project, the concept of centrality gains special significance. The planner, who, along with the project manager, is one of the few people to see the project from beginning to end, moves steadily to a more central and influential position in the informal organization. Functional managers, involved for shorter periods or with only one phase of the project, may never equal the planning engineer's power, even though they outrank him in the formal hierarchy.

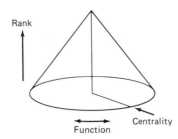

Figure 14-2. Schein's model of an organization.

The Dynamics of the Planner's Power

The concept of the planner as a centrally-placed information officer explains his source of power in the organization but does not tell us how he exercises this power. Kotler (1977) identifies four types of power over others: obligation, reputation, identification and dependence. All four are evident in the way that the planning engineer establishes power in his relationships with other members of the project team.

Firstly, acting as a 'misinformation' system, the planner may choose not to report all variances. This leaves the initiative with the delinquent part of the organization, and creates an obligation for it to take remedial action before the problem is passed up through the organization.

Secondly, the planner, through his reputation and position, can influence others through intimidation. Believing in his expertise in planning and his inside knowledge of the project, other managers may defer to him on matters that have to do with the schedule.

Thirdly, the planning engineer can become a champion for later phases of the project, and gain power from his identification with them. Thus at the early design stage of a construction project before the site personnel have been appointed, the planner can champion their priorities for the production of drawings and orders. The site organization, when it develops, will find it already has an ally in the business of time allocation. This is a process that the planner can repeat over and over again: supporting the mechanical engineers' requirements for early civil access, or the start-up function's requirements for early completion of key systems. In each case he fulfils an important integrative role in the balance of power, and gains influence through his identification with forthcoming phases of the work.

Finally, the planner gains power through the dependence he creates. Intelligence is a drug. When the project manager finds that intelligence bestows an ability to influence the project, then generally he cannot get enough of it. The more effective the planning becomes, the greater the demand and support for it. The planning engineer must consciously manage this dependence, because there is a danger of overdependence. It is essential that the project manager participates in the planning process, and does not abdicate his overall responsibility for the program.

To sum up, we have looked at the planner's source of power and at the dynamics of his exercise of power in project relationships. In practice, on large construction projects, a triumvirate may develop: the project manager becomes a statesman, primarily concerned with the management of external stakeholders in the project; the construction manager becomes a chief operating officer; and the planning engineer becomes a third manager of the project, an integrator and strategist. Whether or not this happens depends upon the human dynamics of the project organization, and depends most critically upon the planner's ability to capture the imagination of the project team members and his ability to move them to action on the strength of his perception and integrity.

IMPLICATIONS FOR PROJECT MANAGEMENT

Willingness to Evaluate Network Planning

Although project managers are justifiably suspicious of network planning, there is a remarkable unwillingness to evaluate its contribution to the success of a project. Network planning provides a comfortable discipline for rational analysis, and is now institutionalized in the planning procedures of many major companies. Yet rarely are the results of project network analysis measured. Unconsciously managers seem to want to be able to say they are doing something about planning, but are reluctant to evaluate the outcome, because they do not want to change.

Though network planning has been sold as an essential element in effective project management, the value of network planning has been challenged in the academic literature. Thus Marquis, studying the use of network planning in industry in 1969, found that project managers who use it are more likely to be highly regarded than those who do not. However, he also found no relationship between this judgment on the excellence of project managers and the outcome of their projects, either technically or administratively. Davis (1972), in one of the few studies on the use of network analysis in large construction firms, found that, although 80% of companies used network planning, only 13% of the users felt that they were very successful in achieving the numerous benefits attributed to it.

The technique itself has come under fire. Elmaghraby (1977) has emphasized the need for probabilistic planning methodology to cope with the uncertainties of the project environment, but has exposed serious flaws in PERT (the most widely used probabilistic variant of network analysis). Unfortunately Elmaghraby's proposed alternative, a generalized activity network, has proved infeasible for large-scale application. Numerous authors have questioned the validity of the network model of reality. Birrell (1980), for example, argues that network planning is an inappropriate model of construction processes, and suggests a return to the earlier line-of-balance technique.

Other authors raise questions that touch upon the very axioms of network planning. Allison (1971) demonstrates that decision-making is not merely a process of rational choice, but the outcome of organizational and political forces. Brooks (1975) shows that time and resources are not interchangeable in complex situations (assigning more people to a task can make it take longer), although he does recommend cautious use of network planning tools. Finally, Pascale (1978) makes a case for ambiguity rather than confrontation in the resolution of resource-allocation conflicts: it may sometimes be more effective not to stress the critical path.

I am not arguing for an abandonment of network planning but for a more deliberate evaluation of its application and contribution. These criticisms of network planning deserve attention because too often the methodology has become a substitute for a deep understanding of the project. The project manager is ultimately responsible for the success of the project and, if he is truly determined to meet budgets and schedules, he must be realistic about the contribution of planning. Otherwise he is likely to get the quality of planning that he is prepared to tolerate.

The Dilemma of the Project Manager

Planning, as we have seen, is a double-edged sword. It generates real problems for the project manager by creating a new power base within the organization. In tackling this dilemma, the project manager must answer three major questions:

1. Does he really want effective planning?
2. If so, what should be the role of the planning engineer?
3. What planning tools should be used?

If the project manager cannot face the threat of a powerful planning function, then he must develop some alternative information systems. If he wants effective planning, then he must invest enough of his time and energy in the planning process to maintain his leadership of the project. Similarly, he must encourage active participation in planning at all levels of the project organization.

In addition, the project manager must consider the role of the planning engineer in the project organization. The project manager can define this role effectively through his choice of individual for the job. Since personal qualities are so critical to the success of the planner, the project manager must look for someone whose exceptional experience and dedication to the project will be tempered by equally exceptional maturity and self-control.

Finally, the project manager must think about the planning tools to be used, because a rigid adherence to prescribed procedures or sophisticated methodologies can easily stifle flexible and creative planning.

In conclusion, planning is not a remote intellectual exercise but a practical discipline that is based upon a deep understanding of the human dynamics of the project organization. Planning can be a powerful force for change and control, but it poses difficult problems for project management. The way that a project manager resolves these problems provides a significant insight into both his stature and his ability.

BIBLIOGRAPHY

Allison, G. T. *Essence of Decision,* (Boston, Mass.: Little, Brown & Company, 1971).

Birrell, G. S. "Construction Planning—Beyond the Critical Path." *Journal of the Construction Division,* Proceedings of the American Society of Civil Engineers, Vol. 106 No. CO3 (September 1980).

Brooks, F. P. *The Mythical Man-Month,* (Addison-Wesley, 1975).

Davis, E. W. "CPM Use in Large Construction Firms—A Top Management Survey." *The Practical Application of Project Planning by Network Techniques,* Ed. Mats Ogander, (New York: John Wiley, 1972).

Elmaghraby, S. E. *Activity Networks: Project Planning and Control by Network Models,* (New York: John Wiley, 1977).

Horwitch, M. "Designing and Managing Large-Scale, Public-Private Technological Enterprises: A State of the Art Review." *Technology in Society,* Vol. 1 (1979), pp 179–192.

Kottler, J. P. "Power, Dependence and Effective Management." *Harvard Business Review,* (July–August, 1977).

Marquis, D. "A Project Team + PERT = Success, Or Does It?" *Innovation,* No. 5, (1969).

McGregor, D. M. *The Human Side of Enterprise,* (New York: McGraw-Hill, 1960).

Pascale, R. T. "Zen and the Art of Management." *Harvard Business Review* (March–April, 1978).

Peters, T. J. "Symbols, Patterns and Settings: an Optimistic Case for Getting Things Done." *Organizational Dynamics,* (Autumn, 1978).

Sapolsky, H. M. *The Polaris System Development, Bureaucratic and Programmatic Success in Government,* (Harvard University Press, 1972).

Schein, E. H. *Organizational Psychology,* 3rd Ed., (Prentice Hall, 1980).

Stout, R. *Management or Control? The Organizational Challenge,* (Indiana University Press, 1980).

15. Developing and Using the Work Breakdown Structure

Garry D. Lavold*

INTRODUCTION

During the last two decades the emergence of projects with diverse ownership, long time spans, integral government involvement, and requirements for large quantities of diverse resources has put new strains on project management capabilities and project communication requirements. This growth in project size and complexity has, in addition, strained previously used communication channels to such an extent that a new approach to information systems and communication channels is required. This chapter proposes that a properly designed and implemented Work Breakdown Structure (WBS), with associated coding structure and dictionary, forms an effective basis for project control systems, policies and procedures for all projects. The WBS helps in organizing and planning all phases of a project.

Project management requires effective, precise information throughout all phases of the project and between all personnel involved with the project. A well designed WBS provides the basis for the design of these project control information systems (either manual or automated). The definition of the WBS as supplied by the Department of Energy in its Performance Measurement Systems guidelines is:

Work Breakdown Structure. A product-oriented family tree division of hardware, software, services, and other work tasks which organizes, defines, and graphically displays the product to be produced, as well as the work to be accomplished to achieve the specified product.[1]

---

*Mr. Garry Lavold holds a Bachelor of Sciences in Chemical Engineering and a Master of Business Administration from the University of Alberta. A process engineer with Gulf Oil Canada from 1969 to 1974, he was involved in all phases of the construction and startup of an 80,000 BPD grass roots refinery. From 1974 to 1978, Mr. Lavold worked as special projects engineer with NOVA, an Alberta Corporation, with special emphasis on new projects and the project control of construction. At present he is Manager of Project Control for Husky Oil Operations with responsibility for control of cost, schedule, and budgets on all major projects.
[1]"mini-PMS Guide," Performance Measurement System Guidelines, Attachment 1 (Dept. of Energy. Washington, D.C., 1977), pp. A1–4.

The "product to be produced" is the completion of a project within a specified time frame and budget while conforming to the constraints of public interest groups and governments. Having the WBS as a discipline applied to the project ensures that all participants, both owners and contractors, are fully aware of the work required to complete the project. This utilization of the WBS as the foundation for which all estimates, schedules and project outlines are developed ensures the WBS will become the central device through which all groups communicate information with one another.

Essential to the management of the project is the establishment of the WBS early in the project life. This will enable all participants to implement effective information channels at the beginning of the project life cycle. By utilizing the WBS for information basis with outside groups, such as governmental agencies, the regulatory process will be simplified in that all communication regarding the project will be via a common basis, thereby enabling both industry and governmental personnel to communicate on a common basis of understanding.

This chapter presents an overview of the environment within which the WBS should operate, the essential elements and concepts to be included during the design of the WBS and one example of WBS currently being used on a pipeline project.

COMMUNICATION—USERS OF THE WBS

In the environment of large projects involving large cash expenditures, requiring multi-owners, multi-contractors, and in most cases, government involvement with high technology facilities, the requirement for information integration and communication is an order of magnitude greater than encountered in the past. These large projects deal with millions of dollars over a multi-year span; which means that as the projects proceed, the environment within which the project was conceived is quite often very different from the environment in which the project is completed. The requirement of government regulation, government involvement, and governmental watching and monitoring requires that all groups have a common information basis despite changing environments. This chapter proposes that for projects, the WBS should become the common information basis, the common language, the device whereby diverse users can communicate back and forth from the very inception of the project to its final completion. These users include: owners, project management personnel, contractors, designers and government agencies. The integration of the users and their information is illustrated in Figure 15-1.

The left side of Figure 15-1 illustrates the functional groups (prime users), either in the owner's organization, contractor's organization, or a mixture thereof, that must perform the work required to design and construct the project. These users responsible for the work exchange information with each

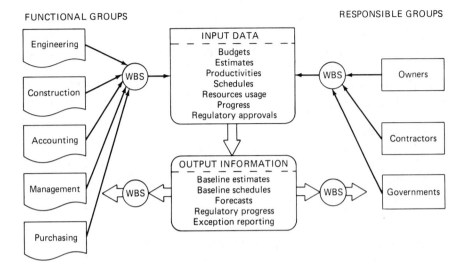

Figure 15-1. Work breakdown structure information inegration.

other, using the WBS as a common basis of understanding. A properly designed WBS will enable these functional groups to have a precise communication linkage by which all the data illustrated as "input data" can be gathered and distributed. Key input data, normally required, is illustrated as follows:

- Budgets—which represent the expected yearly cash flows.
- Estimates—which provide the cost of the project on a facility basis.
- Productivities—the expected production rates to be achieved by design groups, drafting groups and the construction crews.
- Schedules—the expected timing and sequence of all the activities necessary to complete the project.
- Resource Usage—the expected quantities of manpower, equipment and consumables required over the life of the project.
- Progress—as the project proceeds, the progress of activities is measured and compared to the base estimate to ascertain the project status.
- Regulatory Approvals—most projects require a variety of government approvals. These approvals must be scheduled and form part of the overall project plan.

All the above information is prepared, using the WBS to define all the required elements. This use of the WBS enables all of the elements to be correlated on a common basis. The interrelating of cost, schedule and productivity on a consistent basis is essential for accurate progress measurement and project control. Having all information collected on a common basis ensures that all work to be done is comparable to a well defined baseline.

All input data would be collected from the functional groups, using the WBS to define all the elements. Shown in the middle section of Figure 15-1 is the Output Information. The data from all the groups is consolidated to provide overall project budgets, schedules and estimates. This provides a baseline estimate and schedule for the construction of the project, using the WBS; and as the project proceeds, forecasts against these baselines are made utilizing the WBS. The regulatory progress and exception reporting are also done, utilizing WBS as the common basis and the device by which all progress reporting and forecasting is done. Thus, the WBS is an integral part of all project reporting and project planning.

The original groups who prepare the outline and the concept of the project define it to a stage from which the WBS can be prepared. Thus, the first phase is the complete definition of a project and its associated WBS. The WBS works as an effective tool in organizing the work into logical groupings.

The next phase is to report against the baseline, and finally, to prepare a reconciliation against the estimate to measure overall performance on the project. The *use* of a common coding, a common structure and a common language, from the start of the project life to the finish, enables problems and their solutions to be readily definable by the common WBS.

The right side of Figure 15-1 illustrates the responsible groups—the people who require the project, who are involved in building the project, or who are involved in approving the project. The owners, the contractors and, on the larger projects, the government agency must be communicated with. This communication or information flow will use the WBS at a summary level, whereas the functional groups on the left side communicate normally at a detailed level of the WBS. The output information from the consolidated baseline format at a summary level of WBS will be utilized by the owners and the contractors for preparing the proposals to shareholders and/or for submissions to the government. Later, this WBS breakdown will be used in preparing the original bid documents and, as the progress proceeds, in preparing the progress to date and forecast to completion reports.

Thus, as can be seen, the WBS should be used from the start to the finish of the project for planning, tracking and reconciliation. It is the device by which the users such as owners, contractors, and the government can organize information among themselves and with the people who are performing the work required to complete the project successfully.

SYSTEM INTEGRATION—USING THE WBS

The user community, as described in the preceding section, communicates with each other using a common language defined by the WBS. To give the users the information they require involves support from project control systems and accounting systems. Typical project control systems include scheduling, progress and performance measurement, manpower, equipment, material tracking, cost monitoring and forecasting systems. Project accounting systems usually include ledgers such as accounts receivable, accounts payable, capital assets and a project cost ledger. Each one of these systems in both accounting and project control may be independent, automated or manual, although for most large projects, these systems would be automated. By grouping all the systems above as project control and/or accounting, systems information transfer between the respective systems can be analyzed.

As the explanation proceeds describing the project control and project accounting information transfer, it must be realized that this transfer would be applied to all other subsystems as well. By highlighting the two overall systems, the principles, ideas and concepts will be explained on an overall basis.

Figure 15-2 illustrates the project accounting and project control systems which both collect data using the WBS. These systems receive data on the common basis of the dictionary and code structure directly associated with the WBS. The Project Control Systems, whether manual or automated, always serve the purpose of collecting as precisely as possible, timely information which is current and which can be used for management reporting and forecasting. The Project Control System's key function is to warn management early of any impending problems which, with management's decisions, can be solved or at least have their impact reduced. These systems do not have precise cost information but supply vital current key information to manage the project. All information is collected, sorted and reported via the WBS code structure. The Project Control Systems use this code for all aspects of monitoring cost, schedule and productivity and future planning.

The use of the WBS code for entering all information into the project control systems ensures that all progress data collected is comparable to a baseline.

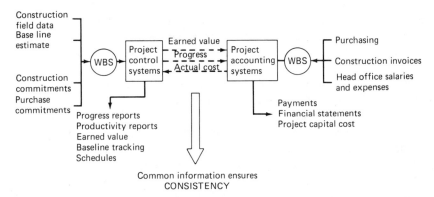

Figure 15-2. Work breakdown structure system integration.

Use of actual progress and resource data compared to the baseline allows forecasts of anticipated problems to be analyzed. These results from the systems can be used for control in a meaningful manner through the use of WBS, since all references to the information are made via a uniform and consistent referencing method. Thus the WBS forms an integral part of the control process.

The project accounting systems, which by design are precise but not normally as timely as the project control systems, collect the official or auditable information for cost and resource usage on the project. The resource usage or cost is collected via invoices from contractors, time sheets from personnel working on the project, and expenses of the personnel doing the work. This information is collected by WBS, with payments being recorded for the WBS elements. Having the project accounting system able to verify the actual costs that were spent against the estimate and against the budget by common means allows the actual cost of the progress to date to be tracked precisely against the estimate of cost as well as against the forecast to complete. The more this common tie, (i.e. WBS), between the accounting and the project control systems is used, the better it is for the management of the project since it is possible to analyze results not system discrepancies. With all information collected on a common basis, it ensures that the engineer, the accountant, and management are all referring to the same information with the same meaning. One of the problems typically present in many projects is that the accounting and project control systems are not using identical coding. By utilizing the WBS in conjunction with the existing accounting coding, or if you have the luxury of using it uniquely for the project without having to adapt to the existing accounting code, you are ensured that as the project proceeds, estimates can be verified and sound projections can be made. This is essential to proper management of the project because it ensures that explanations of cost or schedule problems will be made on an organized basis. The key to providing proper explanations is the disciplined usage, by every person involved in both systems, of the WBS which is a dictionary of definitions and a fixed coding structure that is unique for all project activities. The precision of this type of reporting ensures that as the project proceeds, every individual involved is well aware of the project problems, their proposed solutions, the cost estimate, and the actual cost of these problems.

The method of integration using the WBS as described above, between the project accounting and the project control systems, is also applicable to the purchasing system, which may feed either project control or project accounting, and any other systems that are utilized within the project. Each system, whether manual or automated, should include the WBS as part of its system definition. The WBS works in manual or automated systems or any combination thereof. It is a discipline and an information organizer which applies equally well whether the information systems are automated or manual, but it must be present in all applicable systems to ensure that the required common linkages are available.

WBS—RESPONSIBILITY RELATIONSHIP

The WBS provides an information organizer between both the users and the systems. This was previously illustrated in Figures 15-1 and 15-2. Communication utilizing the WBS is based on a facility basis or a contract basis. The WBS defines the project in a structured format via the facilities and the items required to build the facilities, or the contracts required to complete construction of the facilities. The WBS structure should reflect as accurately as possible on paper the physical project to be completed. Utilizing the WBS in this format requires that the management structure or organization responsibility centres which are responsible for the various components of the project be defined separately. The relationship between the management structure and the WBS is illustrated in Figure 15-3.

The right side of Figure 15-3 illustrates the WBS or the project tree which

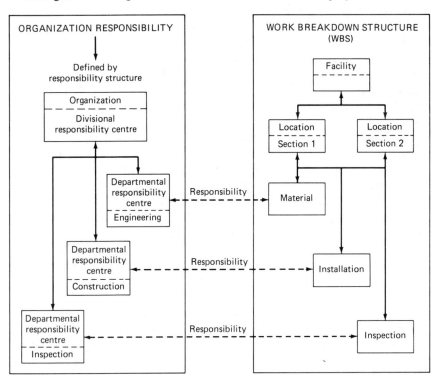

Figure 15-3. Responsibility/WBS relationship.

defines the project. On the left side is the organizational responsibility as defined by a responsibility structure. The overlay of this organizational responsibility on the WBS creates the management matrix. This management matrix is designed specifically to allow for the case of the large project where there may be many organizations involved in the project. Usually, the basic facility definition does not change through time; whereas organizational responsibilities will, as the project progresses through the project life cycle. The WBS will be designed to provide the total precise project definition on a facility basis, with the major responsibility assignments being overlayed as required to allow assignment of responsibility centres for managing parts of the project, without upsetting the project records, the information exchanges, and systems required to manage the project.

The concept of using the management matrix is essential to effectively manage projects where costs, schedules and resource usage need to be tracked from project inception through to its completion, which can be several years later. The common fixed basis is the WBS which will not change with organizational responsibility, but can only be revised with a scope change in the project definition. At that time the WBS is normally added to or augmented with the basic structure and the basic definitions of the WBS remaining. The WBS provides stability to the information for the cost control and accounting systems as well as to the personnel involved with the project for the life of the project. As the organization responsibility assignments change, the responsibilities for the various segments for the WBS will change; but by having the WBS tied to the facilities, this changing organizational responsibility will not interfere with cost, schedule and progress reporting. The key to this will be that the information from the WBS data base will be provided to different people at different times, but the base information remains the same and is collected on that basis.

The consistency in tracking information through the use of the WBS allows for consistent reporting to governments, senior management, owners, contractors and other participants. This is a key factor in project control. It is therefore important in designing the WBS not to build the organization-responsibility structure as part of the WBS, because if the organization structure is built into the WBS, the end result, due to rapidly changing definitions, will be a non-useful project control tool. Therefore, the WBS should be designed, structured and coded to the facility being built, regardless of the organization managing it.

The organization structure should be considered in light of how the project is to be managed on an overall basis but not on what is to be built. Next must be considered the design and development of a WBS, as a key project control tool to be used between the groups responsible for the project and systems utilized to measure project progress.

WBS DEVELOPMENT

Overview

In developing the project plan, the WBS must be defined with regard to all the elements that are required to make it a working entity. The base elements are:

1. Structure.
2. Code.
3. Reporting.

Before integrating these elements, one must first look at each one separately, then their relationship to each other.

In the design of the project WBS, the "management philosophy" must be considered. The WBS can be a facility-oriented tree or a contract-oriented tree representing the hierachical components of the project to be managed. The approach to the design of the WBS and its development will depend upon the management philosophy adopted. If it is contract-oriented, it must be related to the facilities to be built.

WBS Structure

The structure of the WBS must be such that each level is significant and meaningful, both from a data collection and an overall reporting point of view. This means that every level of the structure developed has significance and relates to a facility contract actually being built or managed within the project, and can be used to generate a required or meaningful report.

The overall design of the structure of the WBS is the key to an effective working system. Therefore, it must be studied very carefully from an input and output of information point of view. Since the WBS serves as a common information exchange language, it is the language, the code and the structure by which all information on the project is gathered, and it is also the device by which all information of the project is disseminated. Therefore, the structure will be built in a hierarchical manner, or as a tree, such that the bottom level will represent the detailed information, and will be large in scope. The base level of the WBS structure is the lowest level of information required to manage the project. This is the lowest level of information at which a user can foresee a need to communicate or monitor. It is the lowest level that the line managers, the construction personnel will require to manage the project.

The next level up the structure will be narrower and will supply information to another level of users. These higher levels will supply significant information for management—significant from the point of view of providing information that is meaningful to various levels of management. This significance ensures that too many levels are not built into the structure. The structure must be designed so that it is meaningful and hierarchical. Twenty levels are too many to manage effectively. Four, five, up to six generally appears to be an adequate number of levels in a large project. (In some cases two sets of the five levels may be used—a base set of five for the detailed collection of data rolling up to a contract level or a major facility level; and five as a superstructure or overlay which ties together the larger components of the facility or the larger contracts.) This would allow up to a total of ten levels, but with two distinct purposes. This double level structure of the WBS works very well and does not restrict the WBS development.

In designing each level of the structure, consideration must be made as to how information will flow upwards to the next level. This transition from one level to another should happen in a natural manner. It should not be forced so that it is difficult, or, as the information flows upward, becomes meaningless. As a new structure is being designed, it should be based on the most likely case and should have some flexibility for additions, although this flexibility for additions will come mainly from the coding once the structure has been set. A simple example of such a structure would have the facilities of the top level followed by the items to build the facility at the lower levels.

In designing a WBS, provision should be made so that when the structure is translated into code, the coding is meaningful to the user. This means that the user can identify the WBS as a facility tree of physical assets which he can recognize when he goes out in the field. It is of paramount importance that the usage of the WBS be designed such that it becomes THE project language. Thus, in a project, items that the user understands and sees as major physical units become elements of the WBS.

The structure is the essential base around which the coding is built and the reporting capabilities of the WBS determined. Thus the structure design is key to an effective WBS.

Code Design

The design of the coding is the key to establishing the WBS as the device to be used by the accounting and project control systems. An effective meaningful code will assist the user and will complement the structure design described above. Whether the user be the field accountant, the field clerk or senior management, the code should have common meaning to all. The top level of the code could be the facility to be constructed such as a pipeline, compressor stations and meter stations or the process plant, buildings and off-sites. It would be a level above this which would represent the project. The code is the ingredient which the user and the functional groups building the project must work with on a daily basis. In designing the code, consideration must be given to the information collected and the methods used to collect it. The user, who analyzes the raw data collected and puts the paper code on it so that the information can be entered into the applicable recording system via the WBS code, must understand the code.

The code design is directly related to the structure development. Each level of the structure represents a segment of the code. The code design is the assimilation of a group of digits to represent a physical facility to be built. At the top level the project does not need to be coded; at the next level the key facilities to be built are coded utilizing the first digit of the code. If the number of key facilities to be managed is nine or less, the code would typically be a one digit code, assuming only numerics are used for coding. If alphas and numerics are used, then the level could have thirty-five different items. The next level below the facility in the structure represents the key items or key contracts to be utilized in building the facility. This level would typically be a two digit code which gives the flexibility to define ninety-nine or, if alphas are used, more than ninety-nine different items. In designing the code, the level above always determines the meaning of the level below. An example of this is illustrated using Figure 15-4 which illustrates a WBS utilized for pipeline construction.

Figure 15-4 illustrates the code which can be used in a four-level WBS. The top level, "Pipeline Construction" is one digit (2), the next level, "Mainline Location" is three digits (212). These three digits represent the type of facility to be built and its physical location. The next two levels, shown as 3 and 4, provide a breakdown of all the items required to build the facility. Note that each level of the code hierarchy is dependent on the levels above to determine the complete definition of a given level. This allows elements in level 4 to vary according to the type of facility to be built as defined in levels 1, 2 or 3. If at all possible, at a specific level, identical coding should reference similiar information. This will facilitate a more understandable code. This ability for lower levels of the WBS to have different meanings depending on the upper levels allows for more project scope to be accommodated without adding unnecessary digits to the code. Although the code is developed in a hierarchical manner, it is desirable within the structure for the code at a given level to be the same in as many places as possible across the project. The code illustrated in Figure 4 always uses the same level 3 code of _ _ _ 1 for Materials, _ _ _ 2 for Installation and _ _ _ 3 for Inspection for all facilities on the project. This provides the capability for material, installation and/or inspection costs, schedules or productivity information to be produced.

As the code is designed, the users must be considered. The users are the people who must code all the information that is to be utilized by the systems. Developing the code should occur in such a way that the user can understand

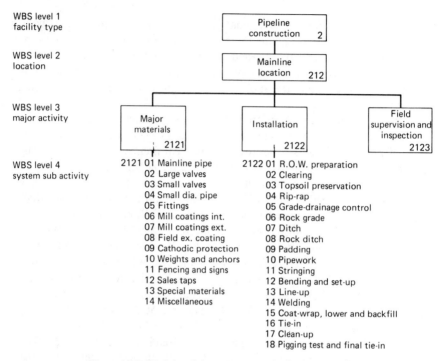

WBS level 1
facility type

WBS level 2
location

WBS level 3
major activity

WBS level 4
system sub activity

Pipeline
construction   2

Mainline
location   212

Major
materials
2121

Installation
2122

Field
supervision and
inspection
2123

2121 01 Mainline pipe
02 Large valves
03 Small valves
04 Small dia. pipe
05 Fittings
06 Mill coatings int.
07 Mill coatings ext.
08 Field ex. coating
09 Cathodic protection
10 Weights and anchors
11 Fencing and signs
12 Sales taps
13 Special materials
14 Miscellaneous

2122 01 R.O.W. preparation
02 Clearing
03 Topsoil preservation
04 Rip-rap
05 Grade-drainage control
06 Rock grade
07 Ditch
08 Rock ditch
09 Padding
10 Pipework
11 Stringing
12 Bending and set-up
13 Line-up
14 Welding
15 Coat-wrap, lower and backfill
16 Tie-in
17 Clean-up
18 Pigging test and final tie-in

Figure 15-4. Work breakdown structure pipeline construction.

its meaning and significance. Many companies have used alpha characters to give this meaning in a simple form. For example, they may code M for manpower, E for equipment and C for consumables.

Integration of the code and the structure is such that every level of the structure has a specific number of digits of code assigned to it. This is where the structure hierarchy becomes important in the code design. If the structure has twenty levels, this necessitates that the coding have a minimum of twenty digits, which is too long; thus a compact structure which gives compact coding will supply a system that the people will use. It is paramount in the design of the code and the structure that usage and simplicity be kept upmost in mind. The "nice-to-have" information should be of secondary importance in the design ensuring that required information can be retrieved from a simple effective structure and related coding.

Reporting Considerations

In designing the WBS, all levels of reporting should be looked at from senior management, or overall project management, down to the lowest level of the person recording the information and the project engineer who wants to know in detail exactly what is happening on his project. The WBS should be designed so that all reports generated from the WBS are automatic without requiring extravagant report writing methods to extract the information collected. The reports required should be looked at and checked to see that both the WBS and the reports are meaningful and representative of what is really required. Once this has been determined, the WBS design should reflect the reports that will be produced for the various levels of management who are involved in the project. Thus, a level in the structure often becomes a level in the reporting hierarchy to the various project management personnel. By incorporating the structure, the reporting and the usage considerations into the coding, the first part of the code supplies the management report and as the code expands it supplies the detailed project reports.

The consideration of the reporting requirements in the WBS design also helps to define the exact reports that will be available to management as the project proceeds. In going through this design phase, management will be able to review the reports they expect to see from the appropriate project management people, and on the detail level, the personnel doing the estimates and the schedules of the baseline work will be able to review exactly the level of detail they will see later for verifying their estimates. In working on the output side of the WBS, the structure and code design will be influenced by the requirements of the different groups responsible for different areas of management. This is not to be confused with the responsibility overlay matrix.

In designing the reports, the prime requirement is to generate the applicable management information required on a facility basis and not the responsibility information required for functional or organizational responsibility reporting. It must be kept clear in designing the reports that they are not the departmental or functional reports but the progress reports for the progress to date for the completion or construction of a particular facility. It must be clearly stated to the users that the WBS only applies to facility related reports.

Co-ordination of Structure, Code and Report Requirements in WBS Design

The preparation of the WBS requires the integration of the structure, code and reporting requirements. Initially, the scope of the project is outlined through a pictorial representation of the WBS which should be prepared. This illustration, note Figure 15-4 for example, should be circulated without coding to the user community both at the worker level and the management level.

At this formative stage, it is important that much forward looking or insight into the project be considered. The structure should be simple, clear and have meaning, and then this should be linked to the code after the structure has been finalized. The coding should then be prepared. Sample reports using the

WBS should be drawn up and circulated for review. These reports should be generated using test data and the proposed code.

The design of the structure, the code and the reports should contain as much input as possible from the groups that will be using it, given whatever time, cost or system constraints which are applied to the particular project. In many cases existing systems such as accounting, or existing policies and procedures within the company may dictate the shape of the WBS. These constraints must be worked around, and an effort should be made to make the WBS as close as possible to the "ideal" required. These constraints should not be the primary determinants of the structure but must be considered in the design. These stumbling blocks and the hurdles must be overcome because this project control tool (WBS) is an absolute necessity in any project with multi-owners, multi-contractors and/or government intervention.

When the WBS is completed, it must be presented and explained to all the users. It should be in book form, which can be readily updated. The first section in the book should illustrate the WBS structure with pictorial drawings, the next section should illustrate the code, either pictorially or graphically, and the final section should be a dictionary of definitions defining the content of each WBS element. These definitions are necessary in projects, ensuring that when a term is used, it is used as the project means it to be used, not with historical meanings which vary from group to group. A careful documentation of the meaning in the dictionary of each WBS element with regard to cost, schedule and resource requirements for the activity ensures that all users will gather and supply information with common meaning to personnel involved with the project. The WBS manual containing coding, definitions and explanations for usage is the last key step in the development of the WBS. A supplement to the manual may contain samples of the report formats to be utilized by the groups and illustrations as to how these tie into the WBS.

Upon completion of the manual, it should then be the responsibility of the project manager's staff to explain it to all users and personnel involved in the project. They should explain why it is necessary, and when and what it is required for. The why is to ensure that all information collected, reported, and forecast against has common meaning, regardless of the information source. It should be explained for usage in all communications (the what) on budgets, estimates, schedules, productivities, performance and items associated with management of the project and should be done with reference to the applicable WBS element. This reference should be used and maintained from the very first day (the when) the project is clearly defined to the final reconciliation of the project. WBS should be used by the engineers, project control, and accounting. The WBS is used everywhere that information on the project's progress is collected.

EXAMPLES OF A WBS

Background

The previous section described the required elements for the preparation of the WBS as the foundation for establishing project control. The characteristics to be considered in WBS development and usage are:

1. Management philosophy.
2. User groups.
3. System integration.
4. WBS—Responsibility Relationship.
5. WBS Components:
   —structure
   —code
   —reporting.

The development process described was used for the preparation of a WBS for the Canadian section of the Alaska Highway Gas Pipeline Project (AHGPP). This project has a WBS which is currently being used by seven companies to manage an estimated expenditure in excess of 8 billion dollars during the 1980 to '85 time span.

Figure 15-5 illustrates the Overall Project, which starts from Prudhoe Bay through Alaska down through the Yukon, British Columbia, Alberta and Saskatchewan. Thus the project covered a large geographical area. Overall, as can be seen by the map, there were many companies and governments involved. The major companies involved were the Northwest Alaska Pipeline Company, the Foothills Pipeline Companies (as shown), and for their part in the southern States, the Northern Border Pipeline Company and the Pacific Gas Transmission Company. This meets the criterion of multi-ownership. The time span for the project was also long, with the start of construction in 1980 and completion in 1985.

Management Philosophy

The management philosophy for the project required a WBS designed on a facility basis.

User Groups

The planned Canadian line was over 2,000 miles with pipe sizes varying from 36" to 56" in diameter. Along this section of the route were approximately 21

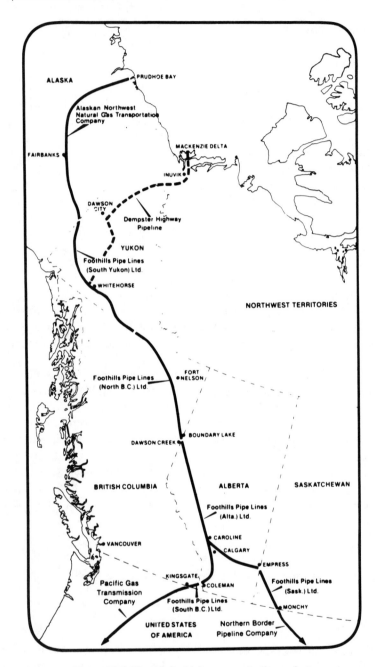

Figure 15-5. The Alaska highway gas pipeline project.

compressor stations each with over 25,000 horsepower. The user community for this project, as shown on Figure 15-1, had functional groups which were part of four companies with the responsible groups including two owner companies, government agencies and contractors. This diverse owner community with the multi-functional centres required a very precise WBS to ensure effective project information flow.

Systems Integration

The functional groups in all six Canadian companies used the WBS as part of their budgeting, estimating, accounting and scheduling systems utilizing both manual and automated systems. All information collected by these systems was summarized using the WBS and then forwarded to management on a common basis using both manual and automated interfaces.

WBS Development

The WBS was developed to meet the needs of all the users described previously. A segment illustrating the WBS structure developed is shown as Figure 15-4. This illustrates the different levels of the structure with their applicable coding. As can be seen from Figure 15-4, the first level is facility, the second location, the third prime activity, and the fourth describes sub-activity. For each of these levels, there are specific reports. The top level—facility type—supplies cost, productivity and schedule information on a facility basis, which is a top management report. To provide additional detail, the reports for each specific facility will be generated for cost, schedule, productivity, manpower, and equipment usage for each level of the WBS shown. The final two levels of activity—the prime activity and sub-activity—enable the designer, the cost engineer, and the scheduler to monitor specific items required to build a particular facility. These levels represent the engineering technical level which is required for the detailed mangement of the project. As can be seen on Figure 15-4, the hierarchical rollup is natural in that each level rolls to the next level in a meaningful fashion.

The code is shown on Figure 15-4 and is graphically illustrated on 15-6. On the left of Figure 15-6 is a map of Alberta showing the facilities to be constructed. The section highlighted is a section of pipeline to be built at the particular location shown. Code 2 is always pipeline with 212 being pipeline at location 12. Also on the drawing are locations 363 etc., which are compression facilities at designated locations. This figure illustrates a portion of the code and its meaning. This type of illustration is very useful in training staff in the usage of the WBS.

An example of the usage of this coding is presented on Figure 15-7. This is

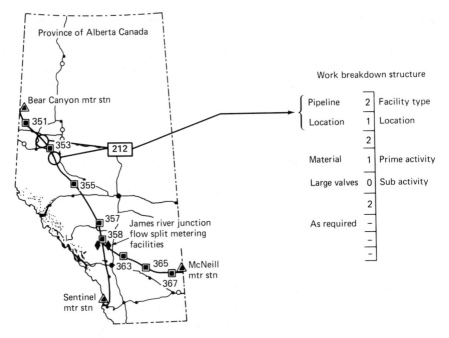

Figure 15-6. Work breakdown structure pipeline construction.

the standard commitment report on a WBS basis for a particular location. The left side of the figure is the WBS code, six digits in this case. The capability of nine digits is allowed to supply future flexibility as the project proceeds. If more information is needed in a particular area, then the WBS can expand to receive the information without redesigning the code or structure, while maintaining the flow of information in a hierarchical manner. The first three digits identify the facility type and its location, as shown on Figure 15-6. Then come the materials as the next digit, which is represented by a "1". The materials code for the items required for pipeline are next. The authorized dollars illustrated are for the items authorized for purchase for the particular location. As the project proceeds, the incurred costs will be recorded as well as committed costs. In addition, estimates to complete will be done so that an estimated final total cost can be determined for this part of the project. This report shown in Figure 15-7 is only one of many which can be generated within the WBS framework. This example of the Pipeline project illustrated a WBS which is utilized in the multi-company environment for a large project where the WBS is a key project control tool. Thus as illustrated, a properly designed WBS is the basis for effective project control tools.

WBS Code	WBS Description	Current authorized	Incurred cost this period	to date	Committed cost this period	to date	Estimate to complete	Estimated final total
212100	Unallocated							
212101	Mainline pipe	37,505						
212102	Large valves	420						
212103	Small valves	21						
212104	Small diameter pipe	2						
212105	Fittings	47						
212106	Mill coating internal	329						
212107	Mill coating external							
212108	Field coating external	460						
212109	Cathodic protection							
212110	Weights and anchor	785						
212111	Fencing and signs							
212112	Sales taps							
212113	Special materials — coating	54						
212114	Miscellaneous	88						
	Sub-total materials	39,711						

Figure 15-7. Work breakdown structure commitment report.

CONCLUSIONS

It appears that for now and the foreseeable future, projects with long time spans from the conceptual stage to operation, large capital expenditures, complex ownership and government involvement will become more common. In this complex environment, it is absolutely essential to have a precisely defined methodology for the WBS with which all involved personnel can exchange information, plan the project and organize reporting. This paper has outlined the reasons why a properly designed WBS becomes the essential tool for effective project management in a project environment. The paper illustrates the components and requirements to prepare the required WBS. The prime reasons the WBS should be used are:

1. Developing the WBS early in the project life cycle provides a method for clear definition of the project scope and the process of WBS development helps all participants to clearly understand the project during the initial stages.
2. The use of the WBS code for monitoring and forecasting of all cost, schedule and productivity information ensures that project management personnel will have a baseline to which comparison can be made. By establishing a common definition for all information on the project, effective and logical management decisions can be made.
3. With multi-participants and changing personnel, it is essential that all terms used mean the same to all participants. This consistency of defini-

tion is established through the development and use of the WBS with associated code and dictionary.

4. The WBS becomes the basis from which all information flow between information systems can be established, and upon which all facility type reporting is available.

Thus a properly designed and developed WBS with its structure, code and dictionary, supplies the common base for project management by having cost, schedule and productivity information all using WBS definitions forming the foundation of quality project control for any project.

16. Network Techniques in Project Management

Joseph J. Moder*

Project management involves the coordination of group activity wherein the manager plans, organizes, staffs, directs and controls, to achieve an objective with constraints on time, cost and performance of the end product. This chapter will deal with the planning and control functions. *Planning* is the process of preparing for the commitment of resources in the most economical fashion. *Controlling* is the process of making events conform to schedules by coordinating the action of all parts of the organization according to the plan established for attaining the objective.

It can also be said that project management is a blend of art and science: the art of getting things done through and with people in formally organized groups; and the science of handling large amounts of data to plan and control so that project duration and cost are balanced, and excessive and disruptive demands on scarce resources are avoided. This chapter will deal with the science of project planning and control that is based on a network representation of the project plan; also referred to as critical path methods.

It is appropriate at this point to elaborate on the term *project*. Projects may, on the one hand, involve routine procedures that are performed repetitively, such as the monthly closing of accounting books. In this case, critical path methods are useful for *detailed* analysis and optimization of the operating plan. Usually, however, these methods are applied to one-time efforts; notably construction work of all kinds; maintenance operations; moving, modifying, or setting up a new factory or facility of some sort; etc. Critical path methods are applicable to projects which encompass an extremely wide range of resource requirements and duration times.

*Joseph J. Moder is Professor in the Department of Management Science at the University of Miami, Coral Gables, Florida. He received his B.S. degree from Washington University, his Ph.D. from Northwestern University, and he did Post Doctoral work in Statistics and Operations Research at Iowa State University and Stanford University. He was a Visiting Professor of Engineering Production at the University of Birmingham, England. His research interests include applied statistics and project management methodology. He has published numerous articles and several books in these fields, and has conducted short courses and research projects in these areas.

In project management, although similar work may have been done previously, it is not usually being repeated in the identical manner on a production basis. Consequently, in order to accomplish the project tasks efficiently, the project manager must plan and schedule largely on the basis of his experience with similar projects, applying his judgment to the particular conditions of the project at hand. During the course of the project he must continually replan and reschedule because of unexpected progress, delays, or technical conditions. Critical path methods are designed to facilitate this mode of operation.

HISTORY OF THE EARLY DEVELOPMENT OF CRITICAL PATH METHODS

Until the advent of critical path methods, there was no generally accepted formal procedure to aid in the management of projects. Each manager had his own scheme which often involved the use of bar charts originally developed by Henry Gantt around 1900. Although the bar chart is still a useful tool in production management, it is inadequate as a means of describing the complex interrelationships among project activities associated with contemporary project management.

This inadequacy was overcome by the significant contribution of Karol Adamiecki in 1931 (1).* He developed a methodology in a form that he called a Harmony graph. This is essentially a bar-chart, rotated 90 degrees, with a vertical time scale, a column (movable strip) for each activity in the project, and a very clever means of showing the interrelationship among project activities. This work was evidently completely overlooked. It was not until 1957–1958 that a more formal and general approach toward a discipline of project management occurred. At this time several techniques were developed concurrently, but independently. The technique called Critical Path Method (CPM) was developed in connection with a very large project undertaken at Du Pont Corporation by Kelley and Walker (5). The objective here was to determine the optimum (minimum total cost) duration for a project whose activity durations were primarily deterministic variables.

A similar development occurred in Great Britain where the problems of overhauling an electricity generating plant were being studied (6). The principal feature of their technique was the determination of what they called the "longest irreducible sequence of events."

A somewhat different approach to the problem, called Project Evaluation and Review Technique (PERT), was developed in conjunction with the Polaris weapons system by Malcolm and others (7). The objective here was to develop an improved method of planning, scheduling, and controlling an extremely

---

*Numbered references are given at the end of this chapter.

large, complicated development program in which many of the activities being conducted were at or beyond the state of the art, and hence the actual activity duration times were primarily random variables with considerable variance.

DEVELOPMENT OF THE NETWORK PLAN CONCEPT

Although all of the above developments were conducted independently, they are essentially all based upon the important concept of a *network* representation of the project plan. The network diagram is essentially an outgrowth of the bar chart which was developed by Gantt in the context of a World War I military requirement. The bar chart, which is primarily designed to control the time element of a program, is depicted in Figure 16-1(a). Here, the bar chart lists the major activities comprising a hypothetical project, their scheduled start and finish times, and their current status. The steps followed in preparing a bar chart are as follows:

1. Analyze the project and specify the basic approach to be used.
2. Break the project down into a reasonable number of activities to be scheduled.
3. Estimate the time required to perform each activity.
4. Place the activities in sequence of time, taking into account the requirements that certain activities must be performed sequentially while others can be performed simultaneously.
5. If a completion date is specified, the diagram is adjusted until this constraint is satisfied.

The primary advantage of the bar-chart is that the plan, schedule, and progress of the project can all be portrayed graphically together. Figure 16-1 shows the five-activity plan and 15-week schedule, and current status (end of 3rd week) indicates, for example, that activity B is slightly behind schedule. In spite of this important advantage, bar-charts have not been too successful on one-time-through projects with a high engineering content, or projects of large scope. The reasons for this include the fact that the simplicity of the bar-chart precludes showing sufficient detail to enable timely detection of schedule slippages on activities with relatively long duration times. Also, the bar-chart does not show explicitly the dependency relationships among the activities. Hence, it is very difficult to impute the effects on project completion of progress delays in individual activities. Finally, the bar-chart is awkward to set up and maintain for large projects, and it has a tendency to quickly become outdated and lose its usefulness. With these disadvantages in mind, along with certain events of the mid-fifties such as the emergence of large technical programs, large digital computers, general systems theory, etc., the stage was set for the develop-

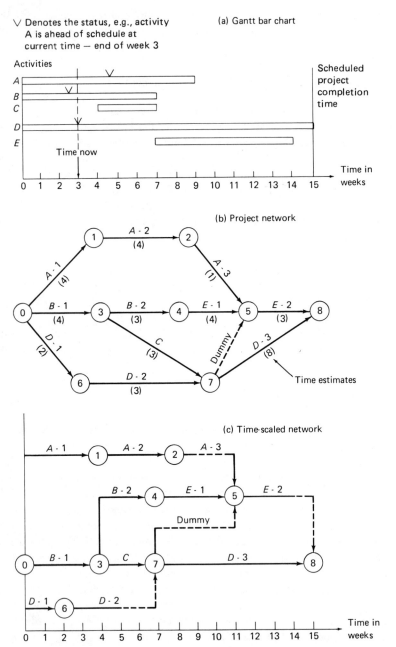

∨ Denotes the status, e.g., activity A is ahead of schedule at current time — end of week 3

(a) Gantt bar chart

(b) Project network

(c) Time-scaled network

Figure 16-1(a),(b),(c). Comparison of bar chart, project network, and time-scaled network. (From *Project Management with CPM and PERT.* J. J. Moder and C. R. Phillips, © 1970 by Litton Educational Publishing, Inc. Reprinted by permission of Van Nostrand Reinhold Co.)

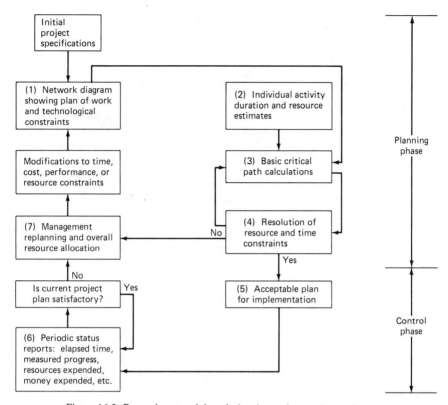

Figure 16-2. Dynamic network-based planning and control procedure.

ment of a network-based project management methodology. Something like the critical path method literally had to emerge.

Before taking up the logic of networking, it will be useful to preview the scope of critical path methods as the basis of a dynamic network-based planning, scheduling, and control procedure, as shown in Figure 16-2.

Step 1, which is the representation of the basic project plan in the form of a network, will be treated in the next section. Steps 2 and 3 will then be considered to estimate the duration of the project plan and determine its critical path. Considered next are the techniques which comprise Step 4; they are designed to modify the initial project plan to satisfy time and resource constraints placed on the project. Finally, the control phase of project management, Step 6, will be considered.

THE LOGIC OF NETWORKS AS MODELS FOR PROJECT PLANS

The first step in drawing a project network is to list all jobs (activities) that have to be performed to complete the project, and to put these jobs in proper technological sequence in the form of a network or arrow diagram. Each job is indicated by an arrow, with nodes, called events, placed at each end of the arrows. Events represent points in time and are said to occur when all activities leading into the event are completed. In Figure 16-3, for example, when the two activities "select operators" and "prepare training material" are completed, the event numbered 10 is said to occur. It should be pointed out that the two predecessor activities of Event 10 need not be completed at the same time; however, when they are both completed, Event 10 occurs, and only then may the activity "train operators" begin. Similarly, when this activity is completed, Event 15 occurs, and the successor activities "test process A" and "test process B" each *may* then begin. It is important to note that the ordering of these activities is based on the "technology" of the resources being utilized.

Activities require the expenditure of time and resources to complete; eight time units and three instructors in the above example. The length of the arrow is not important, but its direction relative to other activities and events indicates the *technological constraints* on the order in which the activities making up the project may be performed.

There is also a need for what is called a *dummy* activity, which requires neither time nor resources to complete. Activity 7-5 in the middle of Figure 16-1 is an example of such an activity. Its sole purpose is to show precedence relationships, i.e., that activities C and D-2 must (technologically) precede activity E-2.

The project network is then constructed by starting with the initial project event which has no predecessor activities and occurs at the start of the project. From this event, activities are added to the network using the basic logic described above. This process is continued until all activities have been included in the network, the last of which merge into the project end event which has no successor activities. In carrying out this task the novice must be extremely careful to avoid the common error of ordering the activities arbitrarily according to some preconceived idea of the sequence that the activities will probably take when the project is carried out. If this error is made, the subsequent scheduling and control procedures will be unworkable. However, if the network is faithfully drawn according to technological constraints, it will be a unique project model which only changes when fundamental changes in

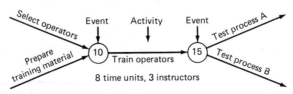

Figure 16-3. An example arrow diagram activity.

the plan are made. It will also present maximum flexibility in subsequent scheduling of the activities to satisfy resource constraints.

The preparation of the project network presents an excellent opportunity to try out, or simulate on paper, various ways of carrying out the project, thus avoiding costly and time-consuming mistakes which might be made "in the field" during the actual conduct of the project. At the conclusion of the planning operation, the final network presents a permanent record giving a clear expression of the way in which the project is to be carried out so that all parties involved in the project can see their involvement and responsibilities.

The Time Element. After the planning or networking, the *average duration* of each job is estimated, based upon the job specifications and a consideration of the resources to be employed in carrying out the job. The best estimates will usually be obtained from the person(s) who will supervise the work or who has had such experience.

These time estimates are placed beside the appropriate arrows. If we were then to sum the durations of the jobs along all possible paths from the beginning to the end of the project, the longest one is called the critical path, and its length is the expected duration of the project. Any delay in the start or completion of the jobs along this path will delay completion of the whole project. The rest of the jobs are "floaters" which have a limited amount of leeway (slack) for completion without affecting the target date for the completion of the project.

These concepts are illustrated at the bottom of Figure 16-1 where the network activities have been plotted to scale on a time axis. This diagram shows the critical path quite clearly. It consists of activities B-1, C-1, and D-3, and has an overall duration of 15 weeks. The slack along the other network paths is shown by the dashed portion of the network arrows. For example, the path D-1 and D-2 has 2 weeks of slack, that is, 7 weeks are available to carry out these two jobs which are expected to require only 5 weeks to complete.

The above time-scaled network can be considered as a graphical solution to what is called the *basic scheduling computations*. This is not an operational procedure; it was used here primarily for illustrative purposes.

The objective of the scheduling computations is to determine the critical path(s) and its duration, and to determine the amount of slack on the remaining paths. It turns out that this can best be accomplished by computing the earliest start and finish, and latest start and finish times for each project activity.

BASIC SCHEDULING COMPUTATIONS

A programmable algorithm for the basic scheduling computations is given by Equations [1] and [7] below, in terms of the following nomenclature.

D_{ij} estimate of the mean duration time for activity $(i-j)$
E_i earliest occurrence time for event i
L_i latest allowable occurrence time for event i
ES_{ij} earliest start time for activity $(i-j)$
EF_{ij} earliest finish time for activity $(i-j)$

LS_{ij} latest allowable start time for activity $(i-j)$
LF_{ij} latest allowable finish time for activity $(i-j)$
S_{ij} total slack (or float) time for activity $(i-j)$
FS_{ij} free slack (or float) time for activity $(i-j)$
T_s schedule time for the completion of a project or the occurrence of
          certain key events in a project

Earliest and Latest Event Times

Assume that the events were numbered (or renumbered by a simple algorithm) so that the initial event is 1, the terminal event is t, and all other events $(i-j)$ are numbered so that $i < j$. Now let $E_1 = 0$ by assumption, then

$$E_j = \max_i (E_i + D_{ij}), \qquad 2 \le j \le t \qquad [1]$$

$E_t =$ (expected) project duration, and
$L_t = E_t$ or T_s, the scheduled project completion time. Then,

$$L_i = \min_j (L_j - D_{ij}), \qquad 1 \le i \le t - 1 \qquad [2]$$

Earliest and Latest Activity Start and Finish Times and Slack

$$
\begin{aligned}
ES_{ij} &= E_i, & \text{all } ij & \qquad [3] \\
EF_{ij} &= E_i + D_{ij}, & \text{all } ij & \qquad [4] \\
LF_{ij} &= L_j, & \text{all } ij & \qquad [5] \\
LS_{ij} &= L_j - D_{ij}, & \text{all } ij & \qquad [6] \\
S_{ij} &= L_j - EF_{ij}, & \text{all } ij & \qquad [7]
\end{aligned}
$$

The above equations embody two basic sets of calculations. First, the *forward pass calculations* are carried out to determine the earliest occurrence time for each event $j(E_j)$, and the earliest start and finish times for each activity $i-j(ES_{ij}$ and $EF_{ij})$. These calculations are based on the assumption that each activity is conducted as *early* as possible, i.e., they are started as soon as their predecessor event occurs. Since these calculations are initiated by equating the initial project event to time zero ($E_1 \equiv 0$), the earliest time computed for the project terminal event (E_t) gives the expected project duration.

The second set of calculations, called the *backward pass calculations,* are carried out to determine the latest (allowable) occurrence times for each event $i(L_i)$, and the latest (allowable) start and finish times for each activity $i-j$ (LS_{ij} and LF_{ij}). These calculations begin with the project end event by equating its latest allowable occurrence time to the scheduled project duration, if one is specified ($L_t \equiv T_s$), or by arbitrarily equating it to $E_t(L_t \equiv E_t)$ if no duration is specified. This is referred to as the "zero-slack" convention. These calculations then proceed by working backwards through the network, always assuming that each activity is conducted as *late* as possible.

Role of Hand Computation Procedure

The misuse of computers is not uncommon in the application of critical path methods. This occurs notably in making the above scheduling computations during the initial development of an acceptable project plan; an operation pre-

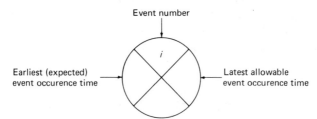

Reading earliest expected and latest allowable activity start and finish times and slack from the special symbols

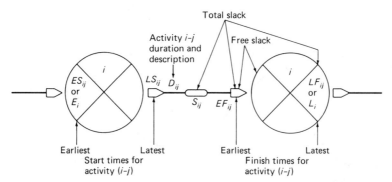

Figure 16-4. Key to use and interpretation of space symbols. (From *Project Management with CPM and PERT*, J. J. Moder and C. R. Phillips, © 1970 by Litton Educational Publishing, Inc. Reprinted by permission of Van Nostrand Reinhold Co.)

viously described as Steps 3 and 4 in Figure 16-2. At this stage it is important that the momentum of a project planning session must not be broken by the requirement for a computer run, and furthermore, it is more economical to perform these computations once by hand, regardless of the size of the network.

For this purpose a set of special networking symbols is useful to avoid making arithmetic errors. The key to these symbols is given in Figure 16-4, and their application is given in Figure 16-5, where the network employed is essentially the same as that used in Figure 16-1.

The start of the project at time zero is noted by setting $E_0 = 0$ in Figure 16-5. Then, equation [4] gives the early finish time for activity $[0 - 1]$ as $EF_{01} = E_0 + D_{01} = 0 + 2 = 2$. Since event 1 has but one predecessor, activity $[0 - 1]$, its early occurrence time is given by $E_1 = EF_{01} = 2$. The application of equation [1] occurs at all "merge" events [5, 7 and 8]. For example, at event 5 the early event time $E_5 = 11$ is computed as follows:

$$E_5 = \max_{i=2,4} (E_2 + D_{25} = 6 + 1 = 7;\ E_4 + D_{45} = 7 + 4 = 11) = 11$$

The backward pass is initiated by using the zero-slack convention, i.e. letting $L_8 = E_8 = 15$. Working backwards from here, the latest start time for activity $[5 - 8]$ is obtained from eq. [6] as $LS_{58} = L_8 - D_{58} = 15 - 3 = 12$. Since event 5 has but one successor, activity $[5 - 8]$, its latest occurrence time is

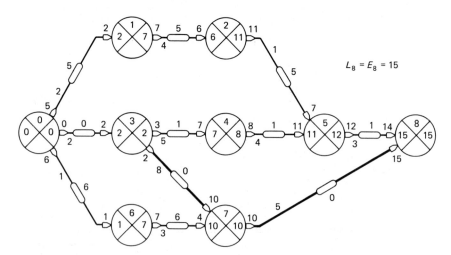

Figure 16-5. Illustrative network employing the special activity and event symbols, showing completed computations. (From *Project Management with CPM and PERT*, J. J. Moder and C. R. Phillips, © 1970 by Litton Educational Publishing, Inc. Reprinted by permission of Van Nostrand Reinhold Co.)

given by $L_5 = LS_{58} = 12$. The application of equation [2] occurs at all "burst" events [0 and 3]. For example, at event 3 the latest event time $L_3 = 2$ is computed as follows:

$$L_3 = \min_{j=4,7} (L_4 - D_{34} = 8 - 5 = 3, L_7 - D_{37} = 10 - 8 = 2) = 2$$

The Critical Path and Slack Paths

Among the many types of slack defined in the literature, two are of most value and are discussed here: they are called total activity slack, or simply total slack, and activity-free slack, or simply free slack. They are also referred to as total float and free float, with the same definitions.

Total Activity Slack.   *Definition:* Total activity slack is equal to the difference between the earliest and latest allowable start or finish times for the activity in question. Thus, for activity $(i-j)$, the total slack is given by

$$S_{ij} = LS_{ij} - ES_{ij} \quad \text{or} \quad LF_{ij} - EF_{ij}$$

Activity-Free Slack.   Merge point activities, which are the last activities on slack paths, have what is called activity-free slack.

Definition: Activity-free slack is equal to the earliest occurrence time of the activity's successor event, minus the earliest finish time of the activity in question. Thus, for activity $(i-j)$, the free slack is given by

$$FS_{ij} = E_j - EF_{ij} \quad \text{or} \quad ES_{jk} - EF_{ij}$$

Critical Path Identification.   *Definition:* The critical path is the path with the least total slack.

We will point out later that whenever scheduled times are permitted on intermediate network events, the critical path will not always be the longest path through the network. However, the above definition of the critical path always applies.

If the "zero-slack" convention of letting $L_t = E_t$ for the terminal network event is followed, then the critical path will have zero slack. This situation is illustrated in Figure 16-5, where $L_8 = E_8 = 15$. However, if the latest allowable time for the terminal event is set by T_s, an arbitrary scheduled duration time for the completion of the project, then the slack on the critical path will be positive, zero, or negative, depending on whether $T_s > E_t$, $T_s = E_t$, or T_s

$< E_t$, respectively. The last situation indicates, of course, that the completion of the project is expected to be late, that is, completion after the scheduled time, T_s. This is generally an unsatisfactory situation, and replanning (Steps 3 and 4 in Figure 16-2) would be required.

To carry out this replanning, it is quite helpful to be able to determine the critical path and its duration with a minimum of hand computation. This can be accomplished from the *forward pass computations alone.* Referring to Figure 16-5, start with the end event, 8, which must be on the critical path. Now trace backwards through the network along the path(s) with $EF_{ij} = E_j$. In this case we proceed to event 7 because $EF_{78} = E_8 = 15$, while $EF_{58} = 14 \neq E_8$. In like manner we proceed backwards to event 3 and then to the initial event zero. Thus the critical path is 0-3-7-8, with a duration of 15 time units, determined from the *forward pass computations alone.*

If the backward pass computations are also completed, then total slack and free slack can also be computed. For example, path 0-1-2-5 has a total slack of 5. This is the amount of time by which the actual completion time of this path can be delayed without causing the duration of the overall project to exceed its scheduled completion time. When the critical path has zero slack, as in this example, then the total slack is equal to the amount of time that the activity completion time can be delayed without affecting the earliest start time of any activity or the earliest occurrence time of any event *on the critical path.* For example, activity 0-1 has a total slack of 5 and a free slack of 0. If its completion time is delayed up to 5 time units, it will affect the early start times of the remaining activities on this slack path; however, it will not affect any event on the critical path (event 8 in this case). On the other hand, activity 2-5 has a total slack of 5 and a free slack of 4. Its completion can be delayed up to 5 time units without affecting the critical path (event 8), and it can be delayed up to 4 (free slack) without affecting *any* other event or activity in the network.

Multiple Initial and Terminal Events, and Scheduled Dates

In certain projects there may be several key events, called milestones, which must occur on or before an arbitrary scheduled date. To handle these situations, the following conventions are usually adopted.

Conventions: A scheduled time, T_s, for an initial project event (one without predecessor activities) is interpreted as its earliest expected time, i.e., $T_s \equiv E$ for initial project events. A scheduled time, T_s, for an intermediate (or terminal) project event is interpreted as its latest allowable occurrence time, i.e., $T_s \equiv L$.

To illustrate the effect of a scheduled time for an intermediate network event, suppose that $T_s = 10$ for event 5 in Figure 16-5. In this case, with L_5

$= T_s = 10$, the critical path would become 0-3-4-5, since it would have the least slack of -1 time units. The longest path through the network would, of course, continue to be 0-3-7-8.

Another network complication is the occurrence of multiple initial and/or terminal events. For example, suppose there are several projects, each with their own networks, that are competing for a common set of resources. Since a number of algorithms require single initial and terminal events, a procedure is needed to combine these projects into one network with a single initial and terminal event. This can be accomplished by the use of dummy initial and terminal events to which each project connects with dummy activities. Duration times are assigned to the latter to impute the correct project start time relative to the early start time assigned to the initial event, and the correct finish time relative to the late finish time assigned to the terminal event.

TIME-COST TRADE-OFF PROCEDURES

The determination of the critical path and its duration was described above. This constitutes Step 3 in Figure 16-2. Moving on to Step 4, if the earliest occurrence time for the network terminal event exceeds the scheduled project duration, then some modification of the network may be required to achieve an acceptable plan.

These modifications might take the form of a major change in the network structure. For example, changing the assumption that one set of concrete forms is available to the availability of two sets may result in a considerable change in the network and reduction in the project duration.

A different procedure that is frequently employed to handle this problem is referred to as time-cost trade-off. Referring to Figure 16-5, we might ask the question, how can we most economically reduce the duration of this project from its current level of 15 time units, say weeks, to 14 weeks. To accomplish this, the critical path, i.e., 0-3, 3-7, 7-8, must be reduced by 1 week. The decision in this case would be to buy a week of time on that activity(s) where it is available at the lowest additional (marginal) cost. If this turns out to be activity 3-7 or 7-8, then the resulting project will have two critical paths, each of 14 weeks duration, i.e., 0-3, 3-4, 4-5, 5-8, and 0-3, 3-7, 7-8. Thus further reductions in this project duration will be more complicated because both paths must now be considered. One must also constantly consider buying back time previously bought on certain activities. This problem very rapidly reaches the point where a computer is required to obtain an optimal solution.

The Critical Path Method (CPM)

The CPM procedure, developed by Kelley and Walker (5) to handle this problem, arises when we ask for the project schedule, which minimizes *total project costs.* This is equivalent to the schedule that just balances the marginal value of time saved (in completing the project a time unit early) against the marginal cost of saving it. The total project cost is made up of the indirect costs, determined by the accounting department considering normal overhead costs and the "value" of the time saved, plus the *minimum* direct project costs, determined as follows by the CPM procedure.

The CPM computational algorithm is based on an assumed linear cost vs. time relationship for each activity. With this input, this problem can be formulated as a linear programming problem to minimize the total project *direct* costs, subject to constraints dictated by the activity time-cost curves, and the network logic.

Although this is an elegant algorithm, it is rarely applied, primarily because of the unrealistic basic assumption of the unlimited availability of resources. Nevertheless, it is an important concept that is frequently applied in the simple manner illustrated at the beginning of this section. The important consideration of limited resources is treated in the next section.

SCHEDULING ACTIVITIES TO SATISFY TIME AND RESOURCE CONSTRAINTS

To illustrate how Figure 16-5 can be used to solve resource allocation problems, suppose that activities 1-2, 3-4, and 5-8 require the continous use of a special piece of equipment during their performance. Can this requirement be met without causing a delay in the completion of this project?

With the aid of Figure 16-5, it is very easy to see that the answer to this question is yes, if the following schedule is used. The reasoning proceeds as follows. First, activities 1-2 and 3-4 must preceed 5-8, so the first question is which of these two activities should be scheduled first. Reference to Figure 16-5 indicates that both have an early start time of 2, and since the floats are 5 and 1 for activities 1-2 and 3-4, respectively, the activity ordering of 1-2, 3-4, and 5-8 follows.

One can, of course, ask more involved questions dealing with the leveling of the demand for various personnel skills. From a computer standpoint, these questions are the most important ones involved in the use of critical path methods.

A Heuristic Resource Scheduling Procedure

Resource allocation problems in general can be categorized as the determination of the scheduled times for project activities which:

1. Level the resource requirements in time, subject to a constraint on the project duration; or

2. Minimize the project duration subject to constraints on the availabilities of resources; or
3. Minimize the total cost of the resources and the penalties due to project delay—the long-range planning problem.

A popular scheduling procedure to solve the first and second problems consists of scheduling activities one day at a time, working from the first to the last day of the project. Each day, the activities that are ready to start (all predecessors complete) are ordered in a list with least slack first. Then, working through this list, as many activities as possible are scheduled (resource availability permitting). At the end of each day, the resources available are updated, as well as the early start and finish times of all delayed activities. This process is then repeated until the entire project has been scheduled.

The combinatorial nature of this problem has prevented it from yielding to the optimal solution techniques of mathematical programming. Because of this lack of success with optimization procedures, major attention has been devoted to developing heuristic procedures which produce "good" feasible solutions. The procedure described above is a popular example of such heuristic procedures and is known as the "least slack first rule," or its equivalent name, the "minimum late start time rule." Collectively, they are essentially schemes for assigning priorities to the activities that are used in making the activity sequencing decisions required for the resolution of resource conflicts.

EVALUATION OF SEVERAL SCHEDULING HEURISTICS

Two categories of heuristics that have been found most effective are those incorporating some measure of time, such as activity slack or duration, and those incorporating some measure of resource usage. Davis [3] has made an extensive comparison of eight heuristics on some 83 network problems for which the optimal solutions were obtained using his bounded enumeration procedure. The rules tested included:

1. *Minimum Late Start Time* (LST)—order by increasing LST.
2. *Minimum Late Finish Time* (LFT)—order by increasing LFT.
3. *Resource Scheduling Method*—order by increasing d_{ij}, where d_{ij} = increase in project duration resulting when activity j follows i; = $\max[0; (E_i - L_j)]$, where E_i and L_j denote the early finish time of activity i and the late start time of activity j, respectively. The above activity comparison is made on a pairwise basis among all activities in the eligible activity set.
4. *Shortest Imminent Operation*—order by increasing activity duration.
5. *Greatest Resource Demand*—order by decreasing total resource demand.
6. *Greatest Resource Utilization*—priority is given to that combination of

activities which results in maximum resource utilization in each scheduling interval; a rule which requires the use of zero–one integer programming to implement.

7. *Most Jobs Possible*—similar to Rule 6, except the number of active jobs is maximized.

8. *Select Jobs Randomly*—order the eligible activities by a random process.

The first four rules above were studied because they are very popular in the open literature on scheduling. The next three rules were included because they have been reported to be used in some of the many computer programs available for project scheduling on a commercial basis. The detailed workings of these programs have been kept secret. The last rule was included as a benchmark of human performance—presumably an experienced scheduler can outperform this rule.

The primary evaluation made in this study was based on the average percentage increase in project duration over the optimal schedule. On this basis the first three rules, having percentages of 5.6, 6.7, and 6.8, respectively, were considerably better than Rule 8, based on random selection, which had a percentage of 11.4. Also, Rules 5, 6, and 7, having percentages of 13.1, 13.1 and 16.0, respectively, gave poorer schedules than Rule 8.

While average performance is a reasonable guide in selecting scheduling rules, it should be pointed out that it is the nature of heuristics that no one rule will always give the best schedule. For this reason, one can argue that if the problem warrants a near optimal schedule, then several different heuristics should be applied. It also suggests that an important research area is to relate heuristic rule performance with simple parameters that describe the network and its resource constraints.

A Realistic Scheduling Procedure

Although the above heuristic scheduling procedure is oversimplified for most practical applications, it has three important properties. First, it can handle any number of resources. Second, it can handle any number of projects as long as their scheduled start and finish times are given. Finally, the procedure can be used as the basis for a more generally applicable scheduling procedure, such as that developed by Wiest (10). Some of its features include:

1. Variable crew sizes are permissible.
2. Splitting or interrupting an activity is permissible.
3. Assignment of unused resources is incorporated.

The application of Wiest's procedure to solve Problem 2 cited in the section entitled A Heuristic Resource Scheduling Procedure is obvious. It can also be used to solve the long-range planning problem, 3 above, by evaluating the total cost of alternative levels of available resources and the penalties associated with delays in the completion of certain projects.

PROBABILISTIC CONSIDERATIONS IN NETWORKING

There are two probabilistic aspects of critical path methods that are of some importance. The first involves those projects in which special milestone events occur, such as the end of test or evaluation activities. The special nature of these events is that they may have several *possible* successor activities, but only one will be selected and the others will be ignored. This situation is referred to as probabilistic branching. For example, in a space vehicle project, an evaluation activity may result in the choice of a solid or a liquid fuel engine, but not both. Also, as a result of a "failure" in some test, such projects may require recycling to an earlier network event, forming a closed loop. Neither of these situations is permissible according to the network logic assumed above.

The occurrence of these situations can be handled by drawing the network in general rather than specific terms. For example, the network plan for the above situation would be drawn up without reference to whether the engine was liquid or solid fuel. Also, the loop situation would be handled by omitting the loop, and including its time effect in other network activities. Where more refined planning is required, a special simulation language called GERT (Graphical Evaluation and Review Technique) has been developed by Pritsker (9) which permits the above situations to be built into the network.

The second stochastic aspect of critical path methods deals with the fact that the actual duration of a project activity is usually a (hypothetical) random variable rather than a deterministic constant. Up to now, the effects of the variance in activity performance times on the procedures we have discussed have either been assumed to be negligible or have been neglected. The initial consideration of this problem led to the development of PERT, as cited in the opening section.

The PERT Statistical Approach to Project Management

One of the chief concerns in the development of PERT was meeting the schedules placed on key milestone events, where considerable uncertainty in actual activity performance times existed. Because of this emphasis on events, which is a long-standing United States government practice in controlling projects by monitoring milestones, the activity labels were placed inside the event symbols. This convention, however, has no effect on the network logic described above, and thus represents a minor difference from the networking procedures described above. A major difference in procedures arises, however, from the efforts to estimate, from the project plan, the probability that the milestone schedules would be met.

The approach to this problem, which is frequently taken in developments of this type, was to collect input information on the basic elements of the system, and from it synthesize their effects on system performance. In this case the input information consisted of a measure of the uncertainty in activity duration times, and from this the uncertainty in meeting schedules was computed.

PERT Three Time Estimates

In the PERT approach, the actual activity performance time, t, is assumed to have a hypothetical probability distribution with mean, t_e, and variance, σ_t^2. It is referred to as hypothetical because its parameters must be estimated before any actual observations are made. When the activity is finally completed, the actual time can be regarded as the first (and last) sample from this hypothetical distribution. Estimates of t_e and σ_t^2 must therefore be based on someone's judgment, which in turn is based on a "sampling" of prior work experience.

The PERT activity input data is in the form of three time estimates, called a, m, and b. They denote the optimistic, most likely, and pessimistic estimates of t, respectively. Statistically, these are the zero percentile, the mode, and the 100 percentile of the hypothetical probability distribution.

A rule of thumb in statistics is that the standard deviation can be estimated roughly as ⅙ of the range of the distribution. This follows from the fact that at least 89% of any distribution lies within three standard deviations from the mean, and for the Normal distribution this percentage is 99.7+%. Thus the estimate of the variance is given by

$$\text{variance of } t \equiv \sigma_t^2 = [(b - a)/6]^2 \qquad [8]$$

While the above formula is a part of the original PERT procedure, the author prefers to define a and b as the 5 and 95 percentiles, which in turn calls for replacing the divisor 6 in Equation [8] by 3.2.

To derive an estimate of the mean requires an assumption about the shape of the probability distribution of t. In the development of PERT, it was assumed that a plausible (and mathematically convenient) distribution for t is the Beta distribution whose standard deviation was ⅙ of its range. For this distribution, Equation (9) gives a linear approximation to the true (cubic) relationship between the mean, t_e, and the mode, m:

$$\text{mean of } t \equiv t_e = (a + 4m + b)/6 \qquad [9]$$

PERT Probability Calculation

At this point the scheduling computations described in the section entitled Basic Scheduling Computations can be carried out using only the mean values computed from Equation [9] for each activity. The PERT procedure then considers the activities on the critical path(s) through the network, and ignores all others; a rather strong simplifying assumption. If there are several critical paths, then the one with the largest variance is chosen to represent the network. Assuming the actual activity performance times for these activities to be *independent random variables* with means, t_{ei}, and variances, σ_{ti}^2, the statistical properties of the "project" duration follows directly from the Central Limit Theorem. Assuming the critical path consists of N activities, and denoting the sum of their actual durations by T, this can be written as follows:

$$T = \sum_{i=1}^{N} t_i$$

$$\text{mean of } T \equiv T_e = \sum_{i=1}^{N} t_{ei} \qquad [10]$$

$$\text{variance of } T \equiv \sigma_T^2 = \sum_{i=1}^{N} \sigma_{ti}^2 \qquad [11]$$

shape of distribution of T: Normal

probability of meeting schedule T_s $\qquad [12]$

$$= P\{T \le T_s\} = P\left\{ Z \le \frac{T_s - T_e}{\sigma_T} \right\}$$

where Z has a Normal distribution with zero mean and unit variance, so that the last probability is read from the standard table of the cumulative normal distribution. By varying T_s over a range of times of interest, one can obtain a graph giving the cumulative probability of meeting the project schedule for alternative scheduled completion times.

The basic assumption that the t_i's above are independent random variables must be emphasized. Since a project manager will normally expedite a project when it falls behind schedule, the independence is violated. Hence the interpretation of the probability given by Equation [12] is *the probability that the project will meet the schedule without having to be expedited.* This, of course, is very useful for planning purposes since it is computed at the outset of the project. If the calculated probability is low, say <0.75, then the project manager can anticipate the need to expedite the project and can exercise convenient or inexpensive options early in the project.

The simplifying assumption made above, that is, basing the probability computation on the critical path and ignoring all others, warrants further discussion. It is possible for a subcritical path, with a relatively high variance, to have a lower probability of meeting a schedule than the "longer" critical path. A more bothersome point is that the effect of this assumption at every network merge event is to introduce a negative bias in the estimated earliest expected time for the event. While these effects can assume practical significance, it is surprising to the author how accurate the PERT estimates are in most cases.

There are ways of estimating when the above assumption will cause a significant error. The most appropriate solution, where the refinement is called for, is to use simulation. The GERT language cited earlier is very easy to use for this purpose. The output of the simulation includes, among other things, the probability that each activity will be on the actual critical path through the network. This notion replaces the idea of a fixed critical path and slack on the remaining paths. An alternative practical solution is to use a method called PNET (11). It involves a relatively simple procedure of determining a *set* of (assumed) statistically independent paths that "represent" the project network. The probability of meeting a scheduled data is then approximated by the product of the separate probabilities that each path in the *set* will meet the schedule. This method works surprisingly well.

Applications of PERT

PERT is much like the CPM time-cost trade-off algorithm in that it is seldom used. However, the reasons are different. It is the author's opinion that most project managers either have not learned to use PERT probabilities effectively, or they have no confidence in them. This is unfortunate because there are legitimate situations where PERT probabilities can be a useful tool, and there are also some basic advantages in the three time estimate system.

Several studies have shown that when the variance of t is high, the mean activity duration time can be estimated more accurately using the three time estimate PERT procedure, than the one time estimate system which is now used quite widely. Also, a project manager's attention should be drawn to the high variance activities as potential problem areas in the conduct of the project.

NETWORK TIME AND COST CONTROL PROCEDURES

Having completed the presentation of planning and scheduling techniques, the attention now turns to project control as depicted by Step 6 in the dynamic project management procedure outlined in Figure 16-2. To periodically assess how well the plan is working, actual progress information regarding time and cost performance of activities is entered into the system, and the network is updated.

Network Time Updating

Updating a network to reflect current status is similar to the problem introduced in the section entitled Multiple Initial and Terminal Events, and Scheduled Dates, in that a project underway is equivalent to a project with multiple start events. After a project has begun, varying portions of each path from the initial project event to the end event will have been completed. By establishing the status on each of these paths from progress information, the routine forward pass scheduling computations can then be made. No change in the backward pass computation procedure is necessary, since progress on a project does not affect the network terminal event(s), unless the scheduled completion date is revised.

Additional updating information is required if changes in the project plan are made which require revisions in the network or in the activity duration time estimates. Also, if an activity has not started, but its predecessor event has occurred since the last network update, then a scheduled start time or some "built-in" assumption about its start time must be entered into the system.

One additional convention is needed for network updating in the case where scheduled dates are associated with intermediate network events.

Convention: The latest allowable time for an intermediate network event on which a schedule time, T_s, is imposed, is taken as the earlier (smaller) of the scheduled time, T_s, and the latest allowable time, L, computed in the backward pass.

An update may indicate that the critical path has shifted, or more important, that the slack on the critical path has become negative. In this case, replanning will be in order to bring the project back onto schedule.

To illustrate this updating procedure, consider the network presented in Figure 16-6, which indicates an expected project duration of 15 days. Suppose we have just completed the fifth work day on this project, and the progress is as reported in Table 16-1.

The actual activity start and finish times given in Table 16-1 have been written above the arrow tails and heads, respectively, in Figure 16-6. Events that have already occurred have been cross hatched, and activities that are in progress have been so noted by a flag marked 5 to denote that the time of the update is the end of the fifth working day.

Having an actual, or assumed, start time for the "lead" activities on each path in the network, the forward pass calculations are then carried out in the

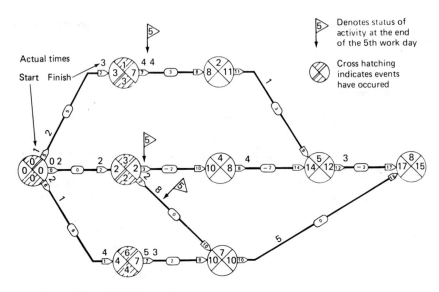

Figure 16-6. Illustrative network showing time status of project.*

usual manner. The original times are crossed out, with the new updated times written nearby. These calculations indicate that the critical path has shifted to activities 3-4-5-8, with a slack of minus two days. Assuming we were scheduled to complete the project in 15 days, the current status indicates we are now two days behind schedule.

Table 16-1. Status of Project Activities at the End of the Fifth Working Day.

ACTIVITY	STARTED	FINISHED
0–1	1	3
1–2	4	—
0–3	0	2
3–7	2	—
0–6	2	4
3–4	5	—
6–7	5	—

NOTE: all times given are at the *end* of the stated working day.

---

*Moder, J. J. and C. R. Phillips *Project Management with CPM and PERT,* 2nd Ed., (Van Nostrand Reinhold, New York, 1970), p. 82.

Network Cost Control

Network cost control considers means of controlling the dollar expenditure as the project progresses in time and accomplishment. While network-based expenditure status reports may take many forms, they are primarily directed at the following basic questions.

1. What are the actual project costs to date?
2. How do the actual costs to date compare with planned costs to date?
3. What are the project accomplishments to date?
4. How do the actual costs of specific accomplishments compare with the planned costs of these same accomplishments?
5. By how much may the project be expected to overrun or underrun the total planned cost?
6. How do the above questions apply to various subdivisions and levels of interest within the project?

The major problem in the development of systems to answer these questions is the conflict between traditional functionally oriented accounting and a system based upon network activities. One solution to this problem is the use of groups of activities, called "work packages," in the coding of cost accounts. For example, in the construction industry a work package is often taken as a separate bid item. This, however, still does not solve all of the problems of allocating overhead and sharing various joint costs.

The use of network activities as an accounting base lend themselves to major increases in the amount of detail available to and required of the manager. This is both the promise and the inherent hazard of such systems, and it is one of the primary tasks of the system designer to achieve the level of detail that provides the greatest return on the investment in the system.

Network cost control employs an "enumerative cost model" in which activity costs are assumed to occur linearly in time. Thus, if the project budget is apportioned among the activities, cumulative cost vs. time curves can be computed based on the earliest and latest allowable activity times. These two curves will bound the curve based upon the scheduled times for each activity. The latter is then taken as the plan against which progress is measured. Such a curve is shown as the middle curve in Figure 16-7, and is marked "Budgeted Cost and Work Value." Using the nomenclature shown below, two important control variances can be defined.

T_{Now} = Time of Update or Time Now
T_S = Scheduled Project Completion Time
T_F = Forecasted Project Completion Time

$ACWP$ = Actual Cost of Work in Place at T_{Now}
$BCWS$ = Budgeted Cost of Work Scheduled for Completion at T_{Now}
$BCWP$ = Budgeted Cost of Work in Place at T_{Now}.

$$\text{Cost Variance at } T_{Now} = \left(\frac{ACWP - BCWP}{BCWP} \right) 100\% \qquad [13]$$

$$\text{Cash-Flow Variance at } T_{Now} = \left(\frac{ACWP - BCWS}{BCWS} \right) 100\% \quad [14]$$

The cost variance given in equation [13] is computed at each update time. It gives the total percent project cost over (under) run up to time T_{Now}, and is used to aid in forecasting the eventual total project cost.

The cash-flow variance given in equation [14] is used to compare planned vs. actual expenditure *rates* to aid the evaluation of *time* status. For example, a zero cost-variance and a negative cash-flow variance would indicate project cost is currently on budget, but resources are not being applied to the project at the planned rate. This in turn may indicate that man-power limitations may not allow making this up in the future, and hence completion of the project may be delayed.

Each of the major computer firms, plus a number of other corporations, have

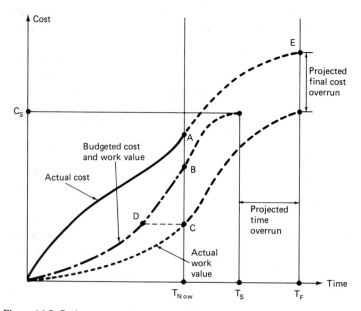

Figure 16-7. Project cost vs. time curve to illustrate cost and cash flow variances.

developed cost control computer packages of varying complexity. They may include:

1. Separate progress report outputs for three or more levels of indenture in the organization, e.g., a program manager report, subproject manager reports, and finally task manager reports under each subproject.
2. Elaborate computer printed graphical type outputs of resource requirements vs. time; actual and planned expenditures vs. time; bar chart type outputs showing activity early start, late finish, and scheduled times; etc.
3. Data base reports for cost estimating, labor standards, etc.
4. All too infrequently they include a resource leveling subroutine.

Although it is technically possible to only elect those options of a program that are desired, most users find that these elaborate packages are quite difficult to implement in this way.

OTHER NETWORKING SCHEMES

The activity-on-arrow networking logic presented above was the system utilized in the development of PERT and CPM, and is today still widely used. However, it is not the easiest for the novice to learn. For this reason, another scheme, called activity-on-node, has gained considerable popularity.

The Activity-on-Node Networking Scheme

The activity-on-node system is merely the reversal of the other, that is, the nodes represent the activities and the arrows become the connectors to denote the precedence relationships. Neither of these networking schemes, however, can cope with the problem of rapidly escalating numbers of activities when two or more jobs follow each other with a lag. Since this situation occurs quite frequently, particularly in construction work, the networking scheme called precedence diagramming is gaining considerable attention.

Precedence Diagramming

An extension to the original activity-on-node concept called precedence diagramming appeared around 1964 in the User's Manual for an IBM 1440 computer program (4). Extensive development of this procedure has since been conducted by K. C. Crandall (2). This procedure extends the PERT/CPM network logic from a single type of dependency to include 3 other types, illustrated in Figure 16-8. It is based on the following nomenclature.

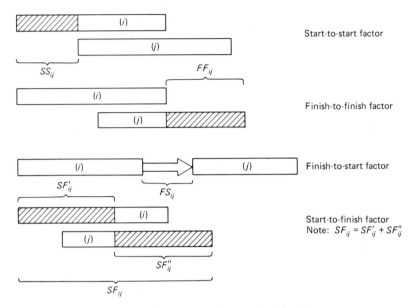

Figure 16-8. Precedence diagramming lead/lag factors.

SS_{ij} denotes a start-to-start constraint, and is equal to the minimum number of time units that must be complete on the preceding activity (i) prior to the start of the successor (j).

FF_{ij} denotes a finish-to-finish constraint, and is equal to the minimum number of time units that must remain to be completed on the successor (j) after the completion of the predecessor (i).

FS_{ij} denotes a finish-to-start constraint, and is equal to the minimum number of time units that must transpire from the completion of the predecessor (i) prior to the start of the successor (j). (Note, this is the sole logic constraint used in PERT/CPM, with $FS_{ij} = 0$).

SF_{ij} denotes a start-to-finish constraint, and is equal to the minimum number of time units that must transpire from the start of the predecessor (i) to the completion of the successor (j).

The above constraint logic will be applied in the next section to illustrate the powerful features of precedence diagramming. It will also point up an anomaly that can occur that needs explanation.

Precedence Diagram Anomalies

Consider a construction subcontract consisting of *Framing* walls, placing *Electrical* conduits, and *Finishing* walls, with the duration of each task estimated to be 10 days, using standard size crews. If the plan is to perform each of these tasks sequentially, the equivalent arrow diagram in Figure 16-9(a) shows that a project duration of 30 days will result.

To reduce this time, these tasks could be carried out concurrently with a convenient lag of say 2 days between the start and finish of each activity. This plan is shown in Figure 16-9(b), in precedence diagram notation. The equivalent arrow diagram shown in Figure 16-9(c), indicates a 14 day project schedule. One important advantage of Figure 16-9(b) over 16-9(c) is that each trade is represented by a single activity instead of 2 or 3 subactivities. Also note how the $SS = 2$ and $FF = 2$ lags of Figure 16-9(b) are built into the equivalent arrow diagram in Figure 16-9(c). For example, the first two days of the Electrical task in Figure 16-9(c) must be separated from the remainder of this task to show that 2 days of Electrical work must be completed prior to the *start* of the Finishing task. Similarly, the last 2 days of Electrical work must be separated from the remainder of this task to show that Framing must *finish* 2 days before Electrical is finished. Thus, the 10 day Electrical task must be broken up into 3 sub-activities of 2, 6, and 2 days duration, respectively.

So far, precedence diagramming is easy to follow and is parsimonious with activities. But let us see what happens if the duration of the 3 tasks in this project are unbalanced by changing from 10, 10, 10, to 10, 5, and 15 days, respectively. These changes are incorporated in Figures 16-9(d) and 16-9(e), along with appropriate new lag times. Note that $SS = 2$ was chosen between Framing and Electrical to insure that a full days work is ready for Electrical before this task is allowed to start. Similarly, $FF = 3$ was chosen between Electrical and Finishing because the last day of Electrical work will require 3 days of Finishing work to complete the project. The other lags of 1 day each were chosen as minimal or convenience values needed in each case. These lags define the activity breakdown shown in Figure 16-9(e) where we see the critical path is the *start* of Framing (1-2), then the *start* of Electrical (4-5), and finally the *totality* of Finishing (8-9-10). This is also shown in the precedence diagram, Figure 16-9(d), where $ES = LS = 0$ for the *start* of Framing, $ES = LS = 2$ for the *start* of Electrical, and finally $ES = LS = 3$ and $EF = LF = 18$ for the totality of Finishing. Since the precedence diagram shows each of these tasks in their totality, $EF \neq LF$ even though $ES = LS$ for the Framing and Electrical tasks. For Framing in Figure 16-9(d), $LF - EF = 14 - 10 = 4$ days of float, which corresponds to the 4 days of float depicted by activity 7-9 in Figure 16-9(e). Similarly, for Electrical in Figure 16-9(d), $LF - EF = 15 - 11 = 4$ days of float which is also depicted by activity 7-9 in Figure 16-9(e). The middle Electrical activity (5-6) in Figure 16-9(e) *appears* to have an additional path float of 4 days, or a total of 8 days. This attribute is not shown at all in Figure 16-9(d) because it depicts only the beginning and end points of each activity, but not intermediate subactivities such as 5-6.

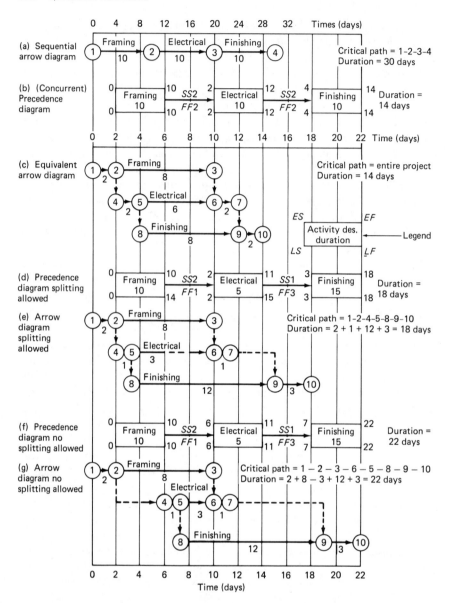

Figure 16-9. Arrow and precedence networks to illustrate splitting vs. no splitting.

Closer examination will show, however, that any delay in the start of activity 5-6 exceeding 3 days would cause the Finishing crew to run out of work, and hence the critical path would be delayed. This problem is shared by both arrow and precedence diagrams, and the user should understand this. It does not, however, present a real problem in the applications since the job foreman generally has no difficulty in the day-to-day management of this type of interrelationship among concurrent activities. It is generally felt that it is not worthwhile to further complicate the networking and the computational scheme to show all interdependencies among activity segments, since these tasks can be routinely managed in the field.

A very important difference between Figures 16-9(c) and (e), other than the 4 day difference in the project durations, lies in the Electrical task which is represented by 3 sub-activities in both diagrams. In Figure 16-9(c) these 3 sub-activities are expected to be conducted without interruption. However, in Figure 16-9(e) this is not possible. Here, the last day of the Electrical task (6-7) must follow a 4 day interruption because of the combination effect of constraint $SS = 1$ depicted by activity 5-8, and constraint $FF = 1$ depicted by activity 3-6. This forced interruption will henceforth be referred to as *splitting* of the Electrical task.

If necessary, *splitting* can be avoided in several ways. First, the duration of the Electrical task could be increased from 5 to 9 days. But this is frequently not desirable in projects such as maintenance or construction because it would decrease productivity. The second way to avoid *splitting* would be to delay the start of the Electrical task for 4 days, as shown in Figure 16-9(g), where it is assumed that activity splitting is not allowed. At first, it may seem that there is no difference between these two alternatives, but this is not so. Reflection on Figure 16-9(g) shows that delaying the start of the Electrical task to avoid *splitting* will delay the start of the Finish work, and hence the completion of the project is delayed by 4 days. But increasing the duration of the Electrical task will not have this effect. Actually, we have described an anomalous situation where an *increase* of 4 days in the duration of an activity on the critical path (starting 4 days earlier and thus running 4 days longer), will *decrease* the duration of the project by 4 days, from 22 to 18. If you are used to dealing with basic arrow diagram logic ($FS = 0$ logic only), this anomaly will take some getting used to. It results from the fact that the critical path in Figure 16-9(g) goes "backwards" through activity 5-6, and thus *subtracts* from the total duration of this path. As a result, the project duration *decreases* while the duration of an activity on the critical path is *increased*. This anomalous situation occurs whenever the critical path *enters* the *completion* of an activity through a *finish* type of constraint (*FF* or *SF*), goes backwards through the activity, and leaves through a *start* type constraint (*SS* or *SF*).

The precedence diagram in Figure 16-9(f) shows that the entire project is critical, since $ES = LS$ and $EF = LF$ for each task. While it appears that the Electrical task has float in Figure 16-9(g), this is not true since *splitting* is not allowed. No-splitting is a constraint not explicitly incorporated in the arrow diagram logic.

Critical Path Characteristics

Wiest (12) describes the anomalous behavior of activity 5-6 in Figure 16-9(g) picturesquely by stating that this activity is *reverse* critical. Similarly, in Figure 16-9(d) and (e) both Framing and Electrical are called *neutral* critical. They are critical because their $LS = ES$, but they are called *neutral* because their $LF > EF$, and the project duration is independent of the task duration. A task is *neutral* critical when a pair of start time constraints result in the critical path entering and exiting from the starting point of the task, or a pair of finish time constraints enter and exit from the finish point of a task. These situations could also be referred to as *start* or *finish* critical. In Figure 16-9(d) and (e), the Framing and Electrical tasks are both *start* critical, while Finishing is *normal* or *increase* critical. That is, a delay in the completion of the Finishing task will have a *normal* effect on the project duration, causing it to *increase*. Wiest (12) suggests that precedence diagram computer outputs would be more useful if they identified the way in which tasks are critical. The author suggests that the following nomenclature be considered for this purpose:

IC— denotes an activity that is critical to an *In*crease in its duration.

DC— denotes an activity that is critical to a *De*crease in its duration.

BC— denotes an activity that is *Bi*-critical, both to an *In*crease or *De*crease in its duration.

SC— denotes an activity that is critical to its *S*tart Time.

FC— denotes an activity that is critical to its *Fi*nish Time.

MIC— denotes an activity whose *M*iddle portion is critical to an *In*crease in its duration.

MDC— denotes an activity whose *M*iddle portion is critical to a *De*crease in its duration.

MBC— denotes an activity whose *M*iddle portion is *Bi*-critical to both an *In*crease or *De*crease in its duration.

NC— denotes an activity that is *N*on-critical.

To conclude this discussion, it should be noted that the critical path always starts with a job (or a job start), it ends with a job (or a job finish), and in between it consists of an alternating sequence of jobs and precedence arrows. Although the critical path may pass through a job in any one of the many ways listed above, it *always moves forward* through precedence constraint arrows. Hence, any *increase* in the lead-lag times associated with SS, SF, FF, or FS constraints on the critical path, will always result in a corresponding *increase* in the project duration.

Following the suggestion of stating the nature of the criticality of activities on the critical path, for Figure 16-9(d) this would consist of the following alternating activities and precedence constraints: Framing (*Start Critical—SC*); $SS2$; Electrical (*Start Critical—SC*); $SS1$; Finishing (*Increase Critical—IC*). Similarly, for Figure 16-9(f) it would be: Framing (*IC*); $FF1$; Electrical (*DC*); $SS1$; Finishing (*IC*). It should be noted here that Electrical is labeled decrease critical (*DC*), which puts the manager on notice that any *decrease* in the duration of this activity will increase the duration of the project. As stated above, it is *decrease* critical because its predecessor constraint is a *finish* type (*FF*1), and its successor constraint is a *start* type (*SS*1).

Computational Procedures

Obviously the forward and backward pass computational problem becomes more complex with precedence diagramming, and it calls for establishment of somewhat arbitrary ground rules which were unnecessary with the unique nature of basic arrow diagram logic. In the computational procedures to follow, we will assume that the specified activity durations are fixed, e.g., because of the productivity argument cited above. This assumption can be relaxed, of course, by varying the activity durations of interest, and repeating the calculations. Regarding task splitting, three basic cases will be treated.

Case 1: Activity splitting *is not* allowed on any activities, such as shown in Figure 16-9(g).

Case 2: Activity splitting *is* allowed on all activities, such as shown in Figure 16-9(e).

Case 3: Combination of 1 and 2; activity splitting is permitted only on designated activities.

Figures 16-9(g) and (e) represent Cases 1 and 2, respectively. The effect of not allowing splitting (of the Electrical task) is a 4 day increase in the project duration. Here, the choice must be made between the (extra) cost of splitting the Electrical task, and the cost of a 4 day increase in project duration. Case 3 is provided to allow the project manager to take the possible time (project duration) advantage concomitant with splitting on those activities where it can be tolerated, and to avoid splitting on those activities where it cannot be accommodated.

The computational procedure for Case 1 is reasonably simple and will be described below. The procedure for Case 2 is considerably more complex; it is given in Reference 8. The computational procedure for Case 3 merely amounts to the application of the Case 1 *or* the Case 2 procedure to each activity in turn, depending on whether the activity is designated as one where splitting *is not* allowed, or *is* allowed, respectively.

Computational Assumptions

The computational procedure for Case 1—No Splitting Allowed, is analogous to the arrow diagram procedure described above. In making the forward pass calculations, one must consider *all* constraints leading into the activity (j) in question, i.e., the start time constraints (SS_{ij} and FS_{ij}) *as well as* the finish time constraints (SF_{ij} and FF_{ij}). For *each* constraint, the early start time for activity (j) is computed, and the maximum (latest) of these times then becomes the early start time (ES_j) for activity (j). Because some project activities may only have finish time constraints, it would be possible for the above procedure to lead to a negative ES_j time, or a time earlier than the specified project start time. For example, referring to Figure 16-10, we see that activity D has no *start* time constraint. If the duration of activity D was 22 (instead of 12), then its early start time would be $EF - D = ES$, or $19 - 22 = -3$ (instead of 7). This would be an erroneous negative value. To prevent the occurrence of this error, an additional time, called the INITIAL TIME, is introduced. It is usually set equal to zero, or else to an arbitrarily specified (non-zero) project scheduled start time, and it overrides the start times computed above if they are all negative, or less (earlier) than the specified project start time.

The backward pass computations follow a similar procedure to find the late finish times for each activity, working backwards along *each* constraint leaving the activity (i) in question. In this case, an additional time, called TERMINAL TIME, is required to prevent the occurrence of a late finish time (LF_i) *exceeding* the project duration, or the scheduled project completion time. As usual, the project duration is taken as the maximum (latest) of the early finish times computed for each activity in the forward pass computations. For example, this is equal to 42 units in Figure 16-10, which is the largest of all activity early finish times.

The computational procedure given below has the same requirement that prevailed for arrow diagram computations. It requires that the activities are topologically ordered. That is, activities are arranged so that successors to any

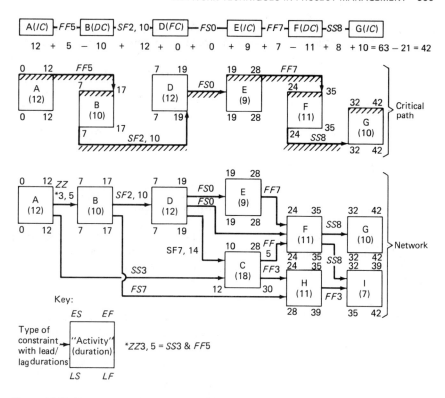

$$12 + 5 - 10 + 12 + 0 + 0 + 9 + 7 - 11 + 8 + 10 = 63 - 21 = 42$$

Figure 16-10. Example Network with Forward and Backward Pass Times Shown—No Splitting Allowed.

activity will *always* be found below it in the ordered list. The two step computational procedure is then applied to each activity working the list from the top down. When the computations are performed by hand on a network, this ordering is accomplished automatically by working one path after another, each time going as far as possible. Again, this is the same procedure required to process an arrow diagram.

Forward Pass Computations—No Splitting Allowed

The following two steps are applied to each project activity, in topological sequence. The term called INITIAL TIME is set equal to zero, or to an arbitrarily specified project scheduled start time.

STEP 1: Compute ES_j, the early start time of the activity (j) in question. It is the maximum (latest) of the set of start times which includes the

INITIAL TIME, and one start time computed from *each* constraint going to the activity (j) from predecessor activities indexed by (i).

$$ES_j = \underset{\text{all } i}{\text{MAX}} \left\{ \begin{array}{l} \text{INITIAL TIME} \\ EF_i + FS_{ij} \\ ES_i + SS_{ij} \\ EF_i + FF_{ij} - D_j \\ ES_i + SF_{ij} - D_j \end{array} \right\}$$

STEP 2: $EF_j = ES_j + D_j$

Backward Pass Computations—No Splitting Allowed

The following two steps are applied to each project activity in the reverse order of the forward pass computations. The term called TERMINAL TIME is set equal to the project duration, or to an arbitrarily specified project scheduled completion time.

STEP 1: Compute LF_i, the late finish time of the activity (i) in question. It is the minimum (earliest) of the set of finish times which includes the TERMINAL TIME, and one finish time computed from *each* constraint going from activity (i), to successor activities indexed by (j).

$$LF_i = \underset{\text{all } j}{\text{MIN}} \left\{ \begin{array}{l} \text{TERMINAL TIME} \\ LS_j - FS_{ij} \\ LF_j - FF_{ij} \\ LS_j - SS_{ij} + D_i \\ LF_j - SF_{ij} + D_i \end{array} \right\}$$

STEP 2: $LS_i = LF_i - D_i$

Example Problem

To illustrate the application of the above algorithm, a small network consisting of 9 activities with a variety of constraints, is shown in Figure 16-10. The forward pass calculations are as follows, based on the assumption that the project starts at time zero, i.e., INITIAL TIME = 0.

Activity A
$ES_A = \{\text{INITIAL TIME} = 0\} = 0$
$EF_A = ES_A + D_A = 0 + 12 = 12$

Activity B

$$ES_B = \overset{\text{MAX}}{A} \left\{ \begin{array}{l} \text{INITIAL TIME} = 0 \\ ES_A + SS_{AB} = 0 + 3 = 3 \\ EF_A + FF_{AB} - D_B = 12 + 5 - 10 = 7 \end{array} \right\} = 7$$

$$EF_B = ES_B + D_B = 7 + 10 = 17$$

Activity D

$$ES_D = \overset{\text{MAX}}{B} \left\{ \begin{array}{l} \text{INITIAL TIME} = 0 \\ ES_B + SF_{BD} - D_D = 7 + (2 + 10) - 12 = 7 \end{array} \right\} = 7$$

$$EF_D = ES_D + D_D = 7 + 12 = 19$$

Activity C

$$ES_C = \underset{A,D}{\text{MAX}} \left\{ \begin{array}{l} \text{INITIAL TIME} = 0 \\ ES_A + SS_{AC} = 0 + 3 = 3 \\ ES_D + SF_{DC} - D_C = 7 + (7 + 14) - 18 = 10 \end{array} \right\} = 10$$

$$EF_C = ES_C + D_C = 10 + 18 = 28$$
ETC.

The backward pass calculations are as follows, wherein the TERMINAL TIME is set equal to the project duration, determined from the forward pass calculations to be 42, i.e., the EF time for the last critical path activity G.

Activity G
$$LF_G = \{\text{TERMINAL TIME} = 42\} = 42$$
$$LS_G = LF_G - D_G = 42 - 10 = 32$$

Activity I
$$LF_I = \{\text{TERMINAL TIME} = 42\} = 42$$
$$LS_I = LF_I = 42 - 7 = 35$$

Activity H
$$LF_H = \underset{I}{\text{MIN}} \left\{ \begin{array}{l} \text{TERMINAL TIME} = 42 \\ LF_I - FF_{HI} = 42 - 3 = 39 \end{array} \right\} = 39$$
$$LS_H = LF_H - D_H = 39 - 11 = 28$$

Activity F
$$LF_F = \underset{G,I}{\text{MIN}} \left\{ \begin{array}{l} \text{TERMINAL TIME} = 42 \\ LS_G - SS_{FG} + D_F = 32 - 8 + 11 = 35 \\ LS_I - SS_{FI} + D_F = 35 - 8 + 11 = 38 \end{array} \right\} = 35$$
$$LS_F = LF_F - D_F = 35 - 11 = 24$$
ETC.

From the computational results shown in Figure 16-10, the critical path consists of activities A — B — D — E — F — G. The nature of the criticality of each activity is indicated at the top of Figure 16-10, along with the critical constraints between each pair of activities. Activities A, E and G are *increase* (normal) critical, activities B and F *decrease* critical (noted by the reverse direction cross hatching), and activity D is only *finish* time critical. The duration of the critical path, 42, is also noted, with the net contributions of the activity durations being $(12 - 10 + 0 + 9 - 11 + 10) = 10$ and the contributions of the constraints being $(5 + 12 + 0 + 7 + 8) = 32$, for a total of 42 time units. The early/late start/finish times for each activity have the conventional interpretations. For example, for the critical activity E, both the early and late start/finish times are 19 and 28; the activity has no slack. But for activity H, the early start/finish times are 24 and 35, while the late start/finish times are 28 and 39. In this case, the activity has 4 units of activity slack or free slack, because the completion of activity H can be delayed up to 4 units without affecting the slack on its successor activity I.

CONCLUDING REMARKS

Critical path methods represent a modern tool to aid the project manager. But they are only models of the dynamic real world interplay of money, people, materials and machines, directed in time to accomplish a stated goal. Starting with the simple logic of the deterministic arrow diagram, they can be embellished to capture the stochastic elements of the problem; the random duration of the activity times by PERT, and the random nature of the network by GERT. More recently, Precedence Diagramming has been added to this array of models to depict more closely how many projects are actually conducted, without the proliferation of project activities. Finally, the role of the computer looms large when sophisticated resource allocation or general management information systems development questions are asked. Or, when large projects extending over a long period require frequent updating, possibly for several levels of management, to control both time and cost. Network techniques form the vehicle for the conduct of these important management developments.

REFERENCES

1. Adamiecki, Karol, "Harmonygraph." *Przeglad Organizacji* (Polish Journal of Organizational Review), (1931).
2. Crandall, Keith C. "Project Planning with Precedence Lead/Lag Factors." *Project Mngt. Quarterly,* 6(3), 18–27 (1973).
3. Davis, E. W., and J. H. Patterson "A Comparison of Heuristic and Optimum Solutions in Resource Constrained Project Scheduling," *Manage. Sci.* (1974).
4. IBM. *Project Management System, Application Description Manual* (H20-0210). IBM. 1968.

5. Kelley, J. F. "Critical Path Planning and Scheduling: Mathematical Basis, *Oper. Res.*" **9**(3). 296–320 (1961). J. Kelley and M. Walker. "Critical-path planning and scheduling" in *Proceedings of the Eastern Joint Computer Conference,* 1959.
6. Lockyer, K. G., *An Introduction to Critical Path Analysis,* 3rd ed., Pitman. London. 1969. p. 3.
7. Malcolm, D. G., J. H. Roseboom, C. E. Clark, and W. Fazar "Applications of a technique for R and D program evaluation (PERT)". *Oper. Res.* **7**(5), (1959), pp. 646–669.
8. Moder, J. J., and C. R. Phillips, *Project Management with CPM and PERT.* 2nd ed., Van Nostrand Reinhold. New York. 1970. 3rd edition in preparation.
9. Pritsker, A. B., and R. R. Burgess, *The GERT Simulation Programs.* Department of Industrial Engineering. Virginia Polytechnic Institute, 1970. (See also the section on GERT in this encyclopedia.)
   Pritsker, A. B., et al., "GERT: Graphical Evaluation and Review Techniques, Part I. Fundamentals—Part II. Probabilistic and Industrial Engineering Applications." *J. Ind. Eng.* 17(5), and 17(6), (1966).
10. Wiest, J. D., "A Heuristic Model for Scheduling Large Projects with Limited Resources." *Manage. Sci.* **13**(6), B359–B377 (February 1967).
11. Ang, A. H-S, J. Abdelnour, and A. A. Chaker, "Analysis of Activity Networks Under Uncertainty." *J. of the Eng. Mech. Div.,* (Proc. of Am. Soc. Civil Eng.), Vol. 101, No. EM4, (August 1975), pp. 373–387.
12. Wiest, Jerry D. "Precedence Diagramming Methods: Some Unusual Characteristics and Their Implications for Project Managers." *Journal of Operations Management,* Vol. 1, No. 3, (February 1981), pp. 121–130.

17. Stochastic Network Analysis

Robert S. Sullivan*

Jack C. Hayya †

INTRODUCTION

A major event in the history of management science occurred during 1957–58 when network analysis was introduced as a tool for planning, scheduling, and controlling large scale projects. During that time, James Kelly and Morgan Walker developed the Critical Path Method (CPM), and the U.S. Navy's Special Projects Office initiated a program to develop a new system for evaluating large scale, complex projects. The Navy's program culminated in the development of Program Evaluation and Review Technique (PERT), which became renowned for its successful application to the Pollaris ballistic missile project. PERT originally stood for Program Evaluation Research Task. Many different acronyms for variants of PERT have subsequently been developed.

The numerous books and articles dealing with stochastic PERT network analysis attest to the impact that this approach has had upon projected management. Furthermore, applications of network analysis have extended to all types of institutions, private and public, profit and non-profit, and service and manufacturing.

Because of theoretical errors inherent in the PERT procedure (Mac-Crimmon and Ryavec, 1964), several alternatives to PERT have been proposed in recent years. Three of these command attention and are the subject of this article. They are network reduction (Martin, 1965) (Hartley and Wortham,

---

*Robert S. Sullivan is an Associate Professor of Management at the University of Texas at Austin. His research interests lie in stochastic network theory. Dr. Sullivan has authored numerous articles that have appeared in such journals as *Operations Research* and *Project Management Quarterly*. He also is the coauthor of the textbook *Service Operations Management* (McGraw-Hill, 1982). Dr. Sullivan received his Ph.D. Degree from the Pennsylvania State University.

†Jack C. Hayya is Professor of Management Science at Penn State University. He obtained his Ph.D. from the University of California, Los Angeles. He holds an M.S. in Management from California State, Northridge and a B.S. in Civil Engineering from the University of Illinois. He has been a contributor to *Decision Sciences, Management Science, The Accounting Review,* and *The Journal of Financial and Quantitative Analysis.* He is a member of AIDS, the American Statistical Association, and the Institute of Management Sciences.

1966) (Ringer, 1969), the method of bounding distributions (Kleindorfer, 1971), and Monte Carlo Simulation (Van Slyke, 1963) (Burt and Garman, 1970) (Burt, Gaver, and Perlas, 1970) (Kleijnen, 1975). But although these methods have many good features, they have not received the publicity or acceptance of PERT. The most popular textbooks in operations management discuss the details of PERT, but give at best a cursory treatment of Monte Carlo simulation. Network reduction and the method of bounding distributions are generally ignored. For example, see (Shore, 1973), (Chase and Aquilano, 1973), and (Buffa, 1977). Because of their popularity, these textbooks influence the syllibi of operations management courses and consequently the management tools used by many organizations.

The newer methods are perceived to be computationally sophisticated and consequently more costly to use than PERT. But because of tremendous advances in computer technology over the last two decades, the potential value of these methods has been enhanced. Larger, faster, and cheaper computers are more readily available, thereby making computationally sophisticated techniques economically practicable.

STOCHASTIC PERT

To provide a framework for our discussion, we shall define terms often used in stochastic PERT network analysis. We define a network as a set of nodes (circles) connected by a set of directed arcs (arrows). More formally, a network can be described by the couple (N, A), where N is a nonempty set of nodes and A is a set of arcs. A connected network in which every arc has an orientation (direction) with no cycles or loops and which contains exactly one source and one sink is called a directed acyclic network. If $s \epsilon N$ has no arcs entering it, then s is the source of the network. If $z \epsilon N$ has no arcs leaving it, then z is the sink of the network.

For a project network, we adopt the convention of letting arcs represent discrete activities. An alternative approach is to let nodes represent activities and arcs represent the sequencing of activities. The term "discrete" refers to the separateness of the activities in terms of starting and completion time. The start and the completion of activities are represented by nodes and are referred to as project events. The orientation of the arcs indicates the technological sequence in which the activities are to be performed. In project networks, it is generally assumed that the networks are acyclic.

Associated with each arc $a_i \epsilon A$ is a non-negative random variable, t_i, which has a known cumulative probability distribution, $F_i(t)$. The random variable t_i is the duration of the ith activity. Define P_j as the jth complete path from s to z. The completion time of all activities on the jth path, $j = 1, \ldots, m$, is given by

$$Y_j = \sum_{i \epsilon P_j} t_i \qquad\qquad [1]$$

Since there are m complete paths from s to z, the project completion time, T, is

$$T = MAX(Y_1, Y_2, \ldots, Y_m) \qquad\qquad [2]$$

where T is a random variable whose distribution is generally difficult to evaluate because of the complex geometry of networks and the intractable form of activity distributions. We shall let $G_T(t)$ be the cumulative distribution function (c.d.f.) of T. We shall also let $E(T)$ and σ_T^2 be the mean and variance of the distribution of T.

Assumptions

There are several assumptions that underlie PERT network models. One is that a project can be decomposed into a set of predictable, discrete activities. That is, all the activities required to accomplish a project are known with certainty, and the starting time of one activity can be discerned from the completion of preceding activities.

Another assumption is that the durations of project activities can be estimated and that these durations are statistically independent of each other. This means that the duration of one activity does not influence the duration of other activities in the project. For stochastic networks where the activity durations are random variables, it is assumed that the probability distributions of the durations are known. Acyclic networks possessing the above characteristics are often referred to as stochastic PERT networks.

In using PERT, it is assumed that activity durations are beta distributed. It is also assumed that three time estimates determine the mean and variance of an activity duration. These are:

1. An optimistic time estimate, t_o: this is the time required to perform an activity if no unusual or unexpected difficulty arises. It is the shortest time in which an activity can be performed.
2. A pessimistic time estimate, t_p: this is the time required to perform an activity if unusual difficulties arise. It is the longest time in which an activity can be performed.
3. A most likely time estimate, t_m: this is the time required to perform an activity that has the highest probability of being realized. It is the mode of the distribution of activity completion time.

PERT assumes that the optimistic and pessimistic times are six standard deviations apart. That is,

$$\hat{\sigma}_t = \frac{t_p - t_o}{6} \qquad\qquad [3]$$

where $\hat{\sigma}_t$ is the PERT estimator of the standard deviation of an activity duration, σ_t. Grubbs (1962) shows how these assumptions lead to the familiar PERT estimator of the expected activity duration

$$\hat{t}_e = \frac{t_o + 4t_m + t_p}{6} \qquad\qquad [4]$$

The PERT Approach

The following summarizes the familiar PERT approach:

1. Calculate $\hat{\sigma}_t$ and t_e for every activity in the network, using Equations [3] and [4].
2. Determine the critical path, P_c, in the network. P_c is the longest complete path in the network based upon expected activity durations.
3. Calculate the estimated expected project completion time, $\hat{T}$, and variance, $\hat{\sigma}_T^2$, by

$$\hat{T} = \sum_{i \epsilon P_c} \hat{t}_{ei} \qquad\qquad [5]$$

and

$$\hat{\sigma}_T^2 = \sum_{i \epsilon P_c} \hat{\sigma}_{ti}^2 \qquad\qquad [6]$$

4. Assume that P_c consists of enough activities such that the Central Limit Theorem holds. The distribution of project completion time, T, would then be normal with estimated mean $\hat{T}$ and variance $\hat{\sigma}_T^2$. Thus, we can calculate the probability of completing a project within a specified time using the standard normal tables.

An Example. We use an example from Hillier and Lieberman (1980, p. 264) to illustrate the PERT approach. Consider the project network and activity

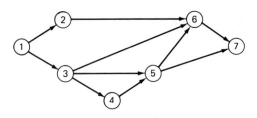

	Time Estimates		
	Optimistic	Most Likely	Pessimistic
Activity	t_o	t_m	t_p
1 → 2	14	16	18
1 → 3	11	14	16
2 → 6	13	18	23
3 → 4	7	8	9
3 → 5	16	16	16
3 → 6	20	26	37
4 → 5	6	8	12
5 → 6	8	10	13
5 → 7	13	17	21
6 → 7	6	8	15

Source: Hillier, Frederick S. and Lieberman, Gerald J. *Introduction to Operations Research.* San Francisco: Holden-Day, Inc., 1980, p. 264.

Figure 17-1. Project network and PERT three estimates.

time estimates given in Figure 17-1. PERT calculations using Equations [3], [4], [5], and [6] yield $1 \rightarrow 3 \rightarrow 6 \rightarrow 7$ as the critical path with mean 49.5 and variance 5.167. Hence, the probability of completing the schedule within, say, 52 periods is

$$P(T \le 52) = P\left(z \le \frac{52 - 49.9}{\sqrt{5.167}} \right) = P(z \le 1.10) = 0.86$$

Errors of the PERT Approach

PERT is easy to use, but the errors introduced by its numerous assumptions can be significant. MacCrimmon and Ryavec (1964, pp. 22–24) show that in extreme cases these errors may be as large as 33% for $E(t)$ and 17% for σ_t. In more realistic situations, however, they concede that these errors will be about 5% to 10%. Hartley and Wortham (1966, p. B-479) give an example where the PERT estimate of the expected project completion time is biased downward by 172%. Although this bias is always optimistic, its magnitude is a function of the network geometry, the number of project activities, and the form of the activity distributions.

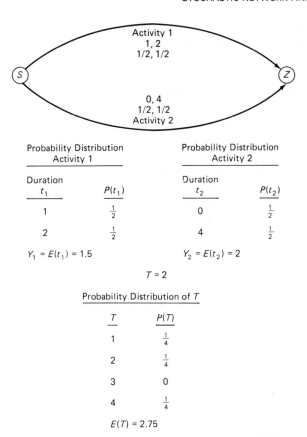

Figure 17-2. An illustration of downward bias in stochastic PERT analysis.

An Example. An illustration of the downward bias in stochastic PERT analysis is provided by the two-activities network given in Figure 17-2. Calculating the critical path by means of expected values of activity durations yields $\hat{T} = 2$. This, of course, is the expected completion time of activity 2, which comprises the critical path. But if we list the actual probability distribution for completing the network, we see that $E(T) = 2.75$. Clearly, there is a bias in expected completion time of $\dfrac{2 - 2.75}{2.75}$ or -27.3% using the PERT procedure.

NETWORK REDUCTION

Network reduction methods have been suggested for evaluating stochastic PERT networks. These rely upon identifying subnetworks whose probability distributions are analytically tractable; that is, subnetworks where it would be possible to determine the probability distribution of their completion times. In that case, the subnetwork can be treated as a single activity, thereby reducing the size of the network. Nevertheless, simulation or analytical approximations to activity distributions are needed to make these network reduction methods practicable.

Several network structures can be evaluated analytically. J. J. Martin (1965) suggested an algorithm to determine the distribution of completion time for series-parallel subnetworks. He also indicated an approach for restructuring any acyclic network into series-parallel geometry. This means that any stochastic PERT network can be analyzed using Martin's algorithm.

The analysis of a series-parallel subnetwork is straightforward. First, the series activities are evaluated in pairs using the relationship

$$F(t) = \int_0^\alpha F_{i-1}(t - r)A_i(r)\ dr \qquad [7]$$

where activities $i - 1$ and i are in series, and $F(t)$ is the c.d.f. of completion time for the series. For discrete distributions, [7] becomes

$$F(t) = \sum_{r=0}^{r=\alpha} F_{i-1}(t - r)A_i(r) \qquad [8]$$

Once the series activities have been evaluated, they are treated as single activities. Next, the parallel activities are evaluated using the relationship

$$F(t) = \prod_{i=1}^{i=n} F_i(t), \qquad [9]$$

where n is the number of parallel activities. The resulting c.d.f. is associated with the completion time of the series-parallel subnetwork.

An Example. Consider the series-parallel subnetwork given in Figure 17-3. The probability distributions for activity durations are given in Table 17-1.

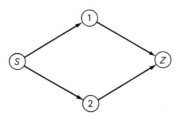

Figure 17-3. An example of a series-parallel subnetwork.

Table 17-1. Probability Distributions for Activity Durations.

ACTIVITY	TYPE OF DISTRIBUTION	PARAMETERS		
$S \rightarrow 1$	Triangular	1	2	3
$S \rightarrow 2$	Triangular	2	3	4
$1 \rightarrow Z$	Triangular	2	3	4
$2 \rightarrow Z$	Triangular	1	2	3

Table 17-2. Evaluation of Activities in Series.

ACTIVITY SERIES	COMPLETION TIME	CUMULATIVE DISTRIBUTION FUNCTION
$S \rightarrow 1 \rightarrow Z$	2	.000
	3	.063
	4	.313
	5	.688
	6	.938
	7	1.000
$S \rightarrow 2 \rightarrow Z$	2	.000
	3	.063
	4	.313
	5	.688
	6	.938
	7	1.000

Table 17-3. Evaluation of Activities in Parallel.

COMPLETION TIME	CUMULATIVE DISTRIBUTION FUNCTION
2	.000
3	.003
4	.098
5	.473
6	.879
7	1.000

Table 17-2 gives the c.d.f.'s associated with the completion times of each of the two series of activities. These were determined using Equation [8]. Next, the two c.d.f.'s are evaluated using Equation [9] to yield the c.d.f. of completion time for the subnetwork. This is given in Table 17-3. The subnetwork consisting of four activities can now be replaced with a single distribution of completion time.

Hartley and Wortham (1966) proposed an algorithm for evaluating a so-called "Wheatstone bridge" subnetwork, an example of which is shown in Fig-

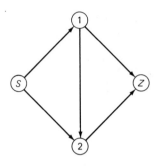

Figure 17-4. "Wheatstone bridge" subnetwork.

ure 17-4. A similar approach was developed by Ringer (1969) for evaluating a subnetwork consisting of two adjacent Wheatstone bridges as shown in Figure 17-5. Hartley-Wortham and Ringer suggest that a network first be reduced using their algorithms. The reduced network then can be analyzed economically using Monte Carlo simulation.

While network reduction methods are theoretically appealing, it is not clear whether they are computationally efficient or practical, except for extremely small networks. For example, Ringer (1969) notes that it took thirty seconds on the IBM 360-65 to recognize and evaluate a double Wheatstone bridge subnetwork. This is the CPU time needed to reduce the network by only seven activities. Concern over computation cost may then deter the widespread adoption of network reduction methods.

BOUNDING DISTRIBUTIONS

G. B. Kleindorfer (1971) developed a method for determining bounds on $G_T(t)$, $E(T)$, and σ_T^2 when activity distributions are discrete. The method of bounding distributions (MBD) begins with the first activity of the project and succes-

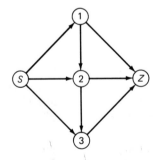

Figure 17-5. "Double Wheatstone bridge" subnetwork.

sively calculates activity bounding distributions based upon the distributions of predecessor activities. Again, let $F_i(t)$ be the probability that the ith activity would be completed on or before time t. Let $P_i(t)$ be the probability that the ith activity would be started on or before time t and $A_i(r)$ be the probability that the activity requires r units of time. Let B_i be the set of activities that immediately precede activity i. By assuming independence of activity durations, it follows that for any t,

$$F_i(t) = \sum_{r=0}^{r=\alpha} A_i(r)P_i(t - r) \qquad [10]$$

Now let $P_i'(t)$ and F_i' be the respective upper bounds for $P_i(t)$ and $F_i(t)$. Also, let $P_i''(t)$ and $F_i''(t)$ be the lower bounds. Kleindorfer shows that

$$P_i'(t) = min_{b \epsilon B_i} F_b'(t) \qquad [11]$$

where

$$F_i'(t) = \sum_{r=0}^{r=\alpha} A_i(r)P_i'(t - r) \qquad [12]$$

and

$$P_i''(t) = \pi_{b \epsilon B_i} F_b''(t) \qquad [13]$$

where

$$F_i''(t) = \sum_{r=0}^{r=\alpha} A_i(r)P_i''(t - r) \qquad [14]$$

Equations [11], [12], [13], and [14] are evaluated successively beginning with the initial project activity. The first activity duration is assumed to be deterministic with duration zero. Consequently,

$$P_1(t) = P_1'(t) = P_1''(t) = F_1'(t) = F_1''(t) = F_1(t) \qquad [15]$$

Kleindorfer shows how bounds on $E(T)$ and σ_T^2 can be easily determined by differencing the bounds on $G_T(t)$. For example,

$$E'(T) = \sum_{t=0}^{t=\infty} t[G'_T(t) - G'_T(t - 1)]$$

[16]

$$E''(T) = \sum_{r=0}^{r=\alpha} t[G''_T(t) - G''_T(t - 1)]$$

An interesting result is that the lower bound for $E(T)$ is at least as precise as the PERT estimator.

The MBD requires more computation effort than PERT. However, there are several obvious advantages to using it. First, the method provides a 100% probability interval for $G_T(t)$. Second, it does not rely upon simplifying assumptions concerning network geometry and the probability distribution of activities. The only assumption is that activity distributions are discrete.

Another advantage of the bounding distribution method is that it can readily yield upper and lower bounds on the mean and standard deviation of flows through the network. Such flows might be time, cost, or resource utilization. Finally, the method is well-suited for computer implementation.

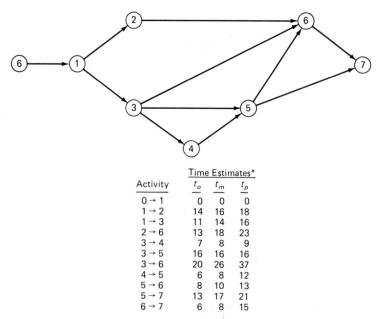

	Time Estimates*		
Activity	t_o	t_m	t_p
0 → 1	0	0	0
1 → 2	14	16	18
1 → 3	11	14	16
2 → 6	13	18	23
3 → 4	7	8	9
3 → 5	16	16	16
3 → 6	20	26	37
4 → 5	6	8	12
5 → 6	8	10	13
5 → 7	13	17	21
6 → 7	6	8	15

*Activity durations are assumed to be triangularly distributed.

Source: Hiller, Frederick S. and Lieberman, Gerald J. *Introduction to Operations Research*. San Francisco: Holden-Day, Inc., 1980, p. 264.

Figure 17-6. Project network with three time estimates.

An Example. Consider the network given in Figure 17-6. This problem from Hillier and Lieberman (1980, p. 264) was used previously to demonstrate PERT. But we have added a deterministic first activity that has zero duration. Also, we have assumed that activity durations follow the triangular distribution, with the three parameters indicated for each.

Table 17-4 gives the upper and lower bounds for the completion of activities $1 \rightarrow 2$, $1 \rightarrow 3$, and $5 \rightarrow 6$. Table 17-5 presents the bounds for the completion of the network. The bounds given in Table 17-6 are used to develop bounds for $E(T)$ and σ_T. These are [50.414, 51.272] for $E(T)$ and [3.016, 3.386] for σ_T. Observe the tightness (closeness) of these bounds. We know that the actual values for $E(T)$ and σ_T lie between the bounds calculated.

Table 17-4. Bounds on Distributions of Completion
Times for Activities $1 \rightarrow 2$, $1 \rightarrow 3$, and $5 \rightarrow 6$.

ACTIVITY	COMPLETION TIME	LOWER BOUND	UPPER BOUND
$1 \rightarrow 2$	13	.000	.000
	14	.111	.111
	15	.333	.333
	16	.667	.667
	17	.889	.889
	18	1.000	1.000
$1 \rightarrow 3$	10	.000	.000
	11	.021	.021
	12	.214	.214
	13	.429	.429
	14	.714	.714
	15	.905	.905
	16	1.000	1.000
$5 \rightarrow 6$	34	.000	.000
	35	.001	.007
	36	.006	.034
	37	.025	.095
	38	.080	.195
	39	.188	.327
	40	.349	.478
	41	.534	.627
	42	.706	.756
	43	.837	.857
	44	.922	.926
	45	.967	.967
	46	.988	.988
	47	.996	.996
	48	.999	.999
	49	1.000	1.000

Table 17-5. Bounds on Distribution of Completion
Times for Network.

COMPLETION TIME	LOWER BOUND	UPPER BOUND
41	.000	.000
42	.000	.003
43	.001	.011
44	.004	.031
45	.015	.067
46	.043	.125
47	.099	.204
48	.186	.302
49	.298	.412
50	.425	.526
51	.552	.635
52	.669	.733
53	.769	.815
54	.850	.879
55	.910	.926
56	.951	.958
57	.975	.978
58	.989	.990
59	.995	.996
60	.998	.998
61	.999	.999
62	1.000	1.000

A Comparison of the Method of Bounding Distributions (MBD) and Monte Carlo Simulation

Sullivan and Hayya (1980) investigated experimentally the relative efficiency of the MBD and Monte Carlo simulation. The MBD and simulation were compared in estimating the cumulative distribution function (c.d.f.) of network completion time, $G_T(t)$, and the expected completion time, $E(T)$. The MBD and simulation differ in two aspects that are important when comparing efficiency. First, the MBD gives an interval within which a parameter is certain to fall. Consequently, there is no uncertainty associated with this interval. The interval estimate calculated using simulation, by contrast, is affected by the sample size and by the confidence coefficient. It was assumed that a 99 percent confidence coefficient is close enough to certainty in most applications. Consequently, we compare the 100 percent confidence interval obtained by the MBD with the corresponding 99 percent confidence interval obtained by simulation.

The second difference relates to computation time. The computation time required by the MBD increases linearly with the number of network activities

Table 17-6. Experimental Results for Estimating $G_T(t)$ and $E(T)$.

NUMBER OF NETWORK ACTIVITIES	$\sigma_T^{(a)}$	Δ_g	n_1	Δ_e	n_2
10	2.59	.319	105	2.27	35
20	2.73	.382	73	2.28	39
30	4.29	.451	53	4.78	22
40	2.29	.298	120	1.97	36
50	2.50	.402	66	2.37	30
60	5.19	.413	62	5.19	27
70	3.41	.585	30	5.03	13
80	2.62	.422	60	2.61	27
90	6.11	.391	70	5.45	34
100	3.28	.372	77	3.18	29
110	3.77	.500	43	5.14	15
120	3.13	.468	49	4.47	14
130	3.21	.333	96	2.80	35
140	2.29	.580	30	3.67	11
150	4.24	.551	34	6.27	13
160	4.49	.593	29	8.61	8
170	4.74	.577	30	7.06	12
180	5.04	.491	45	6.35	17
190	3.18	.471	48	4.00	16
200	3.99	.404	66	4.15	25

[a] σ_T is estimated from 1,500 simulations of each network.

(Kleindorfer, 1971, p. 1600), whereas for simulation it increases linearly with the number of network activities and also the number of simulations (Van Slyke, 1963, p. 848). It is possible, therefore, to determine the number of simulations such that computation times for both methods are equal, ie., the breakeven point. In this experiment, the breakeven-point was 139 simulations.

The breakeven point depends upon programming efficiency and the choice of computer and compiler. But experimental studies comparing the efficiencies of techniques have traditionally reported computational experience on a particular computer. See Burt and Garman (1971, p. 213), and Carter and Ignall (1975, p. 615). It should be noted, therefore, that the breakeven point may vary depending upon the computational resources available.

The networks used in this experiment were acyclic and stratified according to the number of activities. The strata are 10, 20, 30, . . . , 200 activities, with one network in each stratum. The duration of activities are uniformly distributed random variables whose parameters are selected at random from the interval [0, 9]. Also, the networks are structured randomly.

For each network, the MBD was used to calculate bounds for $G_T(t)$ and $E(T)$. Standard statistical procedures were then used to determine the number of simulations required to provide 99 percent confidence intervals that have the same ranges as those of the MBD. The efficiency of the MBD vis-á-vis simulation for estimating $G_T(t)$ and $E(T)$ was analyzed by testing the hypothesis H_o: $\mu_n \geq 139$ versus the alternative H_1: $\mu_n < 139$, where μ_n was the mean number of simulations required to give 99 percent confidence intervals whose ranges were the same as those of the MBD. A five percent level of significance was used.

The relationship between the number of simulations required to provide equal precision and network size was examined. This was accomplished by testing H_o: $\rho_s = 0$ versus the alternative H_1: $\rho_s < 0$, where ρ_s was the rank correlation coefficient for the number of simulations and the number of network activities.

Recall that the MBD determines the interval $[G_T''(t), G_T'(t)]$ such that $G_T(t)$ is contained within it. Define Δ_g to be the maximum that $G_T(t)$ can deviate from either bound. Thus,

$$\Delta_g = \sup_t [G_T'(t) - G_T''(t)] \qquad [17]$$

We want to determine the number of simulations, n_1, such that

$$D_{.01, n_1} = \Delta_g/2 \qquad [18]$$

where $D_{.01, n_1}$ is the Kolmogorov-Smirnov statistic associated with a 99 percent confidence interval. The value of n_1 satisfying [18] can be read from available tables; for $n_1 > 40$, it can be estimated using $n_1 \simeq 10.63 \, \Delta_g^{-2}$. See Conover (1971, p. 397).

Let Δ_e be the range of the MBD interval estimate for $E(T)$. It follows that the number of simulations required to provide a 99 percent confidence interval for $E(T)$ with range Δ_e is

$$n_2 = (4z_{.995}^2 \sigma_T^2)/\Delta_e^2 \qquad [19]$$

The Experimental Results. The MBD was applied to the 20 test networks; Δ_g, n_1, Δ_e, and n_2 were calculated for each. Table 17-6 summarizes the results. Sullivan and Hayya (1980, p. 616) report the following analysis and conclusions:

Estimating $G_T(t)$. The sample mean and standard deviation of n_1 are: $\overline{X}_n = 59.30$, $s_n = 25.86$. These are used in testing H_o: $\mu_n \geq 139$ versus H_1: $\mu_n < 139$, yielding a test statistic of $t = -13.78$. The latter is significant at approximately the zero level. Consequently, simulation is more efficient than the MBD for estimating $G_T(t)$.

Let r_s be the sample rank correlation coefficient for n_1 and number of network activities. In testing H_o: $\rho_s \geq 0$ versus H_1: $\rho_s < 0$, $r_s = -0.41$, which is significant at the .038 level. Therefore, in estimating $G_T(t)$, the relative efficiency of the MBD vis-à-vis simulation decreases for larger networks.

Estimating $E(T)$. The sample mean and standard deviation of n_2 are: $\overline{X}_n = 22.90$, $s_n = 9.91$. Testing H_o: $\mu_n \geq 139$ versus H_1: $\mu_n < 139$ yields the statistic $t = -52.4$, which is significant at the zero level. Thus, simulation is far more efficient than the MBD f estimating $E(T)$.

Furthermore, for n_2 and number of network activities, $r_s = -.45$. This is significant at the 0.024 level. Hence, for larger networks, the MBD becomes progressively less efficient than simulation for estimating $E(T)$.

Comments. This experiment suggests that simulation is more efficient than the MBD for estimating both $G_T(t)$ and $E(T)$. It also suggests that the relative efficiency of simulation is enhanced for larger networks. This means that simulation may provide the same or better precision than the MBD and can achieve this with less computational cost.

Other arguments also favor simulations over the MBD. First, a simulation program for network analysis can be written quite easily, but gaining an understanding of the MBD and programming it may be time-consuming and difficult. Second, simulation is flexible in that we can choose the number of replications to provide a desired level of confidence, whereas the MBD is inflexible, always yielding a fixed interval. Third, the simulation program we used did not take advantage of variance-reducing techniques. Burt, Gaver, and Perlas (1970, p. 452), for example, have shown that the antithetic variate method can reduce the variance of the simulation estimator of $E(T)$ by one-half. Consequently, the use of such variance-reducing techniques would further add to the superiority of simulation over the MBD. In the next two sections, we shall take a close look at Monte Carlo simulation and the antithetic variate method.

MONTE CARLO SIMULATION

One of the earliest attempts to avoid the bias problems of PERT was made by R. M. Van Slyke (1963). Van Slyke recommended assigning to an activity a duration randomly drawn from an appropriate probability distribution. Random values selected in this manner are then used to determine the longest complete path through the network. By simulating this process many times, a series of realizations of T is generated. A histogram or a goodness-of-fit of these realizations would then provide an approximation to the actual distribution of T.

Assume that a network comprised of M activities is simulated n times. The duration assigned to the ith activity during the jth simulation is

$$t_i = F_i^{-1}(R) \qquad [20]$$

where $F_i^{-1}(\cdot)$ is the inverse of $F_i(t)$ and R is a uniformly and independently distributed random variable such that $0 \leq R \leq 1$. Similarly, all activities are randomly assigned durations based upon their c.d.f.'s, and the longest complete path for the jth simulation is determined. Let T_j be the completion time of this path. Then, for all n simulations we have the realizations $T_1, T_2, T_3, \ldots, T_n$. A histogram or a goodness-of-fit of these leads to an estimate of $G_T(t)$. A confidence interval for $G_T(t)$ can be constructed using the Kolmogorov-Smirnov (K-S) statistic. Let $\hat{G}_T(t)$ be the Monte Carlo estimate of $G_T(t)$ based upon n simulations. Then a $1 - \alpha$ confidence interval for $G_T(t)$ is

$$[\hat{G}_T(t) - D_{\alpha,n}, \hat{G}_T(t) + D_{\alpha,n}] \qquad [21]$$

where $D_{\alpha,n}$ is the K-S test statistic. Also, unbiased estimates of $E(T)$ and σ_T^2 can be calculated, and this is a distinct advantage over PERT.

Let $\overline{T}$ a d and s_T be the sample estimates of the mean and standard deviation of completion time based upon n simulations. Then a $1 - \alpha$ confidence interval for $E(T)$ is

$$[\overline{T} - z_{\alpha/2} S_T / \sqrt{n}, \overline{T} + z_{1-\alpha/2} S_T / \sqrt{n}] \qquad [22]$$

where $z \sim N(0, 1)$.

Another advantage of Monte Carlo simulation is that a "criticality index" can be associated with every activity in the network. If a particular activity were on the longest (i.e., the critical) path k times in n simulations, then its criticality index is

$$\hat{I} = \frac{k}{n} . \qquad [23]$$

This is an estimate of the probability that an activity is on the critical path. In terms of project implementation, those activities with large indices deserve the most managerial attention.

Often, the number of simulations required is large. For an M activity network simulated n times, $M \times n$ activity durations would be randomly generated. Authors such as Ringer (1969, p. B-136) indicate that the computation time required to simulate large networks can be prohibitive. We might expect, for example, that Monte Carlo would require approximately n times as much CPU time as PERT, since critical path analysis is performed for each simulation. This problem was particularly acute in 1963 when network simulation was first suggested because computer capabilities were still at a low level. Today, however, computers with tremendously increased capability are readily available, making network simulation a more practical alternative to PERT.

In recent years, the potential for using simulation to analyze stochastic networks has increased tremendously. In addition to advances in computer technology, new network-based simulation languages have been developed. For example, SLAM (Simulation Language for Alternative Modeling) can be easily used to simulate conventional PERT networks. Furthermore, this language allows for additional complexities to be included in the model. These might involve conditional branching, where only one of a set of subsequent activities will be realized. Or it might involve cycles of activities that repeat depending upon the realization of certain events. The new simulation languages such as SLAM should hasten acceptance of Monte Carlo simulation for analyzing stochastic networks. See Pritsker and Pegden (1979).

VARIANCE REDUCTION

Concern over computation time in Monte Carlo simulation led Burt and Garman (1970) to recommend variance-reducing techniques for simulating stochastic networks. These methods are well developed in the general theory of Monte Carlo, and are shown to enhance the precision of Monte Carlo simulation while at the same time reducing the time required for computation. See, for example, Hammersley and Handscomb (1965).

As an example of a variance-reducing technique, consider the antithetic variate method (AVM). This approach relies upon generating pairs of simulated realizations of T which are negatively correlated. Let R be a uniformly distributed random variable such that $0 \le R \le 1$. Define R' as the complement

$$R' = 1 - R$$

Consequently, R' is uniformly distributed with $0 \le R' \le 1$.

If $F_i(t)$ is the c.d.f. of the ith activity duration, then two negatively correlated randomly sampled values of the activity's duration are

$$t_i = F_i^{-1}(R)$$

and

$$t_i' = F_i^{-1}(R')$$

All activities in the network are sampled in this fashion, yielding two negatively correlated realizations of completion time, T and T', where T' is known as the antithetic variate. Therefore, n simulations of a network yield the stream of realizations, $T_1, T_1', T_2, T_2', \ldots, T_n, T_n'$. A histogram of these values leads to an estimate of $G_T(t)$.

The antithetic variate method can also be used to calculate an unbiased estimator for $E(T)$. Burt and Garman (1970) give an example where the variance of the antithetic variate estimator for $E(T)$ is one fifth that provided by straightforward Monte Carlo. This clearly indicates that the number of simulations required to provide the same precision can be greatly reduced by using this method.

Burt and Garman (1971) have suggested several other techniques for reducing the computation time of network simulation. These include conditional sampling and the control variate method. Such techniques are directed at making simulation a practical, less costly approach for stochastic network analysis. In this section, we shall look more closely at the relative efficiency of the antithetic variate method.

A Comparison of the Antithetic Variate Method (AVM) with Straightforward Monte Carlo

By straightforward Monte Carlo we mean simulation without the use of variance-reducing techniques. We would like to know the statistical efficiency of the antithetic variate method (AVM) in estimating the expected completion time of stochastic networks. In comparing AVM with straightforward Monte Carlo, we consider both computation effort and the variance of the estimators. We first develop an efficiency ratio which is the generally accepted criterion for comparing Monte Carlo methods. Experimental analysis of the efficiency ratio is then carried out using test networks that are randomly structured and whose activity distributions are randomly assigned. An unbiased estimator of $E(T)$ determined from n independent Monte Carlo simulations is $\overline{T} = \sum_{i=1}^{n} T_i / n$, where T_i is the project completion time realized during the ith simulation. The precision of this estimator is measured by its variance, $\sigma_{\overline{T}}^2 = \sigma_{T}^2 / n$, where σ_T^2 is the variance of T.

The antithetic variate estimator for $E(T)$ is

$$\overline{T}_a = \sum_{i=1}^{n} (T_i + T_i')/2n$$
$$= (\overline{T} + \overline{T}')/2$$

[24]

It can be shown that the variance of $\overline{T}_a$ is given by

$$\sigma_{\overline{T}a}^2 = (\sigma_T^2/2n)(1 + \rho)$$

[25]

where ρ is the correlation between T and T'. Therefore, the antithetic variate estimator based upon n pairs of simulations is more precise than the Monte Carlo estimator based upon $2n$ independent realizations when $\rho < 0$. Kleijnen (1975) observes that for complicated simulations, negative correlations cannot be proven. However, experiments with moderately complex systems show that such correlations occur, indeed.

Efficiency Ratio. The efficiency of a Monte Carlo estimator should consider both computation time and the variance of the estimator. See, for example, Shreider (1964) and Hammersley and Handscomb (1965). The relative efficiency of the antithetic variate estimator of $E(T)$ compared to the straightforward Monte Carlo estimator is measured by the efficiency ratio

$$\epsilon(\overline{T}:T_a) = (\tau_m \sigma_T^2)/\tau_a \sigma_{\overline{T}_a}^2 \qquad [26]$$
$$= 2(\tau_m/\tau_a)/(1 + \rho)$$

where τ_m and τ_a are the computation times required by straightforward Monte Carlo and the AVM, respectively.

Sullivan, Hayya, and Schaul (1982) have estimated bounds on τ_m/τ for a given network. Note that the AVM involves n replications of T and T'. The time required for the replications of T is τ_m. The time required for the replications of T' is less than τ_m, since they use only the complements of random numbers. Therefore, $\tau_a > \tau_m$ and $\tau_a < 2\tau_m$ yield

$$\tfrac{1}{2} < \tau_m/\tau_a < 1 \qquad [27]$$

Extensive computational experience on the IBM 370-168, FORTRAN IV G level compiler, at The Pennsylvania State University indicates that $0.75 < \tau_m/\tau_a < 0.90$. This range, of course, will vary depending upon the computational resources available and the distributions from which the samples are drawn.

Relationships [26] and [27] are used to develop the conservative bounds:

$$1/(1 + \rho) < \epsilon(\overline{T}:\overline{T}_a) < 2/(1 + \rho) \qquad [28]$$

These bounds are plotted as a function of ρ in Figure 17-7. We see that so long as ρ is negative, the antithetic variate estimator will be more efficient. With strongly negative correlation, this method can result in tremendous gains in efficiency. For example, when $\rho = -.75$, we expect the antithetic variate method to be between five and ten times better than straightforward Monte Carlo. Looked at in another light, AVM can provide the same precision as Monte Carlo with between one-tenth to one-fifth the computation time.

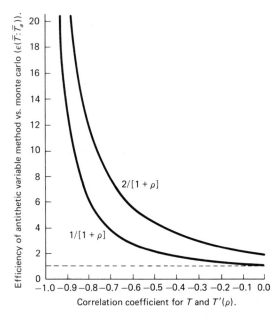

Figure 17-7. Bounds on the relative efficiency of the antithetic variate method versus Monte Carlo ($\epsilon(\overline{T}:\overline{T}_a)$).

The value of ρ is sensitive to network characteristics. For example, when activity distributions are symmetric, then ρ is strongly negative, and the antithetic variate estimator is extremely efficient. For the trivial case of a series network with symmetric activity distributions, it is easy to show that $\rho = -1$. Therefore, one replication of both T and T' will yield the exact value of $E(T)$.

Sullivan, Hayya, and Schaul (1982) experimentally investigated the effects of network characteristics upon ρ and upon the efficiency ratio. Test networks were randomly structured, and activity durations were assumed to be distributed normally, uniformly, or exponentially. The exponential distribution was used to investigate the impact of thick-tailed, skewed distributions.

Statistical analysis of the results of the experiment indicates the following:

1. The AVM is always superior to straightforward Monte Carlo for stochastic network analysis.
2. On the average, the AVM was 3.66 times more efficient than straightforward Monte Carlo.
3. When all activity durations are symmetrically distributed, the AVM is far superior to straightforward Monte Carlo (on the average, 10 times more efficient). But even when activity durations are exponentially distributed, the AVM is more efficient, with an average efficiency ratio of 1.94.

4. ρ is insensitive to the number of activities in a network, but it is sensitive to the number of activity durations having exponential distributions. The sample mean value for ρ was $-.51$.

Discussion

The efficiency of Monte Carlo simulation can be enhanced through the use of the antithetic variate method. Burt, Gaver, and Perlas (1970) give examples where the precision of the Monte Carlo estimator of $E(T)$ is improved by as much as 50%. Sullivan, Hayya, and Schaul (1982) demonstrate that 50% is very conservative. On the average, the antithetic variate method can provide the same precision as straightforward Monte Carlo, but with approximately one-fourth the computation effort. Furthermore, when activity durations are distributed symmetrically about their means, we can expect the antithetic variate method to require less than one-tenth the computation effort.

Other issues naturally present themselves when dealing with variance reduction techniques. For example, Burt, Gaver, and Perlas (1970, pp. 451–55) give some sample results from a combined antithetic variate and control variate simulation of stochastic networks. The precision of the estimators for $E(T)$ was better than when either method was used independently. Kleijnen (1975, p. 1177), on the other hand, challenges the efficacy of combining variance reduction techniques. He notes that while the antithetic variate method generates negative correlations, the control variate method generates positive correlations and these tend to offset the negative correlations.

SUMMARY

A lttle over twenty years ago, stochastic network analysis was suggested as a tool for planning, scheduling, and controlling large-scale projects. The first approach used was PERT, which relies upon simplifying assumptions and which gives rise to biased estimates for project completion times. More recently, three alternative approaches have been espoused: network reduction, the method of bounding distributions, and Monte Carlo simulation. These methods are computationally more sophisticated than PERT, and this may have impeded their use. However, tremendous advances in computer technology over the past twenty years have made these techniques economically feasible. Therefore, the alternatives to PERT deserve serious reconsideration as practical approaches to stochastic network analysis.

We began this chapter by reviewing the conventional PERT procedure, stressing the inherent biases in estimated completion times. We then provided a brief discussion of network reduction, along with an example to help guide the practitioner.

We also provided a numerical example in the section on bounding distributions. In that section, we undertook a comparison of the method of bounding distributions with that of straightforward Monte Carlo, using the criterion of efficiency. We measured efficiency in terms of computation time and the precision of the estimates. The results indicated that simulation is more efficient than bounding distributions. Also, the relative efficiency of simulation vis-à-vis bounding distributions is further enhanced as networks become larger.

We next described Monte Carlo simulation in more detail, and then developed the rationale for the variance reduction technique known as the antithetic variate method. In the section on variance reduction, we investigated the efficiency of antithetic variate simulation for estimating the expected completion time of stochastic networks. We compared the antithetic variate method with Monte Carlo simulation and considered both computation effort and the variance of the estimators. We developed and investigated an efficiency ratio and carried out an experimental analysis of it using test networks that were randomly structured and whose activity distributions were randomly assigned. We showed that on the average, the antithetic variate method can provide the same precision as Monte Carlo simulation, but with approximately one-fourth the computation effort. Furthermore, when activity distributions are symmetric, we can expect the antithetic variate method to require less than one-tenth the computation effort.

Thus, we see that straightforward Monte Carlo is superior to the method of bounding distributions; also, that the antithetic variate method is superior to straightforward Monte Carlo. We have, however, not compared the network reduction technique, nor have we by any means discussed all the issues related to stochastic network analysis.

REFERENCES

Buffa, E. S. *Modern Production Management.* (New York: John Wiley and Sons, Inc., 1977).

Burt, J. M., and Garman, M. B. Monte Carlo Techniques for Stochastic PERT Network Analysis. *Proceedings of the Fourth Conference on Applications of Simulation.* (New York, December, 1970), pp. 146–153.

Burt, J. M., and Garman, M. B. Conditional Monte Carlo: A Simulation Technique for Stochastic Network Analysis. *Management Science* 18: 207–17 (1971).

Burt, J. M., Gaver, D. P., and Perlas, M. Simple Stochastic Networks: Some Problems and Procedures. *Naval Logistics Quarterly* 17: 439–59 (1970).

Carter, G., and Ignall, E. J. Virtual Measures: A Variance Reduction Technique for Simulation. *Management Science* 21: 607–16 (1975).

Conover, W. F. *Practical Nonparametric Statistics.* (New York: John Wiley and Sons, 1971).

Chase, R., and Aquilano, N. *Production and Operations Management.* (Homewood, Illinois: Richard D. Irwin, Inc., 1973).

Grubbs, F. E. Attempts to Validate Certain PERT Statistics or 'Picking on Pert'. *Operations Research* 10: 912–15 (1962).

Hammersley, J. M., and Handscomb, D. C. *Monte Carlo Methods.* (New York: John Wiley and Sons, Inc., 1965).

Hartley, H. O., and Wortham, A. W. A Statistical Theory for PERT Critical Path Analysis. *Management Science* 12: 469–81 (1966).

Hillier, F. S., and Lieberman, G. J. *Introduction to Operations Research.* (San Francisco: Holden-Day, Inc., 1980).

Kleijnen, J. P. Antithetic Variates, Common Random Numbers, and Optimal Computer Time Allocation in Simulation. *Management Science* 21: 1176–85 (1975).

Kleindorfer, G. B. Bounding Distributions for Stochastic Acyclic Networks. *Operations Research* 19: 1586–601 (1971).

MacCrimmon, K. R., and Ryavec, C. A. *An Analytical Study of the PERT Assumptions.* Operations Research 12: 16–37 (1964).

Martin, J. J. Distribution of the Time Through a Directed Acyclic Network. *Operations Research* 13: 46–66 (1965).

Pritsker, A. A. B., and Pegden, C. D. *Introduction to Simulation and SLAM.* (New York: Halsted Press, 1979).

Ringer, L. J. Numerical Operators for Statistical PERT Critical Path Analysis. *Management Science* 16: 136–143 (1969).

Shore, B. *Operations Management.* New York: McGraw-Hill, Inc., 1973.

Shreider, Y. A. *Method of Statistical Testing Monte Carlo Method.* (New York: Elseiver Publishing Company, 1964).

Sullivan, R. S., Hayya, J. C., and Schaul, R. Efficiency of the Antithetic Variate Method for Simulating Stochastic Project Networks. *Management Science* 28, (1982).

Sullivan, R. S., and Hayya, J. C. A Comparison of the Method of Bounding Distribution (MBD) and Monte Carlo Simulation for Analyzing Stochastic Networks. *Operations Research* 28: 614–617 (1980).

Van Slyke, R. M. Monte Carlo Methods and the PERT Problem. *Operations Research* 11: 839–860 (1963).

18. Linear Responsibility Charts in Project Management

David I. Cleland*
William R. King†

The organizational model which is commonly called the *organization chart* is much derided in the literature and in the day-to-day discussions among organizational participants. However, organizational charts can be of great help in both the planning and implementation phases of project management.

In this chapter we shall explore a systems-oriented version of the traditional chart. Initially, we shall do this in the context of a chart which will be helpful to managers in aligning the project organization, i.e., the implementation function. We shall then present an adaptation of the concept of the systems-oriented chart which has proved to be useful in the planning phase of a project.

THE TRADITIONAL ORGANIZATIONAL CHART

The traditional organizational chart is of the pyramidal variety; it represents, or models, the organization as it is *supposed* to exist at a given point in time.

At best, such a chart is an oversimplification of the organization and its underlying concepts which may be used as an aid in grasping the concept of the organization. Management literature indicates various feelings about the value of the chart as an organization tool. For example, Cyert and March say:[2]

---

*Dr. Cleland is Professor of Engineering Management in the Industrial Engineering Department at the University of Pittsburgh. He is author/co-author of eight books and has published numerous articles appearing in leading national and internationally distributed technological, business management and educational periodicals. Dr. Cleland has had extensive experience in management consultation, lecturing, seminars, and research.

†Dr. William R. King is Professor of Business Administration in the Graduate School of Business at the University of Pittsburgh. He is the author of more than a dozen books and 100 articles in the fields of strategic planning, information systems and project management. Additional biographical material may be found in the current editions of *Who's Who in the World, Who's Who in America,* and other standard references.

1Portions of this chapter have been paraphrased from *Systems Analysis and Project Management,* 2nd Edition, by David I. Cleland & William R, King, (McGraw-Hill Book Company, New York, 1975).

2Richard M. Cyert and James G. March, *A Behavioral Theory of the Firm* (Prentice-Hall Inc., Englewood Cliffs, N.J., 1963), p. 289.

Traditionally, organizations are described by organization charts. An organization chart specifies the authority or reportorial structure of the system. Although it is subject to frequent private jokes, considerable scorn on the part of sophisticated observers, and dubious championing by archaic organizational architects, the organization chart communicates some of the most important attributes of the system. It usually errs by not reflecting the nuances of relationships within the organization: it usually deals poorly with informal control and informal authority, usually underestimates the significance of personality variables in molding the actual system, and usually exaggerates the isomorphism between the authority system and the communication system. Nevertheless, the organization chart still provides a lot of information conveniently—partly because the organization usually has come to consider relationships in terms of the dimensions of the chart.

Jasinski is critical of the traditional, pyramidal organizational chart because it fails to display the nonvertical relations between the participants in the organization. He says:[3]

Necessary as these horizontal and diagonal relations may be to the smooth functioning of the technology or work flow, they are seldom defined or charted formally. Nonetheless, wherever or whenever modern technology does operate effectively, these relations do exist, if only on a nonformal basis.

LINEAR RESPONSIBILITY CHARTS (LRCs)

The linear responsibility chart (LRC) goes beyond the simple display of formal lines of communication, gradations of organizational level, departmentation, and line-staff relationships. In addition to the simple display, the LRC reveals the task-job position couplings that are of an advisory, informational, technical, and specialty nature.

The LRC has been called the "linear organization chart," the "linear chart," and the "functional chart." None of these names adequately describes the device. The LRC (or the table or grid, as Janger calls it)[4] shows who participates, and to what degree, when an activity is performed or a decision made. It shows the extent or type of authority exercised by each executive in performing an activity in which two or more executives have overlapping authority and responsibility. It clarifies the authority relationships that arise when executives share common work. The need for a device to clarify the authority relationships

---

[3]Frank J. Jasinski, "Adapting Organization to New Technology," *Harvard Business Review* (January–February 1959.), p. 80.
[4]Allen R. Janger, "Charting Authority Relationships," *The Conference Board Record* (December 1964).

is evident from the relative unity of the traditional pyramidal chart, which 1) is merely a simple portrayal of overall functional and authority models and 2) must be combined with detailed position descriptions and organizational manuals to delineate authority relationships and work-performance duties.

The typical pyramidal organizational chart is not adequate as a tool of organizational analysis since it does not display systems interfaces. It is because of this inadequacy that a technology of position descriptions and organizational manuals has come into being. As organizations have grown larger and larger, personnel interrelationships have increased in complexity, and job descriptions and organizational manuals have grown more detailed. Typical organizational manuals and position descriptions have become so verbose that an organizational analysis can be lost in semantics. An article in *Business Week* reflected on the problem of adequate organizational tools in this manner:[5]

> The usual way to supplement it [the pyramid organization chart] is by recourse to a voluminous organizational manual prescribing the proper relationships and responsibilities. But the manuals—cumbersome and often outdated—rarely earn much attention.

Position descriptions do serve the purpose of describing a single position, but an executive is also concerned with how the people under his jurisdiction relate to one another. On many occasions, executives are confronted with the task of examining and explaining relationships. Project management, corporate staff organization, concepts of product planning, the development of a corporate plan—all these lead to highly complex working relationships. A dynamic organization is often—even continually—redefining large numbers of positions and establishing new responsibility and authority patterns.

Structure and Philosophy of the LRC

Typically, the LRC shows these characteristics:

1. Core information from conventional organizational charts and associated manuals displayed in a matrix format.[6]
2. A series of position titles listed along the top of the table (columns).
3. A listing of responsibilities, authorities, activities, functions, and projects down the side of the chart (rows).
4. An array of symbols indicating degree or extent of authority and explaining the relationship between the columns and the lines.

---

[5]"Manning the Executive Setup," *Business Week* (Apr. 6, 1957), p. 187.
[6]For example, one writer proclaimed: "On one pocket-size chart it shows the facts buried in all the dusty organizational manuals—plus a lot more."

Such an arrangement shows in one horizontal line all persons involved in a function and the extent and nature of their involvement. Furthermore, the one vertical line shows all functions that a person is responsible for and the nature of his responsibility. A vertical line represents an individual's job description: a horizontal line shows the breakout of a function or task by job position.

One potential value of such a chart is the analysis required to create it, i.e., the necessary abstracting and cross-referencing from position descriptions and related documentation manuals. The LRC in Figure 18-1 illustrates the authority interrelationships of a series of positions composing a definable unit. This chart conveys the same message by extensive organizational manuals, position descriptions, memorandums of agreement, policy letters, etc. It shows at a glance not only the individuals' responsibilities for certain functions but, what may be even more valuable, the way a given position relates to other positions within the organization.

But why not use the more conventional procedure of position analysis and position description for this sort of thing? There are two primary advantages to this mode of presentation. First, position descriptions and position guides are better at laying down responsibilities and authority patterns than at *portraying relationships*. Second, this type of charting depicts the work of top management as an *integrated system* rather than as a series of individual positions. The chart makes it easy to compare the responsibilities of related executives; in the coordination of budgets, for example, six individuals share the responsibility, ranging from "must be consulted" to "may be consulted" and "must be notified." The filled-in chart provides a quick picture of all the positions involved in the performance of a particular function.

In the words of Allen R. Janger, concerning the chart of Figure 18-1:[7]

> The top line . . . shows that the *president* is responsible for establishing basic policies and objectives. He works under the general supervision of his *board of directors*, and with the consultation of his corporate staff. Responsibility for coordinating engineering, research and development . . . is parceled out in a bit more complicated fashion. The *vice president, engineering, research, and development* carries the actual responsibility. He operates under the general supervision of the *president*, but must carry on close consultations with the *vice president, marketing and advertising* and the *director of manufacturing*. Consultation with the *vice president, finance* on R&D matters is not mandatory but may be required. It is also understood that the *board of directors* will be informed of significant developments.
>
> By reading down the chart it is possible to summarize rapidly a position's salient responsibilities. As depicted, the *president* has actual responsibility

---

[7]Op. cit.

	Board	President	Vice-president marketing-advertising	Vice-president engineering and R&D	Director of manufacturing	Vice-president finance	Secretary-treasurer	Vice-president foreign operations
Establish basic policies and objectives	2	1	3	3	3	3	3	3
Direct operations, control and planning functions	2	1	4	4	4	4	4	4
Fix relationships between central office and operating divisions	2	1	3	3	3	3	3	3
Control expansion — merger — acquisition plans	2	1	3	3	3	3	3	3
Administer merger — acquisition operations		2	1	3	3	3	3	3
Establish marketing policies and procedures		2	1		4			4
Coordinate sales forecasts and projections	5	2	1		5			3
Coordinate advertising plans	5	5	1					4
Coordinate engineering, research and development	5	2	3	1	4	4		4
Coordinate new product programs		2	3	1	4	3		4
Administer research and development center		3		1				
Establish accounting policies and procedures		2				1		
Administer financing, borrowing, equity	2	2				1	3	
Coordinate budgets	5	2	3	4	1	3		
Administer legal and tax matters		2				1		
Utilization of manufacturing facilities		3			1			
Coordinate training and safety programs		2	1		1			
Coordinate and administer capital expenditures	2	2	4	4	3	1	3	
Administer insurance plans and stockholder relations		2			4		1	
Coordinate foreign and export operations		2	4	4				1

Code
1 Actual responsibility   4 May be consulted
2 General supervision   5 Must be notified
3 Must be consulted

Figure 18-1. Authority interrelationships in a unit. (*From Allen R. Janger, "Charting Authority Relationships,"* The Conference Board Record, *December* 1964.)

PURCHASING ACTIVITIES

	Corporate						Division				Plant				
	Director of purchasing	V.P. manufacturing	Controller	Manager, engineering	Manager, trade relations	General manager of division	Manager, construction purchasing	Division purchasing	Division engineer	Manager of division	Plant purchasing	Plant purchasing agent	Plant manager	Plant controller	Plant engineer
PURCHASING-OPERATIONS															
A. Raw materials (controlled commodities)															
1. Development of annual plan for purchases of major raw materials.	O	▲						△	●						
2. Purchase or requisition of raw materials according to annual plan.										O	△	●			
3. Revisions in annual plan as to supplier, quantity, and (or) price.	O	▲						△	●		O	O			
4. Selection of appropriate suppliers.	O	△					O		●		O	O			
5. Conducting of any contract or other negotiations with suppliers.	O	▲						O	△	●					
B. Maintenance contracts															
1. Under $10,000 and on standard contract form.											△	●			●
2. Over $10,000 or a nonstandard contract (also approved by Legal Department and Trade Relations Department).	O	▲							△		▲	●	O		●
C. Surplus disposal															
1. Request for disposition of fixed assets.	▲	▲	▲	▲		▲	O				▲			▲	●
2. Disposition of surplus construction materials, equipment and supplies.	▲			▲					▲		▲	▲	●	O	O
3. Disposition of self-generated scrap (other than metal), supplies, and waste materials up to $100,000.	▲			▲					▲		▲	▲	●	O	O
D. General stores and supplies															
1. Determination of minimum inventory requirements.										O	△	●			
2. Ordering of stores and supplies.										O	△	●			
E. Rental agreements — equipment (under the authorization to execute contracts and purchasing policy).	▲	▲							▲	▲	▲	●			
PURCHASING-CONSTRUCTION															
A. Buildings and equipment															
1. Development of process designs and equipment specifications.				O			△		▲	O	O				●
2. Request of and appropriation of capital funds (RFI procedure in accordance with dollar authorizations).	▲	▲	▲	▲		▲			▲		▲	O	●	●	
3. Determination of the bid list — items over $10,000.	▲	▲							▲		▲	▲	▲	▲	●
4. Selection of the successful bidder — items over $10,000.	▲	▲							▲		▲	▲	▲	▲	●
5. Follow up on the rate and amount of expenditures of the appropriated capital funds (capital expenditures report).	O			▲			O		●		O			●	●

KEY:

△ Authorizes and (or) actuates
▲ Approves
O Recommends and (or) reviews and counsels
● Does the work (personally or within the department)

Figure 18-2. Functional authority relationships (*From Allen R. Janger,* "Charting Authority Relationships," The Conference Board Record, *December* 1964.)

for establishing basic policies and objectives, direction of operating control and planning functions, fixing relationships between the corporate headquarters and the product divisions, and control of expansion, merger, and acquisition plans. Other top management functions are the direct responsibilities of other corporate executives, although the president generally exercises supervision over them. He must at least be consulted on the administration of the R&D center and the utilization of manufacturing facilities. The *vice president, marketing and advertising* need only notify him about advertising plans.

Staff-line and project-functional relationships pose some of the more challenging problems of project management, particularly in light of the desirability of the deliberate conflict between the functional managers and the project manager. The deliberate conflict must be planned so that respective prerogatives are recognized and protected. The use of a chart similar to that shown in Figure 18-2 can do much to define and postulate the functional-project relationships, as well as the staff-line, staff-staff interfaces in the project environment.

The chart shown in Figure 18-2 is different from the chart for top management shown in Figure 18-1 in that the starting point is different. Figure 18-2 emphasizes the purchasing function and its subfunctions. The essence of the analysis is the determination of the sphere of each executive's authority in each of the key purchasing activities and of the extent of that authority. When these facts are ascertained, the relevant positions are listed at the top of the chart, and the appropriate symbols are added. The chart shows the roles of the various executives in manufacturing-related purchasing activities.

Figure 18-1 does more than clarify authority relationships; it can double as a collection of position guides. Its perspective is adequate to permit it to be used as an organizational chart of the top management of the organization. Figure 18-2, on the other hand, cannot serve as an organizational chart since it is not possible to get an overall picture of a position or a unit and its responsibilities from the chart. Figure 18-2 shows only the purchasing activities related to manufacturing; the nonpurchasing activities of the positions, which could be significant, are not shown.

Limitations of LRCs

Charts such as those shown in Figure 18-1 and 18-2 are not a panacea for all organizational difficulties. The LRC is a pictorial representation, and it is subject to the characteristic limitations and shortcomings of pyramidal organizational charts. The LRC does reveal the functional breakout of the work to be done and the interrelationships between the functions and job positions; however, *it does not show how people act and interact.*

It is doubtful that any contemporary management theorists would deny that organizational effectiveness is as dependent on the informal organization of human actions and relations as it is on the structured, formal organization. The LRC, as we have so far discussed it, is limited to showing the man-job relationships that constitute the formal organization; it does not purport to reveal the infinite number of variations in human relations arising out of the informal organization. The LRC technique simply extends the scope of charting formal organizations wherever they are located in the hierarchical order. Thus, a note of caution is in order about the IRC. But, as Karger and Murdick have implied, we still must give it a vote of confidence:[8]

> Obviously, the LRC chart has weaknesses, of which one of the larger ones is that it is a mechanical aid. Just because it says something is a fact does not make it true. It is very difficult to discover, except generally, exactly what occurs in a company—and with whom. The chart tries to express in specific terms relationships that cannot always be delineated so clearly; moreover, the degree to which it can be done depends on the specific situation. This is the difference between the formal and informal organizations mentioned. Despite this, the Linear Responsibility Chart is one of the best devices for organization analysis known to the authors.

The LRC In Input-Output Terms

The LRC can be visualized as an input-output device. For example, if the job positions of the managing-subsystem are considered to be the inputs, task accomplishments the outputs, and matrix symbols the specific task-to-job relationships, then the overall LRC can be looked upon as a diagram of the managing-subsystem from a systems viewpoint (Figure 18-3 diagrammatically illustrates this idea).

If two additional steps are added to this charting scheme, the systems viewpoint can be made more explicit. First, if systems terminology is used to structure the LRC matrix symbols and if the personnel affected are indoctrinated in the philosophy of an LRC, then many of the facets of the informal organization[9] can be formalized and assimilated along with the formal organization into the managing-subsystem structure. The second step is to use the *systems symbols* from one row (one task) of the LRC to draw a schematic

---

[8]Delmar W. Karger and Robert G. Murdick, *Managing Engineering and Research* (The Industrial Press, New York 1963), p. 89.

[9]The informal organization is not what the name implies, i.e., a casual, loosely structured community of people who have similar interests. The informal organization can be most demanding on its members. Its standards of performance and loyalty and its authority patterns can be anything but loose. It can be the most powerful of alliances existing between people having vested interests.

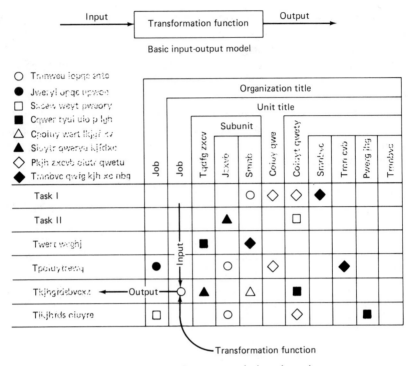

Figure 18-3. Input-output-device schematic.

diagram, as indicated by the symbols of that row; this would show the inter-relationships or intercouplings between the persons involved in accomplishing a task (see Figure 18-4).

The organization's work-subsystem chart could yield another advantage if the titles for the tasks and activities of the LRC were used. If this were done, the managing-subsystem schematic could also be used for diagrammatically integrating the work subsystem and the managing subsystem. A third step would be to superimpose a string of managing-subsystem schematics on the *total* work-subsystem chart to give an overall analytical view of how the organization operates; this would show the stream of interpersonal relations that serve to control, change, and otherwise facilitate the accomplishment of the tasks essential to the realization of the organizational goals.

The Systematized LRC

A systemized LRC could be structured to serve as the basis for drawing a managing-subsystem schematic diagram by following the three steps.

Task/Job Relationships Symbol titles

O Work is done
● Direct supervision
□ General supervision
■ Intertask integration
△ Occasional intertask integration
▲ Intertask coordination
◇ Occasional intertask coordination
◆ Output notification mandatory

Task/Job Relationships	Test management and plans branch						Test operations branch										
								Data A & A section		Elec. mach. testing section			Electronic testing section				
	Division manager	Branch manager	Test-activity integrator	Test-facility manager	Test-data planner	Test and documents coordinator	Branch manager	Section supervisor	Instrumentation engineer	Section supervisor	Test-equipment engineer	Test-article engineer	Section supervisor	Electrical-systems engineer	R. F. systems engineer	Cmd and C+I systems engineer	Test-equipment engineer
Major functional area: test program activities																	
Approve test-program changes	O	▲					▲	◇									
Define test objectives	●	O					■	▲		▲			▲				
Determine test requirements	□	●	O	▲	▲	▲	■	◇		◇			◇				
Evaluate test-program progress	●	O	▲	◇			▲										
Make test-program policy decisions	O	▲					▲										
Write test-program responsibility doctrine	□	●	O				■			◇			◇				
Major functional area: integration of test-support act																	
Chair-test working group	□	●	O				■			◇			◇				
Prepare milestone-test schedules		●	O				■	◆		◆			◆				
Write test directive		●	O	▲	▲	▲	△			◇			◇				
Write detailed test procedures			◇	◇	◆	◆	□	■	△	●	■	O	●	O	O	O	■
Coordinate test preparations			△	■	◇		●	O	▲	O	▲	▲	O	▲	▲	▲	▲
Verify test-article configuration			◆		▲		■					O		O	O	O	
Major functional area: all systems test																	
Certify test readiness	●	■	△	△			O	▲		▲			▲				
Perform test-director function	O	▲	▲	◇			■										
Perform test-conductor function	●						O	■		■			■				
Analyze test data				▲	◇		■	■		●	O	O	●	O	O	O	O
Resolve test anomalies	□			◇			●	▲	▲	O	▲	■	O	■	■	■	▲
Prepare test report	□	■	◇		◇	◆	●	O		O			O				

Figure 18-4. Systems LRC for equipment test division.

Arrangement and Form of Inputs: Job Positions. The job positions involved in the analysis are listed across the top of the LRC matrix. As can be seen from the sample in Figure 18-4, these job positions are arranged in such a manner that the line structure around them indicates the administrative ordering of the job positions. This method of showing job positions provides a means

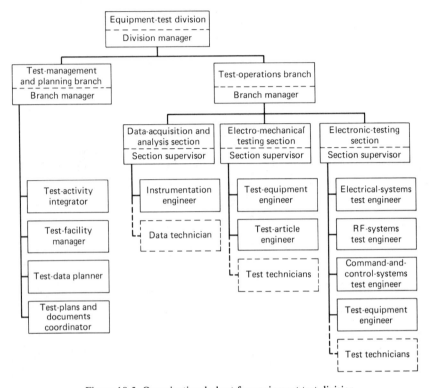

Figure 18-5. Organizational chart for equipment test division.

of integrating the pyramidal organization chart into the LRC. This can be seen by comparing the top portion of the LRC in Figure 18-4 with the corresponding traditional organizational chart in Figure 18-5. The chart should show only the jobs being analyzed. If the analysis concerns only the executives and engineers of an organizational unit, for example, nothing would be gained by including jobs such as those of secretaries, clerks, and draftsmen, even though they are vital parts of the organizational effort. The LRC, like any other chart, must be brief and simple to be effective.

Listing Outputs: Tasks and Activities. The tasks and activities related to the job positions are listed on the left side of the matrix. These tasks and activities should be listed in groupings and subgroupings that would facilitate the analysis and enhance the perspective view of the chart. If the tasks are extracted from the organization's work-subsystem chart, this scheme would enable the work subsystem to be integrated into the managing subsystem. Whether this method or some other is chosen, it is very important that complete, accurate, and agreed-upon descriptions of the tasks are selected. The relative ease of accomplishing the analysis and the subsequent usefulness of the LRC will depend strongly on the adequacy of the task statements.

Description and Definition of Matrix Symbols: Task-Job Relationships. There are a number of ways in which a person (a job position) can be related to a task. For example, he may be the person who takes some direct action concerning the task, he may be the person's supervisor, or perhaps he is an adviser on how to do the work. Perhaps he advises as to what needs to be done from a standpoint of intertask sequencing, e.g., as a production scheduler. He may even be someone in the system who only needs to be notified that an operation on the task has been completed. In each case, there exists what may be called a *task-job relationship* (TJR).

From a systems viewpoint, each TJR can be visualized as falling into one of three major categories: 1) transfer function, 2) control loop, or 3) input-output stream. The LRC shown in Figure 18-4 for the equipment test division of an electrical equipment company uses the eight TJRs defined below. The first three of these are usually found in papers and articles about the LRC; the other five have been retitled and changed so as to be more meaningful for a systems treatment.

Transfer Function: Work Is Done/TJR (WID/TJR). The WID/TJR is the transfer-function aspect of the managing-subsystem model. It is the actual juncture of the managing and the work subsystems. The given inputs of information, matter, and energy (i/m/e) are transformed into predetermined outputs of i/m/e in accordance with the program of instructions (policies, rules, procedures) furnished to the person for this job position.

Control Loop: Direct Supervision/TJR (DS/TJR). The DS/TJR constitutes the prime operational control element in the WID/TJR control loop. The person in the DS job position is considered to be the administrative supervisor of the person in the WID job position. The DS/TJR evaluates the quantity, quality, and timeliness of the WID/TJR outputs through the use of policy guidance information, program directives, procedures, WID input-output comparisons, schedules, and other managerial feedback, measurement, and control devices. The omission of this TJR from a row (task) indicates that the WID/TJR is of such a routine, stable nature that frequent contact with the DS/TJR is not normally required in operation of the transfer function.

General Supervision/TJR (GS/TJR). The GS/TJR is a second-order operational-control element and a first-order or prime source of policy guidance for the WID/TJR. The person in the GS job position is the administrative supervisor of the person in the DS job position. The primary role of the GS/TJR is to furnish the DS and WID job positions with a framework of policies and guidance of a scope that permits as much *closed-loop* decision-making flexibility as possible in attainment of the desired WID/TJR outputs. The exclusion of the GS/TJR from a given WID/TJR control loop indicates that WID actions are seldom taken that involve questions of conformance to, or exceptions from existing GS policy.

Intertask Integration/TJR (II/TJR).   The II/TJR is placed in the WID/TJR control loop to indicate the need for consideration of functional compatibility between this WID/TJR and other WID/TJRs. The extent of the involvement of the II/TJR in the control loop is the extent to which the transfer functions of the tasks concerned are interlocked or functionally interdependent. The person in the II job position does not have an administrative role in the WID/TJR control loop.

Occasional Intertask Integration/TJR (OII/TJR).   The OII/TJR is similar in concept and definition to the II/TJR, discussed above. The principal difference is the specialty nature of this TJR as opposed to the general or routine nature of the II/TJR. The omission of this TJR and (or) the II/TJR from a control loop indicates that the WID/TJR is, as a rule, functionally independent of, and hence decoupled from, other transfer functions in the work subsystem.

Input-Output Stream: Intertask Coordination/TJR (IC/TJR).   The IC/TJR is an information *input* to the WID/TJR and hence does not appear in the control loop; it has nothing to do with the "shape" or "how" of the transfer function. Intertask sequencing, schedule compatibility, quantities, qualities, and other matters of a "what" and "when" nature are indicated by the use of the IC/TJR.

Occasional Intertask Coordination/TJR (OIC/TJR).   The OIC/TJR is similar to the IC/TJR, discussed above, except that its use indicates only specialized instances of coordination instead of being a routine input.

Output Notification Mandatory/TJR (ONM/TJR).   The ONM/TJR is placed in the *output* of the WID/TJR transfer function when it is essential or critical that the ONM job position receive some specialized, exact, or timely information concerning the WID/TJR outputs. The concept of this TJR is one of passive transmission of information only and is not coordinative.

The LRC format, as discussed to this point, consists of job positions administratively ordered, tasks and activities grouped in some meaningful way, and TJRs defined along the lines of systems terminology. The subsequent analytical process involves the findings and determinations that lead to inserting the TJRs in the boxes of the LRC matrix. If a TJR symbol does not appear in a box, the analyst has concluded that the job position is not intercoupled with the WID job position of the task.

The completed analysis is then a systematized LRC model of the managing subsystem. This model displays the following characteristics of, and information about, an organizational unit:

The pyramidal organizational chart is incorporated into the top of the matrix through the use of lines to partition the job positions administratively.

The tasks and activities of the work subsystem are listed according to some functional flow plan.

The TJR symbols in the LRC matrix show the types of intercouplings between the person that offsets the work subsystem—the WID job position—and other persons with an interest in the task.

The TJRs also serve to show how the managing and work subsystems are integrated.

The overall model yields a perspective view of how the *static* formal organization is combined with the *passive* work subsystem to become a *dynamic* functioning entity that maintains a continuous balance with its environment while transforming its information-matter-energy inputs into the outputs that satisfy the everchanging goals and objectives of the organization.

System Model Schematic Diagrams

One additional diagram can be constructed that will further illustrate the systems nature of the managing subsystem. If a WID/TJR and its associated task

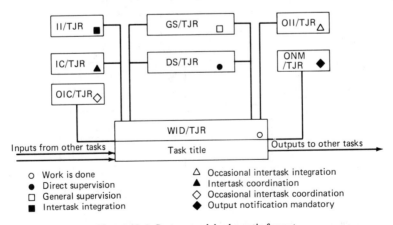

Figure 18-6. System model schematic format.

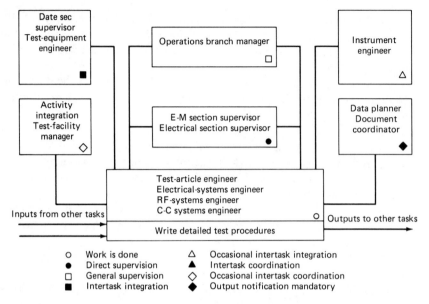

Figure 18-7. System model schematic of the task, "Write detailed test procedures."

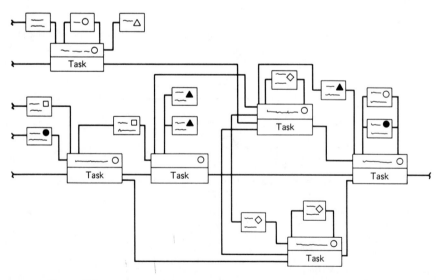

Figure 18-8. Integration of an organization's work and managing subsystems.

title are combined in one rectangle, and if the remaining TJRs are then inter-coupled with that WID/TJR, and if each is enclosed in separate rectangles arranged about, and interconnected with, the WID in accordance with their respective TJRs, the resulting schematic diagram will convey a systems con-cept of the interpersonal relations involved in accomplishing a given task. Fig-ure 18-6 shows the arrangement of TJRs in a system model schematic format. Figure 18-7 is a system model schematic of the task "Write detailed test pro-cedures," which appears in Figure 18-4. If all tasks of the organization's work subsystems are properly analyzed and charted and if the system model sche-matic for each task is shown with its respective tasks and interconnections with the other schematics, the results should give an overall portrayal of the orga-nization's integrated work subsystem and managing subsystem, such as is shown by the sketch in Figure 18-8.

THE LRC IN PLANNING

While the primary focus of the LRC has been descriptive, it may also be used in a prescriptive mode to aid in the systems design aspect of planning. This approach has been developed by the authors within the context of a Depart-ment of Justice study in the Buffalo, N.Y., Police Department.[10]

The approach utilizes both a descriptive and normative LRC-like model of the organization as the basis for developing a "consensus" model through negotiation.

Figure 18-9 depicts a descriptive chart which characterizes one aspect of policy planning—policy formulation.

The entries in the chart represent a number of organizational characteristics with regard to the planning decision area:

1. Authority and responsibility relationships.
2. Initiation characteristics.
3. Input-output characteristics.

The codes used to describe these characteristics for internal units are:

I-Initiation
E-Execution
A-Approval
C-Consultation
S-Supervision

[10]See William R. King and David I. Cleland, "The Design of Management Information Systems: An Information Analysis Approach," *Management Science,* Vol. 22, No. 3 (Nov. 1975), pp. 286–297.

	1	2	3	4	5	6	7	8	9	10	11	12
	City council	Mayor	Comptroller commissioner budget director	Police commissioner	Deputy commissioner	Inspector	Captain	Uniformed patrolman	Police administrator	Other city departments	Boards and agencies	Federal government
Routine complaints				A	C_4	S	E	C_7				
Observation of field practices				A	S	E						
Crime analysis												
Court decisions												
Analysis of social problems												
New legislation				A	S	E						
Issue clarification definition				A	S	E						
Selection of alternatives				A	E	C_5						
Obtaining relevant facts												
Analysis of facts												
Review		A		E						$2^{1.0}$		
Formulation				E	C							
Articulation				A	S_4	S	E					
Training for implementation					A	S	E					
Execution and control				A	S	E	C_4					

Figure 18-9. Model of existing policy-making process.

Subscripts on these coded symbols describe with whom the relationship exists. For instance, the simplified macro-level chart of Figure 18-9 shows on the first row that the analysis of routine complaints (E) is handled at the police captain level under the supervision of an inspector (S) with the police commissioner having approval authority (A). In performing this function, the captain has the consultation of uniformed patrolmen (C_7 where the subscript 7 indicates with whom the consultation takes place). Another consultation takes place when the deputy commissioner consults with the commissioner (C_4) at the approval stage.

Various informational linkages with interfacing environmental organizations are also depicted in these charts. Figure 18-9 shows only one such linkage— that involving "other city departments" who both provide input (i) to and receive output (o) from the mayor (2) in his approval role.

The model of Figure 18-9 is a descriptive one in that it depicts authorities, responsibilities, initiations, inputs, and outputs *as they actually occur in the organization.*

A descriptive model of the organizational and environmental system such as that provided by Figure 18-9 and other associated charts is a useful "road map" for guiding information analysis. It provides insights into "who does what," the interactions among organizational units and between internal and external units, the general nature of information required, the direction of information flow, and the manner in which information requirements are generated.

However, the use of a model of this variety alone as a basis for system design would represent an abrogation of the information analyst's proper role. Instead of creating a system to serve an existing organizational system, he should attempt to restructure the decision-making process so that the system may be oriented toward the support of a more nearly "optimal" process.

To do this, the analyst must call on the best of the knowledge and theory of management to construct a normative model of the organization. For instance, a police department which is not already using a program budget structure should be aided in developing one. A *normative* for the same "policy formulation" area to which the descriptive model of Figure 18-9 applies may be developed. Most organizations will not find it desirable to directly adopt such a prescriptive model. However, an "open minded" organization will usually find some elements of the model which it wishes to adopt.

The development of a consensus model hinges on an objective comparison of a descriptive model, such as the of Figure 18-9 with a normative model. This comparison and evaluation must be done by managers, with the aid and advice of analysts.

One possible medium for this process, which has been used successfully by the authors, is that of a "participative executive development program." The program involved the system participants as "students" and the analysts as "teachers." The normative model was developed and discussed in lecture-discussion sessions. After it had been communicated fully, workshops were used to facilitate the detailed evaluation and comparison of the descriptive and normative models. Recommendations emanating from the workshops were reviewed by top management, and those which were approved were incorporated into a consensus model of the system.

SUMMARY

This chapter demonstrates the values and limitations of traditional organizational charts and introduces a variety of charts—all based on the *linear responsibility chart* (LRC)—which can aid in both the planning and implementing phases of management.

BIBLIOGRAPHY

Allen, Louis A. *Charting the Company Organization Structure,* Studies in Personnel Policy, no. 168, (National Industrial Conference Board, Inc., New York, 1959).

Barnard, Chester I. *The Functions of the Executive,* (Harvard University Press, Cambridge, Mass., 1938).

"Changing the Company Organization Chart," *Management Record,* November 1959.

Cooper, W. W., et al. (eds.) *New Perspectives in Organization Research,* (John Wiley & Sons, Inc., New York, 1964).

Dale, Ernest *Planning and Developing the Company Organization Structure,* (American Management Association, New York, 1952).

Higgans, Carter C. "The Organization Chart: Its Theory and Practice," *Management Review,* (October 1956).

Janger, Allen R. "Charting Authority Relationships," *The Conference Board Record.* (December 1964).

Karger, Delmar W., and Robert G. Murdick *Managing Engineering and Research.* (The Industrial Press, New York, 1963).

Landsberger, Henry A. "The Horizontal Dimension in Bureaucracy," *Administrative Science Quarterly,* (December 1961).

"Linear Responsibility Charting," *Factory,* vol. 121, March 1963.

Litterer, Joseph A. *The Analysis of Organizations,* (John Wiley & Sons, Inc., New York, 1965).

"Mapping the Executive Setup," *Business Week,* (Apr. 6, 1957).

Mesarovic, Mihajlo D. *Views on General Systems Theory,* (John Wiley & Sons, Inc., New York, 1964).

Munsey, Virgil W. *An Empirical Demonstration of the Systems Characteristics of Complex Organizations,* Research Report, (Air Force Institute of Technology, School of Engineering, 1966).

Patton, John A. "Make and Use an Organization Chart," *Business Management,* (May 1963).

Randall, Clarence B. "The Myth of the Organization Chart," *Dun's Review and Modern Industry,* (February 1960).

Terry, George R. *Principles of Management,* 4th ed., (Richard E. Irwin, Inc, Homewood, Ill., 1964).

19. Pricing Out the Work

Harold Kerzner*

The first integration of the functional unit into the project environment occurs during the pricing process. The total program costs obtained by pricing out the activities over the scheduled period of performance provides management with a fundamental tool for managing the project. During the pricing activities, the functional units have the option to consult program management for possible changes to work requirements as well as for further clarification.

Activities are priced out through the lowest pricing units of the company. It is the responsibility of these pricing units, whether they be sections, departments or divisions, to provide accurate and meaningful cost data. Under ideal conditions, the work required (i.e., manhours) to complete a given task can be based upon historical standards. Unfortunately for many industries, projects and programs are so diversified that realistic comparison between previous activities may not be possible. The costing information obtained from each pricing unit, whether or not it is based upon historical standards, should be regarded only as an estimate. How can a company predict the salary structure three years from now? What will be the cost of raw materials two years from now? Will the business base (and therefore the overhead rates) change over the period of performance? The final response to these questions shows that costing out performance is explicitly related to an environment which cannot be predicted with any high degree of certainty.

Project management is an attempt to obtain the best utilization of resources within time, cost and performance. Logical project estimating techniques are available. The following thirteen steps provide a logical sequence in order to obtain better resource estimates. These steps may vary from company to company.

*Dr. Harold Kerzner is Professor of Systems Management and Director of The Project/Systems Management Research Institute at Baldwin-Wallace College. Dr. Kerzner has published over 35 Engineering and Business Papaer and six texts: *Project Management: A Systems Approach to Planning, Scheduling and Controlling; Project Management for Executives; Project Management for Bankers; Cases and Situations in Project/Systems Management; Operations Research; and Proposal Preparation and Management.*

STEP 1: PROVIDE A COMPLETE DEFINITION OF THE WORK REQUIREMENTS

Effective planning and inplementation of projects cannot be accomplished without a complete definition of the requirements. For projects internal to the organization, the project manager works with the project sponsor and user (whether they be executives, functional managers, or simply employees) in order for the work to be completely defined. For these types of inhouse projects, the project manager can wear multiple hats as project manager, proposal manager and even project engineer on the same project.

For projects funded externally to the organization, the proposal manager (assisted by the project manager and possibly the contract administrator) must work with the customer to make sure that all of the work is completely defined and that there is no misinterpretation over the requirements. In many cases, the customer simply has an idea and needs assistance in establishing the requirements. The customer may hire an outside agency for assistance. If the activity is sole-source or perhaps part of an unsolicited effort, then the contractor may be asked to work with the customer in defining the requirements even before any soliciting is attempted.

A complete definition of project requirements must include:

- Scope (or statement) of Work.
- Specifications.
- Schedules (Gross or Summary).

The scope of work or statement of work (SOW) is a narrative description of all the work required to perform the project. The statement of work identifies the goals and objectives which are to be achieved. If a funding constraint exists, such as "this is a not-to-exceed effort of $250,000," this information might also appear in the SOW.

If the customer supplies a well-written statement of work, then the project and proposal managers will supply this SOW to the functional managers for dollar and manhour estimates. Unless the customer maintains a staff of employees to provide a continuous stream of RFP/RFQ's*, the customers must ask potential bidders to assist them in the preparation of the SOW. As an example, Alpha Company wishes to build a multi-million dollar chemical plant. Since Alpha does not erect such facilities on a regular basis, Alpha would send out inquiries instead of a formal RFP. These inquiries are used not only to identify potential bidders, but also to identify to potential bidders that they will have to develop an accurate SOW as part of the proposal process. This process may appear as a feasibility study. This is quite common especially

---

*RFP (Request for Proposal); RFQ (Request for Quote)

on large dollar-value projects where contractors are willing to risk the additional time, cost and effort as part of the bidding process. If the proposal is a sole-source effort, then the contractor may pass this cost on to the customer as part of the contract.

The statement of work is vital to proposal pricing and should not be taken lightly. All involved functional managers should be given the opportunity to review the SOW during the pricing process. Functional managers are the true technical experts in the company and best qualified to identify high risks areas and prevent anything from "falling through the crack." Misinterpretations of the statement of work can lead to severe cost overruns and schedule slippages.

The statement of work might be lumped together with the contractual data as part of the terms and conditions. The proposal manager may then have to separate out the SOW data from the RFP. This is vital for the pricing effort.

This process is essential because misinterpretation of the statement of work can cause severe cost overruns. As an example, consider the following two situations:

- Acme Corporation won a Navy contract in which the Government RFP stated that "this unit must be tested in water." Acme built a large pool behind their manufacturing plant. Unfortunately, the Navy's interpretation was the Atlantic Ocean. The difference was $1 million.
- Ajax Corporation won a contract to ship sponges across the United States using aerated boxcars. The project manager leased boxcars that had doors on the top surface. The doors were left open during shipping. The train got caught in several days of torrential rainstorms and the boxcars eventually exploded spreading sponges across the countryside. The customer wanted boxcars aerated from below.

The amount of money and time spent in rewording the technical data in the SOW for pricing is minimal compared to cost of misinterpretation.

The second major item in the definition of the requirements is the identification of the specifications, if applicable. Specifications form the basis from which manhours, equipment and materials are priced out. The specifications must be identified such that the customer will understand the basis for the manhour, equipment and materials estimates. Small changes in a specification can cause large cost overruns.

Another reason for identifying the specifications is to make sure that there will be no surprises for the customer downstream. The specifications should be the current revision. It is not uncommon for a customer to hire outside agencies to evaluate the technical proposal and to make sure that the proper specifications are being used.

Specifications are in fact standards for pricing out a proposal. If specifications either do not yet exist or are not necessary, then work standards should be included in the proposal. The work standards can also appear in the cost volume of the proposal. Labor justification backup sheets may or may not be included in the proposal, depending upon RFP/RFQ requirements.

For R&D proposals, standards may not exist and the pricing team may have to use educated guesses based upon the estimated degree of difficulty, such as:

- Task 02-15-10 is estimated to be 25% more difficult than a similar task accomplished on the Alpha Project which required 300 manhours. Hours needed for Task 02-15-10 are therefore 375.
- Task 03-07-02 is estimated at 450 hours. This is 20% more than the standard because of the additional reporting constraints imposed by the customer.

The standards mentioned here are usually the technical standards only.

The technical standards and specifications may be called out by the customer or, if this is a follow-on project, then the customer will expect the work to be performed within the estimate on the previous activity. If the standards or specifications will be different, then an explanation must be made or else the customer (and line managers) may feel that he has been taken for a ride. Customers have the tendency of expecting standards to be lowered on follow-on efforts because the employees are expected to be performing at an improved position on the learning curve.

The key parameter in explaining the differences in standards is the time period between the original cost estimate and the follow-on or similar cost estimate. The two most common reasons for having standards change are:

- New technology requiring added effort.
- Key employees with the necessary skills or expertise have either left the organization or are not available.

In either event, justifications of the changes or modifications must be made so that the new ground rules are understood by all pricing and reviewing personnel.

The third item in the identification of the requirements is the gross schedule. In summary, the gross schedule identifies the major milestones of the project and includes such items as:

Start date.
End date.
Other major milestone activities.
Data Items and reports.
If possible, all gross schedules which are used for pricing guidelines should

contain calendar start and end dates. Unfortunately, some projects do not have definable start and end dates and are simply identified by a time spread. Another common situation is where the end date is fixed and the pricing effort must identify the start date. This is common occurence because the customer may not have the expertise to accurately determine how long it will take to accomplish the effort.

Identifying major milestones can also be a tedious task for a customer. Major milestones include such activities as long-lead procurement, prototype testing, design review meetings and any other critical decision points. The proposal manager must work closely with the customer or inhouse sponsor to either verify the major milestones in the RFP or to identify additional milestones.

Major milestones are often grossly unrealistic. Inhouse executives of the customer and the contractor occasionally identify unrealistic end dates because either resources will be idle without the completion at this point in time, not enough money is available for a longer project, or management wants the effort completed earlier because it affects management's Christmas bonus.

All data items should be identified on the gross schedule. Data items include written contractual reports and can be extended to include handout material for customer design review meetings and technical interchange meetings. Data items are not free and should be priced out accordingly. There is nothing wrong with including in the pricing effort a separate contingency fund for "unscheduled or additional" interchange meetings.

STEP 2: ESTABLISH A LOGIC NETWORK WITH CHECK POINTS

Once the work requirements are outlined, the project manager must define the logical steps necessary to accomplish the effort. The logic network (or arrow diagram as it is more commonly referred to) serves as the basis for the PERT/CPM diagrams and the Work Breakdown Structure. The arrow diagram simply shows the logical sequence of events, generally at the level which the project manager wants to control the program. Each logic diagram activity should not be restricted to specific calendar dates at this point because line managers should price out the work initially assuming:

- Unlimited resources.
- No calendar constraints.

If this is not done during the initial stages of pricing, line managers may commit to unrealistic time, cost and performance estimates. After implementation, the project manager may find it impossible to force the line manager to meet his original estimates.

STEP 3: DEVELOP THE WORK BREAKDOWN STRUCTURE

The simplest method for developing the work breakdown structure is to combine activities on the arrow diagram. If each activity on the arrow diagram is considered to be a task, then several tasks can be combined to form projects and the projects, when combined, will become the total program. The WBS may contain definable start and end dates in accordance with the gross schedule at this point in time, although they may have to be altered before the final WBS is firmly established. Most project managers prefer to work at the task level of the WBS (Level 3).* The work is priced out at this level and costs are controlled at this level. Functional managers may have the option of structuring the work to additional levels for better estimating and control.

Often the arrow diagram and WBS are considered as part of the definition of the requirements, because the WBS is the requirement that costs be controlled at a specific level and detail.

STEP 4: PRICE OUT THE WORK BREAKDOWN STRUCTURE

The project manager's responsibility during pricing (and even during execution, for that matter) is to establish the project requirements which identify the "What," "When," and "Why" of the project. The functional managers now price out the activities by determining the "How," "Who," and "Where" of the project. The functional managers have the right to ask the project manager to change the WBS. After all, the functional managers are the true technical experts and may wish to control their efforts differently.

Once the Work Breakdown Structure and activity schedules are established, the program manager calls a meeting for all organizations which will be required to submit pricing information. It is imperative that all pricing or labor costing representatives be present for the first meeting. During this "kickoff" meeting, the Work Breakdown Structure is described in depth so that each pricing unit manager will know exactly what his responsibilities are during the program. The kickoff meeting also resolves the struggle-for-power positions of several functional managers whose responsibilities may be similar or overlap on certain activities. An example of this would be quality control activities. During the research and development phase of a program, research personnel may be permitted to perform their own quality control efforts, whereas during production activities, the quality control department or division would have overall responsibility. Unfortunately, one meeting is not sufficient to clarify all problems. Follow-up or status meeting are held, normally with only those parties concerned with the problems that have arisen. Some companies prefer to have all members attend the status meetings so that all personnel will be famil-

---

*see chapter 15

iar with the total effort and the associated problems. The advantage of not having all program-related personnel attend is that time is of the essence when pricing out activities. Many functional divisions carry this policy one step further by having a divisional representative together with possibly key department managers or section supervisors as the only attendees to this initial kickoff meeting. The divisional representative then assumes all responsibility for assuming that all costing data be submitted on time. This may be beneficial in that the program office need only contact one individual in the division to learn of the activity status, but may become a bottleneck if the representative fails to maintain proper communication between the functional units and the program office or if the individual simply is unfamiliar with the pricing requirements of the Work Breakdown Structure.

During proposal activities time may be extremely important. There are many situations where a Request for Proposal (RFP) requires that all responders submit their bids no later than a specific date, say 30 days. Under a proposal environment, the activities of the program office, as well as those of the functional unit, are under a schedule set forth by the proposal manager. The proposal manager's schedule has very little, if any, flexibility and is normally under tight time-constraints in order that the proposal may be typed, edited and published prior to date of submittal. In this case, the RFP will indirectly define how much time the pricing units have to identify and justify labor costs.

The justification of the labor costs may take longer than the original cost estimates, especially if historical standards are not available. Many proposals often require that comprehensive labor justifications be submitted. Other proposals, especially those which request almost immediate response, may permit vendors to submit labor justification at a later date.

In the final analysis, it is the responsibility of the lowest pricing unit supervisor to maintain adequate standards, if possible, so that almost immediate response can be given to a pricing request from a program office.

The functional units supply their input to the program office in the form of manhours. The input may be accompanied by labor justifications, if required. The man-hours are submitted for each task, assuming that the task is the lowest pricing element, and are time-phased per month. The man-hours per month per task are converted to dollars after multiplication by the appropriate labor rates. The labor rates are generally known with certainty over a 12-month period but from there on are only estimates. How can a company predict salary structures five years hence? If the company underestimates the salary structure, increased costs and decreased profits will occur. If the salary structure is overestimated, the company may not be competitive. If the project is government funded, then the salary structure becomes an item under contract negotiations.

The development of the labor rates to be used in the projection are based upon historical costs in business base hours and dollars for either the most recent month or quarter. Average hourly rates are determined for each labor unit by direct effort within the operations at the department level. The rates are only averages, and include both the highest-paid employees and lowest-paid employees together with the department manager and the clerical support.* These base rates are then escalated as a percentage factor based upon past experience, budget as approved by management, and the local outlook and similar industries. If the company has a predominant aerospace or defense industry business base, then these salaries are negotiated with local government agencies prior to submittal for proposals.

The labor hours submitted by the functional units are quite often overestimated for fear that management will "massage" and reduce the labor hours while attempting to maintain the same scope of effort. Many times management is forced to reduce man-hours either because of insufficient funding or just to remain competitive in the environment. The reduction of man-hours often provides heated discussions between the functional and program managers. Program managers tend to think in the best interests of the program while functional managers lean toward maintaining their present staff.

The most common solution to this conflict rests with the program manager. If the program manager selects members for the program team who are knowledgeable in man-hour standards for each of the departments, then an atmosphere of trust can develop between the program office and the functional department such that man-hours can be reduced in a manner which represents the best interests of the company. This is one of the reasons why program team members are often promoted from within the functional ranks.

The ability to estimate program costs involves more than just labor dollars and labor hours. Overhead dollars can be one of the biggest headaches in controlling program costs and must be estimated along with labor hours and dollars. Although most programs have an assistant program manager for cost whose responsibilities include monthly overhead rate analysis, the program manager can drastically increase the success of his program by insisting that each program team member understand overhead rates. For example, if overhead rates apply only to the first forty hours of work, then, depending on the overhead rate, program dollars can be saved by performing work on overtime where the increased salary is at a lower burden.

The salary structure, overhead structure and labor hours fulfill three of four major input requirements. The fourth major input is the cost for materials and support. Six subtopics are included under materials/support: materials, purchased parts, subcontracts, freight, travel and other. Freight and travel can be

---

*Problems can occur if the salaries of the people assigned to the program exceed the department averages. Also, in many companies department managers are included in the overhead rate structure, not direct labor, and therefore their salaries are not included as part of the department average.

handled in one of two ways, both normally dependent on the size of the program. For small dollar-volume programs, estimates are made for travel and freight. For large dollar-volume programs, travel is normally expressed as between three and five percent of all costs for material, purchased parts and subcontracts. The category labelled other support costs may include such topics as computer hours or special consultants.

The material costs are very time-consuming, more so than the labor hours. Material costs are submitted via a bill of materials which includes all vendors from whom purchases will be made, project costs throughout the program, scrap factors and shelf lifetime for those products which may be perishable.

Information on labor is usually supplied to the project office in the form of manhours/department/task/month. This provides a great degree of flexibility in analyzing total program costs and risks, and is well worth the added effort. Costs can be itemized per month, task, or even department. Computers, with forward pricing information, will convert the manhours to dollars. Raw materials are always priced out as dollars per month with the computer providing the forward pricing information for escalation factors.

STEP 5: REVIEW WBS COSTS WITH EACH FUNCTIONAL MANAGER

Once the input is received from each functional manager, the project team integrates all of the costs to ensure that all of the work is properly accounted for, without redundancy. An important aspect of this review is the time-phased manpower estimates. It is here where the project manager brings up the subject of limited rather than unlimited resources and asks the line managers to assess the various risks in their estimates.

As part of the review period, the project manager must ask the following questions:

- Was sufficient time allowed for estimating?
- Were the estimates based upon history or standards, or are they "best guesses?"
- Will the estimates require a continuous shifting of personnel in and out of the project?
- Will there be personnel available who have the necessary skills?

Obviously, the answers to these questions can lead into a repricing activity.

STEP 6: DECIDE UPON THE BASIC COURSE OF ACTION

After the review with the functional managers, the project manager must decide upon the basic course of action or the base case. This is the ideal path that the project manager wishes to follow. Obviously, the decision will be based upon the risks on the project and the projected tradeoffs which may have to be made downstream on time, cost and performance.

The base case may include a high degree of risk if it is deemed necessary to satisfy contractual requirements. This base case approach and accompanying costs should be reviewed with the customer and upper-level management. There is no point in developing finalized detailed, PERT/CPM schedules and the program plan unless there is agreement on the base case.

STEP 7: ESTABLISH REASONABLE COSTS FOR EACH WBS ELEMENT

Since the project will be controlled through the WBS, the project manager must define, with reasonable accuracy and confidence, his target costs for each WBS element, usually at level 3. Once the project is initiated, these costs will become the basis for the project targets. The problem here is that the costs were based upon unlimited resources. Limited resources may require overtime or perhaps the work will have to be performed during higher cost escalation periods. These factors must be accounted for.

STEP 8: REVIEW THE BASE CASE COSTS WITH UPPER-LEVEL MANAGEMENT

Once the base case is formulated, the pricing team member, together with the other program office team members, perform perturbation analyses in order to answer any questions that may come up during the final management review. The perturbation analysis is designed as a systems approach to problem solving, where alternatives are developed in order to respond to any questions that management may wish to consider during the final review.

The base case, together with the perturbation analysis costs, are then reviewed with upper-level management in order to formulate a company position for the program as well as to take a hard look at the allocation of resources required for the program. The company position may be to cut costs, authorize work or submit a bid. If the program is competitive, corporate approval may be required if the company's chief executive officer has a ceiling on the dollar bids he can authorize to go out of house.

If labor costs must be cut, the program manager must negotiate with the functional managers as to the size and method for the cost reductions. Otherwise, this step may simply entail the authorization for the functional managers to begin the activities or to develop detailed plans.

STEP 9: NEGOTIATE WITH FUNCTIONAL MANAGERS FOR QUALIFIED PERSONNEL

Once the base case costs are established, the project manager must begin the tedious effort of converting all estimates to actual calendar dates and time frames based upon limited resources. Detailed schedules cannot be established without some degree of knowledge as to exactly which employees will be assigned to key activities. Highly qualified individuals may be able to accomplish the work in less time and may be able to assume added responsibilities.

Good project managers do not always negotiate for the best available resources because either the costs will be too great with those higher paid individuals or the project priority does not justify the need for such individuals.

Accurate, detailed schedules cannot be developed without some degree of knowledge as to who will be available for the key project positions. Even on competitive bidding efforts, customers require that the resumes of the key individuals be included as part of the proposal.

STEP 10: DEVELOP THE LINEAR RESPONSIBILITY CHART

Once the key employees are assigned to the activities, the project manager works with the functional managers in assigning project responsibilities. The project responsibilities may be assigned in accordance with assumed authority, age, experience on related efforts, maturity and interpersonal skills.

The linear responsibility chart, if properly developed and used, is an invaluable tool not only in administering the project, but also in estimating the costs.* The linear responsibility chart permits the project manager the luxury of assigning additional work to qualified personnel, of course upon approval of the functional managers. This additional work may be assigned to lower salaried individuals so that the final costs can come close to the departmental averages, assuming that the work was priced out in this fashion.

The linear responsibility chart development has a direct bearing upon how the costs are priced out and controlled. There are three methods for pricing out and controlling costs.

- Work is priced out at the department average and all work performed is charged to the project at the department average salary, regardless of who performed the work.
- Work is priced out at the department average but all work performed is billed back to the project at the actual salary of those employees who are to do the work.
- The work is priced out at the salary of those employees who will perform the work and the costs are billed back the same way.

Each of these methods has its advantages and disadvantages as well as a serious impact on the assignment of responsibilities.

---

*see chapter 18

STEP 11: DEVELOP THE FINAL DETAILED AND PERT/CPM SCHEDULES

Work standards are generally based upon the average employee. The assignment of above or below average employees can then cause the schedules to be shifted left or right. These detailed schedules are now based upon limited resources and provide the basis for accurate cost estimating. If at all possible, "fat" and slack time should be left in the schedules so as to provide some degree of protection for the line managers. Fat and slack should be removed only as a last resort to lower costs, such as in the case of wanting to remain competitive or on buy-ins.

It should be obvious at this point that project pricing is an iterative process based upon optimization of time, cost and performance together. After the detailed schedules are developed, the entire pricing process may have to be reaccomplished. Fortunately, the majority of the original estimates are usually salvagable and require only cosmetic modifications unless the customer provides major changes to specifications or quantity revisions because initial cost estimates were grossly unacceptable.

STEP 12: ESTABLISH PRICING COST SUMMARY REPORTS

Although the pricing of a project is an iterative process, the project manager must still burden himself at each iteration point by developing cost summary reports so that key project decisions can be made during the planning. There are at least two times when detailed pricing summaries are needed; in preparation for the pricing review meeting with management and at pricing termination. At all other times it is possible that "simple cosmetic surgery" can be performed on previous cost summaries, such as perturbations in escalation factors and procurement cost of raw materials. The list identified below shows the typical pricing reports.

- A detailed cost breakdown for each WBS element. If the work is priced out at the task level, then there should be a cost summary sheet for each task, as well as rollup sheets for each project and the total program.
- A total program manpower curve for each department. These manpower curves show how each department has contracted with the project office to supply functional resources. If the departmental manpower curves contain several "peaks and valleys," then the project manager may have to alter some of his schedules so as to obtain some degree of manpower smoothing. Functional managers always prefer manpower-smoothed resource allocations.
- A monthly equivalent manpower cost summary. This table normally shows the fully burdened cost for the average departmental employee car-

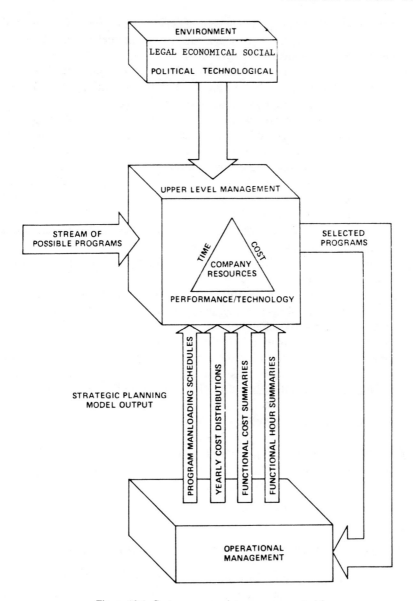

Figure 19-1. Systems approach to resource control.*

*Kerzner, Harold: *Project Management: A Systems Approach to Planning, Scheduling and Controlling,* Van Nostrand Reinhold Company, New York, NY, p. 405.

ried out over the entire period of project performance. If project costs have to be reduced, the project manager performs a parametric study between this table and the manpower curve tables.

- A yearly cost distribution table. This table is broken down by WBS element and shows the yearly (or quarterly) costs that will be required. This table, in essence, is a project cash flow summary per activity.
- A functional cost and hour summary. This table provides top management with an overall description of how many hours and dollars will be spent by each major functional unit, or division. Top management would use this as part of the forward planning process to make sure that there are sufficient resources available for all projects. This also includes indirect hours and dollars.
- A monthly labor hour and dollar expenditure forecast. This table can be combined with the yearly cost distribution, except that it is broken down by month, not activity or department. In addition, this table normally includes manpower termination liability information for premature cancellation of the project by outside customers.
- A raw material and expenditure forecast. This shows the cash flow for raw materials based upon vendor lead times, payment schedules, commitments and termination liability.
- Total program termination liability per month. This table shows the customer the monthly costs for the entire program. This is the customer's cash flow, not the contractor's. The difference is that each monthly cost contains the termination liability for manhours and dollars, on labor and raw materials. This table is actually the monthly costs attributed to premature project termination.

These tables are used both by project managers and upper-level executives. The project managers utilize these tables as the basis for project cost control. Top level management utilizes these tables selecting, approving and prioritizing projects, as shown in Figure 19-1.

STEP 13: DOCUMENT THE RESULTS INTO A PROGRAM PLAN

The final step in cost estimating is to document all of the results into a project plan. The cost information will also be the basis for the cost volume of the proposal. The logical sequence of events leading up to the program plan can be summarized as in Figure 19-2. Pricing is an iterative process, at best. The exact pricing procedure will, of course, differ for projects external to the organization as opposed to internal.

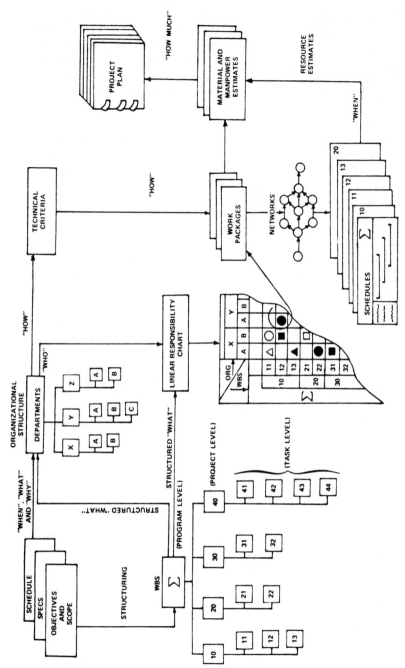

Figure 19-2. Project planning.*

*Kerzner, Harold: *Project Management for Executives*, Van Nostrand Reinhold Company, New York, NY. p. 366.

Regardless of whether or not you are managing a large or small project, cost estimating must be accomplished in a realistic, logical manner in order to avoid continuous panics. The best approach, by far, is to try to avoid the pressures of last minute estimating, and to maintain reasonable updated standards for future estimating. Remember, project costs and budgets are only estimates based upon the standards and expertise of the function managers.

20. Unique Issues of Multiple-Project Management

James H. Reedy*

OBJECTIVE AND SCOPE

This chapter will focus on the issues, problems, and solutions of managing a group of smaller simultaneous projects in contrast to the issues involved with managing a single major one. While the primary emphasis in the field of project management has been placed on improving control over the major projects, there are some unique techniques required to effectively manage a multiproject effort. A knowledge of project management problems and tools used on major projects is helpful in understanding the contrasts drawn in this chapter, but it is not essential.

The chapter begins with a background on the development of formal project management techniques and tools such as CPM**. Next, the multiproject environment is defined and highlighted with some descriptive examples. The special problems of multiproject management are brought into sharper focus in the next section, followed by a discussion of suggested conceptual solutions. In the final section, some specifications for management tools to help solve some of these problems are presented, including an example of a computer-driven CPM package designed specifically for this purpose.

BACKGROUND

The discipline of project management as a recognized science had its beginning in the 1950s, roughly coincident with the development of one of its major tools;

---

*James H. Reedy is a Senior Associate with Theodore Barry & Associates (TB&A), a management consulting firm based in Los Angeles. He has performed many corporatewide organizational and operational reviews and specializes in project management for major projects. Prior to joining TB&A, he headed project control departments for several major construction efforts including two nuclear plants. Additionally, he has broad experience in the areas of corporate planning, engineering, and finance. He is co-developer of a commercially available cost and scheduling system. Mr. Reedy holds an Engineering degree from University of Florida, and an M.B.A. from the University of Washington.
**see also chapter 16

Critical Path Method (CPM). The "necessity" that spawned this invention and the broader management discipline was the increasing complexity of major system projects. Not only were the interrelations of project elements outstripping the ability of managers to manage "in their heads," but the resources of time and money were also becoming more critical. It seemed inevitable that project management had to develop a better tool.

CPM was invented as this tool and demonstrated successfully on a major project (the Navy's Polaris program, using a CPM approach termed PERT).* Initially, it was touted as the panacea for all project management ills, but inexperience and overzealous application to inappropriate projects severely dimmed its bright outlook. Refinements and the development of resource management techniques in CPM brought a degree of sophistication so that now we view CPM as a seasoned and invaluable tool in the management of large and complex projects.

The point to be highlighted here is that project management science in general and CPM specifically were born, raised, and almost died in the context of major, monolithic development projects—monolithic in the sense of being large, singular, and stand-alone in nature. (Today, a major project can cost more than 1.5 billion dollars, span 15 years, and induce the formation of an independent organization solely to design, build, and manage it) While these projects are certainly worthy of the effort expended to improve their management, there is a class of projects that have largely been ignored, or worse, treated in the same manner as monolithic projects.

MULTIPLE-PROJECT ENVIRONMENT

This other class of projects is the multiple-project—a group of smaller jobs interconnected by somewhat tenuous physical requirements or by virtue of common budgetary and resource considerations. These subprojects can be quite diverse in their nature and have varying degrees of complexity. Preservation of the identity of each individual subproject is necessary because they are typically conceived, budgeted, and controlled individually. Management is prevented from rolling these subprojects together rigidly into a monolithic project because the interrelations and interdependencies are so weak. Cancellation of one project may have no physical effect on the rest, or else merely cause a shift in other loose interdependencies.

Another major distinction between a monolithic and multiple-project environment is found in the organizational structures of each. Monolithic projects warrant a fully dedicated project management team or "matrixed" organization containing all the various required functions reporting to a project manager. Figure 20-1 shows a typical project organization within a company. On

---

*see chapter 16

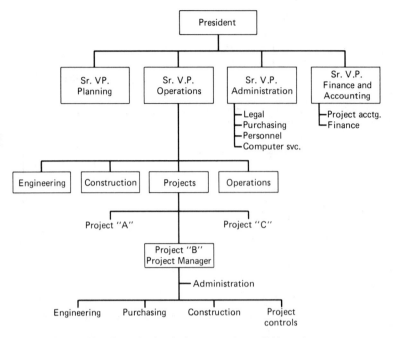

Figure 20-1. Organizational placement of monolithic project team.

the other hand, because of smaller scope, multiple-projects are completed by separate permanent functional departments, each performing only a specialized piece of the subproject, and each doing that function for all subprojects in the company. Figure 20-2 shows typical functional departments responsible for smaller projects. As many as ten departments can be involved with completing each subproject and often a few departments have to deal with the same project more than once at different stages of development. Figure 20-3 depicts a rep-

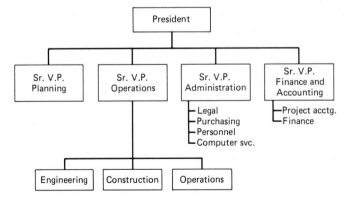

Figure 20-2. Typical functional departments involved with multiple projects.

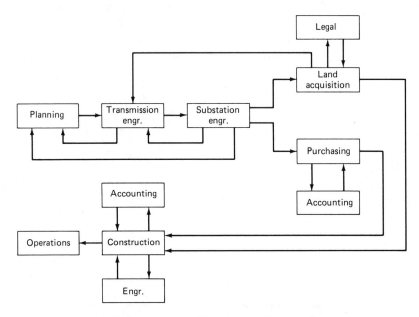

Figure 20-3. Representative work-flow in multiple project environment.

resentative flow of work through various departments, giving an idea of the number of times responsibility is passed from one group to another. It is evident that coordination and resource planning are special problems in the multiproject arena.

An example of the distinctions between multi and monolithic projects can be found in the electric utility industry. Power plant design and construction is a paradigm of monolithic undertakings; a nuclear plant is the epitome of complexity and high cost in this country today. Here, project management organizations are formed (either within the company or sometimes as an independent subsidiary) with the sole purpose of designing and building *one* plant or unit. Even the personnel function is often incorporated into the team. Resources (money, labor, tools, equipment and materials, clerical aids, etc.) are acquired in a build-up/wind-down pattern that attempts to optimize the time required for completion rather than the administrative problems of changing resource levels. Of course there are recognized limits to all resources in a monolithic project, and optimality is desirable, but a constant level of resources is definitely not the major objective of managers of power plant construction projects.

This same utility must also build and maintain miles of transmission and distribution lines and numerous substations, constrained usually by a pool of resources that is relatively fixed. This is representative of a multiproject situation. A new transmission line may be required to feed a new distribution sub-station, but the interdependencies are only in the siting and real estate choices and the final energization dates. Alternatively, they might not be electrically or physically related at all, but the legal and real estate department can handle only a limited amount of land purchases in a year with their current staff and hiring new lawyers would be impractical because of uncertain work load next year. Similar problems can exist in each of the 6–10 different permanent departments typically involved in the completion of a single subproject.

There are numerous other examples. Building of chain stores or hamburger stands around the country, development of a "planned living" community, or management of a multifaceted defense project are several others.

UNIQUE PROBLEMS OF MULTIPROJECT MANAGEMENT

In this section, the management problems that are uniquely associated with the multiproject environment are discussed in order to draw a contrast to the ones experienced in a monolithic project. As a general statement it can be said that most of these problems stem either directly or indirectly from the organizational structure typically responsible for designing and building these projects, as discussed earlier. The secondary root cause of these problems emanates from the relatively small size of each subproject which precludes heavy investment in management and management tools.

Intradepartment Resourcing

Because there were not enough lawyers to handle the work load in our previous example, some projects would have to be deferred from one year to the next. This will occur either by discrete management choice or by happenstance as the law staff works on those projects that are the most interesting or easiest to complete. This latter process is going on in other departments at the same time as well—lawyers have not been maliciously singled out—with chaotic effects on planning and management of the projects if indeed there exists a project management function at all in the overall organization. Often there is none, or at best the Planning or Engineering Departments informally perform what can be described as a coordination role in attempting to usher the projects through to completion. However, priority setting, contingency planning, and resource management are usually lacking in this approach.

The problem of proper resource allocation is indeed an especially difficult and eclectic one in the multiproject management environment; in fact, more so than in the monolithic project milieu. In effect, the degree of complexity is twice that for a single project because two constraints must be observed as each department attempts to optimize resources: 1) the needs of each project that comes through the department must be met and; 2) resource levels in the department, especially labor, must be stable. (While not an absolute premise, this condition is nevertheless observed in most organizations as a practical matter. To hire and fire people in a functional department to keep step with small or temporary changes in the work load is deemed to be worse than having occasional project delays or staff underutilization).

Interdepartment Resources

A companion problem to lack of resource allocation within an individual department is lack of balanced resource planning *between* departments. The "weak link in the chain" situation can and often does prevail in a multiproject environment due to the independent organizational authority and staffing policies. Each department builds its staff based upon its own perception of the work load and in its own arena of department and division politics. Quite often, the perception and politics of one differs from the others, and both may differ from the true need. This creates a situation in which projects are bottlenecked in one area while staff underutilization exists in others, with little hope of appropriate corrections.

Coordination, Priority Setting, Contingency Decisions

As a direct result of the fragmented nature of the various departments involved in completing a multiproject effort, tactical coordination and communication is a rather severe problem. Interdepartmental barriers seem to prevent the simplest of discourse even if it involves only a walk down the hall or a telephone call. This can be expanded to include related problems such as lack of priorities set for the best interest of corporate objectives and lack of an effective function to replan, restructure, and reprioritize all projects as a result of unexpected disruptions of the original plan. Within a department, projects are usually worked on in a first-in/first-out manner; when the department experiences excessive work loads due to prior tasks, work usually stops on new projects. This order is often preempted by short or "easy" projects which get preferential treatment. This is due to human nature that desires to show accomplishment as subjectively measured by numbers of completed tasks, irrespective of the length, difficulty, or importance of the tasks. In fact, difficult and long tasks tend to be constantly postponed, especially if there is a steady flow of simpler ones to assume "priority." It is evident that these criteria do not relate to the priorities of the organization.

Another related problem is the lack of an effective status and progress reporting function necessary for project control and contingency management. In fact, interdepartmental barriers tend to withhold important and timely status assessments, exacerbating an already difficult management task.

Visibility

As every experienced manager has discovered, there are some subtle but important benefits to be gained by keeping all project team members briefed on the high level objectives, project progress, and interfaces even if they do not directly involve each person. Due to the fragmented nature of the various departments involved in a multiproject environment, visibility of the "big picture" is easily lost because a comprehensive, highly visual plan and status report is usually not maintained. Furthermore, it is difficult for a department involved in the early stages of a project to have the prescience to understand accurately the effect its actions have on "downstream" departments involved in the same project. Often blame is placed on downstream departments for missing a completion date when, in fact, an upstream department caused the delay but was not as visible as its successor in the chain. Typically the construction department, being the last group to get responsibility for a project, is left "holding the bag" when the in-service date is missed. An analysis will show that just as typically, the Engineering Department or Land Department failed to give it to Construction in time, not due to malice but a lack of understanding of construction time requirements. This misunderstanding is perpetuated by lack of a comprehensive plan which shows all projects together. For example, Engineering may estimate that Project A will require 6 weeks to construct, so they give it to Construction 7 weeks ahead of the completion date. While this time estimate may be ample if Project A were the only one in the queue, Construction also has to build Projects B, C, D, E, and F at the same time. Engineering usually is not aware of these other projects (they may come from sources other than Engineering) and to further complicate matters, construction problems usually necessitate many shifts in priorities.

Budgeting

Commensurate with the previously discussed problems of resource planning (especially personnel), the multiproject environment suffers from special difficulty in forecasting and maintaining an accurate budget. The reason stems not necessarily from lack of accurate cost estimates on any one project, but more from the timing and mistiming aspects of the budgeting process. Because subprojects can have loose ties to one another and because there is greater chance of unplanned bottlenecks than in a monolithic situation, large budget variances seem to be a common occurrence. Moreover, overruns in long range aggregate budgets (usually one year or greater) are experienced due to chronic underbudgeting in the latter portion of the budget period. This in turn is caused by failure to carry the planning and estimating horizon, however sketchy, far enough beyond the end of the budget period to capture "spill-back" effects into the current period.

Management Overhead

It is obvious that many of the problems already discussed could be solved by techniques commonly practiced by managers of large projects, including, possibly, CPM applications. The assignment of project managers and the use of these tools has not been rapid in acceptance for two major reasons. The first stems from fragmented organizational authority structures as already discussed. The second relates to the relatively small size and cost of the projects themselves. When viewed individually, they do not warrant costly managers, manager's staff and expensive computer systems. Also, historically, the projects have been simple enough to manage by committee action as a secondary duty of the department managers. This situation is rapidly changing today, creating a need both for project managers and project management tools.

Accomplishment Measures

In the past, a common relationship that was used to evaluate project status (for both monolithic and minor projects) was dollars expended over time. It has since been accepted that this method has little merit because physical accomplishment is not recognized in the dollar figure—e.g., although costs might be higher than planned at a certain point in the project, it could be caused by construction being well ahead of schedule, turning an ostensibly alarming situation into merely a false alarm. Therefore, in the monolithic project management field earned-value techniques, based on quantities of materials installed, were developed which embody physical accomplishment. Now, earned-value plots (in terms of dollars or man-hours) vs. time *do* have significance and are an effective reporting tool for major projects. However, in the smaller projects, the earned-value approach is more troublesome because construction materials, as measured in homogeneous physical units (pipe, concrete, wire, steel, etc.), are not used in the huge quantities that they are in major projects. When smaller quantities of materials are used on a smaller project, the earned-value becomes a lesser part of the total work than in larger projects.

It must be emphasized that although earned-value is troublesome in strict application on small projects, the approach is still the only valid one known. The concept must be applied, however modified (there are valid application methods for small projects), because the misleading effects of any other reporting parameters are too pernicious to ignore.

CPM Application

Turning our attention now from a general management discussion to the primary technical tool, we find that there are several impediments to applying conventional CPM techniques in a multiproject situation. The first is cost, not only of the computer system and hardware, but more significantly cost of the personnel and time required to support it. Someone must review each project, create a logic network for it, label all activities, estimate activity durations and resources, debug logic and other problems, and finally maintain and update the network. For anyone who has actually experienced this process, the impracticality of using conventional CPM for hundreds of small projects is evident. Solutions to this problem are emerging, however, that promise to make modified CPM techniques feasible. One such system that is currently in existence is described in the section on "CPM Solutions."

A significant shortcoming of all CPM systems known to this author (except the one described in the "Solutions" section), used on large and small projects alike, is the inadequacy of "total float" and "early/late" date pairs.* Every CPM program will give "early" and "late" dates for a series of dependent activities in a chain (called a "path"), and will calculate the difference between any "late" date/"early" date pair (called "total float"). This float is shared by all activities on a path. Using a conventional "early" start/"late" start range of dates, the manager of a downstream activity may be planning to start his activity on the "early" start date, while *at the same time,* an upstream activity may be planned to begin on the "late" start. By virtue of his plan, the upstream department manager has consumed all available float on the path and hence the plan for downstream activities is invalid from the beginning. The downstream manager usually will not discover the problem until his portion of the work has slipped. Figure 20-4 graphically demonstrates this problem using two in-line activities as an example. This situation is less of a problem (although not nonexistent) for a monolithic project under the coordination of a project manager, but it is quite pernicious in the multiproject milieu when independent departments are shifting work in an attempt to levelize their own resources. An effective solution to this problem, called a "plan-date pass," is described in the section on CPM solutions.

Another serious deficiency in most CPM applications is the failure to produce a profile of resources required to achieve a certain schedule plan. This is a universal problem on monolithic as well as smaller projects. One cannot say anything conclusive about the feasibility of a certain schedule until and unless the commensurate resource level (especially manpower) required to achieve that schedule is examined and deemed practical. Further, this profile must be built up from the composite of detailed activities, not merely a broadbrush estimate of manpower made independent from the schedule. The problem has long been recognized and sound solutions do exist in a number of CPM packages,

---

*see chapter 16 for definitions of these terms

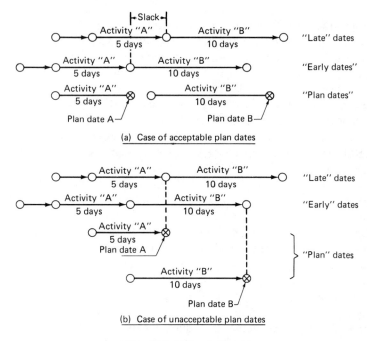

Figure 20-4. Plan date usage.

however, appropriate application of the solution is rare. A process for building this profile is described in the "CPM Solutions" section.

A final inadequacy of conventional CPM technology in the multiproject setting arises from the nature of the work and the organizational structure. In a major project, there are definite start and end dates for the project; a project organization is created and Engineering begins on a specific date (usually under contract). Work proceeds as fast as possible due to the high time cost of capital and replacement opportunities. In a multiproject setting, however, the situation is different. Many projects are handled at once in Engineering, some faster, using more department resources than others depending upon priorities. A small project does not have a clear-cut start in Engineering or Purchasing or Land Acquisition, but rather a sort of nebulous beginning of activity. What is clear-cut, however, is usually the construction start date in which work is optimally handled by a dedicated crew working full time until construction is completed. Therefore, in order to be useful, a CPM system must be able to use "construction start" (or any other designated point) as a fixed point in the network and work in both "directions" to calculate the schedule dates. In addition, it must allow any input date to be fixed (called "plug" dates) and the downstream dates consequently be a function of the plug dates (many systems will merely print out dates but the system ignores them in the calculations). This is needed to handle the myriad external constraints that are a significant facet of life in multiproject management.

SOLUTIONS

In this section, solutions to the problem previously outlined will be presented. Most have been developed through actual experience and are in existence today, although not necessarily widespread. The discussion is divided into two parts. First, organizational structures and management processes necessary to permit effective multiproject management are discussed in a general manner. Following this, the major features of a currently available CPM package designed specifically for multiproject management (called MPM) are highlighted to demonstrate that solutions do exist for the CPM problems outlined above.

Organization and Management Solutions

Not surprisingly, a vast majority of the management ills in the multiproject environment can be cured by the establishment of a project management function. The structure and relationships of the functional departments should remain as is because they have evolved for good reason. But an independent project manager with a small staff of planners should be assigned to each project at its inception. Each project manager could be responsible for several projects simultaneously according to project size and complexity. Further, the project manager and staff could all belong to a single department, probably labeled "Project Management Department."

It is improbable to expect these managers to have the degree of authority and responsibility that their counterparts in the major projects have; undoubtedly the functional manager would retain more power. Hence coordinating, planning, and communicating would be the major thrust of the multiproject manager's duties, but these can be most effective in solving the problems outlined in this article. To facilitate these processes, it is *essential* that the Project Management Department report at a high level in the organization, preferably to a Senior Vice President. Further, they should be placed in as independent a position as possible. For example, the effectiveness of project managers in dealing with Purchasing would be severely limited if the project manager reported to the same Vice President as Engineering. Figure 20-5 is a suggested organizational structure.

The duties of each project manager would be to first organize and plan the

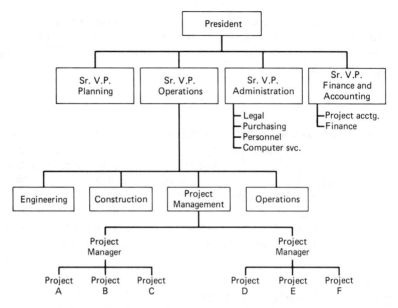

Figure 20-5. Suggested placement of multi-project managers.

project in accordance with corporate objectives in terms of budget and in-service date. Then this plan must be validated with each functional manager as it impacts the resource burden of his department. After numerous revisions of the plan to make it simultaneously realistic across all departments, then the commitments of project scope, schedule, and budget are published. As the project progresses through the departments, status is regularly reported by the project manager. Any snags or potential problems are quickly reviewed by the project manager and if necessary, the problem project and possibly all others are replanned and rescheduled according to corporate priorities.

CPM Solutions

After the organizational structure and management processes are in place, the main planning, coordinating and reporting tools must be implemented. These can be manual tools (even CPM can realistically be manual). Then, only after an analysis of the cost and benefits to be gained by going to a computer system should this step be taken.

Assuming that the numbers of projects and activities creates a sufficiently complex environment to warrant a computer system, it is important to acquire one that is simple and inexpensive to operate yet incorporates the features described below. These features are found in the Multiproject Management

System (MPM) currently available through General Electric Company, Information Services Division, and co-developed by this author. (Other developers are R. W. Weishaupt, Florida Power Corporation, and C. A. Seibold, General Electric Company, Information Services Division) The description of this system in this discussion is intended to serve as an example of possible solutions to the inadequacies of conventional CPM applied in a multiproject environment.

MPM has been demonstrated with 400 simultaneous projects, some logically interdependent, most of them independent. It has been used as an integral part of cost forecasting and budgeting procedures by providing a schedule based rolling budget for all projects. It is a system in which the emphasis is placed on flexibility, capturing the entire scope of all projects involved rather than any one single job. The structure is such to permit the operators a reprieve from handling volumes of data and yet allows direct access to all facets of the system.

MPM possesses six addressable levels of work organization, none of which is required, but when used will remain discreet for control and identity purposes. Figure 20-6 depicts this structure. In conventional fashion, ACTIVI-TIES are the basic unit of work, with several activities forming a discernible WORK ITEM. It is at this work item level that RESOURCES (both estimated and actual) are entered into the system. Associating resources with a

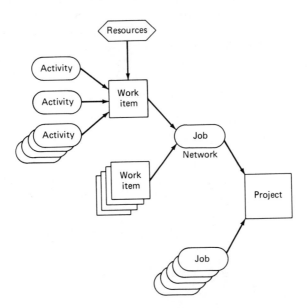

Figure 20-6. MPM structure.

work item, rather than an activity, permits a more natural interface with the accounting and estimating functions, as the work item can be defined by the user to conform to any work division that may already exist in the organization. This relation also permits resources to be "tied" to the schedule via activities while not being restricted to this element when such a relationship would be improper.

Several different work items can then be linked together to form a uniquely identified JOB which is represented, in conventional CPM terminology, as a network. The job is usually a stand-alone work unit (such as the construction of a single aircraft) that may be related to other jobs (such as the construction of a squadron). Projects may be separated into BUDGET TYPES as might occur under a parent holding company situation.

This type of structure permits essential flexibility, allowing adaption of the MPM system to various corporate organizations that may exist. Since the only element *required* by MPM is a job identification (name), work with little definition can be factored into the total corporate picture with a minimum of effort.

Multinetworking

MPM treats the job or network as the basic stand-alone unit of work, therefore, the identity of a job must be maintained for storage and reporting purposes. However, a unique multinetworking feature will permit the user to define relationships that may exist between several jobs (thus forming a project) for the purposes of calculating dates and processing resources as a function of a rela-

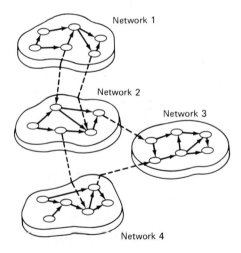

Figure 20-7. Multi-network concept.

tionship between these jobs. Figure 20-7 illustrates this concept. Each job is then stored and reported separately but the results are a product of the entire project.

This permits another degree of flexibility, as a network in the MPM context could be thought of as merely a subnetwork where separate or independent control is a significant desire. Networks containing large numbers of activities are often structured with a series of subnetworks.

It is noteworthy that the multinetworking feature will allow each network to have the same collection of nodes and activities, thus allowing any particular activity of interest to be sorted out and reported on a project level or even a corporate level (an area manager might be interested in a consolidated summary of the dates for building permits for all jobs). Such summaries, or milestone reporting, are based on activities with common identification numbers. This feature also permits the use of another extremely important technique in the multiproject environment, which is master or standard networks.

Master Networks

The problem of constructing, without error, a network for each one of a large number of projects is staggering. Delays encountered in constructing the network can cause updates to be less than complete in reflecting the total corporate picture. In a multiproject environment, it is essential that a network for each job be generated from standardized or master networks that contain the basic logic and standard durations with resources for as many activities as possible. MPM will automatically copy a designated master from several master types and give the new "blank" network a job identification. Then, by way of the periodic updates, this job is "filled in" with its unique durations and resources as the information becomes available.

Although some detail might be lost in using standard logic, this is insignificant in light of the benefit gained when one considers that the concern is placed on the entire collection of all jobs and projects rather than a specific activity. It can be demonstrated that uniqueness through increased detail reaches a point of diminishing return from the standpoint of better project control. For jobs that are planned for the future, and as yet have little definition, the use of the standard network will help portray resources more accurately for that future time period.

With all activity numbers being generated automatically from a master, there is assurance that all repetitive or common activities will have the same number and thus may be sorted out and reported if so desired. The use of master networks is also required to support the standard processing of networks (such as changing and/or correcting), an important feature of MPM and an essential element of multiproject control.

Standard Processing

In further pursuit of handling ease, the MPM system will allow any element of a job or a network to be automatically changed for all jobs created from a given master. Thus, as procedures are modified, organizations changed, or previous errors discovered, standard changes are processed. Schedule data including durations or resources or process control parameters (which control the calculation of the schedule dates, resource allocation, and executive functions) are applied to all similar networks.

Plan Date and Plan Date Pass

"Plan Dates" are used by MPM to augment the inadequacies of "early start/ late start" and "early finish/late finish" dates as discussed earlier. A plan date is a feedback mechanism supplied by the person responsible for the particular activity in question after he has reviewed the early and late dates. If his plan date is within the calculated schedule early and late dates, it is accepted unless the plan date of an activity earlier in the network has violated the calculated constraints, thus making the downstream plan date unrealistic. (Figure 20-4) A plan date pass is made through the network to correlate all plan dates and to verify that the relationship between them is valid. Once verified, the plan dates then form the basis for the distribution and allocation of the resources associated with this network, as well as schedule reporting. Such features introduce a high degree of reality into the schedule plan as well as encourage closer coordination between functions that are represented within a network. This realistic schedule plan, in turn, is the basis for a realistic resource picture as discussed in the following sections.

Resource Allocation and Profiles

Resources on a project can be of a variety of types. A resource type might be manpower required over a particular phase or activity of a job expressed as crews or number of men; it may be the dollar cost estimate for a particular function expressed as a continuing expenditure or as a periodic payment required; it may be specialized types of equipment necessary for work between jobs or networks, it could be material consumed as a work activity proceeds; or it may be expendable items, such as tools, or expendable equipment actually consumed through a job process. In each case, the resource and its units of identification has an estimated amount, an associated amount of actuals expended and a resulting forecast of a remaining estimate. The resource is generally associated with and physically placed with an activity in the MPM system according to one of four allocation modes of "spreading" resources over activities.

The first mode of allocation places the total input resource estimate on a selected date. A common use of this mode is in the representation of a cash payment on a specified date or dates.

The second mode assumes the estimated input as a daily quantity, calculating a total resource estimate based on the number of work days of the resource involvement. The total calculated is then spread equally over that involvement using selected dates. An example of the use of this mode is in case of a specified work force available where the total number of man-days expended will be strictly a function of the estimated duration of the work.

The third mode assumes the estimated input to be spread equally over the work duration using selected dates. An example of this use would be the situation where the manpower or cost total is estimated in lump total and it is desired to simply apply the total to all or part of the activity duration resulting in a daily allocation.

The fourth mode assumes the estimated input to be a daily quantity and calculates a total estimate using the activity work duration, placing the total on a selected date. This mode is effectively a combination of the first and second mode, where unit cost installation per day may be the known quantity and a payment date is specified for the total involvement.

The system allows simulation of resource patterns for each work item utilizing a series of step functions for a given resource class. This effectively allows one resource class to be broken into individual segments, each being allocated individually so that the sum total represents a required resource profile. This eliminates the need for specialized spreading functions which in themselves are quite limited and substantially inflexible. A series of step functions permits more versatility in the area of profile simulation, especially in the light of the available standard processing procedures which permits common profiles to be applied and controlled across a large number of projects. Figure 20-8 demonstrates how a resource profile is created for a particular work item using steps. These individual work item profiles are then automatically summed for all work items, all networks, and all jobs to create an overall resource profile that

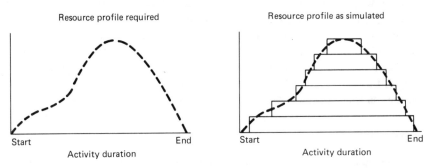

Figure 20-8. Profile simulation for a single work item.

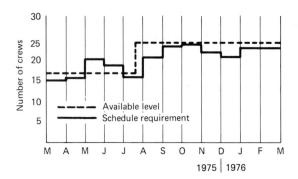

Figure 20-9. Composite resource profile.

is a direct result of schedule requirements. As shown in Figure 20-9, this requirement can then be compared to resource availability to assess the workability of the current schedule.

Rolling Budget

As a consequence of the fragmented characteristic of a multiproject environment, it is difficult to compile a total corporate picture with regard to the forecast, especially in the later portion of the budget period. This is due to the relative independence of smaller jobs which may move about in time; being cancelled, rescheduled, redesigned, reestimated, or postponed continuously so that actual attainment of an approved budget, goal, or objective for a long fiscal period is exceedingly elusive. The features of the MPM system can be used to better portray this dynamic situation and better direct the course of the projects to attain the approved budget. The process is essentially a form of budgetary planning which requires some type of cost and manpower estimate regardless of the degree of work definition or network development that may exist for distant projects. As time proceeds and preliminary planning on future jobs provides better definition and more detail becomes available, then the resource allocation results become more refined. (Although more and better detail provides more realistic allocation, that detail is not mandatory as a part of the allocation procedure in MPM)

This process is performed on a continual rolling basis as depicted in Figure 20-10, thereby assuring that early work on projects scheduled for completion in the following period is properly represented in the current period.

CONCLUSIONS

Management of a number of smaller, simultaneous projects can present some difficult challenges not encountered by managers of large single projects. Most

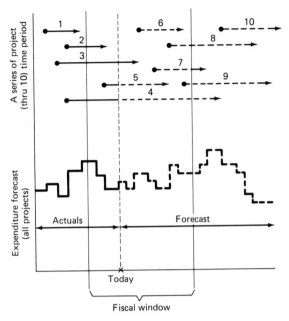

Figure 20-10. Rolling budget concept.

of these problems stem from the organizational structures in which permanent functional departments are established to perform the various duties of the project. This introduces a second order of resource constraints which, combined with noncoherent objectives and interdepartmental politics, makes coordination and management difficult. Most often, a well defined project management function is completely absent from the organization.

The tools that project managers traditionally have used on large projects have some drawbacks when applied to a multiproject situation. Basically, the cost, time, and effort required to maintain conventional CPM outstrips the benefit derived from its application. However, by modifying the approach somewhat, and installing some unique features, certain systems can greatly facilitate multiproject management. Naturally the system is not the entire solution, for the appropriate management processes must be in place in order for any degree of success to prevail.

Section VI

Project Control

This section focuses on the project control process that complements project planning.

In Chapter 21, James A. Bent develops the project control concept as it relates to project planning. He emphasizes project control ideas in the construction context, but his ideas are widely applicable in other situations as well.

In Chapter 22, F. A. Hollenbach briefly describes project control concepts as they are applied in Bechtel Power Corporation.

Kenneth O. Chilstrom provides in Chapter 23, the framework for the management audit of projects—a diagnostic tool that can serve important control objectives.

In Chapter 24, Harold Kerzner presents various techniques for assessing the performance of project personnel. Project control is thereby conceived as not only involving *project* assessments, but also assessments of people.

In Chapter 25, John Tuman, Jr. discusses the development and implementation of an effective system for the control of a project. He relates the control function to the information that is necessary if control is to be exercised and provides information flow models and modular configurations for a project management information and control system. (The systems development methodology that he prescribes is related to that described in terms of the linear responsibility chart in chapter 18).

21. Project Control: An Introduction

James A. Bent*

General

Philosophical discussions on defining "control" are never ending. There is the long stated opinion that actual control is only exercised where the right of decision is vested—in this case, the decision-making of the project manager, line supervisors and design engineers.

It is stated that cost and schedule engineers only provide information and, therefore, have no exercise of control. This is partly true. Often, a staff function does become one of reporting and accounting. However, reporting, trending and analysis are essential ingredients for forecasting which, in turn, is an essential ingredient of control.

It is also true that control is minimal where there is little creative analysis and only reporting and accounting.

The fundamental elements of control are the cost estimate and project schedule.

Planning the Project

One of the most important functions in the life cycle of a project is project planning, especially in the preliminary phases when basic decisions are being made that will affect the entire course of the project. The purpose of project planning is to identify the work that must be done, to gain the participation of those best qualified to do the work, and to develop appropriate project cost and schedule objectives. Sound planning will minimize lost motion and clearly define for all participants—owner, contractor, associated corporate departments and outsiders—their role in the project. Sound planning will also provide

---

*James A. Bent is President of James Bent Associates, Inc., consultants in project management and project control. Mr. Bent was with Mobil Research and Development Corporation for 12 years, where he was Supervisor of Cost and Schedule Control for Mobil's worldwide capital projects program. He is a member of the British Institute of Design Engineers (MI DESIGN E), a certified member of the American Association of Cost Engineers (CCE) and a member of the Project Management Institute. Mr. Bent has developed training courses in planning and scheduling, cost control, subcontract administration and project control and is the author of *Applied Cost and Schedule Control.* New York: Marcel Dekker, May 1982.

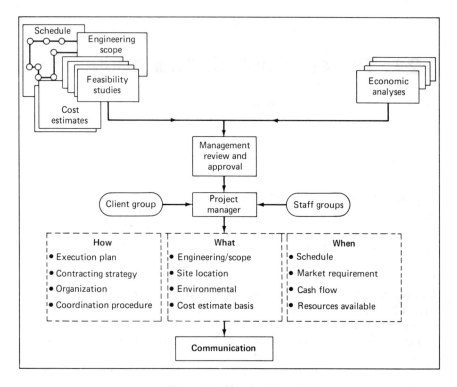

Figure 21-1. Planning the project.

adequate consideration of all project elements, and will ensure a proper effort to meet the completion date. Figure 21-1 illustrates the major elements of project planning.

The project manager should personally supervise this effort with the support of business, cost and schedule specialists. Project planning should consider such items as organization, communication channels, personnel skills, client requirements, business-political environment, project execution strategy and draw up a plan to set in motion these operations. The project manager should develop a *Project Coordination Procedure,* after consulting with client and others, as necessary. This document will identify all principals concerned with the project, define their functions and responsibilities, and indicate appropriate contacts for each. The purpose of the document is to provide an effective basis for coordinating company activity and communications on the project, especially in the early stages of project execution when project scope and other elements are being defined. *Effective communication channels are essential for successful control.*

Who determines the organization, control systems and resource requirements?

Too often, project managers will set up projects without seeking the support, advice and assistance of staff personnel. On large projects this can be disastrous, particularly for the project control and estimating function. Resource requirements, control systems, and organizational arrangements should be matters of consultation and discussion with staff groups prior to decision by the project manager. This will also ensure that anticipated manpower requirements and resources are adequately reflected in the early conceptual estimates.

Apart from project size, the proposed execution plan and contracting strategy are the most significant elements for determining the control basis and associated organizations for the project. Figure 21-2 shows the typical phases of a project from an owner's feasibility and front end studies to full implementation by a prime contractor. This typical life cycle is for a large process plant and shows durations of 8 months for a Phase I and 33 months for a Phase II operation. The durations for the front end vary widely.

There are many possible variations of project life cycles, this particular configuration is a typical routine of large oil corporations. Many owners use a phased approach, rather than a straight-through approach. This provides the owner with less risk on capital investment and also the ability to fully investigate the feasibility and financial viability of multiple projects at the same time.

A phased approach, particularly of large projects, also provides for more control by corporate management as the project is being developed in the feasibility, scoping and design phase. However, it may add costs and will increase the overall project duration.

The following brief explanations cover the various phases as illustrated in Figure 21-2.

Owner Front End is the feasibility stage when a design specification is produced by engineering, economic and market evaluations by the affiliate and capital cost estimate and schedule by the cost group. The design specification is sometimes produced by a contractor, in greater detail than an owner engineered design specification, but not to the detail of a Phase I operation. The control basis will be set by overall corporate objectives, mainly in the form of a development budget.

Phase I generally covers conceptual design, process selection, optimization, upgrading of estimate/schedule, environmental/governmental studies and finalization of the process design. The "authorization for funds" for the Phase II work is then prepared, presented, and when approved, a contractor is selected to carry out the work. The Phase I work is carried out by a contractor, normally on a reimbursable basis with a small Owner Project Task Force (PTF) in attendance. There are two basic objectives for a Phase I operation. For large projects and revamps, it provides greater definition of scope, schedule

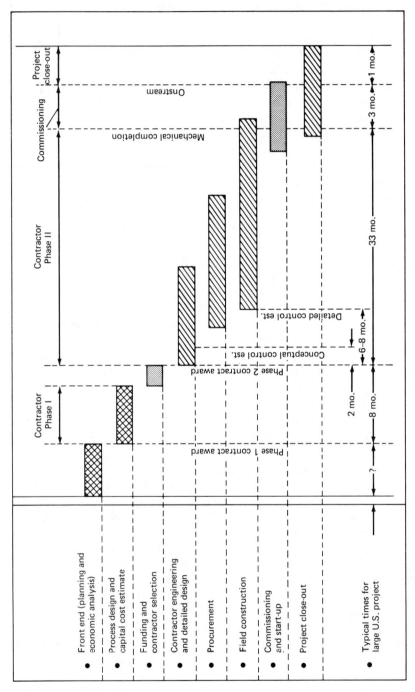

Figure 21-2. Project life cycle—typical.

and cost. On small projects, it provides a design package suitable for lump sum bids. An important element of a Phase I operation is to provide an execution plan for Phase II. The control basis will be the expenditure and cost of the contractor manhours and a milestone project master schedule.

Phase II is full execution of the project by a contractor. The normal project philosophy is that of a prime contractor with single responsibility for engineering, procurement and construction. Most large projects are executed on a reimbursable basis with an Owner PTF directing/monitoring the work. This will require a complete project control system.

There are variations of a Phase II, where engineering and construction responsibilities are split and awarded to different contractors. This is the method usually adopted by utility companies where architect-engineers provide the design and construction contractors manage the field work on a subcontract basis. This approach does not provide a single responsibility and the designer and constructor can blame each other for errors of design and installation.

As outlined, the phased approach requires different control methods for each phase. A front end (feasibility study), usually carried out within the owner's organization, is authorized by an operating affiliate from its own development budget. As these budgets are developed in one year and five year cycles, there is rarely a need for detailed cost and schedule control at this stage. Expenditures can range from $100,000 for a small project, to $5,000,000 for a very large project.

A contractor phase I, on a reimbursable basis, requires a monthly monitoring of engineering manhours and associated costs. Controls will be manual expenditure curves and progress measurement of engineering design. Expenditures can range from $1,000,000 for small projects to $20,000,000 for very large projects.

A contractor phase II will require full schedule control for reimbursable and lump sum bases, but minimal cost control if on a lump sum basis.

A further variable on control requirements is the question of technology. New technology, such as synthetic fuels and offshore facilities, will generally require additional controls due to the lack of an existing data base. The past decade of the Alaska Pipeline, nuclear power plants and North Sea platforms has clearly shown that prototype engineering, project size, hostile environments and lack of data have produced poor cost estimates and schedules. This type of project will generally require a phased approach in order to develop data for a detailed project execution plan.

It cannot be emphasized too strongly that poor cost estimates and unrealistic project schedules can only result in an "out of control" project.

Project Execution Plan

Figure 21-3 shows major elements of a project execution plan. This plan is developed during phase I and covers all aspects of scope, associated services,

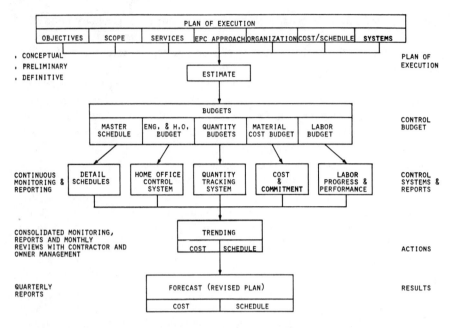

Figure 21-3. Project execution plan.

infrastructure, approach to engineering—procurement—construction (EPC), resources, organization structure and project control requirements.

This detailed execution plan is essential for developing a quality control estimate and project schedule. Large overseas projects with remote jobsites require that the execution plan consider logistics and material handling, local infrastructure and resources, camp facilities, training, expatriate conditions, national and governmental requirements. A quality execution plan will provide a good estimate, control budgets, detailed schedules and a breakdown of the project into controllable areas and cost centers. The project organization will be similarly structured, as will trending, control and reporting systems.

Key Items of Execution Plan (this list is not all-inclusive):

- *Objectives*—reach agreement with owner on broad objectives.
  —National engineering and construction content.
  —Limits of authority.
  —Community responsibility/town planning.
  —Public relations. T.V., press, jobsite tours.
  —Contractual relationship/responsibilities.
- *Scope*
  —Process decisions/engineering specifications.

  —Capacity/feed stock and product slate.
  —Owner products for use during construction.
- *Services*—contractor and owner responsibilities.
  —Subcontracts.
  —Procurement.
  —Commissioning and start up assistance.
  —Training. Management and craft labor.
- *Engineering—Procurement—Construction (EPC) Approach*
  —Licensors and other third parties.
  —Location of design offices.
  —Purchasing, procedures and practices.
  —Infrastructure. Local area and jobsite interface.
  —Project procedures.
  —Work week for engineering and construction.
  —Contractor employee conditions and procedures.
  —Preassembly/modularization.
  —Constructability analysis.
  —Labor relations and recruiting strategy.
  —Construction equipment plan/rigging studies.
  —Construction preplanning. Path of construction, field facilities.
- *Infrastructure*
  —Camp. Messing and personnel facilities.
  —Local resources. Banks, postal, religious, etc.
  —Transportation. Jobsite and local area.
  —Rest and recreation.
  —Security.
- *Organizations*
  —Size and complexity. Integration and project management.
  —Breakdown of project. Cost and management.
  —Engineering and construction management.
  —Third party integration.
  —Owner organization. Relationship with contractor.
  —Organization development (OD).
  —Communication system.
  —Matrix, task force and functional considerations.
  —Decision process. Delegation, strategic, tactical.
- *Cost and Schedule*
  —Resource evaluation. Manpower and manufacturing.
  —Control estimate/work breakdown structure.
  —Project control system.
  —Trending systems/quantity control.
  —Schedule milestones and owner interfaces.
  —Long lead items.

—Logistics and material handling.

—Environmental, governmental regulations and permits.

- *Systems*
  —Manual versus computer.
  —Owner requirements.
  —Level of detail and distribution.
  —Flexibility requirements. Contraction and expansion.
  —Frequency of reports.
- *Auditing System*
  —Terms of reference.
  —Evaluations and reports.
  —Procurement and financial.
  —Documentation.
- *Procurement*
  —World-wide operation.
  —National requirements.
  —Purchasing procedures and strategy.
  —Centralized buying/field purchasing.
  —Owner approvals.
  —Negotiation practices.
- *Subcontracting*
  —Content. Work category and contract type.
  —Organization and control requirements.
  —Pre-quotation meetings.
- *Material Control*
  —Material take off. Control and reporting.
  —Freight consolidation.
  —Marshalling yards.
  —Jobsite controls.
  —Weather protection and maintenance.
  —Documentation.
- *Project Run-Down and Demobilization*
  —What to control and at what point.
  —Level of control and reporting.
  —Personnel demobilization.
  —Material surplus program.

Contract Strategy

The current market environment plus the project cost and schedule objectives will generally determine the contracting strategy. Lump sum work is generally the most efficient method, however, a well defined engineering package and stable market conditions are essential. There are several alternatives for the reimbursable project and a phased approach, though lengthy, can reduce the financial risk of a "straight-through" project.

Lump sum (fixed price) bids are expensive to produce and contractors are not anxious to pursue this course without a reasonable expectation of success. A poor owner definition can cause a low contractor estimate, resulting in continuous claims and extras by the contractor. It can also result in a large contingency being applied by the contractor.

Under lump sum contracts, control of time and money is the primary concern of the contractor, as his performance directly affects his profits. Here, the owner is concerned with checking contractor's compliance with project requirements, with evaluating cost extras, and with periodic analyses of the project schedule.

Under most cost-plus contracts, however, the contractor has limited incentive for controlling time and money beyond professional responsibility. In such cases, the owner is more deeply involved in the project control function than on lump sum projects. Here, owner personnel must supervise closely contractor's preparation of the definitive cost estimate and control system. This is necessary to ensure that the estimates and evaluations are prepared for facilities that are adequate for owner's needs, and to provide the owner with a better insight and understanding of the reliability and accuracy of the contractor estimates.

Target cost and schedule incentives can produce improved performance. However, the owner thereafter faces a contractor program to inflate the cost target with high estimates of engineering changes and extras.

A fixed fee, based on a percentage of the total cost, can reward poor performance. The higher the cost, the greater the fee.

Omnibus-type fees for portions of engineering and construction can result in the lack of necessary services. A fee for engineering can result in lack of optimization, poor design, over generous specifications and poor equipment engineering, resulting in high priced equipment. Material costs are reimbursable. Similarly, a fee for construction equipment can result in excessive use of labor, leading to higher labor costs and schedule extension. Labor costs are reimbursable. A fixed fee for construction management can result in lack of supervision and services, particularly if construction conditions change from those anticipated.

The above problems can be magnified with projects on a "fast-track" approach where there is a greater element of the unknown.

The Control Estimate

Most owners develop an estimate at the front end and feasibility stage. This conceptual estimate would generally fall in the $\pm 30\%$ accuracy level and would be based on cost-capacity curves or equipment and bulk ratio breakdowns.

This estimate could be updated as the design is developed, or the control could be transferred to the contractor's estimate, which is probably being developed on a different basis. Using the contractor's estimate will generally produce a greater sense of commitment and responsibility by the contractor. Whichever estimate is used to control the project costs, it is not recommended that the contractor be forced to structure his estimate to the same work breakdown and account codes of the owners.

The Project Schedule

In addition to a conceptual estimate, an overall schedule is developed by the owner at the front end of a project. This schedule is developed on a summary basis as scope and execution plans are still in a preliminary stage. As the project develops, it is recommended that daily control and detailed planning be transferred to the contractor's scheduling operation. Overall monitoring should be maintained by the owner of the contractor's schedules and planning operation.

This early schedule provides the time basis for the estimate and presents to management an overall program showing the major decision points. At this stage, it is vital that this information be easily and clearly communicated to management.

The best format for this summary schedule is a time-scaled network. It will provide an excellent picture of time and the major phases and dependencies of the project. From a technical viewpoint, time-scaled networks are inefficient as they can require considerable rework and redrafting, but from a communication viewpoint, they are outstanding.

Figure 21-4 is a typical example of a summary schedule. This schedule, of a synthetic fuel plant, shows a phased approach, the major scope elements of a process plant and a coal mine, environmental requirements, contracting decision points, mechanical completion and plant start-up.

With an adequate scheduling data base, the following significant information can be easily developed with this schedule:

- Escalation mid-points for material and labor.
- Progress curves for engineering and construction (Phase II).
- Manpower histograms for engineering and construction (Phase II).
- Owner manpower and project team requirements.

Activity durations are determined by judgment, past experience (data base) or a combination of both.

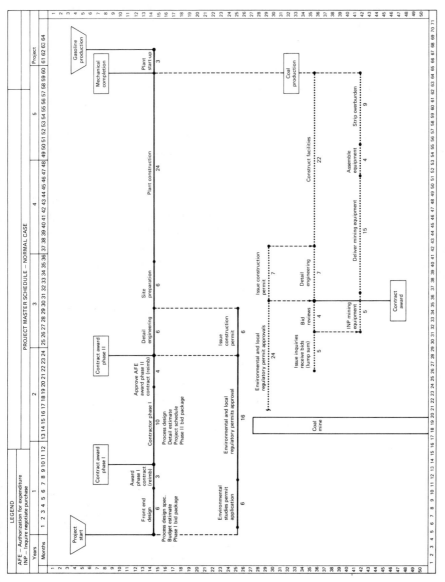

Figure 21-4. Project master schedule.

A Project Control Organization

Figure 21-5 illustrates a typical organization for project control. It is recommended that the project control section be part of the project management division, whereas estimating and its associated functions can be a separate group.

The project control section would have three main project support groups and one staff support group: cost control and scheduling support groups organized on a geographic or manufacturing basis; a central group for methods development, training, manpower planning; and a specialist group to handle subcontract administration and construction management.

Rotational assignments and career development objectives should ensure the movement of personnel through the project control and project management groups. This would improve manpower utilization, provide greater training opportunities and increase individual skill levels.

Personnel in the cost and schedule support groups should be developed to handle both cost and schedule work. Capability in both functions would be beneficial for providing home office "suitcase" services and also personnel for control manager positions.

Due to high workload, large projects would require separate functions of cost and scheduling.

A significant organization problem of project management and a staff project control group is the "we and they" attitude. When the project control

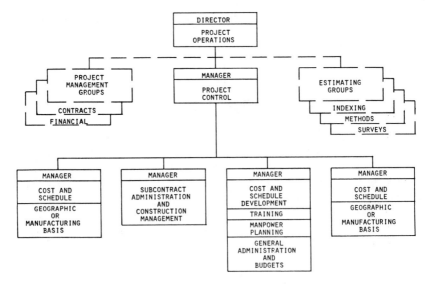

Figure 21-5. A project control organization.

group is part of the project management division, the "we and they" attitude is greatly reduced. In addition, the "audit image" is also reduced.

Alignment in project management divisions can sometimes stifle independent and adverse evaluations by project control personnel.

SECTION 2. A CONTROL ENVIRONMENT

General

Without question, *it is the project manager's responsibility to create an environment which will enable "control" to be exercised.* This means he will seek counsel, accept sound advice and stretch control personnel to the extent of their capability.

A key element for effective control is timely evaluation of potential cost and schedule hazards and the presentation of these evaluations with recommended solutions to project management. This means that the Control Engineer must be a skilled technician and also be able to effectively communicate to management level. Sometimes, a skilled technician's performance is not adequate because he is a poor communicator. *Technical expertise will rarely compensate for lack of communication skills.* As in all staff functions, the ability to "sell" service can be as important as the ability to perform the service. Project teams are mostly brought together from a variety of "melting pots" and the difficulty of establishing effective and appropriate communications at all levels should not be underestimated. In this regard, the project manager is responsible for quickly establishing a positive working environment where the separate functions of design, procurement, construction and control *are welded into a unified, cost-conscious group.* Project managers who relegate the control function to a reporting or accounting function are derelict in their duties.

Project control can be defined as the process which:

- Forecasts and evaluates potential hazards prior to occurrence so that preventive action can be taken.
- Reviews trends or actual situations to analyze their impact and, if possible, proposes action to alleviate the situation.
- Provides constant surveillance of project conditions to effectively and economically create a "no-surprise" condition.

Task Force versus Functional Organization

The question of a functional organization versus a task force approach is a much debated subject. It is the writer's opinion that a task force approach is more efficient for large projects, whereas the functional organization can be adequate for small projects. The task force approach brings a greater concentration of resources and fewer levels of management as the reporting line to the functional departments becomes one of personnel allocation and advice, rather than direction.

Many owners now use task forces to monitor contractor performance. Some contractors are of the opinion that this approach increases schedule durations and project costs. However, in today's volatile market place with associated contractors' reluctance to bid on a lump sum basis, owners believe task forces are necessary, and that they make a clear, positive contribution to meeting owner objectives. In addition, owner's project control expertise, in many instances, is equal to contractor's capability.

Figure 21-6 illustrates a typical owner task force organization. This shows an owner operation with a central engineering department having responsibility for the corporation capital project program. The operating company, or client group, is responsible for funding the project and, in a sense, hires the central engineering department to manage the project. This requires that the project director have two reporting lines: a functional line to the engineering project division and a financial line to the client manager.

The dual relationship can cause conflict. This mostly occurs when the client manager attempts to manage the project director in functional project business. The most common situation of conflict is when the client manager works directly with the contractor.

The focal point for instructions to the contractor must be through the project director and then flow from the owner task force to the contractor organization. Owner and contractor must structure their task force organizations to harmonize. The better the coordination and communication of owner and contractor personnel in this joint task force operation, the greater the prospect for successful project execution. *Systems and procedures do not build projects— People do.*

Owner-Contractor Relationships

A significant feature of a successful project control operation is the relationship between contractor and owner personnel. One item in the initial phase of a capital project is the "screening and qualifying" of contractors prior to contract award. During this activity, owner control requirements can be clearly explained, and an implementation program obtained from the contractors being evaluated. Some owners have a formal system for evaluating contractors.

After contract award, the reality of the implementation program will be tested during detailed discussions in setting up a mutually acceptable system. These should be conducted in a spirit of equal partnership. *The owner control specification will be the basis of discussions on control organization, proce-*

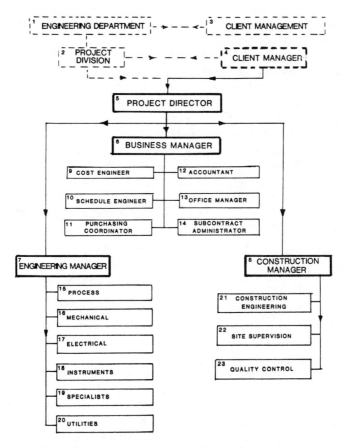

Figure 21-6. Typical task force organization (large project).

dures, systems and controls. These early reviews can prevent later system changes, costly reorganizations, and personnel reassignments. Such discussions should be promptly followed by meetings with the contractor's engineering, procurement, construction and project services groups to verify mutual understanding and acceptance of a common approach to planning, scheduling and cost control. At this stage, the discussions must necessarily be brief and to the point. Everybody is busy. But they are essential to ensure the contractor's control system meets owner's requirements.

Detailed planning, scheduling and cost control are the contractor's responsibility, and it is his responsibility to see that they are efficient operations, effectively utilized. This is an equal partnership operation.

Apart from estimating systems, many owners have established control data such as the following:

- Engineering manhours per piece of equipment and manhours per drawing.
- Construction manhours per work category.
- Standard engineering and construction productivity profiles.
- Standard engineering and construction progress profiles.
- Overall milestone durations and dependent relationships.
- Standard procurement and subcontract relationships.
- Typical manhour expenditure curves.
- Typical material commitment curves.
- Standard engineering discipline relationships.
- Home office and construction indirect relationships.
- Standard engineering and construction rate profiles.
- Typical breakdown of engineering by discipline and section.
- Typical breakdown of construction by craft and prime account.
- Domestic and worldwide productivity factors.
- Typical manpower buildup and rundown.
- Construction manpower density/productivity curves.
- Domestic and worldwide labor and material escalation rates.

Data, as indicated above, enables owners to check contractor's estimates and continuously monitor performance through all phases of a project. Many contractors have invested heavily in the development of PERT, CPM techniques and control systems. In spite of this investment, and resulting sophisticated systems with their associated heavy running costs, owners continue to comment on poor execution of the contractor project control function. In turn, contractors complain that owners do not clearly identify their project objectives, change their minds on scope causing costly recycles of engineering and are often disorganized. A major complaint by contractors is that owners monitor their activities too closely. It is essential that owner's cost and schedule representatives refrain from continuously getting into "too much detail." This, invariably, causes an adverse relationship. Contractors should be allowed freedom of action and an occasional error.

There are two significant procedures which attempt to clearly establish the detailed working relationship of owner and contractor: The coordination procedure, outlined earlier, which covers organizational and functional relationships, and a "document action schedule" which specifies the owner involvement in all documents produced by the contractor. This covers engineering drawings, specifications, inquiry packages, bid tabulations, purchase orders, subcontracts and all control and reporting documents.

When too tight a level of approval is imposed by the owner, it can result in additional costs and lengthening of the schedule.

A major complaint by owners is in contractor scheduling. Rarely does the

See Chapter 16.

owner encounter a contractor's performance where the planning, scheduling and control of engineering, procurement and construction phases are effectively bound into one system. Too often, rigid departmentalization of contractors has forced owners' representatives to act as catalysts and coordinators to achieve efficient execution.

Over-departmentalization is evident when separate groups of a contractor's organization operate to an appreciable degree to the exclusion of the interests of associated groups and departments. In particular, owners experience too many instances where engineering, design, procurement, project and construction departments act as separate companies. Corporate politics sometimes are allowed to override project objectives and the true long-range objectives of the engineer-contractor. Unless engineering, procurement and construction groups operate as a team, with differing functions but common objectives, project execution will be inefficient and costly.

All contractors emphasize in sales presentations the unified application of their resources to the owner's project. Departmental flexibility and coordination are stated as being strengths of the company organization. In practice, the owner too often finds that planning, scheduling and control are exercised only within compartmented contractor departments. While it is highly desirable that individual departments and departmental sections participate in the setting of schedules, and in controlling to these schedules, overall progress scheduling and control are the owner's prime concern. For this reason, final schedule authority must rest in a strong, active project management, supported by adequate staff schedule personnel.

Alternatively, owners sometimes find scheduling operations consolidated in autonomous groups, the output of which is voluminous, but unused. If the engineer-contractor is to meet the owner's objectives, and in the long run, his own objectives, the output of planning and scheduling groups must be both usable and used by the project team.

An Integrated System

Like any control function, effective project control requires that all efforts be fully integrated; that status be fully and accurately reported; that costs, programs and engineering scope be compared against budget estimates, schedules and specifications (the norms); and that the loop be closed either by modifying and correcting the control system, or by changing the control methods. This cycle of events is necessary, and should be continual for successful project execution. The owner's interest and participation in these events will vary from project to project and depend primarily on the type of project contract. In short, for effective project control, a project team (not an individual) must concentrate on anticipating and detecting deviations from project norms, and then take full and timely action to handle such deviations. Project norms should only

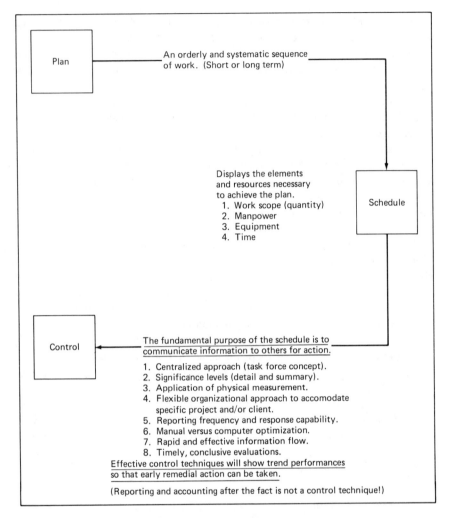

Figure 21-7. Planning/scheduling/control—an integrated system.

be revised when it is absolutely certain that they are beyond achievement; *however, prompt reports should indicate deviations as they become apparent,* even though no immediate action is taken.

Figures 21-7 and 21-8 illustrate major elements of integrated scheduling and cost control systems.

Figure 21-7 is a flowchart indicating the elements necessary for an integrated schedule system. It is the writer's opinion that owners and contractors need to achieve fully integrated and coordinated control systems along these

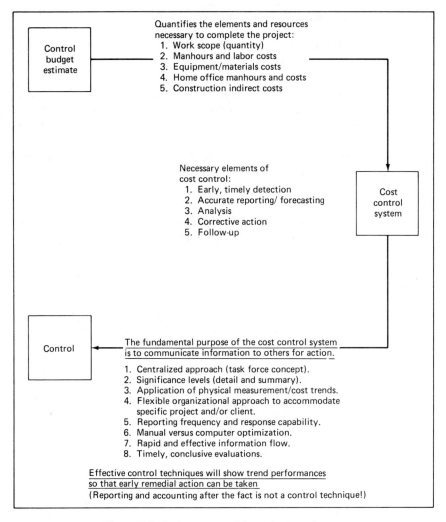

Figure 21-8. Project cost control—an integrated system.

general lines. To do so will require, in many instances, a thorough re-thinking of schedule-related operations, and upgrading of personnel. In some instances, judicious "headknocking" is going to be required to call attention to out-moded practices and attitudes, and failures to conform to stated management policies.

Figure 21-8 is a flowchart indicating the elements necessary for an integrated cost control system. The major items are a quality estimate, based on quantities, an effective trending system and qualified personnel working on a task force basis.

Communication—Manual or Computer

Figure 21-9 is a flowchart of a typical management information system, or, in other words, the operating levels of the project control system.

Again, the key word is communication.

The project control system must generate summary and detailed information for different levels of management. Information must be current, timely and accurate. This flowchart shows four levels of detail, which are typical for most large projects.

Information is generally a combination of computer programs and manual reports. It is difficult to conclude that computer programs are better than manual systems. There are obvious advantages with the computer, but many systems prove ineffective due to the tremendous level of detail.

Scheduling systems with tens of thousands of activities are rarely effective. Alternatively, it is very time-consuming to produce a detailed field progress report without a computer program.

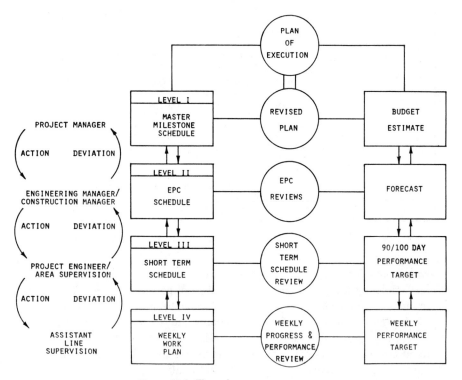

Figure 21-9. Flow of management system.

Each project and each contractor operation should be thoroughly investigated for application of a computer approach to project control.

As most owners work in a monitoring role, it is unlikely that owners would need their own extensive computer programs for control purposes.

Owner Review of Contractor Control System

On large projects, early after contract award, a team should be established to review, in detail, the contractor's cost and schedule system, organization and assigned personnel. The purpose is to recommend to the Project Manager a complete project control system for the project. The team should be led by a senior member of the home office control group and consist of task force and staff cost and schedule personnel. As this review will take four to six weeks, the addition of home office personnel is generally necessary as the workload of the project assigned personnel is very heavy at this time. The team leader must be very experienced in order to understand and handle the complete range of a contractor's project control operation. Hence, a supervisor from the home office is generally required.

Personnel should be nominated by the manager of project control, and a timed execution plan presented to the project manager for approval prior to commencement of the work.

Specific objectives of this review are:

- To investigate the project control systems and organization of prime contractor, joint venture or management contractors and prepare a recommended total project control system. *The investigation should be based on maximizing the use of existing contractor systems and resources. Changes should be minimal and only significant deficiencies should require modification.*

    Should a contractor system or organization have significant deficiencies, it is recommended that the contractor modify his system by supplementing it with the appropriate owner procedure and formats. However, it is important that changes be kept to a minimum and the contractor be permitted full use of procedures and methods with which he is familiar.
- To prepare a detailed report covering the investigation and recommendation.
- To prepare a schedule for the implementation of the above recommendations, extending to the point where the control system is fully operational.
- To present the plan and recommendation to the owner and contractor executive management to obtain full understanding and endorsement by management at an early stage in the project.

Implementation Schedule—Project Control System

It is essential to establish a quality Project Control System at the earliest possible date. As an aid to meeting this objective, it is recommended that a detailed "Implementation Schedule" be prepared showing the completion dates agreed to with the contractor. This schedule should be developed in summary and detailed form and will outline all facets of the proposed control system, showing deadlines for completion and personnel allocations for the work.

Contractor should list and provide "duration-estimates" for all procedures, such as Schedules, Reports, Estimates, Computer Programs and Organization Charts, etc., which constitute the overall Project Control System. It is suggested that a flowchart(s) showing the major elements of the system be prepared by the contractor.

The contractor should provide schedules and details of resource for completion of the Project Control System.

This owner review and preparation of associated implementation schedule can be a frustrating time for contractors. It could be doubly so if owner personnel lack experience and the contractor has to spend considerable time in education as well as explanation. The process is time-consuming and could require time of key contractor control personnel who are already heavily engaged in the project.

However, this is the time for contractors to fully explore owner control requirements, provide effective and detailed explanations of their systems, accept obvious improvements and defend "poor" programs which they believe are effective and which they have proved out on projects.

Owners should have a "minimal change" policy and contractors should encourage owner personnel to live up to this policy.

Figure 21-10 illustrates a segment of a typical implementation schedule.

This schedule should cover major categories of procedures, schedules, cost, computer, measurement and reporting. It should be updated weekly or biweekly for progress and status.

Jumbo Projects

A significant aspect of project work in the 1970's has been the increasing size and complexity of projects.

Major examples are the Trans-Alaska pipeline, offshore platforms in the North Sea, gas gathering facilities in the Middle East, the Sasol synthetic fuel plant in South Africa and the Syncrude Tar Sands plant in Alberta.

These are termed Jumbo or Mega projects.

New and changing technology, a hostile environment (Alaska and the North Sea), construction on a massive scale, plus the minimum of experience and

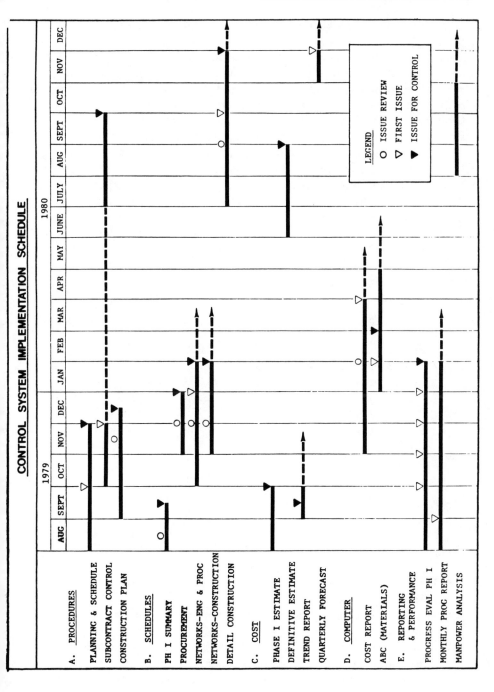

Figure 21-10. Segment of a typical implementation schedule.

data, provide the background to estimating, planning and scheduling of these facilities.

The oil industry was breaking new technological barriers in terms of size and complexity of production facilities. The resultant first-generation jumbo projects experienced a considerable degree of last minute innovation, and were built without full scope definition and little appreciation of offshore construction. Because of the urgent need to bring these facilities on stream, companies were tackling many of the problems during the construction and installation stages. Therefore, cost and schedule overruns were common occurrences.

It was not until about 1976 that realistic criteria and appropriate techniques had been developed to control these very large and complex projects. It was discovered that current concepts and practices of functional and task force organizations were not very effective. In particular, a task force with centralized decision-making was not adequate. Management layers stretched out communication channels and decision-making.

The following size parameters give a general breakdown of projects into small, medium, large and jumbo:

		Small	Medium	Large	Jumbo
(a)	Engineering Manhours	100,000	600,000	1,500,000	6,000,000
(b)	Engineering Manpower	100	200	400	1,000
(c)	Construction Manhours	500,000	400,000	8,000,000	50,000,000
(d)	Construction	400	1,500	3,000	10,000
(e)	Construction Staff	50	150	500	1,000
(f)	Schedule (Months) (Detailed engineering to completion of construction)	25	30	35	50/60

Comparing the jumbo projects of the 1970's with conventional plants, the major lessons learned were:

- The desirability of a decentralized approach to place decision making as close to the work as possible.
- The need to combine owner and contractor project teams into one operating unit.
- Reduce management layers so that decentralized project teams could communicate quickly with overall project management.
- The increased effect that basic organization changes can have on a very large project.

- The importance of leadership, as opposed to managerial skills, in an effective project management organization.
- The increased importance of a quality execution plan prior to the start of detailed engineering, procurement and construction (phase II). The execution plan is to provide a base for the estimate, as well as a plan for executing the project.
- The significance of greatly increased influence of governmental agencies and joint venture partners.
- The inadequacy of existing data base and assumptions of size effect. It is possible that the traditional "scale effect," where increased size and units reduce unit costs, does not apply on jumbo projects. Pioneer projects are likely to experience unit-cost increases as their technology advances. Extreme caution must be exercised in scaling up capacity-cost ratios of conventional plants for jumbo projects requiring new technology and prototype engineering.

The following comments further amplify a new approach to a jumbo project:

Decentralization.   During Phase II, the project should be divided into major cost centers, to an approximate value of ±$200MM, each with its own budget, schedule and complete project organization. Jumbo projects would then have 15–20 of such individual cost centers.

Decision making should be by the individual project organization, constrained only by its budget and schedule and objectives set by the central project management group. The central project group would be responsible for coordination of resources and common services, overall cost and schedule objectives and interfaces with client, corporate and government groups.

Cost, schedule, procurement and engineering specialists of the individual project group would report directly to their project manager and functionally to the specialist manager of the central group. They would receive their day-to-day direction from their project manager and technical guidance from the functional manager of the central group.

Phase I (conceptual process design) and the commissioning and start-up phases should be organized on a central project group basis. As the major decisions of a phase I operation are comparatively few, mainly process design and selection, execution plan and contracting strategy, the decision making process should be in the hands of a few people. Similarly, construction at the 95–98% point will move into the commissioning and start-up phase. This requires the reuniting of the individual projects for a common approach to start-up and operations.

Owner-Contractor Partnership.   An adversary or stand-alone relationship between owner and contractor will add costs and extend the schedule on jumbo projects. The amounts of money are large. Decision making requires greater evaluation and analysis. Fast decision making requires that owner and contractor work as a team during the evaluation process to prevent loss of time with major reviews and presentations.

As most jumbo projects are built on a "fast-track" basis, fast decision making is essential if the schedule is to be achieved.

Continuous agreement at working levels between owner and contractor will generally require owner personnel additional to the traditional levels of the past.

Even though there will be a united team approach, it is vital that the contractor be allowed to freely operate at the daily working level.

A new concept is the completely integrated owner-contractor project team, where owner personnel may have supervisory and subordinate roles. The major problems of this approach are questions of contractor responsibility, professional pride, personnel relationships and proprietary information.

The concept has much to offer and is one that deserves considerably more study, analysis and development.

Organization Changes.   The need for organizational and procedural changes can be recognized and the problem reduced with an organization development group.

The O.D. group.   This group would be established to unblock decision making bottlenecks and improve inadequate procedures. Its objectives would be to constantly monitor and evaluate organization, communications, procedures and methods. This function requires specialized personnel with experience to cover all phases and functions of the project.

Due to the wide range of experience required, it is probable that two groups would be required. One group for the home office covering engineering and procurement; the second group for the field covering construction. About four to six personnel, at peak, would be required for an effective O.D. group.

Leadership versus Managerial Skills.   People skills are essential in the management and control of jumbo projects. With task forces ranging in size from 500 to 1,000, the importance of people skills cannot be over-emphasized.

It is possible that leadership skills are more important than managerial skills. Personnel motivation is an essential ingredient of a successful project team.

Control Estimate.   As a quality estimate is vital to the project control effort, an owner-contractor team should be established to develop the estimate. This will provide continuous working agreement on such significant elements as escalation, productivity levels, unit rates, work breakdown structure, control areas and individual cost centers.

A detailed estimate could be produced about 12–16 months after Phase II contract award and would probably require 40 contractor and 10 owner personnel. With this approach, management review and approval could take one week instead of the months of review and reconciliation which is the more normal case.

Planning and Scheduling.   The size of the activity network is not the major consideration. The quality of the weekly construction program is the main concern. Construction manhours will be in the range of 40MM–100MM. With peaks of 10,000–15,000 men, a quality weekly work program is absolutely essential.

It is likely to be a manual system and should be based on quantities, unit manhour rates, varying productivity adjustments and be reconciled against the objectives of the overall schedule. Productivity goals should be preplanned and then reported against on a weekly basis.

Quantity Control.   This technique is rarely used. On jumbo projects, where the amounts of money are so large, a quantity tracking system is essential for effective cost control.

Appropriate "bulk quantities" (earth, concrete, piping, etc.) should be selected and tracked, by a random sampling technique, from the process design of phase I through detailed engineering of phase II.

Rundown Control.   This method is rarely used in present day project work. Again, due to size, this is an essential technique for jumbo projects.

As engineering and construction commence their rundown (about 80% complete), individual budgets, schedules and manpower histograms should be developed to separately control the remaining work.

Governmental Agencies and Joint Venture Partnerships.   Many of today's jumbo projects have governments as partners. Governmental regulations and agencies, partner and joint venture relationships add a further dimension that must be recognized by the planning, scheduling and cost effort.

Governmental energy companies may require "preferred purchasing" (buying in the host country), extensive training programs for supervisory staff and craft labor and the development of an infrastructure local to the project jobsite.

Joint venture partners require a vote in major decisions. This takes time. Major purchases can require approval of partners prior to purchase. Again, this takes time. Periodic reviews and presentations can be required by partners. This takes effort and costs money.

All above aspects should be carefully considered when developing the project execution plan and schedule.

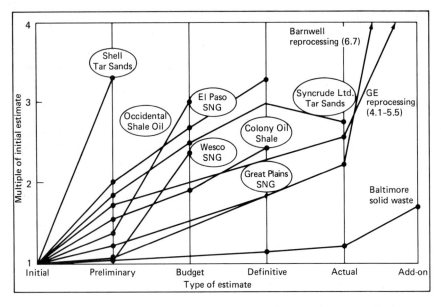

Figure 21-11. Cost growth in pioneer energy process plants (Constant Dollars).

Figure 21-11 vividly illustrates the effects of problems outlined in the opening paragraph of this subsection. This study (R-2481-DOE) by Rand Corporation for Department of Energy shows final costs versus initial feasibility estimates for many jumbo projects. As can be seen, the cost growth is 200–300%. This is caused by either bad estimates, poor performance or a combination of both. Major changes causing significant cost additions can be classed as poor performance. Concern is being expressed that current estimates for jumbo synthetic fuel projects will follow the same patterns as above chart.

Project Levels of Control and Reporting

Levels of control and reporting vary widely in the industry. They can be dependent on:

- Recognition, understanding and need for control.
- Company commitment to control.
- Personnel resources and capability.
- Size and complexity of projects.
- Owner/contractor contractual arrangements.
- Owner/contractor control relationship/expertise.

- Acceptance of cost control.
- Cost effectiveness of control.

Most major contractors have comprehensive project control systems. However, very few owners have a similar capability, or even detailed control specifications which would enable contractors to thoroughly understand owner's project control requirements.

As already outlined, an early, effective project control program is an essential requirement. It is difficult to achieve this objective on reimbursable projects if owners are not able to specify, in detail, their requirements. Even on lump sum projects, a similar approach is necessary, as effective planning, scheduling and progress measurement should be an owner requirement. Apart from an adequate change order procedure, cost control reporting is the contractor's sole responsibility on lump sum projects.

Figure 21-12 lists typical project control requirements for the following project categories:

- Feasibility Study (0–10,000 engineering hours).
- Small Project (10,000–100,000 engineering hours).
- Medium Size Project (100,000–500,000 engineering hours).
- Large Size Project (500,000–1,500,000 engineering hours).

In an attempt to quantify project size, engineering manhours have been allocated to these categories. *This can only be a guide as project size is dependent on the size of the company.*

It is generally recognized that as project size increases, additional control procedures are necessary. Obviously, control for control's sake should be avoided. Typical examples of costly and inefficient control systems are very large activity network programs, duplication of effort by owner and contractor on reimbursable projects and some governmental reporting procedures.

The outlined control procedures are divided into the major phases of a project. They are additive as the project category increases in size. A small project would require the items listed in categories 1 and 2. Similarly, a large project would require all the listed items.

Manpower Planning—Engineering Department

One of the more difficult areas of project control is in-house company planning of engineering personnel. The major uncertainty, causing difficulty, is forecasting the amount and type of future project work. The difficulty is usually greater for owners.

The contracting industry has two major considerations: an annual estimate

PROJECT LEVELS OF CONTROL & REPORTING — REIMBURSABLE PROJECTS

For the designated project size, the outlined techniques, reports and procedures are additive to the previous level lump sum projects would require most of the scheduling procedures. See project control manual for details of method and procedure.

PROJECT	OVERALL	ENGINEERING	PROCUREMENT	CONSTRUCTION	SUBCONTRACTS
1. FEASIBILITY (10,000 eng. hours)	Summary schedule	Project master schedule	Delivery lead times	Site survey	Licensor packages
	Execution plan		Logistics evaluation	Soil report	
	Estimate	Manhour curve			
	Cost report	Manhour rate curve			
	Monthly report	Manpower histogram			
2. SMALL PROJECT (100,000 eng. hours)	Trend report	Discipline schedule (milestones)	P.O. commitment register	Pre-planning program	Overall schedules (by subcontract)
	Project status report			Manforce report	
	● Engineering	Engineering manhour curve	Material status report	Three month schedules	Progress/status report (by subcontract)
	● Material commitment		Overall commitment curve ($)	Construction progress barchart (overall)	Summary cost report
	● Construction	Home office manhour curve	Vendor dwg. report	Manpower histogram	
	Contingency rundown curve	Bid evaluation program		Overall manhour curve	
	Cash flow curve			Overall rate curve	
3. MEDIUM PROJECT (500,000 eng. hours)	Contractors evaluation program	Engineering change log	Equipment commitment curve ($)	Field estimate (quantities)	Subcontract commitment curve ($)
		Material requisition curve			
	Detailed control specs.		Bulk material commitment curve ($)	Construction area progress barcharts	Subcontract preparation schedule
		Document and action schedule			
	Task force approach		Material requisition curves	Weekly work program	Unit price subcontracts
	Computer scheduling program	Progress measurement program (discipline)	Inspection — expediting reports	Progress measurement program	● Cost report
		● Quantities/hours		● Quantities/hours	● Quantity report
	Coordination procedure	● Progress curves		● Progress curves	● Performance evaluation
		● Manpower curves		● Manpower curves	● Progress curve
	Extra work/change order procedure	● Productivity curves		● Productivity curves	● Manpower histogram
				Status report	
		Front end schedules (3 mo.)		● Progress	
				● Productivity	
		Dwg. schedules		● Manpower	
		H.O. Expense expenditure curve ($)		Indirects expenditure curve ($)	
				Staff schedule	
				Equipment schedule	
				Backcharge register	
				Cost report	
4. LARGE PROJECT (1,500,000 eng. hours)	Contractors screening program	Account requisition curves	Account commitment curves ($)	Work lint tracking curves ● earthwork	Independent bid analysis program
		Piping design program	Account requisition report	● concrete	Sensitivity analysis
	Project control implementation schedule	Drawings tracking curves (P&r's) (foundations) (isometrics)	Critical purchasing list	● piping	Performance curve and report
				Area status reports	
	Weekly manforce report		Material delivery histogram	Staff manhour & rate curve	
		Quantity tracking program	Surplus material report	Equipment manhour rate profile	
		Rundown control program		Field office expense expenditure curve ($)	
		● Drawings		Indirect manhour and rate curve	
		● Manhours			
		● Dates		Rundown control program	
		● Manpower		● Manhours	
		● Progress		● Manpower	
		● Productivity		● Progress	
				● Productivity	
		Punch lists		Punch lists	

Figure 21-12. Project control requirements.

450

of owner's capital projects program and an assessment of their ability to obtain a share of that work.

Owner's engineering department can face the following:

- Amount of feasibility studies.
- Technical service requirements.
- Methods development and technical research.
- Actuality of probable or anticipated projects.

Many owner central engineering departments act as a non-profit service company to operating divisions of the corporation. As such, their workload is largely dependent on the capital projects program of the operating divisions. It is not too difficult to assess technical service requirements, methods development and technical research based on past experience. But assessments of feasibility studies and capital projects depend on factors often outside the control of the engineering department:

- Quality of corporate strategic planning program.
- Corporate financing.
- Project economic viability.
- Communication channels with operating divisions.
- Relationships with operating divisions.
- "Project charter" of engineering department.
- Image/credibility/capability of engineering department.

Even though there can be many uncertainties in workload, one thing is certain: Quality evaluations of workload and associated manpower planning are essential—particularly with the typical shortfall of engineers and the industry prediction that the shortfall will increase for the long-term.

The following exhibits outline a systematic approach to engineering manpower planning.

Planning by Individual.   Individual planning is the lowest level of detail. Not only does it provide an assessment of manpower needs to meet a projected workload, it also provides a program of career development for each engineer.

Figure 21-13 illustrates a three year plan for project services personnel (estimating, cost control, scheduling). This shows feasibility work, project assignments (home office and task force), methods development, rotational assignments, transfers, replacements and recruiting requirements. This should be a "dynamic document" as conditions/requirements can quickly change. The control sheet should be constantly updated and issued monthly.

It is recommended that all section personnel "plans" be evaluated and sum-

COLOR CODE:	HOME OFFICE	PROJECT ASSIGNMENT		TRANSFER OUT		
Activity PROJECT SERVICES		Staff Assignments and Personnel Planning			PAGE: ——— DATE: ———	
NAME	SCHEDULE					REMARKS
ESTIMATING						
1. EVANS	GEN. | ABC PHASE I | XYZ FEASIBILITY	TASK FORCE (XYZ) COST CONTROL		GENERAL EST'G		
2. DAVIES	GENERAL ESTIMATING • BUDGETS • FEASIBILITY					
3. JONES	A.F.E. ESTIMATING					
4. WILLIAMS	METHODS DEVELOPMENT | PRODUCTIVITY FACTORS | LABOR & MATERIAL ESCALATION			TRANSFER TO SCHEDULING		
COST CONTROL						
5. PRICE	TASK FORCE | TRANSFER TO PROJECTS					
6. BENNETT	"SUITCASE" PROJECTS 103|201|430	XYZ PROJECT TASK FORCE				
7. GRAHAM	"SUITCASE" PROJECTS 120|150|250|310					
SCHEDULING						
8. ROBERTS	FEASIBILITY SCHEDULES & "SUITCASE" PROJECTS			TRANSFER TO DESIGN		
9. JENKINS	FEASIBILITY SCHEDULES & "SUITCASE" PROJECTS	XYZ PROJECT TASK FORCE				
10. LONGDEN	METHODS DEVELOPMENT | FEASIBILITY SCHEDULES					
RECRUITING						
11. COST ENGINEER	RECRUIT | TRAINING	GENERAL COST CONTROL (SUITCASE)	TASK FORCE			TO REPLACE PRICE
12. ESTIMATOR		RECRUIT | TRAINING	GENERAL ESTIMATING			TO REPLACE WILLIAMS
13. SCHEDULER		RECRUIT | TRAINING	GENERAL SCHEDULING			TO REPLACE ROBERTS
14. ESTIMATOR	RECRUIT | TRAINING	GENERAL ESTIMATING				TO REPLACE EVANS
	JAN. FEB. MAR. APR. MAY JUN. JUL. AUG. SEPT. OCT. NOV. DEC. 1980	JAN. FEB. MAR. APR. MAY JUN. JUL. AUG. SEPT. OCT. NOV. DEC. 1981		JAN. FEB. MAR. APR. MAY JUN. JUL. AUG. SEPT. OCT. NOV. DEC. 1982		

Figure 21-13. Project services—personnel.

marized by the project services group into a monthly engineering department manpower report. It is probable that this would be a computer-based program so as to provide overall manpower reports by individual listing, project assignments, feasibility work, sections, etc.

As manpower plans are only as good as assessments of workload, it is vital that work projections be evaluated each month. This requires close liaison/coordination between project, engineering, construction and project services groups to ensure that current and future work assessments are adequate.

Planning by Project.   The following report format is mostly used by contractors as it concentrates on project manpower allocations.

Figure 21-14, usually a computer report, assesses manpower allocations and requirements based on budget manhours, forecast, manhours to date, schedule and manhour allocations for the past six weeks. Only three months of the schedule are shown and continuation sheets would provide requirements for the complete schedule. The past six weeks show current trends and also a base to assess the viability of future requirements. The computer program will take the manhour forecast, to date manhours, schedule, hourly workweek assessment and forecast the weekly scheduled manpower requirement.

The bottom two lines show men required against men available and the difference provides the necessary recruiting program.

This particular report illustrates an overall engineering manpower report. A similar report could be produced for each section.

Planning by Work Category.   Figure 21-15 illustrates a report format generally used by owners. It is similar to the previous contractor project report, but has additional categories: probable projects, feasibility studies, technical service, and etc. Also, it separates technical from non-technical and managers/secretaries. Obviously, some managers are technical. But this provides a continuous assessment of number of managers to engineers and relationship of technical to non-technical. Both relationships need to be evaluated for an efficient operation. This report shows an annual plan. Additional years could be developed based on the quality of the individual plan cycle.

As previously stated, assessments for feasibility studies and probable projects can be difficult.

The outlined numbers illustrate a large, international operating company having a central engineering department of some 300 engineers. Evaluation of these manpower relationships should bear in mind that detail drafting and other services can be outside contracts. A typical relationship of draftsmen to engineers can be about 3.5 to 1.

This report should be issued monthly and would undoubtedly be derived from a computer program.

Use continuation sheet for rest of schedule ⟶

Engineering Department — Manpower Planning

Project number	Manhours			Manhours for past six weeks						Men weeks to go	Weekly scheduled men		
	Budget	Forecast	To date								Jan	Feb	Mar
1	2	3	4	5	6	7	8	9	10	11	12	13	14
Total above projects													
Miscellaneous projects													
Development work													
Total manhours													
Total men available													
Total men required													

Figure 21-14. Manpower planning.

ENGINEERING DEPARTMENT – MANPOWER PLANNING – WORK CATEGORY

NOTES:
1. DRAFTING IS OUTSIDE CONTRACT.

% FIGURES ARE AS OF MIDYEAR — AS OF MARCH

CODE	WORK CATEGORY	%	ANNUAL PLAN												% FIGURES AS OF MARCH						
			J	F	M	A	M	J	J	A	S	O	N	D	J	J	A	S	O	N	D
	TECHNICAL PERSONNEL																				
	CURRENT AFE PROJECTS	48	188.7	197	197	192.1	188.6	180.4	184.1	183.3	181.1	179.4	159.6	159.6							
	PROBABLE PROJECTS	5	0	0	0	1	3.3	18.6	26.6	35.3	41.8	44.3	55.4	55.6							
	FEASIBILITY STUDIES	12	43.2	43	43	43.5	44.6	44.8	45.8	46	46	46.1	45.3	44.9							
	TECHNICAL SERVICE	4	14.2	14.2	14.2	14.2	14.2	14.2	14.2	14.2	14.2	14.2	14.2	14.2							
	TECHNICAL METHOD DEVELOPMENT	12	42.8	42.8	43.8	43.8	43.3	43.4	43.6	43.5	43.5	43.5	43	43							
	START UP/OPERATIONS	1	2	2	2	2	2	2	2	2	2	2	2	2							
	SUB TOTAL TECHNICAL	82	290.9	299	300	296.6	296	303.4	316.3	324.3	328.7	329.5	319.5	319.3							
	MANAGERS & SECRETARIES	7	27.2	27.2	27.2	27.2	27.2	27.2	27.2	27.2	27.2	27.2	27.2	27.2							
	OTHER INDIRECTS (SERVICES ETC.)	11	42.9	42.9	42.9	42.9	42.9	42.9	43	43	43	43	43	43							
	MISCELLANEOUS	0	0	0	0	0	0	0	0	0	0	0	0	0							
	REQUIRED TOTAL	100	361	369.1	370.1	366.7	366.1	373.5	386.5	394.5	398.9	399.7	389.7	389.5							
	ACTUAL PAYROLL		319	327																	

Figure 21-15. Manpower planning—work category.

ENGINEERING DEPARTMENT – MANPOWER PLANNING – BY SECTION

NOTES:
1. DRAFTING IS OUTSIDE CONTRACT.
% FIGURES ARE AS OF MIDYEAR

CODE	SECTION	%	ANNUAL PLAN						AS OF MARCH					
			J	F	M	A	M	J	J	A	S	O	N	D
	EMPLOYEE RELATIONS	1	4.5	4.5	4.5	4.5	4.5	4.5	4.8	4.9	4.9	5	5	5
	PROCUREMENT	1	4.2	4.4	5	5.3	5.7	4.8	4.7	4.8	5.4	5	5.2	5.4
	PROJECTS – U.S. REFINING & CHEMICAL	5	14.6	15.9	15.9	16.7	17.3	19.7	19.8	20.1	21.4	20.8	19.7	20.1
	– OVERSEAS R & C	6	17.6	18.3	17.6	17.4	17.3	21.7	23.4	24.7	24	23.2	23.2	22.6
	– MIDDLE EAST	3	9.5	9.5	9.5	9.5	9.5	9.5	9.5	9.5	9.5	9.5	9.5	9.5
	– OFFSHORE/SYNFUELS	12	45.2	45.2	45.2	46	45.8	46.2	46.1	45.2	44.3	44.3	44.3	44.3
	PROJECT SERVICES (EST'G./COST & SCHED.)	11	40	40	40.5	40.5	40.5	40.5	42.5	44.3	46	47	45	45
	CONTRACTS	1	4.5	4.5	4.5	4.5	4.5	4.5	5.5	5.5	5.5	5.5	5	5
	GENERAL SERVICES (NON TECH.)	5	22.4	22	21.9	21	21	20.2	22.4	23.5	21.6	21	21	21
	PROCESS ENGINEERING	14	52.6	55.8	55.8	54.5	52.7	53.2	48.8	49.2	48.3	48.7	46	45
	FACILITIES ENGINEERING	26	93.3	96.1	98.2	94.8	94.7	97	104.5	108.8	114.1	115.6	111.2	112.3
	OFFICE & PLANT SERVICES	5	17.7	17.7	17.7	17.7	17.7	17.7	17.8	17.8	18	18.1	18.2	18.3
	OVERSEAS ENGINEERING OFFICES	10	34.9	35.2	33.8	34.3	34.9	34	35.7	36.6	35.9	36	36.4	36
	REQUIRED TOTAL	100	361	369.1	370.1	366.7	366.1	373.5	386.5	394.5	398.9	399.7	389.7	389.5
	ACTUAL PAYROLL		319	327										

AS OF MARCH

Figure 21-16. Manpower planning—by section.

Planning by Section.   Figure 21-16 is a report for the same company, as previously illustrated. Whereas the previous report showed manpower by work category, this report shows manpower by section. The construction group is part of the project management groups.

Individual section reports would clearly indicate a "shortfall" or "overmanning" of personnel by engineering classification. Adequate recruiting and training programs could be developed from this information.

Manpower requirements based on physical assessments can only be made for design groups where drawing/document take-offs and manhour assessments can be made. Historical relationships, engineering department "charter"/responsibilities, control requirements and company policy can determine allocations of service personnel to project work.

22. Project Control in Bechtel Power Corporation

F. A. Hollenbach*

In the Bechtel Power Corporation, project control activities begin as soon as company management and the client define the job requirements, the scope of work, overall schedules, and the project's magnitude. A project parameter guide is used to help determine early in the life of the project some of the essential parameters required for project definition. It is used during contract negotiations and initial project mobilization to identify client preferences, plant operating characteristics, plant appearance, client involvement, project timing, and priorities.

After the project parameters have been defined, important control documents are prepared. These are used to monitor the project during its planning and implementation phases. These documents include:

- Scope of Services Manual—which establishes a baseline for identifying changes in services and a definition of engineering, home office support, and field non-manual services that will be performed by the company in execution of the contract.
- Division of Responsibility Document—which describes the responsibilities of the company, the client, and the major suppliers.
- Project Procedures Manual—which defines the procedures involved in interface activities among the company, the client, and the major suppliers with respect to engineering, procurement, construction, preoperational services, quality assurance, quality control, project control, and communication.
- Technical Scope Document—which describes the project's physical plant, establishes the design basis, and provides input to the civil/structural,

*Fred Hollenbach is vice president and deputy division general manager in Bechtel Power Corporation's San Francisco Power Division. He holds a Bachelor of Science degree in chemistry and physics from Muhlenberg College. He is a member of the American Nuclear Society, the Commonwealth Club of California, is a past president of the Northern California Chapter of the Project Management Institute, and is on the Board of Directors of the Engineers Club of San Francisco. He is a registered professional engineer in the state of California.

architectural, plant design, mechanical, electrical, and control systems disciplines.

- Project Activity Control Guide—which aids in the administration of project activities by identifying and timephasing the development and execution of project plans, programs, procedures, controls, and other significant activities required for effective operation of the project.

After the project has been defined and the preliminary control documents prepared, the project manager and his team develop the project control system that will be used through the remainder of the project.

The main objectives of the project control system are to develop a monitorable plan that reflects expected performance of the contract work and to establish a work control system that provides the information necessary for the team, the company management, and the client to identify problem areas and initiate corrective action.

The essential elements of the control system (as shown on Figure 22-1) are:

- A project plan covering expected scope, schedule, and cost performance.
- A continuous monitoring system that measures the performance against the plan through the use of modular but interrelated monitoring tools.
- A reporting system that identifies deviations from the plan by means of trends and forecasts.
- Timely actions to take advantage of beneficial trends or correct deviations.

Action taken by the company and client teams is the most critical aspect of the control cycle.

Figure 22-2 shows the various control programs through which actual per-

ELEMENTS OF PROJECT CONTROL

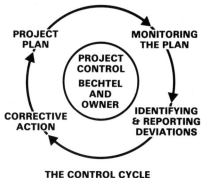

THE CONTROL CYCLE

Figure 22-1. The control system.

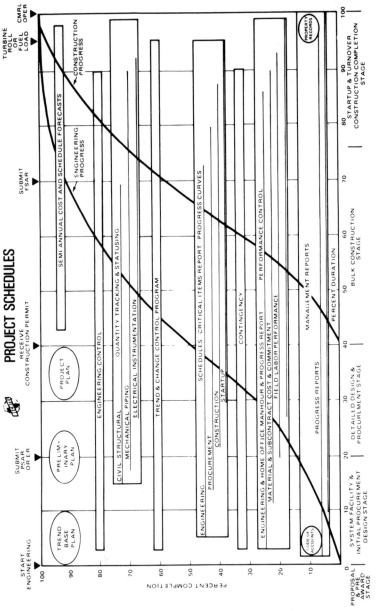

Figure 22-2. Project schedules.

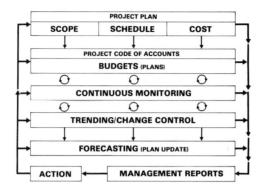

Figure 22-3. The essential elements of project control.

formance is continuously monitored, and their duration in relation to the various project stages for a typical project. Overlaid on this chart are progress curves depicting the relationship of engineering and construction progress relative to these project stages.

The essential elements of project control are shown on Figure 22-3.

PROJECT PLAN

The first objective in project control is the development of a well-conceived project plan that adequately defines the project scope, schedule, and cost. This plan is developed in four stages as the project evolves. It begins with a proposal schedule and cost estimate based on the scope obtained from the client showing type, size, location, and required services. Following project award, a front-end schedule is implemented to identify activities for the first 12 to 18 months. The process plant layout, major equipment, and key operating parameters are developed during this peroid.

The trend base schedule and estimate are established as the second stage plan. It is used to establish early project budgets (such as engineering and home office costs) for reporting and control.

A trend program, based on this plan, is implemented to provide a mechanism for identifying changes in project technical scope, scope of services, and the current plan of engineering, procurement, and construction. A monthly trend report is developed for the project team, company management, and client management. The trend program also identifies scope changes for potential contract changes. It extends through the life of the project.

In the third stage, the preliminary plan is developed on the basis of a project technical scope document containing actual project data. It updates the trend

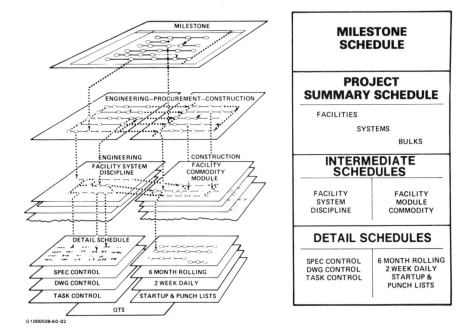

Figure 22-4. Schedule hierarchy and sequence.

base schedule and estimate and ensures that the current plan is consistent with the scope of work.

The more comprehensive project plan is the fourth stage. Based on established minimum criteria, it forms the basis for all detailed cost and schedule budgets; therefore, it is necessary that the company and the client concur that the defined scope accurately reflects what will be built. This plan is usually the basis for contractual cost and schedule goals.

Each plan has as its basis for cost, schedule, and material control a definition of the technical scope of the project and the scope of services to be provided. Milestone dates to be achieved and project procedures to be followed by the client, the company, and major suppliers are also identified.

The project plan is scheduled in a hierarchal and sequential manner as shown in Figure 22-4. The milestone summary schedule, comprising about 50 lines of major project milestones, is the basic schedule. It is expanded into engineering, construction, and startup summary schedules of approximately 500 activities each. Intermediate and detail schedules follow. The intermediate schedules contain about 3000 activities. As each plan develops, the elements of scope, schedule, and cost are integrated by a standard numbering system and are displayed in budgets that are used as a frame of reference for continuous monitoring.

CONTINUOUS MONITORING

Manual or computerized continuous monitoring tools are used to monitor project progress and identify potential deviations from established budgets (see Figure 22-5). These tools monitor engineering and home office manhours and cost, quantities, schedules, commitments, and the cost of project materials as well as contracts/subcontracts and construction performance.

Work process flow charts and quantity take-offs are used to monitor the design, procurement, and installation of commodities; to identify commodity status; and to identify responsibilities for work functions. These flow charts depict the information flow from conceptual design through construction and startup. Deviations from the project plan are identified and reported to management for corrective action. This continuous monitoring of quantities is called quantity tracking and is generally computerized.

After the project plan has been prepared, forecasts are made semiannually that reflect the current scope, schedule, and cost of the project. They are the bases for planning the remaining work and updating the schedule. They provide an up-to-date evaluation of project costs and a current basis for project monitoring and control.

MANAGEMENT REPORTS AND ACTION

The project plan, budgets, continuous monitoring tools, trending/change control, and forecasting produce the necessary information needed by manage-

BUDGETS ARE CONTINUOUSLY MONITORED THROUGH THE USE OF THESE MAJOR TOOLS

DESCRIPTION	MONITORS
ENGINEERING CONTROL	ENGINEERING MANHOURS & SCHEDULE, DRAWINGS, SPECS, & TASK
QUANTITY TRACKING	COMMODITY, QUANTIFICATION & STATUS
INTERMEDIATE SCHEDULE	ENGINEERING, PROCUREMENT & CONSTRUCTION ACTIVITIES
HOME OFFICE COST	MANHOURS & COSTS OF SERVICES
MATERIAL AND (SUB)CONTRACTS	COSTS, COMMITMENTS & FORECASTS, MATERIAL, EQUIPMENT & (SUB)CONTRACTS
FIELD MANHOUR CONTROL	PRODUCTIVITY & FORECASTS
CONTINGENCY	COSTS & SCHEDULE
CASH FLOW	DOLLAR EXPENDITURES

Figure 22-5. Budget monitoring tools.

ment to evaluate the current situation and take appropriate action. Client management reports, prepared periodically, include project status, an executive summary, a production summary, and detailed reports about cost, commitments, subcontracts, and work progress.

Project planning and monitoring identify beneficial trends and detrimental deviations; however, the action taken by the company-client team is the most critical aspect of the control cycle.

23. Project Management Audits

Kenneth O. Chilstrom*

VALUE OF AUDITS

Management audit of projects provides top management a means of independent appraisal in determining the effectiveness of the organization to successfully accomplish a project. This has become more important in recent years where most projects have matrix management requiring the functional organizations to meet the needs of many projects. Project success requires a capable project team that has responsive support from functional areas, and it is management's task to allocate needed resources and achieve the integration of all elements. In addition, the project team will directly benefit from the results of the audit, since findings and recommended actions will concentrate on both internal and external factors that are preventing the achievement of the project goals and plan.

Experience in project management has revealed that periodic audits of project status and operation are one effective way to promote full conformance with contract requirements; to supplement cross-fertilization of both technical and non-technical practices and solutions; and to insure that the project is receiving the necessary priorities, skills, and resources.

In summary, project management audits have served the following purposes:

- As catalytic tools for the manager.
- Foster self appraisal.
- Mirror operation for self analysis.
- Stimulate total program thinking.
- Exchange good practices.
- Provide top management another means of appraisal.

*Kenneth O. Chilstrom's management auditing experience has been extensive in both government and industry. He has had a variety of assignments in the Air Force, including experimental test pilot, program manager and R&D officer. His industrial experience includes program management surveys within the General Electric Company and the auditing of projects and functional areas. He is presently employed with the Government Products Division, Pratt & Whitney Aircraft Group.

AUDIT POLICY

Authority Established

Every business has corporate policies formally established in writing for essential business functions. It is also necessary that audit policy be established at company level. This identifies the technique and use of audits with the boss—the President or General Manager. Unless this occurs, the likelihood of having the support required to conduct successful audits will be greatly reduced. The policy should be adequate in scope to cover responsibilities and the general approach for conduct of project audits. This would include: how projects are selected for audit; who selects the projects and the audit team; the support responsibilities of the project team and functional organizations; and how the audit team will report their findings.

Process for Selection of Project Audits

Audit policy established at corporate level should identify the President or General Manager as the final authority in the selection of a project for audit. He may choose to make his own selection, however the approach found most successful is when he and his immediate subordinates mutually agree as to which projects need an audit and when best to accomplish this. This procedure then commits these individuals to the support of the audit since they have agreed to its necessity. Support from the functional organization is absolutely essential to the successful conduct of an audit. When this does not exist, the individuals involved will clam up, compromising the availability of facts, and thus extend the time required to complete the audit.

PLANNING FOR THE AUDIT

Scope and Subject Areas Defined

At the time the decision is made to have a management audit of a project, there is usually a reason why top management has selected the particular project. This reason or purpose will most often establish the scope of the audit. Since this indicates the area of major concern, it generally is not necessary to accomplish a full scale review of all areas of project management. However if it is early in the schedule, such as 6 months from go-ahead, it is usually considered necessary to examine all areas. The most important factor is to have the areas of audit, which may limit the scope, well defined and understood at the beginning; so there can be no misunderstandings about the objective and expectations of top management and what the audit team members will concentrate on. An example which may typify a very limited scope audit would be a project in early qualification testing of the hardware which is experiencing some failures although other areas of technical, schedule, and cost performance are in good control. Experience of many companies has shown that most new projects deserve a thorough review of all technical and non-technical areas in their first year. It should be obvious that the early phase of a project is where weaknesses will show up in estimating, scheduling, interface relationships, and cost control. Also the more complex the project, the more people involved, and where past experience is limited, the greater the opportunity for management problems in all areas.

Organization of Audit Team

In a majority of companies, which have a 1000 employees or more, there is often a staff function of internal management specialists who form the nucleus of the audit function. In large companies there may exist a good size office of 10 persons or more whose sole activity is operational auditing of projects, or reviews/surveys of special subject areas.

It is desirable and recommended that a professional staff be responsible for the organization and planning of audits, and then augmented with other specialists as required to conduct the audits. These full time management auditors would be experienced specialists in functional areas as well as seasoned operational auditors, and would individually complement and supplement each other. It is the team chief/chairman who must decide on the makeup of the team. The number of persons required to cover the areas of the audit and the technical or non-technical expertise and experience required are critical considerations bearing on the audit success. Criteria in the selection process would generally include but not be limited to the following:

- Specialist vs. generalist (need good mix).
- Must have professional acceptance at all levels.
- Technical competence in specialized areas.
- Analytical mind, articulate, and personable.
- Writing ability.
- Listening ability.
- Maturity and adaptability.
- Line, staff, supervisor experience.
- No project involvement—increasing objectivity.
- Enthusiasm and support of audit assignment.

The results of the audit will always be compared to the caliber of the team and its individual members. As is true in other tasks—one should not send out a boy to do a man's job. The audit payoff will always be directly relatable to the qualifications of the audit team.

Development of Audit Plan

Preparing a plan for the conduct of a project audit not only assists the audit team members, but helps the project team and functional areas in knowing what the audit team needs and where the audit will concentrate its attention. The audit plan should not be a detailed voluminous coverage of how to do an audit, but rather a detailed outline of the subject areas to be covered. The audit team members who have not had recent experience in the actual conduct of the audit should be coached in the technique prior to the auditing phase by the team chief and other members who have had past experience.

In the development of an audit plan, the problems and shortcomings of other projects can provide an insight or a yardstick to judge the project performance. These "lessons learned" are worth identifying in order to determine if they are being repeated and are the source of problems or a successfully applied benefit. It is also important to identify, during the course of the audit, those activities that are performing well. Too often audits concentrate solely on the trouble areas which may compromise the true perspective in judging the overall health of the project and the performance of the project team. However, as an example of where many projects incur pitfalls, the experience of others may identify such typical deficiencies as these:

- Techniques of estimating are poorly developed. They reflect an unvoiced assumption which is quite untrue—that all will go well.
- Estimating techniques confuse effort with progress, hiding the assumption that men and months are interchangeable.
- Schedule progress is poorly monitored.
- When schedule slippage is recognized, the natural response is to add manpower. This can make matters worse, particularly for the budget.
- Planners are optimists, so the first false assumption that underlies the scheduling of projects is *that all will go well, that each task will take only as long as it ought to take.*

The plan for a project audit that includes all areas of project management would include the following:

- Organization of Project Team.
- Functional support and relationships.
- Master plan.
- Contract committments.

- Work definition and assignment.
- Work progress reporting and control.
- Technical plan and capabilities.
- Manufacturing plan and capabilities.
- Product integrity/quality control.
- Logistic support plan.
- Customer relationships.
- Company/corporate policies and procedures applicable.

Initial data review

Upon completion of preparing the audit plan and selection of the full audit team, the team chief should conduct an initial meeting with the project manager. This will enable the project manager to understand the scope of the project and the subject areas to be covered, and would identify the first need and request for the audit team. The team chief with the assistance of the project manager can then develop a listing of project data to be provided for the audit team as soon as possible. This data package which would include such items as the i.e., contract, project operating plan, technical and management progress reports, etc., would provide the audit team background information in order to get well acquainted with the details of the project. This step is essential in order to avoid going in cold when starting the interviews with the project team. An adequate understanding about the project, its status, customer, etc., is important for the audit team member to prepare himself for the interviews and further pursuit of data. The ability to ask the right question, to find the trail, to penetrate to the right depth, is a measure of the auditor's effectiveness; and to a great extent will depend upon the amount of preparation given before the actual auditing begins.

GAINING ACCEPTANCE FOR THE AUDIT

Establishing the Environment

Audits of a project, or any area of an organization, can either be accomplished by an internal team or by hiring an outside management consultant firm. In most cases, an internal team should have advantages since they have the benefit of inside knowledge of why things are the way they are, including organization politics and personalities. However, in some situations, an outside person or team can be more effective for not having any bias and are able to see the issues or reasons for problems in better focus. However, regardless of the use of either approach, it is essential that the organization know that top management is supportive of the audit and should make it known both in writing and vocal opportunities. When this is done, the individuals at working levels should be more willing to recognize and accept the audit in a constructive way than judging it to be an investigation or a witch hunt. When audits are seldom used, they will be more suspect and people less cooperative than if routinely used on all projects and looked upon as a normal way of business.

Top Management Support

In those instances that outside auditors are hired, it is usually undertaken by top management. When this is done, the reasons for the audit should be made known and may include an explanation for the advantages of having an outside group. In addition to this expressed support at the beginning, it may require frequent assessments to ascertain the progress of the audit team and those factors which may be hindering their activity. The success of an audit team can be severely handicapped if it finds an environment which is relating the way things should be done rather than what is actually being done, or only answering Yes or No without offering any information. In most cases the responsiveness of the working levels will depend upon the support that supervision and top management provides the audit on a day by day basis.

In the situation where a business routinely has internal auditors review all projects and functional areas for management effectiveness and efficiency, the problem of top management support is minimized. Where audits have become a way of life, the reason for their being has been overcome and generally accepted. Although top management support is a continuing requirement, the communication problem is less in this circumstance.

Again experience has proven that in most cases management auditing is a tool for the boss and his top management team and requires their support.

Team Credentials

There is a distinct difference between the known credentials of an auditor who is hired from an outside firm as compared to those persons assigned to auditing from within the organization. As expected, the outside person is only known by his written resume of experience along with the reputation of his company, and this must be sufficient to impress management. However, when persons from internal resources are assigned either full time or temporary to an audit team then everyone judges them on many years of personal observations and assessments of character as well as job performance. It is well known that it may be easier to accept a person that you do not know too well. When this situation is recognized it becomes most important that the best people with related experience be selected for audit team assignments. Some companies have a small permanent audit staff who provide the nucleus of the team and who are augmented on a temporary assignment with others from within the organization. It is normally the responsibility of the team chief to identify his team needs and then recommend individuals from through-out the organization who could meet the requirements. It is very important that not only the best qualified people are identified but that they are recognized by top management as having the needed qualifications and have top management's approval. If top management does not select and approve the audit team, then their confidence in the team's findings will not exist and the final payoff may be drastically affected. The criteria for individual selection must always recognize the need for specialists in functional or technical fields. However, other factors are equally important in selecting those that are broad thinkers, but still analytical, and who understand the human behavioral aspects of job performance. It is most unfortunate to accept the fact that too often ad hoc or other than normal assignments will often be given to those persons who are more available rather than selecting individuals on a criteria basis. There must be a general consensus that the findings of an audit team will generally reflect the qualifications of the auditors. If significant results are needed and expected, then the quality of the audit team is essential, therefore each individual's qualifications are important.

Announcements

Communication of audit activity from top down is an essential factor influencing the success of an audit. Usually the President or General Manager of the company should sign the internal memorandum which announces the audit, the reason for it, the support required, and identifies the team members. In addition, verbal announcements should follow from the President to his staff, and from each level down to that of first supervision. It is hoped and desired that discussions at each organizational level be an affirmation that all will cooperate and support the audit, and that there will not be any negative expressions which would promote withholding of information or foot dragging. People at the working levels can usually discern the true feelings of those providing direction and may then exercise a choice of full, some, or no support to the auditors.

It cannot be over-emphasized that when top management decides to have an audit they select the best audit team possible, and provide evidence of their support in written and vocal form to all within the organization.

CONDUCTING THE AUDIT

Protocol

It is very important as a step of gaining further acceptance for the audit team, that normal protocol be observed in the early phase of interfacing with the project team and the supporting functional areas. The initial point of contact and arrangements for interviews must start with the project manager, and it is most appropriate to have the entire team meet with the project manager, his deputy and other key staff members. Such a meeting should include the discussion and outline of the contact plan for the individual interviews to follow. The best procedure is to have a member of the project team assigned to the task as the interface or focal point for arranging all interviews. This has several advantages in that it allows the project team to exercise their prerogative in identifying the sequence of audit areas; provides an organized approach for each day's activities; and ensures that each individual is notified in advance that an interview has been scheduled.

Audit interviews should generally follow the organization structure, starting at the top and proceeding to lower levels. This gives those in charge the first opportunity to provide data which they view as important, and to point out areas which they judge as impacting the success or failure of project activities; therefore, talking to a subordinate should not occur before talking to the subordinate's boss. Since auditors are outsiders to the project team, but are having an opportunity to observe the inside operation, they must observe ethics and politeness. If an auditor disregards this approach and instead acts as a privileged superior who barges in when and wherever he pleases, then the doors will be hard to open, and data and knowledge will be difficult to obtain.

A rule for an auditor's conduct is to treat each person the way one would like to be treated if the roles were reversed.

Team Operation

The results of a project audit are the accomplishments and product of the individual auditors; however, their performance can best be directed by the team chief/chairman. He shoulders the ultimate responsibility for the audit success, therefore his involvement in the planning and the conduct of the audit is absolutely essential. Once the scope of the audit is decided, the plan outlined, and area assignments made then the team chief becomes a manager of the audit team to make sure they are ready for the job at hand and that daily performance is as a team rather than a mix of individual efforts. There must be a close working relationship between audit team members during the interview phase. Often the findings of one auditor overlap into another auditor's area and may have an unforeseen impact. A sharing of knowledge and data is needed on a daily basis, therefore "end-of-day" meetings pay off and the audit team chief will insure that communications occur for mutual benefits. As the audit progresses, the individual auditors begin to arrive at preliminary conclusions or findings. These need to be identified as the interview phase continues for each major subject area that is being reviewed. Once they surface, they need to be challenged and discussed by the audit team to ascertain the validity and sufficiency of data. This will assist the auditor in writing his portion of the report.

Since audit teams may have persons with experience in both auditing and specialized areas, it stands to reason that individual capability is enhanced. The team achieves the most benefit when these areas compliment and supplement each other. At the start of an audit, it is often best to have a person who has never conducted an audit interview get his feet wet by accompanying an experienced auditor. Although the audit team chief continually works to get the working interface established early, experience has revealed that the individual auditors are so preoccupied with their own areas that during the early phase they fail to see the need for exchange. As the audit progresses, this attitude usually changes and each auditor becomes a better team player.

Selection of Audit Areas

The development of an audit plan, regardless of the amount of detail contained in the plan, is essential at the start. The team chief will have a general agreement with those in authority who have directed that an audit be performed. The scope along with the reason or purpose of the project audit has been included in the initial announcement which sets the stage for outlining the audit plan. The contents of this plan should include, but need not be limited to, the following subject areas:

Audit Plan for Project XX

   I. Purpose
  II. Scope
 III. Approach for Conduct
     A. Team Assignments
     B. Schedule/Itinerary
 IV. Audit Areas
  V. Interview Questions by Area

In the case of a new project, an audit plan is usually developed to cover all management areas that could affect the success of the project. In this event, a typical plan would include the following areas to be audited:
Example:

IV—Audit Areas for Project XX

A. Organization
B. Policies and Procedures
C. Master Planning and Control
D. Work Authorization
E. Contract Administration
F. Engineering
G. Manufacturing

H. Quality Control
I. Test
J. Logistics Support
K. Customer Requirements
L. Vendor Support

The assignment of individual auditors to specific areas is usually done according to the background and experience of the auditor. On a large scale project it may be necessary to have more than one auditor per area and whenever possible this is desirable since the combined talents of two may be needed. The scope, size, and sophistication of the project will dictate the number and assignment of auditors to review the many subject areas involved.

Interview Techniques

Interviews for the auditors should be made at least one day in advance. As discussed above, this is best accomplished by having one person arrange all interviews for the project team. Schedules always require some negotiating and last minute changes may occur, however, it is expected that people will make themselves available when the auditors request. The time scheduled for an interview should usually be not less than one hour and no more than two. In many cases the best practice is to have a return interview rather than extend the time to a half a day. Auditors often need time to assess the information and data provided or to confer with other members of the audit team before deciding what additional data is needed.

Prior to the actual interview, the auditor should make preparations by familiarizing himself with both background data and information on the responsibilities of the individual involved. In addition, it is necessary to be aware of the status of progress in the area as well as any known problems. The auditor, of course, will only have enough knowledge to be conversant during the early interviews, however, as time goes by, he will be continually adding to his own knowledge and his proficiency at interviewing will improve. For those auditors who are interviewing for the first time, the development and use of a list of interview questions are a must. As expected for those persons who have been auditing projects for several years, their need of a check list of questions is more for reminders than being dependent upon the use of such a tool. The following examples of check lists of interview questions are presented only to encourage their development by the audit team members before the interviews.

Example: Interview Questions
    for: *Organization and Management*
1. Request organizational charts for the project, delineating relationships between operations.

    a. Clearly indicate who reports to whom?

    b. How does structure reflect dept. management emphasis on the project?

    c. Where and how are project management responsibilities defined?

    d. How many people are actually managing the project effort and what authority and responsibilities are delegated to each?

2. Does the project have its own policies and procedures for assignment of responsibilities and work accomplishment?

Example: Interview Questions
       for: *Logistics Support*

1. What method is used to assure the timely delivery of spare parts?

2. What method is used to assure that instructions in manuals will allow the accurate operation and maintenance of equipment.

During the interview the auditor is a listener, asking only those questions necessary to keep the discussion on track. Requesting copies of a document needed is the best approach rather than taking time to write lengthy descriptions. The use of a list of interview questions will enable the auditor to keep the interview moving along a logical path, and will permit the taking of short notes on the replies to questions asked. In addition to the modus operandi of the auditor in pursuing the subject material, the auditor's style is important. Since he is not an investigator looking for violation of law, it is essential that the tenor of the conversation be friendly. When a healthy rapport develops between the auditor and interviewee, the likelihood of productive results increases dramatically. In contrast, an adversary situation will make it difficult to get the data needed and will also be a mutually unpleasant experience. If at all possible, it pays to be a nice guy.

Development/Preparation of Findings

As the interviews are completed, and data are assembled and analyzed, the auditor will have reached conclusions which can then be identified as Findings. This represents the culmination of the auditor's work and requires concerted effort to ensure that each Finding is accurately stated, fully supported, and will stand up to challenge. The format for documenting the Findings is simple and provides the framework to report the auditor's efforts. This approach and format has been used by many auditors.

FINDINGS

Subject: (Use a short descriptive title)
Finding No.: (Number by subject area)
                The Finding should be brief but include a statement

that describes the problem or outstanding condition, the cause, and the effect.

Discussion: Present as thorough and comprehensive analysis of the condition as is necessary to prove the statements in the Finding. Include corrective actions at end.

Recommendations: State what Action must be taken and by what office or position in the organization.

This phase of analyzing and writing the Findings often requires as much time as was spent in the planning, preparation, and undertaking of the interview. Seldom is an initial draft of a Finding adequate in statement of the problem or in the supporting evidence of the Discussion. This is not a quick and easy task and deserves whatever time it takes to do it justice. The involvement of other team members is a good practice, for their view and perspective should help in the writing and the final acceptance by the team chief and other members.

Validation of Findings

In the preparation of the Findings, and before they are finalized, it is good to go back and discuss them with those individuals directly involved. Most frequently the people involved and concerned the most are really the first to realize what may have gone wrong and what is necessary to correct the situation. In addition, since the individuals involved have had a hand in revealing the situation, they are more willing to accept the Findings, and may assist in determining what the recommended solutions should be. There may be times when it seems impossible to discuss the Findings without a confrontation; but this is usually the exception. In most instances, all levels of management will cooperate and appreciate a post mortem critique. This has a double effect, for if they accept the Findings, they have now become a part of the solution—which you want them to be. Taking the Findings and achieving confirmation of them on up to the Project Manager is the goal, and it will mean more when the complete audit results are presented to General Management.

REPORTING RESULTS OF THE AUDIT

Report Preparation

A report is the end product of the combined efforts of the audit team. The payoff of the audit effort and the effectiveness of follow-up actions will depend upon the manner in which the report is written and presented. Findings must be clearly stated, and discussions must contain only factual information to support each Finding. Avoid lengthy philosophies, opinions, and observations. Where credit is deserved it should be recognized and receive equal treatment in comparison to problem areas and deficiencies. The team chairman should hold frequent coordination meetings to review progress and accomplish the inter-exchange of information. Drafts of Findings should be made as early as possible since considerable review is usually necessary to get agreement within the team, accomplish validation with those involved, and finally satisfy the team chairman. Experience has shown that preparing the audit results in report and briefing form will take as many or more hours as conducting the interviews and analysis. Another rule of thumb when writing the Findings, is that most often it may take five iterations before achieving the final version for use in the report. There is a natural tendency to rush this final phase of the audit since those on temporary assignment will be anxious to return to regular jobs. At this point, it is the team chairman who must hold to accepting nothing less than a well expressed, accurate, and complete report that all can be proud of.

Report Format

The results of the project audit must be presented to the person or persons that originally directed and requested its accomplishment. This usually requires a verbal briefing/presentation and a written report. Typically, the briefing would be a summary of the written report. The following outline is recommended for a project audit report:

AUDIT REPORT FORMAT

PART I—INTRODUCTION
    Section I—Purpose
        (Give a brief explanation of any special reasons that audit is being conducted.)
    Section II—Scope
        (Give a description of scope of audit including limitations imposed.)
    Section III—Audit Team
        (List team membership by name, title, and organization.)
    Section IV—Audit Interviews
        (List all persons interviewed, by name, title, and organization.)
PART II—AUDIT RESULTS
    Section I—Summary and Recommendations
        The summary of results will be a one-page abstract of the major findings and recommendations. Following each specific recommendation will be the action office responsible for that recommendation.
    Section II—Findings, Discussion, Recommendations
        This portion of the report will contain the detailed Findings, discussion and recommendations that pertain to the program.

(1) Subject: Use a short descriptive title, e.g., "Overtime."

(2) Finding: The Finding should be brief but include 1) a statement that describes the condition, i.e., problem or outstanding condition, 2) the cause or reason for this condition or problem, and 3) the effect or impact resulting from the condition. *Summarized, the Finding should reflect a condition, a cause, and the effect.*

(3) Discussion: Mention the pertinent factors collected during discussion with others or revealed through your personal investigations. Present as thorough and comprehensive an analysis of the condition as necessary to prove the statements in your Finding.

(4) Recommendations: If corrective action(s) are suggested by the Finding, they should be recorded at the end of the discussion. Following each recommendation, note the action assignments.

PART III—SUPPLEMENTARY DATA

Note: The appendices listed are for guidance only and will not necessarily apply to each audit report. Conciseness should be employed. As an example, data under appendices for program history and description of system should not normally exceed one page each.

Appendix A—Project history

B—Description of system

C—Documentation and reporting

D—Programming and funding history

E—Customer organization

F—Program organization and management controls

Briefings to Management

This is another time for respecting protocol and recognizing prerogatives. Just as it was important during the audit to start at the top and work down, it is now important to start at the bottom and work up. Early discussion of Findings with the working persons involved will establish credibility and ensure that data is accurate and complete. When the report is essentially complete and a briefing structured, there may be an opportunity to have a dry run with a second level of the project team which could provide a shake-down and then the chance for a final tune-up before a more formal review with the project manager and his staff. At this preview, the report should be 98% solid, with no holes or obvious shortcomings, and hopefully the project manager will not only endorse the report but say it's a job well done.

Since project managers seldom have all the resources under their control, the need to reach top management is absolutely necessary. It is most likely that a majority of the Findings will require decisions and actions by the functional managers. Further, it is the man at the top who can make sure it all happens—

if he is convinced of the project's needs. A good briefing is the best way to get the audit results to the top management team. The team chairman may elect to do the entire briefing or to include members of the audit team to cover their specialized areas. If at all possible, members of the audit team should be included for it provides them an opportunity for recognition which is due. Copies of the briefing charts should be provided to all recipients of the report for they serve as good summaries and ready references. This last step of the audit process which requires effective written and verbal communication becomes the final measure for judging the degree of success of the entire audit effort.

FOLLOW-UP ACTIONS

Responsibilities

The auditor in the recommendations for the Findings should make every effort to determine the organization and person responsible for taking corrective action. In some instances there may be shared assignments, and others that are not absolutely clear cut. Experience has shown that final assignment of responsibilities for each and every recommendation may occur during the briefing to management. This level makes the final decisions and their acceptance and involvement are an important step to the follow-up activity to the project audit.

It has been known that some audit operations report only the conditions, and are not required to make recommendations nor identify responsibilities for corrective actions. As a general practice, this is not recommended for it does not take full advantage of the audit team's capabilities and tends to shackle their initiative and limit their contribution.

Close Out of Report

The audit team as a part of the audit plan should present a follow-up and close out plan at the time of final briefings. This provides an organized means to get actions underway by the responsible individuals. When top management accepts the plan requiring a 30 day report and a 90 day final report from all involved in action assignments, then management direction has occurred and there is a control system to ensure response. At the time of these two reports to management, the audit team chairman and other appropriate team members should be present. This has several benefits, for if actions described are not adequate to correct the condition entirely, then the audit team member should have the opportunity to express his concern. Also this enables him to see the completion of his efforts, and to see a job completed is a part of the final reward.

EVALUATION OF AUDIT FUNCTION

Management Assessment

Since the use of the audit function of projects or other specialized subject areas is a tool that best serves the interests of management, it stands to reason that they should periodically question the value it serves. In the event that the audit results are not sufficient to warrant the use of this tool, management should determine what is required to make it more effective or do away with it. Experience has shown that the audit tool has been successful when top management has actually used it and supported it. This is also true for other internal management consultant functions which are staff support activities. A good example of the right environment was the approach used by a top executive of a high technology firm who immediately after winning a new contract would assess past performance for needed improvements. Sometimes he would ask for an assessment by his entire team so that the next project could benefit from the lessons learned. The alternative is to continue either getting by or even repeating the same mistakes.

Applying "Lessons Learned"

The greatest opportunity for payoff from project management auditing may often occur for the next project in order to avoid early shortcomings in applied manpower, policies and procedures on the next project. The results of a project audit during any phase will reveal problems which, if given visibility and understanding, can assist the next project manager and top management, to avoid or reduce the probability of similar deficiencies occurring again. Although there is universal lip service in recognizing the potential of lessons learned, the action needed to correct such conditions is too often lacking. Here is where top management can take direct action and change people, resources, policies and procedures, and their own involvement. For example, the lessons learned from one project audit could provide the basis for the following plan to be required on the management of new projects:

- More frequent management reviews in the first year of the project.
- More careful selection of key people with proven experience.
- Early assessment of customer satisfaction.
- Early assessment of test results.

As can be expected, people and methods are slow to change, therefore it is the responsibility of management to make changes happen. Results of each project audit will enable the project manager to better see himself and his team and determine the immediate needs and changes to be initiated. Response to such needs may work best when self-initiated, so top management should permit and encourage corrective actions whenever possible. However, there are other times when only management direction gets things done.

Whereas the impatience and daring of a new project manager are often to be admired, it is concluded that as a great philosopher—George Santayana—said, "Those who cannot remember the past are condemned to repeat it."

24. Evaluating the Performance of Project Personnel

Harold Kerzner*

In most traditional organizations, the need for project management is first recognized by those functional, resource or middle managers who have identified problems in allocating and controlling resources. The next step is the tedious process of trying to convince upper-level management that such a change is necessary. Assuming that upper-level management does, in fact, react favorably toward project management, the next step becomes critical. Many upper-level managers feel that project management can be forced on lower-level subordinates through simple directives together with continuous upper-level supervision.

This turns out to be a significant turning point in the implementation phase. Upper-level management must obtain functional employee support before total implementation can be achieved. Functional employees have two concerns. Their first concern is with their evaluation. Who will evaluate them? How will they be evaluated? Against what standards will they be evaluated? Who will help them put more money into their pockets through merit increases or promotions?

The employee's second concern is centered about the resistance to change. Functional employees, especially blue collar workers, have a strong resentment to changing their well-established occupational life styles. They must be shown enough cases (i.e. projects) in order to be convinced that the new system will work. This could easily take two to three years to accomplish. It is therefore imperative that the first few projects be successful. Most upper and middle-level managers agree to the necessity for initially demonstrating success, but often forget about the importance of looking at the evaluation procedure problems.

*Dr. Harold Kerzner is Professor of Systems Management and Director of The Project/Systems Management Research Institute at Baldwin-Wallace College. Dr. Kerzner has published over 35 engineering and business papers, and six texts: *Project Management: A Systems Approach to Planning, Scheduling and Controlling; Project Management for Executives; Project Management for Bankers; Cases and Situations in Project/Systems Management; Operations Research; and Proposal Preparation and Preparation and Management.*

UNDERSTANDING THE NATURE OF THE PROBLEM

In pure project management, the functional employee reports to at least two bosses: a functional manager and a project manager. If the employee happens to be working on three or four projects simultaneously, then he or she can have multiple project managers to whom they must report, either formally or informally. This concept of sharing functional employees is vital if project management is to be successful because it allows better control and use of vital manpower resources by allowing key functional personnel to be shared.

In almost all cases, the relationship between the employees and their superior is a "solid" line where the manager maintains absolute employee control through the use of promotions, job assignments, merit and salary increases. The ability of the manager to motivate personnel is easily achieved through the use of the employee's purse strings.

The project manager, on the other hand, will probably be in a "dotted" line relationship and be less able to motivate temporarily assigned project personnel by using monetary rewards. Therefore, what types of interpersonal influences can a project manager use to motivate people who are assigned temporarily for the achievement of some common objective and who might never work together again? The most common interpersonal influence styles used by project managers are:

- Formal authority.
- Technical expertise.
- Work challenge.
- Friendship.
- Rewards (and punishment).

Formal authority is the ability to gain support from the functional employees because they respect the fact that the project manager has been delegated a certain amount of authority from upper-level management in order to achieve a specific objective. The amount of delegated authority may vary with the amount of risk that the project manager must take. Formal authority is not a very effective means of motivating and controlling employees because every employee knows that he or she has come to the project recommended by their manager.

Technical expertise is the ability to gain support because employees respect the fact that the project manager possesses skills which they lack or because he or she is a recognized expert in their field. If a project manager tries to control employees through the use of "expert power" for a prolonged period of time, conflicts can easily develop between the project and functional managers as to who is the "true" expert in the field.

Work challenge is an extremely effective means of soliciting functional support. If the employees find the work stimulating and challenging, they tend to become self-motivating with a strong desire for achievement in hopes of attaining some future rewards.

Friendship, or referent power, is a means of obtaining functional support because the employee feels personally attracted to either the project manager or the project. Examples of referent power might be when:

- The employee and the project manager have strong ties, such as being in the same foursome for golf.
- The employee likes the project manager's manner of treating people.
- The employee wants specific identification with a specific product line or project.
- The employee has personal problems and believes that he can get empathy or understanding from the project manager.
- The employee might be able to get personal favors from the project manager.
- The employee feels that the project manager is a winner and that the rewards will be passed down to the employee.

Rewards, or reward power, can be defined as the ability to gain support because the employee feels that the project manager can either directly or indirectly dispense those rewards which employees cherish. If the employee is assigned directly to the project manager, such as project office personnel, the project manager has the same direct rewarding system as does a functional manager. However, they may have only indirect reward power with regard to the employees that are assigned to the project but are still attached administratively to a functional department. This chapter focuses on those problems of rewarding the temporary functional employees. The last two items under friendship are examples of reward power as well as referent power. Project managers prefer work challenge and rewards as the most comfortable means for soliciting functional support. Unfortunately, project managers are somewhat limited as to what rewards they can offer directly to the employee. What commitment should or can the project manager make in the way of:

- Salary?
- Grade?
- Responsibility?
- Evaluation for promotion?
- Bonus?
- Future work assignment?
- Paid overtime?

- Awards?
- Letters of commendation?

The major problem with project management is that, in theory, the project manager can *directly* provide only paid overtime rewards, and even this can be questionable. If the project manager cannot directly provide the necessary organizational rewards in order to motivate temporary employees, then what inducement is there for the employee to do a good job? Employees believe in the equity theory which states that a fair day's work should receive a fair day's pay. The difficulty lies in the fact that employees occasionally perceive themselves as working for a project manager who cannot guarantee them any of these rewards.

A special note need be mentioned concerning a project manager's ability or authority to provide an employee with additional responsibility. Most companies that adopt project management have rather loose company policies, procedures, rules and guidelines. To illustrate this point, a functional employee can be performing the same task on three separate projects, yet his responsibilities might be quite different.

The problem appears when the project manager attempts to upgrade an employee. As an example, a Grade 7 employee does a good job on a Grade 7 task and receives an excellent evaluation. The project manager, having established a good working relationship with this employee, and not wanting to see it end, decides to let this employee assume the responsibilities of a Grade 8 on a follow-on task. The employee again performs above average and receives an outstanding evaluation by the project manager. The employee then demands that his manager promote him since he has now successfully performed the work of a Grade 8. The manager now becomes overly upset and claims that the project manager had no right to upgrade an employee without prior approval from the manager.

THE INDIRECT REWARDING PROCESS

Under the definition of rewards, we stated that the project manager could either directly or indirectly dispense the valued organizational rewards. Each project, although considered as a separate entity within the company, is still attached administratively to the company through policies and procedures. These policies and procedures dictate the means of administering the wage and salary program. It is operationally disastrous for the project manager and functional manager to be administering different wage and salary policies at the same time.

When employees are assigned to a new project, their first concern is with the identification of the mechanism by which they can be assured that their manager will be informed if they perform well on their new assignment. A good project manager will make it immediately clear to all new employees that if they perform well on this effort, then he (the project manager) will inform their manager of their progress and achievements. This assumes that the manager is not providing close supervision over the employee and is, instead, passing on some of the responsibility to the project manager. This is quite common in project management organizational structures. Obviously, if the manager has a small span of control and/or sufficient time to monitor closely the work of subordinates, then the project manager's need for indirect reward power is minimal.

Many good projects as well as project management structures have failed because of the inability of the system to properly evaluate the employee's performance. This problem is, unfortunately, one of the most often overlooked trouble spots in project management.

In a project management structure there are basically six ways that an employee can be evaluated on a project.

- *The project manager prepares a written, confidential evaluation and gives it to the functional manager.* The line managers will evaluate the validity of the project manager's comments and prepare their own evaluation of the employee. The employee will be permitted to see only the evaluation form filled out by the line manager.
- *The project manager prepares a non-confidential evaluation and gives it to the functional manager.* The project manager prepares his own evaluation form and both evaluations are shown to the functional employee. This is the technique preferred by most project and functional managers. However, there are several major difficulties with this technique. If the employee is an average or below average worker, and if this employee is still to be assigned to this project after the evaluation, the project manager might rate the employee as above average simply to prevent any repercussions or ill-feelings down stream. In this situation the manager might want a confidential evaluation instead knowing that the employee will see both evaluation forms. Employees tend to blame the project manager if they receive a below average merit increase, but give credit to the manager if the increase is above average. The best bet here is for the project manager to periodically inform the employees as to how well they are doing, and to give them an honest appraisal. Of course, on large projects with vast manpower resources, this approach may not be possible. Honesty does appear to be the best policy in project management employee evaluation.
- *The project manager provides the functional manager with an oral evaluation of the employee's performance.* Although this technique is com-

monly used, most functional managers prefer documentation on employee progress.

- *The functional manager makes the entire evaluation without any input from the project manager.* In order for this technique to be effective, the functional manager must have sufficient time to supervise each subordinate's performance on a continual basis. Unfortunately, most functional managers do not have this opportunity because of their broad span of control.
- *The project manager makes the entire evaluation for the functional manager.* This technique can work if the employee is assigned to only the one project or if the project is physically located at a remote site where he cannot be observed by his functional manager.
- *The project and functional managers jointly evaluate all project functional employees at the same time.* This technique may be limited to small companies with less than fifty or so employees, otherwise the evaluation process might be time consuming for key personnel. A bad evaluation is known by all.

In five of the above six techniques the project manager has either a direct or indirect input into the employee's evaluation process.

WHEN AND HOW TO EVALUATE

Since the majority of the functional managers prefer written, non-confidential evaluations, we must determine what the evaluation forms look like and when the employee will be evaluated. The indirect evaluation form should be a relatively simple tool to use or else the indirect evaluation process will be time consuming. This is of paramount importance on large projects where the project manager may have as many as 200 employees assigned to various activities.

The evaluation forms can be filled out either when the employee is up for evaluation or after the project is completed. If the evaluation form is to be filled out when the employee is up for promotion or a merit increase, then the project manager should be willing to give an *honest* appraisal of the employee's performance. Of course, the project manager should not fill out the evaluation form if the employee has not been assigned long enough to allow a fair evaluation.

The evaluation form can be filled out at the termination of the project. One problem with this technique is that the project may end the month after the employee is up for promotion. One advantage of this technique is that the project manager may have been able to find sufficient time both to observe the employee in action and to see the complete output.

Figure 24-1 represents a rather humorous version of how project personnel perceive the evaluation form to look. Unfortunately, the evaluation process is very serious and can easily have a severe impact on an individual's career path with the company even though the final evaluation rests with the manager.

Figure 24-2 shows a simple type of evaluation form where the project manager identifies the box that best describes the employee's performance. The project manager may or may not make additional comments. This type of form is generally used whenever the employee is up for evaluation, provided that the project manager has had sufficient time to observe the employee's performance.

	Excellent (1 out of 15)	Very good (3 out of 15)	Good (8 out of 15)	Fair (2 out of 15)	Unsatisfactory (1 out of 15)
Performance factors	Far exceeds job requirements	Exceeds job requirements	Meets job requirements	Needs some improvement	Does not meet minimum standards
Quality	Leaps tall buildings with a single bound	Must take running start to leap over tall building	Can only leap over a short building or medium one without spires	Crashes into building	Cannot recognize buildings
Timeliness	Is faster than a speeding bullet	Is as fast as a speeding bullet	Not quite as fast as a speeding bullet	Would you believe a slow bullet?	Wounds himself with the bullet
Initiative	Is stronger than a locomotive	Is stronger than a bull elephant	Is stronger than a bull	Shoots the bull	Smells like a bull
Adaptability	Walks on water consistently	Walks on water in emergencies	Washes with water	Drinks water	Passes water in emergencies
Communications	Talks with God	Talks with angels	Talks to himself	Argues with himself	Losses the argument with himself

Figure 24-1. Guide to performance appraisal.

EMPLOYEE'S NAME   DATE

PROJECT TITLE   JOB NUMBER

EMPLOYEE ASSIGNMENT

EMPLOYEE'S TOTAL TIME TO DATE ON PROJECT   EMPLOYEE'S REMAINING TIME ON PROJECT

TECHNICAL JUDGEMENT:

☐ Quickly reaches   ☐ Usually makes   ☐ Marginal decision   ☐ Needs technical   ☐ Makes faulty
sound conclusions   sound conclusions   making ability   assistance   conclusions

WORK PLANNING:

☐ Good planner   ☐ Plans well with   ☐ Occasionally   ☐ Needs detailed   ☐ Cannot plan at
                     help   plans well   instructions   all

COMMUNICATIONS:

☐ Always   ☐ Sometimes needs   ☐ Always needs   ☐ Needs follow-up   ☐ Needs constant
understands   clarification   clarifications   instruction
instructions

ATTITUDE:

☐ Always job   ☐ Shows interest   ☐ Shows no job   ☐ More interested in ☐ Does not care
interested   most of the time   interest   in other activities about job

COOPERATION:

☐ Always   ☐ Works well until ☐ Usually works   ☐ Works poorly   ☐ Wants it done
enthusiastic   job is completed   well with others   with others   his/her way

WORK HABITS:

☐ Always project   ☐ Most often   ☐ Usually   ☐ Works poorly   ☐ Always works
oriented   project oriented   consistent with   with others   alone
                                          requests

ADDITIONAL COMMENTS: _____

_____

Figure 24-2. Project work assignment appraisal.

Figure 24-3 shows a typical form that can be used to evaluate an employee at project completion. In each category the employee is rated on a scale from one to five. In order to minimize time and paper work, it is also possible to have a single evaluation form at project termination for all employees. (Figure 24-4). As before, all employees are rated in each category on a scale of one to five. Totals are obtained to provide a relative comparison between employees.

Even though the project manager fills out an evaluation form, there is no guarantee that the functional manager will give any credibility to the project manager's evaluation. There are always situations where the project and functional managers disagree as to either quality or direction of work. This can easily alienate the project manager into recommending either a higher or lower

	Excellent	Above average	Average	Below average	Inadequate
EMPLOYEE'S NAME			DATE		
PROJECT TITLE			JOB NUMBER		

EMPLOYEE'S NAME   DATE

PROJECT TITLE   JOB NUMBER

EMPLOYEE ASSIGNMENT

EMPLOYEE'S TOTAL TIME TO DATE ON PROJECT   EMPLOYEE'S REMAINING TIME ON PROJECT

	Excellent	Above average	Average	Below average	Inadequate
Technical judgement					
Work planning					
Communications					
Attitude					
Cooperation					
Work habits					
Profit contribution					

Additional comments_____

Figure 24-3. Project work assignment appraisal.

evaluation than the employee's work justifies. If the employee spends most of his time working alone, then the project manager may have difficulty appraising quality and give an average evaluation when in fact the employee's performance is superb or inferior. There is also the situation where the project manager knows the employee personally and may allow personal feelings to influence the evaluation.

Another problem situation is where the project manager is a "generalist," say at a Grade 7 level, and requests that the functional manager assign their best employee to the project. The functional manager agrees to the request and assigns his best employee, a Grade 10. Now, how can a Grade 7 generalist evaluate a Grade 10 specialist? The solution to this problem rests in the fact that the project manager might be able to evaluate the expert only in certain categories as communications, work habits, problem solving and other such topics but not upon his technical expertise. The manager might be the only person qualified to evaluate personnel on technical abilities and expertise.

EMPLOYEE'S NAME	DATE
PROJECT TITLE	JOB NUMBER
EMPLOYEE ASSIGNMENT	
EMPLOYEE'S REMAINING TIME ON PROJECT	EMPLOYEE'S TOTAL TIME TO DATE ON PROJECT

CODE:

Excellent   = 5
Above average = 4
Average   = 3
Below average = 2
Inadequate   = 1

NAMES	Technical judgement	Work planning	Communications	Attitude	Cooperation	Work habits	Profit contribution	Self motivation	Total points

Figure 24-4. Project work assignment appraisal.

It has been proposed that employees should have some sort of reciprocal indirect input into a project manager's evaluation. This raises rather interesting questions as to how far we can go with the indirect evaluation procedure.

From a top management perspective, the indirect evaluation process brings with it several headaches. Wage and salary administrators readily accept the necessity for utilizing a different evaluation form for white collar workers as opposed to blue collar workers. But now, we have a situation in which there can be more than one type of evaluation system for white collar workers alone. Those employees that work in project-driven functional departments will be evaluated directly and indirectly, but based upon formal procedures. Employees that charge their time to overhead accounts and non-project driven departments might simply be evaluated by a single, direct evaluation procedure.

Many wage and salary administrators contend that they cannot live with a

I. Employee information
1. Name _____ 2. Date of evaluation _____
3. Job assignment _____ 4. Date of last evaluation _____
5. Pay grade _____
6. Employee's immediate supervisor _____
7. Supervisor's level: ☐ Section ☐ Dept. ☐ Division ☐ Executive

II. Evaluator's information:
1. Evaluator's name _____
2. Evaluator's level: ☐ Section ☐ Dept. ☐ Division ☐ Executive
3. Rate the employee on the following:

	Excellent	Very Good	Good	Fair	Poor
Ability to assume responsibility					
Works well with others					
Loyal attitude toward company					
Documents work well and is both cost and profit conscious					
Reliability to see job through					
Ability to accept criticism					
Willingness to work overtime					
Plans job execution carefully					
Technical knowledge					
Communicative skills					
Overall rating					

4. Rate the employee in comparison to his contemporaries:

Lower 10%	Lower 25%	Lower 40%	Midway	Upper 40%	Upper 25%	Upper 10%

5. Rate the employee in comparison to his contemporaries:

Should be promoted at once	Promotable next year	Promotable along with contempories	Needs to mature in grade	Definitely not promotable

6. Evaluator's comments: _____
_____
_____

Signature _____

III. Concurrence section:
1. Name _____
2. Position: ☐ Department ☐ Division ☐ Executive
3. Concurrence ☐ Agree ☐ Disagree
4. Comments: _____
_____
_____
_____

Signature _____

Figure 24-5. Job evaluation.

IV. <u>Personnel Section</u>: (to be completed by the Personnel Department only)

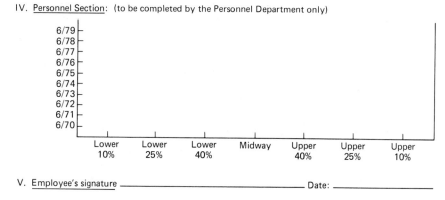

V. <u>Employee's signature</u> _____ Date: _____

Figure 24-5. Job evaluation. (*continued*)

dual white collar system and therefore have tried to combine the direct and indirect evaluation forms into one, as shown in Figure 24-5. Some administrators have even gone so far as to utilize a single form company-wide, regardless of whether an individual is a white or blue collar worker.

The last major trouble spot is the design of the employee's evaluation form. The designs must be dependent upon the evaluation method or procedure. Generally speaking, there are nine methods available for evaluating personnel:

- Essay Appraisal
- Graphic Rating Scale
- Field Review
- Forced-Choice Review
- Critical Incident Appraisal
- Management by Objectives (MBO)
- Work Standards Approach
- Ranking Methods
- Assessment Center

Descriptions of these methods can be found in almost any text on wage and salary administration. Which method is best suited for a project-driven organizational structure? To answer this question, we must analyze the characteristics of the organizational form as well as those of the personnel who must perform there. As an example, project management can be described as an arena of conflict. Which of the above nine evaluation procedures can best evaluate an employee's ability to work and progress in an atmosphere of conflict? Figure 24-6 compares the above nine evaluation procedures against the six

	Essay appraisal	Graphic rating scale	Field review	Forced-choice review	Critical incident appraisal	Management by objectives	Work standards approach	Ranking methods	Assessment center
Conflict over schedules	•	•		•	•		•	•	
Conflict over priorities	•	•		•	•		•	•	
Conflict over technical issues	•			•			•		
Conflict over administration	•	•	•	•			•	•	•
Personality conflict	•	•		•			•		
Conflict over cost	•		•	•	•		•	•	•

Figure 24-6. Rating evaluation techniques against types of conflicts.

most common project conflicts. This type of analysis must be carried out for all variables and characteristics which describe the project management environment. Many compensation managers would agree that the MBO technique offers the greatest promise for a fair and equitable evaluation of all employees. Unfortunately, MBO implies that functional employees will have a say in establishing their own goals and objectives. This might not be the case. In project management, the project manager or functional manager might set the objectives and the functional employee is told that he has to live with it. Obviously, there will be advantages and disadvantages to whatever evaluation procedures are finally selected.

Having identified the problems with employee evaluation in a project environment, we can now summarize the results and attempt to predict the future. Project managers must have some sort of either direct or indirect input into an employee's evaluation. Without this, project managers may find it difficult to adequately motivate people with no upward mobility. The question is of course, how this input should take place. Most wage and salary administrators appear to be pushing for a single procedure to evaluate all white collar employees. At the same time, however, administrators recognize the necessity for an indirect input by the project manager and, therefore, are willing to let the project and functional managers (and possibly personnel) determine the exact method of input which can be different for each employee and each project. This implies that the indirect input might be oral for one employee and written for another, with both employees reporting to the same functional manager. Although this technique may seem confusing, it may be the only viable alternative for the future. A process of good employee evaluations is essential to project success.

25. Devolopment and Implementation of Effective Project Management Information and Control Systems

John Tuman, Jr.*

INTRODUCTION

Today's large projects are characteristically expensive, complex and involve considerable risk to the sponsor. These characteristics will become even more pronounced in the future because inflation, government regulations, and the increasing interdependency of national economies all work to produce an environment of dynamic uncertainty. And, of course, right in the middle of this environment we find the project manager planning, scheduling, measuring, evaluating, informing, and directing a myriad of organizations, complex tasks and expensive resources to accomplish some predefined undertaking. The project manager's situation is made particularly demanding because he functions for the most part outside the traditional line organization structure. He is attempting to complete a difficult job by a certain date with limited resources and he is trying to accomplish this goal with people who for the most part do not work for him. In addition to this, the project manager is expected to be the fountainhead for all knowledge and information about the project. In this type of environment it goes without saying that the project manager's only hope for survival rests with some type of well developed system for the systematic management of project information and action. Without such a system, the project manager and the project participants will soon be lost in a quagmire of conflicting plans, schedules, reports, activities, and priorities.

The assumption being made at this point is that as projects become larger,

*John Tuman, Jr. is manager of the Special Projects Department of Gilbert/Commonwealth Companies, Reading, Pennsylvania. He is responsible for directing a staff of project managers and system specialists in providing consulting services to clients in project and program management. For over 20 years, Mr. Tuman has been involved in all facets of project and program management. He has been a program manager for several major aerospace R&D programs, as well as a project manager for development and production of commercial equipment. Mr. Tuman is a registered professional engineer with an M.S. degree in Computer Science from the University of New Haven, and a B.S. in Mechanical Engineering from Lafayette College.

their requirements become more complex, the number of people, organizations and functions involved become more interdependent, and the project manager becomes further and further removed from day-to-day problems and changing requirements. Therefore, the effectiveness of the project manager tends to be inversely related to the size and complexity of the program. However, this process can be minimized if we provide the project manager with "systems" which enable him to increase his range of control and effectiveness over project activities. Thus, in the following we will briefly examine why it is necessary to design unique systems for project management, how to actually design and develop these systems and, finally, how to implement the systems to ensure that they perform as intended.

WHY DEVELOP A SYSTEM?

Before we consider the approach to defining, designing, and developing a system we must clearly establish that there is a need for such a system. In view of the large investments that have been made by corporations in the development of management information systems in recent years, one would question the need for development of yet another system within the corporate environment. And yet, this is exactly what is proposed here. The soundness of our rationale becomes evident if we examine the role of the project manager and his function within the traditional corporate hierarchical structure.

Traditionally, management information systems have been designed primarily to support functional units within the corporate structure. The computerized accounting system, the payroll system, the general ledger system, and so on, provide systematized approaches to handling the corporate financial functions. In similar fashion, computer supported systems for marketing and sales exist to aid and improve the efficiency of these functions, and personnel subsystems have been developed to aid the human resource functions of the corporation. In the operational or production areas (manufacturing, construction, services, tests, etc.) there are a myriad of computer supported systems available to aid the product/service producing end of the business. By and large, all of these systems have been designed to perform as efficiently as possible to collect and process data to produce information for their respective organizational functions. In more advanced management information systems designs, we have even seen utilization of Data Based Management System (DBMS), where there is an attempt among other things to efficiently share information between functions. However, for the most part management information systems in today's corporate environment are designed to support decision making in the traditional organizational structure.

Unfortunately, by the very nature of project management, the project manager must cut across functional organization lines to accomplish his goal of integrating and directing specific resources of the organization(s) toward a particular goal. The question naturally arises, can he do this effectively utilizing the traditional available management information resources?

In the earlier days of project management, and in fact, even today, for relatively small projects, the project manager acts either in a staff capacity to top management or in a line capacity within a functional organization. As a staff function, the project manager strives to coordinate in the name of top management certain capabilities of the functional organization. In this role, the project manager relies on the functional departments for the detailed planning, scheduling, budgeting, and control of their specific tasks. The project manager's information needs are limited and, generally, are of a summary nature. Even in the line function, the project manager is working in an environment where he can rely on the information system already in place. However, as projects become larger and more complex, companies have established large project organizations which are functioning either deliberately or indirectly in a matrix fashion with the total organization. In this environment project managers have attempted to carry out their responsibilities utilizing the information systems already in place. However, for the most part these project managers have found that their information resources were severely limited. Some of the more typical problems encountered by project managers in trying to do their job while relying on existing or the traditional management information systems resources of the corporation are:

1. *Usefulness*—Existing corporate management information systems do not generate the specific information required by the project manager and other project participants. The needed information is not generally available in a useful form and it requires considerable time and money to revise the existing systems to get the needed data in a timely manner.
2. *Quality vs. Quantity*—Too much detailed information is generated. It is necessary to pour through reams of computer print-outs to extract the required data. It is difficult to get exception reports especially when several functions may be involved.
3. *Integration*—There is little uniformity between corporate systems. Hence, it is difficult to develop a total project picture where several different companies are involved. Even within one organization's management information system it's difficult to reconcile information between diverse functions like finance, personnel, and operations to develop an integrated project status report.
4. *Responsiveness*—Whenever top management requests an answer to a specific question or problem, it initiates a mad scramble to obtain the required data. The existing information systems are not structured to integrate across functions to produce timely exception reports.

The essence of all of the above problems is that the traditional corporate management information systems cannot be efficiently and effectively used by the project manager simply because these systems were designed for another purpose, namely, that of enabling the functional organizations to efficiently carry out their responsibilities. This is now a fairly well recognized fact. Many companies with projects sufficiently large to warrant the cost, are now making the effort to design and implement computer-based project information and control systems specifically suited to their *unique* project management requirements.

CHARACTERISTICS OF THE PROJECT MANAGEMENT SYSTEM

Before getting into the methodology of designing a project oriented information and control system, it is necessary to examine some of the basic characteristics of these systems. For, in order to design a system which is truly effective, we must have a clear idea of what these systems should do both for the project manager and executive management.

Let us begin by examining the basic concept of the project. A project is an organization of people dedicated to a specific purpose or objective. Projects generally involve large, expensive, unique, or high risk undertakings which have to be completed by a certain date, for a certain amount of money, within some expected level of performance. At a minimum, all projects need to have well defined objectives and sufficient resources to carry out all the required tasks. All of the important aspects of a project can be depicted by the simple cybernetic diagram shown in Figure 25-1.

As shown in Figure 25-1, the project is responsible for accomplishing certain specific objectives or outputs. Those outputs can be defined in terms of activi-

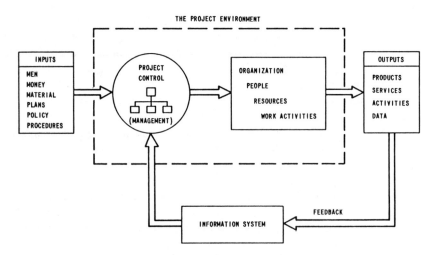

Figure 25-1. The total project management process.

ties, products, services, or data generated by the project. In order to accomplish these objectives (outputs), the project needs appropriate inputs or resources. These can be defined as men, money, or material which the project will expend in the process of accomplishing its objectives.

The control function in this process is management. Management's responsibility is to allocate to the project only those resources required to do a good job, no more and no less. And, of course, management is also concerned that these resources are used in an optimum manner. The question is, how does management determine the quantity of resources to allocate to the project and whether or not these resources are being used effectively in terms of the project goals and accomplishments? The answer is, through the information system. The primary function of the information system is to enable management to assess how the project is performing against its established goals and thereby formulate timely decisions for the effective utilization of valuable resources.

This simplified view of the project is useful to highlight two important elements which must be carefully considered in the design of any project management system. These two elements are: 1) the information system, and 2) the control system. It is particularly important to note that these two distinct and different elements are mutually related and dependent on each other. The reasons for this are obvious if we examine Figure 25-2. Note that the *information* element of the system concerns itself primarily with the task of pro-

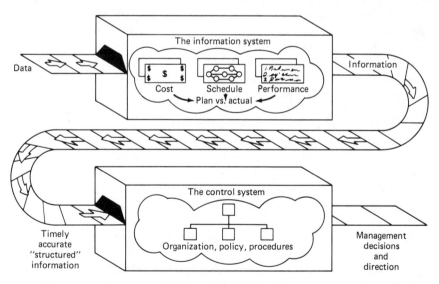

Figure 25-2. Information and control. The Information System must be designed and matched to the control system such that management decisions are a natural output of the process. This means that the right kinds of information must go to the appropriate levels of management at the right time and the decision making process must be initiated as a direct result of established procedures and routines.

cessing data to produce timely, accurate, structured information regarding the cost, schedule, and performance aspects of the project. On the other hand, the *control* element of the system is concerned primarily with using the information supplied to formulate decisions and give direction relative to future utilization of resources and/or resolution of problems. Unless the control element and the information element are designed to be mutually compatible and dependent on each other, they will not function as an integrated system.

With this brief view of the "system" we can define the project management information and control system as the people, policies, procedures, and systems (computerized and manual) which provide the means for planning, scheduling, budgeting, organizing, directing, and controlling the cost, schedule, and performance accomplishments of a project. Implicit in this definition is the idea that *people plan and control projects,* and *systems serve people by producing information.* The design and implementation of the procedures and methodologies which integrate people and systems into a unified whole is both an art and a science. Some of the more pragmatic aspects of these procedures and methodologies are considered next.

GETTING STARTED

Once the need to develop a system has been established, there is generally a great temptation to make an industry-wide survey to find out what everyone else is doing. These whirlwind tours usually result in a mind boggling collection of facts and philosophy on computer hardware, data base management systems, CPM packages*, classification schemes, programming concepts, etc. At best, a survey of other systems will give the uninitiated a feel for the magnitude and complexities of the undertaking.

The other extreme is to call in the computer or systems consultants who, in most cases, recommend the purchase of a particular set of software packages. Unfortunately, instant implementation of these packages is generally not possible. Extensive customizing is normally required to enable usage of the system for a particular project. Even more important, however, software packages are designed for specific purposes and unless the buyer knows exactly what he is going to do with these packages, they are unlikely to be used to their fullest potential.

The only sure way to develop a project information and control system is to first formulate a step-by-step system program plan. This master plan or program plan should fulfill two needs. First, it should be sufficiently detailed to serve as a long range blueprint for the total program and secondly, it should serve as a mechanism for obtaining continued top management support. The

---

*See Chapter 16.

development effort will have a much greater chance of survival if top management has more than just a vague understanding of what the system will eventually do for the organization.

The system program plan should be a living document which is updated frequently and circulated to those who are involved in or provide support to the program. At a minimum, the system program plan should contain the following:

1. *System Objectives*—System objectives should give a concise description of what the system is supposed to accomplish, and for whom. The system objectives should define the functions, disciplines and levels of management to be served by the system, as well as the types of information to be provided. One reason for establishing system objectives is to determine the scope and complexity of the system to be developed. It is especially important to avoid glittering generalities such as, "The system will provide management with all the information necessary to carry out their responsibilities." In some instances it is valuable to define the areas that *will not* be served by the system. This will help avert potential misunderstandings in the future, especially with organizational entities not directly involved in the project.

2. *The System Criteria*—Fairly comprehensive criteria must be established to define the system parameters. All the disciplines to be included in the system (i.e., planning, scheduling, estimating, accounting, cost management, material management, etc.) should be defined, as well as the level of detail of information that will be addressed by these disciplines. In effect, the system criteria establishes the philosophy by which the projects will be managed and defines, or provides boundaries for, the information and level of control needed to effectively manage these projects. *This criteria should accurately reflect the project management environment in which the system will operate.*

3. *The Work Plan*—The basic segments of work related to the design, development, implementation and maintenance of the system should be spelled out in broad terms. Also, the organizational groups responsible for doing the work must be identified.
   In the early stages of conceptualizing the system, development of a detailed work plan is of little value. This can be done after a comprehensive study is made to identify the system resources that currently exist in the organization and the new ones that must be developed.

4. *Schedule and Budget*—A general phasing schedule covering the major blocks of work and a gross overall budget should also be included in the system program plan. Here again, the main emphasis should focus on establishing the time and cost boundaries for the total program. Attempting to define more detailed schedules and budgets at this stage would be, for the most part, an exercise in wishful thinking.

It cannot be overstated that the most important step in the successful development of an effective information and control system is defining the nature of the system itself and the environment it must operate in. Establishing the program plan, as outlined above, is a good start in this direction; however, the real effort required to develop a comprehensive set of system objectives and system criteria will begin following a thorough study and analysis of the organization's *existing* system resources and project management methodology. This type of study will set the stage for development of the detailed work plans, budgets and schedules that will be used to carry out the program through actual system design, development and implementation.

PROGRAM SCOPE

A typical program for the development of a new or improved computer-based project information and control system will involve three distinct phases of work including:

- Phase I —Study and Analysis (Determining what we have now and what we need for the future.)
- Phase II —Design, Development and Implementation (Specify the system, build it, and actually apply it to a project.)
- Phase III—Documentation, Training, Test and Support (Ensure people know how to use the system; make it work using actual project data; and improve it as needed.)

The first phase of effort involves a study of the organization's existing information and system resources to determine what is presently available for use in building a computer-based project information system. Out of this analysis should come a list of systems and procedures that will need to be procured or developed. In addition, the project management approach or mode of operation for management of future projects should be established to identify the types of information resources that must be made available. This analysis must produce very comprehensive system criteria, as well as a preliminary description of the total project information system concept. The final output of the Phase I study and analysis effort should be the action plan which specifies how the recommendations should be carried out, by whom, when, and at what approximate cost. The flow chart given in Figure 25-3 shows the major activities and accomplishments to be realized in the three phases of the program. These will be discussed in detail later.

In the second phase of the program, efforts will concentrate on design, development, and implementation of the software, hardware and related procedures for the total system. Typically, during this phase of the program, studies are made of commercially available software and hardware which will meet specific project requirements. Appropriate analyses and cost trade-off studies will

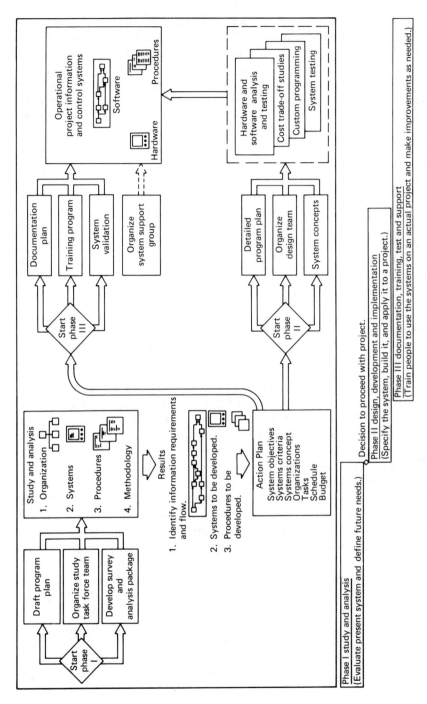

Figure 25-3. Major phases in development of a project information and control system.

be made to select those systems which lend themselves to the total project system concept. In addition, specific software packages will be defined and the related programming and coding will be accomplished. To the maximum extent possible, these systems will be operated in parallel with existing systems in order to subject them to real-life project environments. Generally, all new systems are tested in parallel with existing systems until such time as these systems are debugged, documented and the results verified. Only then will the systems be formally turned over to the using project organizations.

The third and final phase of the program, which will overlap the second phase, involves training all personnel who will use or be served by the system. Appropriate training sessions must be organized and seminars scheduled for all levels of management. In addition, all documentation should be finalized after each element of the system completes its validation test. Once the user's organizations are satisfied that the system fulfills their needs, the development team will phase out of the program.

This is a brief overview of the total program scope; however, to get a feel for the problems that must be faced in actually carrying out such an undertaking, it will be necessary to examine each program phase in some detail.

PHASE I—STUDY AND ANALYSIS

The Study Team

Determining the extent and value of the organization's existing systems and defining the system requirements in detail requires that personnel be designated to organize, direct and accomplish this effort. Obviously, a team of some type is in order. In most companies this assignment falls upon a committee which is organized for that specific purpose. This committee is most often comprised of part-time members from various departments including engineering, data processing, finance, and the project office.

Almost without exception, this committee will do a poor job, and for good reason! They have other, more immediate responsibilities, and are generally unschooled in the art of making a system survey and analysis. Experience has shown that the most successful approach is to organize a full-time task force team dedicated specifically to making a study, and providing recommendations and a proposed implementation plan. A typical team (see Figure 25-4) would include a program manager, who is specifically *responsible* for the work of the team, and several specialists with expertise in systems analysis, planning, scheduling, estimating, cost management, material management, etc. The size of the team can vary as new members are added to focus on specific topics; but, at a minimum, a core group of individuals should be identified as part of the project team until the study is completed. The team's program manager

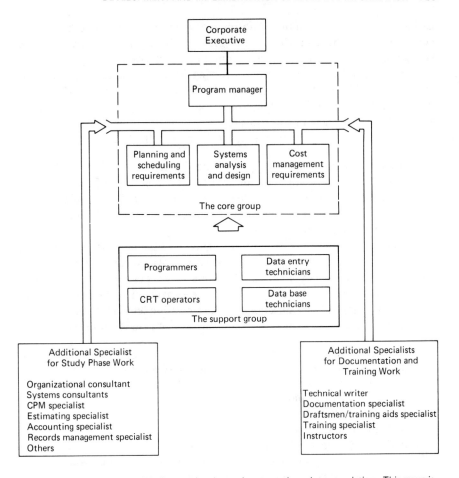

The Core Group is responsible for carrying the total program through to completion. This group is augmented by various specialists during all phases of the program. In addition, a support staff is organized to bring the system into actual operation. Selected members of the core group and the support group can be designated to maintain the system once it becomes operational.

Figure 25-4. The program team organization.

should report to a high level of management, in most large companies a Senior Vice President. The Senior Vice President should, in turn, be held *accountable* for the work of the study team.

Study Methodology

Once a program team is organized and committed to making the study, preparatory work is needed to ensure that the team will make an objective evaluation and collect the required information in an organized, systematic manner. To this end, the team will need to: map out the organizational elements to be included in the study; develop appropriate interview and questionnaire forms; and establish a mechanism for sorting out and evaluating all the information that will be collected. As shown in Figure 25-3, in Phase I the team's study and analysis work will focus on the organization, systems, procedures, and methodologies now in place to support project management.

A well organized survey plan would include the following:

1. *Memo of Introduction*—A brief memo should be directed to all those to be included in the study to advise them of the purpose of the study, the topics to be covered, and the length of time required. The memo should advise all participants of the importance of the effort and should be signed by top management.

2. *Survey Questionnaire*—A well designed questionnaire is invaluable for ensuring that all the appropriate topics are covered consistently from one interview to the next interview. The interviewers can utilize an outline or checklist, see Figure 25-5, to keep the conversation flowing along the required topics. The questionnaire can be completed after the meetings and, if necessary, follow-up discussions can be held to fill in the gaps.

The questionnaire should be designed to capture information on the following topics from the individual being interviewed:

- Responsibilities and functions of the unit.
- Interfaces with the unit.
- Primary work tasks.
- Data inputs needed to perform these tasks.
- Data outputs generated as a result of performing these tasks.
- Problems, requirements and suggestions.*

In addition, the questionnaire should investigate at least three major aspects of the organization including: a) information requirements and information flow, b) methods and procedures, and c) systems used by the organization. For all three of these major areas, specific questions should be developed. Inasmuch as a project information and control system is concerned primarily with the information that a unit needs in order to carry out its function, much effort must be devoted to mapping out this requirement. Simple input/output charts (see Figure 25-6) can be developed for each of the organizational units surveyed. These charts can then be connected (since the information outputs of one unit become the inputs

---

*Chapter 18 describes the way in which a linear responsibility chart may be used as a basis for obtaining this information in the systems design process.

INTERVIEWER		
NAME _____		WORK ORDER _____
DEPT. _____	PROJECT _____	FILE NO. _____
DATE _____		PAGE _____ OF _____
TIME START _____	CLIENT _____	
TIME STOP _____		

SURVEY OUTLINE & INSTRUCTIONS
(CHECK BLOCKS TO MONITOR PROGRESS OF THE DISCUSSION)

I. ORGANIZATIONAL ANALYSIS & INFORMATION FLOW

☐ 1. IDENTIFY ORGANIZATIONAL LEVEL & LOCATION

☐ 2. PRIMARY RESPONSIBILITIES OF THIS ORGANIZATION AS UNDERSTOOD BY THE INTERVIEWEE.

☐ 3. STRONGEST CAPABILITY AND/OR TALENT OF THIS ORGANIZATION

☐ 4. INTERFACES (INTERNAL & EXTERNAL)

☐ 5. ROUTINE TASKS PERFORMED (LIST)
　　SPECIAL ASSIGNMENTS (WHAT AND HOW OFTEN)

☐ 6. PROBLEMS

☐ 7. INPUTS (DATA/INFO) REQUIRED

☐ 8. OUTPUTS (DATA/INFO) PRODUCED

☐ 9. NEW IDEAS – PROBLEM SOLUTIONS

☐ 10. OTHER AREAS TO LOOK INTO

II. PROCEDURES ANALYSIS

☐ 1. WHAT PROCEDURES ARE USED (FORMAL AND/OR INFORMAL) HOW CLOSELY UTILIZED

☐ 2. EFFECTIVENESS OF THESE PROCEDURES

☐ 3. PROBLEMS

☐ 4. ADDITIONAL PROCEDURES REQUIRED (IDENTIFY)

☐ 5. IDEAS & SUGGESTIONS

III. SYSTEMS & METHODOLOGY

☐ 1. DEFINE SYSTEMS NORMALLY USED – COMPUTER BASED
　　　　　　　　　　　　　　　　 – MANUAL SYSTEMS

☐ 2. SYSTEMS UNDER DEVELOPMENT OR BEING CONSIDERED

☐ 3. MAJOR PROBLEM AREAS

☐ 4. IDEAS & SUGGESTIONS FOR SYSTEMS

IV. SPECIFIC QUESTIONS (SEE ATTACHED LIST)

Figure 25-5. Survey questionnaire.

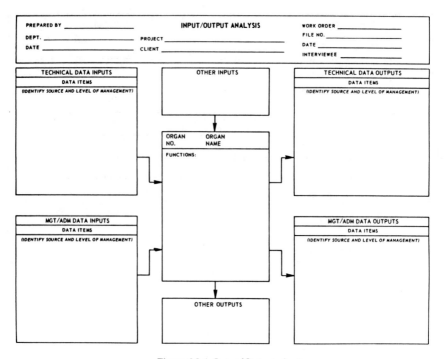

Figure 25-6. Input/Output chart.

of another unit) to develop a composite system information flow (see Figure 25-7). This total system information flow chart will then become an excellent tool for designing the total system logic.

3. *Survey Timetable and Score Card*—Every individual and/or area to be covered in the study should be identified and a fairly comprehensive timetable developed to be sure that the survey effort does not exceed the time allotted. It is important that the study team talk to everyone while management's interest in the project is still strong. Also, it is equally important that the results of the survey be catalogued while still fresh in the interviewers' minds. Thus, a simple matrix will not only ensure that all required areas are covered, but will also provide an evaluation of the effectiveness of the coverage.

Compiling the Findings

Armed with a well organized survey plan, the study team can proceed to conduct their interviews and review the organization's current systems, procedures and methodology for managing projects. As might be expected, information or systems studies are, at best, very subjective. The problem will be to separate

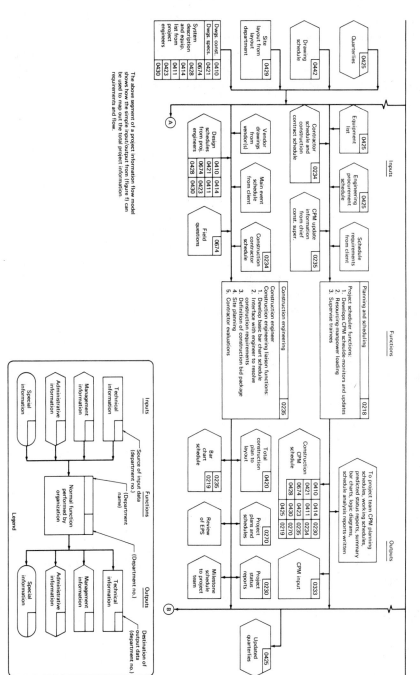

Figure 25-7. Constructing an information flow model for the project.

facts from opinions. To have some degree of confidence in the final results, efforts must be directed at evaluating all interview data on a consistent basis; otherwise, the investigators will fall into the trap of devising systems which respond to what the interviewers think people said, and not what the people actually did say. The following approach will help to minimize the subjective influences:

1. *Compile and Structure the Findings*—To ensure a high degree of consistency in evaluating information collected, the information should first be compiled by discipline and then by level of management. Once this is done, the information requirements should be further subdivided according to technical, management and administrative types of information needed to support each level of management and each discipline.
2. *Categorize the Results*—It is especially important to categorize the inputs obtained during the study to make a clear distinction between those things which are applicable to management information system (MIS) requirements and those which are not. The following three categories are suggested:
   a) Problems and requirements for the information system.
   b) Problems and requirements which are procedural in nature.
   c) Problems and requirements which are management or organizational in nature.
3. *Analysis*—After compiling the information and carefully categorizing all the facts, an analysis should be made from two distinct viewpoints. First, from the viewpoint of the organizational element (and the disciplines within these elements) and secondly, from the viewpoint of the different levels of management. The results of these two analyses should be consolidated to identify all common requirements that must be addressed by the system to be developed. From this, a priority list can be developed to specify the system development sequence.

Making Recommendations

If the study team has carefully organized and documented their efforts as outlined above, the team should be in a position to define the concept for a project information and control system which reflects the personality and unique requirements of their company. At a minimum, the study recommendations should identify:

1. The specific information resources required by:
   a) Each organization or function involved in the project.
   b) Each level of management within the company that will contribute to, or be affected by the project.

2. The new systems (hardware and software) that may have to be developed.
3. The existing systems that may have to be modified.
4. The existing systems that will be utilized.
5. The organizations that must contribute to the development effort.
6. The timetable for developing the total system.
7. A budget estimate.
8. An overview (pictorial flowchart) of the system concept.

The final recommendations should include some discussion of what the system will do to increase the effectiveness of the project management organization. Often there is an attempt to identify cost savings as a means for justifying system development. However, the value of a good project information and control system lies in its ability to enable a small team to manage something large and complex. Unfortunately, this is extremely difficult to quantify in terms of dollar savings.

From the foregoing it should be obvious that the Phase I Study and Analysis is the key to the eventual development of a truly effective project information and control system. Successful development of these systems can be assured to a large degree if the study team follows a well established approach of the type outlined here. Equally important, however, is the need to have a team composed of people who have worked in the project environment and know from experience the value and need for systems. These types of individuals, armed with a structured study and analysis methodology, should be able to produce the detailed information and plans necessary to start actual design of our project management information and control system.

PHASE II—DESIGN, DEVELOPMENT AND IMPLEMENTATION

In the first phase of our program considerable effort has been expended to carefully establish parameters for a project management information and control systems which will effectively function within a particular organizational environment. In addition, we have inventoried the existing systems and procedures and have attempted to evaluate these in terms of their effectiveness in supporting present and future project management requirements. Thus, we have developed a fairly detailed blueprint of what the future system will look like, what it will do for management, and how long and how much it will take to get there. To the system analyst, most of this work would be categorized under the heading of the functional specification. Regardless of what it is called, the purpose is the same, namely to spell out as meticulously as possible all of the user requirements prior to actually designing the system. These user requirements should identify the particular features and capabilities of the systems which must function within a given industry, organization, and management

PROJECT MANAGEMENT FUNCTIONS		BASIC ACTIVITIES INVOLVED IN THESE PROJECT MANAGEMENT FUNCTIONS
1. Project Objectives	—	Define the cost, schedule and performance goals for the project.
2. Work Definitions	—	Define work task to be done and the organizations responsible.
3. Scheduling	—	Define the sequence for doing the work and the time constraints.
4. Budgeting	—	Define the resources (men, money, material available for doing the work.
5. Baseline	—	Define the parameters for measuring cost, schedule, performance accomplishments.
6. Monitoring/Reporting	—	Define how progress will be tracked (the events and level of detail) and how this will be reported.
7. Analysis	—	Define how and who will assess progress against plans.
8. Corrective Action	—	Define who is responsible for corrective action, how it is to be implemented and when.

The Project Management System must provide the people, policies, procedures, systems (manual and computer) to accomplish the basic task involved in each of the eight Project Management functions.

Figure 25-8. Minimum requirements for project management systems.

environment. However, in spite of the wide range of applications for these systems, all project management systems should have the capabilities to support the basic requirements given in Figure 25-8.

It should be noted that the requirements identified in Figure 25-8 hold true for large sophisticated computer based systems as well as simple manual systems. Irrespective of the degree of sophistication of the system, it must be designed to support the project management process.

Design Concepts for Project Management Information and Control Systems

As noted earlier the "systems" discussed here involve people, procedures, computer software and hardware integrated into a unified approach to processing data to produce information to effect a timely management decision process. Note that we do not merely talk about generating information to support the

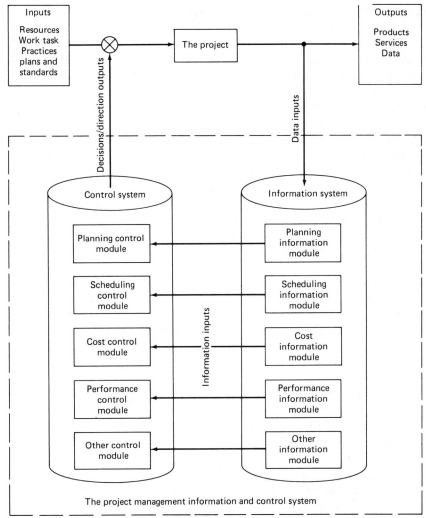

The information system receives data from the project and evalutes the plans, schedules, cost, and performance of the project against established plans and goals. Information is developed relative to the variance between what the project planned to do and what it has actually done. This information is fed to the control system. The control system evaluates the variances for various project parameters against established standards to determine if progress to date is acceptable. The outputs of the control system are decisions/directions which redirect resources, work task, practices and plans and standards of the project.

Figure 25-9. Project information flow.

decision making process, but rather we infer that the decision making process must be forced to take place as a result of the systems information outputs. The implication here is quite important, because for the system concept to truly work for the project management process, the people involved in the process must be an integral part of the input, output, feedback cycle depicted in the cybernetic diagram shown back in Figure 25-1. This means that our project management information and control system must include, in addition to the procedures and systems for generating information, procedures and systems which ensure that decisions or actions are generated as a result of the information inputs. A general concept for doing this is depicted in Figure 25-9.

The system concept for project management information and control given in Figure 25-9 utilizes a one-for-one modular concept to integrate information and management control. That is to say, for every specialized module we create (computer-based or manual) to process data and generate information relative to a specialized discipline or topic, we also create a module for project control action. These control modules identify the people (organizational functions) involved and the process that must be initiated as a result of the outputs of the information module. Thus, in designing our "systems" we must focus on the two unique requirements of information and control. Some suggestions for the methodology to follow in designing these elements of our system are discussed in the next section. However, an advantage of using a modular approach to our design is that we can build a system which can eventually support a wide range of project management requirements.

The system shown in Figure 25-10 addresses a wide range of project management requirements. These include the technical requirements (Group I Module), the usual cost, schedule, performance requirements (Group II Module), and the predictive requirements (Group III Module) of a project. In this example we show the type of system which might need to be developed for a project environment dealing with large scale, high risk, high cost, technical or business development undertakings. By utilizing the modular building block approach, the design effort can focus on the priority areas and make these operational in tune with management's needs and availability of resources. The point that needs to be stressed here is that it is extremely important to conceptualize the total system in the beginning, before starting actual design, otherwise there is a high possibility that the resulting product will be a hodge-podge of poorly related systems. The design process should begin only when the objectives and the design concepts have been carefully defined, understood and agreed to by all.

Design of the Information System

A modern management information system normally consists of two major elements, see Figure 25-11. The first is a data management system, which is the

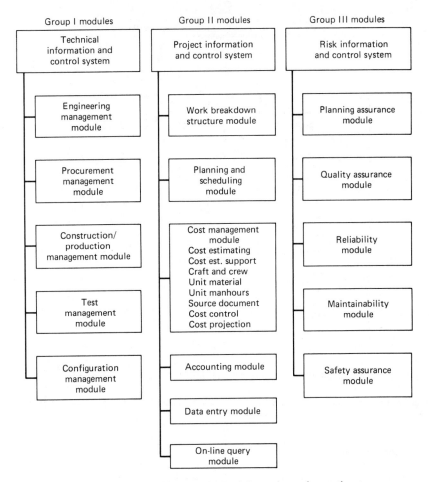

Figure 25-10. The project management information and control system.

heart of the system, and is comprised of a series of data base-related software packages which "manage" (store and retrieve) the project's data on an integrated and logical basis. The second major element of the system consists of a series of computer software packages, or modules, which provide the means for generating information on specific functions of the project. For a project management application these modules will typically address planning, scheduling, estimating, cost management, project accounting, and so on. Additional modules can be utilized to produce information on almost any aspect of the project that management may wish to control. The primary objective of the information system module is to organize, collect, store and process data quickly and efficiently to produce meaningful information which will advise management on the project's status, trends, and potential problem areas.

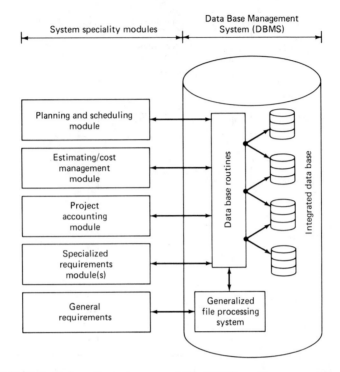

Figure 25-11. Project information system concept. The DBMS provides a convenient method for managing all Project Data on a logical basis. The individual application programs process the data to produce "information" or new data. This "information" is directed to management and/ or to the DBMS for use by other modules.

Elements of the Information System

For project management some of the basic elements of the information system that will need to be designed are described as follows:

1. *Planning and Scheduling Module*—Effective management of a large or complex project calls for a systematic method of depicting the time sensitive relationships and the interdependency between such functions as engineering design, procurement, operations, testing and so on. Normally, the Planning and Schedule Module utilizes Critical Path Method (CPM)* scheduling techniques with resource leveling and target scheduling to provide the tools for planning and monitoring the project. The information generated by the project CPM also provides the keys for more detailed monitoring and analysis of subtasks within various disci-

---

*See Chapter 16.

plines. This is done by creating data base files for specific work tasks or requirements of individual project disciplines. Because of the integrated nature of the data base files themselves, the information can be used to support other modules. Thus, drawing lists, specification lists, purchasing schedules and all types of cost information can be interrelated and used by all the project's organizations (engineering, purchasing, operations, tests, etc.) to manage their specific tasks as well as by the project management organization to overview the total effort.

2. *Project Accounting Module*—The project will require a formalized method to monitor, record and report all costs, and to develop the final cost records upon completion of the project. In the Project Accounting Module this is accomplished through computer-based systems which, together with predefined operating procedures, produces periodic reports and provides for development of actual cost records as the project progresses. Typical outputs for this type of module might be:

a) *Commitments and Invoice Record of Purchase Orders and Contracts*—Used to determine the cost status of each purchase order and contract, and through appropriate coding techniques, to keep track of change orders against these orders.

b) *Statement of Commitments and Recorded Expenditures*—Provides a quick reference to the status of all purchase orders and contracts including base amounts, change orders, recorded cost, remaining commitments and retentions.

c) *Project Ledger*—Detailed cost record for the project.

d) *Change Order Status Reports*—Provides information relative to all change orders associated with each purchase order and contract.

e) *Statement of Recorded Expenditures by Account*—A list, at the account code level, of all actual expenditures, current estimates and current balances for the project.

3. *Estimating/Cost Management Modules**—Effective cost management for the project requires that the system provide an efficient method for making comparisons between current and budget estimates and scheduled and actual cash flow. This is accomplished through the computer-based Estimating/Cost Management Modules and the interface which this module maintains through data base with the Accounting and Planning and Scheduling Modules. Typical outputs of the Estimating/Cost Management Modules are:

a) *Detailed Estimates*—Detailed estimates in account code sequences.

b) *Summary Estimates*—Detailed estimates summarized into work packages.

c) *Updated Estimate/Cost Report*—Updated estimate, at the account

---

*See Chapter 19.

level, providing a comparison of the new estimate with the previous estimate for each account.

d) *Functional Cost Report*—Cost reporting by major functional categories, i.e., material purchase orders, installation purchase orders, field purchase orders, etc.

e) *Outstanding Commitments Report*—A comprehensive profile showing the total, actual and outstanding commitments against each purchase order.

f) *Forecast of Cash Requirements (Summary and Detail)*—Cash forecast reports at various levels and detailed at monthly, quarterly, and yearly increments.

In addition to the above basic modules, many other modules may be developed to address specialized needs of a project, such as labor resources, materials inventory and controls, document indexing and retrieval, health, safety and environmental records, etc. Any requirement that can be defined by tangible data elements can be designed and integrated into the total system in building block fashion. Since a data base management approach is at the heart of the system, the system designers can address all future project needs with relative ease, once these needs are identified.

The actual design and development work involved in the system described above requires a combination of activities including study, evaluation, selection and procurement of commercially available software packages, as well as custom design and programming of specialized modules or application packages. Because large projects require fairly sophisticated computer-based systems to collect, process and disseminate the desired information and because these projects involve many management functions, the system must handle information on an integrated, logical basis. This is why data base management system selection is the first step in system development.

There are a number of excellent data base management systems (DMBS) currently available on the market. The goal is to select the one most suited to the user's needs. To this end, the user will have to develop some type of evaluation criteria. At a minimum, these criteria must address in detail the following:

1. *Technical Capabilities and Requirements of the DBMS*—core requirements, interfaces, security, performance statistics, editing features, utilities available, batch/on-line, maintenance, etc.

2. *Flexibility of the DBMS*—control feature, data access, languages supported, data storage devices, linkage capabilities, search capabilities, etc.

3. *Standardization*—comply with various standards that have been developed for data bases.

4. *Resource Support Requirements*—internal and external support requirements, documentation, etc.
5. *Design Features*—data levels, indexing techniques, networking features, etc.

It is strongly recommended that the user carefully establish his criteria prior to consulting with vendors or other users. Otherwise, the user will be barraged by bewildering terminology and an array of philosophies on DBMS. It is difficult to provide specific guidelines in this area because individual needs vary so widely. However, common sense dictates that the user should not purchase a DBMS more sophisticated than he needs or has the *capability* to use and maintain.

The same situation is true with respect to development of the Planning and Scheduling Modules. For large projects involving design, procurement, and construction, CPM (Critical Path Method) networks are a very popular (and very effective) way of depicting all of the project's major requirements. For large research and development projects involving activities whose outcomes are doubtful, PERT (Program Evaluation and Review Technique) can be utilized most effectively. Since PERT can establish the probability of meeting deadlines it can be helpful in the development of alternative plans. Fortunately, there are many excellent CPM/PERT software packages on the market today to satisfy a variety of requirements. Here again, the goal is to define the needs of the individual project, develop an appropriate criteria and begin an investigation to choose the package which offers the features, options and capabilities most closely suited to management's needs.

The decision to procure and modify software packages to meet a project's individual requirements versus the prospect of developing a system from scratch will depend on the uniqueness of the system requirements and the availability of system design and programming support. Certainly, it does not pay to design a DBMS or a CPM/PERT software package, in view of the number of well designed systems currently on the market. But, by the same token, it may not be practical to try and modify someone else's estimating system to suit a particular project's cost control requirements.

Design of the Control System

The design of the information modules for our system essentially involves the development of procedures for collecting, storing and processing data to produce useful information in a timely manner. Many of these procedures will be instructions for the computer (programs). Hence a good portion of our information system design efforts deal with selecting the appropriate software packages or designing new packages. Unfortunately, when it comes to the control element of our system, there are few in the way of "canned" packages that are available for our use, primarily because it is generally assumed that if managers are given the information they need, they will automatically initiate the appropriate action to "control" the situation. If we are going to devise a project management system which informs and controls as an integral part of the total project function, we cannot rely on a tacit understanding of what management is expected to do. The mechanism for control must be built into the system and it must be activated automatically by the appropriate system stimuli. To establish the parameters for design of the control modules of our system, it is necessary to define exactly what we mean by control.

Control

The purpose of control is to ensure that events conform to plan. Controlling involves locating or identifying deviations from plan and taking appropriate action to ensure desired results. Furthermore, control is concerned with the present and involves regulation of what is happening *now*. In a large measure we are concerned with regulating present activities in order to influence future outcomes.

For a project manager, the importance and the need to control are quite clear. The project manager is the one individual totally responsible for accomplishing project objectives on time and within budget. However, to be able to control, the project manager must have some frame of reference to measure against and he must have some way of determining when he deviates from this reference. This brings us to the essential elements of control.

Elements of Control

There are four essential elements involved in control, and these provide the framework for any good project control system. These elements of control are:

1. Setting Objectives.
2. Reporting.
3. Evaluating.
4. Corrective Action.

Obviously, when we talk of controlling something we assume that we have some predefined target or goal. For a project these targets or goals are usually defined in terms of schedule, cost, technical and quality objectives or requirements. Certainly, the project manager must know what he is trying to accomplish (i.e. get a power plant designed and constructed; design and implement an MIS system, etc.). His problem is to regulate the activities, resources and events to accomplish the technical, cost and schedule goals defined in the project plan. This can be done with appropriate status visibility and timely feedback. Thus, he needs an information system which reports on all the important facets of a project, which brings us to the second element of control, which is reporting.

Since the act of controlling is concerned with the present, the project manager needs a reporting system which is time sensitive. That is, the reporting system must identify problems and requirements in a manner which enables the project manager to make decisions and give direction while there is still time to make a positive change. If the reporting system can only provide feedback considerably after the fact, as a matter of history, then the project manager cannot control his project. Thus, at the heart of control is an information system which gives timely visibility to significant project events. This is why it is so important to have an information system specifically for the project management process.

The third essential element of control is the interpretation and evaluation of the information generated by the information system. This is extremely important because it is the basis for taking corrective action. We know from experience that problems in their early stages of development are seldom black or white. Thus, careful evaluation of indicators, or trends, in project cost, schedule or technical parameters is extremely vital to the whole process of control. Here again a comprehensive project information system can provide the project manager with a powerful tool for spotlighting early problem areas and requirements. Of course, once having identified a problem, the project manager must take prompt corrective action. This is the fourth and final element of control.

Corrective action means that the project manager has identified a situation which is going to cause a deviation from a desired goal and does something about it. Thus, the project manager must develop a number of alternative approaches to solving the problem and he must select the best approach. In effect, the project manager will examine his options and implement a course of action that best utilizes the resources at his command.

Our interest in designing the control system is to ensure that we have established the appropriate interface between the information modules and those who control and that we have put into place the procedures which will ensure that appropriate action is taken as a result of the information process.

Overview of the Control System

A general scheme for the control element of our system is given in Figure 25-12. The basic function of the control module is to receive inputs from the information system relative to the current status of project activities and accomplishments. Generally, these inputs will be in terms of the cost, schedule and performance aspects of the project. Each discrete status input is measured against the previously established project goal, for that measurement period,

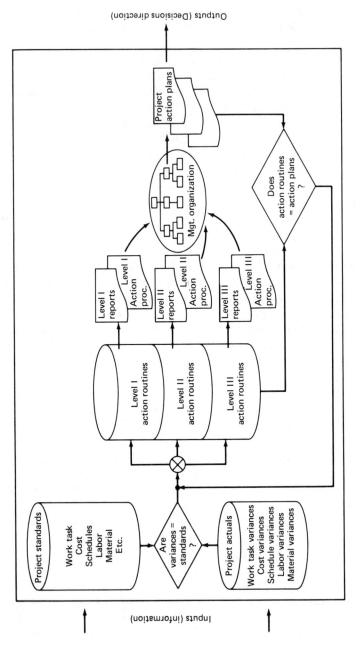

Figure 25-12. Project control system concept.

to determine if a variance exists. In simple terms the control module is asking: "How well are we doing against what we had planned to do?" When deviations are identified they are compared against standards which have been established by management. Again, a new set of deviations are identified. We shall call these deviations "action level deviations." That is, the magnitude of the deviations from our standards will automatically identify the level of management responsible for taking corrective action and the time available for initiating this action. Routines are built into the control module so that, if action is not taken, or is not satisfactory by the next reporting period, the module automatically triggers the problem up to the next level of management. The whole process is repeated until the problems are resolved or the problem reaches the highest level of management.

The tangible actions that can be initiated by a project manager to change the course of events of his project are surprising few. Basically, these actions involve manipulation or controlling the following:

1. *Resources*—The allocation of resources (men, money, material, facilities, and time) to the project participants (a powerful mechanism for control).
2. *Scope of Work*—Increasing or decreasing the amount of work or the type of work to be done.
3. *Practices*—Establishing or changing the methods, techniques, policies, procedures, systems or tools used on the project.
4. *Plans and Standards*—The degree and level of effectiveness of control is determined by the project plans and standards established. These may be changed or modified during the life of the project.

Thus, the final outputs of the control module are decisions by project management (at all levels) which essentially deal with one or more of the above four factors.

Once having designed the information modules and the control modules so that they contain the systems and procedures which enable them to function as a unified system within a specific project environment, consideration must be given to the methodology for implementation.

Implementation

Management information system text books offer a variety of schemes for putting a new system into operation. These include: a) running parallel systems, b) operating a pilot system, c) using the phase-in/phase-out technique, or d) employing the cut-off method (burning the bridges). In most project environments, it is usually a matter of operating parallel systems until the new system proves itself. If no computer-based system presently exists, the other alternative is to run a pilot system until all the refinements are made. This then becomes the real system.

In any event, the system must be implemented in a real project environment and the test of the system effectiveness is whether or not management is able to use it to *make decisions.* Unfortunately, experience has shown that this has not been the case for most new systems. And this is why the next phase of the program is the most important of all.

PHASE III—DOCUMENTATION, TRAINING, TEST AND SUPPORT

Documentation Requirements

One task generally disliked by system designers is documentation. Yet, in terms of the effective utilization of the total system, this is probably the most important task to be accomplished. It is especially important that proper system documentation be developed to meet the needs of the system users and those who will maintain and, more than likely, eventually enhance the system. In this regard, four distinct levels of documentation have been identified as follows:

1. *System Documentation*—These documents are designed to provide management with an understanding of how the computer system works at all levels. It will summarize all interfaces, files, and the logic connecting all jobs, providing an overview of the general concepts, features, capabilities and constraints.
2. *Program Documentation*—Program Documentation provides the programmers and analysts with an understanding of the relation between their own work and the entire effort. This procedure provides a definition of the step-by-step logic developed within each program.
3. *Operations Documentation*—The Operations Documentation dictates the relationship between the functional tasks and the procedures, and establishes a time sequence. It dictates the responsibility for each task, providing a procedure to determine all action taken following a request. This procedure must contain the necessary information to process job steps.
4. *User Documentation*—This section provides a formal description of all functions necessary to input data into the system. Relevant information for the control and processing of source documents and reports should be described.

Actual development of the above required documentation should start quite early in the design effort. In fact, documentation should be a mandatory effort in parallel with system design and development. Ideally, the program manager should devise a documentation checklist which specifies the four levels of documents associated with each major system element or module and provides a timetable for the rough draft, final draft, and fully released documents. Generally speaking, the rough draft documents, which may consist of simple outlines, will suffice throughout the early design effort. However, by the time the systems are fairly well defined (during the program development and implementation stages), this documentation should begin to evolve into descriptive manuals. Once the validation and demonstration tests of the systems have been completed, the revision and publication of final system documentation manuals should be a routine, straight-forward task.

A special note of caution is in order relative to documentation. In any program requiring a year or more to complete, it is highly unlikely that the original team will remain intact. Personnel turnover among programmers is inevitable; therefore, it is absolutely vital to maintain a consistent, strong documentation trail throughout the project.

Training Considerations

In similar fashion, training should start very early in the program. A common error is to wait until all the bugs are totally out of the system before attempting to train system users. The system will have greater acceptance and be utilized more effectively if all levels of management are gradually made to understand the philosophy and mechanics of the system. This can be accomplished by handling the training program in stages as follows:

- *1st Stage Training—System Philosophy.* A series of orientation seminars should be planned to explain to management the role of computer-based information and control systems in the management of large projects. These seminars should focus on the types of information that can be provided to all levels of management and dwell on how the system is used to tie together all the project functions. It is particularly appropriate to organize workshop sessions to get the various levels of management to critique prototype reports and system approaches. This feedback can be used to enhance the actual system design work.
- *2nd Stage Training—System Capabilities.* This stage of training will discuss the "nuts and bolts" of the system and focus on middle management and project specialists. Training will deal with specifics and should address such items as development of the CPM network schedule and the report outputs of the Planning and Scheduling Module, Estimating Module and so on. Those organizations that will depend on the system for regular data and reports must be made to understand what type of information they can and cannot get from the system.

- *3rd Stage Training—System Operations.* Formalized training must be provided to those who will operate and maintain the system. Generally, this type of training is directed to technicians and system engineers and will include specialized courses offered by equipment manufacturers and software vendors. This portion of the training program should also focus on standard operational procedures associated with the system that may be developed by the in-house MIS organization.
- *4th Stage Training—System Utilization.* This stage of training should be a natural follow-up from the first stage or System Philosophy training discussed above. A very strong attempt should be made to get project management, selected middle management and top management involved in seminar-type sessions to give them an opportunity to see first hand how the system can be used to enhance their functions and capabilities. Very carefully structured "what if" type problems can be used to illustrate use of the computer-based information system in the quick evaluation of a number of alternatives or options to arrive at practical project decisions.

Obviously, the scope and level of the training to be provided will be somewhat dependent on budget restrictions and time availability. Nevertheless, money spent for training purposes will help to dispel the mystique surrounding the computer-based system and increase the likelihood that the system will be implemented and utilized successfully.

System Validation

The last major milestone in the project information and control system development should be a validation test. This test should not be confused with the unit test that system designers or programmers will perform to check out the software packages. A validation test should cover all aspects of the system operation and utilization in a real life project environment. This includes everything from data collection, receipt and utilization of the final output report, and subsequent management action. A formal test plan should be written and, at a minimum, this test plan must address all of the system criteria defined in the system program plan. If the program manager has been conscientiously keeping his program plan up to date, this should be a fairly straightforward effort.

Actual formal validation testing may be spread over a long period of time, especially if the system is developed and brought into actual use one module at a time. The program manager and system designers must objectively assess the results of each test and determine if they are within the established criteria. Obviously, there will always be some revisions and improvements that are desirable, but the program manager must be resolute and selective and ensure that the system is useable in a timely manner.

System Support

A final word is in order relative to the long term use of computer-based project information and control systems. While these systems are complex and costly to develop, this cost is small in comparison to the cost of the projects to be managed and the benefits to be derived from proper use of the systems. To ensure that the system is used effectively, management must take an additional step and provide a full-time staff of personnel dedicated totally to maintaining, supporting, improving and constantly educating the user with regard to system capabilities. Otherwise, the system's effectiveness will diminish and reams of unread computer reports will begin to pile up on the corner of the project manager's desk.

SUMMARY

As projects become larger and more complex, the need increases for systems which provide for the systematic management of project information and action. These systems should be designed to function within a particular organizational environment and must reflect the unique project management requirements of that organization.

It is important to address the information system and the control system as two separate but highly dependent components of a total integrated computer-based project management system. In the design of the information system, the focus is on the procedures and techniques for collecting, storing and processing data to produce information concerning project plans, schedules, cost, and performance parameters. In the control system the goal is the development of procedures and routines for evaluating plans against actuals to define the deviations or variances in plans, schedules, cost, and performance, the assessment of the acceptability of these variances (evaluated against some predefined standards) and the systematic development and implementation of action plans by the appropriate organizational units to produce decisions and/or directions which attempt to correct the project's deviations from plan.

Actual design, development and implementation of an integrated system should follow a well defined project methodology. The first step in this process involves making a comprehensive analysis of what is required in the way of information resources and control procedures to make project management function successfully within a particular organization environment. Once this analysis is completed, the actual design and development of the system(s) can be initiated. Design and development involves procurement of specialized software packages and/or design of new packages, as well as the development of the procedures for management action. The eventual success of the new systems will depend to a large degree on how accurately they meet the requirements specifications (as defined in the initial study), how well the systems have been documented, and how adequately the using organizations have been trained to apply these systems to the actual project environment. The true value of a project information and control system will be realized only when it enables a relatively small project management organization to successfully plan, direct and control a complex, expensive, high risk undertaking.

BIBLIOGRAPHY

Articles

Baugh, Eddie W., and Scamell, Dr. Richard W. "Team Approach to Systems Analysis." *Journal of Systems Management* (April 1975) 32–35.

Brown, Foster. "The Systems Development Process." *Journal of Systems Management* (December 1977) 34–39.

Chapman, Charles H. et al. "Project Cost Controls for Research, Development And Demonstration Projects." *PMI Proceedings* (October 1979) 53–63.

Clarke, William, "The Requirements For Project Management Software: A Survey Of PMI Members." *PMI Proceedings* (October 2979) 71–79.

Cullingford, Graham; Mawdesley, Michael J.; and Chandler, Robert L. "Design And Implementation Of An Integrated Cost And Schedule System For The Construction Industry." *PMI Proceedings* (October 1977) 390–397.

Finneran, Thomas R. "Data Base Systems Design Guidelines." *Journal of Systems Management* (March 1978) 26–30.

Gildersleeve, Thomas R. "Optimum Program Structure Documentation Tool." *Journal of Systems Management* (March 1978) 6–11.

Herzog, John P. "System Evaluation Technique For Users." *Journal of Systems Management* (May 1975) 30–35.

Mattiace, John M. "Applied Cybernetics Within R&D." *Journal of Systems Management* (December 1972) 32–36.

Miller, Earl J. "Chapter 9—Project Information Systems And Controls." in *Planning, Engineering, and Construction of Electric Power Generation Facilities,* edited by Jack H. Willenbrock and H. Randolph Thomas. (New York: John Wiley & Sons, Inc., 1980).

Niwa, Kiyoshi et al. "Development of A 'Risk' Alarm System For Big Construction Projects." *PMI Proceedings* (October 1979) 221–229.

Ramsaur, William F., and Smith, John D. "Project Management Systems Tailored For Selective Project Management Approach." *PMI Proceedings* (October 1978) IV-A.1–IV-A.7.

Ross, Ronad G. "Evaluating Data Base Management Systems." *Journal of Systems Management* (January 1976) 30–35.

Tuman, Jr., John. "The Problems And Realities Involved In Developing An Effective Project Information And Control System." *PMI Proceedings* (October 1977) 279–293.

Wilkinson, Joseph W. "Guidelines For Designing Systems." *Journal of Systems Management* (December 1974) 36–40.

Books

Archibald, Russel D. *Managing High-Technology Programs And Projects.* (New York: John Wiley & Sons, Inc., 1976).

Ashby, W. Ross, *An Introduction To Cybernetics.* (London: Methuen & Co. Ltd., 1964).

Carlsen, Robert D. and Lewis, James A. *The Systems Analysis Workbook: A Complete Guide To Project Implementation And Control.* (New Jersey: Hall, Inc., 1980).

Cleland, David I., and King, William R. *Systems Analysis And Project Management.* 3rd edition (New York: McGraw-Hill, 1983).

Fuchs, Walter Robert. *Cybernetics For The Modern Mind*. Translated by K. Kellner. (New York: Macmillan Co., 1970).

Katzan, Jr., Harry. *Computer Data Management And Data Base Technology*. (New York: Van Nostrand Reinhold Company, 1975).

Kerzner, Harold. *Project Management: A Systems Approach To Planning, Scheduling and Controlling*. (New York: Van Nostrand Reinhold Company, 1979).

Martin, Charles C. *Project Management: How To Make It Work*. (New York: AMACOM, 1976).

Murdick, Robert G., and Ross, Joel E. *Information Systems For Modern Management*. (New Jersey: Prentice-Hall, Inc., 1971).

Myers, Glenford J. *Reliable Software Through Composite Design*. (New York: Petrocelli/Charter, 1975).

O'Brien, James J. *Scheduling Handbook*. (New York: McGraw-Hill, 1969).

Orlicky, Joseph. *The Successful Computer System Its Planning, Development, And Management In A Business Enterprise*. (New York: McGraw-Hill, 1969).

Prothro, Vivian C. *Information Management Systems Data Base Primer*. (New York: Petrocelli/Charter, 1976).

Section VII

Behavioral Dimensions of Project Management

This section focuses on the important behavioral dimensions of project management.

In Chapter 26, David H. Morton relates the behavioral sciences to the pragmatic job of the project manager, who must accomplish objectives by working through others in the absence of the legal authority to order them to do as he wishes.

In Chapters 27 and 28, Dennis P. Slevin discusses motivation and leadership in relation to the project manager. In these chapters he provides diagnostic tools that enable an individual to assess his own "motivation to manage" and style of leadership.

In Chapter 29, Raymond E. Hill addresses the management of social conflict from the standpoint of the personality conflicts that inevitably arise when important activities are being pursued. He uses the Myers-Briggs Type Indicator (MBTI) to address differences in problem-solving styles and how differences in such styles also affect the effectiveness with which project teams function.

In Chapter 30, Thomas E. Miller discusses the management of change in terms of teamwork. He views resistance to change as a failure of teamwork and describes a case study of a large urban fire department.

In the last chapter of this section, David L. Wilemon and Bruce N. Baker discuss some major research findings regarding the human element in project management. This chapter is particularly useful to the project manager who is experiencing some problems managing this aspect of the project.

26. Project Manager, Catalyst to Constant Change, A Behavioral Analysis

David H. Morton*

INTRODUCTION

The Project Manager finds himself in most instances in a unique position, with limited budgets, a tight time frame, a complex organizational environment of many disciplines and functions. This chapter investigates the ramifications of the Project Manager's position as catalyst acting, interacting and reacting to the constant changes which come to him from his province, his people, his position and his project.

Management is the art of accomplishing physical objectives through people. Technical knowledge is not enough, for every managerial decision has behavioral consequences. McGregor (1)† states that successful management depends significantly upon the ability to predict and control human behavior. The Project Manager must manipulate the technical elements through the human elements to obtain his project objectives.

The environment of project management has constantly expanded—as the size and complexity of projects has increased. High inflation, speed of new technology changes, greater variables due to increased short falls, and other unpredictables have made the impact on any project a constant changing factor. Project Management is defined by Jenett (2) as the managing and directing of timing and quantity of resources, skills and knowledge to complete a particular endeavor in an orderly, economical manner and meet established objectives in time, dollars and technical results. The project element has been delineated as crossing organizational lines, having a specific beginning and end-

*David H. Morton is the Director of Design and Construction in CF Southern Region, Inc., Houston, Texas. His experience includes working as a general contractor for 8 years in engineering and Sales with Bethlehem Steel, and in project management on the Houston Center project for ten years. Mr. Morton has a Bachelor of Architectural Engineering degree from the University of Pennsylvania, and an M.B.A. from the University of Houston.
†Numbered references are given at the end of this chapter.

ing, and is unique rather than a repetition of a previous effort which can work against budgets and schedules. Management, in its purest element, is the planning, organizing, control, command and coordination of the activities of the human system to achieve objectives.

The Project Manager must turn his staff into a real team, a group which works well and is enthusiastic and responsive and which pulls for the company and the project and not merely each for himself. How can team members be led to understand their joint as well as their individual functions in the enterprise so that responsibility is best met and authority most effectively exercised? How can this be done in terms of managerial control and the carrying out of company plans and policy? The more new people, the more problems of coordination, communication and cooperation. In the past, managerial control rested on the authority-obedience relationships between the manager and his subordinates. The executive had full authoritarian control. However the Project Manager must provide an environment for productivity. However, tight control has the effect of limiting rather than stimulating productivity. The Project Manager must learn the limiting powers of control by coercion, for such control can cause conflict, apathy and resistance. Productivity and profits require teamwork and the management of people—not just the handling of machines, materials and money. The task is one of reshaping the team's policy and managerial approach to fit the body of knowledge produced by the behavioral science in researches which show how people can be motivated to perform their best. The use of this body of knowledge means looking into the authoritarian attitudes of most organizations. It means changing present practices so that conflict will give way to cooperation. The first step is for the manager who manages others to take a close look at himself. He must examine his attitudes, recognize his inadequacies and failings and then reshape them into new insight and skill.

Into the team effort of project management, each individual brings a predetermined set of values, attitudes and beliefs that control the actions and reactions to their own motivation and the perception of their part in the team efforts. It is through the human elements that the day-to-day operations are or are not accomplished. It is the human elements that are the source of most problems. Individuals' needs, perceptions, motivations and satisfactions influence how well they perform, how loyal they are to the organization or team and how valuable they become. Successful management depends on the employees' good will which, in turn, depends upon the relationship between the individual and the organization, and must take into account employees' natural motives and desires.

What are the behavioral sciences? A definition of behavioral science is a body of systemized knowledge concerning how humans behave, the relationship between that behavior and the total environment, and why people behave as they do. When the term scientific is used, the connotation is that there are available some definite laws that can be applied to substitute for hunch and guesswork.

Management is more properly concerned with the behavior of people. This concept can be simplified if we use the same line of thinking as that used in the physical sciences: the relationship of cause and effect. When it is found through experimentation that with certain causes, the same effect is obtained and variations in the causes bring about different effects, a law can be developed. Cause and effect also relate to management problems, but the number of variables is much greater. The problem is to identify both cause and effect and their interrelationships. Much of the confusion in management applications comes from the prolixity of causes and effects. It is the development and analysis of cause and effect that is the new frontier of management.

The most important single factor that has led to the interest in the behavioral sciences is the need for the development of a management science. As a science, it has to be of universal significance in its processes, models and methods. Hence, the emerging management will be an applied science, standing approximately in relation to the behavioral sciences and certain social sciences, as medicine stands with respect to the biological and certain physical sciences.

Most of the important developments in the field of Project Management have been in the technical aspects of the organizational system. The tools and techniques developed have greatly aided in the success of many projects. However, management in general and project management in particular, is the obtaining of desired results through people. Recent surveys by Alderman (3) show that top management places the human aspects of management as the second highest "should have element" in their work requirements. Middle management places working efficiently with individuals as their top requirement. Engineers in the same survey place human relations skills as second in their development needs. Baker, Fisher and Murphy (4) list the factors affecting success of project management and note many behavioral aspects from the perceived success of the project, to how the manager related to people, client and team members. Industry Week (5) noted that the future would see great increases in professional workers and managers with a decrease in non-technical and manufacturing personnel. Most of the research referred to in this chapter is directed toward the professional worker.

Looking ahead in business, major trends that affect human resources appear to include improving of economic position of employees who have climbed the ladder of status, extending the role of government; the growing role of union block power; exploding technology revolution, and larger and more complex projects. For a greater knowledge of human behavior, it is necessary to study all of the inter-personal relationships of individuals, groups, leaders and their environmental situations.

SITUATION

The situation in which the Project Manager may find himself is rarely clear and concise. Internally, depending on the project, the team members and the organization, and externally depending on the environments which can exert change on his operation—including governments (local, state, national or international), communities, clients, stockholders, unions, employees, managers—the Project Manager is surrounded by environments that are dynamic and constantly changing.

The functional areas of many companies, such as engineering, manufacturing (whether a product or a construction project), finance, research and development or marketing, each are within themselves complex and dynamic. Changes within the smallest functional subdivision can, as it expands through the compounded dynamic environmental situation, cause a change upon the Project Manager's project. Gordon (6) lists the management of project contingencies as engineering, material and equipment deliveries, component reliability, quantity variances, extended work weeks, productivity, workmanship, labor relations, and escalated interest rates.

Bass (7) notes that the organizational goals are constantly dynamic with time and are subject to such things as the influence of the economy (maximum production during wartime), special events (such as a serious accident causing safety to become more important), cultural influences (such as the recent attitude toward air pollution), labor versus machinery (advantages of automation as labor unions have grown stronger) and finally, who are setting goals for the company (background of the executives will influence their choice of company goals). Still within the environment, Gross (8) suggests the global matrix which must be satisfied by the organization and their managers. These are listed as satisfaction of interest, output of services or goods, efficiency, investment in viability, mobilization of resources, observance of codes and rationality. Each organization will place a different weight on the different elements within this global matrix in order to accurately reflect the purpose of the particular organization.

With so dynamic a situation, the Project Manager must act as a catalyst to these constant changes to obtain the degree of planning necessary to achieve his goals; insure clarity of definition of responsibility for performance; act in decision making, and maintain a high level of visibility of the contingencies so that trouble can be spotted early enough for corrective action to be taken.

ORGANIZATION

In addition to the external environment which acts upon the situation, the Project Manager must also act and interact with the organizational structure in which he finds himself. He must not only deal with the formal organization of the company but the informal or social organization as well.

Organizational structure is the chart that should clearly define the lines of authority and responsibility of each individual and coordinate their efforts to harmoniously obtain the predetermined objectives.

The formal organization itself can take many shapes and sizes, depending upon the operation. The formal organization has been designed to relate man and jobs in a formal hierarchy of authority. It is from this hierarchy that the Project Manager must build not only his internal project team but the total project team. Depending upon the type of project management organization, the ramifications of the formal organization take on greater or lesser importance.

A number of project management organizations have been defined and do affect the leadership, methods of motivation, authority structure and power of the Project Manager. In a pure project management operation, all of the people on the project team are directy under the command of the Project Manager. He not only has the authority of a manager, but also the legitimate power of reward and punishment.

In a weak matrix organization, the Project Manager is the focal point of control and the focal point of direction. Project size and the most essential elements of the project are directly under him within the matrix project management. The Project Manager picks his people from the functional departments and returns them to that location at the end of the project. In a loose project management team the Project Manager is merely a focal point for communications and he has no authority to direct people other than by persuading, coercing and reporting to his superiors. This is strictly a monitoring authority type of project management with the Project Manager using expert and referent power.

Building an effective project management team, the Project Manager must discover and understand the interacting elements which are necessary to restructure the existing organizational patterns. He must provide an environment conducive to his team's motivational needs. The manager's location on the organizational chart readily identifies him by activity, status, and location. Although the organization must be considered as an interactive network, each position consists of a pattern of expectations from which roles, activities and beliefs are generated. The Project Manager must override almost everybody's self-interest to establish and accomplish the goals set forth by his project. Project orientation is not all consistent with the formal organization or with personal stability and security. The goal of most organizations is survival, yet the very nature of project management is that a project be accomplished within a given period of time and the project team be dismantled at completion. Thus, the Project Manager is involved in making up a new group of people, establishing new perspectives and maintaining order. Project atmosphere can prove quite unpredictable when interfacing with the existing corporations. Short term project aims may not be necessarily compatible or consistent with other long range goals. Personal motivations for taking part in the project or the challenge of the sense of accomplishments, however, if not constructively channeled, can cause uneven performance, finger pointing and even, in the end, real bitterness and dissention.

The Project Manager must frequently ask the functional manager to share resources and employ them in a fashion that is risky in the eyes of the functional manager who is evaluated according to his own use of those resources. As his project grows in size, the Project Manager is faced with the additional problem of social subsystems or cliques which can develop, and this intergroup combination must be dealt with as well as the formal project organization. The Project Manager can help in determining these social subsystems by raising such questions as which members of the project team will have to spend the most time together in getting the project done and which portion of the team is involved in greater contact during business hours. In this way the Project Manager can aid the relationships within the organization by attempting to prescribe what subsystems and social systems might be developed. However, it is the individual's perception which generally dictate the success or failure of these relationships. Vroom (9) notes in his study on perception of organizational goals that the more positive a person's attitude toward an organization, the greater the tendency for him to perceive a similarity between the organizational goals and his own goals for that organization. Also, a person will accurately perceive agreeable organizational goals to the extent that he has positive attitudes towards that organization.

One of the major essentials of the project team organization is the flow of communications. And depending on the perception of those within the team, communications can be delayed and feed-back can be distorted. Carzo (10) notes that information which is passed on to the manager can be distorted if the subordinate may not wish self-discrediting data to go to the manager, or the manager may be told only what it is believed he wants to hear. Again, a subordinate may try to impress his boss and therefore distort the information. Distortion can also occur (and delays result) in information which is being passed both to the functional and project managers. Reliability and accuracy become important in the distribution of communication data. Steps can be taken to increase reliability but these must be weighed against the costs of not getting the data. When time is of the essence, multiple channel communications, which may be sufficient for the formal organization, may not be swift enough for the project organization.

March (11) reflects that the stronger an individual's identification with the group, the more likely that his perception of the group goals will conform to his own, group pressure being the main stimulant. If we succumb to letting our goals and our values color what we are observing, chances are that our diagnosis will stop short of the level of understanding how interdependent forces relate to each other. Lewin (12) notes that success and failure does not depend upon achievement of a given goal but rather upon the relationship between achievement and the person's expectation in a business or project management operation.

Indik (13) also notes that where many individuals are placed in one location, non-sickness absenteeism increases. Thus smaller work groups are satisfactory and tend to produce greater motivation.

Conflict may arise between the Project Manager and his top management. If there is conflict of interest between the Project Manager and the Functional Manager top management should attempt to review and approve long range decisions in favor of the Functional Manager. If top management is indifferent to the project, this attitude may leave a general impression of indifference throughout the company which will result in a loss of support for the Project Manager. A firm position with judicial intervention when required is more appropriate but more difficult to fix and maintain.

Lawrence (14) sees three dimensions in the changing of behavior of individuals within an organization. They are the achievement of the organizational purpose, self-maintenance and growth, and the achievement of social satisfaction. Any attempt at behavioral change which does not to some extent include all of these dimensions will ultimately fail. An organization can successfully initiate change in such a way that progress is made on all three dimensions simultaneously. An effective Project Manager must constantly seek multidimensional solutions and in so doing is forced into many paradoxical situations. He must strive to maintain a consistency in his own behavior while accepting the fact that his behavior may appear inconsistent from any simple one dimensional frame of reference. He must constantly seek solutions that resolve conflict between the interests of several dimensions but accept the fact that such conflicts are inevitable and never ending. He must constantly seek to change the behavior of the social system he is a part of, but to never break up or destroy the systems as a viable entity until the project objectives are reached.

PROJECT MANAGER

Leadership, situation and the interaction of the two have long been the crucial catalysts required for the success of any organization or project team. The project environment in which the leader finds himself is becoming larger, more costly, as more complex and more and more unpredictable elements are being added. They are all under constant rapid change.

The Project Manager and the Functional Manager work in two different environments. Steinmetz (15) notes the strategic differences in that the typical Functional Manager has been taught to standardize all operations while the Project Manager must learn that adaption and implement change to control over the work. The manager must be able to understand, utilize and manage the technicological complexities of the project systems. He must also be able to think in terms of integrating various disciplines and even innovating a cross fertilization and exposure of his personnel to different disciplines. Such activity will in itself foster and promote continuous ability on the part of his personnel to adapt to the continuing changing work involvement. Thus the Project Manager is faced with the critical problem of integrating a variety of disciplines into his project team.

The Project Manager must, therefore, think in terms of living with constant change rather than existing on standard methods. He must think in terms of effective utilization of several subsystems within his total system rather than demanding that his employees comply with established principles, guidelines, rules and techniques. He must think about individual persons, their feelings, emotions and drives rather than viewing them as warm bodies, or mere machines. Finally, he must be result orientated rather than overly concerned with the method and techniques which technical personnel use in accomplishing this work. Although this can result in some problems, the Project Manager must be willing to break up his work organization into subsystems or subgroups and he must be able to fit effectively into the overall system. As previously mentioned, the individual is himself a subsystem and cliques have to be coped with by the Project Manager.

In dealing with leadership, we would have to explore the leader, his influence, his power, his authority, the type of group he is leading and the situation in which he finds himself. Within the functional organization the authority and power of the leader is usually closely tied to the position and the expectations and roles that are perceived by the position. Within the project management environment, the location of the Project Manager does in many respects give the same type of perceived power and authority. The full scope of this authority and power can be seen by reviewing where in the organization the Project Manager reports, the scope of commitment which he is allowed to make, the level at which these orders can be countermanded and the area in which he can give rewards and punishments.

Throughout the life of the project the Project Manager, finds himself in a variety of leadership positions depending on which phase of the life cycle he is managing. In addition, during the complete life cycle he may find his reporting levels, his authority and his legitimate power varying. He must, therefore, be aware of the ramifications of the different types of management leadership styles which are available to him and the expected results that each could produce for him. His leadership is not wholly an individual matter nor are there any set answers or rules of thumb which dictate that given A, B will result.

The variables are human and dynamic and relate to one another in a complex fashion, and results are not always completely predictable. McMurry (16) points out that an understanding of the research findings, together with empirical observations will largely satisfy the scientific prerequisite for achievement. The science of leadership provides the valuable basis, success will not be realized without practice of leadership skills such as appraising the significant variables and displaying the appropriate overt behavior. With the experimental results now available, it is obvious that leadership is something more than a science, it is and will remain in the immediate years ahead, both an art and a science.

Leadership is a supervision style whereby the superior furnishes services that make the subordinates dependent on him. These services take the form of training and advising, being readily available, supplying critical needs, supporting the work group and intergroup conflicts, helping with personal problems, adjusting schedules to fit preferences of the workers. Effective leadership according to Law and Scott (17), is promoted by maintaining some social distance and independence from subordinates, emotional detachment and degree of independence from superiors.

It is necessary for leaders to possess those skills which comprise an ability to lead in a particular situation. Three different styles of leadership have been categorized by the behavoral scientists. First, there is the dictatorship which is characterized by control being centralized and a dominant decision maker who is the undisputed boss. Normally, freedom of individual members is highly restricted, morale is low, agreement and commitment are of little importance, creativity is curtailed, innovations are resisted, participation is low, communications limited, and delegation of authority is rare. The dictator sees himself as a blunt, no nonsense boss. His job is to make the decisions for those under him. He imposes discipline on his subordinates matched by his own obedience and he therefore considers himself a strong advocate of company teamwork. He fancies himself as a put-up or shut-up type, compromise annoys him. Privately he believes in the rule of the strong. The strong and the able succeed, others must take the consequences of their personal limitations. The dictatorial obedience system of the manager is the only one he respects. He makes the rules, criticizes violators and personally tries to follow up on every aspect of the operation. He is a great believer in systems and paperwork and has control of his employees. He does the planning and tells others what must be done. McMurry (16) points out that in this situation the group's own development or improvement is slow. The leader ignores personal needs and interests of members. He avoids being a peer or a member of the group. In his absence the members' production efforts deteriorate. As far as actual productivity is concerned quality is apt to be poor or at its best mediocre. The quantity of production, however, may be quite high.

This kind of his kind of leadership is more likely to be tolerated in large groups because the members value the patriarchs upward influence as essential. In small informal groups, however, they realize that in addition to exerting influence on his superior, he has time to be considerate and member-like in the immediate situation.

Dictatorial decisions are made quickly but the implementation of the decisions may require considerable time. Some researchers have concluded that dictatorial supervision is best suited in situations if an emergency or crisis is being experienced. The dictatorial leadership leads to more productivity than does democratic leadership over a short period of time. However, in the long run democratic leadership seems to tend toward higher productivity. It has also been noted that when the dictatorial leader is absent the group tends to fall apart. The dictatorial leadership is characterized either by the greatest instant of hostility and aggression among members or the greatest apathy, depending upon the group. On the other hand, dictatorial lead groups have the least "talk back" to leaders.

In the democratic or participatory style of leadership, the group has a high member participation. Members share in the decision making process and are thus committed to the goals and tasks of the group. Because consultation and participation require time, democratic decisions take longer to make, however, the decisions are implemented quickly because of commitment and involvement. The actual lapse of time from recognition of a problem to implementation of a decision may be no longer than that required by the dictatorial group. Participation has certain benefits which may be worth pursuing. Creativity is at a high level, group improvement is rapid, communication is open, delegation and planning are effective, morale is good and the quality of work is high. After a group becomes used to this kind of leadership, the quantity of production will normally stabilize out at a high level. One of the major problems with democratic leadership is that it is more difficult for the leader. It is difficult to install this kind of leadership abruptly in a situation where members expect and have experienced only dictatorial supervision. The democratic leader also believes in teamwork. He feels that it is important to understand the personal needs, the wants and goals of his employees. He strives for excellence and aims at the highest results which are compatible with genuine concern for people and their needs. He emphasizes participation. He would like his subordinates to enjoy their work. He believes that they will work better and produce more when they think well of their boss. He expects there will be strong disagreement amongst his people but he encourages them to find areas of agreement. He helps them find points on which they can get together so they can work for further agreement, so instead of suppressing conflict he gets all people involved in it in order to work it through. Whenever possible, he brings his men to a new situation from the beginning. He shares his plans with them and encourages them to participate with him in solving problems on making decisions. He depends on mutual trust and confidence. Members of the democratic group are more satisfied than members of the other groups. The democratic leadership also produces better quality and better quantity over a long period of time.

At another extreme, is the laissez-faire or comprise leader. He is normally considered an easy boss compared to the dominator or dictator. He does not push people. He often finds himself making accommodations. He has a desire to avoid conflict, even though he believes his position is the right one. He sees himself as a practical executive. He avoids setting high goals and takes the middle-of-the-road position. He overlooks mistakes if they don't occur too often. He does the planing, but nullifies his proposals if they are challenged. He believes firmly in teamwork. However, he will give no suggestions unless they are directly asked and neither praises nor punishes the group or his members. The group's effort may result in chaos with this type of leadership. This kind of group is rarely found and not much is known about the consequences of the type of power distribution. There is some evidence, however, which indicates that in some groups, depending on the nature of the task, an effective, information organization will naturally emerge.

The leader should set and communicate a high level of expectations. His expectations should be reasonable but at the same time should require his subordinates to stretch. His expectations are not so unrealistic that the group members see no chance for fulfilling them. Little improvement will be realized. His expectations will constitute a fairly effective floor but not a ceiling on the group's performance.

The Project Manager must keep in mind two distinctions in the idea of leadership: personal quality, and leadership as an organizational function. The first refers to a special combination of personal characteristics; the second refers to the distribution throughout an organization of decision making powers. Depending on his situation, his project and his environment, the Project Manager can mold his style of leadership to obtain the results consistent with his objectives.

PROJECT TEAM

One of the major tasks of the Project Manager is the assembling and putting together of the project team into a cohesive group. Cohesiveness may be thought of as the average results of the forces acting on the group members to remain in the group; the determination of the "we's" as opposed to the "I" feeling within the group. Factors which give rise to group cohesiveness may be classified as those relating to the group itself and those relating to the individual needs within the group. The group itself may act as a source of attraction through the nature of its goal, its activities, its program, composition and its objective. The esteem gained by belonging to the group might satisfy individual needs. Most of these factors must be considered when the group is being created and is being continued. A cohesive group tends to be composed of individuals with similar interests and backgrounds who are able to communicate with each other. It will tend to be more cohesive if formed in the higher status group. Informal grouping tends to be composed of people who work near each other and exhibit some similar characteristics, having common interest, values and close working relationships.

How can you build a winning cohesive team? There is no single magical formula in this combination of techniques. It is based partly on effective communications, partly on sincere interest in the team members, and partly on personal enthusiasm for the future. McMurry (16) summarizes a number of the team members' ramifications by noting that the behavior of a subordinate is influenced by the degree to which he identifies with a cohesive group with a team spirit. A Project Manager should realize that a cohesive group is a powerful force which can work for the good or detriment of the organization. Group cohesiveness results in greater productivity when the organization is seen as supportive rather than threatening to the member's sense of personal worth and status. Pressure usually results in higher productivity, and morale is the highest under moderate pressure within the group. Group members are more likely to accept goals as their own and to work towards those goals when they have participated in setting them. Productivity within the group also depends to a large extent upon the level of the leader's expectations.

The group has certain needs which if frustrated tend to disrupt its effectiveness. Groups have needs which may or may not be apparent on the surface. The members themselves may not realize the importance they ascribe to certain functions, these being categorized as need for accomplishing the task, need for maintaining the status quo and need for development. The group requires certain functions to be performed, encouraging, standard setting, following, compromising, conforming, deviating, initiating, information gathering, information sharing, clarifying, summarizing. These functions may not be performed by the leader hinself. He should, however, feel an obligation to provide for them. The group also tends to look to the leader to exhibit certain functions himself, such as orientating and facilitating new ideas and procedures, resisting some changes, interacting informally with the members, defending against outside pressure, representing the group as its spokesman, exerting influence on higher echelons, reducing conflict, facilitating individual adaptation to the group, defining work, restricting freedom, communicating, using rewards and sanctions, stimulating group progress and assisting in problem solving.

These needs and expectations are generally present in all groups but the degree of importance of each need is highly variable depending upon the severity of the group's frustration. Conflict and anxieties will result if these needs are thwarted. It is just a short step from saying that effective membership performance is synonomous with effective leadership.

Likert (18) notes that the form of organization which will make the greatest use of the human capacity consists of highly effective work teams linked together to an overlapping pattern by other similar effective groups. Groups have values, attitudes and norms. There is nothing implicitly good or bad, weak or strong about a group. Loyalty to the group produces pressure towards conformity. A group may demand conformity to the ideals of supporting, encouraging and giving recognition for the individual creativity or it may value rigidity of behavior with seriously narrowing and dwarfing consequences. Of course, as we expressed the notion of group or team, we mean members of the group. Dorwin Cartwright put it this way: "The relationship between the individual members and the team is analogous to the distinction made in mathematics between the properties of a set of elements and the properties of the elements within the set. Every set is composed of elements but the sets have properties which are not identical with the properties of the elements of the sets."

In many instances in describing an organization, the ideal is not set forth but rather the symptoms which would show poor organization are described. Likert (19) has set forth those properties and performance characteristics of an ideal, highly effective team to include the situation, the leader, the group, the members, their values and goals and their interactions and relationships.

All the interaction, problem-solving, and decision making activities of the group occur in a supportive situation. Suggestions, ideas, information, criticisms are all offered with a helpful orientation. This also aids in stimulating creativity, for the group does not demand narrow conformity as do the work groups under authoritarian leaders. No one has to "yes the boss" nor is he rewarded for such an attempt. The group attaches high value to new, creative approaches and solutions to its problems and to the problems of the organization of which it is a part.

The leader of a highly effective group is selected carefully, however, his leadership ability is so evident that he would probably emerge as a leader in any unstructured situation. The leader exerts a major influence in establishing the tone and situation of the work group by his leadership principles and practices striving for a cooperative rather than a competitive relationship among the members. The members and the leader have a high degree of confidence and trust in each other and believe that each member can accomplish the impossible. These expectations stretch each member to the maximum and accelerate his growth. Likewise, the group, when necessary, will temper the expectation level so that a member is not broken by a feeling of failure or rejection.

The group has been in existence sufficiently long to have developed a well established, relaxed working relationship among all of its members. The group is eager to help each member develop to his full potential, yet when necessary or advisable, will give help to any member to aid in accomplishing the goals set for him. Mutual help is a characteristic of highly effective groups. There is high motivation in the group to use communication process so that it best serves the interest and goals of the group. The group knows the value of "constructive" conformity and knows when to use it and for what purposes. Although it does not permit conformity to affect adversely the creative efforts of its members, it does expect conformity on mechanical and administrative matter to save time of members to facilitate the group's activities.

The members of the group are highly motivated to abide by the major values and to achieve the important goals of the group. The values and goals of the group are a satisfactory integration and expression of the relevant values and needs of its members. They have helped shape these values and goals and are satisfied with them. The more important a value seems to the group, the greater the likelihood that the individual member will accept it. Insofar as members of the group are performing linking functions, they endeavor to have the values and goals of the group which they link in harmony, one with the other. Each member accepts willingly and without resentment the goals and expectations that he and his group establish for themselves. The anxieties, fears, and emotional stresses produced by direct pressure for high performance from a boss in a hierarchical situation is not present.

The members of the group are skilled in all the various leadership and membership roles and functions required for interaction between leaders and members and between members and other members. Each member is attracted to the group and is loyal to its members, including the leader. There are strong motivations to try to influence other members as well as to be receptive to influence by them. This applies to all the group's activities: technical matters, methods, organizational problems, interpersonal relationships and group pressures and processes. This influence ability contributes to the flexibility and adaptability of the group. Ideas, goals, and attitudes do not become frozen if members are able to influence each other continuously. The members are able to exert more influence on the leader and to communicate far more information to him, including suggestions as to what needs to be done and how he could do his job better.

There is strong motivation on the part of each member of the group to communicate fully and frankly to the group all the information which is relevant and of value to the group's activity. This stems directly from the member's desire to be valued by the group and to complete the project. Just as there is high motivation to communicate, there is correspondingly strong motivation to receive communications. Each member is genuinely interested in any information on any relevant matter that any member of the group can provide.

In the highly effective group, individual members feel secure in making decisions which seem appropriate to them because the goals and philosophy of operation are clearly understood by each member and provide him with a solid base for his decision. This unleashes initiative and pushes decisions down while still maintaining a coordinated and directed effort. The important aspect of the highly effective group is its extensive use of the principle or supportive relationships. An examination of the above material reveals that virtually every statement involves an application of this principle.

The Project Manager is constantly striving to have quality people from different disciplines working at peak efficiency in a cohesive group. The manager must be able to understand, utilize and manage the technological complexities of the project system. In many instances, lacking real line authority, the Project Manager must constantly lead, persuade and coerce his peers and his team through a trying period of change. Knowing the ideal for a cohesive work group and faced with an increasing challenge from a changing environment, the Project Manager can successfully put together an efficient, effective, problem solving team.

THE INDIVIDUAL

The Project Manager works with constant change imposed upon him from his environment and in many cases from his own organization and the phase of his project. He must, in forming his cohesive group, keep in constant mind the individuals that make up the group, the team, the organization and the total project. We are in an age where advancement of technology has been astronomical. Unfortunately, these changes have not been accomplished with the necessary revisions in the individual values, customs, attitudes and loyalties. For as technology changes the material aspects of our civilization, so does it change the people involved with those material things.

According to Webber (20), it is the function of the Project Manager to design and adjust the work relationships of the individual so that disturbances do not interfere with their effective performances. The manager must do this by personal transfers, appropriate personal behavior such as maintaining communications and his project team organizational structure.

One of the most difficult responsibilities of the Project Manager is to mediate between the demands of the organization and the environment, which means internal adaptation and goal modifications in response to external conditions. The traditional view of the manager's job is that all outside contacts flow through the manager who feeds them to the firm and the team. The behavioral view reflects the Project Manager's decision making function diluted by specialist activities. The power and the ability to mediate between internal and external worlds no longer are so conveniently concentrated in one position. Actually, most information flow by-passes management. Specialized subordinates respond directly to outside forces, thus circumventing the hierarchy control system. Functional analysis looks at an organization as composed of parts and the whole adapting to an external environment thereby maintaining the interrelated states of the parts.

The Project Manager utilizes the desires, knowledge and aspirations of his team members by allowing them the freedom to express themselves by encouraging their participation in planning, organizing and controlling the team objectives. The manager will utilize the human system factors in a manner which will benefit the organization and the employee. When they have participated in planning and organizing the work to the extent that they perceive that it is self-involving and enhancing, the work goes more smoothly and efficiently. Understanding what motivates a particular individual requires an analysis of many factors; Bass (7) has pointed out the most important: what the team member is capable of doing; what he is interested in doing; and how involved he is in his work and the goals towards to which he strives. The establishment of realistic goals both for the team and for the individual is one of the key ways in which management can contribute to the positive motivation of the worker.

It should be understood that each individual carries into the project team a set of attitudes about authority figures including a set of expectations about what the authority figures should be like and a collection of hopes and fears stemming from his previous experiences with authorities. In reality no Project Manager could hope to measure up to these ideal expectations.

Governmental and many management control systems rely for the strength of their motivation on the attitude and actions management takes in response to reporting performance. Whatever standard of good performance is used, it is likely to be effective as a means of control only if the person being judged agrees that it is an equitable standard. If he does not agree, he is likely to pay no attention to comparisons between his performance and the standard. He is likely to resent and if possible reject an attempt by anyone else to make such a comparison. The best way to secure this agreement is to ask the person whose performance is being measured to participate in the process of establishing this standard. Many times a system is started with loud fanfares, works well for a while and then gradually withers away in effectiveness as the initial stimulus disappears. Incessant arguments can be created about the justice and equity of the reported results in the control system. The method which is most successful is where a general agreement on what basis of measurement is fair. A control system should be adopted by the manager to the personalities of the individuals whom he is supervising. If the people in the organization are not motivated, all reports could just as well be sent to the dead letter file. One other thing is known; the fact that the worker knows that the reports are being made is in itself motivational.

The words to characterize the major aspects of behavior which are the most influential in the management process, according to Scofield (21), are: 1) learning, 2) perception, 3) motivation, 4) communications and 5) attitude formation and change. The formation of new attitudes within the individual is dependent upon the learning process. These attitudes will develop in any event. It would be beneficial if the environmental stimulant situation to be managed is done in such a way that a favorable attitude towards work, colleagues, and self would be formed. To do this means that the work for each individual must be established in such a way that their attainment is to some degree assured. The Project Manager will need to provide the employees with a more pleasant self-rewarding interaction as well as an interesting and self-fulfilling work experience. Each Project Manager must become familiar with the needs, attitudes and desires of those under him if he is to produce the quality product which his team effort has been organized to accomplish.

To most employees, the manager is simply a part of his overall environment and not necessarily the most important part. The employee will make concessions to the manager to the extent that he thinks he must, but he will not necessarily consider it advantageous to do more than that unless it appears that doing so will lead to a lasting significant gain. That gain is not necessarily monetary, it often has more to do with a change in the role that the individual can play. Most of management's actions have motivational effects. The problem is that too often people are motivated to act in unproductive ways. This is usually because they see no advantage to increasing their productivity or because they are actually motivated to thwart the organization if they can.

Today we have a number of motivation theorists who have reported on the varied forms of employee motivation. Maslow's hierarchy of needs, and Herzberg's satisfiers and dissatisfiers are but two.* Maslow (22) notes an ascending order of needs which have to be fulfilled by the individual. They start with the physiological body needs, and ascend to safety-security needs, social relationship needs, esteem needs, and self-actuation needs. This would indicate that when a person is at a level of a particular need his behavior and personality are shaped by the drive to conquer that need. He is little affected by needs higher up on the scale and once a particular need is fulfilled, it no longer remains a need.

Herzberg (23) reflects that those items which give good feelings and motivations have little power to dissatisfy. The dissatisfiers have little power to motivate when removed as a source of dissatisfaction. The motivators are those factors intimately associated with the work itself and are classified as follows: 1) achievement—to succeed in solving a problem, seeing good results of work performed, completing a challenging job, having one's judgement vindicated. 2) recognition—receiving earned praise or acknowledgement from superiors, subordinates, peers, the public, the company or anywhere work is performed. 3) Advancement—an upward change in status or promotion. 4) responsibility—being given a new job, being permitted to work without close supervision, being responsible for one's own work and for the work of others. 5) work itself—like the work being performed, doing challenging or creative work,

---

*See chapter 27 for a detailed discussion.

turning out a complete piece of work. Herzberg also notes that there is a group of maintenance and hygiene items which are dissatisfiers and have to do with the work situation and the fringe area of the job itself. These include such items as: 1) company policy, administration, supervision; 2) interpersonal relationships; 3) supervision and technical relationships, a superior's ability to provide technical guidance, with competence, fairness and willingness to train; 4) salary, all the things involved in compensating, fairness of the wage system, whether increases are given begrudgingly or late and whether differentials are fair and; 5) working conditions, light, space, ventilation, tools, shop, office location, etc. Herzberg concludes that individuals tend to be hygiene minded or motivation minded, responding more readily to one type of factor than another. This phenomenon appears to be related to the individual's personality rather than to the nature of factor itself. The motivation seekers are relatively insensitive to unsavory factors in the environment. The hygiene seekers are preoccupied with the non-job factors, benefit plans, working conditions, pay status, etc. They are normally dissatisfied and show only slight interest at the quality of their work.

Maintenance factors must be kept at an adequate level so they don't surge up as dissatisfiers. Motivation is found in things close to the job and its performance. It is cheaper to achieve the hygiene in terms of dollars but it is much dearer in terms of supervisory and management skills required. Organizations and jobs within the organization must be restructured to provide challenge and opportunity for growth. The engineer will find achievement, recognition, advancement, responsibility and work itself as the big positive motivators.

SUMMARY

Acting as a catalyst, the Project Manager with his single point of responsibility and centralized planning and control can more efficiently and effectively respond to the constant rapid changes in his external and internal environments, molding his individuals into a team to obtain his project objectives. The very nature of the project management organization often produces conflict with the functional organizational setup and in many instances the Project Manager must coerce people into getting the work done since he may not have the legitimate authoritarian power to direct the work.

He must set the objectives and expectations for the team and the individuals and should keep in mind those motivators which will aid in obtaining results in the most efficient manner. The behavioral aspect would indicate that as a democratic leader with participation from his team members he can accomplish the most over the longest period of time. Give people a sense of achievement in their work, opportunity as group members to participate in making decisions and a chance to satisfy their need for recognition. Most people work because they want to. It fulfills the important need of our adult society. Working as a source of fulfillment calls for ego satisfaction, self-esteem and, simply, pride.

In controlling his operations, the Project Manager should not be involved in how the work is done but should see that it is done. This, in many cases, involves management by exception since in a complex organization he is unable to control all the elements that affect his objective. The Project Manager through coercion, by setting of objectives, by including participation of his members and by controlling by exception, can cope with his project and complete it on time, within budget and maintain the technical quality required.

REFERENCES

1. D. McGregor, *The Human Side of Enterprise* (McGraw-Hill, New York, 1960).
2. Eric Jenett, "Guidelines for Successful Project Management." *Chemical Engineering,* pp. 70–82, (July 9, 1973).
3. E. Alderman, S. S. Dublin, H. L. Marlow, "What Bosses Think They Should Know." *Guidelines for Better Management,* H.P.I. Vol. II, pp. 108–112, (1969).
4. Bruce N. Banker, Dalmar Fisher, David C. Murphy, "Factors Affecting Success of Project Management." *P.M.I. Fifth International Seminar Symposium,* pp. 681–684, (1973).
5. "People Management." *Industry Week,* pp. 52–69, (January 5, 1970).
6. R. H. Gorden, "Project Management for Maximum Controls." *AACE Bulletin,* (April 1972).
7. Bernard M. Bass, *Organizational Psychology* (Allyn and Bacon, Inc., Boston, 1965).
8. Bertrom M. Gross, *Organizations and Their Management* (Free Press, New York, 1968).
9. Victor H. Vroom, "The Effects of Attitudes on Perception of Organizational Goals." *Human Relations,* pp. 229–239, (1960).
10. Rocco Carzo, Jr., John J. Yanouzas, *Formal Organizations, A Systems Approach* (R. D. Irwin, Homewood, Ill., 1967).
11. James G. March, Herbert A. Simon, *Organizations* (Wiley, New York, 1958).
12. Kurt Lewin, *Dynamic Theory of Personality* (McGraw-Hill, New York, 1935).
13. Bernard Indik, "Some Effects of Organization Size on Members' Attitudes and Behaviors." *People, Groups and Organizations* (Teachers College Press, New York, 1968).
14. Paul R. Lawrence, *The Changing of Organizational Behavior Patterns* (Harvard University Press, 1958).
15. Lawrence L. Steinmetz, "Systems Approach—Better Management." *Guidelines for Better Management,* H.P.I. Vol. II, pp. 32–36, (1969).
16. Fred D. McMurry, "The Art and Science of Leadership," *Guidelines for Better Management,* H.P.I. Vol. I, pp. 134–142, (1968).
17. Peter M. Blau, Richard W. Scott, "The Role of the Supervisor." *Formal Organizations,* pp. 140–164, Chandler Publishing Co., San Francisco, (1962).
18. Renis Likert, *New Patterns of Management* (McGraw-Hill, New York, 1961).
19. Renis Likert, *The Human Organization* (McGraw-Hill, New York, 1967).
20. Ross A. Webber, David H. Hampton, Charles E. Summer, *Organizational Behavior, and the Practice of Management* (Scott Foreman & Co., Glenview, Ind., 1968).
21. Robert W. Scofield, Dodd H. Bogart, Donald R. Domm, *Human Behavior and Administration,* pre-publication Edition, (University of Houston, Houston, Texas 1968).
22. A. H. Maslow, *Motivation and Personality* (Harper and Row, New York, 1954).
23. Frederick Herzberg, *Work and the Nature of Man* (World Publishing Co., Cleveland, 1966).

27. Motivation and the Project Manager

Dennis P. Slevin[*]

Quentin Thatchley exited his car with a grimace, entered the front door, and dropped his briefcase with a resounding thud on the table.

"Hi," shouted Sarah from the kitchen. "How was your first day in your new position?"

"You wouldn't believe it," said Quentin, "It was awful."

"Awful, already? Tell me about it."

Quentin walked into the kitchen and began without even sitting down.

"Well first they almost allocated our new lab space to Leroy Brown over in sensors. He's got a high priority project and needs additional space as well. I had to raise a tremendous commotion with Sam to make sure that my team got the space that we needed. It was, shall we say, very unpleasant.

"Then, Bill came in with a cockeyed request that he give up lunch hours and leave an hour early during the summer. I just couldn't agree to this because we need him around to answer questions at all times during the working day. Now he's miffed that the first thing that I've done in my new position is to turn down what he thinks is a reasonable request. Then finally I discover that one of my new responsibilities as project manager is the weekly cost report. I've got two hours of tedious, dull, stupid paper work waiting for me this evening in that briefcase."

"Quentin, I'm sure it won't always be this way—just give it a chance."

"Well, I will, Sarah, but so far being a project manager has not been too much fun. I wonder if I'm really cut out to be a manager."

*Dennis P. Slevin is Associate Professor of Business Administration and Director of Executive Development Programs at the Graduate School of Business, University of Pittsburgh. He received his B.A. in mathematics from Saint Vincent College, B.S. in physics from MIT, M.S. in industrial administration from Carnegie-Mellon University and Ph.D. in business administration from Stanford University in 1969. He consults widely and is also the Chief Executive Officer of four companies serving the coal industry in West Virginia. He is published in numerous professional journals and is the coeditor of *Implementing Operations Research/Management Science, The Management of Organization Design,* Volumes I and II, and *The Implementation of Management Science,* and is coauthor of *The Executive Survival Manual.* This chapter is copyrighted by © 1981 Dennis P. Slevin.

INTRODUCTION

Quentin is trying to decide if he has the motivation to manage. Do you? Most chapters on motivation address the issue of how we get other people to do things. We will talk about those issues as well, but first, do *you* have the proper motivational structure to be an effective manager? Some interesting research has been done recently concerning the concept of the motivation to manage and its role in predicting managerial effectiveness. In this chapter we will first explore the concept of the motivation to manage and then look at Maslow's Hierarchy of Needs and Herzberg's approaches to job enrichment as tools for the project manager.

MOTIVATION TO MANAGE DEFINED

Over the past two decades Professor John B. Miner of Georgia State University has been investigating the concept of the Motivation to Manage. He feels that the motivation to manage and its associated attitudes and motives are likely to cause one to:

1. Choose a managerial career.
2. Be successful in a managerial position.
3. Move rapidly up the managerial ladder.

In other words, the motivation to manage is an essential element for managerial success. Let's explore the 6 components of the motivation to manage in Professor Miner's own words:

"1. *Favorable attitude toward those in positions of authority,* such as superiors. Managers typically are expected to behave in ways which do not provoke negative reactions from their superiors; ideally they will elicit positive responses. A manager must be in a position to represent his group upward in the organization and to obtain support for his actions at higher levels. This requires a good relationship between the individual and superiors. It follows that a manager should have a generally positive attitude toward those holding positions of authority over him, if he is to meet this particular job requirement."

"2. *Desire to engage in competition,* especially with peers. There is, at least insofar as peers are concerned, a strong competitive element built into managerial work. Behavior of this kind might not be necessary if the job existed independent of its organizational context, but this is not the case. A manager must compete for the available rewards, both for himself and for his group. If he does not, he may lose ground as he and his operation are relegated to lower and lower status levels. Rapid promotion is certainly very improbable without competitive behavior. Thus managers must characteristically strive to win, for themselves and their groups, and accept such challenges as other managers at a comparable level may offer. On occasion the challenge may come from below, even from among one's own subordinates. In order to meet this job requirement a person should be favorably disposed toward engaging in competition."

"3. *Desire to assert oneself and take charge.* There is a marked parallel between the requirements of the managerial role and the traditional assertive demands of the masculine role as it is defined in our society. Although the behaviors expected of a father and those expected of a manager are by no means identical, there are many similarities. Both are supposed to take charge, to make decisions, to take such disciplinary action as may be necessary, and to protect the other members of their group. Thus, one of the more common role requirements of the managerial job is that the incumbent behave in an assertive, masculine manner. Even when women are appointed to managerial positions they are expected to be able to take charge, at least during the hours spent in the work situation. It follows that a desire to meet requirements for assertiveness should generally lead to success in meeting certain requirements of the managerial job as well."

"4. *Desire to exercise power and authority over others,* particularly subordinates. This is the requirement that a manager must exercise power over his subordinates and direct their behavior in a manner consistent with organizational, and presumably his own, objectives. He must tell others what to do when this becomes necessary, and enforce his words through appropriate use of positive and negative sanctions. The individual who finds such behavior difficult and emotionally disturbing, who does not wish to impose his wishes on others, or who believes it wrong to do so, would not be expected to meet this particular job requirement."

"5. *Desire to behave in a distinctive and different way,* which involves standing out from the crowd. The managerial job tends to require a person to behave in ways differing in a number of respects from the behavior of others in the same face-to-face group. An incumbent must in this sense stand out from his group and assume a position of high visibility. He cannot use the actions of the people with whom he is most frequently associated, his subordinates, as a guide for his own behavior as a manager. Rather he must deviate from the immediate group and do things that will inevitably invite attention, discussion, and perhaps criticism from those reporting to him. The managerial job requires that an individual assume a position of considerable importance insofar as the motives and emotions of other people are concerned. When this prospect is viewed as unattractive, when the idea of standing out from the group, of behaving in an different manner, and of being highly visible elicits feelings of unpleasantness, then behavior appropriate to the job will occur much less often than would otherwise be the case."

"6. *Sense of responsibility in carrying out the numerous routine duties associated with managerial work.* The managerial job requires getting the work out and keeping on top of routine demands. The things that have to be done must actually be done. They range from constructing budget estimates to serving on committees, to talking on the telephone, to filling out employee rating forms and salary-change recommendations. There are administrative requirements of this kind in all managerial work, although the specific activities will vary somewhat from one situation to another. To meet these requirements a manager must at least be willing to face this type of routine, and ideally he should gain some satisfaction from it."

Miner, John B., *The Human Constraint,* (1974, pp. 6–7).

RESEARCH RESULTS

It is this author's opinion that the motivation to manage makes a lot of conceptual sense as a predictive variable in determing whether one is satisfied with the managerial position and successful therein. While it is not the intent of this chapter to do an exhaustive review of research results supporting the relationship between motivation to manage and managerial effectiveness, perhaps some exemplary data are in order. Miner (1974 p. 28) studied the initial motivation to manage and the number of subsequent promotions in the research and development department of an oil company that occurred over a 5 year period. The data were as follows:

Initial Motivation to Manage and Number of Subsequent Promotions Over Next 5 Years in the R & D Department of an Oil Company

MOTIVATION TO MANAGE	NO PROMOTIONS	ONE PROMOTION	TWO OR MORE PROMOTIONS
High Motivation	3 (25%)	6 (38%)	15 (71%)
Low Motivation	9 (75%)	10 (62%)	6 (29%)

Initial Motivation to Manage and Rate of Subsequent Promotion Over Next 5 Years in the Marketing Department of an Oil Company

MOTIVATION TO MANAGE	NO PROMOTIONS	SLOW PROMOTION RATE	FAST PROMOTION RATE
High Motivation	13 (32%)	14 (64%)	16 (89%)
Low Motivation	28 (68%)	8 (36%)	2 (11%)

Miner, John, B., *The Human Constraint,* (1974, pp. 28–29).

Miner has been concerned because his data indicate that the motivation to manage in college students has been declining over the past 15 years and he sees this as producing a potential short fall of competent managers in the next couple of decades.

What is relevance of this for the project manager? Many project managers evolve to their positions out of previous scientific, engineering or technical posts. It is not uncommon to have a highly qualified and very successful engineer move up into the project manager position. The change is dramatic. In his previous role he communicated primarily with things. He now must communicate primarily with people. Previously he could spend long uninterrupted hours reading, reflecting, collecting data and working on technical projects. He now must spend large amounts of time in group meetings, talking on the telephone, being interrupted by subordinates, and the other frenetic activities that encompass a typical manager's day. Before, he could self actualize by coming up with good technical solutions. Now he must engage in the sometimes unpleasant process of exercising power over others and engaging in competition for key resources. Although from the standpoint of status and pay the movement into a project manager's position tends to be viewed as a natural incremental progression, for the talented engineer with a low motivation to manage it may be a traumatic metamorphis indeed. A crucial question that anyone occupying a project manager's position should ask is "Do I have sufficient motivation to manage for satisfaction and success in this position?"

DIAGNOSING YOUR MOTIVATION TO MANAGE (MTM)

On the scale below indicate that extent to which you feel you have below average, above average, or an average amount of the components of making up the motivation to manage. Make a check mark opposite each of the 6 main factors and then total your score.

	Well Below Average				Average				Well Above Average	
Favorable Attitude Toward Authority	0	1	2	3	4	5	6	7	8	9	10
Desire to Compete	0	1	2	3	4	5	6	7	8	9	10
Assertive Motivation	0	1	2	3	4	5	6	7	8	9	10
Desire to Exercise Power	0	1	2	3	4	5	6	7	8	9	10
Desire for a Distinctive Position	0	1	2	3	4	5	6	7	8	9	10
A Sense of Responsibility	0	1	2	3	4	5	6	7	8	9	10

Now that you have looked at the 6 main factors, attempt to assess your perception of your overall motivation to manage.

Overall Motivation to Manage
(Total of above 6 Factor Scores)

Almost None					Average				Very Much Above Average	
0	6	12	18	24	30	36	42	48	54	60

Of course, the assessment that you have just performed is purely your self perception and to do it properly we would want to use a more rigorous device such as the Miner Sentence Completion Scale (copyright 1977). The intent here is to stimulate self insight and critical thinking about the concept. It might even be worthwhile to ask you spouse or co-workers how they would evaluate you on these factors of the motivation to manage.

MTM/JOB FIT

In order for one to be satisfied and successful in an organizational role, you must attempt to match your basic inclinations to the demands of the job. Suppose that you have just concluded that you have a low motivation to manage (MTM) and are yet a project manager. What should you do? You have two alternatives:

1. Select jobs that are more appropriate to your low MTM.
2. Attempt to change your motivation to manage.

The job characteristics that might be appropriate for a high versus low motivation to manage are shown in Table 27-1.

In order for one to be successful and happy in a job, one must be matched to that position. Think carefully about whether or not you have the motivation to manage for ever increasing managerial responsibility and what direction your career should take at varying points. With a bit of self insight and careful thought you should be able to make reasonable career decisions as your project management position progresses through time.

CHANGING YOUR MOTIVATION TO MANAGE

It is generally accepted in psychology that a significant component of motives is learned. McClelland (1965), developing his concept of need for achievement, has claimed the ability to teach individuals techniques for increasing their need for achievement through small group activity, class room lectures, learning more about the concept, and so forth. He has also concluded that successful

Table 27-1. Job Characteristics Associated with High Versus Low Motivation to Manage

LOW MTM	HIGH MTM
Relatively small span of control and small number of total people supervised	Larger span of control and large number of total people supervised
Responsibility should have a high technical/engineering component	Responsibility should have a high people/budgetary component
Maintain "hands on" technical expertise	Surround oneself with competent technical experts
A typical day has a smaller number of total activities with adequate time for reading, analyzing and reflecting	Typical day may consist of as many as 200 different activities including large numbers of interruptions, phone calls and changes of activities
Serve primarily as a facilitator encouraging and supporting your staff	Serve more as a "boss"—saying yes to good ideas and no to bad ones
Career progression consists of becoming the most competent technical expert in your specialty	Career progression consists of assuming more and more responsibility, higher budget authority, more total people supervised, and eventually moving up traditional management ladder
Job requires relatively little exercise of power over the behavior of others	Job requires daily interventions in the lives of others, using legitimate position as well as other power forms
Lower stress position	Higher stress position

managers have a higher need for power than need for affiliation (1976). This seems to be compatible with the motivation to manage in that one must be prepared to exercise power over others in order for managerial success and not let the affiliation needs get in the way.

Would it be possible to increase one's motivation to manage? Researchers are not really sure of the answer to this question; no definitive research has been done on the subject. This author's belief is that in certain cases the answer to this question should be a resounding "yes". Look at the 6 components of the motivation to manage and formulate an action plan for increasing each component. For example, one could read books about great authority figures. One could engage in regular competitive athletic activities. Assertiveness workshops are somewhat in fashion today for changing assertive motivation. One could make a personal commitment that the detail work must be done even if it's not terribly creative and rather tedious. Each individual action plan would be idiosyncratic of the problems faced by that person but this author is optimistic that if one is interested in changing a motivation to manage, movement should be possible. Also, as one gets more project management experience over time it may be possible to expand these 6 factors just through the experience of the job itself. Ask yourself the question, "Do I wish to attempt to change my motivation to manage?" If the answer to this is in the affirmative, formulate your particular action plan.

ACTION PLAN FOR INCREASING MOTIVATION TO MANAGE

Refer back to the instrument that you have already completed diagnosing your current levels of motivation to manage on page 556. Now respond to the same instrument, only this time indicating the desired levels of each motivation to manage factor for your current job position. The difference between the desired level and your actual level gives an indication of the "motivation to manage deficit" that you have on each factor. Specify below an action plan for changing the motivation to manage on those factors in which there is a deficit.

1. Favorable Attitude
   Toward Authority Deficit (Difference between desired and actual 0–10 points) _____
   ACTION PLAN _____
   _____
   _____
   _____

   Probability of Success _____
2. Desire to Compete Deficit (Difference between desired and actual 0–10 points) _____
   ACTION PLAN _____
   _____
   _____
   _____

   Probability of Success _____
3. Assertive
   Motivation Deficit (Difference between desired and actual 0–10 points) _____
   ACTION PLAN _____
   _____
   _____
   _____

   Probability of Success _____
4. Desire to
   Exercise Power Deficit (Difference between desired and actual 0–10 points) _____
   ACTION PLAN _____
   _____
   _____

Probability of Success _____
5. Desire for a
   Distinctive
   Position Deficit (Difference between desired and actual
   0–10 points) _____
   ACTION PLAN _____

   _____

   _____

Probability of Success _____
6. A Sense of
   Responsibility Deficit (Difference between desired and actual
   0–10 points) _____
   ACTION PLAN _____

   _____

   _____

Probability of Success _____
OVERALL MOTIVATION TO MANAGE
   What is your current motivation to manage on a 60 point scale?

   _____

   What is your desired motivation to manage on a 60 point scale?

   _____

   Your 6 month action plan should be able to take you from your current
   to your desired motivation to manage position.

MOTIVATING OTHERS

In the old days it was easier—or it at least appears to have been from today's
perspective. To dramatize this, lets go back to the Bethlehem Steel Company
labor yard in Bethlehem, Pennsylvania in the spring of 1899. Frederick Wins-
low Taylor, the father of scientific management, comes over to the laborer
Schmidt whose job it is to load pig iron onto gondola cars. (His real name was
Henry Noll, but Taylor thought that Schmidt sounded better in his historical
record.) Schmidt's job was quite simple—pick up a 91 lb. pig of iron, walk
horizontally across the yard with it, up an inclined ramp, and deposit it in the
gondola car. He then returned to the pile for another pig of iron and continued
to do this throughout the day. During a typical day Schmidt would load
between 12 and 13 tons (long tons = 2,240 lbs. each), of pig iron per day. For
doing this he earned his daily wage of $1.15. Taylor studied him "scientifi-
cally." He carefully timed how long it took to pick up a pig, the speed with
which one could walk horizontally up the inclined ramp loaded, back down the

ramp unloaded, etc. He then made Schmidt a proposition—"follow my instructions, and increase your output and pay." Schmidt agreed since he was put on a piece-rate system under which he could now earn $1.85 per day providing he reached his target. His target amounted to 45–48 tons of pig iron per day. Schmidt reached his target, and continued to perform at this rate on a regular basis according to Taylor (1903).

The enormity of his task is hard to contemplate in today's world. To accomplish his forty five tons per day, Schmidt had to walk the equivalent of 8 miles each day with a 91 lb. pig of iron in his arms. He then had to run 8 miles back to the pile (Taylor 1911). According to Taylor's reports, Schmidt was not a large man, weighing about 130 pounds but was particularly suited to this work. Based on discussions that this author has had with the Human Energy Laboratory at the University of Pittsburgh, one can conclude that Schmidt's caloric energy output amounted to at least 5,000–6,000 calories per day. The poor man would have had to spend much of his waking hours eating just to keep from slowly disappearing over time.

As an interesting human interest side of this story, although Taylor reported Schmidt as happy with his work, later reports indicate that Henry Noll "later lost his home and job because of excessive drinking" (Nelson, 1980, p 98). Also, as another human interest aside, although Taylor's self reports seem to indicate great success and relative ease of implementation, such was not the case. The excellent history written by Daniel Nelson (1980) demonstrates some extremely difficult problems such as worker resistance, lack of cooperation from top management, political infighting, and other problems reminiscent of the difficulties of implementation of modern day organizational changes.

The moral of this story is that it is much easier to motivate an extremely deprived and hungry worker. Taylor's writings include stories of tremendous accomplishments with "first class men"—individuals that were willing to work at extremely high physical rates. He was able to accomplish these feats because the workers were at near subsistence levels and were willing to work quite hard to get that potential 60% increase in pay. Imagine the difficulties that Taylor might have in a modern day steel yard!

MASLOW'S HIERARCHY OF NEEDS

One very useful model for explaining the changes that have occurred in human motivation over the years is that developed by Abraham Maslow (1943). Maslow's Hierarchy argues that man's needs come in an ordered sequence that is arranged in the following five need categories:

1. Physiological Needs—the need for food, water, air.
2. Safety Needs—need for security, stability, and freedom from threat to physical safety.

3. Love Needs—need for friends with whom one may affiliate.
4. Esteem Needs—need for self-respect and the esteem of others. This includes recognition, attention and appreciation from others.
5. Self-actualization Needs—desire for self-fulfillment, to be able to grow and learn.

Maslow argued that these needs were arranged in a "hierarchy of prepotency". In other words, they must be fulfilled in sequential fashion starting with the lower order needs first and progressing up the need hierarchy. One who is dying of dehydration in the desert is not interested in esteem needs, one who is being threatened by a criminal is not interested in self-actualization, etc. Substantial follow up research (and even Maslow's original speculations) indicate that the needs may not be fulfilled in a lock step fashion and at times the artist may be willing to starve in order to create, etc. But, in general it is a useful managerial model when we consider the problem of how to motivate workers. Over the eight decades since Taylor's initial successes, society at large has moved dramatically up the need hierarchy. It would be quite difficult today to get a worker to triple output in return for a 60% raise in wages. The project manager of today must be able to assess where each of his subordinates and co-workers are in the hierarchy, and attempt to appeal to the appropriate needs. Some people crave status and recognition. Others want strongly to be a member of a cohesive team and "to belong". Others have tremendous needs to be creative, innovative, and learn new skills. If you have a motivational problem with a worker, attempt to answer these two questions: 1) Where is he on Maslow's Need Hierarchy?—what needs will motivate him? 2) How can I help him to satisfy this need?

HERZBERG'S MOTIVATION HYGIENE THEORY

Herzberg (1968) has suggested that there are two types of motivational factors: Hygiene Factors and Motivators. He suggests that the hygiene factors are necessary conditions for a satisfied worker, but do not guarantee satisfaction. If they are absent, you will have an unhappy worker, but their presence does not guarantee contentment. The hygiene factors are:

- Company Policy and Administration.
- Supervision.
- Relationship with Supervisor.
- Working Conditions.
- Salary.
- Relationship with Peers.
- Personal Life.

- Relationship with Subordinates.
- Status.
- Security.

In other words, the hygiene factors satisfy the lower level Maslow Needs. On the other hand, there are motivators which are factors that account for satisfaction in the worker. The motivators are:

- Achievement.
- Recognition.
- Work Itself.
- Responsibility.
- Advancement.
- Growth.

In other words, the motivators are found at the higher levels of Maslow's Hierarchy, see Table 27-2.

Herzberg's model has been challenged on both empirical and conceptual grounds, and we do not have time to critique these issues here. However, it has been demonstrated to be quite powerful as a general guide to the process of "job enrichment". The basic philosophy is that you can enrich someone's job and induce that individual to work harder by making the work more interesting and satisfying.

Table 27-2. Herzberg & Maslow compared.

NEED THEORY		TWO FACTOR THEORY
SELF-ACTUALIZATION	SATISFIERS	WORK ITSELF
		RESPONSIBILITY
		ADVANCEMENT
		GROWTH
ESTEEM AND STATUS		ACHIEVEMENT
		RECOGNITION STATUS
BELONGING & SOCIAL ACTUALITY		INTERPERSONAL RELATIONS
		SUPERVISION
	DISSATISFIERS	PEERS & SUBORDINATES
SAFETY & SECURITY		SUPERVISION
		COMPANY& POLICY
		ADMINISTRATION JOB
		SECURITY WORKING
		CONDITIONS
PHYSIOLOGICAL		SALARY
		PERSONAL LIFE

SOURCE: K. Davis, Human Behavior at Work, 4th Ed., New York: McGraw-Hill Book Company.

If you would like to explore the possibility of job enrichment, perform the following steps: 1) Remove serious dissatisfiers—in other words make sure that the working conditions, the pay and the supervision are satisfactory. 2) Vertically load the job content on the *satisfiers*. This consists of steps such as the following:

- Push responsibility downward.
- Push planning downward.
- Provide meaningful modules of work.
- Increase job freedom.
- Introduce new and difficult tasks.

It is well known that individuals tend to do what is satisfying to them. They are more likely to repeat behaviors that result in rewards and to not repeat behaviors that do not. Consequently, if as project manager you can design a work environment in which individuals are reinforced by the work itself, you will experience much greater effectiveness as a manager.

IN CONCLUSION—MOTIVATING YOURSELF AND OTHERS

You have now had an opportunity to assess in a personal way your motivation to manage. The logical steps in this assessment are portrayed on the flow chart shown in Figure 27-1. Try to accomplish this in as perceptive a way as possible. It's fun to consider your own personal motivational structures and to talk to others about career, job and personal needs. If you can better understand where you are concerning your motivation to manage, you will be in a better position to perform your job at peak efficiency. If your motivation to manage is insufficient for your current or future job prospects, then you must seriously consider changing these needs or changing your career. Millions of people get matched to millions of jobs through ad hoc and almost accidental sequences of events. In this chapter you are provided with a framework for consciously and analytically attempting to assess the match between your motivation structure and the project manager's job.

The second point of this chapter consists of attempting to motivate others. Remember that different people have different motivational needs. You may have to respond in a very contingent manner to individuals on the project manager team. Entire books have been written on this topic, and human motivation is indeed a complex area. In brief, you should try to assume the role of a facilitator that links up need satisfactions with desired job performances. If you can structure an environment in which diverse individual needs are being met through job performance, you will find yourself with a more cohesive and dedicated working work group. If you can master these techniques, you will be

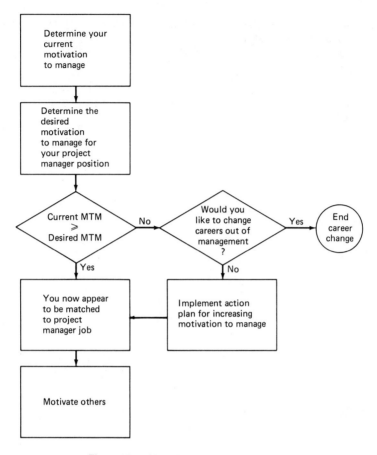

Figure 27-1. Chart for motivating yourself and others.

well on your way to becoming a highly effective and successful project manager.

REFERENCES

Herzberg, Frederick, "One More Time: How Do You Motivate Employees?" *Harvard Business Review,* 46 (1), pp. 53–62, (1968).

Maslow, A. H., "A Theory of Human Motivation." *Psychological Review,* Vol. 1, 1943, pp. 370–396, (1941).

McClelland, David C., "Toward a Theory of Motive Acquisition." *American Psychologist,* Vol. 20, pp. 321–333, (1965).

McClelland, David C., and David H. Burnham, "Power is the Great Motivator." *Harvard Business Review,* (March–April, 1976).

Miner. John B., *The Human Constraint,* (BNA Books, 1974).

Nelson, Daniel, *Frederick W. Taylor and the Rise of Scientific Management,* (University of Wisconsin Press, Madison, WI, 1980).

Rush, Harold M. F., Behavioral Science: Concepts in Management Application, Personnel Policy Study #216, (The Conference Board, Inc., 1969).

Taylor, Frederick W., "Time Study, Work, and First Class Man." Transactions of the American Society of Mechanical Engineers, Vol. 24, pp. 1, 3, 5, 6-1, 3, 6, 4, (June 1903).

Taylor, Frederick, W., *The Principles of Scientific Management,* (W. W. Norton and Company, Inc., 1911).

28. Leadership and the Project Manager

Dennis P. Slevin*

Quentin Thatchley drove more rapidly than usual up his street and into the driveway. He had a spring in his gait as he pushed open the front door. "Sarah, I got it! George just told me today. I finally got it!"

His wife came down the stairs with a puzzled frown. "Got What, Honey?"

"The promotion. Starting Monday I'm the new Project Manager—Mobile Systems—my first management position ever." Quentin was young, 29 years and 6 months, and brimming with enthusiasm at the opportunity to be a "manager" before his 30th birthday. Sarah was a willowy and wise 27 and was curious what this would mean for Quentin and her. She attempted to satisfy her curiosity without dampening his spirits.

"Why Quentin, that's wonderful," she said enthusiastically "Explain it to me."

"Starting Monday I've got a new office—a bigger one—and I share my secretary with only one other guy. I'll get a raise, and finally qualify for the organization's incentive plan."

"More status, huh? I thought you didn't care about status," said Sarah as she playfully pushed him backwards onto the sofa. "Remember those late night discussions in college about not caring about the trappings of success?"

"I really don't care that much about the status—although it is nice when you get it. But this will give me a chance to show what I can do. I'll have a lot of responsibility."

"You had responsibility before. If your designs didn't work, a lot of people could have gotten into trouble."

*Dennis P. Slevin is Associate Professor of Business Administration and Director of Executive Development Programs at the Graduate School of Business, University of Pittsburgh. He received his B.A. in mathematics from Saint Vincent College, B.S. in physics from MIT, M.S. in industrial administration from Carnegie-Mellon University and Ph. D. in business administration from Stanford University in 1969. He consults widely and is also the Chief Executive Officer of four companies serving the journals and is the coeditor of *Implementing Operations Research/Management Science, The Management of Organization Design,* Volumes I and II, and *The Implementation of Management Science,* and is coauthor of *The Executive Survival Manual.* This chapter is copyrighted © 1981 by Dennis P. Sleven.

"This will be different, Sarah, I'll be responsible for what others do as well."

"Will this promotion change what you do in any other ways?"

"I'll meet with George twice a week to brief him on our status."

"You used to see him everyday."

"I still will, but this will be more formal. And I'll be busier—making sure that things are all going right."

"I still don't see how being a manager is going to differ from what you've done up to now," said Sarah as a combination of curiosity, frustration, and concern showed on her features.

"I'll be in charge! I'll tell our group of five engineers who works on what, what our priorities are, and our scheduling."

"But haven't you been doing the scheduling the past year for the mobile systems group?" asked an inquisitive Sarah.

"Yes, but now I am the formal leader. Don't you understand? I'll tell you what. You get dressed and I'll explain it all to you over a nice leisurely dinner at Victor's," said Quentin as he picked up the evening mail and began to pore over an article entitled "The Manager as a Leader" in his monthly management journal. "I've finally assumed a position of leadership", he muttered.

INTRODUCTION

Quentin Thatchley is trying to come to grips cognitively with what his new job means. Over the next several weeks he will experience the problems and successes that leadership brings. If he is to be a good project manager, he must also be a good leader. And yet the project manager as a leader is faced with significant problems. Two major issues come to mind:

1. The project manager position is typically a low power leadership position. The project manager is often only slightly elevated over his peers in terms of legitimate authority, and as a consequence much of his leadership style must rely on influence and persuasion rather than on authority and commands.
2. The project manager is typically in a heavy information exchange job. As a leader he must continually interact with his team, constantly exchanging large volumes of information of a technical and financial nature.

What this means for Quentin and for you as a project manager is that you are in a challenging leadership position. The better you understand what leadership is and how it relates to the project manager's role, the more successful you will be. The purpose of this chapter is to present you with a leadership framework that you might use in a variety of project manager situations. We will also provide you with a diagnostic instrument to determine your preferred leadership style and whether it fits with your leadership situation. At the conclusion a power audit is presented to enable you to do your best to size up the power realities of the project management leadership role that you face.

LEADERSHIP DEFINED

What is a good leader? How does leadership relate to management? I have asked the following true/false questions of a number of executive groups to demonstrate some of the conceptual problems that we have with leadership in management.

	TRUE	FALSE
1. A good manager is a good leader.	_____	_____
2. A good leader is a good manager.	_____	_____

The overwhelming response to question 1 is "true." Practicing managers seem to feel in strong agreement that an effective manager must also be an effective leader. Question 2 usually produces about a 50/50 split. When students are asked to explain, the following dialogue typically takes place.

Student 1: "The leader decides which way to go and then the manager implements."

Professor: "Does this mean the managers don't make long run strategic planning decisions?"

Student 1: "No but . . ."

Student 2: "A manager uses his formal authority to get things done whereas a leader uses charisma."

Professor: "Does this mean that strong leaders never have strong formal authority and is charisma not a useful management trait?"

Student 2: "I see your point."

Student 3: "Management is more mechanical using quantitative tools, accounting, pert charts and so forth. Leadership is more creative, seeking broad directions and changes of course for society as a whole."

Professor: "That's an interesting distinction, but you are not meaning to imply that good managers lack in creativity are you?"

Student 3: "It still seems to me that the two words have different connotations."

And indeed they do. In this author's opinion, the general public views leadership and management somewhat as demonstrated by the following clustering.

Manager: short run, mechanical, using specific techniques, dealing with smaller problems, using formal authority of position, and in general being somewhat of a robot implementing broader policies that are somehow decided elsewhere.

Leader: long run, charismatic, creative, artistic, brilliant, and in general coming up with new approaches that impact on large numbers of people.

Perhaps the distinction in the connotation of the two terms is overdrawn, but over the past fifty years behavioral scientists have spent a very significant amount of time studying leadership and most of them have attempted to make some sort of distinction between "leader" and "manager." To this author there is no difference between the two concepts and the overlap between leadership and management is 100%. This can be shown if you accept the following two premises:

1. An effective manager modifies other persons' behaviors.
2. An effective leader modifies other persons' behaviors.

This author agrees with Howard Sargent (1978) in his book *Fishbowl Management* in which he lists in the index "leader: alternate term for manager, 352."

By "modify" we don't necessarily mean long term personality or behavior changes, we only mean movement. A manager gets things done through people. A leader gets followers to follow. If you define both terms from the standpoint of getting behavior change in others, they overlap. You may feel that this is much ado about a few definitions, but it has great significance for the project manager. If you are to be successful, you must be an effective leader. You must use creativity, charisma, planning, persuasion, in addition to formal authority and well structured techniques. In the remainder of this chapter we present you with a leadership model that will cover a variety of project management situations. And we provide you with a behavioral instrument to diagnose your leadership style.

After a leisurely dinner, Quentin and Sarah continue their discussion.

"See, Sarah, I've got two important decisions to make this week. Decision one involves whether we make the mobile data collection unit in modules— three separate units—or put them all together in one large unit."

"Which way will work the best and be the least expensive?" asked Sarah.

"Well, it's not that simple. You see the modules are easier to maintain but more expensive to build. They are also easier to ship, but take longer to set up on the site."

"What does your project group think?" asked Sarah.

"Well, Bill is a strong proponent of modules. In fact, he's what I would call a modular nut. If he could, he'd have his automobile with a lift out engine, a plug in transmission, and an interior that you could drive in and have replaced in half a day when it gets a bit worn. But, he's got some good points. Especially about field maintenance problems. Tom and the others want to go with one central unit. They feel that for this first go around it would be simpler, faster and less expensive to put everything in one box."

"Well what are you going to do?"

"I really don't know. Worse," said Quentin, "I not only don't know what I am going to do, I don't even know how I am going to decide what to do."

A confused Sarah replied, "I don't understand."

"Well you see I could play this three ways," said Quentin as he reached for a napkin and penciled out the alternatives: "1. group consensus, 2. consultative, 3. autocrat."

"Using the group consensus approach, I could call my staff together for a half a day or a day, whatever it takes, and we would sit as a group and thrash things out. I would try to be more of a facilitator than a leader and just make sure that all the points get on the table, but leave the responsibility for the decision with the group. This would be time consuming and perhaps generate a lot of conflict, but at least the group would be on board when the decision is made.

"Under alternative two, I could listen to everybody's best recommendations probably in one-on-one meetings with them and then make the decision myself. After all, it is my neck that is on the line if this system doesn't work in the field.

"Then we come to alternative three. I've been living with this project for the past six months and I probably know as much about modularization as anybody, so I could just decide without even talking to any of the guys. I have the right to do that now, don't I, since I am now 'the project manager', he questioned with a wry smile."

TWO KEY QUESTIONS

Quentin, in his back of the napkin analysis, has come up with the two key questions that any leader must ask before he handles a leadership decision. They are:

1. Whom do I ask?
2. Who makes the decision?

These two questions relate to the two key dimensions of any leadership situation, *information input* and *decision authority*, and must be addressed at the front end of a leadership decision.

BONOMA/SLEVIN LEADERSHIP MODEL

Bonoma and Slevin (1978) have used these two dimensions in formulating their graphical model of leadership.

"The first dimension is one of information, the second one of authority. These two critical dimensions can be plotted on a graph, as in the Figure 28-1. The horizontal dimension represents the authority continuum. The vertical dimension represents the information input provided by group members either to the leader or to other group members (exchange of information). The first number indicates the manager's position on the decision authority (horizontal) axis. The second number is his or her position on the information input (vertical) axis" (Bonoma and Slevin, p. 83).

FOUR LEADERSHIP STYLES

"Using this plotting system, we can describe almost any leadership style. However, the four extremes of leaders you have known (depicted in the four corners of the grid) are the following:

1. Autocrat (10, 0). Such managers solicit little or no information input from their group and make the managerial decision solely by themselves.
2. Consultative Autocrat (10, 10). In this managerial style intensive infor-

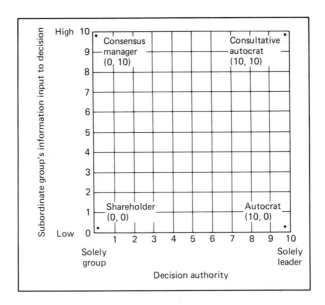

Figure 28-1. Bonoma-Slevin leadership model.

mation input is elicited from the members, but such formal leaders keep all substantive decision-making authority to themselves.

3. Consensus Manager (0, 10). Purely consensual managers throw open the problem to the group for discussion (information input) and simultaneously allow or encourage the entire group to make the relevant decision.

4. Shareholder Manager (0, 10). This position is literally poor management. Little or no information input and exchange takes place within the group context, while the group itself is provided ultimate authority for the final decision" (Bonoma and Slevin, 1978, p. 84).

LEADERSHIP STYLE PRESSURES

Given the four positions in the Bonoma/Slevin model, the leader should be able to move his style around the graph in response to characteristics of himself and

Table 28-1. Three leadership style pressures.

1. PROBLEM ATTRIBUTE PRESSURES	DIRECTION OF PRESSURE ON LEADERSHIP GRID
• Leader lacks relevant information; problem is ambiguous.	North—more information needed.
• Leader lacks enough time to make decision adequately.	South and east—consensus and information collection take time.
• Decision is important or critical to organization.	North—information search maximized.
• Decision is personally important to leader.	North and east—personal control and information maximized.
• Problem is structured or routine.	South and east—little time as possible spent on decision.
• Decision implementation by subordinates is critical to success.	West and north—input and consensus required.

2. LEADER PERSONALITY PRESSURES	
• Leader has high need for power.	East—personal control maximized.
• Leader is high in need for affiliation or is "people oriented."	North and west—contact with people maximized.
• Leader is highly intelligent.	East—personal competence demonstrated.
• Leader has high need for achievement.	East—personal contribution maximized.

3. ORGANIZATION/GROUP PRESSURES	
• Conflict is likely to result from the decision.	North and west—"participative aspects" of decision making maximized.
• Good leader-group relations exist.	North and west—group contact maximized.
• Centrality, formalization of organization is high.	South and east—organization style matched.

Source: Bonoma, Thomas V. and Dennis P. Slevin, *Executive Survival Manual,* Wadsworth Publishing Company, Belmont, CA, 1978, p. 89.

the situation he faces. Bonoma and Slevin (1978) have tabulated the types of pressures that the leader might face and the directions that these pressures might push him. Using the terminology North, South, East and West, you can look at the graph and follow the direction that each pressure might tend to move the leader. (See Table 28-1.)

The key to successful leadership is knowing what your dominant style is and being able to modify that style depending upon the contingencies of the various leadership situations that you face. We will now try to give you some feedback on your personal style.

DIAGNOSING YOUR STYLE

Please answer the questions on the Jerrell/Slevin Management Instrument as listed below. It is intended to give you feedback on your leadership style as it fits the Bonoma/Slevin leadership model.

Jerrell/Slevin Management Instrument

Name _____

	Strongly Disagree	Disagree	Neutral	Agree	Strongly Agree
1. It is easier to make a decision in a group.	1	2	3	4	5
2. Groups usually take up more time then they are worth.	5	4	3	2	1
3. I often ask for information from subordinates.	1	2	3	4	5
4. Groups give a deeper analysis of a problem.	1	2	3	4	5
5. I often use what subordinates have to say.	1	2	3	4	5
6. No one else can know as much about the problem as I do.	5	4	3	2	1
7. I usually make my decision before calling a staff meeting.	5	4	3	2	1
8. Better decisions are made in group situations.	1	2	3	4	5
9. A group is no better than its best member.	5	4	3	2	1
10. Group decisions are the best.	1	2	3	4	5

Total your I score by summing the answers to items 1–10 you have checked above.	I = __43__

11. I don't like it when others disagree with me.

$\bar{1}$ $\quad$ $\bar{2}$ $\quad$ $\bar{3}$ $\quad$ $\bar{4}$ $\quad$ $\bar{5}$

12. I like quick results.

$\bar{1}$ $\quad$ $\bar{2}$ $\quad$ $\bar{3}$ $\quad$ $\bar{4}$ $\quad$ $\bar{5}$

13. I find it hard to accept others' decisions.

$\bar{1}$ $\quad$ $\bar{2}$ $\quad$ $\bar{3}$ $\quad$ $\bar{4}$ $\quad$ $\bar{5}$

14. I have a very strong ego.

$\bar{1}$ $\quad$ $\bar{2}$ $\quad$ $\bar{3}$ $\quad$ $\bar{4}$ $\quad$ $\bar{5}$

15. Once I make up my mind, I stick to it.

$\bar{1}$ $\quad$ $\bar{2}$ $\quad$ $\bar{3}$ $\quad$ $\bar{4}$ $\quad$ $\bar{5}$

16. I enjoy giving orders.

$\bar{1}$ $\quad$ $\bar{2}$ $\quad$ $\bar{3}$ $\quad$ $\bar{4}$ $\quad$ $\bar{5}$

17. The work groups should determine its own vacation schedule.

$\bar{5}$ $\quad$ $\bar{4}$ $\quad$ $\bar{3}$ $\quad$ $\bar{2}$ $\quad$ $\bar{1}$

18. The work group should determine its own work schedule.

$\bar{5}$ $\quad$ $\bar{4}$ $\quad$ $\bar{3}$ $\quad$ $\bar{2}$ $\quad$ $\bar{1}$

19. I feel comfortable being placed in a powerful position.

$\bar{1}$ $\quad$ $\bar{2}$ $\quad$ $\bar{3}$ $\quad$ $\bar{4}$ $\quad$ $\bar{5}$

20. I like working in a group situation.

$\bar{5}$ $\quad$ $\bar{4}$ $\quad$ $\bar{3}$ $\quad$ $\bar{2}$ $\quad$ $\bar{1}$

Total your DA score by summing the answers to items 11–20 you have checked above.	DA = _33_

A note of caution should be interjected here. This instrument, as with even the best and most carefully tested psychometric instruments, has limitations of reliability and validity. You should not seize on any one number that you generate using this instrument. Rather it should be used to stimulate self insight as you attempt to analyze what your dominant leadership style is.

GENERAL PRINCIPLES

The following does not represent carefully tested quantitative research, but rather the author's experience in working with a large number of managers concerning their leadership style. I call them "research results" but they are more the function of clinical experience than large sample research.

1. *You are more autocratic than you think.* If you place yourself on the graph and then have your subordinates place you there also, it is highly likely that they will place you more in the direction of the South East. They view you as more autocratic than you view yourself. Why is this so? This is a function of the job itself. You are "boss" and there is nothing that you can do to stop from being boss. No matter how participative you are, no matter how friendly and open you attempt to be with your staff, you still have the legitimate formal authority to make decisions affecting

Scoring Instructions

Step 1—Total your I scores by summing the answers to items 1–10 which you have checked on the previous page.

Step 2—Total your DA scores by summing the answers to items 11–20 which you have checked on the previous page.

Step 3—Compute your percentile score from the table listed below.

DA		I	
Raw Score	% tile	Raw Score	% tile
16	1	21	1
18	1	22	1
23	3	23	2
24	5	24	3
25	7	26	4
26	12	27	5
27	17	28	7
28	27	29	10
29	34	30	17
30	46	31	22
31	54	32	29
32	65	33	37
33	71	34	48
34	79	35	57
35	85	36	66
36	90	37	72
37	95	38	79
38	96	39	87
39	97	40	90
40	98	41	93
41	99	42	94
43	100	43	97
		44	97
		45	98
		46	99
		50	100

List your % tile I & DA scores here: DA = __71__%

I = __97__%

Step 4—Plot yourself on the grid on the following page.

1% tiles are estimates based on data collected from 188 American managers.

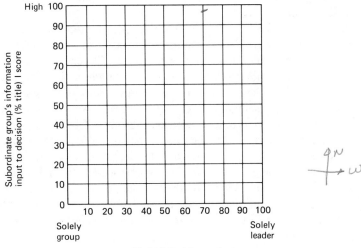

DA score (% title) Decision authority

them. There is nothing that you can do to remove the cloak of authority and responsibility once you agree to take it on.

2. *But it's okay.* If you then ask your subordinates where they would like you to move on the graph, the most probable answer is "things are fine as they are." In other words, even though their perception of you is more autocratic than your self perception, it does not mean that some sort of movement is necessary. They may be quite satisfied with the particular position you assume.

3. *It's easy to move North and South.* If you want to do an interesting experiment concerning your leadership style, attempt to plot on the graph each of your leadership decisions for the next two weeks. I'll bet that you find that most of them cluster on a North/South line and deviate very little to the West. This is because it is easy for managers to collect varying amounts of information. After all, management is an informational job, and if you want to collect additional information, it is quite easy to do.

4. *It is hard to move West.* A movement to the West can really shake up your group and other groups in the organization. By moving Westward, you are changing power realities in your group and in the organization as a whole. When I have asked practicing managers to merely place themselves on the graph without using the Jerrell/Slevin instrument, almost no managers characterized themselves as being lower than 5 on the decision authority dimension. After all, it's their neck on the line if

things don't work out, so why should they move in a more consensual direction?

5. *If your leadership style does not meet your subordinates' expectation, you will generate conflict.* If you make a decision in a more autocratic fashion than your subordinates had expected, it will generate problems of cohesion and morale. I've seen instances occur where the subordinates totally agreed with the decision, but were upset with *the way it was made.* In other words, sometimes decision process in working with small groups becomes as important as decision substance. I believe that this is a very important message for the project manager. You tend to be in a position of minimal power vis-a-vis your subordinates. As a consequence, you are probably going to be pushed to assume leadership styles that you are to the North and the West on the Bonoma/Slevin model. This will be more time consuming than autocratic approaches, but may pay off for you in the long run in terms of higher quality decisions and a mere motivated work group.

POWER DIAGNOSIS

Given that the project manager is often in a low power leadership position, it becomes essential that you analyze the power realities of your position, espe-

In the management situation you are considering, estimate your power on the five dimensions listed below.

	Low									High
---	1	2	3	4	5	6	7	8	9	10
Coercive power: ability to control punishments.										
Legitimate power: "legitimate authority" due to position or office.										
Referent power: others are attracted to and identify with you.										
Expert power: due to specialized knowledge and skill.										
Reward power: ability to control rewards.										

Source: Power Equalization: The Primary Management Constraint, Dennis P. Slevin, 1978.

Figure 28-2. Power diagnosis check list.

cially before taking on new assignments. French and Raven (1959) suggested 5 types of power: coercive, legitimate, referent, expert and reward. Using their definitions, we have developed the power diagnosis check list shown below. (See Figure 28-2.)

In the management situation you are considering, estimate your power on the five dimensions listed below.

Before taking on a project management assignment, attempt to diagnose the power that you will have as a project manager on each of the above 5 dimensions. *Don't be afraid to attempt to negotiate for power in advance of taking on the assignment.* It is much easier to negotiate agreements and understandings before the assignment starts than it is once you have already agreed to do it. After all, it's nice to have power! Although the term power has almost become a "dirty word" in our society and one who lusts for power is viewed with great suspicion, the manager can do nothing without power. Since your project manager position is probably one of relatively low power with respect to the rest of the group, the more incremental increases that you achieve in your power the greater your potential for success.

LEADERSHIP AUDIT

After you have completed the work in this chapter, you should be able to answer the following questions:

1. What is my dominant leadership style?

2. Am I flexible enough—do I modify my style to fit the situation?

3. Do I fit in my organization—does my style have compatibility with the leadership climate in the organization as a whole?

4. Do my subordinates fit? Are their expectations of my behavior in line with my actual style?

And finally, the two fundamental questions that every project manager should be able to answer about his job:

1. Do I get sufficient information? —Am I receiving adequate information now in order to perform my job effectively?

_____

_____

2. Do I have adequate decision authority? Do I have the legitimate authority to make decisions that are necessary for success in my position?

_____

_____

You might even be able to extend the above two questions to the organization as a whole. In an optimally tuned organization each manager receives exactly the information he needs to perform his job effectively and no more, and each manager has adequate decision authority for the decisions that he faces. In future when faced with leadership situations, attempt to analytically decide in advance the leadership style that you are going to use in each situation. The more you critically analyze the style you use, the more effective leader you will be.

REFERENCES

Bonoma, Thomas V. and Dennis Slevin, *Executive Survival Manual,* (Wadsworth Publishing Company: Belmont, CA, 1978).

French, John R. P., Jr. and Bertram Raven, "The Bases of Social Power" in Dorwin Cartwright (ed.) *Studies in Social Power,* (University of Michigan, Ann Arbor, 1959).

Jerrell, S. Lee and Dennis Slevin, "Jerrell/Slevin Management Instrument," copyright 1981, used with permission.

Slevin, Dennis P., "Power Equalization: The Primary Management Constraint," (University of Pittsburgh Working Paper Series #287, 1978).

29. Managing the Human Side of Project Teams

Raymond E. Hill*

INTRODUCTION

A central theme in managing the human side of project teams is the management of social conflict. Conflict in organizations is pervasive, inevitable and ubiquitous; organizations develop specialized, differentiated subunits which then obey many of the principles of general systems theory, not the least of which is the emergence of opponent processes among the differentiated parts. Project teams, by the very act of bringing together representatives of the specialized subunits become a microcosm of the larger organizational dynamics.

There are a variety of issues around which conflict arises. Thamhain and Wilemon (1)† have reduced these issues to seven fundamental areas which include the following: project priorities, administrative procedures, technical opinions and performance tradeoffs, manpower resources, cost estimates, scheduling and sequencing of work, and personality conflict. Thamhain and Wilemon found significant variation in intensity of the seven conflict types over the life cycle of a project. Data from one hundred project managers indicated considerable variation over time in the intensity of conflict from almost all sources *except* personality clashes. Personality conflicts were relatively constant during all phases of a project life cycle including project formation, build-up, main program phase, and phaseout. In discussing personality clashes as a source of conflict, Thamhain and Wilemon suggest that while it is not as intense as some other conflict types, it is nevertheless problematical. In particular, they suggest "Project managers emphasized that personality conflicts are particularly difficult to handle. Even apparently small and infrequent person-

*Raymond E. Hill is Associate Professor of Organizational Behavior in the Graduate School of Business Administration, The University of Michigan. He is a member of the American Psychological Association and the Academy of Management. His research interests are focused on project management with recent interests centered around career choice and development processes, particularly of systems and computer personnel. He has published several articles in professional journals, and has edited a book of readings on Matrix Organization.
†Numbered references are given at the end of this chapter.

ality conflicts might be more disruptive and detrimental to overall program effectiveness than intense conflict over nonpersonal issues, which can often be handled on a more rational basis" (1, p. 39). It is the purpose of the present chapter to relate two frameworks for conceptualizing personality conflict both of which can be diagnosed and assessed using standardized questionnaires and to report on how differences can be managed for more effective project performance.

EMOTIONAL STYLES: THE FIRO FRAMEWORK

It is important to recognize that the location of the problem in most so-called personality conflicts does not reside solely in one person. Most social conflicts are inherently *relational;* that is a problem does not exist until two or more persons have to work together, or live together, etc. The dysfunction then is typically not located in one person or the other, but rather is located in their relationship. Thus any framework which systematically attempts to explain personality conflict must in fact be a theory of interpersonal relationships. The framework used in the present study was developed by W. C. Schutz (2), and is both concise and operational in the sense that it provides for a method of assessing the degree of potential interpersonal strife or incompatibility in any relationship. It is not the only theory of interpersonal behavior extant in the behavioral sciences, but is one which has been found to be useful in a variety of social and work contexts.

In the following discussion, interpersonal incompatibility will be used as synonymous with "personality conflict," whereas interpersonal compatibility suggests harmony and lack of conflict. The basis of Schutz's theory is the individual's *fundamental interpersonal relations orientation,* or FIRO as it is usually abbreviated. One's FIRO is an "interpersonal style" which is hypothesized to be rather stable and to have developed from psychological forces in the person's childhood and developmental history. It reflects a person's central emotional position with respect to other people generally. That is, people learn a way of relating to others along certain dimensions, and they tend to carry that style around with them as a rather stable aspect of their personality which affects their work and social relations. The FIRO is in fact a set of three basic interpersonal needs which are common to all persons in greater or lesser degrees. These three needs are inclusion, control, and affection and are considered to be predictive in a general sense of the fundamental behavior that occurs interpersonally. Inclusion refers to the need to be included in other people's activities, or to include others in one's own activities, and is analogous to the introversion-extroversion dimension of other authors, or to sociability. It entails moving toward or away from people psychologically. Control refers to the need to give and receive structure, directions, influence, power, authority and responsibility.

Affection is concerned with emotional closeness to others, friendship, liking or disliking, and refers to the need to act close or distant toward others.

There are two aspects to each of the three interpersonal needs. One is what we do or have a need to express toward others, and the second is how we want others to behave toward us. This is shown schematically in Table 29-1. That is, people have a need to both give and receive in each need area and this forms the basis for interpersonal harmony or strife. Harmony (compatibility) results when one party has a need to give (or express) what the other party is interested in getting (or wants). If we symbolize the need to express behavior as "e", the need to receive from others as "w", and the three need areas of inclusion, control and affection as I, C, and A, then any individual can be characterized by the six scales: eI, wI, eC, wC, eA, wA. Schutz has developed a questionnaire, referred to as FIRO-B which is designed to measure an individual's need levels in each of the six categories (the "B" indicates the questionnaire is designed to predict behavior). The six categories are measured on a scale from a low of zero to a high of nine. This scaling provides a way of assessing the potential conflict or incompatibility in an interpersonal relationship. Suppose for example that persons, A and B, each have hypothetical FIRO-B scores on the control dimension of eC equal to nine and wC equal to zero as shown in Figure 29-1. Both would be trying to exert control and influence, but would be unwilling to receive influence from the other. A power struggle would be going on under the surface, and would likely be acted out around task issues, often in unproductive ways. In this situation, the parties would be said to be "originator incompatible" in an aggressive way. The example of parties C and D

Table 29-1. The FIRO Framework.
NEED AREA

	INCLUSION	CONTROL	AFFECTION
What I need to express to others (symbolized as e)	eI need to initiate interaction with others—need to reach out and include others in ones activity	eC need to assume leadership, responsibility, control and exert influence	eA need to act close and personal toward others— express friendship
What I need or want from others (symbolized as w)	wI need to be invited to join others—need to be included in interaction	wC need to receive directions, guidance, assume followership roles, receive influence	wA need to be on the receiving end of friendship and personal closeness

	A	B	
orginator	e 9	9	relationship characterized by a competitive
incompatible	w 0	0	power struggle

	C	D	
orginator	e 0	0	relationship characterized by a power vacuum
incompatible	w 9	9	and apathy

	E	F	
orginator	e 9	0	relationship characterized by unilateral
compatible	w 0	9	control (E controlling F)

	G	H	
orginator	e 5	5	relationship characterized by mutual control
compatible	w 5	5	and shared influence

Figure 29-1.* Hypothetical FIRO-B scores in the control area.

*Reprinted from "Managing Interpersonal conflict in Project Teams" by Raymond E. Hill, *Sloan Management Review,* Vol. 18, 45–62, by permission of the publisher. Copyright (1977) by Sloan Management Review Association. All rights reserved.

reflect an opposite problem of unwillingness from either party to exert influence. Thus each would be wanting direction, but none would be present in the relationship. This example also illustrates originator incompatibility, because there is no reciprocity, or complementarity with respect to who originates and who receives. The parties E and F illustrate an example of originator compatibility where E is willing to originate influence and F is willing to receive it. The control would be unilateral in that E would be in practically exclusive command, but nevertheless the relationship would be characterized by compatibility with regard to who originates and who receives influence. Parties G and H would also reflect an originator compatible pair, but control would be shared, and their relationship would be characterized by an exchanging of leadership and followership roles.

These examples serve to illustrate the essential nature of the FIRO framework. Schutz has developed methods for scaling the degree of potential interpersonal incompatibility in a group by combining the FIRO-B scores of all individuals in the group according to certain formulas. The control dimension will be used to explain these formulas since control is often at the heart of difficulties in work settings; control is the dominant need aroused by the necessity to engage in division of labor, take on responsibility, engage in leadership and followership, etc. Accordingly, more illustrative examples are shown below based on Pfeiffer and Heslin's (3, p. 144) work with the FIRO-B instrument in human relations training.*

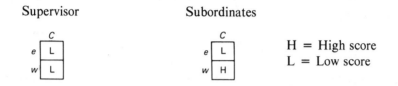

Supervisor   Subordinates

H = High score
L = Low score

Subordinates: "Boss, we're ready to go, tell us what you want us to do?"
Supervisor: "Look over the situation, and do whatever you think is best."
Pfeiffer and Heslin report a situation where the physical education department of a college had this constellation of scores. The employees would say, "Fred, what do you think we should do with the intramural program this year?" Fred would generally respond, "I don't care fellows. Do whatever you want." Needless to say this caused employee frustration, and low performance since the employees wanted (and needed) influence from others to be effective.

The reverse case also occurs:**

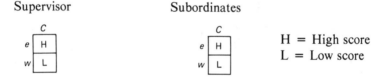

Supervisor   Subordinates

H = High score
L = Low score

Subordinates: "Boss, let us do it our way and we'll give you the best sales department in the country."
Supervisor: "You'll do things the way I say to do them."
This relational constellation represents competitive, aggressive incompatibility wherein it is difficult for the parties to share control and leadership. Since the supervisor has formal authority and can invoke various forms of punishment for non-compliance, the subordinates often lose interest in work, and withdraw their vitality from the job. Or, they may actively express their anger in the form of sabotage, and other counter productive maneuvers.

---

*Used with permission and reprinted from J. W. Pfeiffer, R. Heslin & J. E. Jones, *Instrumentation in Human Relations Training* (2nd Ed) San Diego, CA: University Associates, 1976.
**Ibid.*

Schutz's concept of originator compatibility reflects the degree to which one person's excess of a need to express or receive in a given need area is balanced by the other person's excess in the reverse direction; e.g. if one party's e score is greater than the w score, the other party's w score should be greater than the e score so that one difference counterbalances the other. The originator compatibility formula symbolized as OK for person i and person j is given in equation [1].

$$\text{Originator Compatibility: } OK_{ij} = (e_i - w_i) + (e_j - w_j) \qquad [1]$$

for example, returning to the extreme case illustrated earlier of a competitive, incompatible relationship around control, the two persons, i and j would be:

	i
e	9
w	0

	i
e	9
w	0

$OK_{ij} = (9 - 0) + (9 - 0) = 18$, extreme competitive incompatibility

Two persons who are compatible around initiation-reception might be:

	i
e	7
w	2

	j
e	2
w	7

$OK_{ij} = (7 - 2) + (2 - 7) = 0$, perfect compatibility

Person i's propensity to initiate control is directly counterbalanced by person j's propensity to receive control, and hence they would be compatible with i initiating and j following. One last example will show how originator compatibility is bipolar:

	i
e	0
w	9

	j
e	0
w	9

$OK_{ij} = (0 - 9) + (0 - 9) = -18$, extreme apathetic incompatibility

This pair is at the other extreme of incompatibility, but their relationship would be characterized by a serious absence of leadership. Thus the originator compatibility scale ranges from a negative extreme to a positive extreme.

```
−18 . . . . . . . . . . . . . . . . . . 0 . . . . . . . . . . . . . . . . . . +18
   apathetic              compatibility            competitive
  incompatibility                                incompatibility
```

There must be some complementarity, reciprocity, or "oppositeness" in the relationship for originator compatibility to exist. Schutz (2 p. 118) suggests this aspect of relationships reflects the old maxim "opposites attract."

Another maxim seemingly contradictory to the first about interpersonal relationships is that "birds of a feather flock together," or similarity attracts. The second type of compatibility can be used to assess this dimension of relationships. It is called interchange compatibility (symbolized as *IK*) and refers to whether two persons have a need to be similarly active in a given need area. Incompatibility results where two persons are very different in how much interchange (activity) they prefer in the various need areas.

For inclusion, the typical conflict is between the joiner or participator (high interchange) who likes to be surrounded by people doing things together, and the more withdrawn person who prefers to work alone (low interchange). In the control area, the conflict is between those who like to create a system of rules and clearly delineated roles (high interchange) versus those who prefer to "live and let live" in a more permissive, unstructured atmosphere (low interchange). For affection, interchange incompatibility reflects a conflict between those who want to be close, personal and confiding versus those who prefer cooler, more distant and non-disclosing relations. Interchange compatibility between persons i and j is given by the formula:

$$\text{Interchange Compatibility: } IK_{ij} = |(e_i + w_i) - (e_j + w_j)| \qquad [2]$$

Interchange compatibility ranges from zero (most compatible) to eighteen (least compatible). In our three prior examples, all pairs would be interchange compatible in the sense that within each pair there would be an interest in the same amount of "general control activity" even though not all cases were originator compatible. Thus people may be compatible in one sense, but not the other. Below is an example that would be originator compatible, but not interchange compatible:

```
        i                          j
    ┌──────┐                   ┌──────┐
  e │  9   │                 e │  1   │
    ├──────┤                   ├──────┤
  w │  8   │                 w │  2   │
    └──────┘                   └──────┘
```

$$OK_{ij} = (e_i - w_i) + (e_j - w_j) = (9 - 8) + (1 - 2) = 0, \text{ compatible}$$

however,

$$IK_{ij} = |(e_i + w_i) - (e_j + w_j)| = 17 - 3 = 15, \text{ incompatible.}$$

Thus, person j would usually want to work in an unstructured fashion whereas person i would be very concerned about establishing order, roles, rules, and leader-follower behavior. Control would be a source of friction for this pair; however, if person j could accept the necessity for leader-follower behavior, he or she would likely be the follower in relation to person i. It is no paradox, incidentally to be high in both expressed and wanted control. The ideal military officer, for instance, must take orders from above (be high on wanted control) and turn around and give orders to those below (be high on expressed control). In short, individual i in the last example would be comfortable both as a leader and as a follower.

There is another type of compatibility, referred to as reciprocal compatibility which is rather similar to originator compatibility and will not be discussed here. Interested readers are referred to Schutz (2), Pfeiffer & Heslin (3) and Hill (4) for further information on reciprocal compatibility.

The typical data for a group is displayed in the format shown in Table 29-2, where each compatibility type is shown for each need area. In addition, the rows and columns can be averaged to illustrate compatibility by need area or type. Finally, the entire matrix can be averaged to assess the total group compatibility.

Inspection of this matrix can signal the source and nature of potential conflicts in a group. Schutz indicates that the most frequently occurring types of incompatibility which affect work group functioning usually center around inclusion interchange, control interchange, and control originator.

Inclusion interchange problems in project teams are usually expressed as conflicts between members who prefer to work in groups (high inclusion activity) versus those who prefer to work more individualistically (low inclusion activity). The differences manifest themselves in the group setting, since when-

Table 29-2. Compatibility Types and Areas.

		AREAS OF COMPATIBILITY			ROW AVERAGES
		INCLUSION	CONTROL	AFFECTION	
Type of	O	$OK(I)$	$OK(C)$	$OK(A)$	overall OK
Compatibility	I	$IK(I)$	$IK(C)$	$IK(A)$	overall IK
	column Average	overall K, Inclusion	overall K, Control	overall K, Affection	average K, entire matrix

ever a decision must be made, those high on inclusion prefer working it out together, whereas those low on inclusion attempt to go off on their own in pursuit of the decision.

Control interchange problems tend to pervasively affect a group, since as indicated earlier some members will be satisfied with attempt to create a group structure and definite roles, responsibilities, etc. Those low in the control area will be resisting the high control persons and attempting to create an unstructured group with freedom to play different roles at different times as they see fit.

Control originator compatibility problems, like many interpersonal conflicts, are also expressed through the task all too often. If someone makes a suggestion in a group meeting, it is improbable that someone else would say "Your suggestion is okay, but I want mine accepted because I want to have the most influence here." The person is more likely to say "your idea is okay, but these are its disadvantages, and I think we should do so and so." The merits of suggestions are often secondary to the deeper agenda of who will have how much control over the decision process. This competitive incompatibility often produces a general feeling of struggle and conflict in the group. Apathetic incompatibility on the other hand usually produces feelings of emptiness and boredom with the group process.

Affectional conflicts are perhaps less frequently felt in work settings, but a high interchange person imbedded in a low interchange group would probably complain of an impersonal group in which there was not enough encouragement and support.

Using the FIRO-B in Team Development

The FIRO system then can be used to conceptualize interpersonal strife in any work group or team which must accomplish some objectives. Probably its greatest value lies in diagnosing and defining the kind of conflict likely to occur in a group. By administering the FIRO-B questionnaire to a project team, a profile can be obtained of the potential points of friction, and the manager as well as the entire team can then be more informed as to the likely origin and nature of conflict in the team. This procedure would probably best be carried out with the assistance of a staff specialist, and in an open manner wherein the results were fed back to the entire team, and the meaning and nature of the FIRO system fully explained. In short, all of the usual organizational development ground rules regarding survey feedback (i.e. voluntary participation, disclosure of results, etc.) would ideally be adhered to, and the feedback effort itself would become an intervention to facilitate team development.

The FIRO system is used analogously in marriage counseling where the therapist would like to get to the basic issues quickly (5). It is also used by a variety of human relations trainers in the National Training Laboratories (NTL) network for workshops on interpersonal relations and conflict. The Diamond Shamrock Company has used it in an organization development effort similar to what is being suggested here, except the application was to management groups rather than project teams (6). It has also been used to select submarine crews, police teams, and for personnel placement in various industries.

If the FIRO-B instrument is used to help a team see its conflict areas more clearly, and deal with them more constructively, there are several uses which Pfeiffer and Heslin (3, p. 140) suggest as revelant for group and individual development. These are reproduced below:

1. *Generating a Personal Agenda:* Giving the FIRO-B scale early in a training session can provide participants with insights into their inclusion, control, and affection desires and behavior which they may wish to modify or change by trying out new behaviors within the group setting.
2. *Sensitization to Interpersonal Dimensions:* Scoring and discussing the FIRO-B can make participants aware of dimensions of interpersonal relations with which they will be dealing during a training session. It introduces terminology for understanding inclusion, control, and affection problems.
3. *Checking Self Understanding:* Administering the FIRO-B can be preceded by asking members to estimate how they expect to score (high, medium, or low) on each scale. If the group has been in existence long enough, members can also predict how they expect the other members to score on the instrument. FIRO-B is not a deceptively-worded instrument, so pre-awareness should have little effect on the respondent's scores.
4. *Individual Interpretations:* FIRO-B can be given in a group followed by a general discussion of the subscales. Later the facilitator can meet with members individually to interpret each person's pattern of scores in detail and discuss how this feedback effects the individual's understanding of his or her past and future group behavior.

The upshot of most group interventions with FIRO-B is that it serves to sensitize and educate the members as to the nature of interpersonal conflict. It also serves as a stimulus for an open discussion of problem areas within the group, which when attended by a competent facilitator, can enable a group to work through the problem of interpersonal agendas contaminating the productive efforts of the group.

Managing Conflict Constructively

Prior research with the FIRO-B instrument in relation to project team performance has suggested that moderate levels of conflict are inevitable, and desirable particularly if people are able to constructively utilize conflict. The key is effective conflict management by supervisors and members of the team. Note the key word here is conflict management rather than resolution. Probably the majority of social conflicts are not amenable to complete resolution, and it is probably more realistic to think in terms of managing conflict for productive purposes rather than resolving it. Hill (7) studied the characteristics of project team leaders employed in a large oil company who were selected by their organization as being outstanding project managers, and compared them to a sample of average managers in terms of the leadership practices which distinguished the two samples. The description below borrows heavily from Hill's (7) prior work with project teams.*

There seems immediately to be two general aspects in which high performing managers differed from the lower performing in terms of responding to internal team conflict. First, the high performers reflected a much larger repertoire of responses. They simply had more ideas and choices about how to deal with conflict generally. Second, they seemed much less afraid of disagreements, and intimated much more willingness to approach conflict rather than avoid it. This latter point is a common theme in management literature and has been noted by other authors as a preference for confrontation rather than withdrawal as a conflict handling mode. The lower producing managers had a more prevalent feeling that conflict would "go away" if left unattended.

With these general differences in mind, the next question became what specific behavior did the higher performing managers report which distinguished them from their lower performing counterparts?

Personal Absorption of Aggression.   Being willing to hear subordinates out when they are particularly disturbed by a peer was a common theme. One manager made the following observation, "You have to learn to listen, keep your mouth shut, and let the guy get it off his chest . . . sometimes, it's not that easy though, because you get the feeling the guy is yelling at you, but if you lash back, you're finished . . . it just compounds the problem." The same manager went on to add, "Usually, when someone blows their stack, it is short lived, but at the moment it is pretty important to the guy involved."

A second manager described a situation in which two subordinates were making life rather miserable for a third and had essentially rejected this third subordinate. When confronted on their behavior, one of the two team members launched a brief personal attack on the manager himself. Instead of counterattacking, the manager simply asked the subordinate involved what was really

---

*Parts of this section are reprinted from "Managing Interpersonal Conflict in Project Teams" by Raymond E. Hill, *Sloan Management Review,* Vol. 18, No. 2, by permission of the publisher. Copyright (©) (1977) by Sloan Management Review Association. All rights reserved.

bothering him, as it appeared that some hidden agenda was more responsible for the anger. The subordinate declined to answer, and abruptly walked away. At this point, the manager felt some unease as to whether he had lost respect from the two subordinates. However, the next day, they both came to his office, apologized, and explained their feelings that the third subordinate did not take enough initiative and do his share of work, which subsequently left them carrying most of the load. Whereas the manager had originally feared loss of respect, it now appeared that perhaps he had gained respect. And equally as important, he had started a process of owning up to interpersonal antagonisms which could then be worked on with future benefits to team functioning.

A third manager related an episode in which he was standing between two subordinates who were in the middle of an altercation, while at the same time, all three were late to a meeting with the manager's organizational superior. His response, however, was to remain calm and patient in the face of stress, and in fact to draw out the parties more by asking questions and listening.

The picture which emerged was one of a manager who did not flinch in the fact of negative interpersonal feelings, and who accepted them as a normal part of working life. In short, differences between people were viewed as legitimate and their expression was not inhibited. This is closely related to the next differentiating characteristic.

Encouraging Openness and Emotional Expression.   Interpersonal relationships as well as leadership behavior has long been characterized by at least two fundamental dimensions: instrumental and expressive behavior. Leadership behavior in both areas has been linked with effectiveness (see Likert (8)). In a recent study the author formed impressions relative to the expressive behavior of high and low performing managers. The higher performing managers seemed more concerned with how their subordinates felt about work, the organization, their peers, etc., and reported more initiative in attempting to allow expression of those feelings. More of the high performing managers claimed to have an "open door" policy in which subordinates were free to speak with them anytime. However, there was much more to the picture than just a manager sitting passively in his or her office with the door open. One manager started out by stating that "the guys can talk to me anytime," but then went on to relate a story of how he in effect initiated conversation with them "anytime" and frequently. The same manager ended his story with the idea that "a project leader must show an interest in members (of the project), and let them know he's willing to be open about their concerns . . . I don't like to be in the dark about what's going on out there or what people are thinking."

In addition to encouraging expression and being employee centered directly, a more subtle difference seemed to characterize the high performing managers as a group. One got the impression that they simply enjoyed social interaction more than their less effective counterparts. Although there were exceptions, as a group they talked more enthusiastically, spontaneously, and longer during the interviews. This impression led the author to compare the magnitude of the total interpersonal needs on the FIRO-B scale for the high and low performing project managers. All six FIRO-B scales can be summed to obtain an index of how "active" an individual wants to be interpersonally. The scale would run from a low of 0 to a high of 54 (a score of nine on all six subscales). The higher performing managers averaged 27.2 whereas the lower group averaged 22.9. This was not statistically significant at the usual 5 percent level but was in the direction expected from clinical observation (i.e. the higher performers reflected a greater propensity for interpersonal activity).

Norm Setting, Role Modeling and Counseling.   One of the most fascinating aspects of the study involved managers who, in essence, "taught" their subordinates how to cope with interpersonal conflict in productive ways. Several of the high performing managers felt it was important for them to "set an example" when it came to reacting to personality clashes. They felt it was more legitimate for them to urge a subordinate to listen to his or her emotional rival with more understanding if they in fact did that themselves. One manager noted that "An effective supervisor teaches others to listen by doing it himself. Some analysts have trouble listening . . . they keep talking when it is inappropriate. A good boss will be emulated, though, and I find that is one of the best ways to get across an idea on how to behave."

An interesting correlate of this process was the observation that often a peer would intercede and act out a third party conciliation role much like the manager might normally perform. Thus two parties in conflict would find themselves the target of peer pressure to live up to a norm which involved at least trying to understand the other party's point of view. At the same time, each party would also be likely to find other peers who tried to be impartial, but reassuring that it was okay to feel hostility. The norm seemed to be one of acceptance of conflict rather than suppression, and was apparently felt by members of high producing groups more often than lower producing teams.

Some managers resorted to counseling and in some cases exhortation to try to influence some subordinates to behave differently toward their perceived rival. One manager recounted advice he had given a subordinate, telling him "not to lash back at Eddie . . . all it does is set off another round of charges."

Other comments which reinforced the idea that supervisors served as role models was the observation that managers set the "climate" in the group, and that if conflict was handled poorly in a group, it was usually because people did not feel free to "open up" in front of the supervisor. In fact, one manager observed that many groups seem to take on the personality characteristics of the supervisors. Of course, it is not the "group" which takes on the manager's characteristics, but rather the individuals who comprise it. Lower producing managers seemed to verbally encourage openness with admonishments about the value of keeping people informed, but did not report as many instances where they actually practiced it themselves or taught it by example.

Awareness of the Utility of Conflict.   The higher producing managers seemed to more frequently evidence the attitude that conflict could be harnessed for productive ends. One manager very actively took this stance, and counseled his team with the admonition, "You never know where a good idea is going to come from next," as if to legitimize broad participation and differences of opinion. On the other hand, the lower producing managers seemed to speak more frequently of the disruptive effects of conflict.

Another high producing manager noted that, "You have to break people in to the idea that conflict does not have to be personally destructive, but can be important toward task accomplishment . . . I try to encourage freedom of expression, and consensus on issues with my team."

Pacing and Control of Potential Conflict.   While the prior factors suggest a pattern of high producing managers confronting differences, they also intimated a sense of when to do just the opposite. There were cases when they delayed face to face group meetings because they felt two rival members were on the edge of acrimonious outbursts. The higher producing managers seemed more willing to stop work and socialize with two or three persons over coffee, and on occasion would take the entire team out to lunch as a way of getting away from work pressures. In fact, it seemed that informal work stoppages were more frequent during periods of high work stress such as deadlines and project phaseout. Sometimes, however, the process was more formal and involved allowing team members time off from work (with no pay penalty) because they had recently put in a large amount of overtime. People were becoming exhausted and tempers were getting short.

The extreme of this general containment strategy involved removing people from teams; only one high producing manager had actually done this, although others reportedly threatened it on rare occasions.

The important aspect of pacing and control of conflict as a coping strategy was that high producing managers seemed to be in close enough touch with team members that they could judge whether it was appropriate to approach or avoid conflict. The lower producing managers did not exude the same sense of relatedness to subordinates and interpersonal sensitivity.

Summary of the Effective Project Manager

Table 29-3 summarizes the above discussion by illustrating relative frequencies for six conflict coping responses. Definitive categorization was difficult in some

Table 29-3. Differences between High and Low Producing Project Managers.

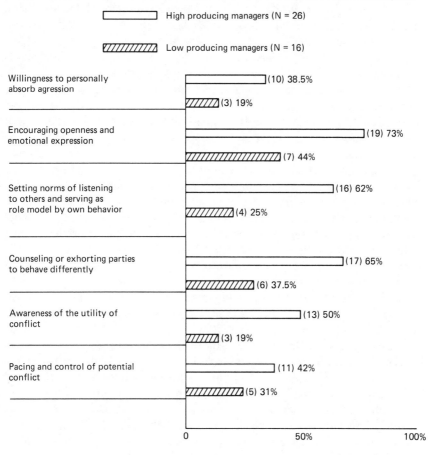

High producing managers (N = 26)

Low producing managers (N = 16)

Reproduced from Hill, R. E., "Managing Interpersonal Conflict in Project Teams." Sloan Management Review, 18: 45–62 (1977).

cases however; for example, willingness to absorb aggression and setting an example of listening sometimes appeared to entail almost identical behavior. These dilemmas were resolved primarily by reliance on the larger context in which the behavior occurred.

The composite picture which emerged was one of a high producing manager who "came on straight" with subordinates and who was open in dealing with their conflicts. He also encouraged subordinates to express their problems, and signaled to all concerned that he was tolerant of negative and hostile feelings. High producing managers also "taught" their team members through example as well as direct counseling how to respond to conflict. This appeared to be a critical phenomenon since it apparently expanded the conflict managing capacity of the entire team. While the high producing manager exuded a belief in approaching conflict, he also had enough knowledge of his subordinates to know when to avoid conflict, and was willing to postpone meetings or confrontations when necessary. Thus while conflict was generally confronted, its expression was also paced and controlled at times.

The composite picture which emerged from the interviews was that the higher producing managers tended to play out a third party conciliation and interpersonal peacemaking role. It is important to re-emphasize, however, that these actions were taken primarily in response to what was perceived to be personality clashes rather than disagreement over substantive issues (even though they are often difficult to separate). As Walton (9, p. 75) notes, "The distinction between substantive and emotional issues is important because the substantive conflict requires bargaining and problem solving between the principals and mediative interventions by the third party, whereas emotional conflict requires a restructuring of a person's perceptions and the working through of feelings between the principals, as well as conciliative interventions by the third party. The former processes are basically cognitive; the later processes more affective."

The particular kinds of third party conciliative roles involved several. First, empathic support and reassurances that hostile feelings are accepted in someone's eyes is important in getting parties to express real differences between themselves. Second, helping parties express their differences by patient listening is crucial to the management or resolution of them. As Walton (9) suggests, differentiation puts a certain reality and authenticity into the relationship of the principals to the conflict. In addition, it provides information as to opinions and attitudes in the relationship which can be checked and corrected as to accuracy. In short, an expressional function is critical to interpersonal conflict because a person cannot begin productive resolution of differences until he or she is clear what the real differences in fact are. In addition, under stress one usually has to be emotional before they can be rational.

Third, superior knowledge of the principal's situation and feelings helped the higher producing managers pace the confrontation of conflict. Confrontation per se is not universally a panacea for conflict management, but rather confrontations in which the principals can exhibit a modicum of rationality and problem solving behavior are what is needed. Fourth, so-called "counseling" tended to place the manager in the role of an interpersonal process consultant.

There are some crucial limitations on the effectiveness of organizational superiors as third party conciliators of subordinate conflict, however, Walton (9) suggests that effective third party consultants should not have power over the fate of the principals, and should also be neutral as to the substantive outcome. This is rarely if ever approximated in most organizational settings. However, the fascinating aspect of the study results suggested that team member peers often acted out third party conciliator roles by modeling and identification with their manager. Peers usually have no formal power over the fate of the principals to the conflict, and are potentially able to be more neutral as to the outcome. Thus, peer members of a conflict pair often supplied a third party influence which the manager could not. This phenomenon, however, appeared to depend critically on whether subordinates identified with the manager. By creating a more open interpersonal climate, the high performing managers apparently leveraged their ability to manage personality clashes by stimulating resolution responses from the conflicted parties peers. This is similar to Likert's (8) observation that participative management systems stimulate leadership behavior from subordinates themselves (or "peer leadership" as he calls it).

A more subtle process may have been operating also through the mechanism of identification with the superior. Heider (10) proposes a "balance theory" of interpersonal conflict which suggests that two parties find it more difficult to maintain negative feelings toward each other when they both feel positively toward a third party. Thus the higher producing managers who created positive subordinate relations may have ameliorated conflict largely by an unconscious process. Levinson [11, pp. 163–164] expands on the dynamics of the process by saying that "A generalized process of learning how to behave and what to become occurs through identification.... By acting as the focal point of unity—the ego ideal of the group of organization—the leader serves as a device for knitting people together into a social system. With such a leader, said Freud, a group is capable of high achievement, abnegation, unselfishness, and devotion to an ideal. Without such a leader, the group falls apart because people then lose their medium for establishing ties through each other—identification with the leader."

PROBLEM SOLVING STYLES: THE MBTI FRAMEWORK

Whereas the prior section examined a framework for understanding the emotional dynamics of groups and individuals, this section will explore a framework for understanding the cognitive or problem solving styles of group members, and how these styles influence team functioning.

Problem solving can be viewed as involving two dimensions: the process of gathering information, and the process of making evaluations, decisions, or judgments based on that information. Information gathering involves finding out about a problem, interpreting the world, inferring meaning from all the complexity which usually surrounds a given event, etc. As Hellriegel and Slocum (12) note, information gathering also involves *rejecting* some data and reducing much of it to a manageable, comprehensive form. Judgment, the process by which information is evaluated and decisions are made, is the second important operation in problem solving.

A framework for conceptualizing and assessing problem solving styles has

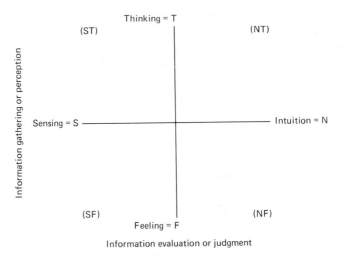

Figure 29-2. Problem solving styles.

Adapted from Hellriegel, D. and Slocum, J. W. "Preferred Organizational Designs and Problem Solving Styles: Interesting Companions," *Human Systems Management*, 1: 151–158 (1980).

been developed by Isabel Briggs-Myers based on Jung's theory of psychological types (13).

The basic dimension of information gathering is referred to as *perception* and takes the two opposing forms of either *sensing* or *intuition*. Information evaluation, or *judgment* takes the opposing forms of either *thinking* or *feeling*. The Myers-Briggs Type Indicator (MBTI) is a questionnaire that assesses which type of perception and judgment an individual prefers to use in problem solving.

An initial categorization of problem solving styles can be depicted as the four quadrants of Figure 29-2 (adapted from Hellriegel and Slocum, 12).

Two Ways of Perceiving: Sensing and Intuition

Sensing types look at the world and see the hard data that is directly available through the senses (seeing, hearing, touching, etc). They tend to be realistic, pragmatic, and focused in the here and now. They prefer problems which lend themselves to standardized solution procedures, and they prefer routine work and enjoy working in structured settings. They dislike unstructured problems, high degrees of uncertainty and change and working with "soft data".

Intuitive types on the other hand look at the world, and see not what is "just there," but rather what might be. They see beyond the here and now into the realm of possibilities, implicit meanings and potential relationships among events. Intuitives often use "soft data," hunches and possibilities which came to them rather sponstaneously. They also tend to see the "big picture" or totality rather than the fine print or details as sensing types do. Intuitive types also enjoy complexity, unstructured problems, and newness, and are burdened by too much routine. Mary McCaulley, president of the Center for Applications of Psychological Type (CAPT, Inc.) in Gainsville, Florida has now taken over applications and development of the MBTI suggests that "In a new and complex venture, a team needs more intuitive types; in a venture which requires careful management of many details, a team needs more sensing types" (14).

Two Types of Judgment: Thinking and Feeling

The second dimension in the model involves making decisions, and again there are two opposing approaches. Those who prefer thinking as their favorite judgment process like putting things into a structured format and using cause-effect logic. Thinking types tend to be uninterested in people's feelings and seem "hard headed" (or hard hearted) and are able to fire or reprimand people when necessary. They enjoy applying data and formulas to problems, and are particularly attracted to the contributions made by operations research, and management science to decisional problems. And they like to think of management as a *science,* not an art. As Hellriegel and Slocum (12) note, there is considerable similarity between thinking types, the scientific method, and work in bureaucratic organizations which emphasize rationality and impersonality in human relations.

Feeling types also make decisions by a rational process. As McCaulley (15, p. 732) notes "Feeling does not refer to emotions, but rather to the process of setting priorities in terms of values, weighing their greater or lesser importance to oneself and others." They tend to become sympathetic, are concerned about their own and others reactions in decision situations, and reflect a concern for the establishment of harmonious interpersonal relations. They do not particularly like to tell others unpleasant things, and often gravitate toward mediator and conciliator roles in team situations. Whereas thinking types approach decisions with abstract true or false judgments and formal logic rules, the feeling type invokes more personalistic judgments of good or bad, pleasant or unpleasant, and like or dislike.

The Composite Styles

Each type of perception can team up with each type of judgment, so that the quadrants of Figure 29-2 represent four basic problem solving styles. The sensing-thinkers (STs) are the traditionalists of organizational life. They can absorb, remember and manage a large number of facts and details. They strive to create and maintain order, structure and control; sensing thinkers are realistic, pragmatic, economically motivated, follow through on assignments and generally represent the "quintessential organization man" (in the positive sense of the term). They are good task leaders.

Sensing-feeling types (SFs) also prefer structured organizations and work, but could be characterized as "loyalists," and gravitate toward social-emotional leadership. They tend to accept people as they are, know a lot of personal things about the people they work with, and are sensitive to the fit between the person and the job.

Intuitive thinkers (NTs) are visonarys. They are innovative, and enjoy creating a new system, rather than maintaining or running an established program. They need to be supported by persons who are good at implementation and maintenance of new programs. They feel burdened by overly structured organizations and jobs, and function best in looser organization designs.

Intuitive feeling types (NFs) could be considered catalysts in a team setting. They focus on possibilities, and can often get other people excited about new projects, or spark new enthusiasm in the face of obstacles on current problems. They prefer democratic, less structured organizations, and are particularly interested in the quality of working life experienced by both themselves and others. Other people are likely to attribute personal charisma in NFs, because they are popular and tend to become personally involved with those around them. Sometimes, this involvement makes them vulnerable since they prefer positive harmonius relations with others.

These four composite styles are shown in Table 29-4 which has been reproduced here from *Introduction to Type* (16, p. 3).

The Myers-Briggs Type Indicator output is somewhat more complex than the two dimensional models shown in Figure 29-2, but the present discussion explicates the central part of the framework. Two more bipolar scales are printed out along with the two dimensions discussed above. The first is an extroversion-introversion scale which indicates whether the individual prefers to operate primarily in the outer world of people, action and objects (extroversion) or in the more contemplative, inner world of ideas and concepts (introversion). The final scale reflects whether a judging or perceiving attitude will be taken toward the outer world. Judging types "tend to live in a planned, decided, orderly way, aiming to regulate life and control it. Perceptive types . . . tend to live in a flexible, spontaneous way, aiming to understand life and adapt to it" (17, p. 2).

For more detailed descriptions of the MBTI, the reader is referred to References (16) and (13).

Implications for Team Functioning

Effective team functioning requires that the psychological and intellectual resources of all individuals be utilized. One of the greatest barriers to effec-

Table 29-4. Composite Styles*
EFFECTS OF THE COMBINATIONS OF PERCEPTION AND JUDGEMENT

Sensing plus Thinking. ST people are mainly interested in facts, since facts are what can be collected and verified directly by the senses—by seeing, hearing, touching, etc. And they make decisions on these facts by impersonal analysis, because the kind of judgment they trust is thinking, with its step-by-step process of reasoning from cause to effect, from premise to conclusion.

Sensing plus Feeling. SF people are also interested in facts, but make their decisions with personal warmth, because the kind of judgment they trust is feeling, with its power to weigh how much things matter to themselves and others.

Intuition plus Feeling. NF people make decisions with the same personal warmth. But, since they prefer intuition, their interest is not in facts but in possibilities, such as new projects, things that have not happened yet but might be made to happen, new truths that are not yet known but might be found out, or, above all, new possibilities for people.

Intuition plus Thinking. NT people share the interest in possibilities. But since they prefer thinking, they approach those possibilities with impersonal analysis. Often the possibility they choose is a theoretical or technical one, with the human element more or less ignored.

The columns below present some of the results of these combinations.

	ST	SF	NF	NT
People who prefer:	SENSING + THINKING	SENSING + FEELING	INTUITION + FEELING	INTUITION + THINKING
focus their attention on:	Facts	Facts	Possibilities	Possibilities
and handle these with:	Impersonal analysis	Personal warmth	Personal warmth	Impersonal analysis
Thus they tend to become:	Practical and matter-of-fact	Sympathetic and friendly	Enthusiastic & insightful	Logical and ingenious
and find scope for their abilities in:	Technical skills with facts and objects	Practical help and services for people	Understanding & communicating with people	Theoretical and technical developments
for example:	Applied science Business Production Construction Etc.	Patient care Community service Sales Teaching Etc.	Behavioral science Research Literature & art Teaching Etc.	Physical science Research Management Forecasts & analysis Etc.

*Adapted from Myers, Isabel B. *Introduction to Type,* Gainesville, Florida: Center for Application of Psychological Type, 1976, 2nd ed., and reproduced by special permission of the publisher, Consulting Psychologists Press, Inc., 577 College Ave., Palo Alto, CA 94306.

tiveness is the truncation of one person's resources by another simply because they perceive and react to problems in quite different ways. Sensing-thinking types, for instance are inclined to want the facts and an explicit statement of the problem before considering possible solutions. Intuitive feeling types (the opposite of STs) must first be inspired by interesting possibilities before they will pay much attention to facts. And even then the "facts" by the NF will more likely be viewed as "soft" impressionistic data to the ST.

As Myers notes (17, p. 3) problem solving generally could be viewed as a sequential use of the various perception and judgment functions: sensing establishes the facts, intuition suggests possible solutions, thinking establishes the probable consequences of different courses of action, and feeling weighs the likelihood of acceptance among relevant persons. Thus all the psychological functions should ideally be brought to bear on problems and well balanced teams which allow broad participation should have greater resources than even the best balanced individual decision maker. In fact, leadership in a team could be defined as insuring that the appropriate functions are brought to bear on problems at the appropriate stage.

The formation of interdepartmental project teams is likely to bring together different types because there is some evidence to suggest type is related to occupational specialization. Mary McCaulley (15, 18) has developed data relating type to engineering specialization among University of Florida students, and has compiled data related to scientists also.

The applied fields of engineering such as civil, industrial and agricultural are more likely to attract sensing types, whereas the more theoretical fields such as chemical, nuclear and aerospace are more likely to attract intuitive types. Also, as one might expect, McCaulley's data indicate engineering is tilted toward thinking types (59% in a sample of 1,060 students) although again the theoretical specialties were more thinking oriented than the applied specialties. McCaulley notes that two important implications flow from this trend (15, p. 732). First, a team heavily weighted with similar types can develop group "blind spots" characteristic of the dominant type. Thinking types often neglect the human aspect of project work because technical work is more appealing to them. Second, if feeling types are in a minority, they may be undervalued and criticized, which causes them to withdraw their vitality and energy from the team effort. Third, thinking types may be inclined to take a laissez-faire attitude toward persuading others to accept their work, believing often erroneously, that "the logic will speak for itself," and that high quality technical work will unquestioningly be accepted by project clients. Fortunately, as McCaulley notes, the engineering professions contain a large number of feeling types who are of great value in gaining acceptance of project work with the client-users. The leadership challenge, however, is to create a climate where thinking judgment can predominate during planning stages and feeling judgment during project implementation.

In conclusion, it has been my purpose to introduce the MBTI framework in its simpler form and to suggest how it can be useful in understanding conflict between team members. Individual team members must come to see others as sources of differing resources, or "differing gifts," rather than as sources of antagonism. Table 29-5 illustrates how complementary functions can be sup-

Table 29-5. Mutual Usefulness of Opposite Types.

The clearest vision of the future comes only from an intuitive, the most practical realism only from a sensing type, the most incisive analysis only from a thinker, and the most skillful handling of people only from a feeling type. Success for any enterprise demands a variety of types, each in the right place.

Opposite types can supplement each other in any joint undertaking. When two people approach a problem from opposite sides, each sees things not visible to the other. Unfortunately, they seldom see each other's point of view. Too much oppositeness makes it hard for people to work well together. The best teamwork is usually done by people who differ on one or two preferences only. This much difference is useful, and the two or three preferences they have in common help them to understand each other and communicate.

When extreme opposites must work or live together, an understanding of type does much to lessen the friction. Disagreement is less irritating when Smith recognizes that it would hardly be normal for Jones to agree. Jones is not being willfully contrary. He is simply being an opposite type, and opposite types can be tremendously useful to each other when given the chance. The lists below show some of the specific ways.

INTUITIVE NEEDS—A SENSING TYPE:	SENSING TYPE NEEDS—AN INTUITIVE:
To bring up pertinent facts	To bring up new possibilities
To apply experience to problems	To supply ingenuity on problems
To read the fine print in a contract	To read the signs of coming change
To notice what needs attention now	To see how to prepare for the future
To have patience	To have enthusiasm
To keep track of essential detail	To watch for new essentials
To face difficulties with realism	To tackle difficulties with zest
To remind that the joys of the present are important	To show that the joys of the future are worth working for

FEELING TYPE NEEDS—A THINKER:	THINKER NEEDS—A FEELING TYPE:
To analyze	To persuade
To organize	To conciliate
To find the flaws in advance	To forecast how others will feel
To reform what needs reforming	To arouse enthusiasm
To hold consistently to a policy	To teach
To weight "the law and the evidence"	To sell
To fire people when necessary	To advertise
To stand firm against opposition	To appreciate the thinker

*Reproduced from Myers, Isabel B. *Introduction to Type*, Gainesville, Florida: Center for Application of Psychological Type, 1976, 2nd ed. and used by special permission of the publisher, Consulting Psychologists Press, Inc., Palo Alto, CA 94306.

plied by opposite types to the benefit of both (adapted from *Introduction to Type,* 14, p. 5). This process could be greatly facilitated by having either an external or internal organization development specialist administer and conduct educational seminars for teams using the MBTI. It is an instrument which is gaining increasing application in the behavioral sciences to a variety of management problems. If this discussion has served to pique interest in its use among project teams, my purpose will have been served. Carl Jung suggested that individual development and maturity involves an integration over time of the four psychological functions of sensing, intuition, thinking and feeling. A team can similarly develop, given democratic leadership, and norms which value the uniqueness and individuality of its members.

REFERENCES

1. Thamhain, H. J., and Wilemon, D. L. Conflict Management in Project Life Cycles, *Sloan Management Review,* Spring: 31–49 (1975).
2. Schutz, William C. *The Interpersonal Underworld,* (Reprint edition) (Palo Alto: Science and Behavior Books, 1966).
3. Pfeiffer, J. William, and Heslin, Richard *Instrumentation in Human Relations Training,* (Iowa City: University Associates, 1973).
4. Hill, R. E. Interpersonal Compatibility and Workgroup Performance, *The Journal of Applied Behavior Science,* 11: 210–219 (1975).
5. Ryan, Leo R. *Clinical Interpretation of the FIRO-B,* (Palo Alto: Consulting Psychologists Press, 1971).
6. Louis, A. M. They're Striking Some Strange Bargains at Diamond Shamrock, *Fortune,* January: 142–156 (1976).
7. Hill, R. E. Managing Interpersonal Conflict in Project Teams. *Sloan Management Review,* 18: 45–62 (1977).
8. Likert, Rensis A. *New Ways of Managing Conflict,* (New York: McGraw-Hill, 1976).
9. Walton, Richard E. *Interpersonal Peacemaking: Confrontations and Third Party Consultation,* (Reading, Mass.: Addison-Wesley, 1969).
10. Heider, F. *The Psychology of Interpersonal Relations,* (New York: Wiley, 1958).
11. Levinson, Harry. *The Exceptional Executive: A Psychological Conception,* (New York: Mentor, 1968).
12. Hellriegel, D. and Slocum, J. W. Jr. Preferred Organizational Designs and Problem Solving Styles: Interesting Companions, *Human Systems Management,* 1: 151–158 (1980).
13. Myers, Isabel B. *Manual: The Myers-Briggs Type Indicator,* (Palo Alto: Consulting Psychologist Press, 1962, 1975).
14. McCaulley, M. How Individual Differences Affect Health Care Teams. *Health Team News* 1: No. 8 (1975).
15. McCaulley, M. Psychological Types in Engineering: Implications for Teaching, *Engineering Education,* 66: 729–736 (1976).
16. Myers, Isabel B. *Introduction To Type,* 2nd ed. (Gainesville, Florida: Center for Application of Psychological Type, 1976).
17. Myers, Isabel B. *Type and Teamwork,* (Gainesville, Florida: Center for Application of Psychological Type, 1974).
18. McCaulley, Mary H. *Personality Variables: Model Profiles that Characterize Various Fields of Science,* (Gainesville, Florida: Center for the Application of Psychological Type, 1976).

30. Managing Change

Thomas E. Miller*

INTRODUCTION

This new work schedule dreamed up by the experts in city hall is for the birds! The men don't like it and are laying down on the job. A lot of them aren't showing up or they're late, or calling in sick. Injuries are up, equipment gets lost or it's in the repair shop half the time, and we chiefs are spending God knows how many hours detailing men from one fire station to another. We've told city hall about our morale problem, but they say if the men refuse to fulfill the contract agreement, we have no recourse but to reprimand, suspend, and in chronic cases, fire them. But, hell, if any of these steps are taken, we just aggravate the manpower shortage. If you were a seasoned firefighter, how would you like to put your life on the line with a raw young recruit next to you?

I'm swamped with paperwork and I have to go to a training course that's supposed to tell me how to handle the men, but I spend most of my time listening to their complaints. I don't have any time for training, equipment inspection, or fire prevention as the plan says I should. I'm lucky to make it to a fire since I'm usually in a meeting trying to iron out the kinks in this schedule. We chiefs have all complained to city hall, but they argue that the new work schedule is a success. The computer says so. Now, if they can only get the computer to fight the fires, we can all go home.

These remarks were made by a middle manager, a battalion chief, some months after a new work schedule had been introduced in his fire department. Any reader of the organizational behavior literature will quickly recognize

---

*Dr. Thomas E. Miller is Professor of Administration and Human Relations at the University of Missouri-Kansas City, where he teaches courses in human relations, organizational behavior, organization theory and communications. He also taught at Northwestern University and the University of Kansas, and was a Training Fellow and instructor in human relations at the Harvard Business School. Dr. Miller has been a consultant and trainer in the private as well as the public sector, has authored several case studies and articles on change, teamwork and management. His current research interests focus on career development, promotions, and leadership, particularly in federal, law enforcement and fire suppression organizations.

many of the familiar "resistance-to-change symptoms," such as restriction of output, sickouts, work slowdowns as well as the more subtle forms of passive indifference, hostility, and "rationalizations" on why the change won't work.[1]

This "change-resistance syndrome"[2] has been well documented in the literature.[3] Roethlisberger believes the syndrome has the properties of reciprocalness, similar to reciprocal relations encountered in mathematical relations.[4] The reciprocal pattern begins when management introduces a change. Immediately, the workers counter with resistance. Anticipating this resistance, managers resort to strategems designed to overcome the workers' objections. These approaches can take many forms such as: 1) elaborate logical explanations as to why the change is necessary, 2) hiring outside consultants to "justify" the change or to help "facilitate" its acceptance, 3) using "feedback" sessions involving managers, union, and/or staff personnel to alert all parties to the "realities" behind the change, and sometimes, as in this case study, 4) sending middle managers, who usually experience the brunt of the change, to training programs to acquire techniques on how to handle resistance.

When all else fails, management proposes *new* (and different) changes to cure the illnesses caused by the original change. Frequently, these new proposals are also resisted, thus reactivating the reciprocal cycle. In frustration and anger, management then forces the change on the workers by utilizing its positional authority. As resistance persists, management punishes the holdouts and rewards the collaborators. This reward-punishment pattern drives wedges among the organizational social groupings and the battle continues until the ringleaders quit or the workers passively accept the change, or management decides to chuck the whole idea. At this point, equilibrium in the organization is restored, except for one major difference: often bitterness and resentment linger between the two parties and make the next innovation and its acceptance that much more difficult. Thus the changes that should be accomplished during

---

[1] Paul R. Lawrence, "How to Deal with Resistance to Change," *Harvard Business Review* 32 (1954): 49.

[2] The phrase is the author's.

[3] For a sampling see: Fritz J. Roethlisberger and William J. Dickson, *Management and the Worker* (Cambridge: Harvard University Press, (1949), pp. 657-68 and 579-80; Kurt Lewin, "Group Decisions and Social Change," in G. E. Swanson, T. M. Newcomb, and E. L. Hartley (Eds.), *Readings in Social Psychology,* Rev. ed., (New York: Holt, 1952), pp. 459-73; Lester Coch and John R. P. French, "Overcoming Resistance to Change," *Human Relations* 1, No. 4 (1948): 512-532; Alvin Zander, "Resistance to Change—Its Analysis and Prevention," *Advanced Management* 15 (1950): 9-11; David Klein, "Some Notes on the Dynamics of Resistance to Change: The Defender Role," in W. G. Bennis, K. D. Benne, and R. Chin, *The Planning of Change* (New York: Holt, Rinehart and Winston, 1976) pp. 117-124; Gary Powell and Barry Z. Posner, "Resistance to Change Reconsidered: Implications for Managers," *Human Resource Management* 17, No. 1 (1978): 29-34.

[4] Fritz J. Roethlisberger, *The Elusive Phenomena* (Boston, Mass.: Division of Research, Harvard Graduate School of Business Administration, 1977) pp. 169-70.

the normal day-to-day work routines are avoided, brushed aside, and minimized by management and the worker until external or internal pressures force them to face the change process again.[5]

In spite of all of our managerial knowledge on how to handle change, the change-resistance syndrome still appears and appears frequently in modern-day organizations. Some writers believe that the symptom-by-symptom attack that management is prone to take in overcoming resistance does not get below the surface to the human factors involved. By failing to recognize the hydra-headed nature of the social situation with which it is faced when introducing technical innovation, management will cut off one head, only to have two new ones appear.[6] Other writers argue that the whole idea of resistance to change needs reconceptualization since management's anticipation of resistance may lead them to the creation of resistance—sort of a self-fulfilling prophecy.[7] Whatever the basis, most writers concede that there is a gap between our existing knowledge (theory) and managerial practice (skill) when introducing change.

The purpose of this chapter is to examine the causes of the change-resistance syndrome by reporting a clinical case study of change in a large urban fire department. The thesis is that resistance to change is a *failure in teamwork*. Where teamwork exists, resistance does not emerge, or if it does, the proactive collaboration between those affected—both management and workers alike—allows them to develop technical and social skills in handling both their logical and social involvement in the change process. Teamwork gets to the core of resistance by facilitating the cooperative interactions between people, irrespective of their status, in the accomplishment of a common task. This is the basic insight from the relay assembly room of the Western Electric Studies, where teamwork existed no special resistance was encountered among the workers in spite of the fact that several major technical changes were introduced. "What actually happened," wrote Mayo, "was that six individuals became a team and the team gave itself wholeheartedly and spontaneously to cooperation in the experiment."[8] The team process held the human situation steady and permitted the participants to develop both technical and social skills in relation to change phenomena.[9] The workers did not view nor experience change as something

---

[5]Larry E. Greiner, "Patterns of Organizational Change," *Harvard Business Review* 45 (1967): 119–30.

[6]Paraphrased from Fritz J. Roethlisberger, "The Foreman: Master and Victim of Double Talk" in *Man In Organization: Essays of F. J. Roethlisberger* (Cambridge: Belknap Press of Harvard University Press, 1968), p. 36.

[7]Powell and Posner, "Resistance to Change Reconsidered," p. 29.

[8]Elton Mayo, *The Social Problems of an Industrial Civilization* (Boston, Mass.: Division of Research, Harvard Graduate School of Business Administration, 1945), p. 72.

[9]Ibid., p. 72.

externally imposed by management; rather, change became a way for them to adapt and experience social complication in their work. Satisfaction came from meeting and coping with the challenge.

More often than not, when teamwork is left to chance, management does not get teamwork; they get instead the kind of resistance behavior which was described by the battalion chief in the opening of this article. Resistance is management's external evaluation of the workers' behavior when they do not accept a technical change; opposition to management's change is the workers' internal response in protecting their social work world. Teamwork bridges the gap between these internal and external processes during change. However, unless both managers and workers diagnostically understand this process and can behaviorally respond to each other in such fashion as to create cooperation, then teamwork will elude them. Before we explore further the worth of this idea and its implications, let us give a brief history of a change introduced in a fire department and its outcome.

INTRODUCTION OF A CHANGE IN A FIRE DEPARTMENT

In a major move from conventional scheduling, the management of a large urban city placed its firefighting personnel on a 40-hour work week consisting of three eight-hour work shifts. This contrasted with the department's former 50-hour week schedule of 24 hours on-duty and 48 hours off-duty. The primary objective of the plan was to maximize the on-duty time of the firefighting personnel, thus providing a better level of fire service to the citizens and taxpayers of the city.

The eight-hour plan was just one component of the city's comprehensive fire protection plan, but was regarded by management as central to the plan and an innovative step forward in fire service. Many advantages seemed to be inherent in the plan: fresh personnel every eight hours rather than every 24 should reduce life risks due to fatigue; an increase in on-duty productivity and communications should result because the men would work their full shifts instead of sleeping part of them; and lastly, round-the-clock attention could be given to fire prevention, training, and equipment maintenance. Also management believed that by putting the men on an eight-hour schedule it would be easier to justify raising their pay commensurate with other protective service personnel in the city. The eight-hour shift was thus negotiated as part of a pay package requested by the local firefighters' union. Pay increases in the contract were tied to a "good faith, best effort" on the firefighters' part in carrying out management's plan.

During the three years that the eight-hour shift was in operation, the department was in considerable turmoil because of the firefighters' steadily mounting resistance to the shift change. Management pointed to the many tactics the firefighters were using to resist the plan: slow-downs, work stoppages, sickouts, and damaging and losing equipment. On their part, the firefighters felt that the city was squandering the taxpayers' money on what was a totally unworkable plan, designed only to "punish" them for their pay demands.

The Fire Chief and his technical assistants held many meetings with the deputy and battalion chiefs in an effort to work out "the bugs" in the implementation of the plan. Several adjustments were made to the plan as a result of these meetings: 313 persons were promoted; relief companies were formed to provide back-up manpower; and a special task force consisting of the deputy chiefs and several battalion chiefs was created to "track" the progress of the plan. But in spite of all of management's efforts, few of the chiefs and even fewer of the rank-and-file firefighters "accepted" the work schedule. A six-months' evaluation of the plan prepared by the special task force concluded that the eight-hour work shift had failed to achieve management's objective of greater productivity and had been devastating to the morale and satisfactions of the firefighters.

When contract negotiations came due three years later, relations between city management and the union were at a boiling point. The union was determined to change the eight-hour work day; management was equally determined to keep the plan intact, but was open to any internal modification to make the work schedule more flexible. When negotiations broke down, the union initiated a massive work slowdown. Management responded by discharging some 40 firefighters for contract violations. Fearing that the discharged firefighters would not be rehired because of the slowdown, the men returned to their jobs and negotiations resumed. When it then became apparent to the union that the city did not intend to rehire the discharged firefighters, it called a strike, leaving the stations virtually unmanned except for the deputy and battalion chiefs. In short order, city management called in the police and the national guard to man the fire stations and their presence naturally inflamed the situation. Before the paralyzing strike was over, an international firefighters' union, the governor of the state, the city council, the mayor, and many prominent citizens had become involved in trying to resolve the crisis. Public opinion was divided. Some citizens believed that the firefighters had failed to honor their agreement with the city and were attempting to usurp the city's authority to run the department. Others felt that the city had "forced" an impractical plan on the firefighters and that the latter were justified in their counteractions.

After the strike was settled, the eight-hour shift was replaced by a 10/14 day work schedule, a schedule regarded by the firefighters as better than the eight-hour shift but not as desirable as the original 24/48 work schedule. The outcome of the situation seemed to be losses for all concerned: the city had spent a great deal of time and money on the innovative plan which they were finally forced to abandon largely due to outside pressures; the firefighters settled for a longer work week with the same pay and few additional benefits; the fire chief with over 30 years of service resigned; the union president was passed over for promotion although he was more than qualified; and many outstanding firefighters left the department either through early retirement or by seeking employment in other fire departments. These were the immediate and apparent consequences—hundreds of thousands of dollars lost, turnover, lowered morale and motivation, and no noticeable improvement in fire service.

Briefly, then, these are the facts of the implementation of a change in a fire department. We now might ask: how did management and the firefighters evaluate their experiences in the presence of the same concrete phenomena? As we saw it, both top management and the firefighters responded to and handled the change process in a similar way—they both assumed that what was happening to them was a rational-logical experience caused by the technical change. Although each drew different inferences from the happenings because of their organizational roles and interpersonal needs, they both pointed to the technical alterations as both the cause and the cure of their problems, (whereas, in truth, it was the internal anxieties and feelings provoked by the change process that each failed to understand sufficiently.) The underlying approach of both managers and firefighters was to translate (convert) the social relationship disturbances into technical phenomena. Using facts and figures, each group confronted the other with its logical shortcomings. Let us explore how this rational approach to non-rational phenomena unfolded in their discussions about the change

How Management Reasoned

To management, obviously, there was nothing basically wrong with the plan and any number of adjustments could be made to eliminate the "bugs." The real problem, they concluded, was the firefighters' refusal to carry out the plan in "good faith." Being good logicians, they were at first reluctant to draw this inference (although they felt it in their guts) until more evidence was in. So, to be consistent at all costs, management spent innumerable hours and inestimable sums of money getting the "bugs" out of the work schedule, hopefully to the satisfaction of the chiefs and the firefighters. In particular, technical specialists, both inside and outside the department, along with a specially appointed associate city manager and the fire chief spent endless hours discussing the chiefs' and firefighters' objections to the schedule and making appropriate modifications only to find that each modification required another, and yet another until at the end of the first six months, a major adjustment was made approximately once a week. Management seemed to be operating on the assumption that the better the firefighters and, particularly, the chiefs, understood the logics of the plan, the more likely it was that they would support it. When this assumption did not come true, management then drew the inference that the chiefs and the firefighters were "unreasonable" because of their stubborn refusal to face the facts.

How the Firefighters and Chiefs Reasoned

In the presence of the same happenings and utilizing the same rational approach, the firefighters, along with the union officers and middle management chiefs, drew just the opposite inference from that of top management: "The plan is not working because it is not suitable to our work situation, and no amount of propping up can save it." The chiefs and the union countered logic with—from their point of view—better logic. Like upper management, they produced lengthy reports—filed with facts and figures—to demonstrate how the plan, not they, had failed. As the firefighters never tired of pointing out to city management, "a firefighter's job is unique and will not fit into a nine-to-five work schedule." The chiefs and the union argued that other cities had tried the eight-hour work schedule and eventually abandoned it as impracticable. The more they talked and tried to explain their position (just like top management), the more they tended to evaluate management as being unreasonable and resisting logic.

A Stalemate Results from the Rational Approach

Because of the circular nature of the rational approach, it is difficult for its practitioner to realize consciously what he is doing at any given point in the reasoning process. Within this framework, the practitioner evaluates as follows: Change → causes consequences (both expected and unexpected) → leading to the need for correction. Since the "unexpected" consequences are, by definition, not anticipated (and therefore not desirable), someone or something is to *blame.* Either the designer of the schedule did not set it up properly, the supervisors did not effectively implement it, or the firefighters did not do what they had been told.

In meeting after meeting each participant pointed to the external, technical phenomena and blamed the other party for its failure to comprehend the "facts." Both assumed they were talking only about the technical shortcomings of the plan, when in reality they were responding to their uncomfortable feelings and disturbed social relationships. Both firefighters and chiefs tried to convey to top management the social confusion which had been brought into their lives by the change, but in management's presence their explanations always came out as logical rationalizations, which management, with its superior set of logic, always succeeded in beating down. Likewise, the chiefs never understood nor were able to accept management's emotional involvement in the change. As one chief put it: "It's the city's plan; let them make it work!" So, in time the positions froze because of a basic misevaluation: that social behavior is not involved in technical change.

The conflict between management and firefighters becomes more phenomenologically understandable when viewed through the membership commitments each had to their respective social groups. Social membership roles were manifested in their meetings and discussions but neither management nor the men understood how they were linked to the success or failure of the work schedule change. It was essentially their *social* world which was threatened by the change and this needed to be placed in perspective along with the technical aspects of the change. Let us now turn to a description of the four major groupings which made up the social system of the fire department and which determined how their members viewed and responded to their work world.

A DESCRIPTION OF THE FIRE DEPARTMENT AS A SOCIAL SYSTEM

As the writers on social systems have stressed, people who work together over a period of time begin to form into collective configurations or groupings. Because of the formal and logical divisions established in an organization, certain people are brought together more frequently than others. Initially, people interact with one another in certain prescribed ways dictated by the wider society and the formal requirements of the work. But, in time, these prescribed patterns are modified, changed, or adapted to accommodate to individual and group differences and needs. And, gradually, groups form among those who share the same values, the same sentiments, and similar needs. Out of these shared interactions, sentiments, and activities, norms of behavior develop. Group members as a whole develop certain ideas about how they should be treated, what their contributions are worth, and what are proper and improper ways of behaving according to their status and job roles. It is these group processes which emerge and feedback on the purposive organization that we point to when we speak of social phenomena.

Although social phenomena are related to technical phenomena, they are also different. Technical phenomena can be created, ordered, modified and even eliminated without consideration of the feelings of people. Technical phenomena can be talked about, pointed to, diagramed, and manipulated far more easily than social phenomena. Social phenomena exist at lower levels of abstraction; they are "relations of interconnectedness which exist among persons" and are part and parcel of concrete natural systems.[10] These phenomena

---

[10]Roethlisberger, *The Elusive Phenomena*, p. 144.

are more difficult to point to, to talk about, and to manipulate. More important, they are *naturally ordered* by individuals and groups to bring stability and meaning to their lives. Technical phenomena are logically ordered to attain the purposes of the organization. Social phenomena are non-logical in origin and seldom can be modified by logic alone.

The social interconnectedness among the members of the fire department was "tight." Firefighting is a most dangerous occupation and literally firefighters depend upon each other for survival. This fact alone would create the need for cooperation among them. In addition, living together "around-the-clock" in the fire stations increased opportunities for social interactions. The men ate, slept, and fought fires together; occasionally, some died together. They thought of their stations as home; many brought television sets and furniture to make the stations more livable, more like home. The family atmosphere and group loyalty was expressed in the elaborate parties given for those who had retired, the large attendance at funerals for "old-timers," and contributions made toward gifts to fellow firefighters at times of noteworthy occasions in their lives.

To illustrate the deep sense of dedication, loyalty, and friendship that bound them together, here is a typical statement from the casewriter's data:

> Our job is different, it isn't just a nine-to-five kind of job. We actually spend more time with each other than with our families. We have trust because of our work. Remember, when you go out on a run, that man next to you can save your life or let you burn. We are all brothers. This feeling is hard to explain to someone who has never been a firefighter. If you make friends with a firefighter, you make it for life.

These sentiments were expressed by a senior battalion chief nearing the end of his career. Most firefighters—from the raw recruit to the fire chief—would share them. However, agreement with these sentiments did not mean that as a consequence all firefighters thought alike, behaved alike, shared the same values and followed the identical norms of social behavior. Depending on their background values, personal needs and social ranking, some firefighters regarded work as more important than friendship, status more important than group respect, competence more important than seniority, and pleasing the boss more important than conforming to his coworkers' expectations.

Four Natural Groups.

The different values brought to the work situation and the values which emerged on the job while they interacted resulted in the formation of several social groups in the fire department. We will briefly describe the four major groups which we delineated from the data, keeping in mind, of course, that not every individual fitted neatly into any one group.[11]

Technical-specialist organizational. As the name suggests, these people are most comfortable relating to technical phenomena and organizational authority. They tend to be "standoffish" in social relations and they are usually regarded by other group members, particularly the social regulars, as isolates, although they may be admired for their technical competence. Their isolation is often self-imposed. If they rise in the management hierarchy—and many do because of their performance—their social isolation is reinforced by their becoming organizationals, namely, "boss oriented." Their values: "Technical competence is foremost. My job is to get the work done regardless of whose toes I step on." Technical specialists can be high producers.

Social-Specialist Regular. Feeling lonely, misunderstood or disliked is the worst thing that can happen to a social regular. Satisfaction is secured not exclusively from doing a good job, but is only secondary to being accepted by one's colleagues. Leaders of this group have great influence with their peers and subordinates because they are people, rather than power, oriented. Their values: "We stick together, and that's how we get the job done. Keep confidences, never hurt a brother." Their production can be on-the-line or high (never low) depending on how established their group membership is and the way their performance is regarded by their colleagues, not by top management.

Underchosen. These men may truly be unhappy isolates, not selfchosen like the technical specialists. They are underchosen by both the technicals and the socials because of some critical value out-of-lineness such as age, competence, ethnicity, education or personality. If they rise in the hierarchy, they are seen as sycophants by their colleagues because of their subservience to management. Around their fellow workers they often behave like "good Joes" but their social influence is limited. By "working both sides of the street" they hope to gain acceptance and status. Their values: "Whatever you desire me, I'll be. I've paid my dues and I want what's coming to me." Their production is often minimal and they usually keep a low profile when conflict emerges because of their unstable organizational status and group membership.

Power Specialist. These people seek recognition and acceptance by exercising power. To enhance their standing with the social regulars, with whom they

---

[11]For some of the ideas and the distinctions in the social groupings, the author is indebted to David Moment and Abraham Zaleznik, *Role Development and Interpersonal Competence,* Division of Research, Harvard Graduate School of Business Administration, Boston, Mass., pp. 122–125.

ultimately identify, they openly confront hierarchical authority in the name of a "good cause." Both their organizational status and group membership can be threatened because of their aggressive activities. On the one hand, they are admired by social regulars—never organizationals or the underchosen—for their accomplishments, but on the other hand, they are feared because of their reckless actions. They often have enormous group influence and power, particularly at times of crisis. Their values: "Go for broke; rock the boat; the cause is everything." Their production is variable like their status and group membership. They have many labels—politicos, power-seekers, do-gooders, troublemakers—depending on where you and they identify in the social system.

The Impact of the Social Groups in the Change Process

The delineation of social groupings could be extended or modified in terms of the many existing social patterns in the fire department. These groups were chosen because they provided a comprehensible framework for viewing and understanding the departmental members' behavior during the change.

As the tensions mounted over the work schedule, group membership became a major determinant of the firefighters' evaluations. The technical-organizational group, composed of the fire chief, an associate city manager, and their assistants, clearly identified with the values of upper management. These members experienced no role conflict within their own group; their frustrations and conflict resulted from their inability to enlist many followers. Since upper management had originally entrusted them with the creation and implementation of the plan, these men had to gain the men's acceptance of the work schedule. But because they were identified with upper management's values and goals, they were regarded with suspicion by other group members and their effectiveness was limited. The target of the technical organizationals was, of course, the chiefs who had strong social ties with both the social regular firefighters and the power specialist union members. In time, the only people the fire chief and his group influenced significantly were a handful of the department's staff personnel and some underchosen low producers and "good Joes."

Explicitly opposed to the work schedule was the power specialist group. Headed by the union officers, this group urged all firefighters to resist the work schedule at all costs or run the risk of forfeiting their "social" membership. Paying the price could mean accusations of group disloyalty and weakness at best or group exclusion and loneliness at worst. The pressure of this group was felt by both the social regulars and the underchosen.

Caught between these two groups, which were both vying for their support, were the critical management line supervisors: the deputy and battalion chiefs. Over the years most of the chiefs had identified with the values of the social regulars, but a few had split loyalties, partly to upper management and partly to the union of which they had historically been members.

Their organizational role placed them right in the middle of the conflict. On the one hand, the chiefs had to enforce the logics of the change to keep their supervisory positions, while on the other, they needed to maintain their group standing in order to hold the firefighters' cooperation. A decision for management could mean rejection by the men; a decision for the men could mean organizational exclusion by upper management.

The chiefs' role conflict erupted into the open at the time of the six months' evaluational report presentation. Intentionally or not, upper management evoked the incident when they selected the members of a steering committee to "track" the results of the change and write up a report. Management "bent over backwards" to appoint a fair and equitable representation of the chiefs, knowing full well that many were not sympathetic to the new schedule. In preparing the written report, the committee solicited reactions from all the chiefs and added their own inputs. The report when completed was signed by all deputy and battalion chiefs.

The Six Months' Evaluational Report. On the day of the presentation, the committee, chaired by a senior deputy chief, met with the fire chief and his assistants. The chairman and most of the chiefs were social regulars and carried the brunt of the interactions; a few were "underchosens" and remained largely silent during the meeting. The power specialists were present as "spectators" along with several members of the news media. (News had leaked out to the press that the report on the work schedule was unfavorable.)

In a tense atmosphere, the chairman opened the meeting:

Chairman: The purpose of this meeting is to review the findings of the six months' evaluation of the plan. (He passes out copies of the report.)

Fire Chief: (Thumbing through his copy.) This is the first time I've seen this report.

Chairman: No one has seen it but the chiefs. Duplication was just finished yesterday. However, it isn't that long. We can all go through it together.

Fire Chief: All the chiefs have seen the report since they all signed it. All officers have read the report except the chief officer of this department. Is that correct?

Chairman: Well, Chief, you were away and ———

Assoc. City
Manager: The report was requested by the city manager's office. Your job was to make an objective appraisal.

Consultant: Just glancing through the report, it seems to contain a number of subjective statements and not much hard data. You must fold into your report the computer data on response times and allocations of equipment and manpower. Your statistics and conclusions must be carefully meshed. We must be guided by the facts in our evaluations.

An Assistant: Who wrote the report?

Senior
Battalion
Chief: We all wrote it. It bears no malice to anyone. We report the concerns of all the chiefs.

Chairman: The report isn't all that bad. It's written from an operational point of view, it isn't very long, and it has several good things to say.

Fire Chief: I will make no comments until I have thoroughly studied the report.

Chairman: (Pause) I accept your decision, of course, but I think it's a sad day when we can't discuss our mutual problems openly.

Firefighter: (Speaking from the back of the room) I think this report should be gotten out and not buried somewhere. The public should be informed about what kind of fire protection they are or are not getting.

Assoc. City
Manager: Of course, when everyone has had time to read the report, we'll certainly go through it carefully and consider every recommendation.

At this point, the meeting turned to other matters, and shortly afterwards was adjourned.

Ostensibly, the committee had met to discuss the report but intergroup relationships and feelings were such that an open discussion was impossible. The report was a "plea for understanding and help," although this was probably an unconscious wish on the part of the chiefs; however, management perceived it as a "slap in the face." Management reacted only to the "slap" and "slapped back." In fact, all committee participants evaluated what happened in the meeting only from their respective group referents.

These were the reactions after the meeting:

Technical
Organizational: The chiefs are just too close to the men. They should support the city. I told the uppers they'd get a bad report from this committee. (He had not read the report.)

Social Regular: Had the report been given first to the city, all the findings unfavorable to them would just have been buried. There's no way in good conscience we chiefs can ignore the men.

Underchosen: I didn't want to sign the report, but what else could I do? I was on the spot.

Power Specialist: After this maybe the chiefs will come over to our side where they belong.

Subsequent communications within each group and between groups only reinforced these perceptions. Upper management immediately came to the defense of the technical organizationals by verbally reprimanding the chiefs for publicly airing departmental differences. (They believed the chiefs were responsible for the leak to the press.) The city officials felt strongly, and understandably, that they had been "set up" to look bad in the public's eye. The chiefs felt misunderstood, but admitted they had mishandled the presentation of the report. At the next meeting, the committee members apologized to upper management; management reciprocated. Following this exchange, a technical organizational commented: "It's good we got this off our chests; now, we can turn to the real work, the facts of the report." In short, he was saying that now they could dismiss the uncomfortable social dimensions of the situation and return to the only feasible task at hand, the logical implementation of the work schedule change.

In the months ahead, staff meetings were concerned exclusively with the technical problems caused by the work schedule. Upper management met less and less with the battalion chiefs until finally all meetings between them ceased. As time went on, management tended to exclude the chiefs from all major decisions, and thereby, consciously or not, reduced their status and authority.

This misevaluation, perpetuated by upper management, and exploited by the power specialists, eventually forced the chiefs to make a choice. In time, they and the other groups—the social regulars and the power specialists—united in "teamwork" against upper management and the technical organizationals. This was teamwork, unfortunately, only in opposition to a perceived external threat. By joining these groups, the chiefs were rendered ineffective in working out any sort of managerial compromise between the city and the firefighters' union.

The technical organizationals totally underestimated the strength of intrinsic group membership values and never really understood how these values were linked to success in achieving extrinsic goals. At least, if they did understand, they were never able to act upon their insights in any effective way. The power specialists learned only to exploit the weaknesses and strengths of the various groups for their own purposes. The social system for all practical purposes became frozen and the change-resistance syndrome intensified between upper management and the union. At contract negotiation time, when the union was free of legal obligations and all communications had broken down between the city and the firefighters, the union called a strike.

SUMMARY

This case study has illustrated once again a breakdown in communications and cooperation between management and workers during a change process. In the fire department, both upper management and the firefighters were quickly swept up in the vicious cycle of the change-resistance syndrome. Both parties evaluated the technical consequences of the change as the problem; both failed to grasp the impact that the technical change had on their interactions and interpersonal feelings. In their meetings and discussions, they responded to breakdowns in communication as though they were only technical misunderstandings which could be corrected through logical coordination and formal rules. By addressing only the logical impact of the change, the vital social group processes which were disturbed by the change went unattended.

This basic misevaluation occurred not because one or both parties was power-oriented, stupid, or illogical. Both intuitively understood and responded to their own needs and their own group involvement; less clearly did each understand the impact that their behavior had on each other as they went about satisfying their needs for security, belonging and status. The fire department situation seemed not a battle for power between opposing forces—as both management and the firefighters evaluated it—but rather a struggle between the logics of change and the sentiments of group membership.

When introducing change, the manager's role becomes crucial. On the one hand, he must determine what changes are necessary for the effective survival of the organization, and on the other, he must secure and maintain the effective cooperation of individuals and groups to insure their acceptance. How is he to achieve this equilibrium?

Implications for Practice

Diagnostic Skills. It may be difficult to accept that we need to improve our understanding of the dynamics of organizations, but all our clinical research points to this need.[12] A manager is a practitioner and requires diagnostic skills similar to those of the clinician. Before a physician can act, he must diagnose the sort of illness he is handling—whether it be a case of measles, mumps, or cancer. Managers often behave as if they require no such equivalent skills in diagnosis. Too often, if we are not careful, we try to solve our problems of teamwork and change intellectually, abstractly, and analytically rather than through the diagnostic identification and sizeup of individual values and group norms in relation to organizational requirements.

To become better diagnosticians requires we understand our own involve-

---

[12]For several ideas in this section, the author is indebted to Roethlisberger, *Man In Organization,* pp. 65, 139, 169.

ment and the impact of our behavior on others. Particularly is this true during an introduction of change when actions on the part of both managers and workers are so critical and subject to such easy misunderstanding. A manager is an involved participant and member of his social system and from this involvement there is no escape. He is both an instrument of change and a recipient of that change; his dilemma is: how can he (a part of a system) affect a change in other parts of the system of a whole of which he is an involved member without destroying cooperative relations in the process? A manager is the bridge between organizational requirements and interpersonal cooperative processes and how well he understands social processes will largely determine whether his change is accepted or rejected.

We might give an example of a simple social process which, because it went unrecognized by upper management, led to much bitterness and deepened the chasm between management and firefighters.

> The social custom of the "cook shack" was a long established practice in the fire stations under the former work schedule. The fire companies took enormous pride in their food preparation and there was considerable vying among the various stations for a reputation as "best house." Deputies and battalion chiefs were often invited as special guests to share a meal and pass judgment on the "table."
>
> On these occasions, the senior ranking officers sat at the head of the table, while the less senior in rank and age took their respective places around the sides. The conversation was not limited to social matters; often, chiefs, captains, and experienced firefighters shared mutual problems about particular fires, equipment, etc., while the younger men listened and added their comments.

According to the "logics" of the new work schedule, firefighters were discouraged from cooking in the stations. They were expected to "brown bag" it or eat at nearby restaurants. Neither the city nor the firefighters properly understood how this alteration in eating habits with the new work schedule impacted upon morale. "Eating together" was a social process which paid off handsomely at the fire site later in terms of strengthening the patterns of company and battalion teamwork.

Distinguishing Fact from Sentiment.   Diagnostic understanding and intuitive familiarity with such social uniformities deters a skillful manager from making a quick size-up when introducing change. He begins not with a theory nor a technique but rather, with the slow, laborious task of observing social behavior in relation to technical behavior. By practicing a diagnostic skill, a manager can begin to improve his communications with others; he can become gradually more proficient at promoting cooperation and participation during the change process.[13]

For example, a skillful manager realizes he cannot express his own feelings without regard to the impact they will have on others, particularly his subordinates, who cannot be expected to distinguish between his expression of feelings and his statements of fact. He must help them to make that distinction. This confusion between fact and sentiment seemed to be at the core of the conflict between managers and firefighters.

Basically, the confusion arises when one participant makes a value judgment of another's behavior from the former's point of view. Not only do people make value judgments, but they also insist that the other person accept these judgments as correct, factual, and true. When this pattern occurred in the case study, all cooperation ceased. A manager needs to practice a skill of communication which distinguishes between fact and sentiment in his dealings with others. He must learn to identify the values, sentiments, and norms which are important for him and others to maintain in their interactions. Simply put, when people are not kept busy defending their personal feelings, they have more time and *desire* to cooperate.

Utilizing Listening Skills to Facilitate Teamwork.   No group was more critical to the successful introduction of change in the fire department than the deputy and battalion chiefs. Both upper management and the union knew this. As we have stated, the chiefs were caught in a role conflict aggravated by a change which they intellectually understood but emotionally found difficult to handle. Their job, organizationally, as seen by upper management, was simply to enforce the change. This placed the chiefs, as they saw it, in the role of being "watchdogs," a role they found personally uncomfortable and virtually impossible to carry out and at the same time maintain their image in the eyes of the rank-and-file firefighters. Time and time again they had to do things that were "disloyal" from upper management's point of view in order to get the work done. On the other hand, with the firefighters in the field, the chiefs frequently had to "distort reality," plead ignorance, or be vague about some happening or regulation in order to maintain their social group standing.

Had upper management recognized more explicitly the chiefs' role dilemma and responded to it more skillfully by listening, two important processes might have been set in motion. First, by listening, upper management would have heard not only the chiefs' *words,* but more importantly, what these words *pointed to*—the chiefs' role conflict. Listening implies we attend to 1) what

---

[13]Fritz J. Roethlisberger, "Conversation," in William Dowling, Ed. *Effective Management and the Behavioral Sciences* (New York: AMACOM, A Division of American Management Association, 1978), p. 207.

people want to tell you, 2) what they don't want to tell you, and 3) what they cannot tell you without help. Listening reduces social distance and softens social status differences between groups. It is a facilitator to understanding and cooperation. By being listened to, the chiefs would have felt more accepted and less defensive in their communications with upper management.

Secondly, the systematic practice of listening gives the manager more phenomenologically useful data to take action upon since such data come to him from an internal as opposed to an external point of view. Had upper management understood that the chiefs' role conflict sprang not from a lack of "management knowledge about logics" but rather from the very nature of the concrete social system of which they were a part, they might have made a more proper evaluation of the chiefs' "double talk" during their meetings. With this insight, management's actions would have been more consistent with the chiefs' internal experiences. This is one of the most important lessons we need to learn when introducing change—that a little difference, such as listening, can make a big difference among organizational members.[14]

Breakdowns in cooperation and communication between management and workers continue to be commonplace in modern organizations. Disillusionment with interpersonal skills such as listening and understanding is also rising among managers, possibly because they expect too much from them too soon. There is no magic nor any guarantees of success in the listening process. However, management's recent shift back to a reliance on organizational structure as a change variable may prove, as it did in this case study, to be costly, disruptive, and self-defeating. Perhaps it is time we take Mayo's admonition seriously: teamwork "is the problem we face in the . . .twentieth century. There is no 'ism' that will help us to solution. We must be content to return to the patient, pedestrian work at the wholly neglected problem of the determinants of spontaneous cooperation."[15]

---

[14]Ibid., p. 217.
[15]Mayo, *The Social Problems*, p. xvi.

31. Some Major Research Findings Regarding the Human Element in Project Management

David L. Wilemon*

Bruce N. Baker†

INTRODUCTION

One of the most significant developments in management thought and practice during the past two decades has been the accelerated emphasis on project management in administering complex tasks and programs. Project management is now a widely utilized management system. The early project management literature tended to be oriented around the development and explanation of the tools and techniques of the project manager (1).‡ Since the late 1960s, however, increased research attention has been placed on the behavioral and organizational dimensions of the project management concept. This research emphasis has resulted in a growing body of knowledge which helps to explain the myriad of complex human factors which contribute to project management effectiveness. This article summarizes the mainstream of research in the human factors of project management. This review should help the user to

*Dr. David Wilemon is a professor and director of the Innovation Management Program in the Graduate School of Management at Syracuse University. He is widely recognized for his work on conflict management, team building, and leadership skills in project-oriented work environments. He has studied various kinds of project management systems in the United States and in several foreign countries.

†Dr. Baker is a Professor of Management at the University of Wisconsin-Oshkosh, and is also President of InterSystems Inc., a management consulting firm specializing in seminars, surveys and consulting work in the fields of planning, project management, alternative futures, and information systems. He received his A.B. degree from Princeton University, his M.B.A. degree from Stanford University, and his D.P.A. degree from The George Washington University. He is currently a consultant to the Food and Agriculture Organization of the United Nations and the U.S. EPA.

‡Numbered references are given at the end of this chapter.

better understand the numerous interpersonal forces found in the project ambience.

A review and synthesis of the most relevant research which has contributed to the understanding of the human element in project management is appropriate at this time in the life-cycle of project management. Although the authors reviewed dozens of articles, some important research may have been neglected. Space limitations preclude a complete coverage of all the relevant research. In some areas, pertinent research dealing with general management problems has been cited to further contribute to the understanding of the interpersonal dimensions of project management.

Five major areas were selected for a review of key research contributions. These areas include: 1) leadership styles/interpersonal skills, 2) conflict management; 3) decision making styles and team building skills; 4) organizational design and project manager authority relationships; 5) communications in project management; and 6) project team relationships with the parent, client, and other external organizations.

LEADERSHIP STYLES/INTERPERSONAL SKILLS

The leadership abilities and interpersonal skills of the project manager are critical to effective project management performance. While there has been much discussion on the role of leadership in project management, only recently has there been a growing interest in empirical investigations of some of the determinants of effective project management leadership.

Lawerence and Lorsch (1967) investigated the differences between effective and ineffective integrators (managerial positions like project managers) in terms of their behavioral styles in dealing with others in their organizations (2). Ten integrators were rated as "effective" and ten were evaluated as "less effective" (superiors' ratings were utilized). It was found that:

- Effective integrators had a significantly higher need for affiliation than the integrators rated as less effective. Differently put, the effective integrators had higher needs for interpersonal involvement, interactions, and demonstrated empathy in dealing with others.
- No statistically significant findings were found between the effective and less effective integrators in their need for achievement. A tendency, however, did emerge which seemed to indicate that the more effective integrators had a lower need for achievement than their counterparts.
- The need for power was rated approximately the same for the effective and the less effective integrators.
- Integrators rated as effective "prefer to take significantly more initiative and leadership, they are aggressive, confident, persuasive, and verbally

fluent. In contrast, less effective integrators avoid situations that involve tension and decisions."(3).
- Effective integrators also were more ambitious, forceful, and effective in communication than those rated as less effective.

Hodgetts (1969) empirically addressed the means of overcoming the "authority gap" in project management (4). Researching project management in aerospace, construction, chemicals, and state government environments, he found the following:

- Negotiation skills were important in aerospace and construction project environments.
- Personality and/or persuasive ability was considered important in all the project management situations.
- The project manager's competence was considered important in aerospace, construction, and in chemicals.
- Reciprocal favors were noted as important as a surrogate for authority in aerospace and construction.
- The combined sample of firms (aerospace, constructions, chemicals, and state government) rated the four authority supplements as "very important," or "not important." The following represents the significance of each technique as rated by the project managers in overcoming authority deficiencies. (Percentages are for those authority surrogates rated as either very important or important.)

—Competence	98%
—Personality and/or Persuasive Ability	96%
—Negotiation Ability	92%
—Reciprocal Favors	47%

Gemmill and Wilemon's exploratory research (1970) on forty-five project managers and supporting project team members focused on identifying several influence bases utilized by project managers in eliciting support (5). Their research suggested the following:

- Authority, reward, punishment, expertise, and referent power are sources of influence frequently utilized by project managers in gaining support for their projects. Each influence mode can have different effects on the organizational climate of the project organization.
- Two fundamental management styles used by project managers were identified. The first style relied primarily on the project manager's authority, his ability to reward, and his ability to block the attainment of objectives by those who support him—punishment. The second style relied on an expert and referent power influence style.

Gemmill and Thamhain's empirical research (1974) of twenty-two project managers and sixty-six project support personnel addressed the relationship of the project manager's utilization of interpersonal influence and project performance (6). Their research revealed the following:

- Support project personnel rank the eight influence methods as follows (1 is most important, 8 is least important):

Influence Method	Mean
Authority	3.0
Work Challenge	3.2
Expertise	3.3
Future Work Assignments	4.6
Salary	4.6
Promotion	4.8
Friendship	6.2
Coercion	7.8

- Project managers who are perceived to utilize expertise and work challenge as influence modes experience higher levels of project performance.
- Project performance is positively associated with high degrees of support, open communication among project participants, and task involvement by those supporting the project manager.
- The use of authority by project managers as means to influence support personnel led to lower levels of project performance.

The work of Fred. E. Fiedler has been a catalyst to much of the current research and literature concerning effective leadership styles under various levels of authority and for various task situations (7). Space limitations preclude describing his model which supports a contingency-oriented approach to leadership but one of his major findings is that:

"Both the directive managing, task-oriented leaders and the nondirective, human relations-oriented leaders were successful under some conditions. Which leadership style is the best depends on the favorableness of the particular situation and the leader. In very favorable or in very unfavorable situations for getting a task accomplished by group effort, the autocratic, task-controlling, managing leadership works best. In situations intermediate in difficulty, the non-directive, permissive leader is more successful" (8). "This corresponds well with our everday experience. For instance:

- Where the situation is very favorable, the group expects and wants the leader to give directions. We neither expect nor want the trusted airline pilot to turn to his crew and ask, "What do you think we ought to check before takeoff?"

- If the disliked chairman of a volunteer committee asks his group what to do, he may be told that everybody ought to go home.
- The well-liked chairman of a planning group or research team must be nondirective and permissive in order to get full participation from his members. The directive, managing leader will tend to be more critical and to cut discussion short; hence he will not get the full benefit of the potential contributions by his group members.

The varying requirements of leadership styles are readily apparent in organizations experiencing dramatic changes in operating procedures. For example:

- The manager or supervisor of a routinely operating organization is expected to provide direction and supervision that the subordinates should follow. However, in a crisis the routine is no longer adequate, and the task becomes ambiguous and unstructured. The typical manager tends to respond in such instances by calling his principal assistants together for a conference. In other words, the effective leader changes his behavior from a directive to a permissive, nondirective style until the operation again reverts to routine conditions.
- In the case of a research planning group, the human relations-oriented and permissive leader provides a climate in which everybody is free to speak up, to suggest, and to criticize. The brainstorming method in fact institutionalizes these procedures. However, after the research plan has been completed, the situation becomes highly structured. The director now prescribes the task in detail, and he specifies the means of accomplishing it. Woe betide the assistant who decides to be creative by changing the research instructions!" (9).

The findings of the others also support a contingency-based view of project management organization design.

CONFLICT MANAGEMENT

It is widely accepted that project environments produce inevitable conflict situations (10). Increasingly, the ability of project managers to handle these conflicts is being recognized as a critical determinant of successful project performance. Researchers have addressed the causes of disagreements in project management and the means by which conflict is managed.

Determinants of Conflict

Wilemon's study (1971) on delineating fundamental causes of conflict in the Apollo Program revealed that (11):

- The greater the diversity of expertise among the project team members, the greater the potential for conflict to develop.
- The lower the project manager's power to reward and punish, the greater the potential for conflict to develop.
- The less the specific objectives of a project are understood by project team members, the more likely that conflict will develop.
- The greater the ambiguity of roles among the project team members, the more likely conflict will develop.
- The greater the agreement on superordinate goals (top management objectives), the lower the potential for detrimental conflict.
- The lower the project manger's formal authority over supporting functional and staff units, the higher the probability that conflict will occur.

Butler's theory-oriented paper (1973) develops a number of propositions on the primary causes of conflict in project management (12). Many of his propositions are supported by prior research on conflict in various organizational settings—not exclusively project management. A few of the propositions advanced by Butler may be summarized as follows:

- Conflict may be either functional (beneficial) or dysfunctional (detrimental).
- Conflict is often caused by the revised interaction patterns of professional team members in project organizations.
- Conflict also develops as a result of the difficulties of team members adapting their professional objectives to project work situations and requirements.
- Conflict often is the result of the difficulties of diverse professionals working together in a project team situation where there is pressure for consensus.
- Role ambiguity and stress by the project managers and supporting functional personnel is more likely to occur when project authority is not clearly defined.
- Competition over functional resources, especially functional personnel, is likely to produce conflict.
- Conflict may develop over the lack of professional incentives derived from functional specialists participating in project-oriented work.

Thamhain and Wilemon's research (1974) focused on the causes and intensity of various conflict sources (13). Utilizing a sample of 100 project managers, their study measured the degree of conflict experienced from several variables common to project environments which were thought particularly conducive to the generation of conflict situations.

- The potential sources of conflict researched revealed the following rank-order for conflict experienced by project managers:
  1. schedules
  2. project priorities
  3. manpower resources
  4. technical conflicts
  5. administrative procedures
  6. cost objectives
  7. personality conflicts
- The most intense conflicts occur with the supporting functional departments followed by conflict with personnel assigned to the project team from functional departments.
- The lowest degree (intensity) of conflict occurred between the project manager and his immediate subordinates.

Thamhain and Wilemon followed their 1974 research with a study focused on measuring the degree of conflict experienced in each of the four generally accepted project life-cycle phases, namely, project formation, build-up, main program, and phase-out (14). Results reported from this research include:

- Disagreements over schedules result in the most intense conflict situations over the entire life cycle of a project.
- The mean conflict intensities over the four life cycle stages reveal the following rank order:
  Project Formation
  1. Project priorities.
  2. Administrative procedures.
  3. Schedules.
  4. Manpower resources.
  5. Cost.
  6. Technical conflicts.
  7. Personality.
  Build-up Phase
  1. Project priorities.
  2. Schedules.

3. Administrative procedures.
4. Technical conflicts.
5. Manpower resources.
6. Personality.
7. Cost.

Main Program Phase

1. Schedules.
2. Technical conflicts.
3. Manpower resources.
4. Project priorities.
5. Administrative procedures, cost, personality.

Phase-Out

1. Schedules.
2. Personality.
3. Manpower resources.
4. Project priorities.
5. Cost.
6. Technical conflicts.
7. Administrative procedures.

Conflict Handling Methods

If recognizing some of the primary determinants of conflict is a first step in effective conflict management, the second step is understanding how conflictful situations are managed in the project environment. Lawrence and Lorsch in their 1967 study examined the methods that "integrators" used in handling conflicts (15). The following items from their study are considered pertinent:

- The uses of three conflict handling modes were examined, namely, the confrontation or problem-solving mode, the smoothing approach, and the forcing mode. The utilization of the latter often results in a win-lose situation.
- The most effective integrators relied most heavily on the confrontation approach.
- Functional managers supporting the integrators in the most effective organizations also relied more on the confrontation approach than the other two modes.
- Functional managers in the highly integrated organizations employed "more forcing, and/or less smoothing behavior" than their counterparts in the less effective organizations.

Thamhain and Wilemon (1974), building on the methodologies of Lawrence and Lorsch (16), Blake and Mouton (17), and Burke (18), examined the effects of five conflict handling modes (forcing, confrontation, compromising, smoothing, and withdrawal) on the intensity of conflict experienced (19). They found:

- When interacting with personnel assigned from functional organizations, the forcing and withdrawal methods were most often associated with increased conflict in the project management environments.
- Project managers experienced more conflict when they utilized the forcing and confrontation modes with functional support departments.
- The utilization of the confrontation, compromise, and smoothing approaches by project managers were often associated with reduced degrees of conflict in dealing with assigned personnel.
- The withdrawal approach was associated with lower degrees of conflict. (This may be detrimental to overall project performance.)

To determine the actual conflict handling styles utilized by project managers, research was conducted by Thamhain and Wilemon (1975) in conjunction with their study on conflict in project life-cycles (20). The results reported included:

- The problem-solving or confrontation mode was the most frequently utilized mode of project managers (70%).
- The compromising approach ranked second with the smoothing approach ranking third. The forcing and withdrawal approach ranked fourth and fifth.
- Project managers often use the full spectrum of conflict handling modes in managing diverse personalities and various conflict situations.

Several suggestions for minimizing or preventing detrimental conflict were also provided by the study.

First, conflict with supporting functional departments is a major concern for project managers. Within the various categories of common conflict sources (schedules, project priorities, manpower resources, technical opinions, administrative procedures, and cost objectives), the highest conflict intensity occurs with functional support departments. The project manager frequently has less control over supporting functional departments than over his assigned personnel or immediate team members, which contributes to conflict. Moreover, conflict often develops due to the functional department's own priorities which can have impact on any of the conflict categories, i.e., manpower resources and schedules.

Minimizing conflict requires careful planning by the project manager. Effective planning early in the life cycle of the project can assist in forecasting and perhaps minimizing a number of potential problem areas likely to produce conflict in subsequent project phases. Consequently, contingency plans should be developed as early as possible in the life of a project. Senior management involvement in and commitment to the project may also help reduce some of the conflicts over project priorities and needed manpower resources and administrative procedures. In the excitement and haste of launching a new project, good planning by project managers is often insufficient.

Second, since there are a number of key participants in a project, it is important that major decisions affecting the project be communicated to all project related personnel. By openly communicating project objectives there is a higher potential for minimizing detrimental, unproductive conflict. Regularly scheduled status review meetings, for example, can be an important vehicle for communicating important project related issues.

Third, project managers need to be aware of their conflict resolution styles and their potential effect on key interfaces. Forcing and withdrawal modes appear to increase conflict with functional support departments and assigned personnel, while confrontation (problem-solving) compromise tend to reduce conflict. Again, it is important for project managers to know when conflict should be minimized and when it should be induced. In some instances project managers may deliberately create conflict to gain new information and provoke constructive dialogue. Provoking open disagreements and dialogue can produce positive results in the decision making process.

Fourth, a definite relationship appears to exist between the specific influence mode of project managers and the intensity of conflicts experienced with interfaces. For example, the greater the work challenge provided by a project manager, the less conflict he experiences with assigned project personnel. Thus, project managers need to consider the importance of work challenge not only in eliciting support but also in assisting in the minimization of conflict. One approach is to stimulate interest in the project and to match the needs of supporting personnel with the specific work requirements of the project.

Conflict with functional departments also may be created by the project manager who overly relies on penalties and authority. Often, the overuse of authority and penalties appears to have a negative effect in establishing a climate of mutual support, cooperation, respect, and thus their use must be guarded by the project manager.

Thus, project managers not only must be aware of the management styles they use in eliciting support but also of the effect of the conflict resolution approaches they employ. For the project leader each set of skills is critical for effective performance. If a project manager is initially skillful in gaining support but cannot manage the inevitable conflict situations which develop in the course of his project, then his effectiveness as a manager will certainly erode.

DECISION MAKING STYLES AND TEAM BUILDING SKILLS

The degree of participative decision making and esprit de corps have considerable impact upon not only the human aspects of the project management environment but also upon the perceived success of projects.

Baker, Murphy and Fisher in their study of over 650 projects, including over 200 variables, found that certain variables were significantly associated with the perceived failure of projects, others were significantly associated with the perceived success of projects, and still others were linearly related to failure/ success (21), e.g..

- Lack of project team participation in decision making and problem solving, lack of team spirit, lack of sense of mission within the project team, job insecurity, and insufficient influence of the project manager were variables significantly associated with perceived project failure.
- In contrast, project team participation in setting schedules and budgets was significantly related to perceived success.
- The relative degree of goal commitment of the project team and the degree to which task orientation (with a back-up of social orientation) was employed as a means of conflict resolution were linearly related to project success.*

Kloman's study contrasting NASA's Surveyor and Lunar Orbiter projects revealed that several elements contributed to the higher levels of actual and perceived success associated with the Lunar Orbiter project:

- Lunar Orbiter benefited from a strong sense of teamwork within both the customer and contractor organizations and in their relations with each other. Surveyor was handicapped by the lack of an equivalent sense of teamwork, particularly in the early years of the program.
- Senior management was committed to full support of the Lunar Orbiter project and was personally involved in overall direction at both the NASA field center and in the prime contractor's organization. There was far less support and involvement in the case of Surveyor (22).

There has been an accelerated use of team building in project management in the last few years. Varney suggests that there are three primary reasons for

---

*These findings are discussed in detail in chapter 33.

the increasing interest in team building (23). First, there are more specialists/ experts within organizations whose talents need to be focused and integrated into the requirements of the larger task. Second, many organizational members want to become more involved in the total work environment rather than just perform narrowly defined roles. Third, there is ample evidence that people working together can create synergy and high levels of creativity and job satisfaction.

In a recent exploratory research study with over 90 project managers, Thamhain and Wilemon identified some of the major barriers project leaders face in their attempts to build effective teams (24). The results of the exploratory field probe revealed the following common major barriers.

- Differing priorities, interests and judgments of team members.
  A major barrier is that team members can have different professional objectives and interests. Yet project accomplishment requires team members to place "what's good for the project" above their own interests. When team members are reluctant to do so, severe problems can develop in building an effective team. This problem is further compounded when the team relies on support groups which have widely different interests and priorities.
- Role conflicts
  Team development efforts are thwarted when role conflicts exist among the team members. Role conflicts are most likely to occur when there is ambiguity over who does what within the project team and between the team and external support groups. Overlapping and ambiguous responsibilities are also major contributors to role conflicts.
- Lack of team member commitment
  Lack of commitment to the project was cited as one of the most common barriers. Lack of commitment can come from several sources, such as: the team members' professional interests lie elsewhere; the feeling of insecurity being associated with projects; the unclear nature of the rewards which may be forthcoming upon successful project completion; and from intense interpersonal conflicts within the team.

  Other issues which can result in uncommitted team members is suspicious attitudes which may exist between the project leader and a functional support manager or between two team members from two warring functional departments. Finally, it was found that low commitment levels were likely to occur when a "star" on a team "demanded" too much deference from other team members or too much pampering from the team leader.
- Communication problems
  Not surprisingly, poor communication was a major barrier to effective

team development efforts. The research findings revealed that communication breakdowns could occur among the members of a team as well as between the project leader and the team members. Often the problem was caused by team members simply not keeping others informed on key project developments. The "whys" of poor communication patterns are far more difficult to determine than the effects of poor communication. Poor communication can result from low motivation levels, poor morale, or carelessness. It was also found that poor communication patterns between the team and support groups could result in severe team-building problems, as did poor communication with the client. Poor communication practices often led to unclear objectives, poor project control and coordination, and uneven work flow.

- Project objectives/outcomes not clear

  One of the most frequently cited team-building barriers was unclear project objectives. As one project leader in the study remarked:

  > How can you implement a team building program if you're not clear on what the objectives for the project are? Let's face it, many teams are muddling along on fifty percent of their potential because no one is really clear on where the project should be headed.

  In R & D and computer systems projects, objectives may be formulated by clients external to the team. Moreover, if objectives are not explicit, it becomes difficult, if not impossible, to clearly define roles and responsibilities.

- Dynamic project environments

  A characteristic of many projects is that the environments in which they operate are in a continual state of change. For example, senior management may keep changing the project scope, objectives and resource base. In other situations, regulatory changes or client demands for new and different specifications can drastically affect the internal operations of a project team. Disruptive operating environments are frequently a characteristic of project teams. Finally, the rate by which a team "builds up" to its full manpower base may present team-building barriers.

- Credibility of the project manager

  Team-building efforts also are hampered when the project leader suffers from poor credibility within the team or with important managers external to the team. In such cases, team members are often reluctant to make a commitment to the project or the leader. Credibility problems may come from poor managerial skills, poor technical judgments or lack of experience relevant to the project.

- Lack of team definition and structure

  One of the most frequently mentioned barriers was the lack of a clearly delineated team to undertake a project. The study found this barrier to be most likely to occur among computer system managers and R & D project leaders. A common pattern was that a work unit (not a project team) would be charged with a task but no one leader or team member was clearly delegated the responsibility. As a consequence, some work-unit members would be working on the project but not be clear on the extent of their responsibilities.

In other cases, a poorly defined team will result when a project is supported by several departments but no one person in these departments is designated as a departmental coordinator. Such an approach results in the project leader being unclear on whom to count for support. This often occurs, for example, when a computer systems project leader must rely on a "programming pool."

- Competition over team leadership
This barrier was most likely to occur in the early phases of a project or if the project ran into severe problems and the quality of team leadership came into question. Obviously, both cases of leadership challenge can result in barriers (if only temporary) to team building. These challenges were often covert attacks on the project leader's managerial capability.

- Project team member selection
This barrier centered on how team members were selected. In some cases, project personnel are assigned to the teams by functional managers, and the project manager had little or no input into the selection process. This, of course, can impede team development efforts especially when the project leader is given "available personnel" versus the best, hand-picked team members. The assignment of "available personnel" can result in several problems, e.g., low motivation levels, discontentment and uncommitted team members. As a rule, the more influence the project leader has over the selection of his/her team members, the more likely team-building efforts will be fruitful.

ORGANIZATIONAL DESIGN CONSIDERATIONS IN PROJECT MANAGEMENT

Several research studies have investigated the impact of organizational arrangements and the authority of the project manager. Baker, Murphy and Fisher found that with respect to organizational and authority arrangements:

- Excessive structuring within the project team and insufficient project manager authority were significantly related to perceived project failure.
- Adequate and appropriate organizational structures and effective planning and control mechanisms were significantly related to perceived project success. (Note that no particular type of organizational structure

or particular type of planning and control mechanism was associated with success. This finding supports the contingency theory of management.)

- Degree of bureaucracy and degree of spatial distance between the project manager and the project site were linearly related to success/failure, i.e., the greater the bureaucracy and the greater the spatial distance, the more likely the project was perceived as a failure (25).*

Marquis and Straight studied approximately 100 R & D projects (mostly under one million dollars) and found that:

- Projects in which administrative personnel report to the project manager are less likely to have cost or schedule overruns (26).
- Projects organized on a functional basis produce better technical results.
- Matrix organizations in which there is a small project team and more than half of the technical personnel remain in their functional departments are more likely to achieve technical excellence and, at the same time, to meet cost and schedule deadlines, than purely functional or totally projectized organizations (27).

Baker, Fisher and Murphy also found that insufficient project manager authority and influence were significantly related to cost and schedule overrun. Chapman found that:

- A matrix structure works best for 1) small, inhouse projects, where project duration is two years or less; 2) where assignments to technical divisions are minimal, and 3) where a field installation has substantial fluctuation in the amount of project activity it is handling.
- A matrix structure begins to lose its flexibility on large, long duration projects, and therefore a more fully projectized structure is appropriate in these circumstances (28).

In contrasting functional organizations with project organizations, Reeser found some unique human problems associated with projectized organizations:

- Insecurity about possible unemployment, career retardation, and personal development is felt by subordinates in project organizations to be significantly more of a problem than by subordinates in functional organizations.
- Project subordinates appear to be more frustrated by "make work" assignments, ambiguity and conflict in the work environment, and multiple levels of management than functional subordinates.

---

*These findings are discussed in greater detail in chapter 33.

- Project subordinates seem to feel less loyal to their organization than functional subordinates (29).

COMMUNICATIONS IN PROJECT MANAGEMENT

Increasingly, effective interpersonal communication is being recognized as a critical ingredient for project success. A study by Tushman, for example, clearly illustrates the role and managerial consequences of effective communication networks with R & D oriented project work environments (30). He notes that for complex problem-solving, "verbal communication is a more efficient information medium than written or more formal media (e.g., management information systems)."

Tushman found the following communication patterns existing for complex research projects conducted in a large corporate laboratory:

- There were high degrees of problem solving and administrative communication within the high performing teams. Further, the frequency of these two types of communication were positively associated with performance.
- The high performance project teams relied more on peer decision making intereaction than on supervisory direction.
- Communication to provide feedback and technical evaluation to areas outside the project but within the host organization tended to be highly specialized for the more effectively managed research projects.
- The high performing research teams made effective use of "gate-keepers" to link with expertise external to the project team, e.g., universities and professional societies.

From his major findings Tushman develops an information processing model to help plan and manage communication requirements for complex projects and programs.

RELATIONSHIPS OF THE PROJECT TEAM WITH THE PARENT, THE CLIENT, AND OTHER EXTERNAL ORGANIZATIONS

The patterns of relationships among the project team, the parent, the client, and other external organizations are extremely important to the perceived success of projects. Baker, Murphy, and Fisher found that:

- Coordination and relation patterns explained seventy-seven percent of the variance of perceived project success. (Stepwise multiple regression analysis with perceived success as the dependent variable. perceived success factor included satisfaction of all the parties concerned and technical performance.)

- Success criteria salience and consensus among the project team, the parent and the client also significantly contributed to perceived project success (second heaviest factor in the regression equation).
- Frequent feedback (but *not* meddling or interference) from the parent and the client, a flexible parent organization, lack of legal encumbrances or governmental red tape, and a minimal number of public governmental agencies involved with the project were pertinent variables significantly related to perceived project success(31).*

These findings supported Kloman's earlier study:

- From a management viewpoint, the greatest contrast between the Surveyor and Lunar Orbiter projects was the nature of the relationships of participating organizations, or what might be called the institutional environment. For Surveyor, there was an unusual degree of conflict and friction between Headquarters, JPL and the prime contractor. For Lunar Orbiter, harmony and teamwork prevailed. Institutions and people worked together in a spirit of mutual respect (32).

CONCLUSIONS

Research regarding the human element in project management has enabled practitioners to formulate strategies which can not only improve the behavioral aspects of project management but which also result in more effective project performance. The many research projects are relatively consistent with each other. Some of the principal findings which should be consistently stressed are:

- There is no single panacea in the field of project management; some factors work well in one environment while other factors work well in other environments;
- It is important to vest a project manager with as much authority as the environment permits; once vested with his authority, the project manager is well advised to utilize his expertise and work challenge as influence modes rather than his formal authority;
- The confrontation or problem-solving approach is generally more successful than the smoothing or the forcing mode of conflict resolution;
- Participative decision making styles are generally more successful than other styles; commitment, teamwork, and a sense of mission are important areas of attention in project management;
- Project organizational design must be tailored to the specific task and the environment, but higher degrees of projectization and higher levels of authority for the project manager result in less probability of cost and schedule overrun;

---

*These findings are discussed in chapter 33.

- To attain high levels of perceived success (including not only adequate technical performance but also satisfaction of the client, the parent, the project team, and the clientele), effective coordination and relations patterns are extremely important; also, success criteria salience and consensus among the client, the parent, and the project team are crucial.

Fully understanding the complexity of the interpersonal network in project management requires an on-going research effort. We hope that research on this crucial area of project management will continue to produce new knowledge in the future.

REFERENCES

1. Such a focus is a natural development in the life-cycle of many management concepts. In the area of systems analysis, for example, the early literature centered on the hardware, software, and technical information handling processes. An earlier version of this paper appeared in the *Project Management Quarterly,* (March 1977) pp. 34–40.
2. Paul R. Lawrence and Jay W. Lorsch, "New Management Job: The Integrator," *Harvard Business Review* (November-December, 1967), pp.142–151.
3. Ibid., p. 150.
4. Richard M. Hodgetts, "Leadership Techniques in the Project Organization," *Academy of Management Journal,* Vol. 11 (1968), pp. 211–219.
5. Gary R. Gemmill and David L. Wilemon, "The Power Spectrum in Project Management," *Sloan Management Review* (Fall, 1970), pp. 15–25.
6. Gary R. Gemmill and Hans J. Thamhain, "Influence Styles of Project Managers: Some Project Performance Correlates," *Academy of Management Journal* (June, 1974), pp. 216–224. Also see, Gary R. Gemmill and Hans J. Thamhain, "The Effectiveness of Different Powerstyles of Project Managers in Gaining Project Support," *IEEE Transactions on Engineering Management* (May, 1973), pp. 38–43.
7. Reprinted by permission of the *Harvard Business Review.* Excerpt from "Engineer The Job To Fit The Manager" by Fred E. Fiedler (September/October 1965). p. 119 Copyright 1965 by the President and Fellows of Harvard College; all rights reserved.
8. Ibid.
9. Ibid.
10. Paul O. Gaddis. "The Project Manager," *Harvard Business Review* (May-June, 1959), pp. 89–97; Richard M. Goodman, "Ambiguous Authority Definition in Project Management," *Academy of Management Journal* (December, 1967), pp. 395–407; John M. Steward, "Making Project Management Work," *Business Horizons* (Spring, 1967), pp. 63–70.
11. David L. Wilemon, "Project Management Conflict: A View from Apollo," *Proceedings of the Project Management Institute* (1971).
12. Arthur G. Butler, "Project Management: A Study in Organizational Conflict," *Academy of Management Journal* (March, 1973), pp. 84–101.
13. Hans J. Thamhain and David L. Wilemon, "Conflict Management in Project-Oriented Work Environments," *Proceedings of the Project Management Institue* (1974).
14. Hans J. Thamhain and David L. Wilemon, "Conflict Management in Project Life Cycles," *Sloan Management Review* (Summer, 1975), pp. 31–50.
15. Paul R. Lawrence and Jay W. Lorsch (same reference as footnote 2), pp. 148–149.
16. Paul R. Lawrence and Jay W. Lorsch (same reference as footnote 2).

17. R. R. Blake and Jane S. Mouton, *The Managerial Grid* (Houston: Gulf Publishing Company, 1964).
18. Ron J. Burke, "Methods of Resolving Interpersonal Conflict," *Personnel Administration* (July-August, 1969), pp. 48–55.
19. Hans J. Thamhain and David L. Wilemon (same reference as footnote 11).
20. Hans J. Thamhain and David L. Wilemon (same reference as footnote 1).
21. David C. Murphy, Bruce N. Baker, and Dalmar Fisher, *Determinants of Project Success,* Springfield, Va. 22151; National Technical Information Services, Accession number: N-74-30392, 1974, pp. 60–69.
22. Erasmus H. Kloman, *Unmanned Space Project Management—Surveyor and Lunar Orbiter,* a Report Prepared by the National Academy of Public Administration and sponsored by the National Aeronautics and Space Administration, Washington, D.C.; U.S. Government Printing Office, (1972), p. 14.
23. Glenn H. Varney, *Organization Development for Managers,* (Reading, Ma. Addison-Wesley Publishing Co., 1977), p. 151.
24. Hans J. Thamhain and David L. Wilemon, "Team Building in Project Management." *Proceedings of the Project Management Institute,* Atlanta (1979).
25. Murphy, Baker, and Fisher (same reference as footnote 21).
26. Donald G. Marquis and David M. Straight, *Organizational Factors in Project Performance,* Washington, D.C.: National Aeronautics and Space Administration, (July 25, 1965).
27. Donald G. Marquis, "A Project Team + PERT = Success or Does It?" *Innovation,* Number Five, (1969), pp. 26–33.
28. Richard L. Chapman, *Project Management in NASA,* a report of the National Academy of Public Administration Foundation, (January, 1973).
29. Clayton Reeser, "Some Potential Human Problems of the Project Form of Organization," *Academy of Management Journal,* (December, 1969), p. 467.
30. Michael L. Tushman, "Managing Communication Networks in R & D Laboratories," *Sloan Management Review,* (Winter, 1979), pp. 37–49.
31. Murphy, Baker, and Fisher (same reference as footnote 21).
32. Kloman (same reference as footnote 22), p. 17.

Section VIII

The Successful Application of Project Management

This section deals with successful applications of project management in the sense of both contextual applications and "success factors" that contribute to project success.

In Chapter 32, Mary B. Hunter and Frank A. Stickney provide an overview of a wide range of project management applications. Their annotated bibliography is an excellent guide to the broader literature describing various such applications.

In Chapter 33, Bruce N. Baker, David C. Murphy and Dalmar Fisher discuss "project success and failure factors"—those factors that have been demonstrated to affect the perceived success or failure of projects. Such factors can provide the project manager with insight into those characteristics that might influence the eventual degree of success that his project is perceived to have achieved.

In Chapter 34, Baker, Fisher and Murphy present a comparative analysis of public-and private-sector projects in terms of their success and failure patterns.

In the concluding Chapter 35, David I. Cleland discusses the cultural ambience of the matrix organization—those "climatic" or cultural factors that appear to be associated with successful matrix organizations.

32. Overview of Project Management Applications*

Mary B. Hunter and†
Frank A. Stickney‡

INTRODUCTION

The purpose of this chapter is to analyze the applications of project management in specific contexts ranging from industry, government and military to education and health service organizations. The authors are convinced that the project management process is the most effective approach to the management of multiple tasks, projects, products, etc. in many contemporary organizational situations. This is exemplified by the fact that project management applications are increasing in number and will undoubtedly continue to do so in the future.

Over the past twenty years many contemporary organizations have adopted and implemented the project management concept for better planning and control of their multiple projects, tasks and/or products. However, project management cannot and must not be considered a universal panacea for contemporary organizations who are encountering problems in the management of multiple tasks. Project management is not relevant to all organizational situations because the implementation and operation of project management requires the use of additional resources. It should be used only where the benefits obtained from its use offset these additional costs. The authors propose that the contingency approach must be followed in determining whether a given organization should adopt and implement project management. In other

*References are denoted by bibliographical entry number followed by page number; i.e., (4:25) denotes bibliographical entry number 4, page number 25.
†Mary B. Hunter graduated from Wright State University, Dayton, Ohio with a Masters Degree in Business Administration in 1981. Her fields of specialization were Systems Management and Strategic Management in which she conducted extensive research. She performed a major project in systems analysis of the Clark County Cooperative Education Service.
‡Frank A. Stickney is a Professor of Management at Wright State University. He received his Ph.D. from the Ohio State University in 1969. In addition to his academic research activity and consulting he has extensive work experience in project management and related activities. His primary areas of research interest are Organizational Design, Job Satisfaction and the Supervisory Process.

words, if an organization designed and operated under the traditional functional structure without project management is achieving its objectives satisfactorily, then there is no reason to adopt project management.

Project management received its earliest and strongest stimulus in organizations functioning in the aerospace, electronics, and communication technologies. The technologies involved in these industries are very dynamic and are characterized by rapid change. However, these technological conditions are spreading at a rapid pace to organizations in many other technological environments. Unstable environments, organizational growth and complexity, and change are evident in the various applications reviewed in this chapter. The effects of these factors are examined.

The structure used in developing this analysis consists of the following chapter sections:

I. A basic overview of the definition of project management and circumstances under which it should be used.
II. A description and analysis of project management applications.
III. Summary and conclusions

A BASIC OVERVIEW OF THE DEFINITION OF PROJECT MANAGEMENT AND CIRCUMSTANCES UNDER WHICH IT SHOULD BE USED

Project management is the application of the systems approach to the management of technologically complex tasks or projects whose objectives are explicitly stated in terms of time, cost, and performance parameters. In reality, a project is one of several subsystems in an organization. All of these subsystems must be managed in an integrative manner for the effective and efficient accomplishment of organizational/system objectives. Project management provides an interfunctional structure for a specific project and has a basic management orientation. It involves a project manager who, through funding control, obtains the required resources from the various functional departments. By the management functions of planning, organizing, directing, and controlling, the project manager coordinates the application of these resources to a given project with specific objectives providing the primary focus for this process.

The project organization is the focal point for all activities on a given project; it provides total project visibility. It is integrative in nature and becomes the hub of all activities, both internal and external, which affect the project. It is a management mechanism and does not replace the functional activities of the various departments; it supplements them. It is emphasized again that it is not applicable to every task, project, product, etc.; i.e., it is not an organizational panacea.

Many qualified "project management" organizations exist which use a "team or task-force approach," "matrix structure," "program structure," and "product structure." Not all of these approaches/structures fully qualify as project management organizations, but all contain characteristics of project management. Specifically, the differences among these recognized subsets of the general project management approach are simply a matter of emphasis. (1:1)* For example, the task-force approach is interdisciplinary, but has no finite termination date. The term "program" structure is usually used to define a multi-"project" structure (basically similar, but more complex).† Since matrix management seems to be the most widely used form of project management, a more complete description will facilitate understanding of the applications to be presented later in the chapter.

Matrix Management

Matrix management may be an effective organizational form when a large number of projects compete for limited resources resulting in extensive demands on the functional units. A matrix organization represents a web of horizontal, diagonal, and vertical relationships rather than the traditional vertical functional relationships through which all tasks are to be performed. Matrix management is a hybrid of project and functional concepts.

The systems approach must be used for the design of a matrix organization, the major emphasis being on the *totality* of all major activities. Organizations functioning in technology intensive environments, experiencing growth and/or complexity and change must be outstanding performers in both their product/project and specialized functional activities to survive and compete effectively. The matrix structure meets the need of these organizations as it is designed on the basis of two primary subsystems, one for projects/products and one for specialized functional activities. Organizational objectives must first be determined and then the objectives of its subsystem must be derived from them. Subsystem objectives must be compatible with each other and supportive of system or organizational objectives.

Figure 32-1 is a model which illustrates the basic relationship between the project/product subsystem and the functional subsystem. This model illustrates the horizontal flow of project authority and responsibility overlaid on the vertical flow of functional authority and responsibility. Where these two flows interface, the organizational relationship of the project and functional manager

---

*Numbered references are given at the end of this chapter.
†A detailed and thorough discussion of the forms of project management is beyond the scope of this paper. For a more thorough discussion, the reader is referred to Adams, John R., Barndt, Stephen E., and Martin, Martin D., *Managing by Project Management* (Dayton, Ohio: Universal Technology Corp., 1979), pages 1–14.

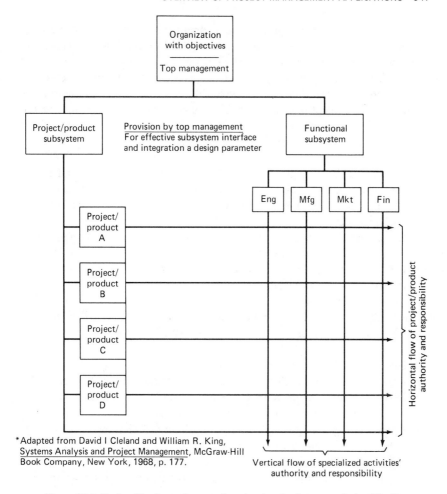

Figure 32-1. Project/Product subsystem functional and subsystem relationships.*

Source: Frank A. Stickney and William R. Johnston, "One More Time: Why Project Management?," *1979 Proceedings of the Project Management Institute* (Drexel Hill, PA: The Project Management Institute, 1979), p. 318.

is consumated. This figure is a conceptual model to analyze and understand the project and functional management relationships and does not reflect actual organizational designs.

The forms of project management should be a function of organizational needs. For example, where much complexity and change prevails with multiple projects, the matrix is adopted; where lesser degrees of such factors prevail, task forces are formed to solve problems, and so on.

The authors propose that project management is a means of managing technological change when organizations are engaged in multiple efforts. It provides the organizational structure required for the successful management of these efforts reflecting both organizational as well as task/project objective achievement. Many authors have developed criteria to use in evaluating the applicability of project management. Davis and Lawrence have listed the following conditions (words in parentheses added by authors) which must exist for a task to qualify for project management (12:15):

- There must be a single, identifiable overall task (innovation and timely completion of these tasks are the primary output of the organization)
- The task must be complex (reciprocal organizational and technological interdependencies)
- It must be interdisciplinary (requires simultaneous coordination of two or more functional departments)
- It must have a distinct life cycle and a termination date (as well as performance and cost objectives)

Cleland and King also list several conditions where project management techniques should be considered. Among these are (9:198–201):

- Existence of multilateral objectives
- Pressures to improve the product and advance the state of the art
- Risks are high; future uncertain (technologically dynamic environment with large volumes of information to be processed)
- Project is a type requiring advanced feasibility studies and development
- A management climate exists which permits the temporary "shorting" of reporting relationships within the organization (horizontal and integrative communication links—rather than vertical and authoritarian—are feasible)

The above are the major factors which an organization must consider in making its decision to adopt project management; it should insure that the benefits of better project planning, control and performance outweigh the additional costs required by the adoption of project management. The following section reviews numerous applications of project management and from an extensive review of the literature it appears that benefits exceeded costs in the examples reviewed.

A DESCRIPTION AND ANALYSIS OF PROJECT MANAGEMENT APPLICATIONS

The applications of project management are clustered by type of technology. To thoroughly describe and analyze all the cited applications is beyond the scope of this chapter because many of them are complex in nature and would require more space than a text of this nature permits. If more information is desired, the reader should review the referenced bibliography item.

Research and Development Activities

Research and development groups are basically concerned with translating intangible concepts, ideas, and theories into specifications, tangible products or processes. Consequently, these groups are different from the other subsystems within an organization and often require a different organizational form (23:24).

Drug development operates in a complex, ever changing environment requiring a dynamic system of operations, and this process at *Searle Laboratories Division of G.D. Searle and Company* in Chicago, Illinois is no exception. Searle utilizes a "collateral" project structure for achievement of both its research and organizational objectives. Included in this structure are the following groups:

1. A corporate *Pharmaceutical R&D Group* which has "goal-setting" responsibility and which interfaces primarily with the Action Council in a strategic administrative capacity.
2. *The Action Council* which is an interfunctional group employing worldwide technical personnel; this group has responsibility for product selection and prioritization and for selection and evaluation of project leaders
3. *Core Committees* which are interfunctional groups interfacing with the Action Council, project teams and project task forces; they are responsible for needed resources, project sites and determining the nature of world-wide technical inputs.
4. *Interfunctional Task Forces* consisting primarily of members from the Core Committee; they are responsible for project planning.
5. *Project Leaders* who are responsible for managing the projects and *Project Management Consultants* who are responsible for monitoring the project progress. Project leaders have personnel assigned based on skill assessment requirements determined by the interfunctional task forces; this comprises the basic project management team.

All of the above groups are in continuous interaction by organizational/system plan and their specific roles and relationships are explicitly specified. The task of these groups is made exceedingly difficult by government regulation and monitoring, by frequent changes and modifications, and by the nature of basic research. Although some interdependencies are more complex than others, all necessitate dynamism and flexibility in organizational structure. The project structure, although seemingly complex, appears to be conducive to achievement of objectives in their environment (18:143).

Battelle Pacific N.W. Laboratories (BNW), a division of Battelle Memorial Institute, is a second example of project management in R&D. While its main purpose years ago was the provision of technical support to the Hanford plant of the Atomic Energy Commission, today it has project contracts from both government and industry (national and international) which are extremely broad in scope, with their size and complexity ranging from the small, single-discipline type to the large multimillion dollar, multidisciplinary type. Internal strengths/resources are widely diversified with R&D capabilities ranging from molecular biology to nuclear waste disposal and within the staff of approximately 2700 persons, most technology-oriented disciplines and many social science disciplines are represented. A Research Project Management System (RPMS) was established which supports a work environment conducive to the creative, innovative output expected from researchers with functional/specified discipline orientations. It also provides for effective performance of the firm's many projects. RPMS is responsive to researchers' needs and is conducive to minimizing uncertainties involved in the management of R&D activities.*

BNW maintains a "functional" structure with an implied "project" structure which operates as a matrix organization. Project managers report to functional managers but maintain the flexibility for temporary assignment to other functional managers as needed within the organization. For example, one project may need input from a chemical engineer, a biologist, a statistician, an economist, an ecologist and a social scientist. The assigned project manager is responsible for obtaining and coordinating these inputs. The project organization is not reflected in the formal organization chart but is created when needed. It is believed by those who have used the Project Management System at Battelle that it has been successful (29:243–245).

Construction

Construction projects requiring interdisciplinary efforts from not one, but two or more separate technologically oriented organizations, by nature, necessitate a project management structure applied contingently to each situation. An example of this is the *James H. Campbell Plant Unit #3,* a coal-fired power plant designed and constructed near Grand Haven, Michigan. This project was under the direction of Consumers Power Company (CPCo), plus two separate

---

*For a thorough discussion on the topic the reader is referred to: Miles, G. Patrick. "Implementing a Project Management System in a Research Laboratory," *1979 Proceedings of the Project Management Institute* (Drexel Hill, PA: The Project Management Institute, 1979), pp. 243–252.

organizations, Townsend and Bottam Engineers and Constructors (T&B), the constructor, and Gilbert/Commonwealth (G/C), the engineer. These two autonuomous organizations joined together in providing the interdisciplinary, single responsibility focus CPCo required. This effort was carried out by integrated project teams (integrating the expertise of both companies) with a single project manager as the individual with key responsibility to CPCo. The magnitude of this project and the complexities involved made this task understandably difficult. Complex channels of communication, distance, and a lack of understanding among the different groups and/or companies were coped with through weekly management meetings. Progress reviews were held first for each functional discipline and these reviews were then followed by a project group meeting where open communication and constructive criticism was the mode.

Communication and information flow are the basic elements affecting the integration of diverse efforts; these meetings facilitated this process which was one major factor contributing to its success. In addition, "Team Building Sessions" were held to promote cooperation between and among all groups. The success of this project is attributable to the project management approach and the resulting integration of effort (37:258).

Over the past few years *electric utility companies* have played an increasingly active role in performing and managing the work activities of their major power plant construction projects. The factors necessitating this participatory role are presented in Table 32-1 (13:313).

As a result of these factors, electric utility companies are becoming more actively involved in construction, and project management has become a common organizational form to deal with the new relationships existing between utility companies and architect/engineer-constructors (A/E's). A/E's were previously the sole operational entities with complete responsibility for design and construction of new plants (13:311). Although utility project management organizations are a variety of structures, the matrix design is the one most commonly used.

Another construction organization which has applied project management to its operations is the *Los Angeles County Flood Control District,* a system of flood control and water conservation facilities (i.e. dams, major channel improvements, spreading grounds, etc.) for Los Angeles County. This system became increasingly subject to problems as the organization grew and expanded from its inception. Inflation caused construction costs to skyrocket and eroded the real purchasing power of dollars allocated to construction projects. Performance targets were not being met while rapid population growth in the area simultaneously dictated a need for further expansion. Community support of flood control projects lessened, thus impairing expansion. Geographic and climatological environmental conditions dictated a need for expan-

Table 32-1. Changed Settings for Utilities.

- Plant costs have increased substantially
    Technological advances
    Increased regulatory requirements
    Larger plant sizes
    Inflation and escalation
- Regulatory setting has changed
    Utilities have direct responsibility for licenses, permits and regulatory approval in:
        Engineering/Design
        Construction
        Operation
- Business environment conditions have changed
    Rising energy costs
    Load growth prediction difficulty
    Increased difficulty in financing capital projects
                        Requirements resulting from changed setting.
- Increased Cost Control
- Increased Schedule Control
- Increased Technical Control

Source: DeLorenzo, Robert A., "The Evolving Role of Electric Utilities Relative to Major Project Management," *1977 Proceedings of the Project Management Institute* (Drexel Hill, PA: The Project Management Institute, 1977), p. 313.

sion and the number of organizations external to the system with which it had to interact increased steadily. Staff was increased (especially engineering) to meet the expansion needs and new divisions were formed creating problems in coordination, suboptimization, and communication among divisions. If change had not been implemented, achievement of not only short-range, but also long-range, strategic objectives would have been threatened causing decreased ability for survival and growth of the system (16:IV–G.1).

In 1966, a small program management effort was adopted and implemented consisting of two men and one secretary with mainly a facilitating responsibility for recommending change. The program management function grew from that state, encountering problems (i.e. resistance to change) and solving problems (i.e. increased systems perspective). Several years later program/project managers were directly assigned to projects, although not all projects now have project managers, and a Management Systems Division (MSD) was formed. (16:IV–G.4) Program/project management had a positive impact on this organization since it increased communication/cooperation with the community and other environmental systems, facilitated timeliness of decision-making, increased a systems perspective, decreased suboptimization within divisions and has facilitated use of computer programming as a management tool. The new organizational structure is believed by many within the Flood Control District to be an appropriate alternative for dealing with complexity and change.

It clearly indicates the use of project management as an integrating mechanism for diverse activities required for achievement of common objectives (16:IV–6.7).

Aerospace Programs—Department of Defense/NASA

Industrial project management has its early origins in the aerospace industry because of government requirements. The experiences with project management in the aerospace industry during the past three decades are numerous and well documented. Therefore they will not be discussed within this analysis. But, the experience of government organizations in aerospace activities will be presented.

NASA's space shuttle program is an extremely complex and immense undertaking. It requires control and motivation of a large number of highly trained and creative personnel, coordination of many diverse contractors, products and their subsystems, and it consists of diverse, national and international locations. NASA is required to meet specific time, cost and performance parameters and is subject to limited availability of resources. The complexity and reciprocal interdependencies of this program necessitate a tremendously dynamic system structure. The structure developed consists of the following four levels:

- *Level I* is NASA Headquarters in Washington D.C. which interfaces directly with Congress and other government agencies. It is responsible for provision of major program direction and planning, basic performance requirements and control of major milestones and funding allocations to NASA field centers
- *Level II* is the Space Shuttle Program Office which has the following divisions:
  Systems Integration—technical orientation.
  Operations Integration—technical orientation.
  Management Integration—management orientation.
  Resources and Schedules Integration—management orientation.
  They all have major interfunctional program management responsibilities.
- *Level III* is the actual projects which are managed through project offices at NASA centers.
- *Level IV* is the level where contractors carry out operational duties[1].

---

[1]Frederick Peters. "NASA Management of the Space Shuttle Program," *1975 Proceedings of the Project Management Institute* (Drexel Hill, PA: The Project Management Institute, 1975), p. 154.

Unity of effort in a program of this scope is seemingly impossible, yet it is an absolute necessity for achievement of program objectives. A project structure to facilitate integration is an essential prerequisite for coordination, control, and task achievement. Integration of these diverse and multiple efforts is a complex process involving the above levels in program management. A smaller and less complex program would have a less complex structure, but this structure facilitates smooth communication flows and processing of information to key decision centers within the constraints of this program.

The *Navel Air Systems Command* uses project management in its defense weapon systems acquisition process. The Command receives approximately $7.7 billion annually, employs technical personnel in many diverse activities throughout the United States, and is responsible for the design, engineering, test, fleet acceptance, production management and logistical support for the life of a weapons system. The following are a few examples of the program responsibilities of the Naval Air Systems Command which reflect the complexity and variety of tasks (33:41).

- Airborne electronics.
- Aeronautical target systems.
- Navy and Marine Corps aircraft.
- Air launched weapons systems.
- Photographic and meteorological equipment.

With these multiple tasks, the Naval Air Systems Command functions most effectively with a matrix organizational design. Project offices are formed for the weapons systems requiring large outlays of R&D and/or production dollars, and project managers are assigned overall project responsibility. The technical and administrative experts from the functional departments are assigned to projects to provide the specialized expertise on an as required basis. However, centralized management direction is provided for each of the major command tasks. The Command's contractors (suppliers) also use the project management concept for managing their portion of the project and for interfacing with the project manager in the Command. With the complexities and interdependencies inherent in major weapon systems development, the matrix structure appears to be working well in this situation (33:45).

The *Aeronautical Systems Division (ASD),* United States Air Force is responsible for the acquisition of aircraft and related support equipment for the Air Force. It is a large, complex organization with many functional and staff activities supporting the acquisition and management operations of approximately fourteen program offices. The technological weapon system acquisition environment within which the Air Force and its contractors function is highly suitable for project/program management. When an organization like ASD is dealing with many projects, a matrix organization is appropriate since there are well established functional departments which have the special skill and capabilities required for performance and support of multiple projects. Rapidly changing workloads and the necessity for capable, highly trained functional specialists have dictated the need for the matrix form of organization. A project office in this matrix organization has three categories of personnel; first, those individuals permanently assigned to the project office for the management of the project; second, those functional specialists co-located in the project office reporting to both the project manager and their respective functional managers; and third, functional specialists who remain in their functional offices and support specified projects when needed by the co-located functional specialists.

In general, matrix management has met the expectations of ASD, i.e. it has aided in the rapid reallocation of functional personnel to meet changing project demands and has enhanced the exchange of innovative management techniques through communication flows. Functional managers are generally better able to insure that program offices have the most effective functional support commensurate with program requirements, and specialized resources are assigned with inherent flexibility where they are most useful. Although problems invariably arise, these positive aspects are greater in importance than the costs of the negative factors (39:469–478).

There are many factors that determine whether or not project management will function in a positive manner. For example, the *F-15 system,* a major program within ASD, was established to develop the world's best air superiority fighter aircraft. It operated with a matrix organizational design which integrated project tasks (airframe, engine, avionics, etc.) and functional tasks (engineering, configuration management, integrated logistics support, production, procurement, etc.) Some of the factors contributing to the success of this program were as follows (22:43).

- The program manager, understood the weapon system acquisition process, and had the necessary authority for carrying out his responsibilities.
- Maximum emphasis was placed on early and definitive planning in an effort to stabilize and control the program in terms of time, cost, and technical performance parameters.
- The production and quality plans were jointly prepared involving the program office and the supplying contractor. Through this process, an understanding of procedures and techniques was reinforced, and communication was enhanced among those involved.
- The program office personnel/contractor interface was a critical point for objective achievement. The personnel in the Air Force project office and

the contractor personnel established open information flow and communication channels through travel to each geographic location on a continuous basis through the major critical milestones in the project.

Industry (Non-Aerospace)

The following is an analysis and discussion of project management efforts in non-aerospace industrial organizations. For an organization to survive, thrive and grow, it must maintain open interaction with its environmental systems, the technological, political, social and economic forces. Those organizations which have not maintained this contact have encountered severe problems. The project management approach has enabled many organizations to maintain this interface.

By the end of 1973, the management of *General Motors* found it necessary to closely examine their corporation and to determine the reasons behind their failure in adapting to environmental and market demands. Mileage had suddenly become the overriding concern in the automobile industry, which required a major turnaround/redesign effort in nearly every product line. The business environment of the automobile industry had become increasingly complex and uncertainty was ever present. The conditions were appropriate for project management and in 1974, the project center concept was adopted to coordinate the efforts of the five automobile divisions. These project centers are temporary in nature and are formed whenever a major effort requiring interfunctional specialities is required. Project centers work on problems common to all divisions (i.e. frames, electrical systems, steering gear, and brakes). The project center concept may well be considered G.M.'s most important tool in development of new body lines; i.e. it has speeded new technological ideas onto the production line and has utilized resources to their best advantage, eliminating much redundancy in efforts (6:96).

At the *Inland Division of General Motors,* a "team approach" was implemented to minimize the suboptimization of organizational objectives that often occur in large, complex, multifaceted organizations. Before the implementation of this approach, there was little cooperation/coordination among the functions of engineering, manufacturing, sales, and other personnel. Now communication and cooperation are vastly improved with the various functions working on common problems using the team approach for products and major components. This approach consists of interfunctional teams who work on one or more major projects, rotating team chiefs with differing technical specialities, and a "board" to oversee the team operations and to provide strategic management direction. It illustrates another positive result of the project management approach to interfunctional problems although it does not meet the exact criteria for a project office (10:89).

In 1967 *Dow Corning* showed the following symptoms (words in parentheses added by authors) of a need for change common in many traditional hierarchial organizations:

- Executives had inadequate financial information and control of operations and cumbersome communications channels existed between key functions (vertical and authoritarian communication links rather than horizontal and integrative were used).
- In the face of stiffening competition, the corporation remained too internalized in its thinking and organizational structure (parts of the organization were closed to the environment which unduly constrained the system).
- Long-range corporate planning was sporadic and superficial causing overstaffing, duplicated efforts and inefficiency (strategic planning and timely completion of tasks were vital for long run organizational survival and growth, but were inadequately accomplished).

Dow Corning exhibits many characteristics indicative of the need for a strong project management structure. For example, they develop, manufacture, and market many diverse, interrelated, technological products; have market interests in virtually ever major industry; have a rapidly expanding global/multinational business; and work within a dynamic, rapidly changing business environment. The organization was ripe for change, and in 1967, Dow Corning began an organizational restructuring into a multidimensional matrix structure that required approximately four years of evolution (21:153).

A full account of the restructuring is beyond the scope of this paper.* Basically the new organizational form integrated profit centers, cost centers and geographic areas worldwide. It consisted of multi-matrices on four major dimensions of:

1. Functions (marketing, manufacturing, research, etc.)
2. Businesses (arbitrarily selected product groups)
3. Areas (geographically—i.e. Europe, U.S., Asia, etc.)
4. Growth, movement and change through time" (20:179).

Has the new structure proven effective? Sales have quadrupled and profits have increased nearly five times, while manpower has grown by less than 35%.

---

*For a complete discussion of these problems the reader is referred to Goggin, William C. "A Decade of Progress: Multidimensional Organization Structure," reprinted in *Matrix Organization and Project Management*. Edited by Raymond E. Hill and Bernard J. White (Ann Arbor, Michigan: The University of Michigan, 1979), pp. 179–188.

In 1974 there were ten separate businesses within Dow Corning and in 1979 there were six which emphasizes the efficient resource utilization facilitated by project management. From a cost/benefit perspective, management at Dow Corning believes that the new structure is a success (20:180).

In 1976, *Litton's Microwave Division* had a problem that many contemporary organizations encounter. It was an inability to grow as rapidly as market opportunities. They were the leading producer of commercial microwave ovens, had enjoyed a 50% per year growth rate since inception in 1963, and had set a strategic, long-range objective of a compound 40% per year growth rate for the next five to seven years. These kinds of criteria clearly required a dynamic organizational structure that would be responsive to change and complexity, with increased flexibility, an ability to absorb rapid growth, maintain stability, efficiently utilize resources, and encourage creativity of personnel (19:72).

William George, then president of the division, realized that if action was not taken, it would become increasingly difficult for functional managers to maintain a systems perspective, i.e. suboptimization of organizational objectives might increase. While change in organizational structure was the most obvious solution, it was believed that the current functional structure provided the necessary foundation and stability for further growth. Therefore, an information "task team" approach was developed to carry out much of the work. It consisted of functional department representatives, team leaders, and corporate management support and direction provided intermittently. Some examples of task team projects included new product development, manufacturing of products, new marketing programs, cost reduction activities, and new business ventures.[2] The informal project structure did not replace the functional structure; it supplemented it. Before reorganization, problems of inadequate communication and assignment of blame to others for product quality, hours per unit, etc. prevailed. Under the new structure, problems were either resolved very quickly, or never developed because of improved communication among functions. Results were tangibly reflected in areas of improved product quality and decreased unit production costs. The team approach has also contributed to increased morale, trust, and mutual respect throughout the organization. It has most importantly enabled this division to grow rapidly with a minimum of growing pains (19:78).

In the *railway industry*, there has traditionally been a lack of management/ labor cooperation, a problem with operations and service reliability, and problems with job security and safety of the work force. To solve these types of problems, a task force approach in Missouri Pacific's St. Louis terminal, the

---

[2]William W. George. "Task Teams for Rapid Growth," *Harvard Business Review*. (March–April, 1977), p. 72.

Chicago terminal, and the Houston terminal has been promoted between management, labor, and government (41:21). The task force approach contains characteristics of project management because it is interfunctional in nature and works toward common goals and objectives. The main difference in this approach from the definition of project management given previously is that there is no finite termination date for the project or task. For example, the basic objectives of this task force were to determine solutions to the above traditional industry problems. Thus, the task force approach depicts an organizational form that is only partially characteristics of project management.

Standard Steel Company of Burham and Latrobe, Pennsylvania, a traditionally functional organization, provides another example of project management application. As product diversity increased into four distinct product lines, each with different processing facilities, management became overwhelmed with detail. The company was increasingly subject to unduly constraining environmental factors such as inflation, excessive foreign competition, and strong, insistent governmental demands regarding pollution control and other matters. Standard Steel, a major producer of open-die forgings and heavy shafting for marine and nuclear reactor applications, produced 300,000 tons of steel per year, employed 2,600 people, and invested in high technology resources. These combined factors resulted in pressure for change and Standard Steel became one of the first companies in the metals industry to employ matrix management. The project structure was integrated with the functional structure, and teams of specialists (i.e. production, finance, metallurgy, etc.) jointly managed a product line or geographic area. Many companies in the metals industry may not find this approach applicable to their situations, but for Standard Steel the approach is working well (8:38).

In 1969, *Scientific Control Systems Ltd. (Scicon),* a management sciences and computer consultancy firm, was experiencing rapid change and complexity in products and markets, difficulty in staffing projects, had acquired a staff of 400 individuals with a differentiated range of activities, and was having difficulty fulfilling career needs and aspirations of the work force. Although an attempt was made to deal with these factors through the creation of a new division in each new major computer development area, such actions caused management control and communications problems. In addition, employees were experiencing career development problems and were leaving at an alarming rate. These symptoms indicated a need for an organizational restructuring and for adoption and implementation of project management. A matrix structure was designed with project groups to provide flexibility overlaid on the hierarchial resource division structure to provide continuity and technical expertise. This new structure was seemingly successful because within the first year improvements were seen in such areas as service clients, quality of work, and satisfaction of the work force regarding career opportunities (26:61).

Educational Organizations, Health Services, and Social Service Organizations

Project management is applicable not only to industry and government, but also to not-for-profit organizations. Depending on the complexity of the technology involved, the organizational interdependencies, the demands of the community and/or clients, and factors previously described which indicate a need for project management, organizations may find interfunctional restructuring a very feasible alternative to promoting coordination/control and achievement of objectives.

In educational organizations the project management concept has been neutralized because it is viewed by many professionals as being administratively promoted for accountability rather than as a concept which also has relevance for the interfunctional considerations of personnel, academic and student development. It is felt that this close-minded attitude exists because those in educational administration perceive a loss of their positions of money, power, and influence with the more participative management approach inherent in project management (5:453).

The *Shawnee Mission (Kansas) Public School System* found in 1969 that the traditional hierarchial organization was unable to meet insistent community demands, criticism, and scrutiny for instant equal educational opportunity in the 65 schools of the then new K-12 district. This school system ranked 90th nationally in size with 45,000 students. The system superintendent recognized a need for a different means of managing work effort, and began instituting a "team management" task force structure, combining school board members, students, parents, and educators. It has been found that the increased communication, feedback, and open relationships facilitated by this approach greatly aided the successful flow of information from the community to the school system and back to the community again. It is believed that this process has resulted in improved system output in the form of children with higher quality education and more equal educational opportunities (2:35).

Since President Kennedy signed the Community Mental Health Act of 1963, and with the 1975 amendments to that act, the services of community mental health centers (CMHC) have become increasingly complex. Governmental funds for operations decreased while the components and complexities of CMHC's responsibilities increased with added service responsibilities and increased caseloads. In 1976, the *Westside Community Mental Health Center* was a traditional functional organization. Problems existed because a limited number of services were offered and service areas exhibited varying degrees of productivity. Coordination among service areas was increasingly complex, communications were poor, often patients were discharged from the Inpatient Department with no follow-up arrangements made in the Outpatient Department, and a systems perspective among personnel became exceedingly rare. These conditions were conducive for change. A matrix organizational structure was adopted, and since then major improvements in operations are evident. In 1978, there were five additional service programs offered employing seven less staff personnel than in 1976. The adoption and implementation of the matrix organizational form was highly conducive to increased coordination, control, and task/objective achievement (42:99–105).

As with community mental health centers, community health service organizations in general have experienced rapid change. These organizations have been traditionally designed within a functional structure, i.e. nursing, pharmacy and other functional departments, and advanced technology has stimulated a strong trend toward an increased number of functional specialities. Clinical doctors, consultants and general practitioners have maintained private contracts with health services and are not organized within hierarchies. These factors indicate a need for differentiation of technical specialists and for coordination of these specialists with the functional hierarchies. Single dimension solutions to problems have become increasingly ineffective. For example, a person may be cured from an illness, but the poor home environment precipitating the problem cannot be "cured". *The British National Health Service* was reorganized in 1974, and involves the overlapping of the functional hierarchial organization with various lateral relationships, some permanent, some ad hoc (a matrix/team structure). The lateral groupings have a variety of responsibilities/tasks ranging from direct provision of services by health service professionals to developing policies and/or plans by both inhouse personnel and non-health agency personnel. This organizational form has in addition, a synergistic effect upon the health service. When those with technical expertise are brought together to solve problems, learning from the skill and knowledge of one another is inherent in the interactions, resulting in greater realization of organizational goals (14:82–85).

It is important to note that establishing team structures within this health service was, and is, a difficult effort. Because the individual professionals perceive the task at hand from their particular sub-system culture which is the basis of their expertise, differences of opinion are often difficult to resolve. Teams interface not only within the organization, but also beyond organizational boundaries because of multidimensional problems. Consequently, team members may be subject to multi-influences from both their team and functional speciality, and from their differing employing authorities as well. These factors make the contingency approach even more vital to efficient/effective achievement of organizational objectives (14:86).

SUMMARY AND CONCLUSIONS

Summary

Several project management applications have been reviewed and the characteristics of organizations which have used project management have been discussed. The major outputs of organizational systems are not of paramount importance. The outputs may be newly developed drugs, methods of nuclear waste disposal, a high powered utility plant, a major weapon system, automobiles, glassware products, or a better educated society with individuals cured of physiological problems. Factors such as a technologically dynamic environment, interdisciplinary tasks, limited availability of resources, and complex and interfunctional decisions requiring real time solutions are some of the major determinants.

A system perspective requires one to think of an organization as a totality with inputs, transformation, and output processes. The principal points of interface of the system with its supra environmental systems must be identified and understood, and the degree of complexity of interdependencies of parts within the system affect the type of system design. Although organizations are very different in their inputs, transformation mechanisms, and output components of the process, they are quite similar with respect to the nature of the environmental forces impacting upon them. The structure to manage their diverse products, tasks, projects, etc. must provide for not only adaptability to their environmental forces but also for a degree of stability. The review of project management applications illustrate how project management provides for this requirement.

The authors believe that organizations which seem to exhibit differences due to differing technologies and dissimilarities of purpose may still benefit from the application of project management. In other words, one must consider the specific aspects of the internal and external organizational environment as previously described. Unfortunately, as contemporary organizations strive to increase specialization to cope with rapidly advancing technology, coordination costs increase. The basic implication of this is that a systems perspective is required and is vital to the strategic health of an organization. This perspective allows the organizational design to be an effective tradeoff of both factors.

The research and development organizations described were subject to technologically complex environments, large specialized staffs requiring interfunctional integration, and differentiated outputs. Because of these similarities, project management was determined to be applicable. Differences in the approach of implementation and problems encountered are understandably different among organizations (i.e. even individual departments within an organization may be given latitude in implementation technique). Resistance to change in organizational processes is usually a common problem among specialized professionals in these organizations.

In the construction areas examined similarities were found in the need for interdisciplinary efforts, rising costs coupled with a need for more and larger plants, and the magnitude and complexities involved in major construction efforts. Aerospace programs in the Department of Defense and NASA are similar in that they usually employ large numbers of individuals with a wide variety of specializations, are subject to many environmental pressures and require interfunctional integration for specific output with time, cost, and performance parameters inherent in the process.

In other industries, organizations in uncertain, technologically dynamic environments with work effort requiring interfunctional coordination and control for production of diverse, interrelated, technological products/services are also prime candidates for project management. Social service and educational organizations are not sheltered from these kinds of factors simply because of their not-for-profit purpose. They are also faced with limited resources, and must more effectively satisfy the expectations of their clientele. It is for this reason that more contemporary service organizations are adopting and implementing project, program, task force, or matrix management when the structure is appropriate and may contribute to more effective achievement of organizational goals and objectives within critical resource constraints.

Conclusions

The purpose of this chapter was not to perform an indepth analysis and review of each selected project management application, but to familarize the reader with the general nature of the applications and any special factors pertaining thereto. The annotated bibliography enables the reader to go directly to the source if a more detailed explanation is desired.

As an organization progresses through the stages of its life-cycle, many short-term operational problems evolve that must be dealt with daily. On the other hand, when major strategic problems vital to the life of the system develop, they must be dealt with in the form of long-term and major strategic changes. The approach that should be taken is termed the contingency approach and the solution should be a direct function of the situation.

More and more contemporary organizations are finding that some form of project management is applicable to them. Although project management cannot and must not be considered a panacea, it does have potential for contribution to more efficient/effective achievement of organizational objectives if internal and external environmental factors justify its use. It is the authors' belief that, because of increasing organizational complexity and the dynamism of today's total environment which this review reflects, these applications are only the preamble to what may be expected in potential project management applications for the future.

ANNOTATED BIBLIOGRAPHY

1. Adams, John R., Barndt, Stephen E., and Martin, Martin D. (eds). *Managing by Project Management* (Dayton, Ohio: Universal Technology Corporation, 1979), pp. 1–13.
   A variety of forms of work effort sharing the same common project management concept (with any differences being a matter of emphasis) are fully described.
2. Ball, Arzell L. and Miller, Ellen W. "The Case for Replacing," *The American School Board Journal* (July 1975), pp. 34–36.
   The concept of "team management" is supported as a positive alternative to the traditional hierarchial organization and an application of this approach at the Shawnee Mission (Kansas) Public Schools is presented.
3. Baumgartner, J. Stanley (ed). "A Discussion With the Apollo Program Director, General Sam Phillips," *Systems Management* (Washington, D. C.: The Bureau of National Affairs, Inc., 1979), pp. 13–25.
   Points out the means through which the Apollo (project management) program was organized, including problems that occurred.
4. ———. "A Discussion With Robert K. Duke of Fluor Corporation," *Systems Management* (Washington, D.C.: The Bureau of National Affairs, Inc., 1979), pp. 95–98.
   A brief discussion giving some interesting insights into project management as it is applied at Fluor.
5. Borland, David T. "Aggressive Neglect, Matrix Organization, and Student Development Implementation," *Journal of College Student Personnel* (November 1979), pp. 452–454.
   Explains the matrix concept applied to education and points out that it has been neglected in education.
6. Burck, Charles G. "How G.M. Turned Itself Around," *Fortune* (January 16, 1978), pp. 87–96.
   Some benefits of the "project-center" idea (formed whenever a major new effort is planned, operating for the duration of the undertaking) are discussed.
7. Carson, John H. (ed). "Teamwork: A Tired Concept Fuels a Turnaround," *Industry Week* (March 1, 1976), pp. 30–33.
   The way in which Standard Pressed Steel Company's Aerospace and Precision Products (A&PP) Division was turned around by utilizing a teamwork approach is discussed.
8. Cathey, Paul. "How Metals Industry Uses Management Tools," *Iron Age* (November 20, 1978), pp. 38–41.
   A matrix management system at Standard Steel of Burham and Latrobe, Pennsylvania is working well. Article points out some reasons for success and some difficulties encountered.
9. Cleland, David I. and King, William R. *Systems Analysis and Project Management,* Second Ed. (New York: McGraw-Hill, Inc., 1975), pp. 198–217.
   Examples are given of the application of project management and of the form in which it is often used in specific situations.
10. Cobbs, John L. (ed). "G.M.'s Test of Participation," *Business Week* (February 23, 1976), pp. 89–90.
    A "teamwork approach" at the Inland Division of General Motors Corporation has solved some problems and caused some others. This article focusses on how the process was implemented and some of the more important results.
11. Curling, David H. "The Canadian Government and Project Management," *1980 Proceed-*

ings of the Project Management Institute (Drexel Hill, PA: The Project Management Institute, 1980), pp. II-G.1-II-G.10.

Reviews outline how project management has become "institutionalized" in the Canadian government over the last two years. The project management team and its relationships with the public and private sectors is clearly described.

12. Davis, Stanley M. and Lawrence, Paul R. (eds). *Matrix* (Reading, Massachusetts: Addison-Wesley Publishing, Inc., 1977), pp. 11–23, 155–181.

General examples are outlined "beyond industry" in which the matrix may be found. Some areas dealt with include insurance, consulting, CPA firms and law firms.

13. DeLorenzo, Robert A. "The Evolving Role of Electric Utilities Relative to Major Project Management," *1977 Proceedings of the Project Management Institute* (Drexel Hill, PA: The Project Management Institute, 1977), pp. 311–319.

Problems arising from environmental forces interfacing with electric utilities and causing them to implement project management organizations while simultaneously experiencing an increase in involvement in project tasks and activities are discussed in depth.

14. Dixon, Maureen. "Matrix Organization in Health Services," in *Matrix Management—A Cross-Functional Approach to Organization,* Edited by Kenneth Knight (Great Britain: Gower Press, 1977), pp. 82–90.

The British National Health Service is used as an example of difficulties in implementing matrix, clarifying responsibility, and reasons for the matrix. This application is exemplified in terms of providing care: doctors, nurses, social workers, etc.

15. Duke, Robert K., Wohlsen, Frederick H., and Mitchell, Douglas R. "Project Management at Fluor Utah, Inc.," *1977 Proceedings of the Project Management Institute* (Drexel Hill, PA: The Project Management Institute, 1977), pp. 28–32.

Deals with task force/department "matrix-type" organization development at Fluor Corporation.

16. Easton, James. "Long-Term Effects of Program and Project Management on a Large Public Works Organization," *1978 Proceedings of Project Management Institute* (Drexel Hill, PA: The Project Management Institute, 1978), pp. IV-G.1-IV-G.19.

Explains the evolution of program and project management, the use of matrix management, and the results and evolutionary changes brought about by such management approaches on the Los Angeles County Flood Control District (a large public works organization).

17. Frankel, D. S. "The Advertising Agency Account Group: Its Operation and Effectiveness as a Matrix Group," in *Matrix Management—A Cross-Functional Approach to Organization,* Edited by Kenneth Knight (Great Britain: Gower Press, 1977), pp. 73–81.

Findings from an investigation of fifteen agencies into certain determinants of effectiveness in a matrix group within the advertising agency structure are thoroughly presented.

18. Gallagher, Susan C. "The Management of World-Wide Pharmaceutical Development Utilizing Geographically Spread Resources," *1975 Proceedings of Project Management Institute* (Drexel Hill, PA: The Project Management Institute, 1975), pp. 143–145.

Steps in project development and functional interdependencies in the "collateral" project management system at Searle Laboratories Division of G. D. Searle and Company are highlighted well.

19. George, William W. "Task Teams for Rapid Growth," *Harvard Business Review.* (March–April 1977), pp. 72–80.

Illustrates how informal task teams operated within a formal functional organization of the Litton Microwave Cooking Division to achieve and manage very rapid growth—thorough article on the topic.

20. Goggin, William C. "A Decade of Progress: Multidimensional Organization Structure," reprinted in *Matrix Organization and Project Managements,* Edited by Raymond E. Hill

and Bernard J. White (Ann Arbor, Michigan: The University of Michigan, 1979), pp. 179–188.

Good discussion of twelve major factors which facilitated effective implementation and resolved some characteristic problems of the matrix at Dow Corning.

21. ———. "How the Multidimensional Structure Works at Dow Corning," reprinted in *Matrix Organization and Project Management,* Edited by Raymond E. Hill and Bernard J. White (Ann Arbor, Michigan: The University of Michigan, 1979), pp. 152–171.

Factors leading to a need for a matrix system at Dow Corning and the workings of the system are fully explained.

22. Guarino, Gilbert B., Lilly, Relva L., and Lindenfelser, James J. "Faith Restored—The F-15 Program," reprinted in *Systems Management,* Edited by J. Stanley Baumgartner, (Washington, D.C.: Bureau of National Affairs, Inc., 1979), pp. 43–52.

Concepts used in the F-15 weapon system acquisition organization based on a matrix integrating project and functional organizational forms are highlighted.

23. Gunz, H. P. and Pearson, A.W. "Matrix Organization in Research and Development," in *Matrix Management—A Cross-Functional Approach to Organization,* Edited by Kenneth Knight (Great Britain: Gower Press, 1977), pp. 23–44.

Summarizes the findings of a study done on approximately forty R&D organizations in the United Kingdom to see how different types of structure, especially co-ordination and leadership matrices, assist people in managing activities.

24. Hey, Anthea M. "Local Authority Social Service Departments: Examples of Matrix Organization," in *Matrix Management—A Cross-Functional Approach to Organization,* Edited by Kenneth Knight (Great Britain: Gower Press, 1977), pp. 91–105.

Five types of matrix relationships are explored in a social service context—coordinating; functional monitoring and coordinating; attachment and outposting; attachment with co-management; secondment.

25. Kunde, James and Stickney, Frank. "An Application of Project Management Concepts to Municipal Organizations: Task Force Management," *1974 Proceedings of the Project Management Institute* (Washington, D.C.: The Project Management Institute, 1974), pp. 36–52.

Describes and highlights the task force approach taken by the city of Dayton in the areas of housing, crime, youth services, racism, Dayton's future, and employment.

26. McCowen, Peter. "Introduction and Operation of a Matrix Organization in Management Consultancy," in *Matrix Management—A Cross-Functional Approach to Organization,* Edited by Kenneth Knight (Great Britain: Gower Press, 1977), pp. 59–72.

Excellent article on the application of the matrix at Scientific Control Systems Ltd. of the United Kingdom. This management sciences and computer consultancy firm has operated with a matrix structure for the last seven years.

27. McCraw, Sammy T. "Problems and Prospects in Managing Communications for Research Projects," *1980 Proceedings of the Project Management Institute* (Drexel Hill, PA: The Project Management Institute, 1980), pp. V–D.1–V–D.8.

Specific applications of project management at the Battelle, Pacific Northwest Laboratories (division of Battelle Memorial Institute) in the area of communication are presented. The R&D project manager is a key information link.

28. Morris, Peter and Reis de Carvalho, Emerson. "Project Matrix Organizations—Or How To Do the Matrix Swing," *1978 Proceedings of the Project Management Institute* (Drexel Hill, PA: The Project Management Institute, 1978), pp. IV–D.1–IV–D.13.

Gives an account of the application of project management as the basis of implementing a huge construction project by Acominas Gerais (a Brazilian steel company). Some general management inferences on project matrix management are drawn.

29. Patrick, Miles G. "Implementing a Project Management System in a Research Laboratory," *1979 Proceedings of the Project Management Institute* (Drexel Hill, PA: The Project Management Institute, 1979), pp. 243–252.
Fully describes the implementation of a Research Project Management System (RPMS) at the Pacific Northwest Division of the Battelle Memorial Institute. (Overall structure resembles matrix form with interdisciplinary specialties interfacing across organizational lines.)

30. Paulson, Boyd C., Jr., Fukuda, Kunio, and Ohbayashi, Yoshihisa. "Project Management in Japan," *1979 Proceedings of the Project Management Institute,* (Drexel Hill, PA: The Project Management Institute 1979), pp. 253–262.
Project management in the construction industry in Japan is discussed and differences between Japanese and American project management practices are pointed out.

31. Peters, Frederick. "NASA Management of the Space Shuttle Program," *1975 Proceedings of the Project Management Institute* (Drexel Hill, PA: The Project Management Institute, 1975), pp. 151–159.
The program/project organization and techniques NASA is using to manage the Space Shuttle Program in response to an altered socioeconomic environment and stringent cost and schedule constraints is dealt with.

32. Rhodes, R. Richard (chairman). "Pharmaceutical Industry R&D Perspectives of Project Management: From the Client," *1980 Proceedings of the Project Management Institute* (Drexel Hill, PA: The Project Management Institute, 1980), pp. V–A.1–V–A.2.
The speeches of three individuals representing R&D management from three pharmaceutical companies, regarding their experience with R&D project management, are reviewed.

33. Robinson, Clarence A., Jr. (ed). "Matrix System Enhances Management," *Aviation Week and Space Technology* (January 31, 1977), pp. 41–58.
Explains how the Naval Air System Command organizes its tasks under matrix management structure to develop, procure, and support serial weapons systems for the fleet. An in-depth description of the reasons behind the success of matrixing in this specific case is covered.

34. Salapatas, J. N. (moderator). "PMI Seminar/Symposium—Utility Panel," *1977 Proceedings of the Project Management Institute* (Drexel Hill, PA: The Project Management Institute, 1977), pp. 323–325.
Panel members (from Commonwealth Edison Co., Tennessee Valley Authority, and Salt River Project) discuss problems and highlight major interest areas of utility managers and executives including matrix management.

35. Sappington, M. H. and Meyer, W. E. "A Program Manager Looks At Program Management," reprinted in *Systems Management,* Edited by J. Stanley Baumgartner (Washington, D.C.: Bureau of National Affairs, Inc., 1979), pp. 53–58.
AEGIS, a medium range, surface-to-air, all-weather system for first line Navy escorts is used as an example of the application of project management; major problems with the application are highlighted.

36. Shepherd, Alan J. "The Evolution of Project Management Concepts from Tools to Realities—Two Case Histories," *1975 Proceedings of the Project Management Institute* (Drexel Hill, PA: The Project Management Institute, 1975), pp. 72–85.
The use of task forces in two specific utilities, one successful (unnamed) is dealt with, with a clear distinction being recognized between the functional and project aspects of the organizations.

37. Shrontz, M. P., Porter, G. M., and Scott, N. L. "Organization and Management of a Multi-Organizational Single Responsibility Project—The James H. Campbell-Power Plant—Unit #3," *1977 Proceedings of the Project Management Institute* (Drexel Hill, PA: The project Management Institute, 1977), pp. 258–264.
Outlines some problems uncovered during the construction project of the James H. Campbell

Plant Unit #3, an 800 MW coal-fired power plant, (the primary objective of the project being better coordination of various functional areas) and offers respective solutions to such problems.

38. Stickney, Frank A. and Johnston, William R. "One More Time: Why Project Management?," *1979 Proceedings of the Project Management Institute* (Drexel Hill, PA: The Project Management Institute, 1979), pp. 305–319.

Fully analyzes the situational factors which strongly support the decision to adopt project management; strongly supports the idea that project management is not a panacea; and provides a model to follow in determining when, how, and why a company should adopt project management.

39. Stickney, Frank A., Johnston, William R., and Harzman, Kem O. "The Application of the Matrix Organization to the United States Air Force Weapon System Acquisition Process," *1979 Proceedings of the Project Management Institute* (Drexel Hill, PA: The Project Management Institute, 1979), pp. 469–478.

Thoroughly analyzes and discusses the application of the matrix organizational structure and concept to the systems acquisition process within the United States Air Force.

40. Walsh, Edward M. "Curriculum Management Using an Interdisciplinary Matrix Structure and a Modular/Credit System," *International Journal of Institutional Management in Higher Education* (May 1977), pp. 32–45.

The operation and results of an experiment on the matrix structure in Ireland (consisting of interdisciplines and departments responsible for academic policy and operation, respectively) are highlighted.

41. Welty, Gus. "The Task Force Approach: Change Comes Slowly—But It Comes," *Railway Age* (June 13, 1977), pp. 21, 24.

Interesting account of specific accomplishments of a joint management-labor-government program developed to deal with rail industry operating problems, forming independent project groups along the way and improving management-labor relations.

42. White, Stephen L. "The Community Mental Health Center as a Matrix Organization," *Administration in Mental Health* (Winter 1978), pp. 99–106.

Phases of the Westside Community Mental Health Center's experience with a matrix organizational design are described. Services were expanded, staff reduced, productivity increased, and morale improved in one year.

43. Wintermantel, Richard E. "Application of the Matrix Organization Mode in Industry," *1979 Proceedings of the Project Management Institute* (Drexel Hill, PA: The Project Management Institute, 1979), pp. 493–497.

Outlined are: the learning experiences of those implementing the matrix organizational structure at General Electric, and situational factors condusive to successful matrix applications.

44. Wolff, Michael F. (ed). "The Joy (and Woe) of Matrix," *Research Management* (March 1980), pp. 10–12.

Highlights 15 years experience of Bruce Merrifield at Hooker Chemical Company (currently at the Continental Group, Inc.). Nine of the "cons" of the matrix as he has experienced them are dealt with.

33. Factors Affecting Project Success*

Bruce N. Baker†
David C. Murphy
Dalmar Fisher

Why are some projects perceived as failures when they have met all the objective standards of success:

- —completed on time,
- —completed within budget,
- —all technical specifications met?

On the other hand, why are some projects perceived as successful when they have failed to meet two important objective standards associated with success:

- —not completed on time,
- —not completed within budget?

*The study reported in this paper was conducted under the sponsorship of the National Aeronautics and Space Administration, NGR 22-03-028. The complete report is entitled, *Determinants of Project Success,* by David C. Murphy, Bruce N. Baker, and Dalmar Fisher. It may be obtained from the National Technical Information Services, Springfield, VA, 22151, by referencing the title and the Accession number: N-74-30392, September 15, 1974.

†Dr. Bruce N. Baker is a Professor of Management at the University of Wisconsin-Oshkosh, and is also President of InterSystems Inc., a management consulting firm specializing in seminars, surveys and consulting work in the fields of planning, project management, alternative futures, and information systems. He received his A.B. Degree from Princeton University, his M.B.A. Degree from Stanford University, and his D.P.A. Degree from The George Washington University. He is currently a consultant to the Food and Agriculture Organization of the United Nations and the U.S. EPA.

David C. Murphy is Chairman of the Administrative Sciences Department and Associate Professor at the Boston College School of Management. His research and publications have been concerned with project and program management, strategy and policy formulation, environmental analysis, and organizational decentralization. He has served as editor of *Project Management Quarterly,* and is an active member of several professional societies including the Project Management Institute. He received the D.B.A. degree from Indiana University.

Dalmar Fisher is Associate Professor of Organizational Studies at the Boston College School of Management, where he teaches courses in organizational behavior and administrative strategy. He has authored several articles and books in the areas of organizational communication, project management and managerial behavior, and has served as associate editor of *Project Management Quarterly*. He received his D.B.A. Degree from Harvard Business School.

WHAT CONSTITUTES SUCCESS FOR A PROJECT?

If project success cannot be considered simply a matter of completing the project on schedule, staying within the budget constraints, and meeting the technical performance criteria, then how should project success be defined?

The research conducted by the authors on some 650 projects supports the following definition of success:

If the project meets the technical performance specifications and/or mission to be performed, and if there is a high level of satisfaction concerning the

Table 33-1. Project Management Characteristics Which Strongly Affect the Perceived Failure of Projects (The absence of these characteristics does not ensure perceived success).

- Insufficient use of status/progress reports.
- Use of superficial status/progress reports.
- Inadequate project manager administrative skills.
- Inadequate project manager human skills.
- Inadequate project manager technical skills.
- Insufficient project manager influence.
- Insufficient project manager authority.
- Insufficient client influence.
- Poor coordination with client.
- Lack of rapport with client.
- Client disinterest in budget criteria.
- Lack of project team participation in decision-making.
- Lack of project team participation in major problem solving.
- Excessive structuring within the project team.
- Job insecurity within the project team.
- Lack of team spirit and sense of mission within project team.
- Parent organization stable, non-dynamic, lacking strategic change.
- Poor coordination with parent organization.
- Lack of rapport with parent organization.
- Poor relations within the parent organization.
- New "type" of project.
- Project more complex than the parent has completed previously.
- Initial under-funding.
- Inability to freeze design early.
- Inability to close-out the effort.
- Unrealistic project schedules.
- Inadequate change procedures.
- Poor relations with public officials.
- Unfavorable public opinion.

The lists in Tables 33-1, 2, and 3 are based on statistic tests in which data about each project management characteristic were grouped according to whether the project's success was rated in the upper third (successful), middle third, or lower third (unsuccessful).

project outcome among: key people in the parent organization, key people in the client organization, key people on the project team, and key users or clientele of the project effort, the project is considered an overall success.

Perceptions play a strong role in this definition. Therefore, the definition is more appropriately termed, "perceived success of a project." What types of variables contribute to perceptions of success and failure? One would certainly assume that good schedule performance and good cost performance would be key ingredients of the perceptions of success and failure. But note that schedule and cost performance are not included in the above definition.

How do cost and schedule performance relate to the perceived failure and success of projects? It was found that cost and schedule overrun were not included in a list of twenty-nine project management characteristics significantly related to perceived project failure. See Table 33-1. Conversely, good cost and schedule performance were not included in a list of twenty-three project management characteristics significantly related to perceived success, Table 33-2. Nor were cost and schedule performance included in the list of ten project management characteristics found to be linearly related to both per-

Table 33-2. Project Management Characteristics Associated with Perceived Success. (The following were found to be necessary, but not sufficient conditions for perceived success.)

- Frequent feedback from the parent organization.
- Frequent feedback from the client.
- Judicious use of networking techniques.
- Availability of back-up strategies.
- Organization structure suited to the project team.
- Adequate control procedures, especially for dealing with changes.
- Project team participation in determining schedules and budgets.
- Flexible parent organization.
- Parent commitment to established schedules.
- Parent enthusiasm.
- Parent commitment to established budget.
- Parent commitment to technical performance goals.
- Parent desire to build-up internal capabilities.
- Project manager commitment to established schedules.
- Project manager commitment to established budget.
- Project manager commitment to technical performance goals.
- Client commitment to established schedules.
- Client commitment to established budget.
- Client commitment to technical performance goals.
- Enthusiastic public support.
- Lack of legal encumbrances.
- Lack of excessive government red tape.
- Minimized number of public/government agencies involved.

Table 33-3. Project Management Characteristics Linearly Related to Both Perceived Success and Perceived Failure. (The presence of these characteristics tends to improve perceived success while their absence contributes to perceived failure.)

- Goal commitment of project team.
- Accurate initial cost estimates.
- Adequate project team capability.
- Adequate funding to completion.
- Adequate planning and control techniques.
- Minimal start-up difficulties.
- Task (vs. social) orientation.
- Absence of bureaucracy.
- On-site project manager.
- Clearly established success criteria.

ceived success and perceived failure, Table 33-3. If the study had been conducted solely on aerospace projects, this might not have been too surprising, but aerospace projects represented less than 20% of the responses. For project managers and project personnel who have constantly lived with heavy emphasis upon meeting schedules and staying within budgets, this finding may be difficult to swallow. A partial explanation may be as follows: The survey was concerned only with *completed* projects. As perspective is developed on a project, the ultimate satisfaction of the parent, the client, the ultimate users, and the project team is most closely related to whether the project end-item is performing as desired. A schedule delay and a budget overrun may seem somewhat unimportant as time goes on, in the face of a high degree of satisfaction and a sound foundation for future relationships. Conversely, few can legitimately claim that "the operation was a success but the patient died." If the survey had been conducted on current, ongoing projects only, the management emphasis upon meeting schedules and staying within budgets would undoubtedly have been reflected more heavily in the research results. Moreover, good cost and schedule performance *were* correlated with success but to a lesser degree than the items listed in Table 33-2.

ANALYSIS OF VARIABLES ASSOCIATED WITH PERCEIVED SUCCESS AND VARIABLES ASSOCIATED WITH PERCEIVED FAILURE

The listings variables associated with perceived success and failure. Tables 33-1, 33-2, & 33-3, are much lengthier than anticipated. For a project to be perceived as successful, many, if not most, of the variables associated with success must be present. The absence of even one factor or inattention to one factor can be sufficient to result in perceived project failure. Similarly, most, if not all, of the variables associated with perceived failure must be absent. To add to the fragility of perceived success, the variables must be present or absent in the right degree. For example, project management is closely associated with the use of PERT and CPM networking systems.* So much so, that many managers consider project management and networking systems as synonymous terms.

Is the use of PERT-CPM systems the most important factor contributing to project success?

No. PERT-CPM systems *do* contribute to project success, especially when initial over-optimism and/or a "buy-in" strategy has prevailed in the securing of the contract, but the importance of PERT-CPM is far outweighed by a host of other factors including the use of project tools known as "systems management concepts." These include work breakdown structures, life cycle planning, systems engineering, configuration management, and status reports. The overuse of PERT-CPM systems was found to hamper success. It was the *judicious* use of PERT-CPM which was associated with success. An important military satellite program was actually hampered by early reliance upon a network that covered four walls of a large conference room. The tool was too cumbersome and consumed too much time to maintain it. Fortunately, someone decided that the network was a classified document and ordered curtains to be placed over the walls. Once the curtains were up, they were never drawn again and the project proceeded as planned. More often than not, however, networking *does* contribute to better cost and schedule performance (but not necessarily to better technical performance).

GENERAL STRATEGIES FOR DIRECTING PROJECTS

Based upon the factors associated with success and the factors associated with failure, a set of general strategies can be developed for directing projects. Some of the strategies tend to be counter-intuitive or counter to traditional practice. The somewhat controversial general strategies are presented in the form of statements which the reader is asked to indicate as true or false.

A matrix form of project organizational structure is the least disruptive to traditional functional organizational patterns and is also most likely to result in project success. True or false?

False. Although there are no clear definitions of the different forms of project organizational structures which have attained widespread acceptance, there are some terms which imply certain patterns. The matrix form of organization is well understood by experienced project management personnel but the authority which goes with such a matrix form of structure varies considerably. In order to provide a spectrum of choices which attempted to avoid preconception of terms, the following organizational patterns were presented

---

*See Chapter 16.

for describing the organizational structure of the project team as it existed during the peak activity period of the project:

- Pure Functional—Project Manager, if any, was merely the focal point for communications; he had no authority to direct people other than by persuasion or reporting to his own superior.
- Weak Matrix—Project Manager was the focal point for controls; he did not actively direct the work of others.
- Strong Matrix or Partially Projectized—Project Manager was the focal point for directions and controls; he may have had some engineering and control personnel reporting to him on a line basis, while remainder of the Project Team was located administratively in other departments.
- Projectized—Project Manager had most of the essential elements of the Project Team under him.
- Fully Projectized—Project Manager had almost all of the employees who were on the Project Team under him.

Each of these organizational arrangements was associated with perceived success in certain situations, but an F-test of these different forms of organizational structure compared with perceived project success revealed that the projectized form of organizational structure is most often associated with perceived success. In general, it is important for the project manager of a large, long duration project to have key functions of the project team under him.

In the early days of the Ranger and Surveyor lunar research programs, the project managers had only a handful of people reporting to them on a line basis. Both of these programs were relatively unsuccessful as compared to the Lunar Orbiter Program, which employed a projectized organization from the start.[1]

The question remains, however, how should the decision making authority of the project manager relate to the decision making authority of the client organization (the organization which sponsored, approved, and funded the effort), and the parent organization (the organization structure above the level of the project manager but within the same overall organization)?

When a project is critical to the overall success of a company and/or it is critical to the client organization, the parent organization and/or the client organization should take a strong and active role in internal project decision making. True or false?

---

[1]Many comparisons between the Surveyor Program and the Lunar Orbiter Program support the findings of this paper. See: Erasmus H. Kloman, *Unmanned Space Project Management—Surveyor and Lunar Orbiter,* a report prepared by the National Academy of Public Administration and sponsored by the National Aeronautics and Space Administration, Washington, D.C.: U.S. Government Printing Office, (1972).

False. It is important for the client organization to establish definitive goals for a project. Similarly, especially for in-house projects, the parent organization must also establish clear and definitive goals for the project. When there is a good consensus among the client organization, the parent organization, and the project team with respect to the goals of a project, then success is more readily achieved. A path analysis revealed that success criteria salience and consensus are especially important for:

- Projects with complex legal/political environments.
- Projects which are relatively large.
- Projects undertaken within a parent organization undergoing considerable change.

Once success criteria have been clarified and agreed upon by the principal parties involved with a project, i.e., the client, the parent, and the project team, then it is essential to permit the project team to "carry the ball" with respect to internal decisions.

Because some decisions require the approval of the client organization, it was found that the authority of the client contact should be commensurate with the authority of the project manager. Projects characterized by strong project manager authority and influence and strong client contact authority and influence were strongly associated with success. Unfortunately, many client organizations and parent organizations tend to believe that the more closely they monitor a project and the more intimately they enter into the internal project decision process, the more likely the project is to be successful. Close coordination and good relations patterns were found to be the most important factors contributing to perceived project success. Nonetheless, there is a very important distinction between "close" and "meddling" and there is just as important a distinction between "supportive" and "interfering" relationships. Many factors and relationships pointed to the need for the client and the parent organization to develop close and supportive working relationships with the project team but to avoid meddling or interfering with the project team's decision making processes. The lesson is clear: The project manager should be delegated sufficient authority to make important project decisions and sufficient authority to direct the project team. In the case of the Polaris Program, for example, the head of the Special Projects Office of the U.S. Navy had extensive authority with respect to contracting arrangements. This level of authority combined with strong levels of authority for the project managers in the contractors' plants, was a major factor contributing to the success of that program. Once given this authority, how should the project manager arrive at decisions and solve problems?

Because participative decision making and problem solving can tend to slow up the decision making and problem solving processes, these approaches should not be employed on complex projects having tight schedules. True or false?

False. First of all, participative decision making and problem solving within the project team was highly correlated with success for the total sample of projects. Second, a path analysis* revealed that under some conditions of adversity, such as a highly complex project, or one where initial over-optimism prevailed regarding the time and cost for completing the project, it was especially important to employ participative approaches to overcome these adversities.

If this pattern is successful, should the public also participate in project decisions affecting the public interest?

Public participation is an essential ingredient of success for projects affecting the public interest. True or false?

Mostly false. Although the trend of the past two decades has certainly been in this direction, i.e., to encourage, or at least to facilitate, public participation in the decision making process for public projects, and although value judgements may lean heavily toward this approach, the facts are that public participation often delays and hampers projects and reduces the probability of success.

Therefore, from a management standpoint (not from a value judgement standpoint), public participation should be minimized, avoided, or circumvented as much as possible. Public participation is, of course, a legal requirement for most public projects but there seems to be little reason for overdoing it.

If too much public participation hampers success, can the cooperation and participation of several agencies help to safeguard the public interest and result in a more successful overall effort than a project undertaken by a single agency?

Public projects involving the cooperation, funding, and participation of several governmental agencies are more likely to be successful than projects undertaken by a single agency. True or false?

False. Again, the trend is certainly in this direction. There has been a great deal of emphasis upon:

- Inter-agency cooperative efforts, e.g., Departments of Labor, Commerce, and Transportation.
- Inter-governmental cooperative efforts, e.g., Federal, state, and local jointly funded efforts.
- The creation of new, integrative agencies, e.g., regional commissions combining the efforts of several states, counties, or cities to attack common problems.

Although the creation of these jointly-funded, jointly-managed organizational mechanisms may be desirable from the standpoint of integration of

---

*A statistical procedure. Path analysis is explained on P. 694.

efforts, they tend to result in less successful projects as compared to projects undertaken by a single source of funding and authority. Such cooperative efforts often result in the creation of elaborate bureaucratic structures, decision delays, red tape, and relatively diminished success. The New England Regional Commission is an example of an agency which consumed millions of dollars for its own bureaucracy but failed to accomplish much of anything for New England.

Many discussions of project management focus upon qualities of an ideal project manager.

It is much more important for a project manager to be an effective administrator than to be a competent technical person or to possess good human relations skills. True or false?

Mostly false. All three types of skills (technical skills, human skills, and administrative skills) were found to be important but technical skills were found to be most important, followed by human skills, and then by administrative skills.

It is true that technically-oriented scientists and engineers who are placed into project manager positions often perform poorly from an administrative and human relations standpoint but, on the other hand, some of the most costly blunders have been made by administrators of proven competence who ventured into unfamiliar areas. During the past decade, much progress has been made in training technical people to acquire effective human relations and administrative skills.

Leadership style has been the subject of a great deal of research.

The most effective project managers are non-directive, human relations-oriented leaders as opposed to directive, managing, task-oriented leaders. True or false?

Mostly false. Fiedler has conducted extensive research on this subject, finding that, "In very favorable or in very unfavorable situations for getting a task accomplished by group effort, the autocratic, task-controlling, managing leadership works best. In situations intermediate in difficulty, the nondirective, permissive leader is most successful."[2]

The research described in this paper supports the concept of a leader who is task-oriented with a back-up social-orientation for *most* project efforts. Does this contradict Fiedler's research and the previous statement that project team participation in decision-making and problem solving is important to project success? The authors believe that there is no contradiction. An effective project manager is generally one who is committed to the goals of the project and constantly stresses the importance of meeting those project goals. Yet, he calls

---

[2]Fred E. Fiedler, "Engineer the Job to Fit the Manager," *Harvard Business Review* (September–October 1965), p. 18.

upon key project team members to assist with problem solving and decision making. In *some* very straightforward or very chaotic settings, a project manager 'may find an autocratic style to be most effective. And, as Fiedler's research suggests, a project manager may need to employ different leadership styles at different times during the project effort.

A more complete list of general strategies is shown on Table 33-4. Strategy guidelines are presented for the client organization, the parent organization, and the project team for three distinct phases of a project. It is important to note 1) the interlocking and interdependent relationships among the three organizational groups involved, and 2) that two of the three phases leading to overall perceived success occur before contract award or go ahead. Although different combinations are needed for success in various situations and environments, these general strategies seem to apply to most situations.

KEY FACTORS TO MAXIMIZE POTENTIAL OF PERCEIVED PROJECT SUCCESS

Up to this point, the ingredients to assure success and to avoid failure have been somewhat overwhelming. This portion of the article will attempt to focus in on the key factors which appear to be most important for achieving high levels of perceived success.

In re-examining Table 33-1, one can see that a large number of the variables associated with perceived failure center about poor coordination and human relations patterns. Therefore, in order to minimize the chances of perceived failure, project managers are well advised to put heavy emphasis on establishing good, effective patterns of coordination and human relations. Such emphasis may eliminate failure but may not necessarily promote success. Table 33-2 sheds light on the need for good tight controls and commitment to the goals that have been established for a project in order to achieve high levels of perceived success.

Tables 33-1, 33-2, 33-3 and 33-4 also point to another important strategy: Effective project planning is absolutely essential to project success. Of the twenty-nine items listed in Table 33-1, over half the variables associated with perceived failure can be avoided through effective project planning. The role of project planning is even more apparent in Table 33-2. Almost every one of the variables associated with success is determined by, or can be significantly influenced by, effective project planning. Finally, every one of the items listed in Table 33-3 is intimately related to the project planning process. As stated previously, two of the three phases of strategies shown in Table 33-4 occur before actual work on the project end-item begins. Therefore, effective project planning is very important to project success.

In addition to the analyses summarized to this point, stepwise multiple

Table 33-4. General Strategies for Directing Projects.

	CONCEPTUAL PHASE (BEFORE THE INVITATIONS FOR BID)	BID, PROPOSAL, CONTRACT DEFINITION, AND NEGOTIATION PHASE (BEFORE CONTRACT AWARD OR GO-AHEAD)	IMPLEMENTATION PHASE (AFTER CONTRACT AWARD OR GO-AHEAD)
The Client Organization and/or Principal Client Contact	Encourage openness & honesty from the start from all participants.		Develop close, but not meddling, work relationships with project participants.
	Create an atmosphere that encourages healthy, but not cutthroat, competition or "liars' contests." Plan for adequate funding to complete the entire project.	Reject "buy-ins."	Avoid arms-length relationships.
	Develop clear understandings of the relative importance of cost, schedule, and technical performance goals.	Make prompt decisions regarding contract award or go-ahead.	Do not insist upon excessive reporting schemes.
	Seek to minimize public participation and involvement. Develop short and informal lines of communication and flat organizational structures.		
	Delegate sufficient authority to the principal client contact and let him promptly approve or reject important project decisions.		

Table 33-4. General Strategies for Directing Projects. (continued)

	CONCEPTUAL PHASE (BEFORE THE INVITATIONS FOR BID)	BID, PROPOSAL, CONTRACT DEFINITION, AND NEGOTIATION PHASE (BEFORE CONTRACT AWARD OR GO-AHEAD)	IMPLEMENTATION PHASE (AFTER CONTRACT AWARD OR GO-AHEAD)
The Parent Organization and/or Principal Parent Contact	Select, at an early point, a project manager with a proven track record of technical skills, human skills, & administrative skills (in that order) to lead the project team.	Do not exert excessive pressure on the project manager to win the contract.	
	Develop clear and workable guidelines for your project manager.	Do not slash or balloon the project team's cost estimates.	
	Delegate sufficient authority to your project manager and let him make important decisions in conjunction with his key project team members.	Avoid "buy-ins."	
	Demonstrate enthusiasm for and commitment to the project and the project team.	Develop close, but not meddling, working relationships with the principal client contact and the project manager	
	Develop and maintain short and informal lines of communication with the project manager.		

The Project Manager and/or the Project Team

Insist upon the right to select your own key project team members.

Select key project team members with proven track records in their area of expertise.

Develop commitment and a sense of mission from the outset among project team members.

Seek sufficient authority and a projectized form of organizational structure.

Coordinate frequently and constantly reinforce good relationships with the client, the parent, and your team.

Seek to enhance the public' image of the project.

Fall upon key project team members to assist in decision-making and proble solving.

Develop realistic cost, schedule, and technical performance estimates & goals.

→ Employ a workable and candid set of project planning and control tools.

Develop back-up strategies and systems in anticipation of potential problems.

Develop an appropriate, yet flexible and flat, project team organization structure.

Seek to maintain your influence over people and key decisions even though your formal authority may not be sufficient.

→ Avoid preoccupation with, or over-reliance upon, one type of project control tool.

Constantly stress the importance of meeting cost, schedule and technical performance goals.

Generally, give highest priority to achieving the technical performance mission or function to be performed by the project end-item.

→ Keep changes under control.

Seek to find ways of assuring the job security of effective project team members.

Plan for an orderly phase-out of the project

Table 33-5. The Relative Importance of the Factors Contributing to
Perceived Project Success.

DETERMINING FACTORS	STANDARDIZED REGRESSION COEFFICIENT	SIGNIFICANCE	CUMULATIVE R^2
Coordination and Relations	+.347	$p<.001$	.773
Adequacy of Project Structure and Control	+.187	$p<.001$	.830
Project Uniqueness, Importance, and Public Exposure	+.145	$p<.001$	.877
Success Criteria Salience and Consensus	+.254	$p<.001$	.886
Competitive and Budgetary Pressure	−.153	$p<.001$	.897
Initial Over-Optimism, Conceptual Difficulty	−.215	$p<.001$	.905
Internal Capabilities Buildup	+.084	$p<.001$	.911

regression analysis was conducted to determine the independent contribution of some thirty-two factors to Perceived Success. It should be re-emphasized that technical performance was integrally associated with success and was part of Perceived Success itself. Beyond technical performance, however, what are the principal factors contributing to project success?

Table 33-5 shows that the strongest seven of the determining factors explained 91% of the variance in Perceived Success. The makeup of these seven factors is shown in Table 33-6. Note the extremely important impact of coordination and relations patterns (77% of the variance). Success Criteria Salience and Consensus and avoidance of Initial Over-Optimism, Conceptual

Table 33-6. Items Included in the Seven Factors of Table 33-5.

Coordination & Relations Factor.
   Unity between project manager and contributing department managers.
   Project team spirit.
   Project team sense of mission.
   Project team goal commitment.
   Project team capability.
   Unity between project manager and public officials.
   Unity between project manager and client contact.
   Unity between project manager and his superior.
   Project manager's human skills.
   Realistic progress reports.
   Project manager's administrative skills.

Table 33–6. (continued)

Supportive informal relations of team members.
Authority of project manager.
Adequacy of change procedures.
Job security of project team.
Project team participation in decision making.
Project team participation in major problem solving.
Parent enthusiasm.
Availability of back-up strategies.
Adequacy of Project Structure and Control Factor.
    Project manager's satisfaction with planning and control.
    Team's satisfaction with organization structure.
Project Uniqueness, Importance and Public Exposure Factor.
    Extent of public enthusiasm.
    Project larger in scale than most.
    Initial importance of state-of-art advancement.
    Project was different than most.
    Parent experience with similar project scope.
    Favorability of media coverage.
Success Criteria Salience and Consensus Factor.
    Importance to project manager—budget.
    Importance to project manager—schedule.
    Importance to parent—budget.
    Importance to parent—schedule.
    Importance to client—budget.
    Importance to client—schedule.
    Importance to client—technical performance.
    Importance to parent—technical performance.
    Importance to project manager—technical performance.
Competitive and Budgetary Pressure Factor (Negative Impact).
    Fixed price (as opposed to cost reimbursement) type of contract.
    Highly competitive environment.
    Parent heavy emphasis upon staying within the budget.
    Project manager heavy emphasis upon staying within the budget.
    Client heavy emphasis upon staying within the budget.
Initial Over-Optimism, Conceptual Difficulty Factor (Negative Impact).
    Difficulty in meeting project schedules.
    Difficulty of staying within original budget.
    Original cost estimates too optimistic.
    Difficulty in meeting technical requirements.
    Project was more complex than initially conceived.
    Schedule overrun.
    Difficulty in freezing design.
    Unrealistic schedules.
    Project was different than most.
Internal Capabilities Build-up Factor.
    Extent to which project built up parent capabilities.
    Original total budget.
    Total cost of project.

Difficulty were the next two heaviest weighted factors in the regression equation. Note also that although the factor, Adequacy of Project Structure and Control, is included in the seven principal factors contributing to Perceived Success, no particular tool, as such, is included in the factor. In other words, PERT and CPM are *not* the be-all and end-all of project management.*

Occasionally, project management personnel adopt a defeatist attitude about a project. One hears such comments as, "The project was doomed to failure from the start," or "There was no way we could make them happy on that project." Table 33-5 does not lend credence to such an attitude. An analysis of Table 33-5 reveals that a very high proportion of the key factors associated with success are within the control of the project manager and the project team. The project manager *can* help to achieve effective coordination and relations; the project manager *can* make certain that there are adequate project structure and control systems; the project manager *can* help to achieve success criteria salience and consensus; the project manager *can* help to avoid initial overoptimism and conceptual difficulty; and, the project manager *can* have some impact upon internal capabilities buildup, the atmosphere of competitive and budgetary pressure, and the project uniqueness, importance, and public exposure.

Therefore, the project manager *can* control the destiny of the project and the perceptions others will have of him/her. Even under extremely adverse circumstances, a project manager can be perceived as doing the best job possible under the circumstances.

CONCLUSIONS

The following conclusions seem to be warranted from the research:

1. Project success cannot be adequately defined as:
   - Completing the project on schedule.
   - Staying within the budget.
   - Meeting the technical performance specifications and/or mission to be performed.
2. Perceived success of a project can best be defined as:
   - Meeting the project technical specifications and/or project mission to be performed.
   - Attaining high levels of satisfaction from:
     - The parent.
     - The client.
     - The users or clientele.
     - The project team itself.

---

*See Chapter 16.

3. Technical performance is integrally associated with perceived success of a project, whereas cost and schedule performance are somewhat less intimately associated with perceived success.

4. In the long run, what really matters is whether the parties associated with, and affected by, a project are satisfied. Good schedule and cost performance mean very little in the face of a poor performing end product.

5. Next to technical performance and satisfaction of those associated with, and affected by, a project, effective coordination and relation patterns are the most important contributors to perceived project success.

6. Project managers can attain high levels of perceived project success even under adverse circumstances.

34. Project Management in the Public Sector: Success and Failure Patterns Compared to Private Sector Projects*

Bruce N. Baker†
Dalmar Fisher
David C. Murphy

INTRODUCTION

How do public sector projects differ from private sector projects? Most people have definite preconceptions about the two. Some of these preconceptions may be summarized by the types of contrasting characteristics listed in Table 34-1. A number of studies have been made of public sector projects which tend to support some of these types of preconceptions. For example, a number of studies regarding cost growth and cost overrun of federal government projects have been conducted during the past two decades.

*The study reported in this article was conducted under the sponsorship of the National Aeronautics and Space Administration, NGR 22-03-028. The complete report is entitled, *Determinants of Project Success,* by David C. Murphy, Bruce N. Baker, and Dalmar Fisher. It may be obtained from the National Technical Information Services, Springfield, VA, 22151, by referencing the title and the Accession number: N-74-30392, September 15, 1974.
†Dr. Baker is a Professor of Management at the University of Wisconsin, Oshkosh, and is also President of InterSystems Inc., a management consulting firm specializing in seminars, surveys, and consulting work in the fields of planning, project management, alternative futures, and information systems. He received his B.A. degree from Princeton University, his M.B.A. degree from Stanford University, and his D.P.A. degree from The George Washington University. He is currently a consultant to the Food and Agriculture Organization of the United Nations and the U.S. EPA.
Dalmar Fisher is Associate Professor of Organizational Studies at the Boston College School of Management, where he teaches courses in organizational behavior and administrative strategy. He has authored several articles and books in the areas of organizational communication, project management and managerial behavior, and has served as associate editor of *Project Management Quarterly*. He received his D.B.A. degree from Harvard Business School.
David C. Murphy is Chairman of the Administrative Sciences Department and Associate Professor at the Boston College School of Management. His research and publications have been concerned with project and program management, strategy and policy formulation, environmental analysis, and organizational decentralization. He has served as editor of *Project Management Quarterly,* and is an active member of several professional societies including the Project Management Institute. He received the D.B.A. degree from Indiana Unviversity.

Table 34-1. Some Preconceptions Regarding Private Sector Projects vs. Public Sector Projects.

Private	Public
Efficient	Inefficient
Effective	Ineffective
On schedule	Behind Schedule
Within budget	Overrun of budget
Well planned	Poorly planned
Competitive	Non-Competitive
Capable managers	Incapable managers
Competent workers	Incompetent workers
Free of Politics	Encumbered by politics
The end-product "works"	The end-product doesn't "work"
Minimum paperwork	Excessive paperwork
Definitive goals	Nebulous goals
Feelings of satisfaction	Feelings of dissatisfaction
People seem to care	People don't seem to care
Good team spirit	Lack of team spirit
Incompetent people are fired	Incompetent people can't be fired
Good performance is rewarded	Good performance is not rewarded

The most sophisticated studies of actual cost performance on Department of Defense programs as compared to original cost estimates were the Merton J. Peck and Frederic M. Scherer studies[1] and several Rand Corporation studies.

Peck and Scherer analyzed twelve typical weapon systems programs of the 1950s. All twelve systems employed cost-plus-fixed fee contracts. The average cost growth was found to be 220% beyond original target cost.[2]

Almost identical results came from a later study of 22 Air Force weapon systems programs involving 68 estimates. The study, entitled *Strategy for R&D: Studies in the Microeconomics of Development* by Thomas Marschak, Thomas K. Glennan, Jr., and Robert Summers of Rand Corporation, showed an average cost growth of 226% beyond original estimated cost.[3] These programs involved mainly the cost-plus-fixed-fee contracts of the late 1950s.

In the 1960s, incentive contracts, rather than cost-plus-fixed-fee contracts, were used for most engineering development efforts in the Department of Defense. One might therefore expect actual program costs to be closer to original cost estimates. Two such studies of the 1960's were undertaken by Rand personnel.

---

[1]Merton J. Peck and Frederic M. Scherer, *The Weapons Acquisition Process—An Economic Analysis* (Boston: Graduate School of Business, Harvard University, 1962).
[2]Ibid. p. 429.
[3](New York: Springer-Verlag New York Inc., 1967), p. 152.

Robert Perry *et al* reported in a study of 21 Army, Navy and Air Force system acquisition programs that " . . . [F]n average, cost estimates for the 1960s were about 25% less optimistic than those for programs for the 1950s. Thus, if reduction in bias (or reduced optimism) is a realistic index of 'better,' there is evidence of improvement in the acquisition process."[4] Even such a statement as this must be hedged considerably as Perry *et al* were careful to do: "Still, the model has little explanatory power (in a statistical sense), and it does not indicate *why* improvements have occurred.[5]

In contrast, a later Rand follow-up study discounted any improvement in the 1960s over the 1950s noting that, " . . . [F]or programs comparable in length and difficulty, 1960s procurements would have resulted in actual costs exceeding estimates by roughly the same proportion as had 1950s procurements."[6]

All objective studies, including more recent ones, have shown that federal government projects, entailing other than firm-fixed price contracts, have overrun the original budget by a considerable percentage, on average. Even firm-fixed price contracts often entail significant overruns or government "bailouts."

Personal experience often reinforces the preconceptions of public sector efforts through one's dealings with the U.S. Postal Service, governmental social service agencies, regulatory agencies, etc. And the situation may be getting worse. Sayles and Chandler, after a thorough study of NASA, conclude that NASA's ambitious, complex projects may represent the good old days compared with the public programs of the future.[7] They note that life was simple in NASA's "closed loop", mission-focused projects, while in today's public programs, operations are increasingly mixed with regulatory functions and missions are interrelated. Goals relating to oceans, pollution, health and urban development interact with one another. The public demands more of a voice. Housing and Urban Development, for example, does not "control" housing as much as it tries to cope with the special interests it encounters wherever it turns. Projects in such areas as housing and environmental protection encounter obstacles and setbacks NASA never dreamed of.

Nor does the U.S. have a monopoly on public sector project difficulties. Martin notes in a recent article that Canada has experienced a plague of failures of large scale public sector projects to reach their targets.[8] He cites the Pan-

---

[4]*System Acquisition Experience,* Memorandum RM-6072-OR prepared for United States Air Force Project Rand (Santa Monica: The Rand Corporation, November, 1969), p. 6.
[5]Ibid.
[6]Alvin J. Harman, *A Methodology for Cost Factor Comparison and Prediction,* Memorandum RM-6269-ARPA prepared for Advanced Resarch Projects Agency (Santa Monica: The Rand Corporation, August, 1970), p. 6.
[7]Leonard R. Sayles and Margaret K. Chandler, *Managing Large Systems* (New York: Harper and Row, 1971), pp. 319–320.
[8]A. P. Martin, "Project Management Requires Transorganizational Standards", *Project Management Quarterly,* Vol. X, No. 3, 1979, pp. 41–44.

artics, James Bay, the Gentilly nuclear reactors, the NORAD defense network renewal, and the Montreal Olympics.

Very few studies have been conducted of private sector projects. For example, cost overrun data is generally not available or at least not publicized by independent sources. Yet, the cost overrun records and fiascos of some major private sector projects are comparable to many public sector projects. See Table 34-2.

Although good data may not be available for a comprehensive comparison of actual cost overrun and actual schedule overrun for private sector projects vs. public sector projects, the authors conducted a study which compares these dimensions as well as overall perceived project success for the two sectors. The study was designed to detail the relationships among situational, structural, and process variables as they related to project effectiveness.

The study is believed to be the largest and most comprehensive investigation to date on the subject of project management effectiveness. A sample of 646 responses to a 17-page questionnaire represented a variety of industries (34% manufacturing, 22% construction, 17% government, and 27% services, transportation and others). Most of the respondents themselves had been directly involved in the particular project they chose to describe in their questionnaire. Of the total sample, 50% had been the project manager, 31% had been in other positions on the project team, and another 10% had been the project manager's direct superior. About one-third of the projects were described as being public in nature, the remaining two-thirds being in the private sector. The types of contracts or agreements involved included cost plus fixed fee (32%), in-house work orders (28%), fixed price (21%), and fixed price with incentives (14%). The major activity or end product involved in the projects included construc-

Table 34-2. Some Notable Failures Among Private Sector Projects.

Ford	The Edsel
Proctor and Gamble	Rely Brand Tampons
General Dynamics	Convair 880 and 990
Lockheed	L-1011 Airbus
Four Seasons	Chain of Nursing Homes
John Hancock Mutual	Windows in Boston Office Building
Polaroid Corporation	Polavision
Firestone	Radial Tires
Dupont	Korfam
Gillette	Digital Wristwatches
Dansk Designs, Ltd.	Gourmet Product Line
BIC Pen Corporation	Fannyhose
General Foods	Burger Chef Restaurants
A & P	WEO Price Reduction Program
National Semiconductor	Consumer Products

Table 34-3. Determinants of Cost and Schedule Overruns.

- Cost underestimates.
- Use of "Buy-in" strategies.
- Lack of alternative backup strategies.
- Lack of project-team goal commitment.
- Functional, rather than projectized, project organization.
- Lack of project team participation in setting schedules.
- Lack of team spirit, sense of mission.
- Inadequate control procedures.
- Insufficient use of networking techniques.
- Insufficient use of progress/status reports.
- Over-optimistic status reports.
- Decision delays.
- Inadequate change procedures.
- Insufficient project manager authority and influence.
- Lack of commitment to budget and schedule.
- Overall lack of similar experience.

tion (43%), hardware or equipment (22%), new processes or software (14%), and studies, services and tests (11%).

DETERMINANTS OF COST AND SCHEDULE OVERRUN

The study revealed the principal determinants of cost and schedule overrun for both public and private sector projects. Cost overruns were found to be highly correlated with the size of the project and the difficulty of meeting technical specifications. However, schedule difficulties and resulting schedule overruns were the primary causal factors leading to cost overruns. Schedule overruns were, in turn, caused by the variables listed on Table 34-3.

In order to prevent schedule and cost overruns, or to minimize the amount of schedule and cost overrun when initial over-optimism or a "buy-in"[9] has occurred, the research points to the need for employing networking techniques, systems management approaches, participative approaches to decision making within the project team, and a task-oriented style of leadership, with a back-up relationship-oriented style.

COMPARISONS BETWEEN PRIVATE SECTOR AND PUBLIC SECTOR PROJECTS

The comparisons between the private sector projects (2/3 of the sample) and public sector projects (1/3 of the sample) were extremely intriguing. Although

---

[9] A "buy-in" is an intentional underestimation of costs in order to obtain a contract or to obtain approval to proceed on an effort with the hope that follow-on contracts, changes, or additional funding will compensate for the original low estimate.

Table 34-4. Variables Significantly Associated with Public Sector Projects.[10]

Delays caused by governmental red tape	(P < .001)
Government overcontrol	(P < .001)
Difficulty in obtaining funding to complete the project	(P < .001)
Length of project	(P < .001)
Scheduled length of project	(P < .001)
Multi-funding	(P < .001)
Percent of R&D budget to the total parent budget	(P < .001)
*Number of times the project manager was replaced	(P < .001)
The extent of use of work breakdown structures	(P < .001)
The extent of use of systems management concepts	(P < .001)
The extent of use of operations research techniques	(P < .001)
*The project manager's authority over merit raises	(P < .001)
*The client contact's influence in relaxing specifications	(P < .001)
*The client contact's authority in relaxing specifications	(P < .002)
The job insecurity of project team members	(P < .002)
The number of governmental agencies involved with the project	(P < .002)
*The legal restrictions encumbering the project	(P < .002)
The need for new forms of government-industry cooperation	(P < .002)
Overinvolvement of the public with the project	(P < .003)
Total project team personnel	(P < .004)
The value of systems management concepts	(P < .004)
*The project manager's authority to select project team personnel	(P < .005)
The amount of politics involved in the contract award	(P < .006)
*The importance to the client of staying within the budget	(P < .006)
The importance to the project manager of obtaining follow-on work	(P < .007)
The difficulty of obtaining funding from the client	(P < .008)
The excessive volume of paperwork	(P < .009)
*The availability of back-up strategies	(P < .010)
The travel time between the project manager and the client	(P < .011)
The importance of state-of-the-art advancement	(P < .012)
The difficulty of keeping competent project team members	(P < .015)
*The degree to which competition was considered cutthroat	(P < .018)
The value of operations research techniques	(P < .020)
The extent to which problems arose because the project was different	(P < .024)
The ratio of the number of parent managers to total employees	(P < .024)
The number of staff-type project team members	(P < .027)
*The influence of the project manager over the selection of project team personnel	(P < .029)
*The client satisfaction with the outcome of the project	(P < .037)
The extent to which bar charts or milestone charts were used	(P < .041)
*The extent to which the project team participated in major problem solving	(P < .043)

*Indicates probable counter-intuitive relationships.

---

[10]This list is based on statistical tests in which data about each project were grouped according to whether the project was a private or a public sector project.

many of the characteristics may seem intuitively obvious and may coincide with our preconceptions, some of the findings appear to be counterintuitive. Moreover, some of the characteristics commonly attributed to public sector projects do not appear on the listings of items that statistically differentiate public from private sector projects. The variables which were found to be highly related to public sector projects are shown in Table 34-4.

Of course, the bulk of the items coincide with our preconceptions and experiences. Such items as red tape, overcontrol, overinvolvement of the public, politics, paperwork, the ratio of parent managers to total employees, the number of staff-type project team members, etc. coincide well with our beliefs and experiences.

As indicated by the asterisks, however, there are at least twelve variables on the list which may not coincide with our pre-conceptions or our intuition. We may tend to believe that the private sector has greater latitude in replacing project managers but the survey clearly shows that project managers on public sector projects are replaced much more often than their private sector counterparts. We may tend to believe that project managers of private sector projects have much greater authority and influence in selecting project team personnel and in determining their raises, but the study shows just the opposite. We may tend to believe that client contacts for private sector projects have greater influence and authority in relaxing specifications, and greater satisfaction with the outcome of the project, but the study shows just the opposite. We may tend to believe that the legal restrictions resulting from OSHA, EPA regulations, etc. result in greater legal encumbrances over private sector projects as compared to public sector projects, but the study shows just the opposite. We may tend to believe that greater emphasis is placed on the availability of back-up strategies for private sector projects, but the study shows just the opposite. And we may tend to believe that cutthroat competition is more prevalent among private sector projects but, again, the study shows just the opposite.

Table 34-5 indicates the variables which are significantly uncharacteristic of public sector projects. As might be expected, unity between the project manager and public officials involved with the public sector effort is generally not high, and the parent organization places little importance upon achieving the technical performance goals of the project (as opposed to staying within the budget and meeting the schedule). Also, the project manager's influence in selecting subcontractors and his authority to permit subcontractors to exceed original budgets or schedules are very low.

Of greater interest than the preceding lists are the characteristics which did *not* show up as significantly different between public sector and private sector projects. Table 34-6 lists some items which did not show statistically significant differentiation. *Note particularly that actual cost and schedule overrun were not found to be significantly different.* Also, satisfaction of the parent organi-

Table 34-5. Variables Significantly Uncharacteristic of Public Sector
Projects.

The degree of unity between the project manager and the principal public officials involved with the effort	(P < .001)
The project manager's authority to permit subcontractors to exceed original budgets or schedules	(P < .009)
The importance to the parent organization of achieving the specified technical performance goals	(P < .016)
*The difficulty in freezing the design	(P < .025)
The project manager's influence in selecting subcontractors	(P < .042)

*This characteristic may be considered counter-intuitive.

zation, the project team, and the ultimate users did not differ significantly. In fact, client satisfaction tends to be *higher* for public sector projects as indicated on Table 34-4.

In general, the comparisons between private sector projects and public sector projects do not support many of our pre-conceptions. Public sector projects certainly have their share of problems but they have been maligned more than the evidence of this study warrants.

STRATEGIES FOR OVERCOMING SOME OF THE PROBLEMS FACING PUBLIC SECTOR PROJECTS

Many of the characteristics which distinguish public sector projects from private sector projects can be considered adverse in nature. These adverse conditions make the probability of success less likely for public sector projects as compared to private sector projects. Should those involved with public sector projects therefore accept their fate and be content with very low levels of relative success? The findings of this study do not support such a defeatist approach to the management of public sector projects.

Table 34-6. Some Variables Which Did Not Differ Significantly Between Private Sector and Public Sector Projects.

Actual cost overrun.
Actual schedule overrun.
Extent of use of networking systems.
Advance in state-of-the-art required.
Difficulty in defining the goals of the project.
Difficulty in meeting the technical requirements of the project.
Satisfaction of the ultimate users, recipients, or clientele with the outcome of the project.
Satisfaction of the parent organization with the outcome of the project.
Satisfaction of the project team with the outcome of the project.

Instead, several strategies have been derived from the research findings which can maximize the success potential of public sector projects. Even when combinations of adversities exist, moderate success levels can be achieved if heavy emphasis is placed upon appropriate strategies for the situation and the environment as well as upon diligent pursuit of the project goals. The strategies which follow are based upon a path analysis diagram which was derived from a series of multiple regressions. Path analysis is a relatively new analytic technique and is not to be confused with networking techniques such as PERT and CPM. The result of a path analysis is a model which explains the interaction of a large number of variables. Such a model illustrates the causal relationships contained in a series of relationships. The strength of these relationships are measured by path coefficients. These coefficients are standardized measures which can be compared to determine the relative predictive power of each independent variable with the effects of the other variables held constant. The particular value of path analysis is that it illustrates the working relationships of many variables in a network of relative predictive powers; thus allowing one to understand the relationships among variables in a systematic manner. The strategies derived from the path analysis are summarized in Figure 34-1, Contingent Strategies for Successful Projects.

The most significant conclusion to be derived from Figure 34-1 is that a *project manager faced with one or more adversities need not and should not adopt a defeatist approach to the management of the project.* Even when combinations of adversities exist, moderate success levels can be achieved if heavy emphasis is placed upon appropriate strategies for the situation and the environment as well as upon diligent pursuit of the project goals.

A project manager can thus use Figure 34-1 as a basis for developing contingent strategies to overcome or circumvent certain adversities. The path analysis diagram was derived from the complete sample of private and public sector projects, but two of the adversities which often face managers of public projects will be analyzed:

- Legal-Political Difficulties, and
- Large Projects

The reader can examine Figure 34-1 to see the basis for the strategies designed to overcome these adversities. Although most of these strategies can be considered general strategies, they should receive added emphasis for public projects facing one or both of these adversities. In situations where these adversities do not exist, these strategies can be played down.

Strategies for Overcoming Legal-Political Difficulties

1. *Encourage openness and honesty from the start from all project participants and specifically seek to avoid and reject "buy-ins."*

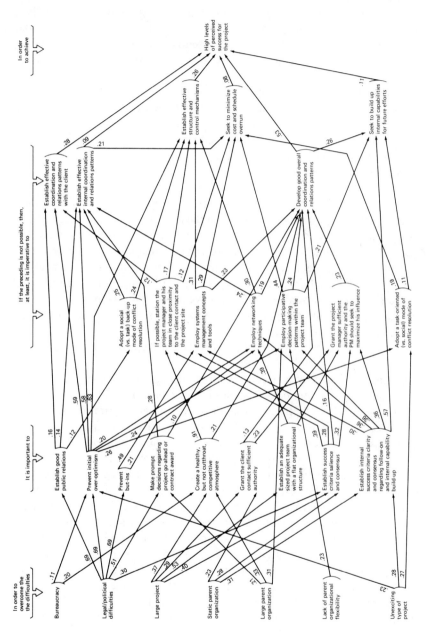

Figure 34-1. Contingent strategies for successful projects.

When legal political difficulties surround a project, these difficulties can only be compounded in the long run by permitting "buy-ins" to occur. In the short run, it may appear advantageous to secure initial program funding and initial contracts in order to enable "the camel's nose to enter the tent," but in the long run such a strategy and/or acquiescence to such a strategy results in:

- Panic reprogramming of public funds.
- Diminished reputation of the agencies and contractors involved with the project.
- Loss of credibility regarding future efforts.
- Poor relations with legislative bodies.
- Poor relations with the public.

In view of these factors, the recommended strategy seems best suited to public sector projects in both the short run and the long run. Such a strategy entails planning for and securing adequate funding commitments to complete the project. If the funding is considered excessive in relation to other deserving projects, then the project may be shelved or rejected, but is not this also the best strategy and the fairest in the long run for all competing interests? The parent organization must also avoid excessive pressure on the project manager to win the contract and the parent must also avoid slashing or ballooning the project team's cost estimates.

2. *Develop realistic cost, schedule, and technical performance estimates and goals.*

This strategy is closely related to the first strategy. It is sometimes difficult to distinguish when intentional overoptimism (or buy-in) has occurred, rather than unintentional overoptimism. Buy-in (or intentional optimism) and unintentional overoptimism were two of the biggest factors contributing to project failure. Cost realism can best be determined by means of an independent cost estimate conducted by a truly independent organization. In most cases, so-called "independent government cost estimates" can hardly be considered independent because of the vested interests of the agencies involved. In practice, the "independent" government cost estimate may be known by the contractors, and conversely, earlier contractor estimates may be known by the independent cost estimating team. When they are not known, the government cost estimates may vary over 100 percent higher or 50 percent lower than the dollar figures proposed by contractors for cost reimbursement contracts. As a result, contracting officers usually ignore the independent government cost estimates. Even if a truly independent cost estimate could be performed by a disinterested party, the question remains how accurate is such an estimate and how far can a contractor's estimate vary from such an estimate to be considered "realistic"?

The answers do not rest in some rules-of-thumb or complicated formulas.

The answers rest in the creation of an appropriate atmosphere and checkpoints to catch unintentional overoptimism and the creation of severe sanctions for intentional overoptimism (buy-in).

3. *Seek to enhance the public's image of the project.*

Project initiators generally are required and/or encouraged to obtain public participation during the planning and approval phases of most types of projects affecting the public interest. Some people believe that the more the public participates in these processes, the more successful the project will be. Although this concept may be appealing in the context of one's value judgments, it is not conducive to project success in a management context. High levels of public participation often result in a "tempest in a teapot." Project delays, poor public relations, and diminished project success are the results of excessive public participation. The most successful strategy from a project management success perspective is to create a good public relations image with only the minimal required levels of public participation. This is not an opinion. It is derived from the study of the hundreds of projects described in this article.

4. *Make prompt decisions regarding project go-ahead or contract award.*

This strategy is obviously directed to the client organization. There is nothing wrong with providing sufficient time for studies, planning, definition, etc. before seeking bids on a contract effort. But, once bids are sought, the schedule of contract award or go-ahead should be adhered to. Otherwise morale of the project team cadre deteriorates, to say nothing of the added costs of the delays.

5. *Seek to establish definitive goals for the project and seek to establish a clear understanding and consensus among the principal project participants (client organization, parent organization, and project team) regarding the relative importance of these goals.*

Although this factor was not quite as important as the previous four in overcoming legal/political difficulties, it was, nonetheless, an important factor on the road to project success.

Strategies for Overcoming the Disadvantages of Large Projects

1. *Establish a project team of adequate size but with a flexible and flat organizational structure.*

Obviously, the larger the project, the larger the project team must be, but this does not necessarily entail the creation of excessive levels of organizational structure. Flexible and flat organizational structures were found to be an essential ingredient for project success.

2. *Seek to establish definitive goals for the project and seek to establish a clear understanding and consensus among the principal project participants regarding the relative importance of these goals.*

Success criteria salience and consensus was found to be an important factor on both paths discussed here, but it was especially important for large projects.

3. *Create an atmosphere that encourages healthy, but not cutthroat, competition or "liars' contests."*

The larger the project, the more likely there will be many contractors who will be anxious to obtain the contract. It is sometimes tempting for a public agency to take advantage of this situation by creating a cutthroat competitive atmosphere, or even a subtle form of auction. In the long run, such a strategy works to the detriment of all parties concerned. A public agency and public officials must be especially careful to support the healthy aspects of the free enterprise system.

4. *Delegate sufficient authority to the principal client contact and let him/her promptly approve or reject important project decisions.*

The best way to overcome the sluggishness of a large organization and the traditional red tape associated with public projects is to delegate a high level of authority to the principal client contact.

Difficulties that Come in Bunches

Unfortunately, when trouble occurs, it does not occur in just one dimension. The expression "a bag of snakes" is commonly heard in meetings involving public projects. In many cases, as Figure 34-1 allows, a project manager is faced not only with legal-political difficulties but also with a buy-in situation, initial overoptimism, poor public relations, delays in contract award go-ahead, and/or lack of success criteria clarity and consensus. Similarly, a project manager confronting the inherent difficulties of a large project cannot always avoid additional major obstacles such as an inadequately sized project team, heavy budgetary pressure, etc. Figure 34-1 points the way to strategies for overcoming such combinations of adversities. For each combination of adversities toward the left of the diagram, it is possible to achieve improved levels of perceived success by placing heavy emphasis on the related strategies to the right. The reader may undertake similar analyses with the aid of Figure 34-1 for the other major adversities, such as a static or large parent organization, which may face a public sector project.

CONCLUSIONS

In general, the comparisons derived from the research of public sector projects and private sector projects do not support many of our preconceptions regarding public sector projects. For example, the study revealed no significant difference between private sector projects and public sector projects with respect to cost and schedule overrun. It is not only possible, but also very common, to attain high levels of perceived success on public sector projects.

In order to prevent schedule and cost overruns, or to minimize the amount of schedule and cost overrun when initial overoptimism or a "buy-in" has occurred, the research points to the need for employing networking techniques, systems management approaches, participative approaches to decision making within the project team and a task-oriented style of leadership, with a back-up relationship-oriented style.

Adverse environmental or "given" conditions do not necessarily affect project success directly, but often may be seen as affecting success through their influence on other intervening conditions and management processes. An adverse environmental or given condition can therefore be avoided or overcome through astute identification of those factors which it tends to affect directly, and through effective management action on those factors.

A project manager cannot afford to set his sights solely on objectively-oriented targets, i.e., meet the schedule, stay within the budget, and meet the technical requirements. Perceived success is in the eyes of all participants and the parties affected by the project. In the long run, perceived success appears to be more important than the traditional objective measures of success, provided that the project meets the technical performance specifications or mission to be performed.

Although many general strategy guidelines, based upon the study of hundreds of projects, have been developed to assist with improving project management, these guidelines must be tailored to the situation and the environment. Certain strategies must be given added emphasis in order to overcome specific adversities, and some strategies must be played down in order to meet the demands of other environments. Overemphasis or underemphasis of just one strategy can lead to failure. Combinations of multiple strategies can afford more frequent project successes in the public sector.

35. The Cultural Ambience of the Matrix Organization*

David I. Cleland†

INTRODUCTION

The concept of matrix management has grown beyond the project management context first introduced by John Mee in 1964.[1] Project management has been the precursor of today's matrix management approach found in diverse uses today. In the multinational corporation product, functional, and geographic managers work in a sharing mode of matrix management. Matrix management is found in a wide variety of other contexts: product management, task force management, production teams, new business development teams, to name a few.

In this chapter, I describe the cultural ambience of the project-driven matrix organization.

Culture is a set of refined behaviors that people have and strive towards in their society. Culture includes the complex whole of a society which includes knowledge, beliefs, art, ethics, morals, law, custom, and other habits and attitudes acquired by the individual as a member of society. Anthropologists have used the concept of culture in describing primitive societies. Modern day sociologists have borrowed this anthropological conception of culture and used it to describe a way of life of a people. I borrow from the sociologists and use the term culture to describe the synergistic set of shared ideas and beliefs that is associated with a way of life in an organization.

---

[1] John F. Mee: "Matrix Organization," *Business Horizons* (Summer, 1964).

†Dr. Cleland is a Professor of Engineering Management in the Industrial Engineering Department at the University of Pittsburgh. He is author/co-author of eight books and has published numerous articles appearing in leading national and internationally distributed technological, business management and educational periodicals. Dr. Cleland has had extensive experience in management consultation, lecturing, seminars, and research.

Nature of a Business Culture

The word culture is being used more and more in the lexicon of management to describe the ambience of a business organization. The culture associated with each organization has several distinctive characteristics that differentiate the company from others. In the IBM Corporation the simple precept, "IBM means service" sets the tone for the entire organization, infusing all aspects of its environment and generating its distinctive culture. At 3M the simple motto "Never kill a new product idea" creates an organizational atmosphere of inventiveness and creativity. In some large corporations such as Hewlett-Packard, General Electric, and Johnson & Johnson, the crucial parts of the organization are kept small to encourage a local culture which encourages a personal touch in the context of a motivated, entrepreneurial spirit of teamwork.

Understanding the culture of the organization is a prerequisite to introducing project management. An organization's culture reflects the composite management style of its executives, a style that has much to do with the organization's ability to adapt to such a change as the introduction of a project management system.

THE ROOTS OF THE MATRIX ORGANIZATION

The cultural ambience of the project-driven matrix organization is unique in many respects. But it should not be strange to us since our first organization, the family, has key features of the matrix design. In the traditional family unit, the child is responsible, to and has authority exercised over him by, two superiors (parents). A perceptive child soon learns that he must work out major decisions and such matters with both his bosses. If his parents have agreed on a "work breakdown structure" where each will exercise authority and assume responsibility over a particular aspect of raising the child, it will make it easier for him to get along with them and his peer group. A child may have to find ways of collaborating with both parents as well as his siblings and peers, adjusting to all groups.

When the child goes to school, another similar matrix design is found. The student is placed in a "home room" with a teacher whose main business is administration, "logistic support," and discipline. The student is taught by other teachers who are the "functional specialists," thus the student has several more "superiors" to whom he is accountable as well as a larger peer group. If the student is active in extracurricula activities, still more bosses come into his life. Success and acceptance in these activities generally require peer acceptance, teamwork, and an ability to communicate with his "superiors" and his peers.

When the student leaves school and seeks employment, he may find more of a hierarchical structure, yet the new matrix is in many ways similar to those already experienced. If his initial job is on a production line, the production foreman becomes boss number one, yet the quality control specialist can shut down the production line. The perceptive individual finds that certain staff specialists (personnel, finance, maintenance, wage and salary) and even the informal leaders in the peer groups temper the "sovereign domain" of the foreman. He soon finds that certain people in the organization exercise power simply because they have control of information (such as the production control specialist) or have become experts in some areas. People look to the expert to make decisions or take a leadership role in certain matters. The role of the union steward as a tempering influence on production techniques and policies soon becomes obvious to him. If he is active in community affairs he finds many other "bosses" telling (or suggesting to) him what to do. Who's really the boss? Well, it depends on the situation—as it does in the matrix organization.

The sharing context of project management should not be foreign to any of us. Our family life, education, and work experience have given us ample exposure to working for and satisfying several bosses and of learning to communicate and work with peers as well. Then why such resistance to matrix design? I believe the resistance has its roots in several cultural factors. First, the concept that authority flows from the top of the organization down through a chain of command. The foundation of this belief springs from the "divine right" of the king, who is delegated to rule the kingdom by a diety. Historically most social institutions have had a strong vertical structure—a chain of command. Ecclesiastical organizations have contributed much to organization theory; many of these contributions have reinforced the vertical structure. Have we not always assumed that "heaven"—by whatever name it is called—is a higher place or state? The Bible speaks of ascending into heaven. (Why not moving to heaven on a lateral basis?)

A good friend of mine who is a competent minister once delivered a sermon on the theme that "Hell was a state of mind, not a place." After the sermon was over I asked him this question: If hell is a state of mind and not a place, then it follows that heaven is a state of mind and not a place. He said: "Perhaps, but we are not ready for that yet!"

Perhaps like heaven, the matrix organization is more a state of mind than anything else!

No one would doubt the strong influence the Bible has had on our thinking. Indeed, the words of St. Matthew are familiar to everyone: "No man can serve two masters: for either he will hate the one, and love the other; or else he will hold to the one, and despise the other" (Matthew 6:24).

Part of the rationalization for the principle of "unity of command" may well be traced back to this verse. In managerial theory, this principle and its corollaries "parity of authority and responsibility," "compulsory staff advice," "line commands, staff advises," "span of control," etc., provide the conceptual foundation of the hierarchial organizational form. Indeed, many times managers and professionals have asked, "How can I work for two bosses?"

Yet Matthew also provides us with the basis for doing so: "Render therefore unto Caesar the things which are Caesar's; and unto God the things that are God's (Matthew 22:21).

I contend that in the light of both pragmatic and cultural experience there is as much a basis for the matrix design with its multidimensional sharing of authority, responsibility, accountability, and results, as there is for the hierarchical style of management.

THE MATRIX ORGANIZATIONAL DESIGN

I use the concept of organizational design in a broad context to include organizational structure, management system and processes, formal and informal interpersonal relationships, and motivational patterns. The matrix design is a compromise between a bureaucratic approach that is too inflexible and a simple unit structure that is too centralized. The design is fluid: personnel assignments, authority bases and interpersonal relationships are constantly shifting. It combines a sense of democracy within a bureaucratic context.

From an organizational design viewpoint, the entire organization must be psychologically tuned to results: the accomplishments within the organization that support higher level organizational objectives, goals, and strategies. The purpose of a matrix design is not only to get the best from its strong project approach and strong functional approach but to complement these by a strong unity of command at the senior level to insure that the balance of power is maintained in the organization. In some companies only one or a few divisions might require a realignment to the project-driven matrix form; the others might be left in the pyramidal, hierarchical form. Indeed a single organizational chart cannot realistically portray the maze of relationships that exist inside a large organization because some elements select project management, others opt for the conventional line-staff design, and still others choose some hybrid form.

The Design is Result-Oriented

The matrix design is result-oriented and information-related. The very design itself says that there is need for someone who can manage a process of cutting across the line functions. A compromise results through the bipolarity of functional specialization and project integration. Out of the lateral relations—direct contact, liaison roles, and integration—comes a faculty to make and implement decisions and to process information without forcing an overburden on the hierarchical communication channels. It is the need to reduce the decision process on the hierarchical channels that motivates the formal undertaking of lateral relations through establishing a design which is bilateral:

1. *Project Managers* who are responsible for results.
2. *Functional Managers* who are responsible for providing resources to attain results.

When implementing a matrix design in the early stages, a poor harmony will usually exist between the behavioral reality and the structural form. It is at this stage that the process of integration become important and a series of critical actions must be initiated and monitored by senior management. Superior-subordinate relationships need to be modified; individual self-motivation leading to peer acceptance becomes critical. The development of strategies for dealing with conflict, the encouragement of participation techniques, and the delineation of expected authority and responsibility patterns are crucial. The complexity of the resulting organizational design, described by Peter Drucker as "fiendishly difficult" reminds us that the matrix design should only be used when there is no suitable alternative. The design lacks the simple model of the conventional hierarchy. The nature of projects each in various stages of its life cycle creates a lack of stability. Key people on the project teams must *not only know* their specialty, but also *how* the specialty contributes to the whole.

The emphasis is on flexibility, peer informality, and minimization of hierarchy. To change an existing design to a fully functioning matrix form takes time—perhaps several years.

The matrix organizational design is the most complex form of organizational alignment that can be used. The integration of specialists along with supporting staff into a project team requires strong and continuing collaborative effort. And the coordination of effort in this kind of design requires a continuing integration of the mutual efforts of the team members. Authority (and consequently power) tend to flow to the individual who has the information that is needed and whose particular skills and knowledge are necessary to make a decision. Many managers are found in the matrix design: project managers, functional mangers, work package managers, general managers, staff managers. The greater the number of project teams, the greater the number of managers that will be used. As a result, the management costs in such an organizational approach are increased.

The introduction of project management into an organization tends to change established management practice with respect to such matters as authority and responsibility, procedural arrangements, support systems, department specialization, span of control, resource-allocation patterns, establishment of priorities, evaluation of people, etc. Performance goals within such organizations tend to be assigned in terms of the interfunctional flow of work needed to support a project. In so doing, established work groups within the functional agencies are often disrupted. In addition, there is a potential for the staffing pattern to involve duplication. The functional manager previously had the freedom to manage the organization in a relatively unilateral fashion, for he carried out integration himself or a higher authority handled it. Now he is forced into an interface in an environment which places a premium on the integration of resources through a project team consensus in order to accomplish project results. He must learn to work with a vocal and demanding horizontal organization.

A cultural characteristic of the matrix design causes two key attitudes to emerge: the manager who realizes that authority has its limits and the professional who recognizes that authority has its place.

THE CULTURAL AMBIENCE

In its organizational context, a cultural ambience for matrix management deals with the social expression manifest within the organization when engaged in managing projects. A cultural system emerges which reflects certain behavioral patterns characteristic of all the members of that organization. This system influences the skills, knowledge, and value systems of the people who are the primary organizational clientele. The clientele are a "team" of people who have some vested outcome in the success of an organizational effort.

Thus, project clientele include those in the organizational society who are the managers and professionals collectively sharing the authority and responsibility for completing a project on time and within budget. Superiors, subordinates, peers, and associates are the primary project clientele who work together to bring the project to a successful completion. The cultural ambience that ultimately emerges is dependent on the way these primary clientele feel and act in their professional roles both on the project team and within the larger organizational context. The integration of these clientele results in an ambience which has the following characteristics: Organizational Openness; Participation; Increased Human Problems; Consensus Decision Making; Objective Merit Evaluation; New Criteria for Wage and Salary Classification; New Career Paths; Acceptable Adversary Roles; Organizational Flexibility; Improvement in Productivity; Increased Innovation; Realignment of Supporting Systems; and Development of General Manager Attitudes. These characteristics are discussed below.

Organizational Openness

A propensity toward organizational openness is one of the most characteristic attributes of the matrix design. This openness is demonstrated through a receptiveness to new ideas, a sharing of information and problems by the peer group.

Newcomers to a matrix organization are typically accepted without any concern. There is a willingness to share organizational challenges and frustrations with the newcomer. This openness characteristic of project team management is described in one company as "no place to hide in the organization."[2]

Participation

Participation in the project-driven matrix organization calls for new behavior, attitudes, skills and knowledge. The demands of working successfully in the matrix design create opportunities for the people as well as for the organization. For the people, there are more opportunities to attract attention and to try one's mettle as a potential future manager. Because matrix management increases the amount and the pattern of recurring contacts between individuals, communication is more intense. The resolution of conflicts is also of a more intense nature than in the traditional organization where conflict can be resolved by talking to the functional boss. In a matrix design, at least two bosses have to become involved—the manager providing the resources and the manager held accountable for results. These two managers, locked in a conflict, may appeal as a last resort to the common line supervisor for resolution. Matrix management demands higher levels of collaboration. But in order to have collaboration, trust and commitment are needed on the part of the individuals. In order to be committed and to maintain trust, the individuals in the organization must take personal risks in sharing information and revealing their own views, attitudes, and feelings.

There is growing evidence that individuals today wish to influence their work situation and to create a democratic environment at their place of work. People expect variety in their life-style in the organization as well as in their private lives. The flexibility and openness of the matrix design can accommodate these demands.

The degree to which people are committed to participate openly and fully in matrix organization effort can influence results. Murphy, Baker, and Fisher, in a study of over 650 projects including 200 variables, found that certain variables were associated with the perceived failure of projects. Lack of team participation in decision making and problem solving was one important variable associated with perceived project failure. In contrast, project team participation in setting schedules and budgets was significantly related to project success.[3]

---

[2]"Texas Instruments Shows U.S. Business How To Survive in the 1980's," *Business Week* (September 18, 1978).

[3]D. C. Murphy, Bruce N. Baker, and Delmar Fisher "Determinants of Project Success," Springfield, VA, 22151, National Technical Information Services, Accession No. N-74-30392, 1974, p. 60669. See Chapters 33 and 34.

Increased Human Problems

Reeser conducted research to examine the question as to whether project organization might not have a built-in capacity of causing some real human problems of its own. This research was conducted at several aerospace companies. Reeser's research findings suggested insecurity about possible unemployment, career retardation and personal development is felt by subordinates in project organizations to be significantly more of a problem than by subordinates in functional organizations. Reeser notes that project subordinates can easily be frustrated by "make work" assignments, ambiguity and conflict in the work environment. Project subordinates tend to have less loyalty to the organization. There are frustrations because of having more than one boss. The central implication of Reeser's findings is that although there may be persuasive justifications for using a matrix design, relief from human problems is not one of them.[4]

Even with formal definition of organizational roles, the shifting of people between the projects does have some noticeable effects. For example, people may feel insecure if they are not provided with ongoing career counseling. In addition, the shifting of people from project to project may interfere with some of the basic training of employees and the executive development of salaried personnel. This neglect can hinder the growth and development of people in their respective fields.

Consensus Decision Making

Many people are involved in the making decisions. Members of the matrix team actively contribute in defining the question or problem as well as in designing courses of action to resolve problems and opportunities in the management of the effort. Professionals who become members of a matrix team gain added influence in the organization as they become associated with important decisions supporting an effort. They tend to become more closely associated with the decision makers both within the organization and outside it. Perceptive professionals readily recognize how their professional lives are broadened.

A series of documents which describe the formal authority and responsibility for decision making of key project clientele should be developed for the organization. If a manger is used to a clear line of authority to make unilateral decisions, the participation of team members in the project decision process makes management more complex. However, the result is worth the effort for the decisions tend to be of a higher quality. Also, by participating in the deci-

---

[4]Calyton Reeser: "Some Potential Human Problems of the Project Form of Organization," *Academy of Management Journal,* Vol 12 (December 1979).

sion process people have a high degree of commitment toward carrying out the decision in an effective manner.

Objective Merit Evaluation

This is an important area of concern to the individual in the matrix design. If the individual finds himself working for two bosses (the functional manager or work package manager and the project manager) chances are good that both will evaluate his merit and promotion fitness. Usually the functional manager initiates the evaluation; then the project manager will concur in the evaluation with a suitable endorsement. If the two evaluators are unable to agree on the evaluation it can be referred to a third party for resolution. For the most part, individuals who are so rated favor such a procedure as it reinforces their membership on the project team as well as insures that an equitable evaluation is given. A project team member who has been assigned to the project team from a functional organization may find himself away from the daily supervision of his functional supervisor. Under such circumstances a fair and objective evaluation might not be feasible. By having the project manager participate in the evaluation, objectivity and equity are maintained.

New Criteria for Wage and Salary Classification.

The executive rank and salary classification of a project manager will vary depending on the requirements of his position, the importance of the project to the company, etc. Most organizations adopt a policy of paying competitive salaries. However, the typical salary classification schema is based on the number and grade of managers and professionals that the executive supervises. In the management of a project, although the project manager may only supervise two or three people on his staff, he is still responsible for bringing the project in on time, at the budgeted cost. In so doing, he is responsible for managing the efforts of many others who do not report to him in the traditional sense. Therefore, new criteria for determining the salary level of a project manager are required. Organizations with successful salary classification schema for project manager's salary have utilized criteria such as the following:

- Duration of project.
- Importance of project to company.
- Importance of customer.
- Annual project dollars.
- Payroll and level of people who report directly to project manager (staff).
- Payroll and level of people whom project manager must interface directly on a continuing base with project manager.
- Complexity of project requirements.

- Complexity of project.
- Complexity of project interfaces.
- Payroll and rank of individual to whom project manager reports.
- Potential payoff of project.
- Pressures project manager is expected to face.

In many companies the use of project managemnt is still in its adolesence, and suitable salary criteria have not been determined. In such cases it is not uncommon to find individuals designated as project managers who are not coded as managerial personnel in the salary classification and executive rank criteria. Word of this will get around and the individual's authority may be compromised. The author has found this situation arising usually because of a failure of the wage salary staff specialists to develop suitable criteria for adjusting the salary grade of the project managers. This problem is not as significant in those industries where project management is a way of life, such as in aerospace and construction.

New Career Paths

The aspiring individual typically has two career paths open to him: to remain as a manager in his technical field or to seek a general manager position. Or he may prefer to remain a professional in his field and become a senior advisor, e.g., a senior engineer. Project management opens up a third career field in management. The individual who is motivated to enter management ranks can seek a position as a project manager of a small project and use this as a stepping stone to higher level management positions. It is an excellent way to learn the job of a general manager since the job of project manager is much like that of a general manager except that the project manager usually does not have the formal legal authority of the general manager. This should not deter the project manager; it should motivate him to develop his persuasive and other interpersonal and negotiation skills—necessary skills for success in general management!

Acceptable Adversary Roles

An adversary role emerges in project management as the primary project clientele find that participation in the key decisions and problems is socially acceptable. An adversary role may be assumed by any of the project clientele who sense that something is wrong in the management of the project. Such an adversary role questions goals, strategies, and objectives and asks the tough questions that have to be asked. Such a spontaneous adversary role provides a valuable check to guard against decisions which are unrealistic or overly optimistic. A socially acceptable adversary role facilitates the rigorous and objective development of data bases on which decisions are made. But the prevailing culture in an organization may discourage the individual from playing the adversary role that will help management to comprehend the reality of a situation. This situation is possible in all institutions of an hierarchical character.

An adversary role presumes that communication of ideas and concerns upward are encouraged. As people actively participate in the project deliberations, they are quick to suggest innovative ideas for improving the project or to sound the alarm when things do not seem to be going as they should. If the adversary role is not present, perhaps because its emergence is inhibited by the management style of the principal managers, information concerning potential organizational failures will not surface. An example of the stifling of an adversary role is found in the case of a company in the management of an urban transportation project.

In the late 1960's this company attempted to grow from a $250-million-a-year subcontractor in the aerospace industry into a producer of ground transit equipment. In pursuing this strategy, it won prime contracts for two large urban rail systems. Heavy losses in its rail programs put the company into financial difficulties. What went wrong?

The company got into difficulty in part because the chief executive dominated the other company executives even though he was unable to face overriding practical considerations. When major projects in the rail systems business were in difficulty, the unrealistic optimism demonstrated by the chief executive prevented any executive from doing much about the difficulties. In the daily staff meetings that were held, the executives quickly learned that any negative or pessimistic report on a project would provoke open and sharp criticism from the chief executive. Project managers quickly learned that in the existing cultural ambience the bringing of bad news would not be tolerated. Consequently, they glossed over problem areas and emphasized the positive in order to please the chief executive.

On one of their large contracts they submitted a bid that was 23% below the customer's own estimate, and $11 million under the next lowest competitive bid. The project manager had felt that this estimate was too low but had not argued against it because, "I didn't want to express a sorehead minority view when I was in charge of the program." The cultural ambience within this company during this period might be summarized as follows: Don't tell the boss any bad news, only report good news—if you bring bad news, you run the risk of being sharply criticized.

Members of a project team need to feel free to ask tough questions during the life of the project. When the members of a team can play an adversary role, a valuable check and balance mechanism exists to guard against decisions which are unrealistic. Within Texas Instruments a cultural ambience exists where an adversary role can emerge. Consequently, "It is impossible to bury a mistake in this company. The grass roots of the corporation are visible from the top . . . the people work in teams and that results in a lot of peer pressure and peer recognition."[5]

Organizational Flexibility

The lines of authority and responsibility defining the structure tend to be flexible in the matrix organization. There is much give and take across these lines with people assuming an organizational role that the situation warrants rather than what the position description says should be done. Authority in such an organizational context gravitates to the person who has the best credentials to make the judgment that is required.

The matrix design provides a vehicle for maximum organizational flexibility; no one has "tenure" on a matrix team. There are variable tasks that people perform, a change in the type of situations they may be working on, and an ebb and flow of workloads as the work of the organization fluctuates. When an individual's skills are no longer needed on a team, they can be assigned back to their permanent functional home.

There are some inherent problems in the flexibility of the matrix organization. The need for staffing tends to be more variable. Both the quantity of personnel and the quality needed are difficult to estimate because of the various projects that are going on in the organization. For example, a structural design group may have a surplus of design engineers at a particular time who are not assigned to any one project. The manpower estimates for oncoming projects, however, may indicate that in several months these professionals will be needed for project assignments. A functional structural design manager has the decision of whether to release the men and reduce his overhead or to assign them to "make work" for the period and forego the future costs of recruitment, selection, and training. The same manager may anticipate assigning these professionals to an emerging project yet, if the emerging project is delayed or even cancelled the project manager may not need these people for some time.

As the work effort nears its end, and perceptive individuals begin to look for other jobs, there can be a reduction in their output level. This reduction can damage the efficacy with which the project is being managed. Paradoxically, although morale takes on added significance in the matrix team, the design itself may result in lowering it.

The organizational flexibility of project management does, therefore, create some problems as well as opportunities.

---

[5]"Texas Instruments Shows U.S. Business How To Survive in the 1980's," *Business Week* (September 18, 1978), pp. 66–92.

Improvement in Productivity

Texas Instruments credits the use of project teams for productivity improvement in the company. Its productivity improvement over a period of years was slightly more than offset the combined impact of its wage and benefit increased (average 9.2% annually) and its price decreases (averaging 6.4% per unit).[6]

At Texas Instruments more than 83% of all employees are organized into "people involvement teams" seeking ways to improve their own productivity. The company views its people as interchangeable—"kind of like auto parts." The culture there is much like the Japanese—a strong spirit of belonging, a strong work ethic, competitive zeal, company loyalty, and rational decision making. The culture of Texas Instruments " . . . has its roots buried deep in a soil of Texas' pioneer work ethic, dedication, toughness and tenacity—it (the culture) is a religion. The climate polarizes people—either you are incorporated into the culture or rejected."[7]

The experience of Litton Industries in its Microwave Cooking Dvision shows that the use of project teams in the manufacturing function has increased productivity. Since the manufacturing organization was grouped into team units, production increased four-fold in fifteen months. Product quality has increased, 1000 new production workers have been added to a base of 400 people, and unit production costs have declined 10–15%.[8] Some other claims of productivity increases that have come to the author's attention are as follows:[9]

- A steel company chief executive states: "Properly applied, 'matrix' management improves profitability because it allows progress to be made on a broader front; with a given staff size, i.e., more programs and projects simultaneously pursued (including those concerning productivity)."
- The chief executive of a company in the microprocessor industry declares that the company's success (15% of the microprocessor market, $1.8 million in revenue, 18.1% ROI) would not be possible without matrix management.
- A chemical company president claims: "Matrix management improves people productivity."

The experiences of these companies suggest that project management techniques can assist in raising productivity.

---

[6]Ibid
[7]Ibid.
[8]William W. George: "Task Teams for Rapid Growth," *Harvard Business Review* (March-April 1977), p. 71.
[9]These are productivity claims cited to the author in correspondence.

Increased Innovation

In the private sector in those industries where a fast changing state-of-the-art exists, product innovation is critical for survival. There is evidence that the use of project teams has helped to further innovation within such organizations. For example, the teams are successfully used in the aerospace industry where the ability to innovate is essential, particularly in the development and production of sophisticated weaponry.

Why does the project team seem to foster innovation in organizations? Innovation comes about because an individual has an idea, a technological or market idea, and surrounds himself with some people who believe in the idea and are commited to it. A small team of people is formed, who become advocates and missionaries for the idea. The team of people represents a diverse set of disciplines who view the idea differently. It's difficult to hide anything in such an environment. The openness, the freedom of expression, the need to demonstrate personal effectiveness, all seem to be conductive to the creativity necessary to innovate. Within such organizations, decision making tends to be of a consensus type. An element of esprit de corps exists. The creativity and the innovative characteristics of small teams can be illustrated by the Texas Instruments situation.[10]

Texas Instruments has been extremely successful with the use of teams in over 200 product-consumer centers (PCC). In each of these centers, the manager runs a small business of his or her own with responsibilities that include both long-term and short-term considerations. These managers have access to functional groups and are able to utilize the enormous resources that the functional organizations can offer. Indeed, what Texas Instruments has done is to create an organization in which the entrepreneur—the innovator—can flourish by making available to him/her the technical resources that are needed to do the job.

Project teams used effectively can take advantage of the scale economics of large organizations and, by their team nature, the flexibility of a small innovative organization is realized. An early research effort in the use of program (project) organizations noted that such organizations seemed to have been more successful in developing and introducing new products than businesses without program organizations.[11]

L. W. Ellis, Director of Research, International Telephone and Telegraph Corporation claims that temporary groups (project teams) that are well orga-

---

[10]See "Texas Instruments Shows U.S. Business How to Survive in the 1980's," *Business Week* (September 18, 1978), pp. 66–92.
[11]E. R. Corey and S. H. Star: *Organization Strategy: A Marketing Approach,* Chapter 6, Division of Research, Harvard Business School, Boston, MA, 1970.

nized and have controlled autonomy can stimulate innovation by overcoming resistance to change. Cross functional and diagonal communication within the project team and with outside interested parties helps to reduce resistance to change.[12]

Jermakowicz found that the matrix design was most effective of three major organizational forms he studied in ensuring the implementation or introduction of new projects, while a "pure" project organization produced the most creative solutions.[13]

Kolodny, reporting on a study of his own and citing some other studies as well comments on the effect that matrix organizations have on new product innovation.[14] Kolodny cites Davis and Lawrence, who points to an apparent high correlation between matrix organization designs and very high rates of new product innovation.[15] In his summary Kolodny notes that there is an apparent relationship between high rates of new product innovation, as measured by the successful introduction of new products, and matrix organizational designs.[16]

There is no question that an organization whose business involves the work of temporary projects is more anxiety-ridden, tension-filled, and demanding of personal competence and equilibrium than a stable, conventionally organized one. The matrix design is complex, yet its successful operation reflects a complementary mode of collaborative relationships in an open ambience. It is an adaptive, rapidly changing temporary management system that can favorably impact on organizational innovation.

Realignment of Supporting Systems

As the use of Project Management grows in an organization it soon becomes apparent that many of the systems that have been organized on a traditional hierarchical basis need to be realigned to support the project team. What initially appears to be only an organizationl change soon becomes something larger. Effective project management requires timely and relevant information on the project; accordingly, the information systems have to be modified to accommodate the project manager's needs. Financial and accounting systems,

---

[12]L. W. Ellis: "Effective Use of Temporary Groups for New Product Development," *Research Management* (January 1979), pp. 31–34.
[13]Wladyslaw Jermakowicz:"Organizational Structures in the R & D Sphere," *R & D Management,* No. 8, Special Issue (1978), pp. 107–113v as cited in Kolodny below.
[14]Harvey F. Kolodny: "Matrix Organization Designs and New Product Success," *Research Management* (September 1980), pp. 29–33.
[15]Stanley M. Davis & Paul R. Lawrence: *Matrix* (Addison-Wesley Publishing Company, Reading, Mass.), 1977.
[16]Kolodny, op. cit. p. 32.

project planning and control techniques, personnel evaluations and other supporting systems require adjustment to meet project management needs.

Development of General Manager Attitudes

An organizational culture is in a sense the aggregate of individual values, attitudes, beliefs, prejudices, and social standards. A change for these individuals
means cultural changes. The matrix design, when properly applied, tends to
provide more opportunity to more people to act in a general manager mode.
With this kind of general manager thinking, the individual is able to contribute
more to organizational decision making and information processing.

The matrix design with its openness and demands for persuasive skills provides an especially good environment for the manager-to-be to test his ability
to make things happen by the strength of persuasive and negotiative powers.
A perceptive general manager knows that there is little he accomplishes solely
by virtue of his hierarchical position; so much depends on his ability to persuade others to his way of thinking. Exposure to the workings and ambience
of the matrix culture brings this point home clearly and succinctly.

Effective collaboration on a project team requires plenty of a needed ingredient—trust. To develop this trust, individuals must be prepared to take personal risks in sharing resources, information, views, prejudices, attitudes, and
feelings to act in a democratic mode. Not everyone can do that, yet executives
in successful companies are able to do so. For example, in the Digital Equipment Corporation where a matrix environment prevails, the ambience is
described as "incredibly democratic" and not for everyone. Lots of technical
people can't stand the lack of structure and indefiniteness. In such an organization bargaining skills are essential to survival.[17] The matrix design is permanent—the deployment of people is changing constantly. In such a transi-
tional situation the only thing that prevents breakdown is the personal
relationships as conflicts are resolved and personnel assignments are changed.
Communication is continually needed to maintain the interpersonal relationships and to stimulate people to contribute to the project team efforts.

SOME CAVEATS

The matrix organizational design is hard to get started and challenging to operate. The more conventional the culture has been the more challenges will

---

[17]Harold Sneker: "If You Gotta Borrow Money, You Gotta," *Forbes* (April 28, 1980), pp. 116–
120.

emerge in moving to the matrix form. A few caveats are in order for those who plan to initiate and use the project-driven matrix design.

1. Realize that patience is absolutely necessary. It takes time to change the systems and people who make the matrix work.
2. Promote by word and example an open and flexible attitude in the organization. Encourage the notion that change is inevitable, and that a free exchange of ideas is necessary to make project management work.
3. Develop a scheme for organizational objectives, goals, and strategies that will provide the framework for an emerging project management culture.
4. Accept the idea that some people may never be able to adjust to the unstructured, democratic ambience of the matrix culture. For these people a place in the organization must be assured when they can remain insulated from the "fiendishly difficult" surroundings of the matrix organization.
5. Be mindful of the tremendous importance that the team commitment plays in managing the project activities. Make use of the winning football team analogy where the commitment to win is an absolute prerequisite to becoming a championship team.
6. Provide for a forum whereby conflict can be resolved before the conflict deteriorates into interpersonal strife.
7. Realize that project management is not a panacea for organic organizational maladies. In fact, the implementing of a project management system will bring to light many organizational problems and opportunities that have remained hidden in the conventional line and staff organization.
8. Be aware that the particular route that an organization follows in its journey to the matrix design must evolve out of the existing culture.
9. Recognize that senior management support and commitment are essential to success.
10. Work for communication within the company that is uninhibited, thorough and complete. Information requirements for project management require definition. Those individuals who have a need to know must have access to the information to do their job. Those in key positions have to understand and use the project-generated information.
11. Be aware that shifting to a matrix form is easier for the younger organization. For large well-established companies where a rigid bureaucracy endures, the shift will be quite formidable.
12. Institute a strong educational effort to acquaint key managers and professionals with the theory and practice of project management. Time should be taken to do this at the beginning using the existing culture as a point of departure.

SUMMARY

The real culture of project management refers to actual behavior—those things and events that really exist in the life of an organization. The introduction of project management into an existing culture will set into motion a "system of effects" which changes attitudes, values, beliefs, management systems to a participative, democratic mode. Thus, a new cultural context for the sharing of decisions, results, rewards, and accountability will ultimately emerge as an organization matures in the use of project management.

REFERENCES

D. I. Cleland and W. R. King: Systems Analysis and Project Management, 3rd Edition, McGraw-Hill Book Co., New York, N. Y., 1983.

E. R. Corey and S. H. Star: *Organization Strategy: A Marketing Approach,* Chapter 6 (Division of Research, Harvard Business School, Boston, MA., 1970).

Stanley M. Davis and Paul R. Lawrence: *Matrix* (Addison-Wesley Publishing Company, Reading, Massachusetts), p. 19.

L. W. Ellis: "Effective Use of Temporary Groups for New Product Development," *Research Management* (January 1979), pp. 31–34.

William W. George: "Task Teams for Rapid Growth," *Harvard Business Review* (March-April 1977), p. 78.

Wladyslaw Jermakowicz: "Organizational Structure in the R & D Sphere," *R&D Management,* No. 8, Special Issue (1978), pp. 107–113v.

Harvey F. Kolodny: "Matrix Organization Designs and New Product Success," *Research Management* (September 1980), pp. 29–33.

John F. Mee: "Matrix Organization," *Business Horizons* (Summer, 1964).

D. C. Murphy, Bruce N. Baker and Delmar Fisher: "Determinants of Project Success," National Technical Information Services, Accession No. N-74-30392 (1974), Springfield, VA, 22151, p. 60669.

Clayton Reeser: "Some Potential Human Problems of the Project Form of Organization," *Academy of Management Journal* (December, 1979), Vol. 12

Harold Seneker: "If You Gotta Borrow Money, You Gotta," *Forbes* (April 28, 1980), pp. 116–120.

"Texas Instruments Shows U.S. Business How to Survive in the 1980's," *Business Week* (September 18, 1978).

Index